THE TRANSFERRED LIFE OF GEORGE ELIOT

Reading George Eliot's work was described by one Victorian critic as like the feeling of entering the confessional in which the novelist sees and hears all the secrets of human psychology—'that roar which lies on the other side of silence'. This new biography of George Eliot goes beyond the much-told story of her life. It gives an account of what it means to become a novelist, and to think like a novelist: in particular a realist novelist for whom art exists not for art's sake but in the exploration and service of human life. It shows the formation and the workings of George Eliot's mind as it plays into her creation of some of the greatest novels of the Victorian era.

When at the age of 37 Marian Evans became George Eliot, this change followed long mental preparation and personal suffering. During this time she related her power of intelligence to her capacity for feeling: discovering that her thinking and her art had to combine both. That was the great ambition of her novels—not to be mere pastimes or fictions but experiments in life and helps in living, through the deepest account of human complexity available. Philip Davis's illuminating new biography will enable you both to see through George Eliot's eyes and to feel what it is like to be seen by her, in the imaginative involvement of her readers with her characters.

PHILIP DAVIS is the author of *The Victorians 1830–1880*, volume 8 in the Oxford English Literary History Series, and a companion volume on *Why Victorian Literature Still Matters*. He has written on Shakespeare, Samuel Johnson, the literary uses of memory from Wordsworth to Lawrence, and authored various books on reading. He is general editor of OUP's new paperback series, The Literary Agenda, on the role of literature in the world of the twenty-first century. His previous literary biography was a life of Bernard Malamud. Davis is editor of *The Reader* magazine, the written voice of the outreach organisation *The Reader*. He is Professor of English Literature, and Director of the Centre for Research into Reading, Literature, and Society (CRILS), University of Liverpool.

Praise for *The Transferred Life of George Eliot*

'How many books of erudite, intellectual biography, and closely argued literary criticism can ever be described as an enthralling, lucid, page-turning read? . . . Philip Davis is the searching, perceptive critic this great novelist deserves.'

Patricia Duncker, *Literary Review*

'The strength of Davis's superbly written work of "the great transmitter," as he calls her, lies in the readings of the fiction and discussion of the impact of George Lewes's work on Eliot . . . Summing Up: Highly recommended. Lower-division under-graduates through faculty; general readers.'

W. Baker, *Choice*

The Transferred Life of George Eliot makes its case with impressive force and eloquence. In doing so, it leaves aside many of the standard elements of a biography: an orderly sequence of life-events, financial affairs, contacts with other cultural figures, and so forth. Davis's narrative sticks to Eliot's emotional and intellectual development, as revealed in her fiction and letters. It presents Eliot's life as the heroic overcoming of the multiple oppressions inflicted on a brilliant but awkward and misunderstood provincial girl.'

Paul Delany, *Los Angeles Review of Books*

'There have been several good new biographies of George Eliot in recent years but none quite like this . . . Davis has a magisterial command of all her writing.'

John Rignall, George Eliot Review: *Journal of the George Eliot Fellowship*

'A dense and revelatory study . . . *The Transferred Life of George Eliot* is the remarkable culmination of a lifetime of reflection on that transformative experience.'

Rohan Maitzen, *Times Literary Supplement*

'In his thoughtful and searching account of the writer we know as George Eliot, Philip Davis undertakes a project of which his subject would have approved . . . [Davis is] acute on the psychology of the novels, both in their content and on their connection to their author's life.'

Salley Vickers, *The Observer*

'Davis's book is a celebration of [Eliot's] "realism", which allows us to see minutely the differences in consciousness of different characters—before we return to our sole selves.'

John Mullan, *The Guardian*

'Anyone who has read and loved *Middlemarch* will appreciate Davis's devotion to his subject.'

Claire Lowdon, *Sunday Times*

'I came away from [Davis's] book more full of admiration and awe for his subject matter than ever before.'

Barney Bardsley, On: *Yorkshire Magazine*

The Transferred Life of George Eliot is an unusual and welcome book . . . What Davis best documents and celebrates . . . is Eliot's determination to deliver the complexity and psychological intensity of intimate relationships as they face crisis and change in recognizably real circumstances.'

Tim Parks, *New York Review of Books*

'Philip Davis comes as close as one could to imagining that mysterious process through which a living historical person becomes a writing voice on a page. Anyone who knows what it means to write for her life will honor his achievement.'

Rosemarie Bodenheimer, *Victorian Studies*

FRONTISPIECE.

George Eliot by Samuel Laurence, 1860
(courtesy of The Mistress and Fellows, Girton College, Cambridge)

The Transferred Life
of George Eliot

THE BIOGRAPHY OF A NOVELIST

PHILIP DAVIS

OXFORD
UNIVERSITY PRESS

OXFORD
UNIVERSITY PRESS

Great Clarendon Street, Oxford, OX2 6DP,
United Kingdom

Oxford University Press is a department of the University of Oxford.
It furthers the University's objective of excellence in research, scholarship,
and education by publishing worldwide. Oxford is a registered trade mark of
Oxford University Press in the UK and in certain other countries

First published 2017
First published in paperback 2018

Impression: 2

Published in the United States of America by Oxford University Press
198 Madison Avenue, New York, NY 10016, United States of America

British Library Cataloguing in Publication Data
Data available

Library of Congress Cataloging in Publication Data
Data available

ISBN 978–0–19–957737–8 (Hbk.)
ISBN 978–0–19–882563–0 (Pbk.)

Printed and bound in Great Britain by
CPI Group (UK) Ltd, Croydon, CR0 4YY

'I never expected happiness... [But] this gift of transferred life which has come to me in loving you, may be a new power to me.'

George Eliot, *The Mill on the Floss*

'Depend upon it, you would gain unspeakably if you would learn with me to see some of the poetry and the pathos, the tragedy and the comedy, lying in the experience of a human soul that looks out through dull grey eyes, and that speaks in a voice of quite ordinary tones.'

George Eliot, *Scenes of Clerical Life*, 'Amos Barton'

'No one ... divined what was hidden under that outward life—a woman's keen sensibility and dread, which lay screened behind all her petty habits and narrow notions, as some quivering thing with eyes and throbbing heart may lie crouching behind withered rubbish.'

George Eliot, *Felix Holt*

'Whereas by speech a man transmits his thoughts to another, by art he transmits his feelings.'

Leo Tolstoy, *What is Art?*

Acknowledgements

It is a pleasure to record my thanks for the kind expertise of John Burton of the George Eliot Fellowship, who has been generosity itself, Louise Essex of Nuneaton Library, Becky Harvey of Nuneaton Museum and Art Gallery, and Ali Wells, Curator of the Herbert Art Gallery & Museum in Coventry.

I am more grateful than I can say to those who have been my own close readers: Josie Billington, Sophie Clarke, Sarah Coley, Jane Davis, Angie Macmillan, Fiona Magee, and Brian Nellist, to a life-saving proofreader in Andrew Hawkey, and to my long-supportive editor at Oxford University Press, Jacqueline Norton.

Table of Contents

List of Illustrations

List of Plates

Abbreviations

Cross J. W. Cross (ed.), *George Eliot's Life*, 3 vols (Edinburgh and London: William Blackwood & Sons, 1885).

Essays Thomas Pinney (ed.), *The Essays of George Eliot* (London: Routledge & Kegan Paul, 1963).

GEL *The George Eliot Letters*, ed. Gordon S. Haight, 9 vols (New Haven, CT: Yale University Press, 1954–78).

Introduction

I have chosen to call this book 'a transferred life' in preference to 'an intellectual biography'.

An intellectual biography is what, for example, Robert D. Richardson called his work on Henry Thoreau in *A Life of the Mind* (1986), on Ralph Waldo Emerson in *The Mind on Fire* (1995), and on William James in *In the Maelstrom of American Modernism* (2006). With each subject the aim, Richardson claimed, was 'to understand his life through his work, not the other way round'.[1] For example, 'Emerson's main project, never realized to his satisfaction,' notes Richardson, 'was to write a natural history of intellect; I have tried to honor this aim by reconstructing the natural history of his enthusiasms.'[2]

This present work is the natural history of a novelist—for me *The* quintessential Novelist, George Eliot, arising out of the culmination of the realist novel in the nineteenth century. In what follows, what will be shown are ways of thinking like a novelist, some inherited, some invented, which go into the novel and its influence for ever after. Above all, George Eliot is offered here as the great representative (to use one of Emerson's own terms) of what it means to be a writer of realist fiction, where 'realist', whatever its complexities, signifies the commitment to do work determinedly between life and art, art and life. 'George Eliot' existed to make that link and to be it. William James described *Middlemarch* as 'fuller of human stuff than any novel that was ever written' (Richardson, *James*, p. 152), but more than that, I argue that in her and as a result of her the realist novel itself is fuller of human stuff than any other form of thinking about existence.

As one of her great admirers, Edith Simcox, put it in an essay written on her death:

> Her own view of the world as a whole was too veracious to be summed up in a phrase. Her mind was a mirror, upon which the truth concerning all human relations was reflected with literal fidelity. What one generalisation can cover so wide a range? You can no more draw one moral lesson from her books than you can from life itself; you may draw a thousand if you will, but merely to read one of her books in an impressionable mood is to see such a portion of the world with her eyes and to share in the multiform influence exercised by the vision.[3]

To see with her eyes, or feel with her heart, or think with her mind: these are shorthand terms for what is at stake when, as Tolstoy put it, art does not simply offer a single idea or a paraphrase-able system but transmits something more than intellect, without ever being less than a way of thinking. Literature is transmitted being: it is only within George Eliot's novels that 'her own view of the world as a whole' is given, in the life and the feel of the envisioning. The aim here is to receive and to retransmit the feeling of what the creation of George Eliot, in and through her work, may stand for in the history of the human search for meaning. First to receive and then to retransmit is the reason why, in what follows, so much is quoted direct from the work, and then in turn worked upon: always starting from, always returning to, always passing on George Eliot's own words and what is immersed within them. 'I care for the finger pointing to the right passage more than for any superlative phrases' (GEL 5, p. 324).[4]

My primary aim is indeed, then, to understand her life through her work because it was to her work that she transferred and dedicated her life, belatedly, in her late 30s. She had been an 'intellectual' before that: to become a novelist meant absorption in a form of thinking that went beyond that term, and that is one reason why this volume cannot be thought of as a wholly intellectual biography if it is to seek to stay true to its subject.

Nor is it simply the biography of Mary Anne Evans, born 22 November 1819, but the biography of George Eliot created by her own writing from September 1856 onwards, though drawing on—to transform and redeem—all she had been and half-been, all she had read and thought and felt, before that. It is a book about the acts that created George Eliot, through memories, ideas, imaginative transformations—but in particular the act of realist writing which, in holding together life and art, made the living creation of the Writer-within-her-Work one of the most important achievements in Literature.

'George Eliot' may begin as a mere male pseudonym, as the narrator of the novels by which their author first came into articulate existence. But increasingly she becomes not only a directing emotional presence within the work but, finally, the most important person in them. Culminating in *Middlemarch*, George Eliot becomes her own greatest character, more important than an Adam Bede or a Maggie Tulliver or a Dorothea Brooke, though only realized through the act of creating them. 'George Eliot', said Edward Dowden, was the creation of a 'second self', needed by Marian Evans but needed also by her readers.[5]

In *Why Read?* and *Why Teach?* the literary critic Mark Edmundson argues against the application of particular 'readings', 'interpretations', 'criticisms' of the writers he most cares about—a Marxist critique, a feminist reading, an historicist's contextual distancing—as if those external 'approaches' know more and know better than their subject. Too often, he says, the theorists read not with their author's eyes but against the work. But 'despite the rhetoric of subversion that surrounds it', Edmundson concludes, 'current humanities education does not teach subversive scepticism': instead, what it really teaches is 'the dissociation of intellect from feeling'. George Eliot stands for precisely the opposite. But 'it is easy to be brilliant,' Goethe said, 'when you do not believe in anything'.[6]

What then is to be said, alternatively, on behalf of 'those of us who imagine that if you give yourself over completely to your subject you'll be rewarded with insight beyond what you individually command?'[7] I say with Edmundson that the reader's natural first duty is to risk attempting to recreate from within him or herself a George-Eliot-like view of George Eliot. In Chapters 2 and 3, for example, I argue that imaginative identification is George Eliot's own chosen way from the first. In short, I want to learn from what George Eliot brings into being, to turn the historical into the literary, and to look for belief and purpose in the uses of reading her now.[8]

This, then, is an attempted imaginative recognition of all that George Eliot was in mind and heart, as though she were indeed a real and achieved person and not just a pseudonym or an omniscient narrator made up out of words and syntax on a piece of paper. 'Who can describe a human being?' she writes sceptically in *Daniel Deronda* (chapter 11): even when he or she is present to us, any degree of real knowledge requires 'innumerable impressions under different circumstances'. But wherever she comes from and whatever she is made of, 'George Eliot' is immediately present to us on the page. That *is* her life, more than the words registered but nonetheless realized through those words. In normal existence, as she puts it in that passage from *Daniel Deronda*, 'We recognize the alphabet; we are not sure of the language.' But with George Eliot we have her vocabulary, her syntax, the language of her, in itself, as primary evidence.

As the life of a writer, this literary biography is about her language in that deeper sense, as constructed from its elements, its alphabet, its sentences, and its signature episodes. So, George Eliot on learning the importance of words: 'We learn words by rote, but not their meaning; that must be paid for with our life-blood, and printed in the subtle fibres of our nerves' ('The Lifted Veil', 1859). So too, on learning the importance of grammar: 'Nature has her language, and she is not unveracious; but we don't know all the intricacies of her syntax just yet, and in a hasty reading we may happen to extract the very opposite of her real meaning' (*Adam Bede*, chapter 15). This is not a matter of style as merely aesthetic accompaniment; it is about trying to learn the meaning of the world through the efforts of one realist novelist within it. Who and what *is* this 'George Eliot' as an embodied, transmittable, inhabiting vision of things human?

That main question, in its attempt to understand the life that is felt in and through the work, involves two other concerns for this book.

One is that, like George Eliot herself, this book, by still being biographical, should not give up on the life of Marian Evans as a continuing presence and influence. I look for the use of her life in her work—to recognize the very fact that such a life, even in its ordinary failures, pains, and disappointments *can* be used, transferred, and transmuted. 'I remember once,' reports her first biographer J. W. Cross, 'when I was urging her to write her autobiography, she said, half sighing, half smiling':

> The only thing I should care much to dwell on would be the absolute despair I suffered from of ever being able to achieve anything. No one could ever have felt greater despair, and a knowledge of this might be a help to some other strugglers'—adding with a smile, 'but on the other hand, it might only lead to an increase of bad writing'.[9]

She told Emily Davies that it was impossible for her to write an autobiography 'but she wished that somebody else could do it, it might be useful—or that she could do it herself'. She could do it better than anyone else, she went on, 'because she could do it impartially, judging herself and showing how wrong *she* was' (GEL 8, p. 465).

She was a novelist finally at the age of 37 when writing fiction might have been the last thing that could have been predicted of her, fifteen, ten, or even two years earlier. Dickens was first published at 24, Charlotte Brontë completed *Jane Eyre* aged 31, Hardy and Thackeray appeared in print in their early 30s; even the slow-starting Trollope had three novels published before he was 37. But she had felt 'the *absolute* despair...of ever being able to achieve anything'. Only time and time's story can show how that absolute turned out at last, in retrospect, to be only relative, not final. As she was to write in *Middlemarch*, 'what we call our despair is often only the painful eagerness of unfed hope' (chapter 51). This is why this present work will not be straightforward. Even her names won't stay still. The story of how Mary Ann or (as she later called herself) Marian Evans became George Eliot is not simply linear or seamlessly progressive but goes backwards and forwards in the unpredictable twists and turns of a significance that may turn out to be fulfilled only in the future or reclaimed creatively in retrospect. This book still stays loyal to that story of struggling emergence in so far as its chapters remain in chronological biographical sequence. But inside each chapter, as within different strands or parts of a life, time moves around, tracing suddenly perceived origins and later unforeseen outcomes.

What Johnny Cross put together in *George Eliot's Life* was a compilation from letters and diaries of her own words at different times, under cover of a limited and dutiful literalism, but with all the gaps, privacies, and emotional silences poignantly left to the reader's imagination. It was a life felt amongst the fragments, beneath or between them, in the gratefulness of a woman eventually finding a vocation that pulled everything together. Though there had been her father, though there was above all George Henry Lewes as her partner, she could hardly tell to whom or to what, finally, she was grateful. Perhaps grateful to art, and to whatever gave her the capacity for it. But the feeling was there as part of a life purpose whose end was, also, not wholly clear or easily known. And so, however much she eschewed the narrow egoism of autobiography, or distrusted the flattened conventionality of second-hand biography, George Eliot thought that a knowledge of her own story might still be 'a help' to equivalent beings in analogous difficulty. It could say to 'some other strugglers' both in the books and outside them: What out of a seemingly ordinary or marred existence can you *make* of yourself, in any way of life? If that risked turning people into bad writers, as she wryly joked to Cross, the true aim was to make them into good readers, harder thinkers, and better doers in the world.

It had been a hard slow process for her. One of her acquaintances, Bessie Parkes, had mentioned to her friend Barbara Leigh Smith in 1852, that Marian Evans still seem underdeveloped, even aged 33:

> I know you will like her for her large unprejudiced mind, her complete superiority to other women. But whether you or I should ever love her, as a friend, I don't know at all. There is as yet no high moral purpose in the impression she makes, and it is that alone which commands love. I think she will alter. Large angels take a long time unfolding their wings; but when they do, soar out of sight. Miss Evans either has no wings, or, which I think is the case, they are coming, budding.   (GEL 2, p. 9)

Although she herself did not wish to tell it, it seemed finally that the life of Miss Evans *did* have a story after all, though recurrently for more than twenty years she had despaired of it ever being anything or ever going anywhere. 'An imperfectly developed stunted creature' she had called herself (GEL 2, p. 145). She thought she was ugly, and she was full of self-doubts and insecurities. She thought she was intelligent but unloveable, and in herself the two—the intelligence and the need for love—were in danger of equivalent separation. She at once hated and kept resorting to her egoism. If hers was then a story after all, along the way it must have been an underlying one, at times utterly unknown to its own lost protagonist; a surprise story emerging after faith in its possibility was well-nigh gone; or perhaps a story created back to front, salvaged in retrospect through the tense burdens of writing. She did not wish to tell her life story because she had already created and retold it in transmuted ways in her fiction. This way her life was remade.

But even authorship had felt odd, as though there were for her always two ways of being 'George Eliot'—one in the continual creating and recreating of the doubtful writer again and again on the page; the other afterwards in the final establishment of the published author, the ostensibly confident sibyl. It was like the difference between handwriting and print. As her publisher John Blackwood wrote to her, quoting from a now lost letter of hers on the 'intellectual fermentation' from which works like *Middlemarch* arose: 'What you tell me...makes me envy the process of disciplined thought which after the "simmering" passes all at once into the "irrevocable"' (GEL 6, p. 91). 'She simmers and simmers, despairs and despairs,' wrote Lewes to Blackwood, 'believes she can never do anything again worth doing etc. etc.

A word from you may give her momentary confidence' (GEL 5, p. 11). But then, even head down in the midst of writing, she often did not know quite where she was between Marian Evans and George Eliot, nor if what she was writing was anything more 'in the doing' than something just 'poor and trivial' compared to real life itself. Only afterwards when it was gone from her did it appear at all good and then it seemed 'no longer my own', but as though 'written by someone else'. 'That,' she said, 'is the history of my life' (Cross, 2, pp. 284, 291). This present book seeks at key points to see, as it were, the handwriting behind the print, the simmering still detectable within the irrevocable. Of course, no one can tell precisely what George Eliot was thinking, remembering, changing at any given moment of her writing. But the texts themselves have their hidden clues and prompts, and however approximate the translation of what it is they stand for, they offer an image of the novelist's working mind. The memory of father and brother, the influence of Feuerbach and Spinoza, the jars and excitements of sudden informal realizations: these are also what are involved in art that aims to be more than art for art's sake.

For despite all that effort to be *more* than just plain, struggling, frustrated Mary Ann Evans, what she loved most was that one of her dearest friends—thus proven as such—recognized her, even through the disguise of the male *nom de plume*. Barbara Bodichon had written her on 4 May 1859 to say she had known, with joy, that the novel was hers merely from extracts in reviews. It was to this same Barbara, now married, that Bessie Parkes had written in 1852, in doubt as to whether anything remotely like this great change might ever happen. The discovered novelist replied to Barbara the following day:

> God bless you, dearest Barbara, for your love and sympathy. You are the first friend who has given any symptom of knowing me—the first heart that has recognised me in a book which has come from my heart of hearts....I am a very blessed woman, am I not? to have all this reason for being glad that I have lived, in spite of my sins and sorrows—or rather, by reason of my sins and sorrows.[10]

In reproducing the letter, Cross cut from his biography the reference to 'sins and sorrows', for fear of prurience. Yet it is that shamefaced past, together with the overcoming and transmutation of it, which is part of the story of George Eliot in her heart of hearts. 'In spite of' and yet 'by reason of' too. To try to retell that story is not merely a result of the prurience that Cross understandably feared. But nor is it only to do with George Eliot's own hope that encouragement might be gained from her story. Above all, it comes out of the act of reading the works—in the sense a reader has of the creation of an exceptional person writing these novels and serving as a sustaining presence in them. And for all the achievement and the success, I will want to suggest that the meaning of that person has not yet exhausted its influence nor the larger future life she should have had, and may still have, in the world.

I follow Cross's principle then: use as much as possible her own words; only here, her own words in her fiction as well as in her letters and essays. And that because we cannot know Marian Evans from the inside as she was at the time, but only something of the meaning of her for George Eliot later. This book argues that it took a George Eliot to know Marian Evans and her equivalent strugglers, and it would take a George Eliot to describe and recreate her, as indeed she does in transferred forms. That is why a biography always offers less, second-hand, than the language of the novel in finding out about human beings. Only, this present version of biography seeks to put the novels to use in experimental thinking—to see what person and what purpose these fictions can offer back to life. For she is still unashamedly of use, a help in the dilemmas of meaning and purpose in a secular world.

Hence my other and final emphasis is one that George Eliot was created precisely to make possible: as a presence within the books that sought to take the books out of themselves. It concerns therefore the transference of the life in her works to the life outside them, the transmission to readers and writers of the decades and centuries following—from Edith Simcox and R. H. Hutton to A. S. Byatt and Salley Vickers.

'To see with her eyes', was Edith Simcox's own aspiration, but what the books do is make readers feel as though they are also seen by them. In life, the gaze of George Eliot had been suddenly arresting, as the teacher and writer W. L. Courtney described:

> It was in some senses a disappointing face. It gave the idea of a woman who had passed through so many different phases of experience that there was little or nothing left for her to learn. But her eyes were a different matter. They were wonderful eyes—eyes that now and again seemed to flash a message or analyse a personality. The eyes had something of all that she stood for in the course of her life. However patient the face might look, the eyes were perpetually in activity, keen and eager, though occasionally sorrowful.[11]

There was the unbeautiful face, tired and experienced, unmoved and patient, set in the pose of all-knowing novelist and renowned celebrity; then suddenly her eyes, their shifting light 'convertible into the keenest flash' saw *you* (*Interviews and Recollections*, p. 37). For some, such as Roland Stuart, son of her friend Elma Stuart, it was wonderful: 'she possessed that magnetic power of looking down into your soul and drawing you out and making you speak of yourself—at the same time giving you the impression she was deeply interested in your doings and all that concerned you. I was a mere schoolboy at the time, but I can remember my intense pride in our friendship, and the feeling that one could open one's heart to her and tell her *everything*, being sure of being understood' (*Interviews and Recollections*, p. 166). For others, the soft smiling look in her eyes could suddenly 'turn to mocking', to the cruelty of 'that contemptuous mood' that seemed to come from some 'demon of scornfulness' (*Interviews and Recollections*, p. 231). Edith Simcox wrote of how George Eliot tried to moderate the shifts in herself but even so,

> to love her was a strenuous pleasure, for in spite of the tenderness for all human weakness that was natural to her, and the scrupulous charity of her overt judgments, the fact remained that her natural standard was ruthlessly out of reach, and it was a painful discipline for her friends to feel that she was compelled to lower it to suit their infirmities. The intense humility of her self-appreciation, and the unfeigned readiness with which she would even herself with any sinner who sought her counsel, had the same effect upon those who could compare what she condemned in herself with what she tolerated in them.   (*Nineteenth Century*, p. 785)

The emphatic demand made of *readers* was, nonetheless, for them to raise their natural standard in virtually every respect. Then the text seems to see them as much as they see it: 'In George Eliot, a reader with a conscience may be reminded of the saying that when a man opens Tacitus he puts himself in the confessional.'[12] Throughout this book, but particularly when looking at the novels themselves, I seek to capture moments which are, as I call it, the very biography of the writing itself in the act of communication: that is, moments when a reader can see sudden traces either of deep past experience coalescing behind the creation of a passage or of an immediate nervous life started in the very act of composing it. Then the text seems, as it were, to open its eyes, and the reader can see and feel George Eliot transmitted. This, then, is my attempt both to look through George Eliot's eyes and to show what it is like to be seen by them.

*

Here is the plan, the basic identikit for what follows, in terms of the stages of the life and the corresponding structure of this book.

Who and what was she is my central question. So very conscious of herself and of what people called her and thought of her, she went by many names, changing, it seemed, with each new epoch in her life. Essentially there are five changes.

Born in 1819 at South Farm on the estate of Arbury Hall near Nuneaton, Mary Anne Evans was the third and last child of Robert Evans and Christiana Pearson; Robert had married Christiana in 1813 following the death of his first wife, Harriet, in childbirth in 1809. Two children from that first marriage, Robert and Fanny, had left home early. Robert Evans (1773–1849) was a self-made man, who, like George Eliot's Adam Bede, had risen from the artisan status of a carpenter to become forester, land agent, and steward to Sir Roger Newdigate's Arbury Estate near Nuneaton in Warwickshire. For Mary Anne, there was a pretty older sister, Chrissey, born in

1814, and a brother Isaac, born in 1816. A school notebook from 1834 shows her trying out her newly acquired French, in the large fancy signature of 'Marianne Evans'.

She left school at Christmas 1835 and her mother died of breast cancer on 3 February 1836. Following her elder sister leaving home on her marriage in 1837, she began to act as her father's housekeeper, while still continuing her studies at home. At this decisive point she began to sign herself Mary Ann (without the fussy 'e').

A third epoch comes after another death, that of her beloved father in May 1849, and follows upon her removal to London in 1851 to act as deputy to John Chapman in his editorship of the *Westminster Review*. At that point, in the most painful transition of her life, she called herself Marian.

When, after various unhappy love affairs, she finally met George Henry Lewes, still a married man, and lived with him as his partner from 1854, she insistently became Marian Evans Lewes, Marian Lewes, or even Mrs Lewes. Intimately, Lewes himself called her Polly, a nickname she had first used back in 1838 with her earliest mentor Maria Lewis, the teacher turned friend who was twenty years her senior. This fourth stage was the major period of her life, lasting twenty-five years, when, of course, from 1856 onwards, she also became George Eliot—though in her last work, a book of essays published in 1878, she called herself 'Theophrastus Such'.

Finally, in 1880, desolate after Lewes's death in 1878, she married John Walter Cross, twenty years her junior and later her biographer, for the remaining few months of her life. The gravestone in Highbury cemetery reads: 'Here Lies the Body of "George Eliot", Mary Ann Cross, Born 22 November 1819 Died 22 December 1880'. All these names and the manifestations that go with them, like the changing faces and expressions of the same person, bear what is called in Chapter 1 a 'family likeness'.

Chapters 1–5 depict the movement from Marian Evans to George Eliot. They focus upon the early life, from being the daughter up to joining with Lewes, phases one to three. Through the struggle of immature experience and the need for ideas, these chapters are concerned with what turned out to be her long emotional preparation for life and her apprenticeship in reading and thinking.

Chapters 6–11 are the other way round, George Eliot from Marian Evans, covering the last two stages of her existence in the writing of the novels, but with flashbacks to previous years and reference points. Some passages from the first movement are repeated in the second to show that they are not just one-off quotations but thoughts in the mind of George Eliot that can be brought back, rethought, and used anew in different contexts. These later chapters depict an increasingly *literary* life and result in two different endings—first, in the culminating width and depth of dimension in *Middlemarch*, many novels in one, a whole dense field of ordinary existence; then again, in the extra reach of *Daniel Deronda* as a vision in extraordinary forward search of a future.

But everywhere, within all the chapters, there is overlap and dual motion in the form—movement both forwards and backwards in time, and movement to and fro between the biography and the fiction. I hope this feels like something of what trying to encapsulate a whole life might be like at any specific node of recall. It is at any rate as W. H. Hudson once described it, when viewing 'the entire wide prospect' of his past, set out almost visibly beneath him during the reflective time of serious illness:

> Over it all my eyes could range at will, choosing this or that point to dwell upon, to examine it in all its details; or in the case of some person known to me as a child, to follow his life till it ended or passed from sight; then to return to the same spot again to repeat the process with other lives and resume my rambles in the old familiar haunts.[13]

The author of a web as formally complex as that of *Middlemarch* at least warrants the attempt.

Yet why, finally, a biography at all, and not just a critical analysis of the novels? Because, as she wrote, 'my books are deeply serious things to me, and come out of all the painful discipline, all the most hardly-learnt lessons of my past life' (GEL 3, p. 187). Because the story of Marian Evans becoming George Eliot shows what is at stake in beginning to learn to think, to have to think, to want to think, like a quintessential novelist. And it is a story that goes on not just up to the writing of the novels but repeatedly within them: the story within a story of the transmutation of ordinary sorrow into human achievement. And again: because the novelist's way of thinking, thus learnt through the early struggling ur-versions of itself, is transmittable and transferrable to readers, to those who may not ever become novelists but want to think like them in thinking about real life. Because indeed those novels were never meant to be separate or aesthetically sacrosanct, nor the property of literary academe alone, but to be useful and used. And the way they subterraneously make use of the life of Marian Evans is analogous to the way they usefully summon the hidden lives of their readers also. The two unite in the raw visceral reactions underlying both the writing and the reading of the majestically sophisticated prose: the roars on the other side of silence, the informal human reality on the other side of formal literature.

CHAPTER 1

Family Likenesses, 1819–42

S he began writing *Adam Bede* on 22 October 1857 and had completed chapter 8 by the end of January 1858. One day, sometime in between those dates, she wrote the following, near the beginning of chapter 4:

> Family likeness has often a deep sadness in it. Nature, that great tragic dramatist, knits us together by bone and muscle, and divides us by the subtler web of our brains; blends yearning and repulsion; and ties us by our heartstrings to the beings that jar us at every movement. We hear a voice with the very cadence of our own uttering the thoughts we despise; we see eyes—ah! so like our mother's—averted from us in cold alienation; and our last darling child startles us with the air and gestures of the sister we parted from in bitterness long years ago. The father to whom we owe our best heritage—the mechanical instinct, the keen sensibility to harmony, the unconscious skill of the modelling hand—galls us and puts us to shame by his daily errors; the long-lost mother, whose face we begin to see in the glass as our own wrinkles come, once fretted our young souls with her anxious humours and irrational persistence.

Immediately before this passage, as the prompting occasion for it, is Adam Bede's irritation with his querulous and foolish old mother, to be followed shortly by his impatient disgust with his feeble drunk of a father who leaves work undone for his son to complete. But undoubtedly beneath it, as we shall see, lie raw and painful memories of Mary Anne Evans's own relationships with father and mother, sister and brother, all of whom were lost to her in various ways during the long slow unrecognized struggle to become the author 'George Eliot' at the age of 37. Yet, equally, within itself, true to its author's lifelong passion for intelligence, the paragraph also creates a resonant holding ground for clarifying generalizations—especially those prompted by the underlying structural insights of science, biological and psychological, amidst the dense, painful, and confusing particularities of ordinary existence. So it is that, in the middle of the ordinary personal concerns of the basic nuclear family, the novel suddenly offers nothing less than a genetic blueprint for the unfolding story of the race's evolved amalgam of connections and divisions, generation after generation. Nature's biological drama is that it 'knits *and* divides', 'blends yearning *and* repulsion', '*ties us* by our heartstrings to the beings that *jar us* at every movement'. Voices, eyes, gestures, hands, wrinkles: out of these physical vehicles of memory and kinship come individual words, looks, thoughts, and acts of unkind disinheritance or separation. It does not feel as though sentences should go this way, beginning with 'eyes—ah! So like our mother's', but ending shockingly in 'cold alienation'. Yet painfully they do proceed like this: each clause has a first half of apparently natural piety—'the father to whom we owe our best heritage'—and a second of almost inevitable betrayal—'galls us, and puts us to shame'. Mind and body, parent and child, old inheritance and new individualism, intellect and emotion, sameness and difference, love and criticism, proud progress and painful loyalty; yet, in each case these are not merely *two* separate forces in simple opposition but are feelings still linked together in one sentence, as by the heartstrings.

This tension of complex relationship recorded in multiple dimensions is what first calls 'George Eliot' into being. It makes her the unseen *third* presence, a mental syntax of equivalent heartstrings and brain fibres, an intelligence defined by its almost superhuman capacity to think more than one thing, more than two or three or four things together, at any one time. For what is described in this passage is not only a series of family relationships but also, mapping onto them through all their twists and turns, a way of thinking within the subtler web of the brain. The relationships in the world, the syntax on the page, the pathways of the brain: through all the obstacles and across the differences, all these networks are held analogously together, inside and out, in the great holistic ambition of George Eliot's realist writing.

And as it is with complex sentences unfolding from their beginning through to their end, so it is in the stories: nothing is straightforward. Whilst the family home is being sold up around her, what the young Maggie Tulliver begins to realize in *The Mill on The Floss* (1860) is the shock and the threat that 'the end of our lives will have nothing in it like the beginning' (book 2, chapter 6). There has to be change and there has to be narrative to try to track that change: there is no staying in the first secure places of life and very little simplicity thereafter. So it is by the end of chapter 4 of *Adam Bede*, when, in a major reversal, Adam and his younger brother Seth take home their father, Thias Bede. This time he has not been found drunk but drowned in the dark after drinking:

> The wide-open glazed eyes were grey, like Seth's, and had once looked with mild pride on the boys before whom Thias had lived to hang his head in shame.

Nature's dramatic blueprint has been activated again in those eyes and the associated memories. If a slow reader—the sort George Eliot preferred—had to say where in that sentence George Eliot exists, it would be implicitly in that tiny connective 'before', painfully linking his pride in them at the start with his shame in their eyes near the end. 'The boys before whom Thias had lived to hang his head in shame':

it is a terrible consequence, to live on almost dying with shame. To learn fellow feeling, to read life and interpret people in the book of the world, is a long and hard lesson, George Eliot writes, 'and Adam at present had only learned the alphabet of it in his father's sudden death' (chapter 19). The novelist existed to build up these alphabets, to assemble scripts and codes, putting together the basic words and traits and memories in new combinations of subtle form and language.

It was this passage from *Adam Bede* on family likeness that was one of the extracts quoted in the *Westminster Review* on first publication. The reviewer was John Chapman, an important figure in this story, who described it as a beautiful description of 'the mysterious blending of antagonistic elements in human character'.[1] It was from reading it in this review that Barbara Bodichon recognized the author as her friend, with all that implicit family past massed behind her. To which Marian Lewes replied, as we saw in the Introduction: 'You are the first friend who has given any symptom of knowing me—the first heart that has recognised me in a book which has come from my heart of hearts' (GEL 3, pp. 63–4). That is our first heartfelt flashback: first to the daughter, and then to the sister.

Mother and Father

In this first epoch, she was, above all, her father's daughter, her brother's sister. Something went wrong on the female side of the family.

First: the father, not the mother.

The mother, Christiana, was never well following the birth of Mary Anne, her third child, in 1819, and became worse after the twin sons born to her in 1821 died within ten days. No one will ever be sure how far the mother's troubles were more, or other, than physical.[2] But, as a result it seems, the children were sent away to boarding school, Isaac at 8 to a school in Coventry, Mary Anne joining Chrissey at Miss Lathom's boarding school in nearby Attleborough at the mere age of 5 where she stayed from 1824 till 1827. Philip Wakem in *The Mill on the Floss* never really knew 'that mother's love which flows out to us in a greater abundance because our need is greater, which clings us the more tenderly because we are less likely to be winners in the game of life' (book 5, chapter 3). The 'more' here is something that should meet the 'less' and lovingly compensate it: it is what the daughter always wanted, the greater the need, the greater still was what was offered to it. Yet even when present, her mother was said to be pithily practical-minded and caustically critical, like Mrs Poyser in *Adam Bede* or Mrs Hackit in George Eliot's first short story 'The Sad Fortunes of the Reverend Amos Barton'.

But for all her severity Mrs Evans had been a kind friend to the wife of the local clergyman John Gwyther. And Mrs Hackit—opinionated, sharp-tongued, austere, with a severe liver complaint—was likewise good to Barton's poor sickly wife, Milly, and the children, in particular, the plump 5-year-old boy Dickey who will be left motherless by the end of the story:

> He was a boy whom Mrs Hackit, in a severe mood, had once pronounced 'stocky'...
>
> 'Now *do* you take nourishing things anuff?' was one of Mrs Hackit's first questions, and Milly endeavoured to make it appear that no woman was ever so much in danger of being over-fed and led into self-indulgence as herself...
>
> While this conversation was going forward, Dickey had been furtively stroking and kissing the soft white hand; so that at last, when a pause came, his mother said, smilingly, 'Why are you kissing my hand Dickey?'
>
> 'It id to yovely', answered Dickey, who, you observe, was decidedly backward in his pronunciation.
>
> Mrs Hackit remembered this little scene in after days, and thought with peculiar tenderness and pity of the 'stocky boy'.   (*Scenes of Clerical Life*, 'Amos Barton', chapter 5)

In *George Eliot's Life*, Cross says that it was the boy, Isaac, who could get to his mother's heart; Mary Anne was the father's pet (Cross, 1, p. 17).

Cross writes of George Eliot still recalling to him with pain, after more than fifty-five years, how she had been sent away to boarding-school, into the cold:

> During one of our walks at Witley in 1880, my wife mentioned to me that what chiefly remained in her recollection about this very early school-life was the difficulty of getting near enough the fire in winter, to become thoroughly warmed, owing to the circle of girls forming round too narrow a fireplace. This suffering from cold was the beginning of a low general state of health: also at this time she began to be subject to fears at night—'the susceptibility to terror'—which she has described as haunting Gwendolen Harleth in her childhood. The other girls in the school who were all naturally very much older made a great pet of the child, and used to call her 'little mamma', and she was not unhappy except at nights; but she told me that this liability to have 'all her soul become a quivering fear', which remained with her afterwards, had been one of the supremely important influences dominating at times her future life.
>
> (Cross, 1, pp. 16–17)

What was to become in her a characteristic mix of emotional neediness and unusual intelligence was here, at least in these early schooldays, met with sympathetic response—the older girls, while making a pet of her, at the same time looked up to the seriousness of this little mamma. Yet there still developed some sort of split between her precocious daytime self and the night self of a less clear and solid world—the lifelong concerns about her health being perhaps at this point the only daytime trace of the deep night-time effect. Gwendolen Harleth was a young woman at once far more beautiful and shallow than the girl who became her creator, but as Cross suggests she was similar at least in this: that Gwendolen desperately wanted those sudden intermittent terrors and insecurities from her own childhood onwards to be no part of what was supposed to be her normal character. She only 'unwillingly recognised what' (in a characteristic piece of George Eliot syntax) 'she would have been glad for others to be unaware of'. But when the light changes suddenly, something can happen to the young woman at almost any moment:

> She was ashamed and frightened, as at what might happen again, in remembering her tremor on suddenly feeling herself alone, when, for example, she was walking without companionship and there came some rapid change in the light. Solitude in any wide scene impressed her with an undefined feeling of immeasurable existence aloof from her, in the midst of which she was helplessly incapable of asserting herself.
>
> (*Daniel Deronda*, 1876, chapter 6)

In character and creator across all their differences, it was a dominant weakness, an underlying insecurity which would not simply disappear in future years.

For example, Mary Anne was to write to Maria Lewis (12 August 1841) of a depression she suffered recurrently in her 20s, which has 'made me *alive* to what is certainly a *fact* though my imagination when I am in health is adept at concealing it, that I am *alone* in the world' (GEL 1, p. 102). Or again, to Sara Hennell the freethinking intellectual who was to replace the evangelical Miss Lewis as Miss Evans's best friend (4 June 1848): 'I feel a sort of madness growing upon me—just the opposite of the delirium which makes people fancy that their bodies are filling the room. It seems to me as if I were shrinking into that mathematical abstraction, a point—so entirely am I destitute of contact that I am unconscious of length or breadth' (GEL 1, p. 264).

Yet the need for the reassertion of ego—the defensive re-assumption of intellect in Mary Anne or of beauty in Gwendolen, the exhibition of maturity or talent, the inflation of relative status or size in the world—went almost as deep as the insecurity and depression it sought to combat, and was just as long-established. Sara Hennell recalls a Mrs Shaw seeing Mary Anne at a children's party,

> aged 9 or 10 years old she thinks. M. A. sat apart from the rest, and Mrs Shaw went to her and said, 'My dear, you do not seem happy; are you enjoying yourself?' 'No I am not,' said M. A. 'I don't like to play with children; I like to talk to grown-up people.'
>
> (GEL 1, p. 41)

An early biographer reported that someone who knew her at school at the age of 13 said it was impossible to imagine her as a baby, her features possessing a seriousness of expression startling for her years.[3] Clearly there was something awkwardly unconventional and uncoordinated in a child who, having virtually lost her own mother, was known in the school where she was the youngest pupil as a little mother. In later life she wryly told her stepson Charles Lewes of a tendency begun even before she left home to board: 'when she was only four years old she recollected playing on the piano, of which she did not know one note, in order to impress the servant with a proper notice of her acquirements and generally distinguished position' (Cross, 1, p. 14). At her next school, Miss Wallington's boarding school in Nuneaton which she attended from 1828 to 1832, a visitor took the 13-year-old girl with serious looks to be one of the teachers. Such was her prowess on piano that she was often asked to play for such visitors, though she felt a painful shyness. Afterwards she would rush to her room and, says Cross, 'throw herself on the floor in an agony of tears' (1, p. 26).

This was where George Eliot herself would be needed to understand such a child beneath the level of contradictory appearances: this old/young girl, at times so scornful of other children but also so lonely and envious and vulnerable; shy and yet attention-seeking; ambivalent about her own gifts, needs, and compensations. It was never to be an easily synchronized life. It would take years for her to try to get the balances right, to become the right age for herself.

At any rate, it was Mary Anne's father, not the mother, who came to visit her at school and arranged the weekends and holidays at home. Robert Evans was 46 when she was born, the indulged child of a now mellowed parent in his second marriage following nearly four years a widower. He was known from his youth as a man of great physical strength and honest practical skill, his trustworthy counsel being sought by several local landowners in the valuing of woods, and his sense of justice frequently employed in the arbitration of contentious disputes. He was a conservative man, instinctively taking his religion and politics direct from his betters at Arbury Hall where he acted as estate manager. Born the son of a village carpenter in 1773, he established his own carpentry business and in 1801 had married Harriet Poynton, the servant of a local landowner, Francis Parker, for whom he began to work as estate manager from 1802. Harriet bore him two children but died in childbirth in 1809. Like Adam Bede, Robert had a younger brother, Sam, who had turned Methodist, and Sam's admirable wife Elizabeth was the model for Dinah Morris in *Adam Bede*, save that in that novel she eventually married the older not the younger brother. Robert Evans's own more conventional second wife, Christiana, came of a better family than he, the Pearsons' yeoman stock making them the models for the strict Dodson family in *The Mill on the Floss*. But like Adam Bede and Caleb Garth in *Middlemarch*, it was work—good strong, decent work—that Robert Evans really believed in, as something more than a job to be learnt and paid for. As Caleb says to the young, feckless, and uselessly overeducated Fred Vincy who loves his daughter and wishes to prove his worth:

> A great deal of what I know can only come from experience: you can't learn it off as you learn things out of a book.... You must love your work, and not be always looking over the edge of it, wanting your play to begin.... You must not be ashamed of your

work, and think it would be more honourable to you to be doing something else....
No matter what a man is—I wouldn't give twopence for him...whether he was the
prime minister or the rick-thatcher, if he didn't do well what he undertook to do.

(*Middlemarch*, 1871–2, chapter 56)

The daughter clearly loved that sheer depth in the man, simply expressing an almost
inarticulate religion.

Nonetheless, for all his strength of body and character, reports Cross, Robert
Evans himself suffered from 'a certain self-distrust, owing perhaps to an early
imperfect education, which resulted in a general submissiveness in his domestic
relations' (1, p. 13). He had received a rudimentary education at the local village
school run by Bartle Massey, the name given to the teacher in *Adam Bede*. Outside
the house Robert Evans was known to the tenants to be firm but fair, hard on the
idle and unthrifty, but remarkably gentle towards those who had unluckily fallen on
hard times. As he rode his horse around the neighbourhood in the course of his
work, the father would take Mary Anne along with him, even when she was very
young: the little girl standing between her father's legs, learning the countryside and
its people in all the variety of kind and class. Robert Evans's position as middleman
between the local nobility and the common tenants meant he—and his daughter
after him—was not 'shut out from the large sympathetic knowledge of human
experience which comes from contact with various classes on their own level'
(*Impressions of Theophrastus Such*, 1879, chapter 2, 'Looking Backward').

Cross at one point imagines her at home with a father 'already very proud of the
astonishing and growing intelligence of his little girl', not least because of Evans's
sense of his own educational deficiencies:

> The powerful middle-aged man with the strongly-marked features sits in his deep
> leather-covered arm-chair, at the right-hand corner of the ruddy fireplace, with the
> head of 'the little wench' between his knees. The child turns over the book with pictures
> that she wishes her father to explain to her—or that perhaps she prefers explaining to
> him. Her rebellious hair is all over her eyes, much vexing the pale, energetic mother
> who sits on the opposite side of the fire... (Cross, 1, pp. 17–18)

It feels like a memory, with clear emotional alignments in this family. Yet for all the
clever forwardness devoted to the father, Cross reports that Mary Anne had been a
slow starter in learning to read—partly because, as her brother said, she preferred to
play, but also added Cross, because 'hers was a large, slow-growing nature' (1, p. 15).
Even so, by the time, aged 9, that she had moved to Mrs Wallington's boarding
school at Nuneaton, books had become 'a passion with the child: she read everything she could lay hands on'—though at home 'greatly troubling the soul of her
mother by the consumption of candles as well as of eyesight in her bedroom'

GEORGE ELIOT'S SCHOOLROOM, NUNEATON.

Fig. 1. Elms Schoolroom: Miss Wallington's school in Nuneaton (courtesy of Nuneaton Library).

(Cross, 1, p. 21). She was also given the run of the extensive library at Arbury Hall, from 1806 the home of her father's employer, now (by inheritance) Francis Parker Newdigate.

Her schoolfellows admired her academic mastery as the clever girl in the school, though she would barely join in games and sports. The default stance of her proud yet vulnerable diffidence vanished whenever she stood up in class. Suddenly she would become very excited and animated, an irresistible state which, it was said, 'found further vent in nervous movements of her hands'.[4]

It was at Mrs Wallington's, characteristically, that Maria Lewis, the devoutly pious teacher-governess who was nearly twenty years her elder, became Mary Anne's friend, rather than her schoolfellows. Looking back at 20 at the height of her puritanical fervour, Mary Anne told Miss Lewis that her childhood reading of fiction had made her romantically dissatisfied with the world around her, living in a world of her own creation. She would carry to the grave, she feared, the 'mental diseases' with which novels had 'contaminated' her: 'We cannot help being modified by the ideas that pass through our minds' (GEL 1, pp. 22–3). But for all that early evangelicalism, whilst the rest of the girls at Mrs Wallington's threw themselves into prayer meetings, she held herself back from the group fervour, even while at the same time reproaching herself for 'her coldness and inability to be carried away with the same enthusiasm as others'.[5]

By 1832 and until 1835 she was boarding at a Coventry school run by the sisters Mary and Rebecca Franklin. They removed what remained of their pupil's broad

Midland dialect and accent. Rebecca, training her in musical tones and careful syntax, instilled in Mary Anne the habit of giving a finished completeness to all her sentences. Again she impressed her schoolfellows with her abilities, as they competed to carry her books, but it is a little image of what lay beneath and within her formal academic superiority that one day an admiring girl, borrowing her German dictionary, was surprised to find within its covers on a blank page secret verses that yearned for sympathy and love.[6] However much Mary Anne impressed others with the toughness of her intellect, this was a girl who back at home in the holidays vexed her mother with her untidy hair and her continual reading, and at school hardly knew what to do with her troublesome emotions except impress her fellows and seek out her teachers. There were frequent relapses into violent tears alone and in secret.

*

'It is invariably the case,' George Eliot writes warningly to her publisher John Blackwood, 28 May 1858,

> that when people discover certain points of coincidence in a fiction with facts that happen to have come to their knowledge, they believe themselves able to furnish a key to the whole. That is amusing enough to the author, who knows from what widely sundered portions of experience—from what a combination of subtle shadowy suggestions with certain actual objects and events, his story has been formed.
>
> (GEL 2, p. 459)

It is a warning, but between the life and the work there is itself a 'family likeness'. It is not that, even in the most autobiographical of the novels, *The Mill on the Floss* (1860), Mr and Mrs Tulliver are the actual Mr and Mrs Evans. The argument is, rather, that the reader can imagine George Eliot writing the following—a combination of shadows and actualities—with something of the kindred memories discussed earlier in this chapter, but more than we can ever know. The mother, here nothing like as sharp as Mrs Evans, does still say this:

> 'You talk of 'cuteness, Mr Tulliver,' she observed as she sat down, 'but I'm sure the child's half an idiot i'some things, for if I send her up-stairs to fetch anything she forgets what she's gone for, and perhaps 'ull sit down on the floor i' the sunshine an' plait her hair an' sing to herself like a Bedlam creatur', all the while I'm waiting for her down-stairs.' (*The Mill on the Floss*, book 1, chapter 2)

The real-life daughter knew she was dreamy. Of the romances and novels she had read at the Miss Franklins she had written to her earlier teacher, Miss Lewis, 'When I was quite a little child I could not be satisfied with the things around me; I was constantly living in a world of my own creation, and was quite contented to have no companions that I might be left to my own musings and imagine scenes in which I was chief actress.' Unrealistic novels offered ideal fantasy material 'for building my castles in the air' (GEL 1, pp. 22–3).

But in those early chapters of George Eliot's own realist novel, what matters most to the dreamy vulnerable girl, hiding from harshness, is that the father takes a more understanding line than the mother, speaking as proudly as any Robert Evans of his daughter's intelligence. Intending to seek a neighbour's advice on where best to send his son Tom for his education, Mr Tulliver finds his thoughts instinctively turning to Maggie again instead, twice as clever as her older brother:

> 'And you should hear her read—straight off, as if she knowed it all beforehand. An' allays at her book! But it's bad—it's bad,' Mr Tulliver added, sadly, checking this blameable exultation, 'a woman's no business wi' being so clever; it'll turn to trouble, I doubt. But bless you!'—here the exultation was clearly recovering the mastery –'she'll read the books and understand 'em, better nor half the folks as are growed up.'
>
> (*The Mill on the Floss*, chapter 3)

These are the sudden emotional alternations and transitions of a man whose feelings do not always fit within the general conservative principles that are his set framework. The very shapes and frames that allow for thinking, or rigidify it, were to become vital to George Eliot.

But here, in this moment, clever young Maggie anxiously asks this neighbour how far away Tom will have to go for his schooling—only to receive the patronizing reply that adults too often provide. It's a long way off, he airily replies: Maggie must borrow the seven-leagued magic boots of commonplace childish folklore to get to him. 'That's nonsense!' said Maggie,

> tossing her head haughtily and turning away with the tears springing in her eyes. She began to dislike Mr Riley: it was evident he thought her silly and of no consequence.
>
> 'Hush, Maggie, for shame of you, asking questions and chattering,' said her mother. 'Come and sit down on your little stool and hold your tongue, do. But,' added Mrs Tulliver, who had her own alarm awakened, 'is it so far off as I couldn't wash him and mend him?'   (*The Mill on the Floss*, chapter 3)

Stories of magic boots! she scoffs, in this context at least no longer interested in building castles. For this is where she is not merely the naughty show-off girl her mother thinks her to be, but speaks from a serious adult potential within her, not taken seriously outside, and reduced accordingly to painfully childish tears. It is one of those unforgettably primal, wounding moments that *The Mill on the Floss* can summon, for it is a novel full of formulations such as 'it was the first time'. 'For the first time in his life [Tom] had a painful sense that he was all wrong somehow' (book 1, chapter 9), 'For the first time Tom thought of his father with some reproach' (book 3, chapter 5), 'for the first time [Maggie] saw the possibility of shifting the position from which she looked at the gratification of her own desires' (book 4, chapter 3). It is the experience of such seemingly first times that etch a difference in the memory that created George Eliot.

But there were also repeated times, reassuring occasions that seemed to guarantee some underlying security after all. A year or so further on, it is still the father who understands Maggie, as no one else does, because of his love. In an impetuous fit of anger, Maggie cuts off that troublesome and much-criticized hair of hers, to the amusement of her brother and the horror of the mother and the assembled Dodson aunts:

> 'She's a naughty child, as 'll break her mother's heart,' said Mrs Tulliver, with tears in her eyes.
> Maggie seemed to be listening to a chorus of reproach and derision.... Her feeble power of defiance left her in an instant, her heart swelled, and getting up from her chair, she ran to her father, hid her face on his shoulder and burst out into loud sobbing.
> 'Come, come my wench,' said her father soothingly putting his arms round her, 'never mind. You was i' the right to cut it off if it plagued you. Give over crying: father'll take your part.'
> Delicious words of tenderness! Maggie never forgot any of these moments when he father 'took her part': she kept them in her heart and thought of them long years after, when every one said that her father had done very ill by his children.
> *(The Mill on the Floss*, book 1, chapter 7)

It was her father who was always the model for 'taking her part', speaking out on behalf of the little wench, again in tears, in the face of harsh interpretations. Maggie needed him to save her, and, whatever she became, Mary Anne Evans, likewise, always needed some alternative loving context of comfort and backing. But finally, through writing rather than speaking, it was George Eliot who in every sense *took the part* of those imagined lonely humans called her characters. 'For my part I am very sorry for him', she writes of the sorriest creature in *Middlemarch* (chapter 29).

It is as though, impossibly of course, Maggie Tulliver in growing seeks that George Eliot, and needs the sort of books she wrote, the sort of person she became. At 16 she is thinking she can no longer be content with Scott's novels or Byron's poems: 'She could make dream-worlds of her own—but no dream world would satisfy her now. She wanted some explanation of this hard, real life ... some key that would enable her to understand and, in understanding, endure' (*The Mill on the Floss*, book 4, chapter 3). But for the girl who actually became George Eliot, the turn away from emotional literature and from what it might stand for took an even more extreme form. She had already been influenced by the puritanical Maria Lewis. Now also encouraged by Martha Jackson, her schoolmate at the Miss Franklins, Mary Anne in her teenage years tried countering the power of her feelings and her insecurities by putting them into the narrow strictness of the evangelical revival of fundamentalist principles of sixteenth-century puritanism. With its hard stress on the total depravity of human nature and the corruption of all its works, its belief in the absolute primacy of the Bible, and its insistence on justification by faith in Christ's cross and God's grace alone, evangelicalism demanded the intense inner seriousness of individual self-scrutiny. It even made Mary Anne worry about being moved by religious music lest the devout feeling be due more to the power of the music than the religion. For all her eventual break with evangelicalism in Mary Anne's renewed and growing need for education and culture, the puritan tradition left in the woman who became George Eliot, even after her movement away from Christianity itself in 1841, a residual fear of the compensation she also wanted: namely, that art might be no more than a flawed replacement for the religion she could no longer believe in; that all too easily it could become frivolous and false, unadult and unreal, and even in attempted realism, a waste of precious time and an abuse of imagination. There remained in George Eliot a suspicious hatred of any form of compensatory secondariness or surrogacy; an ethical concern that however well they served her, education and art might still become substitutes for reality. Hence the anxiety there was always to be not only about her writing but within it— the authorial voice apparently intervening for control, the disciplining of fantasy, the self-checking moral concern, the quest to understand the place of imagination or vision within the work in literary realism.

So it is that in the tensely hidden autobiography of writing, George Eliot could feel what it was that Mary Anne Evans never had, which Maggie experiences with sudden surprise in the very midst of her later sexual disgrace.

Her father dead, her own brother turns on Maggie in bitter blame, even as George Eliot sees the differences unrecognizable to those in the midst of the experience:

> Maggie was half stunned: too heavily pressed upon by her anguish even to discern any difference between her actual guilt and her brother's accusations—still less to vindicate herself.
>
> 'Tom,' she said, crushing her hands together under her cloak, in the effort to speak again—'Whatever I have done—I repent it bitterly—I want to make amends—I will endure anything—I want to be kept from doing wrong again.'
>
> 'What will keep you?' said Tom, with cruel bitterness. 'Not religion—not your natural feelings of gratitude and honour. And he—he would deserve to be shot, if it were not—But you are ten times worse than he is. I loathe your character and your conduct. You struggled with your feelings, you say. Yes! I have had feelings to struggle

with; but I conquered them. I have had a harder life than you have had; but I have found *my* comfort in doing my duty. But I will sanction no such character as yours; the world shall know that *I* feel the difference between right and wrong. If you are in want, I will provide for you; let my mother know. But you shall not come under my roof. It is enough that I have to bear the thought of your disgrace; the sight of you is hateful to me.' (*The Mill on the Floss*, book 7, chapter 1)

No one to take her part now: 'Slowly Maggie was turning away with despair in her heart.' No loving voice or tone, no mitigation offers nuances to that absolutely stark and literal 'difference between right and wrong'. The brother's usual mode of reviewing his past actions was 'I'd do just the same again'; but Maggie 'was always wishing she had done something different' (book 1, chapter 6). Morality for her always seems to be what arrives second, after the mistake, in the disorienting mismatch between present naïve spontaneity and a painful retrospective realization. As she wrote these sentences of imagined disgrace near the end of 1859, Marian Evans knew all too well how her brother Isaac had disowned her when she took George Henry Lewes, a married man, to be her partner in 1854. Yet the union saved her life and gave her the support she had never had since the death of her father—support sufficient finally to enable her to become the author of novels such as this, even now, as she writes *The Mill on the Floss*.

But suddenly in this novel, even as Tom completes his condemnation and the sister takes herself off, there comes an instinctive cry from another voice, quite unexpectedly:

'My child! I'll go with you. You've got a mother.'

It never happened outside the fiction. Was this fantasy and compensation, as arguably it is at the tumultuous end of the novel when brother and sister are finally reconciled only in drowning together, arms round each other, in the great flood? She wanted to rescue Tom, as Isaac had never rescued his sister. Yet here it is also close to the moral axiom so often implicitly at work in the novels: if there is no one else to do what is right, then someone, however unlikely, must be the one who, by seeing the necessity of right, stands in to do it. And if indeed there is no one at all, then at another level there has to be the life transferred to George Eliot instead. Here though there is indeed Mrs Tulliver, as later in his own disgrace Bulstrode finds his unremarkable wife suddenly making herself remarkably heroic.

'You've got a mother.' Those words for the woman writing them spoke for the great missing type, the relationship that within the biological-emotional nexus of family likeness and family kindness was never fully realized. This is not the fantasy of an ideal mother: Mrs Tulliver is a stupid woman. But it is Mrs Tulliver, not George Eliot, who for once *makes* herself a mother, in taking her daughter's part.

Throughout her life, especially after the death of her father, as we shall see in Chapter 2, Mary Ann and Marian kept turning to women who would behave maternally towards her. But in *Adam Bede* there is another key maternal moment in a novel when that tough and upright young carpenter, modelled on the early life of her own father, relents towards the young woman who has deserted him. In the courtroom he can hardly bring himself to see Hetty standing there wretchedly guilty:

> Why did they say she was so changed? In the corpse we love, it is the *likeness* we see—it is the likeness, which makes itself felt the more keenly because something else *was* and *is not*. There they were—the sweet face and neck, with the dark tendrils of hair, the long dark lashes, the rounded cheek and the pouting lips: pale and thin—yes—but like Hetty, and only Hetty. Others thought she looked as if some demon had cast a blight upon her, withered up the woman's soul in her, and left only a hard despairing obstinacy. But the mother's yearning, the completest type of the life in another life which is the essence of real human love, feels the presence of the cherished child even in the debased, degraded man; and to Adam, this pale, hard-looking culprit was the Hetty who had smiled at him in the garden under the apple-tree boughs—she was that Hetty's corpse, which he had trembled to look at the first time, and then was unwilling to turn his eyes from.
>
> (*Adam Bede*, chapter 43)

What is extraordinary here is that it is like a *mother's* love—not, as in chapter 4, 'eyes so like our mother's averted from us in the cold alienation of a brother or sister'; but a seeing of the innocent child still in the debased adult, accentuating not the later differences but the underlying continuity of likeness. Modelled on her own father, the most masculine of George Eliot's protagonists, who has felt himself so sexually drawn to Hetty and so sexually betrayed by her, now feels as a mother to the young woman. It is the completest *type* of love, imaginably transferable even across gender, transferable like everything that is most human in the world of George Eliot. It is Silas Marner, after all, who turns out to be the tenderest mother in the whole of the works. The author knew 'from what widely sundered portions of experience—from what a combination of subtle shadowy suggestions with certain actual objects and events [her] story has been formed'.

Sister and Brother

'What widely sundered portions of experience.' It is in the life that so much of the sundering took place. If it was always the father and not the mother, it was equally the brother not the sister.

She never turned to Chrissey, the older sister. Chrissey had never been truly present as far as Mary Anne was concerned. Cross says she was something of the model for the tidy, pretty, conforming little Lucy Deane in *The Mill on the Floss* and that, in the blending of things, the relationship between her and the younger sister was rather like that between the conventional Celia and the earnest Dorothea in *Middlemarch*.

Chrissey was no candidate for second mother. She left home to marry a general practitioner, Dr Edward Clarke, in 1837, by whom she bore nine babies. Poor Clarke never made much money. Like a good father, Robert Evans bought a small house for them in Attleborough in Nuneaton. But, when Evans died in 1849, the house was passed onto Isaac as head of the family. He let them live on there rent-free, but it was a family now dependent on his rather tough and unforgiving help. After Edward Clarke's death in 1852—his wife left with six surviving children—Isaac characteristically took responsibility for Chrissey, keeping her finances strictly under his own control. As soon as she learnt of Clarke's death, Marian (as she had then become) travelled to Attleborough from London, leaving behind her work on the *Westminster Review* but actually staying for only a week. She wrote to her Coventry friends, the sisters Caroline Bray and Sara Hennell, on her return to London, 31 December 1852:

> I arrived here only yesterday. I had agreed with Chrissey that, all things considered, it was wiser for me to return to town—that I could do her no substantial good by staying another week, while I should be losing time as to other matters. Isaac, however, was very indignant to find that I had arranged to leave without consulting him and thereupon flew into a violent passion with me, winding up by saying that he desired I would never 'apply to him for anything whatever'—which, seeing that I never have done so, was almost as superfluous as if I had said I would never receive a kindness from him.   (GEL 2, p. 75)

As if he had ever recently offered her a kindness—she (you can almost hear Isaac saying) who was leaving her family for her literary friends back in London. She was no longer the 'little mamma'. On 16 April 1853 she wrote again to Caroline ('Cara') Bray:

> My chief trouble is poor Chrissey. Think of her in that ugly small house with six children who are inevitably made naughty by being thrown close together from morning till night. To live with her in that hideous neighbourhood amongst ignorant bigots is impossible to me. It would be moral asphyxia...   (GEL 2, p. 97)

'I dare not incur the *material* responsibility of taking her away from Isaac's house,' she goes on guiltily, fearing that her health might fail in the financial effort, that Chrissey might come to regret the move, or almost anything in anxious extenuation:

Yet how odious it seems that I, who preach self-devotion, should make myself comfortable here while there is a whole family to whom, by renunciation of my egotism, I could give almost everything they want. And the work I can do in other directions is so trivial! (GEL 2, p. 97)

She can't go back to 'that hideous neighbourhood amongst ignorant bigots' but she won't bring Chrissey to London either, and yet still keeps thinking in her comfort 'here' of that family 'there'. What she did was regularly send Chrissey extra money from London. By associating Chrissey in her mind with the two sisters Sara Hennell and Cara Bray, she was able to think of the three of them together as the three women tied to her heart by a cord that could not be broken.

Yet within a year she had joined herself to George Henry Lewes, and had written to her brother and sister to tell them so. Chrissey wrote back only to break off all correspondence at her brother's insistence. Only as Chrissey lay dying in February 1859 did Marian hear from her again, as she related to Cara:

I have just had a letter from my Sister Chrissey—ill in bed—consumptive—regretting that she ever ceased to write to me. It has ploughed up my heart. (GEL 3, p. 23)

Fig. 2. The Landscape, 'mother-tongue of our imagination': Griff Hollows (the Red Deeps of *The Mill on the Floss*) (courtesy of Nuneaton Library).

'Ploughed up my heart' is unusually powerful. Set in Griff House, the farmhouse on the road to Coventry, it had been a country childhood in what to an outsider was nonetheless plain, flat, unremarkable middle England. But 'these familiar flowers, these well-remembered bird-notes, this sky with its fitful brightness, these furrowed and grassy fields, each with a sort of personality given to it by the capricious hedgerows—such things as these are the mother-tongue of our imagination, the language that is laden with all the subtle inextricable associations the fleeting hours of our childhood left behind them' (*The Mill on the Floss*, book 1 chapter 5). The ploughing of the heart comes out of that mother tongue. At this point, Marian decided to go at once to Attleborough again. But Chrissey's daughter wrote to say that her mother was afraid that a reunion would be too much for her. Marian didn't attend the funeral.

*

If Chrissey could never have taken the place of a mother, it was Isaac who, as with the father, was the alternative love. It was the same Isaac who appears in later life so self-righteous and narrow-minded in ways that were not only wounding to the sister but the very converse of what, in the name of sympathy and imagination, becoming a novelist meant to her. In the fiction, equivalently, Maggie as a young woman turns on Tom:

> You have been reproaching other people all your life—you have always been sure you yourself are right: it is because you have not a mind large enough to see that there is anything better than your own conduct and your own petty aims....I know I've been wrong—often, continually. But yet, sometimes when I have done wrong, it has been because I have feelings that you would be the better for if you had them.
>
> (*The Mill on the Floss*, book 5, chapter 5)

She (the combination of Mary Ann and Maggie) was the clever one—Tom knew it, Isaac knew it; but it made her think thoughts that removed clear and easy certainties, just as her emotional neediness left her as impulsively precipitant and overcommitted as someone far less intelligent might be. Intelligence was very important to her pride and her identity, but at another level it did nothing at all, only made things worse. Nothing was co-ordinated or synchronized in the young women who were Mary Ann Evans or Maggie Tulliver. No wonder Miss Evans, in the uncertainties of the mid-1850s, was briefly interested in phrenology, the pseudo-science of interpreting bumps on the cranium as signs of psychological make-up: anything that could plausibly enable her to map and integrate her almost independently powerful or conflicting faculties was of vital concern. 'I never believed more profoundly than I do now,' she wrote 16 July 1855, 'that character is based on organization' (GEL 2, p. 210). But the relationships in her own head had to work with the tangled relations outside.

In terms of early stimulation, it was the youthful relationship with the brother which was a formative centre of her emotional life until both were sent away to school in 1824. Through and despite everything that followed, even in anger and sadness and loss, it remained an unshakeable presence. She loved Isaac and admired that determined integrity and single-minded certainty at the core of him even when it seemed to come out as unfeeling hardness. She remained loyal to the primary memory of him, as to 'the mother-tongue' of her imagination, even when they had parted over what, in conventional terms, was her irregular union with Lewes. In 1869 she was to write a sonnet sequence essentially for the lost Isaac. In variation upon the sonneteer's ancient tradition of lover addressing beloved, they were love poems to her brother and to the shared rural Eden of provincial childhood:

> Thus rambling we were schooled in deepest lore,
> And learned the meanings that give words a soul,
> The fear, the love, the primal passionate store
> Whose shaping impulses make manhood whole.
> ('Brother and Sister', 5)

Even the brown canal seemed 'endless to her thought' ('Brother and Sister', 6).

Griff House was the centre of their unspectacular world, half-manor house, half-farm, opening onto long flat vistas of fields and hedgerows, and yet with the mining village of Bedworth nearby. The great event twice a day was the passing of a stagecoach, from Birmingham in the morning, from Stamford in the afternoon. Her roots, says Cross, were 'in the pre-railroad, pre-telegraphic period—the days of fine old leisure' but at the dawn of 'extraordinary activity in scientific and mechanical discovery' (Cross, 1, p. 10). This was in every sense the Midlands—in the mingling of classes, and in the ever-increasing shift from one phase of English life to another. 'Looking Backward', to quote from a late essay of that title, she still saw what she significantly called a 'family likeness' between that old England and the England of rail and steam and mill:

> Is there any country which shows at once as much stability and as much susceptibility to change as ours? Our national life is like that scenery which I early learned to love, not subject to great convulsions, but easily showing more or less delicate (sometimes melancholy) effects from minor changes. Hence our midland plains have never lost their familiar expression and conservative spirit for me; yet at every other mile, since I first looked at them, some sign of world-wide change, some new direction of human labour has wrought itself into what one may call the speech of the landscape.
> (*Impressions of Theophrastus Such*, chapter 2)

In the great regions of the earth, amidst the indifferent mountains or in the vast deserts, the specks of human change counted for little. But in the flat small-scale provincial landscape, those changes were part of a language even the children could make out. It was a landscape connected to their father, himself a stubborn conservative spirit, temperamentally resistant to innovation and dissent, in a way that Isaac would inherit. But 'the circumstance of my rearing', she wrote in the person of the ageing bachelor Theophrastus Such in 'Looking Backward', 'has at least delivered me from certain mistakes of classification which I observe in many of my superiors': it was those cosmopolitan superiors who would dismiss her father as a mere provincial type of the past because they had 'no affectionate memories of a goodness mingled with what they now regard as outworn prejudices'. What George Eliot loved was the rich intermixture of stability and change, the hidden relation of smallness and significance, the inseparability of goodness from the imperfection out of which it arose. Again, it made for a genuinely human language of feeling, not a mere system of separate abstract classification.

At the heart of this primal language, embedded in what George Eliot was to think of as the brain's very fibres, was a sense of an interrelated sameness and difference, prior to any of the conflicts that came later. 'We had the self-same world enlarged for each / By loving difference of girl and boy', she writes ('Brother and Sister', 9). For once gender seemed complementary rather than disabling. What they were each to other she called remarkably, 'a Like unlike', created from within that subtle web of family likenesses. These *experiences* were her mother, not the person herself, though the type image, and the need for it remained.

She changed Isaac into Tom and moved out of this Eden into the later years of growth and separation, only for E. S. Dallas, reviewing *The Mill on the Floss* in *The Times*, to lump the portrait of the brother together with the rest of the Dodson family on the mother's side: Dallas saw it as one clear depiction of small-minded, self-satisfied provincial meanness. Always thin-skinned in the face of misinterpretation and criticism, George Eliot protested to her publishers that 'Tom is painted with as much love and pity as Maggie' (GEL 3, p. 299). The reviewer in *Macmillan's Magazine* spoke of the author's 'evident yearning over Maggie and disdain for Tom', but claimed Tom's to be in his view the finer character—to which George Eliot responded:

> Pray notice how my critic attributes to me a disdain for Tom: as if it were not *my* respect for Tom which infused itself into my reader—as if he could have respected Tom, if I had not painted him with respect; the exhibition of the *right* on both sides being the very soul of my intention in the story.   (GEL 3, p. 397)

Right on *both* sides, and even right within the *wrong* ('sometimes when I have done wrong, it has been because I have feelings that you would be the better for'). Both of these complications required a novelist, a third presence at the apex of the relationship between two, especially when one was a version of herself. George Eliot knew that within every story there were simultaneously other stories, the story of Tom saying from his own equivalently troubled centre: 'You struggled with your feelings, you say. Yes! *I* have had feelings to struggle with; but I conquered them. I have had a harder life than you have had; but I have found *my* comfort in doing my duty.' He was a man, with a clear purpose and a definite role in the world. And she? Maggie always had an awe of him, against which she struggled uselessly, says George Eliot, 'as something unfair to her consciousness of wider thoughts and deeper motives':

> A character at unity with itself—that performs what it intends, subdues every coun-teracting impulse and has no visions beyond the distinctly possible, is strong by its very negations. (*The Mill on the Floss*, book 5, chapter 2)

And that was the paradox—that she could appreciate him as he could not appre-ciate her, precisely because of what made her at once better and worse than he. He does not know what he has not got; she does know, and knows it not only about him but about herself. He would always do the same again, where Maggie was always thinking she could have acted differently. But she was also afraid of her brother, not merely in the obvious sense, but with that vulnerable fear described in Maggie Tulliver 'when we love one who is inexorable, unbending, unmodifiable—with a mind that we can never mould ourselves upon, and yet that we can never endure to alienate from us' (book 7, chapter 1). That again is the writerly syntax of complex relationship—'never mould upon ... and yet ... never endure to alienate'—with the barriers included within the connections.

And again, only becoming the novelist could transcend the hurt sense of complex unfairness—recreating through her sympathetic imagination a character in Tom who would not value the qualities that comprehended him. Then she who was not a character at unity with herself could become a writer who, even so, could do right by both sides.

But to George Eliot, looking back to the earliest beginnings, there had not initially been 'two sides' in the early childhood of Mary Anne and Isaac Evans. Before the fall into divisions, it had been that 'Like unlike'. As ever, the time sequence is compli-cated. Published in 1874 but contemplated since 1869, the 'Brother and Sister' sonnet sequence is a revision of *The Mill on the Floss* which was published fourteen years earlier. As such, it returns to the early days on which the novel was founded, to rescue again the memory of that prior reality which had been lost and buried in the course of the subsequent story.

It is in the poetry, for example, that there is a better memory of 'our mother' precisely through being able to use the word 'our' at this early stage. Characteristic-ally, the mother tells the two little ones to keep to trodden paths: 'the benediction of her gaze/Clung to us lessening' as they go off into the distance ('Brother and Sister', 3).

As they walk on together, the brother, older by three years, begins to take the lead, especially in the masculine arts and sports. There was the picking of fruit, the naming of the creatures, and, above all, the catching of fish: 'One day my brother left me in high charge / To mind the rod, while he went seeking bait.' It was just a little brown canal on flat provincial land but to her it had seemed endless, a place on the banks for dreamy peace. She, no more than 4 years old, was meant to watch for passing barges and pull in the line: 'Proud of the task, I watched with all my might' adding—'For one whole minute', and then her eyes grew wide:

> Till sky and earth took on a strange new light
> And seemed a dream-world floating on some tide—
> A fair pavilioned boat for me alone
> Bearing me onward through the vast unknown.
>
> ('Brother and Sister', 7)

In its sense of a universe, in sudden interchange between bank and boat dissolving all familiar boundaries, this is like a little touch of Wordsworth even in an ordinary local spot just outside Nuneaton.

But suddenly a barge appears, threatening to snap the line, certainly snapping her out of her dreaminess as 'nearer and angrier came my brother's cry / And all my soul was quivering fear'. Abruptly she pulls in the line—and at the end of it, for a wonder, is a silver perch: 'My guilt that won the prey / Now turned to merit'. She can hardly believe her good fortune, escaping the charge of mere dreaminess:

> When all at home were told the wondrous feat,
> And how the little sister has fished well,
> In secret, though my fortune tasted sweet,
> I wondered why this happiness befell.
>
> (Brother and Sister', 8)

'"The little lass had luck," the gardener said.' In *The Mill on the Floss*, Maggie does the opposite: lets a barge break the line; forgets to look after Tom's rabbits after he goes away to school so that they are dead on his return; without thinking eats the larger half of the jam puff Tom offers her, hoping she wouldn't take it. Too late, 'she would have given the world not to have eaten all her puff, and to have saved some of it for Tom' (book 1, chapter 6). I forgot, I never thought, I didn't mean: these are the remarks of an innocent found thoughtless and made guilty, as if expected to be in a second maturer phase of being whilst still in the dreamily undifferentiated first. For realization comes in the second place: that painfully belated consciousness is like the signal of her being a separate person and a flawed one, almost despite herself. As in the cutting off of her own hair, 'she could see clearly enough now the

31

thing was done that it was very foolish' (book 1, chapter 7). A tiny thing but it was probably the publishing house that inserted the commas after 'enough' and 'done' in the final edition: originally in the manuscript George Eliot didn't have 'now the thing was done' separated off, for the whole realization comes in a confused rush, an unsynchronized fluidity in the midst of what is at once both immediate experience and belated retrospect.[7] No wonder then that the 'secret' thought in 'Brother and Sister' is how close a successful result is to a failed one.

She did not break the line, in fact she caught a fish. The dreamy baffled girl knows in her heart of hearts that she does not deserve the praise, but would not deserve the blame. If it is not a matter of just deserts, if it is not guaranteed by morality, then is what comes about no more than a shock of luck, good or bad? Nothing seems to be straightforward, from inner intention to external outcome, though Tom (that 'character at unity with itself—that performs what it intends') would say it should be. He taught her the world of practical reality, leaving the play of dreams and dolls for the demonstrable calculation involved in marbles and humming tops—the accurate skill:

> That seeks with deeds to grave a thought-tacked line
> And by 'What is', 'What will be' to define.
> ('Brother and Sister', 10)

But she did not really know how one thing led to another. At times she barely knew that there was a difference between her, within, and the world outside; but when she does find it, she does not understand the relation.

Nor will she ever quite understand how the past turned into that future of itself we call the present. It is only in poem 9 of the eleven-poem sequence that we learn that something went wrong later between brother and sister. In the early days, in acts of minor risk, the presence of the little girl made the brother think more carefully: 'This thing I like my sister may not do, / For she is little and I must be kind'. Looking back, the writer can see how this responsibility was good for the boy:

> Thus boyish Will the nobler mastery learned
> Where inward vision over impulse reigns,
> Widening its life with separate life discerned,
> A Like unlike, a Self that self restrains.
>
> His years with others must the sweeter be
> For those brief days he spent in loving me.
> ('Brother and Sister', 9)

'With others' at some other time and in some other place, the better because of their past relationship, but never now 'with her', ironically. She writes this almost despite herself, despite the future that was to part them. 'I must be kind' was what Isaac had had to think.

But Isaac was not kind after she finally found the courage to write to him on 26 May 1857 of her alliance with Lewes, a married man with whom she had gone away to Germany in July 1854:

My dear Brother,
   You will be surprised, I dare say, but I hope not sorry, to learn that I have changed my name, and have someone to take care of me in the world.   (GEL 2, p. 331)

He replied through the family solicitor, Vincent Holbeche, on 9 June, who speaks of the brother being hurt at her not having discussed this with him earlier: 'Permit me to ask when and where you were married and what is the occupation of Mr. Lewes' (GEL 2, p. 346). Lewes could never marry her because he had condoned his wife's adultery, accepting her children by another man as his own. She replied on 13 June:

My brother has judged wisely in begging you to communicate with me. If his feelings towards me are unfriendly, there is no necessity for his paining himself by any direct intercourse with me; indeed, if he had written to me in a tone which I could not recognise (since I am not conscious of having done him any injury) I must myself have employed a third person as a correspondent.
   Mr. Lewes is a well-known writer, author among other things, of the 'Life of Goethe' and the Biographical History of Philosophy. Our marriage is not a legal one, though it is regarded by us both as a sacred bond. He is at present unable to contract a legal marriage, because, though long deprived of his first wife by her misconduct, he is not legally divorced.
   I have been his wife and have borne his name for nearly three years; a fact which has been known to all my personal friends except the members of my own family, from whom I have withheld it because, knowing that their views of life differ in many respect from my own, I wished not to give them unnecessary pain.   (GEL 2, p. 349)

She signed herself Marian Lewes.

There was no hope for anything different from Isaac, a conventional man. She wrote Sara Hennell that she had 'learned to see how much of the pain I have felt concerning my own family is really love of approbation' (GEL 2, p. 342). If she was not going to get that approbation, it might be as well to see it as egoism's insecurity. She could be secure in Lewes. At least and at last, she said to Sara, she was free of concealment: 'I dare say I shall never have any further correspondence with my brother, which will be a great relief to me' (GEL 2, p. 364). But it wasn't true; it wasn't simply a relief: 'We hear a voice with the very cadence of our own uttering the thoughts we despise; we see eyes—ah! so like our mother's—averted from us in cold alienation.'

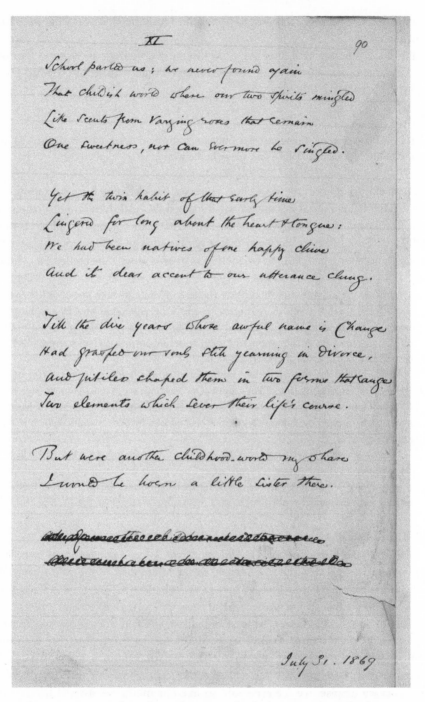

Fig. 3. Manuscript of 'Brother and Sister' xi, the final sonnet (© British Library).

Fig. 4. The Brother: Isaac Evans (1816–1890) in his later years (courtesy of Nuneaton Library).

The novelist decided to delete a passage from the manuscript of *The Mill on the Floss* in which Maggie made up a fictional little world for herself where her mother never bothered her, and Tom was never angry with her, but where 'above all, Tom loved her—oh, so much,—more, even than she loved him, so that he would always want to have her with him and be afraid of vexing her; and he, as well as every one else, thought her very clever'.[8] She cut it, but the brother did recognize her as the author of *Scenes of Clerical Life* and *Adam Bede*, partly because of the use of stories from the neighbourhood, particularly concerning their father in his younger days, but also because of the intelligence they showed, that cleverness that he had always indeed admired.

She did hear from Isaac once again, but more than twenty years later. Lewes was dead; she was to be legally married to John Cross:

My dear Sister

I have much pleasure in availing myself of the present opportunity to break the long silence which has existed between us, by offering our united and sincere congratulations to you and Mr. Cross, upon the happy event of which Mr. Holbache has informed me.

(GEL 7, p. 280)

She replied, 'It was a great joy to me to have your kind words of sympathy, for our long silence has never broken the affection for you which began when we were little ones' (GEL 7, p.287). The only point to be regretted, she added, was that her husband was much younger than she (in fact twenty years younger), signing herself, as if across the years, Mary Ann Cross (GEL 7, p. 287).

The last sonnet in the 'Brother and Sister' sequence speaks of the terrible severing of the two children in later life, the divorce by dire Change, ending even so:

> But were another childhood-world my share,
> I would be born a little sister there.

Out of a sort of loyalty to love, not everything was to be measured by the story of its outcome, by what it had turned into.

*

Isaac did not seem to think he made mistakes, or at least never admitted them. But it was the making of mistakes and the pained realization of them as mistakes that helped create George Eliot. The further baffling complication was that they had not necessarily felt like mistakes at the time; nor did the realization of them feel like simple progress or growth. These were those almost paradoxical 'first times' of reappraisal, the first shocks of second thought.

One such occurred when she was 17 and her gentle Wesleyan aunt, Elizabeth, later to become Dinah Morris in *Adam Bede*, came on an extended family visit. It unwittingly turned into a challenge to the fierce evangelicalism the niece had adopted in an effort to 'shape this anomalous English-Christian life of ours into some consistency with the spirit and simple verbal tenor of the New Testament' (GEL 3, p. 173). There was a dispute—dating back to the Reformation itself— between the young woman's strict Calvinism, committed to the predestined saving of souls solely by God's will, and the aunt's Arminian belief which left more room for human freedom and divine forgiveness. But really it came not so much out of the clash of formal dogmas as from 'the spirit of love which clings to the bad logic of Arminianism' (GEL 3, p. 174). Good feelings despite or in place of consistent principles: that was the sort of thinking which the realist novel was to relish. But the climax to the encounter came at the very end of the stay, with a human particular:

> When my uncle came to fetch her, after she had been with us a fortnight or three weeks, he was speaking of a deceased minister, once greatly respected, who from the action of trouble upon him had taken to small tippling though otherwise not culpable.
>
> (GEL 3, p. 175)

Here was a shocking anomaly, a clergyman who had become a drinker. And despite the mitigation of his 'trouble' the young woman would have been quick to absolute judgement, where, to her indignation, it was not so with uncle and aunt:

> 'But I hope the good man's in heaven for all that,' said my uncle. 'Oh yes,' said my aunt, with a deep inward groan of joyful conviction. 'Mr A's in heaven—that's sure.'

Writing twenty years later, having recently completed *Adam Bede*, she concludes:

> This was at the time an offence to my stern, ascetic hard views—how beautiful it is to me now!

It took time, as so much did for this woman, but that moment with her uncle and aunt was, in retrospect, one of those first times when, crucially, more came into her own mental, moral, and theological framework, in the way of both feeling and complication, than the framework could quite contain: 'I am not without the slower sympathy that becomes all the stronger from a sense of previous mistake' (GEL 3, p. 90).

George Eliot and the uses of the novel were the result of that penitent capacity to let anomalous human content burst its containing theories, to imagine through the perspective of another person a change of view so striking as almost to make the view-taker herself another person too. Such moments made what she would often in her fiction call 'an epoch' in her history. In particular, these were hard lessons in becoming softer, clear feelings for the necessity of a less easy clarity.

It is in the spirit of this turnaround of thought that widely sundered portions and broken fragments of the life are recombined in the writing of the novels, brought back from partial isolation by a renewed family likeness in a different medium. That new medium, the product of second thoughts, was created somewhere between memory and imagination—staying loyal to the real whilst making something more of the given. Its aim was investigatory: to see what the life she had experienced could tell her about itself, when transferred and transmuted. What George Eliot said of *Adam Bede* is true of the principle of organization throughout her work. It shifts or alters the particulars but replicates the pattern of family likenesses, suddenly redis-covered and reappraised:

> The character of Adam, and one or two incidents connected with him were suggested by my Father's early life; but Adam is not my father any more than Dinah is my aunt. Indeed there is not a single portrait in 'Adam Bede'; only the suggestions of experience wrought up into new combinations. (GEL 2, p. 503)

These suggested recombinations then take their own place on a new plane, the rela-tionships there generating further possibilities in the space between characters. 'Every-thing else grew out of their characters and their mutual relationships' (GEL 2, p. 503).

If this is how it goes with the translations of the father and the aunt in *Adam Bede*, it is also how it works with the versions of the father and the brother in *The Mill on the Floss*. There is a great early chapter in that novel which is its first major turning point. It is 'Mr Tulliver Shows His Weaker Side', book 1, chapter 8, where much that we know of Robert Evans and Isaac Evans from the first epoch of the life can be seen being subtly transformed within the shifting movements of the work.

So it is that under financial pressure, not least from his wife's hard, proud family, Mr Tulliver rides off abruptly one morning to see his own soft and affectionate sister, Gritty. Her husband, Moss, is a hopelessly unlucky farmer to whom Tulliver has lent a considerable sum over the years to support the large but loving family: 'Mrs. Moss had eight children, but could never overcome her regret that the twins had not lived.' Now the straitened brother is determined to be strict in thinking about his own immediate family's needs by demanding back his 300 pounds. It is as though George Eliot has taken a version of her father and here associated him with Isaac trying to manage the affairs of Chrissey and Edward Clarke after her father's death; that Isaac who had inherited his father's toughness without his father's later mellowing.

But once reworked within the novel, it is the brother–sister relationship that then reasserts itself. Tulliver acknowledges the likeness between one of his sister's daugh-ters and his own beloved Maggie ('They both take after our mother'), but tries hard to stay in toughened character, like an Isaac Evans in one half of himself at least:

> 'You've got enough o' gells, Gritty,' he added in a tone half compassionate, half reproachful.
> 'Four of 'em, bless 'em,' said Mrs Moss, with a sigh, stroking Lizzie's hair on each side of her forehead, 'as many as there's boys. They've got a brother apiece.'
> 'Ah, but they must turn out and fend for themselves,' said Mr Tulliver, feeling that his severity was relaxing and trying to brace it by throwing out a wholesome hint. 'They mustn't look to hanging on their brothers.'

He, of course, is thinking of *her* being a burden on *him*, and how to get round to his practical object; but Mrs Moss as mother, not sister, is still innocently worrying about her own boys and girls:

> 'No: but I hope their brothers 'ull love the poor things and remember they came o' one father and mother: the lads 'ull never be the poorer for that....
> And the more there is of 'em, the more they must love one another.'

Then, instinctively fearing she is danger of making an unkind mistake, she shifts into a considerate connection:

> 'Not but what I hope your boy 'ull allays be good to his sister, though there's but two of 'em,'

—adding simply:

> 'like you and me, brother.'
> That arrow went straight to Mr Tulliver's heart.

But she had not deliberately shot any such thing. It had come out of her life and her heart. And suddenly, in a further inner shift of dimension, Mr Tulliver is remade not only as brother again but almost simultaneously as a father himself beautifully kin to Gritty as mother, all the roles so emotionally melded as to extend the family connections:

> He had not a rapid imagination, but the thought of Maggie was very near to him, and he was not long in seeing his relation to his own sister side by side with Tom's relation to Maggie. Would the little wench ever be poorly off, and Tom rather hard upon her?

If Mrs Moss had been 'one of the most astute women in the world instead of being one of the simplest', says George Eliot, she could not have done better in propitiating her brother. But George Eliot *is* that most astute of women, doing at a deeper level what she has Mrs Moss do in her own way. It is the very thought of Tom that prevents Tom's father being like Tom becomes; stops him being like that worst part of Isaac on whom for a moment he is tacitly modelled in relation not only to Chrissey but also to Mary Ann herself. 'From what a combination of subtle shadowy suggestions with certain actual objects and events...' Thus the fabric of the novel is woven and interwoven with the threads of family likeness. Parent and child, brother and sister: the principles of relationship that lie behind the novel are allied to the principles of construction within it.

Even so, desperate for simplicity, Tulliver tries to stay unrelentingly hard in his demands upon his sister's useless husband. Single-mindedly he sticks by his intention to demand his due, even when decent Mr Moss mildly responds by saying that if it comes to it he will sell up in order to settle the debt. Tulliver then rides off quickly but he gets only a few yards before stopping abruptly, and repenting: 'Before he reached the next turning, which would take him out of sight of the dilapidated farm-buildings, he appeared to be smitten by some sudden thought, for he checked his horse and made it stand still in the same spot for two or three minutes, during which he turned his head from side to side in a melancholy way, as if he were looking at some painful object on more sides than one.' Returning slowly to his sister, he says to her in a changed and gentler tone that he will somehow manage without the money after all:

> It had come across his mind that if he were hard upon his sister, it might somehow tend to make Tom hard upon Maggie, at some distant day, when her father was no longer there to take her part; for simple people, like our friend Mr Tulliver, are apt to clothe unimpeachable feelings in erroneous ideas, and this was his confused way of explaining to himself that his love and anxiety for 'the little wench' had given him a new responsibility towards his sister.

That is what a novel represents for George Eliot in its multiple dimensions and overlapping stories: the human density of something other than straightforwardly executed intentions or simple ongoing chronologies. Tulliver had come for the money and gone away thankful to be without it; the thought of the young daughter turned back into something new and renewed in relation to his old sister. George Eliot loved the second thoughts that came so humbly in defeat of determined principles, the sudden imaginative turnarounds on the very verge of making terrible mistakes, the humane inconsistencies and confusions that do better, even for wrong reasons, than a more right reasoning might achieve without good feeling.

Her intelligence is to work *within* a Mr Tulliver and a Mrs Moss and not instead or in despite of them. In setting off to claim his money, Mr Tulliver, she concludes, had 'a promptitude in action' inconsistent with 'that painful sense of the complicated puzzling nature of human affairs' that so often came over him subsequently. It was a different sort of impetuosity to Maggie's but analogous. And that impulsiveness and that bafflement were not simply opposite but correlated, 'since I have observed that for getting a strong impression that a skein is tangled, there is nothing like snatching hastily at a single thread'. George Eliot herself was like Mary Ann Evans having second thoughts, thoughts 'on more sides than one', until slowly they became embedded in a second self within a second life writing in the tangled human web of *Middlemarch*. For here in *The Mill on the Floss* she lives in the very thick of the complicated puzzling nature of human reality: as Mr Tulliver, looking forward to the future, worries about Tom being hard upon Maggie when the father was no longer there to take her part; so she, looking backwards after her father's death, knows within another dimension that Isaac had indeed been thus unrelenting.

The Father and the Faith

But there is one other key experience, a final twist, that lies somewhere behind this developed preference for practice overcoming theory, for second thoughts being better than simple principles, whatever a Tom Tulliver might say. And it lies again in the relationship with Robert Evans, at a time when Mary Ann Evans had become his housekeeper in the house they occupied alone together at Bird Grove, Foleshill, from March 1841.

Robert Evans had retired; Isaac had married and taken over Griff House; Mary Ann, unmarried and dependent, felt banished from the old home and trapped in the new. From the moment she learned of Isaac's engagement to Sarah Rawlins, she feared for her own position, writing drily to Maria Lewis back in May 1840:

> I will only hint that there seems a probability of my being an unoccupied damsel, of my being severed from all the ties that have hitherto given my existence the semblance of a usefulness beyond that of making up the requisite quantum of animal matter in the universe. (GEL 1, p. 59)

'An occupied damsel'—with phrases such as 'semblance of usefulness', 'quantum of animal matter'—has all the defensive and self-conscious irony of someone becoming used to external neglect, without a straight voice or a definite role of her own. Though she had insisted on being her father's housekeeper even when he had offered to hire domestic help, equally this 'semblance of usefulness', this need for something to do *and* someone to appreciate what she did had often been a cause for frustration and ambivalent complaint:

> I have lately led so unsettled a life and have been so desultory in my employments, that my mind, never of the most highly organized genus, is more than usually chaotic, or rather it is like a stratum of conglomerated fragments that shews here a jaw and rib of some ponderous quadruped, there a delicate alto-relievo of some fern-like plant, tiny shells, and mysterious nondescripts, encrusted and united with some unvaried and uninteresting but useful stone. My mind presents just such an assemblage of disjointed specimens of history, ancient and modern, scraps of poetry picked up from Shakespeare, Cowper, Wordsworth, and Milton, newspaper topics, morsels of Addison and Bacon, Latin verbs, geometry, entomology and chemistry, reviews

and metaphysics, all arrested and petrified and smothered by the fast thickening every day accession of actual events, relative anxieties, and household cares and vexations.   (GEL 1, p. 29)

In *The Mill on the Floss* Maggie desperately wanted to know what, if any, was the connection between her books and the world outside those books, what was the link between her inner mental life and her external physical existence? This is what a realist novel might do eventually: investigate that desperately needed integration between within and without, while testing also its own relation to the world it sought to represent; seeking therefore within the vital multifariousness of things the possibility of some nonetheless holistic order. For the moment, Mary Ann Evans had no such field of endeavour: hers felt more like a life of scattered fragments and petrified layers, ruefully defended only by a heavily self-mocking scholarly vocabulary. She could neither do one thing thoroughly nor make a whole of the many things she was doing. The intellectual within her was always having to fit her extraordinary range of reading within the ordinary life of meals, preserves, cheese-making, and other 'important trivialities' as she called them (GEL 1, p. 57).

It was not as if she was a poor or careless manager. She knew enough of her responsibilities to those who worked for her, and the practical realities of their situation, to rebuke her beloved friend Barbara Bodichon years later for thought-lessly borrowing from a servant what was to her a trifling sum and not promptly repaying it. Even while still adopting the life of a student—studying everything from Italian and Latin and Greek to chemistry, biology, and botany, as well as the history of religion—she was remarkably efficient at managing the house and the farm and its people. One of her hands in later years, it was claimed, was permanently larger than the other as a result of her practised skill in butter-making—though Isaac's son said his father dismissed this claim, saying she would never touch a cheese or go near a pound of butter. The novelist, at any rate, relished the process in Mrs Poyser's dairy in *Adam Bede*. Meanwhile the young woman was intelligent enough to know how contradictorily she grumbled at being the housekeeper, and moaned again if she was not: 'We are so apt to complain of the weight of duty, but when it is taken from us, and we are left at liberty to choose for ourselves, we find that the old life was the easier one' (GEL 1, p. 334). What was she to do in the world? Neither freedom nor duty seemed to offer a solution.

But at least the move to Foleshill in 1841 had brought her closer to the intellectual world of provincial Coventry. In particular, there was the freethinking circle of Charles and Cara Bray, of Cara's sister Sara Hennell and brother Charles Hennell, all of them keen on challenging philosophic and religious orthodoxy. The evangelicalism of her teenage years and early 20s was about to end.

It was the books as well as the people that characteristically influenced Mary Ann, and in particular two books. Charles Hennell's *Inquiry Concerning the Origin of*

Christianity (1841) provided a humane account of why the apostles created out of the sudden death of their messianic leader the idea of the miraculous resurrection of Christ. It was a belief formed not out of mere wanton fantasy or a desire to deceive, but was a product of disappointment, loss, and need, a beautiful fiction that came out of real feelings and concerns, in spite of the facts, to produce nonetheless the living reality of a moral and spiritual revolution. Charles Bray's *Philosophy of Necessity*, also published in 1841, offered in place of the supernatural and the miraculous an insistence on the existence of fixed laws for the human mind as well as for inanimate matter. Creatures could hardly go against their own natures; acts had irrevocable consequences. Scientific enquiry was to replace otherworldly fantasies, and rational tolerance was necessary as opposed to unrealistic expectations. It was a new secular, critical, scientific world-view suddenly on offer in the advanced thinking of provincial Coventry. What it came to mean to her, in taking the Coventry influence finally to London, will be discussed further in Chapter 3.

But for the moment it was a sudden and radical un-conversion from orthodox religion that offered a new freedom to purpose. Yet for this new version of Mary Ann Evans in her passion for ideas, the intellectual excitement also brought, along with its release from domestic claustrophobia, its own trouble. On Sunday 2 January 1842, while the devout Maria Lewis was paying a visit to her friend and former pupil, something happened which Robert Evans merely noted in his journal in these bare terms: 'Went to Trinity Church in the forenoon. Miss Lewis went with me. Mary Ann did not go.' Two weeks later, after Miss Lewis had gone away, her evangelicalism no longer wanted by her protégée, the father was still writing, without comment: 'Went to Church in the forenoon Mary Ann did not go to Church' (GEL 1, p. 124). It was not really 'did not go' but 'would not go'. It was what the young woman of 22 was to call, ruefully and ironically, her 'Holy War'.

It was Robert Evans who had always encouraged his daughter's education, bought her every book she wanted, and supplemented her school education in languages, with further tuition in Latin and Greek from the Reverend Thomas Sheepshanks, headmaster of Coventry Grammar School, and in Italian and German through Joseph Brezzi, a language tutor in Coventry (whom, in addition, she had found personally attractive). Now it seemed she had used her intellect to turn against her father's inarticulately conservative Church of England faith, with all the zeal of a secular convert.

He had taken her part against others but when she refused to accompany him to church he could not take her part against himself. He hardly knew how to speak to her—though Isaac did and, as the father put in his journal, tried to 'school' her in her duties; while she herself complained of being on the receiving end of 'cooled glances and exhortations to the suppression of self-conceit' (GEL 1, p. 127). Fanny, her older sister by Robert Evans's first marriage, thought much the same as Mary Ann in relation to the old Christian pieties, but 'thinks M.A. very foolish not to keep her notions snugly to herself' (GEL 1, p. 157). Yet after painful weeks under the same roof, the young woman had to spell out her cause and assert her principles, handing her stubborn and hurt father a letter of rational clarification on 28 February 1842 (GEL 1, pp. 128ff). Her writing would always begin where speaking had failed, trying to rewrite the botched scripts of life:

My dear Father,

    As all my efforts in conversation have hitherto failed in making you aware of the real nature of my sentiments, I am induced to try if I can express myself more clearly on paper so that both I in writing and you in reading may have our judgements unobstructed by feeling, which they can hardly be when we are together.

'Together' was a painful word now. Still she went on to insist that she wasn't going to join some other Christian sect like the Brays with the Unitarians, as Evans had feared. But the reassurance was only a prelude to her conscientiously explaining how hers was a complete renunciation of Christianity in any form and a denial of the divine authority of the Bible:

    I regard these writings as histories consisting of mingled truth and fiction, and while I admire and cherish much of what I believe to have been the moral teaching of Jesus himself, I consider the system of doctrines built upon the facts of his life and drawn as to its materials from Jewish notions to be most dishonourable to God and most pernicious in its influence on individual and social happiness. In thus viewing this important subject I am in unison with some of the finest minds in Christendom in past ages, and with the majority of such in the present...

Here, you might say, is an exceptional yet vulnerable young woman painfully standing her lonely and heroic ground against the forces of conventional Victorian England. But here also is a young woman who is as excitedly self-righteous an unbeliever as she had been an evangelical. She was backed by some of the world's finest minds, she said, but this in opposition to a father who was in no way her intellectual equal, and on the issue of whether she went to the local church with him or not. Amidst the ensuing emotional turmoil in the house, it was hardly possible to gauge what was the right proportion between major and minor issues at this time. She went on in her letter, pompous but nervous:

    Such being my very strong convictions, it cannot be a question with any mind of strict integrity, whatever judgement may be passed on their truth, that I could not without vile hypocrisy and a miserable truckling to the smile of the world for the sake of my supposed interests, profess to join in worship which I wholly disapprove. This and *this alone* I will not do even for your sake—anything else however painful I would cheerfully brave to give you a moment's joy.

Even in those italics no reader could miss the pride of new-found conviction, any more than the continuing love for the father beneath it. But, whatever her lingering ambivalence, the unsympathetic pressure on Mary Ann Evans left her no room to take the by now heated and exaggerated views of others into her own view of herself, except defensively. The males had begun to threaten her with the loss of her home:

> From what my Brother more than insinuated and from what you have yourself intimated I perceive that your establishment at Foleshill is regarded as an unnecessary expence having no other object than to give me a centre in society—that since you now consider me to have placed an insurmountable barrier to my prosperity in life this one object of an expenditure held by the rest of the family to be disadvantageous to them is frustrated—I am glad at any rate this is made clear to me, for I could not be happy to remain as an incubus or an unjust absorber by your hardly earned gains which might be better applied among my Brothers and Sisters with their children.

She was the unmarried one: Foleshill had been meant to offer her an entrée into Coventry society but not in the way it turned out. If her intelligence, as well as her lack of good looks, had left her a spinster, the irreligious use of that intelligence made her even more ineligible (except perhaps to working-class Chartists and extreme radicals), and an ever-continuing financial drain. Robert Evans said that, for his own part, he would have been content living less expensively in a cottage he owned at Packington: not caring about money or position, she responded that she would be perfectly content to serve him there—unless he did not want her. She was ready for anything, even if the removal was meant as a punishment for the pain she had caused him—anything but one thing: 'I fear nothing but voluntarily leaving you.'

But to be thrown out unless she changed her position, and to have no home… As she wrote to a friend, 'I must have a *home*, and not a visiting place' (GEL 1, p. 134). Her friends, including her old teacher Rebecca Franklin, tried pleading with the father, interceding on her behalf as her own letter of explanation had failed to do. She was looking ill, pale, depressed, and wasted, telling Cara Bray that it seemed not one of her family cared what became of her. Yet, for all her pain and fear and bitter hurt, nothing could make her more morally intransigent than the demand for a change of mind accompanied by threatening appeals to her worldly interests. She hated the implication that that was what finally could break her resolve, in the same way as in her conversion to secularism she resisted the idea that good should be done not for its own sake but only to escape eternal damnation or win eternal reward. No threats, no deals, no ulterior motives.

Yet for once Isaac was less harsh than his father and came to the rescue, claiming 'she did not wish to set herself up against the family, only wished for liberty to act according to her present convictions' (GEL 1, p. 132). On 23 March she was sent back to Isaac in Griff House for a cooling-off period. As Isaac had anticipated, the father could not bear the house alone after what had happened, and needed to send for her again. Cara Bray writes to a friend:

> The poor old gentleman, it seems, has been quite puzzled about this new case of conscience, and has not known how to act. Miss Rebecca and Mrs Pears have a little enlightened him by telling him how wrong he has been, and how the world would condemn him. He expressed a fear that Mrs Bray had influenced his daughter, but Miss Rebecca said she did not think Mrs. B had shown any disposition to proselytize—so Satan has all the credit, and it is well he should perhaps.   (GEL 1, p. 132)

By 30 April her father had asked her to come home. In his journal for 15 May, he wrote, 'Went to Trinity Church. Mary Ann went with me to day.' The whole dramatic and explosive incident had taken no more than five months. A reconciliation, perhaps closer to avoidance than forgiveness, was achieved, to her considerable relief. It was a damaged and imperfect settlement, its issues not wholly resolved like so much else in her world. But even as such it made an epoch in her life, precisely by not being clear cut.

Its name was human compromise. For it was not just her father who was forced to compromise his rigid principles out of need for his daughter, but she too. She resumed accompanying him to church the second time around. Yet this was no longer simply the 'vile hypocrisy and miserable truckling to the smile of the word' she had feared and despised in her letter to her father. Nor was it like going to church as it had been before. She was now going to church not for the Almighty Father, she knew, but for her own flawed father. The religion was not only or essentially in the church, any more than the principle lay in merely not attending it: whatever value was in the religion and the principle now lay in the going to church for complex human reasons, beyond or beneath the claims of absolute justice or theoretic causes.

Only eighteen months after her crisis, Mary Ann Evans was writing to Sara Hennell about the change she had now made to what she had thought 'in the first instance' of rebellion. It had taken place in the time that allowed for second thoughts, and more general thoughts, in a life lived backwards:

> The first impulse of a young and ingenuous mind is to withhold the slightest sanction from all that contains even a mixture of supposed error. When the soul is just liberated from the wretched giant's bed of dogmas on which it has been racked and stretched ever since it began to think there is a feeling of exultation and strong hope. We think we shall run well when we have the full use of our limbs and the bracing air of independence, and we believe that we shall soon obtain something positive which will not only more than compensate to us for what we have renounced, but will be so well

worth offering to others that we may venture to proselyte as far as our zeal for truth may prompt us.   (GEL 1, p. 162)

Up until then Mary Ann Evans had hardly ever been young. Her reaction against dogmatic Christianity was perhaps the youngest, the most precipitately adolescent, she had ever been. Looking back, only a little older, she knew she was cleverer than her family: she now thought that should have meant more than just having more intelligent beliefs; it should have meant the responsibility, could she have fulfilled it, to avoid or solve the issue. Yet manifestly part of her had wanted to defy Robert Evans in their new home together. It was only the realization of the dangerously looming closeness to permanent damage that had enabled her to reimagine him. Cast away the old props of religion had been the initial simplification of the liberating battle-cry:

> But a year or two of reflection and the experience of our own miserable weakness which will ill afford to part even with the crutches of superstition must, I think, effect a change. Speculative truth begins to appear but a shadow of individual minds, agreement between intellects seems unattainable, and we turn to the truth of feeling as the only universal bond of union.   (GEL 1, p. 102)

The intellectual errors involved in the popular adoption of religious belief were not unnecessary additions that were easily removed, as they seemed to be to abstract intellectualism. They had grown into the living body of people such as her father, and in the relationships: 'we cannot wrench them away without destroying vitality'. She began to think that progress had to be slow, preparing the ground not rooting up the crop, and still sympathizing with feelings in others we may have outgrown ourselves. And even in oneself there had to be time for overly reactive ideas to shake down again into reassembled character. This was not merely unthinking conservatism or guilt-ridden cowardice on Mary Ann Evans's part, on the rebound from her moment of failed defiance. It was, more personally, more feelingly, the fear of doing harm to others in vulnerable need: 'The results of non-conformity in a family are just an epitome of what happens on a larger scale in the world' (GEL 1, pp. 162–3). In the world as in the family, then, 'ought we not on every opportunity to seek to have our feelings in harmony though not in union with those who are often richer in the fruits of faith though not in reason, than ourselves?' (GEL 1, p. 162). It is a fine but crucial distinction between 'harmony' and 'union' which she felt secretly within her whilst outwardly continuing to go with her father to his church: 'In more than one case a person's happiness may be ruined by the confusion of ideas which took the form of principles' (GEL 1, p. 163). Was it worth breaking the relationship with her father, with all those ties of family likeness undercut by family differences? The emphasis was now as it had also become in relation to her aunt and her apologetics: it was underlying human *feelings*—not consciously fixed principles and abstract dogmas, nor notional opinions and rationalized theories—that contained what was vitally real, especially when those feelings could be so easily dismissed as unheroic, sentimental, or weakly compromising. The work eventually was to make what was at stake in those feelings a part of a different form of thinking.

It was George Eliot who was to do that work. She, of course, knew infinitely more of Mary Ann Evans than anyone else would ever know, biographers included; more than that, she was formed out of her, in both her strengths and her failings; and further still, she seemed, to devoted readers of the novels, to know more about human beings than anyone in the century. To begin imaginably to know the novelist and to know what made her is also to ask questions such as: What would *George Eliot* think when she thought back to the holy war of 1842?

Characteristically, what she felt was sorry for *both* the 22-year-old daughter and the ageing father. 'In the last year of her life,' Cross wrote, 'she told me that, although she did not think she had been to blame, few things had occasioned her more regret than this temporary collision with her father, which might, she thought, have been avoided by a little management' (Cross, 1, p. 113). It was second thoughts like this one that were so important to George Eliot. No wonder hers was a slow evolution: she herself was the second thought, the second life of Mary Ann Evans. And it was in the holy war with her father that Mary Ann Evans learnt more about second thoughts than ever before.

Even when Mary Ann Evans was quick and impulsive, it was increasingly the second and subsequent thoughts that mattered to her; it was those that she could grow to tolerate; those that, above all, showed what thought itself was for, in the evolution of a human being. But this was not because second thoughts were merely to be instead of her first strong impulses. Rather, she wanted time to get the second thoughts *in amongst* those first instincts, to create a somewhat different mind and a more integrated person. Mr Tulliver's way of thinking again was more like the human norm in such things—the way of alternation, in stages. His first impulse was changed even by the time he had reached the corner of the road, then came the return backwards for the sake of inarticulate feelings—fatherly and brotherly—that lay deeper and broader than his consciously avowed principles. The second thoughts of Mary Ann Evans seemed even wider and kinder and harder to achieve than this, more general and less egoistical, but almost impossible to deliver immediately and in the thick of things. It was as though they were the product of someone more just and more generous than is often possible in a normal life.

CHAPTER 2

The Valley of Humiliation

The Single Woman, 1840–51

The Need to Utter and to Think

It should not have seemed so important to others or to her, but she was always plain, even ugly. Henry James called her a great horse-faced bluestocking, magnificently ugly. Herbert Spencer disliked her overlarge nose and jawline. Writing in 1883, her first biographer Mathilde Blind mentions a watercolour of her done by Cara Bray in 1842, when she was 23:

> In those Foleshill days she had a quantity of soft pale-brown hair, worn in ringlets. Her head was massive, her features powerful and rugged, her mouth large but shapely, the jaw singularly square for a woman, yet having a certain delicacy of outline. A neutral tone of colouring did not help to relieve this general heaviness of structure, the complexion being pale, but not fair.

Nevertheless, this early biographer goes on:

> [T]he play of expression and the wonderful mobility of the mouth, which increased with age, gave a womanly softness to the countenance in curious contrast with its framework. Her eyes, of a gray blue, constantly varying in color, striking some as intensely blue, others as of a pale, washed-out gray, were small and not beautiful in themselves, but, when she grew animated in conversation, those eyes lit up the whole face, seeming in a manner to transfigure it. So much was this the case that a young lady, who had once enjoyed an hour's conversation with her, came away under its spell with the impression that she was beautiful, but afterward, on seeing George Eliot again when she was not talking, she could hardly believe her to be the same person. The charm of her nature disclosed itself in her manner and in her voice, the latter recalling that of Dorothea, in being like the voice of a soul that has once lived in an Æolian harp. It was low and deep, vibrating with sympathy.[1]

This is the story of a life that did not match with its ostensible outer 'framework', indeed did not believe that most lives did, and sought to 'transfigure' itself from within. Yet it may have been her fame in later years as 'George Eliot' that made some of the difference in impression. Beautiful women at any rate were more naturally fortunate: young Hetty Sorrel's face 'had a language that transcended her feelings... just as a national language may be instinct with poetry unfelt by the lips that use it', her looks making her seem more loveable than she truly was (*Adam Bede*, chapter 26). For the plain-looking the converse is true, in terms of the falseness of appearances. Yet Mathilde Blind believed that the face changed in the course of the woman's learning to become herself: when fully formed, the inner self 'modified the expression, and to some extent the features, to its own likeness' (Blind, p. 54). But at any stage of life, sudden inlets of feeling, bursts of life and interest, would transform her.

In learning the subtler language of herself and of others, George Eliot knew very well how expression, through tone and voice, transformed word and meaning. She might be notionally dutiful to her ageing father, say, but 'when the tones of our voice have betrayed peevishness or harshness we seem to be doubly haunted by the ghost of our sins' (GEL 1, p. 247). Mathilde Blind quotes an observer saying of a later portrait by Samuel Laurence that, though showing her underlying melancholy, it gave no indication 'of the infinite depth of her observant eye, nor of that cold, subtle, and unconscious cruelty of expression which might occasionally be detected there' (Blind, p. 276). You could almost see her inner criticism, feel her judgement. Yet when emotions of kindness and sympathy came into that face, it was changed again by a kind of love. It would make a novelist think: What was it that lay within bodies, looking out through the eyes? George Eliot, in the age of Charles Darwin and Herbert Spencer, was a biological thinker. When I say 'I love thee,' writes the apparently plain and sickly spinster, Elizabeth Barrett to her unexpected lover Robert Browning, then 'what I *feel*, across the inferior features / Of what I *am*, doth flash itself' ('Sonnets from the Portuguese', 10). She becomes lovely in love.

But for a long time, the fate of Mary Ann Evans seemed more like that of Lucy Snowe, the spinster-protagonist of likewise 'inferior features' in *Villette* (1853). It was the novel by Charlotte Brontë she most admired (GEL 2, p. 87). For what Lucy Snowe cannot bear is the thought that, humiliatingly, she might be waiting and waiting in vain for some man to love her, and that that indefinite wait might itself be her whole life, a wasted present in hopeless search of a non-existent future. Better to think of the unmarried state, which never simply begins but only continues, as a definitely settled fate than the endless uncertainty of hoping against hope: 'I had wanted to compromise with Fate: to escape occasional great agonies by submitting to a whole life of privation and small pains' (*Villette*, chapter 4). Easier to be fated and accept it than to suffer the continual rise and fall of hope and disappointment.

But emotionally Mary Ann Evans was not the sort of person stoically to convert what has not happened into what can never happen. At best she could only offer wry defences. Mathilde Blind refers to a comic letter she wrote to Sara Hennell as late as October 1846. It purports to tell of a visit from a German professor who has come over to England to secure a wife who will also serve as the translator of his voluminous writings. It would be an added advantage if the woman had a little capital of her own and, to guarantee her undemanding gratitude, be possessed of a considerable amount of personal ugliness. 'In Miss Evans,' she reports of herself, 'the aspiring professor finds his utmost wishes realized' (Blind, p. 62). If the wit of this little fiction was still rather heavy, it nonetheless was a sign of what writing could do, in a shift of level such as at once tonally to ameliorate and yet substantially not alter the essential predicament. Sara Hennell nicely replied as though herself the professor, declining the engagement because 'she was not ugly enough after all' (GEL 1, p. 226).

In her late teens and early 20s, Mary Ann Evans used her evangelicalism as a religious defence that was meant to go beyond Lucy's stoic acceptance of Fate. Earthly ties, 'the marrying and giving in marriage', she writes to Maria Lewis back in August 1838, are powerful enough to detach the heart from heaven, and yet so fearfully 'brittle' they may snap in any breeze. Give up those ties. There may be those who can love the world and still live in supreme communion with God; but she herself, she says single-mindedly, is not one such. 'In my short experience and narrow sphere of action,' she writes, trying to place herself in context, 'I have never been able to attain this; I find, as Dr. Johnson said respecting his wife, total abstinence much easier than moderation' (GEL 1, p. 6). For her at this stage it had still to be one thing *or* its opposite, no possible in-between position. But it was not some throng of potential suitors she was trying to give up on, it was her own inner desires.

'I am a negation of all that finds love and esteem,' she writes to Maria Lewis in May 1840, quoting Isaiah in a way far more specifically sexual than the prophet had in mind: '"Cease ye from man" is engraven on my amulet' (GEL 1, p. 51). To destroy temptation, she continuously tried to think it would be best to see her lack as God-given—as she writes to her former school-friend, Martha Jackson, five months later in what was becoming a terrible year:

> Every day's experience seems to deepen the voice of foreboding that has long been telling me, 'The bliss of reciprocated affection is not for you under any form. Your heart must be widowed in this manner from the world, or you will never seek a better portion; a consciousness of possessing the fervent love of any human being would soon become your heaven, therefore it would be your curse...' (GEL 1, p. 70)

'Widowed': she felt old at 21, a widow as much as a spinster, without ever having been a wife. 'Not for you,' said the harsh inner voice, not quite her own but drowning out her own.

Yet there had been some sort of infatuation earlier in that year with a young man who had not shared her evangelical faith. It is not clear how far it had progressed, but on the advice of Maria Lewis, it seems, she had dropped even the thought of him. The 'image' of him seldom now arises, she reports to her mentor 30 March 1840, for she belongs again to God. But her writing is so stilted and oblique, it is as though she could hardly speak of him:

> I endeavoured to pray for the beloved object to whom I have alluded, I must still a little while say *beloved*, last night and felt soothingly melted in thinking that if mine be really prayers my acquaintance with him has probably caused the *first* to be offered specially in his behalf. But all this I ought not to have permitted to slip from my pen.
>
> (GEL 1, pp. 46–7)

Yet she couldn't *not* speak of him either. Guiltily praying had to do instead.

Being torn in this way is of a piece with her constant self-references in the self-conscious, awkwardly moaning letters of her youthful lonely years. She cannot stop either talking of herself or apologizing for her own egotism in so doing. 'I am ashamed to send a letter like this,' she writes to Maria Lewis, complaining of her own 'too frequent use of the personal pronoun', 'as if I thought more highly of myself than I ought to think, which is alas! too true' (GEL 1, pp. 23–4). 'Neither do I like to see that I have scribbled so much about myself,' she writes Miss Lewis on another occasion, '—a self so bountifully provided for [compared] to you, my dearest friend, who have substantial difficulties wherewith to combat' (GEL 1, p. 103). Maria Lewis was an impoverished governess, part of a class of single women subject to lonely indignities: there were 'substantial' material and financial problems for her. As secure daughter-housekeeper, Mary Ann Evans had instead problems to which she could hardly point, to do with what *wasn't* there—frustrations that seemed humiliatingly close to over-enlarged self-indulgences. Again like Lucy Snowe, she lived in a world without due proportions, feeling too much about what was too little, 'yearning for what is more than in sober reason and real humility I ought to desire' (GEL 1, p. 137). Before I got your letter, she writes to her new Coventry friend Cara Bray, I kept thinking 'you did not love me well enough to bestow any time on me more than I had already robbed you of' (GEL 1, p. 137). In her embarrassed but unstoppable demandingness, she could not break out of the circle of an almost uselessly intelligent self-consciousness, moaning against moaning. In a mix of saddened narcissism and self-dislike, she desperately needed to show she existed. But at the same time she sought to anticipate, and thus pre-emptively soften, her correspondent's judgement of her.

'No one was more aware of the conflation of writing and egotism than Mary Ann Evans herself.'[2] Yet, equally, no one was more aware of the unavoidable conflation of egotism and loneliness: how impossible to avoid the first in the predicaments of the second. And no one was more aware of writing as serving the need for an emotional understanding of herself, a sympathetic context that was apparently lacking in the world immediately around her. Was there a way of writing—indeed, a way of being—that wasn't egotistical? Even the desire to get *out* of the ego—that point of view from which she must experience everything that affected her—was still expressed within it.

Fast-forward to the fiction that, almost twenty years later, came out of this past and looked back upon it. It was because of this burden of egotism that it was a great relief to Maggie Tulliver, in the midst of her own family troubles, to come across *The Imitation of Christ* written by Thomas à Kempis in the early fifteenth century. On reading it, it flashed through her 'that all the miseries of her young life had come from fixing her heart on her own pleasure, as if that were the central necessity of the universe'. This devotional work suddenly offered her a strong alternative framework of understanding and within it 'the possibility of shifting the position from which she looked at the gratification of her own desires, of taking her stand out of herself, and looking at her own life as an insignificant part of a divinely guided whole' (*The Mill on the Floss*, book 4, chapter 3). That shift from centre to circumference, in reappraisal of what was part and what was whole, was vital to the achievement of adulthood. Everyone thought himself, herself, the god or centre of their own little world in which everyone else was peripheral; but to recognize one's own self-centredness was also to imagine the equivalent centre within others simultaneously, and to know better how little one could count for in their eyes. Maggie Tulliver did not have to go through the almost violent twists and turns of Mary Ann Evans's conversion to evangelicalism and subsequent reaction against it. The old language of God speaks to her direct in teaching her what should be her unregretted place in a world.

Maggie picks up the battered old religious book by chance. It was the same book Mary Ann Evans read throughout her life in a more complicated way, most especially after the death of her father and again in the midst of her affair with John Chapman—and long after the cessation of her formal beliefs. For both women even so, it came out of the cry which William James was to say that religion essentially stood for: Help! Help![3] For Maggie, some reader's hand 'now for ever quiet' had made marks in the margin 'long since browned by time' against certain passages—passages which actually, of course, were marked also by the novel's author:

> Know that the love of thyself doth hurt thee more than anything in the world...thou shalt never be quiet nor free from care: for in everything somewhat will be wanting, and in every place there will be some that will cross thee...It is but little thou sufferest in comparison of them that suffered so much, were so strongly tempted, so grievously afflicted, so many ways tried and exercised. Thou oughtest therefore to call to mind the more heavy sufferings of others, that thou mayst the easier bear thy little adversities. And if they seem not little unto thee, beware lest thy impatience be the cause thereof....
>
> (*The Mill on the Floss*, book 4, chapter 3)

This young woman Maggie, and the different young woman she was partially in memory of, badly needed an orientation that allowed her to know herself young in comparison with an old book handed down through many hands, and small in comparison with the larger sufferings of the world and its generations. And what is more, to feel that this quietist perspective offered relief not belittlement. Of course, Maggie youthfully rushes into it, in her own version of Mary Ann Evans's excited seriousness: 'Here then was a secret of life that would enable her to renounce all other secrets.' Of course, her sudden conversion to selflessness still contains within it all those impulses of the self that drove her to it in the first place: 'Maggie was still panting for happiness, and was in ecstasy because she had found the key to it.' But 'she had not perceived—how could she until she had lived longer?—the inmost truth of the old monk's outpourings, that renunciation remains sorrow, though a sorrow borne willingly'. George Eliot said that her life, in its own unconventional way, was a parallel secular version of the religious life of John Henry Newman, through a series of spiritual changes and developments going in the opposite direction. But in his autobiography *Apologia Pro Vita Sua* (1864), Newman said, 'Great acts take time.'[4] 'How could she until she lived longer?' was the formulation for George Eliot.

In the meantime, Mary Ann Evans always needed, as she put it, to '*utter*': in the very etymology of that verb, to get whatever was within out—to *outer* all of it, if only she could. It was not just a psychological, it was an ontological need, and from it began her compulsion to write if she could not otherwise speak or be heard. Ontological: because to keep her troubled thoughts trapped inside was barely tolerable in so far as it also implied there was no place for them, or for her, in reality, in the outside world. She was writing to Maria Lewis and to Martha Jackson before her Holy War with her father; to Sara Hennell and Cara Bray increasingly during and after it. She had to employ letter-writing as a form of articulate crying, with someone in imagined receipt to bear it sympathetically with her—even if it risked exploiting these friends, and even when it involved replacing one with another. 'Help! Help!'

What she believed in was close and direct communication—as though, originally, thoughts were always *meant* to be spoken out loud. As Max Müller, the language scholar she admired, was to put it, 'To think is to speak low.'[5] When thoughts were thrown back inside, separateness, pain, and loneliness resulted. It was like her omnivorous reading in the attempt to absorb everything altogether and at once: whether it was getting the matter in or getting it out, she almost resented at times the slow necessary indirectness of the medium of communication in her urgent desire for the message:

> When a sort of haziness comes over the mind making one feel weary of articulated or
> written signs of ideas, does not the notion of a less laborious mode of communication,

of a perception approaching more nearly to intuition seem attractive? Nathless I love words... (GEL 1, p. 107)

For the most part there was no such magical transmission or musical transfusion of meaning, no intuitive harmony of immediate understanding. There were fault-lines instead, misunderstandings and misinterpretations, egos, separations, and gaps even between those meant to be close. And hard work through words was needed to get over these obstacles or reach across these chasms:

> It is necessary to me, not simply to *be* but to *utter*, and I require utterance of my friends. What is it to me that I think the same thoughts? I think them in a somewhat different fashion. No mind that has any *real* life is a mere echo of another. If the perfect unison comes occasionally, as in music, it enhances the harmonies. It is like a diffusion or expansion of one's own life, to be assured that its vibrations are repeated in another and words are the media of those vibrations. (GEL 1, p. 255)

There may be people in the world who can simply 'be', 'happy souls who ask for nothing but the work of the hour, however trivial—who are contented to live without knowing whether they effect anything, but who do really effect much good, simply by their calm and even *maintien* [maintenance]' (GEL 1, p. 313). She was not one such: she could take little for granted but needed knowledge, explanation, justification, reassurance, kind feeling, and therefore all the complex paraphernalia of words for what she called '*real* life'. But to try to make words almost physical things in influential and responsive action within the very fibres of the brain: that, as we shall see, is the ambition of the idea of 'vibrations' in George Eliot, as a sort of neural music of thinking and feeling as close as possible to the intuition she could not immediately summon.[6] She had read the German Romantic, Novalis: 'It is certain my conviction gains infinitely the moment an other soul believes in it.' She wanted those other souls and wanted them to be as close and sympathetic as possible.

These, then, were for her the great experiential surprises and excitements which more literal-minded people might simply ignore or deny. That words and thoughts could connect people at a subterranean mental level. That an internal belief felt more true, more objective when freely found and independently held—and not simply repeated or re-enforced—by another person. That genuine alliances were not achieved through pre-concerted agreements or imitation but were most authentically realized through the *differences* between people. It was the translation across those differences, not just despite them, that made for the wonderful overcoming of what otherwise had often seemed an inescapable loneliness. That was how Thomas à Kempis spoke to Maggie across the ages.

This was where affinities began, and suddenly recognized affines and sympathies were what Mary Ann Evans was always searching for, in deeper society. She admired

Goethe's *Elective Affinities* (1809), which she read while studying German with Cara Bray, for just that reason: the idea of chemical attraction translated into the realm of human passions and relations. But it was the unpredictable and almost anomalous connections arising out of particular conditions that most interested her. And it was fiction finally—first Goethe's, then her own—that could best depict the achievement of sudden, unlikely human connection.

Here, from *Scenes of Clerical Life* (1858), is a woman, Janet Dempster, bringing food to a poor consumptive girl called Sally Martin, when suddenly, at the entrance to the bedroom, she hears the voice of the radical evangelical minister, who, in the religious controversies of the neighbourhood, is her husband's enemy: 'Her first impulse was to set down her plate and go away...' On second thought, however, she hesitates as to what to do with the food, and 'was obliged to hear what Mr Tryan was saying':

> He was interrupted by one of the invalid's violent fits of coughing.
> 'It is very hard to bear is it not?' he said when she was still again. 'Yet God seems to support you under it wonderfully. Pray for me, Sally, that I may have strength too when the hour of great suffering comes. It is one of my worst weaknesses to shrink from bodily pain, and I think the time is perhaps not far off when I shall have to bear what you are bearing. But now I have tired you. We have talked enough. Good-bye.'
> Janet was surprised, and forgot her wish not to encounter Mr Tryan: the tone and the words were so unlike what she had expected to hear. There was none of the self-satisfied unction of the teacher, quoting, or exhorting, or expounding, for the benefit of the hearer, but a simple appeal for help, a confession of weakness. Mr Tryan had his deeply-felt trouble, then? Mr Tryan, too, like herself...   ('Janet's Repentance', chapter 12)

George Eliot by then was scarcely more the friend of evangelicalism as a theoretic doctrine than Janet was the friend of her husband's foe; but it was the individual person who made the transcendent difference. It was the separable voice and overheard tone of that person, Tryan, that got through to the mind, making Janet forget her customary theoretical position in a way not possible if she had been directly, physically confronting him. When George Eliot herself spoke in sympathy, said Mathilde Blind, hers was 'like the voice of a soul...low and deep, vibrating with sympathy'. In such communication the encounter is not one of minister and patient, or teacher and congregant, but mortal with fellow-mortal: 'It is like a diffusion or expansion of one's own life, to be assured that its vibrations are repeated in another and words are the media of those vibrations.' In this different medium, hearing without seeing, Janet becomes a third presence to pick up those resonances. It is like the equivalent in life of the literary medium itself; indirect in one sense, direct in another. So it was with Maggie in relation to Thomas à Kempis, 'hardly conscious that she was reading—seeming rather to listen' (*The Mill on the Floss*, book 4, chapter 3). In this privileged space, the space that George Eliot most cared about and most sought to create, Janet is witness to a briefly transmitted communication between a pair of little-known human beings for a few short minutes. It is a quiet private communication which, in lieu of God, only the writing of a poem or novel—and a narrator such as George Eliot herself—could save from being lost or neglected in the wider world. 'Too', used twice, is the appropriately great-but-tiny connective word that vibrates gently in that passage: Tryan's 'Pray for me that I may have strength too', Janet's 'Mr Tryan had his deeply-felt trouble too, like herself.'

For Mary Ann Evans, outside that space, existence of itself was dumbly insufficient, baffling, and lonely. There had to be cries, there had to be responses, there had to be a language for transmission. Across the unhelpful barriers and resistant media of life, verbal recognition and acknowledgement and communication were necessary. What Mary Ann Evans could hardly bear was to think of her friends and not to hear from them. 'I can't help losing belief that people love me—the unbelief is in my nature and no sort of fork will drive it finally out' (GEL 2, p. 397):

> It is an old weakness of mine to have no faith in affection that does not express itself, and when friends take no notice of me for a long while I generally settle down into the belief that they have become indifferent or have begun to dislike me.   (GEL 2, p. 402)

Yet again, this was not only to do with her psychological insecurity—her admittedly anxious, unconfident sense of being unloveable and impermanent amidst the distant busy lives of those who could not care for her as much as for someone daily present. But it was also true that, for her, verbal expression was necessary to any faith in existence. References to faith, belief, and unbelief—'no faith in affection', 'the belief they have become indifferent'—are the clue to something more metaphysical, an insecurity to do not just with herself but with the very nature of *thought*. She could think of someone very intensely indeed and still at that very moment know that the person was separate from her, thinking something utterly different, doing well or doing badly without her knowing it. To most people this would be an obvious fact of reality in the separation of inside and outside, of self and the existence of others. But to Mary Ann Evans it felt almost maddeningly like a paradox.

Mathilde Blind, who consulted Charles and Cara Bray and Sara Hennell as well as Isaac Evans, wrote that in the contradictory nature of this young woman there was one feature that increasingly affected and transmuted her egotism, and that was her power of identification: 'She flung herself, as it were, into other lives, making their affairs, their hopes, their sorrows her own. And this power of identifying herself with the people she came near has the effect of a magnet in attracting her fellow-creatures' (Blind, p. 57). She wanted to feel their feelings, think their thoughts, become them imaginatively and sympathetically, just as she had hoped for this from others in regard to herself. For her, thought might be lodged in one person or another, trapped even to distortion within this or that body; but it was of itself a distinct force and presence in the world, a third possibility as alternative to self or to others. As in a poem or a piece of music, or like Janet witnessing Tryan in the sickroom, thought was set free from the ego-bound person in whom it originated:

> Poor and shallow as one's own soul is, it is blessed to think that a sort of transhumanation is possible by which the greater ones can live in us. Egotism apart, another's greatness, beauty or bliss is our own—and let us sing a Magnificat when we are conscious that this power of expansion or sympathy is growing just in proportion as the individual satisfactions are lessening.   (GEL 1, p. 280)

Transhumanation was the emotional process by which great value in a person or a work or an idea could expand the powers of those who received it beyond what they could normally command. Once a thing of value was transmitted and receptively felt, you were in it, it was in you, till you did not know precisely the difference between the two. The dying Tryan lives in Janet, the woman as the legacy he has saved for the world, just as she lives in him and, later, in memory of him. In a late short poem, Life says to Self of childhood happiness:

> Was it person? Was it thing?
> Was it touch or whispering?
> It was bliss and it was I:
> Bliss was what thou knew'st me by.

There were moments when *life* was in a person; others, when it was in a thought or feeling—a 'thing'—hardly distinguishable from a person.

As Philip Wakem puts it, 'I don't think any of the strongest effects our natures are susceptible of can ever be explained.' Whether those effects are achieved through personal attraction, art or music, 'we can neither detect the process by which they are arrived at nor the mode in which they act on us' (*The Mill on the Floss*, book 5, chapter 1). The felt thought would come to you, and further, as Mordecai was to say in *Daniel Deronda*, what found you stayed with you (chapter 40). That was why George Eliot was the product of Mary Ann Evans being a thinker, not just an ego but a passionate intellectual—where intellectual, I am arguing, means much more in its struggle for extended life than is commonly understood by the merely abstract or arid. It meant 'thing' as well as 'person', but (to keep the shorthand) 'thing' as also like 'person'. Years later George Eliot wrote, as an older woman to a younger, on the possibility of a woman's life being made *more* than personal—by thought working in aid of feeling—and yet still being a life possessed of personally felt qualities:

> I think it is possible for this sort of impersonal life to attain great intensity,—possible for us to gain much more independence, than is usually believed, of the small bundle of facts that make our own personality.... We women are always in danger of living too exclusively in the affections; and though our affections are perhaps the best gifts we have, we ought also to have our share of the more independent life—some joy in things for their own sake. It is piteous to see the helplessness of some sweet women when their affections are disappointed—because all their teaching has been, that they can only delight in study of any kind for the sake of a personal love. They have never contemplated an independent delight in ideas as an experience which they could confess without being laughed at. Yet surely women need this sort of defence against passionate affliction even more than men. (GEL 5, p. 107)

This was not about the proud cleverness she had had from youth. It was not learning sought as a mere female accomplishment, or in imitation of supposedly male-dominated rationalism. It was the absorption and transmutation of learning into a way of being. In her essay 'Silly Novels by Lady Novelists', October 1856, she was scathing about women who merely wanted to make a showy parade of superficial smatterings of culture. This was not simply because she felt vulnerable to being classed among them or held some unsisterly conservativism as to the effect of learning upon traditional female virtues. It was because the education of women demanded a renewal of the actual principles and priorities at stake for both genders:

> A really cultured woman, like a really cultured man, is all the simpler and less obtrusive for her knowledge; it has made her see herself and her opinions in something like just proportions; she does not make it a pedestal...In conversation she is the least formidable of women, because she understands you, without wanting to make you aware that you can't understand her. She does not give you information, which is the raw material of culture,—she gives you sympathy which is its subtlest essence.[7]

Again it is the intrinsic and the integrated effect of experience that is sought, the matter, however initially raw and literal, assimilated over time into feeling and character.

It was a complex, dialectical process. She would lose herself, or get hurt out there in the world, and then have to retreat back inside herself and think hard—only to have to venture back out again. 'Life,' as she was to put it her translation of Feuerbach, 'involves the contradiction of an existence at once dependent and independent,—the contradiction that its possibility lies both in itself and out of itself.'[8] As Mary Ann Evans knew only too well, Life takes existence out of oneself, scatters a young woman such as she was in practical involvements and emotional entanglements. But Thought, says Feuerbach, 'is existence in self': 'life is to give from oneself; thought is to take into oneself' (Feuerbach, p. 40). To move from thinking to living, from living to thinking, however deeply connected were the two, was like moving from one world into another. But what was nourishing to her, not least when her living went badly, was the experience of ideas, how ideas took you out of yourself in one sense but returned you to a larger impersonal self in another, and, more than that, offered an alternative 'transhumanated' model of reality which individuals could tune into.[9]

Hence the frequent deployment in George Eliot of an acoustic language of echoes, harmonies, vibrations, offering, by a kind of osmosis, a different dimension to reality from that of material separateness. It was the dimension Janet occupied when blindly, impersonally, she overheard Tryan. Thoughts, like musical sounds, crossed solid bodies and physical boundaries; you became what you thought of: that was imagination, intuitive sympathy. The novella 'The Lifted Veil' (1859) is a Gothic analogue to that imaginative sensitivity, crucial to the future novelist but also close to a terrifying sense of possession or receptive telepathy.[10] Its protagonist feels 'the obtrusion on my mind of the mental process going forward in first one person, and then another' (chapter 1). 'Obtrusion' marks how the mind feels the brain inside itself as something physical, but also sensitively permeable and invaded. And yet by the same sensitivity, if you were thinking of someone you cared about, worrying about them, then even the smallest imaginable gap between the thought of them and them as they were by themselves was the clue to a reality that was severingly mundane again. Here, for example, she writes to another friend, Bessie Parkes:

> I had several times thought during the last three weeks that some cause of coolness or disgust towards me had arisen to prevent you from writing, to tell me how you were, as you volunteered to do. But I said—Ah well, I have told her that I shall always love her *quand même*, and I resigned myself to having no other satisfaction than that of thinking about you affectionately.   (GEL 2, p. 151)

She had to become able to tolerate, within one person, the experience of moving between the two reality levels of imaginative connection and physical separateness. But still to think something *about* a person and not be able to say it *to* that person, because they were too distant *or* too close—that sudden realization of limitation and boundary, in contracting what should have been expansive, was internally well-nigh unbearable to her.

It was so hard to make the great clunky gear-changes, as it were, between one realm and another, one level and another. Again it is the fiction that becomes the later form of uttering what could hardly be fully expressed at the time. 'I want to tell you everything,' Maggie Tulliver says in *The Mill on the Floss* to her equivalent of Janet's Tryan. 'Do tell me everything' replies Dr Kenn, the vicar of St Ogg's (book 6, chapter 2). In that impossible 'everything', it did not matter what was the denomination of the minister, or whether it was indeed a minister who was involved. For what Mary Ann Evans intuitively remembered and really needed was confession, not just expression. Her need to utter had within it still all the human needs and fears that the ancient practice of confession contained, in attempting to make a life more open and known, more wide and truthful and whole. That is why George Eliot's people often turn to priests for help when they need someone outside the family, whereas after her Holy War Mary Ann Evans herself could not. In this way, the woman who became George Eliot stands on the very cusp of a crucial historical shift from a religious to a secular world-view, from a complete theology to a psychology bearing the weight of what previously had found satisfaction in God. By her writing she makes that transition more than a passing epoch in history but a recognizably recurrent human element in the continuing crisis of the need for truth and meaning and belief, however partial.

It is a need found, even reluctantly, in the realism of quite small and common occasions. In *Adam Bede*, Arthur Donnithorne, fearing sexual temptation, comes to confess the danger to his easy-going mentor, the Reverend Irwine. But in the freer modern setting, this can seem no more than a casual and informal visit. That is the difference, writes George Eliot, from the ancient way now only hidden within it:

> There was this advantage in the old rigid forms, that they committed you to the fulfilment of a resolution by some outward deed: when you have put your mouth to one end of a hole in a stone wall, and are aware that there is an expectant ear at the other end, you are more likely to say what you came out with the intention of saying, than if you were seated with your legs in an easy attitude under the mahogany, with a companion who will have no reason to be surprised if you have nothing particular to say. (*Adam Bede*, chapter 16)

There were now, in the transitional re-founding that made a modern world, fewer set forms, more liberties. What you did not do, or what you got away with, there might be no one ever to know. It was not that George Eliot had leanings towards Catholicism itself, though she had come to repent of the savage tones of anti-popery of her own early evangelicalism. It was, as ever, to do with the culture contained within the dogma, the psychological needs that confession had served and disciplined. But Arthur keeps the secret sexual temptation to himself—and that is what allows him later to succumb to it: 'The mere fact that he was in the presence of an intimate friend, who had not the slightest notion that he had had any such serious internal struggle as he came to confide, rather shook his own belief in the seriousness of the struggle. It was not, after all, a thing to make a fuss about; and what could Irwine do for him that he could not do for himself?' (chapter 16). Not to *believe* in his own seriousness, not to want to believe in the intangible reality of the serious conflict inside that will have serious consequences later in external life: in this there is nothing stopping him, no one to tell him—and that frightened Mary Ann Evans about herself too. For the religious framework could give way to the psychological such as to leave the moral realm unrecognized or unenforced.

It was only by further investigation of the psychological subconscious and unconscious that the idea of telling everything, or of everything being told, could become imaginable again, at a different, more hidden and subterranean level. It was to become in the novels not the direct authorial report of 'She thought this', 'He wondered if that', but what has become known as free indirect discourse—the blending of author and character in the deep unspoken language of a secret interior voice of which the character might not even be fully conscious. This is what confession became in the wide-open, deep-delving language of the novel—free indirect discourse, involuntary and exposing. It is frightening to see undeliberated thinking apparently transcribed into bald print, without any of what George Eliot repeatedly calls 'screenings'. It is like the frighteningly secret presence of that phrase 'slightest notion' in Arthur's subconscious: 'The mere fact that he was in the presence of an intimate friend, who had not the slightest notion that he had had any such serious internal struggle as he came to confide, rather shook his own belief in the seriousness of the struggle.' The solid 'presence' is played off against the invisible and immaterial 'notion': which is to say, that Arthur could look Irwine in the face and at the same time see that his old friend had not the faintest suspicion of what was on his mind and in his conscience. That is how he escapes confession as such and, with it, a still looming reality.

'Was it person? Was it thing?' Mary Ann Evans needed both. Otherwise she could not live with her own inner seriousness. And she could not live without it.

In *Daniel Deronda* there were people who were both, 'half persons and half ideas' (chapter 35). It was they who might convince the normal strugglers that ideas and thoughts were real, could have a voice and a place, and, more, a great consequence in life. Half-person, half-idea was what Tryan was to Janet Dempster, in her unhappy marriage:

> Ideas are often poor ghosts; our sun-filled eyes cannot discern them; they pass athwart us in thin vapour, and cannot make themselves felt. But sometimes they are made flesh; they breathe upon us with warm breath, they touch us with soft responsive hands, they look at us with sad sincere eyes, and speak to us in appealing tones; they are clothed in a living human soul, with all its conflicts, its faith, and its love. Then their presence is a power... ('Janet's Repentance', chapter 19)

To a passionate intellectual, seemingly abstract thoughts could make themselves felt in their own right. Ideas could have a presence, a near-physical being of their own to Mary Ann Evans: they seemed bigger and more dignified than the humiliating psychological problems, the commonplace personal dissatisfactions, the barely remembered non-happenings they spoke to. But to the majority of people, a saving idea might be recognizable only by being transmitted through another human, or else its serious reality might be too easy to discount or avoid, or too hard to believe and follow. Otherwise abstract thinking came into mundane existence only through hard repeated experience, as though a familiar block or renewed crisis were trying still to tell you something. As her own fictional character Felix Holt was to put it in his 'Address to Working Men', where thought is called wisdom:

> Wisdom stands outside of man and urges itself upon him, like the marks of the changing seasons, before it finds a home within him, directs his actions, and from the precious effects of obedience begets a corresponding love.
> But while still outside us, wisdom often looks terrible, and wears strange forms, wrapped in the changing conditions of a struggling world.   (*Essays*, p. 429)

Thought as a presence and a fact, physical and moral, has (says Holt) to 'enter into' the voluntary consciousness and actions of human beings even through those strange or terrible forms of experience in which it is first felt. Even Mary Ann Evans, being young and alone, still wanted the mental support of a guide to re-convince and strengthen her, to remember that there were, in reality, serious laws working their way even within an apparently formless modern world. She still needed to make these thoughts and ideas of hers fully human again, 'transhumanated', through the sympathy and the reality of others. This process of thought finding 'a home' in herself, of her truly being a home to herself, was arduous and slow, only gradually evolving from the feeling of external pressure—like, as Felix Holt puts it, external obedience finally becoming inner love. And, even then, the woman who was George Eliot had to go back and do it again as a writer: 'going through again and again the severe effort of trying to make certain ideas thoroughly incarnate, as if they had revealed themselves to me first in the flesh and not in the spirit' (GEL 4, p. 300).

Finally, in *Daniel Deronda*, George Eliot was to quote Shelley in *Prometheus Unbound*:

> As thought by thought is piled, till some great truth
> Is loosened, and the nations echo round.
> (*Daniel Deronda*, chapter 42)

Thoughts recognized within persons and situations; persons and situations recognized within books and thoughts; those thoughts made into ideas; ideas established as truths; truths echoing around the world, not least through art translating them back again into feelings: that was the ideal mounting movement.

The Need for Adult Love

Even in seeking to pursue that ideal, there was also something the matter in Mary Ann Evans's desire for a guide.

It is picked up, as ever, in the fiction, when, in the midst of her sexual disgrace, the 19-year-old Maggie Tulliver 'felt a child-like, instinctive relief' when she saw Dr Kenn looking at her with a 'middle-aged face' that had 'a grave, penetrating kindness in it'. It was a look that seemed

> to tell of a human being who had reached a firm, safe strand, but was looking with helpful pity towards the strugglers still tossed by the waves...The middle-aged, who have lived through their strongest emotions, but are yet in the time when memory is still half-passionate and not merely contemplative, should surely be a sort of natural priesthood whom life has disciplined and consecrated to be the refuge and rescue of early stumblers and victims of self-despair.   (*The Mill on the Floss*, book 6, chapter 9)

This 'natural' priesthood that Dr Kenn provided for Maggie was what George Eliot offered to the readers of her novels: 'Most of us at some moment in our young lives, would have welcomed a priest of that natural order.' Mary Ann Evans at times could hardly wait, it seemed, to become middle-aged, imagining herself safely established as an identity, a real person in her own right in the midst of life, and not just a mess. But in the meantime she could barely manage her emotional insecurity and loneliness—was 'not fitted to stand alone', as Charles Bray famously reported. 'Always needing someone to lean upon', she took as her mentors a series of older men, many of them married (GEL 1, p. 265). The relief of trying to say everything to someone might be child-like, as Maggie was, but the danger in it was adult and sexual. Dr Kenn, a recent widower, offers Maggie a home as governess to his younger children, but almost immediately town gossip makes him have to ask her to leave.

Mary Ann Evans sporadically knew all too well how vulnerably inauthentic she could be in all this. Often she would find herself confessing precisely in order not to feel what she was trying to rid herself of. 'I am always inclined to make a father-confessor of you,' she writes to the Reverend Francis Watts, a professor of theology at a college in Birmingham, 'probably because I augur that you have no heart for inflicting heavy penances' (GEL 1, p. 142). She worries about the impression she has made. She fears the disturbing intrusion of feelings—unruly affections 'which have shaken my intellect from a steady direction to the object you and my better self would make my pole-star' (GEL 1, p. 142). What could come out of that chaos of mixed motives, relationships that would not stay purely formal and impersonal? She would not try artificially to split off some better self from other ostensibly less noble promptings: she needed to carry everything through together, however ignominiously or dangerously.

*

Something in her was always spilling over set boundaries.

After the 'Holy War' with her father in 1842, Mary Ann Evans spent increasing time with the Brays at Rosehill. Centring around the Bray household—Charles and Cara Bray, Cara's sister Sara Hennell, her brother Charles Hennell and his wife Rufa—the so-called Rosehill Circle received visits from radicals as various as Robert Owen, Richard Cobden, Herbert Spencer, J. A. Froude, John Chapman, and the American visionary Ralph Waldo Emerson. It was that circle that encouraged Mary Ann Evans to become a writer, albeit starting as no more than a learned translator of radical revisionist writings on Christianity: Spinoza, Strauss, later Feuerbach. During the seven-year period from her religious unconversion to the death of her father, this dutiful work and her holidays with the Brays offered her relief from her life alone with the increasingly ailing Robert Evans in their semi-detached villa at Foleshill.

But the free thinking in her intellectual escape group also included the possibility of unconventional relationships. Charles Bray himself—Coventry ribbonmanufacturer, philanthropist, would-be intellectual, lively, handsome, and warmly enthusiastic—had a mistress and second family. It may have been no more than jealous pique that led the now displaced Maria Lewis to speak of he and Mary Ann, in their incessant talk, walking about together like lovers. True to the governess she

Fig. 5. Charles Bray (1811–1884), photograph of 'the Don Juan of Coventry' (on account of his sexual life); his purchase of the *Coventry Herald* in 1846 gave Mary Ann Evans the opportunity to contribute articles (George Eliot Fellowship).

had always been, Maria Lewis was often critical of what was potentially imprudent or unorthodox, too open or too needy, in her protégée's manners. At any rate, the final break, as reported by Sara Hennell, came in a face-to-face quarrel when it was as if 'Miss Lewis had reproached her with seeming to take too much interest in somebody—of the opposite sex'. Feeling wronged and unfairly corrected once again in her life, Mary Ann boldly retorted, 'It might as well be said that you have an "interest" or are interested in your friendship for me.'[11]

Nonetheless, for all the denials, a repeatedly messy and muddled pattern of need and humiliation, of intellectual mentorship and confused emotion, was beginning to emerge. Mary Ann had already been attracted to Joseph Brezzi who came from Leamington each week to the Evans household in 1839 to teach her Italian and then more crucially, from March 1840, German. To Maria Lewis she confessed that Brezzi was 'anything but uninteresting, all external grace and mental power': that is why she needed the injunction from Isaiah, 'Cease ye from man' (GEL 1, p. 51). But the pattern did not cease, and the relation of learning and Eros was established.

Mary Ann Evans first met Elizabeth Rebecca Brabant at the Brays' in 1842 and the four of them went off on various excursions together the following year. Rufa, as she was known, had undertaken to translate Strauss's *Das Leben Jesu* but passed it over to her fellow intellectual Mary Ann in 1844. By then Rufa had married Cara Bray's brother, Charles Hennell, and given up on the project, though Strauss was himself an admirer of her husband's work. Immediately after the wedding in November 1843, Rufa's father, Dr Brabant, a physician, had invited Mary Ann Evans to stay with him and his blind wife in their house in Devizes in Wiltshire 'to fill the place of his daughter'. He was nearly forty years older than she, and called her by the pet name 'Deutera', from the Greek, meaning 'second' but sounding like 'daughter'. It was the prelude to another episode in ambiguity, of misinterpretations and muddled boundaries, and clear types of relationship undermined by needy personal forces within them.

Like his new son-in-law, Brabant was engaged in critical work on the Bible, disputing the status of the supernatural. But also like some early version of the impotent scholar Casaubon with whom Dorothea falls deludedly in love in *Middlemarch*, the apparently learned old scholar, constantly assembling notes and revising opening chapters, never finished his so-called great work. This newly adopted daughter aged 24, on holiday from her actual father, wrote excitedly to Cara Bray on 20 November 1843, of kind looks and kind words—'I am in a little heaven here, Dr. Brabant being its archangel':

Mrs. Brabant is a most affectionate amiable being, too forgetful of herself to talk of her loss [of her daughter to marriage], but really feeling it as much as any one. Of the Dr. what shall I say? For the time would fail me to tell of all his charming qualities. We read, walk and talk together, and I am never weary of his company. I have just written to

Father to beg for a longer leave of absence... I am petted and fed with nice morsels and pretty speeches until I am in danger of becoming even more conceited than ever, and I shall want a month's mortification to make me endurable.   (GEL 1, pp. 165–6)

The tone is that unstable one of hers when she veers between needy triumph and overdone apology—'Dr. Brabant spoils me for every one else' (GEL 1, p. 167); 'The people here are all so ugly! almost as ugly as I am' (GEL 1, p. 165). She adds to Cara, 'He really is a finer character than you think.'

Though she liked having such insights, he probably wasn't better than Cara thought. Looking back three years later, she admitted, 'If I ever offered incense to him it was because there was no other deity at hand and because I wanted some kind of worship pour passer le temps' (GEL 1, p. 225). But she writes on in a way that might seem wincingly unworthy of her unless there was something behind it painful to her pride: 'I always knew that I could belabour my fetisch if I chose, and laughed at him in my sleeve. Even that degree of mock reverence has long since passed away.' A recent renewal of their correspondence is, she insists, a favour she has conferred, not received, and 'I shall certainly take an opportunity of certifying him on which leg the boot was.' Then, self-consciously in the face of how this reads, comes the more characteristic second-thought apology at the end of a paragraph: 'You see I am getting horribly vulgar as well as proud' (GEL 1, p. 225).

What seems to have happened on that visit in 1843 was reported by the real daughter, Rufa Hennell herself, years later in 1851. The sightless Mrs Brabant was not entirely blind as to what might be going on; there was a cuckoo in the nest. Mary Ann was innocent, claimed Rufa: she

in the simplicity of her heart and her ignorance of (or incapability of practising) the required conventionalisms, gave the Doctor the utmost attention; they became very intimate; his Sister-in-law, Miss S. Hughes, became alarmed, made a great stir, excited the jealousy of Mrs. Brabant. Miss Evans left. Mrs. B vowed she should never enter the house again, or that if she did, she, Mrs. Brabant, would instantly leave it. Mrs. Hennell says Dr. B. acted ungenerously towards Miss E., for though he was the chief cause of all that passed, he acted towards her as though the fault lay with her alone. His unmanliness in the affair was condemned more by Mrs. Hennell than by Miss E. herself when she (a year ago) related the circumstances to me.   (GEL 1, p. lvii)

The recorder of this account of Rufa's is John Chapman, writing in his diary 27 June 1851—a man himself embroiled in sexual entanglements which by then began to include the involvement of this same 'Miss E' in his own dubious household affairs.

Asked to leave the Brabant house like a blunderer, Mary Ann Evans went back home again to her father and her laborious translation work, set firmly within the boundaries of limitation. The Brays would try to introduce her to young men nearer her own age, and for a brief week or so in March 1845 there was actually a marriage proposal. Cara Bray writes to her sister Sara:

> She says she was talking to you about a young artist she was going to meet at Baginton. Well, they did meet and passed two days in each other's company, and she thought him the most interesting young man she had seen and superior to all the rest of mankind.   (GEL 1, pp. 183–4)

On the third morning he made a proposal through a mutual friend, Henry Houghton, the husband of her older half-sister, Fanny—'the most fascinating creature he had ever beheld...a person of such superior excellence and powers of mind'—and sought permission to write to her. The artist in him loved her. Mary Ann, Cara goes on, 'came to us brimful of happiness':

> though she said she had not fallen in love with him yet, but admired his character so much that she was sure she should; the only objection seemed to be that his profession—a picture-restorer—is not lucrative or over-honourable.   (GEL 1, p. 184)

'What should you say to my becoming a wife?' she wrote to Martha Jackson (GEL 1, p. 188). But her world always seemed to have its mundane side, and to earn a living, the artist was also a mere picture-restorer. Not having fallen in love with him 'yet'— the little word revealing that characteristically mixed-up and unsynchronized state of hers—she at least tempered her excitement by refusing an immediate engagement. It was fortunate she did, for there was almost immediately a further mundane turn, again on second thought:

> he came to see her last Wednesday evening, and owing to his great agitation, from youth—or something or other, did not seem to half so interesting as before, and the next day she made up her mind that she could never love or respect him enough to marry him and that it would involve too great a sacrifice of her mind and pursuits. So she wrote to him to break it off—and there it now stands.   (GEL 1, p. 184)

'Too great a sacrifice of her mind and pursuits.' It was her powers of mind that had attracted him and it was now that mind, in its suddenly cooled judgement of the poor youth, that turned her off him. It made her doubt his artistic abilities, for all her emotional susceptibility, and the whole thing became an 'it'—'it' would involve to great a sacrifice, she wrote to break 'it' off, there 'it' now stands. 'My unfortunate "affaire",' she wrote Sara Hennell wryly, 'did not become one "du coeur"' (GEL 1, p. 185). Writing to Sara, full of the headache that was constantly plaguing her, she now signed himself 'your loving wife' as though in search of some easier emotional proxy, just as Martha Jackson had been in the past (GEL 1, p. 187)—the female friend as a fallback, when, as she later insisted to Edith Simcox in the midst of her protestations of love, the primary relationship for her was always that between man and woman. But she had moved almost at once from thinking this male suitor the most interesting young man she had ever met to finding him not half so interesting as before, and Cara thought she may have been as 'over-hasty in giving it up' as she had been overenthusiastic at the beginning. Cara wrote to her sister Sara:

> This affair of M. A.'s is much on our minds; although it is given up irrevocably, she is so extremely wretched about it, and we know, wants it to come on again—not that she cares much for him, but she is so grieved to have wounded his feelings and he has behaved so well and unselfishly that he deserves pity, if not more. (GEL 1, p. 186)

After the passionate excitement, then the almost immediate disillusionment, and finally the guilt, but guilt mixed with hankering regret in half-wanting some version of the relationship to resume. It made it worse that the modest young painter never reproached her for the damage caused. Mary Ann told Cara she would not let the incident interfere with her now tiresomely laborious translation of 1500 pages of Strauss. But Cara concluded: 'poor girl, everything seems against the grain with her' (GEL 1, p. 186). One of the simple but fundamental shifts of experience for Mary Ann Evans was that move from her own point of view to her imagination of the point of view of others, particularly some other whom she had hurt.

This became a terrible repetitive pattern for her. As she wrote to Sara Hennell, when, by 1850, their own relationship began to falter in favour of male alternatives:

> The other morning as I was lying in bed I had a clear revelation of my own deficiencies towards you and of the justice of your feelings. This, like all other self-insight, comes too late but it is an irresistible impulse to tell you of it. (GEL 1, p. 337)

Deficiencies on one's own side, underappreciated feelings on the other. Lying in bed, less egotistically involved in the daytime world, she found sudden extricated thoughts coming to mind, as if she were seeing no longer from a first-person perspective but looking at herself as a she, a her, too late. The Victorian critic Peter Bayne selected as vital to an understanding of George Eliot one favourite quotation from All's Well That Ends Well, concerning the unprincipled Parolles: 'Is it possible he should know what he is, and be that he is?'[12] When, unexpectedly, she got clear sight of her own mistakes from some point of view not normally available to her, Mary Ann Evans was painfully involved in such basic paradoxes of knowing and being. How could she think of some discreditable thing in herself and still continue to be—and bear to remain being—that same person? Yet, alternatively, how could she not still remain so? That was what conscience was—belated regret. It was not as if knowing of itself what was wrong could put wrong right. Feeling guilty did not miraculously create a fresh start or reduce the damage. Yet equally, if she *was* still that same person, she could nonetheless manage to sustain within her the capacity to think these painful things of herself. Where did that moral capability come from and what could be done with it?

Back home with her ageing father, amidst her labours as a translator, much of her life went on through letters. But there, even if she could barely resist her own moaning, she could hardly prevent herself criticizing one friend in writing to another. It had been at its worst, understandably, during the Holy War when the complaints were of her own father and her family. She had complained to Cara Bray but by the end of the day was writing of her feelings of disloyalty, 6 March 1842:

> I must relieve my conscience before I go to bed by entering a protest against every word or accent of discontent that I uttered this morning. If I have ever complained of any person or circumstance I do penance by eating my own words. When my real self has regained its place I can shake off my troubles 'like dewdrops from the lion's mane'[13] and then I feel the baseness of imputing my sorrows to others rather than to my own pitiful weakness.   (GEL 1, p. 130)

Sometimes it was easier to blame herself rather than those others whom she was supposed to love. Sometimes it was much harder—to look back, to hear her very tone of voice again, to have to eat her own words. But what was hardest was to establish a just balance. She felt sure there was in her a 'real self' that could regain its place, but how to *be* it more consistently, or at least to activate it at the right time rather than too late, was her predicament. What was psychology in her—its distorted demands, incoherent impulses, and bitter regrets—sought thought, needed protective morality, but also wanted something else still. As it was with confession, 'relieving my conscience before I go to bed', so it was with 'doing penance': what she needed against the psychological pressure was the old religious language of practice and discipline—a language which, ever increasingly, was becoming unavailable to her.

So it is explicitly when she writes to her half-sister, Fanny, in protest against that constant tendency to criticize others, reappearing again 4 February 1849:

> I have been holding a court of conscience, and I cannot enjoy my Sunday's music without restoring harmony, without entering a protest against that superficial soul of mine which is perpetually contradicting and belying the true inner soul. I am in that mood which, in another age of the world, would have led me to put on sackcloth and pour ashes on my head, when I call to mind the sins of my tongue—my animadversions on the faults of others, as if I thought myself to be something when I am nothing. When shall I attain to the true spirit of love which Paul has taught for all the ages?

I want no one to excuse me, dear Fanny—I only want to remove the shadow of my miserable words and deeds from before the divine image of truth and goodness, which I would have all beings worship. I need the Jesuits' discipline of silence, and though my 'evil-speaking' issues from the intellectual point of view rather than the moral,— though there may be gall in the thought while there is honey in the feeling, yet the evil speaking is wrong. We may satirize character and qualities in the abstract without injury to our moral nature, but persons hardly ever.   (GEL 1, p. 276)

This was like the unconscious or silently suppressed cruelty that some observers could see at moments in her eyes. And her own reaction against it is the origin of the George Eliot who cannot have the old religion but must have something equivalent to it; who must think anything and say everything, and yet, knowing from bitter experience the cruelty of unfeeling intellect and the injustice of emotional moodiness, also wants the discipline of silenced criticism and tempered judgement; who hates false distinctions and abstract systems, yet fears mixed motives and emotional chaos. In constant process of dissolving old categories, only to have to reinvent them in a different modern form, she has to reinterpret the categories of the intellectual, the emotional, and the moral, and the shifting relationship of conflict and co-operation between them.

It was like repeatedly trying to recreate a whole person, even out of the tension between parts of it: 'I must relieve my conscience before I go to bed by entering *a protest against* every word or accent of discontent that I uttered'; 'I cannot enjoy my Sunday's music without restoring harmony, without entering *a protest against* that superficial soul of mine.' That puritan language and syntax in protesting *against* herself was the reflexive attempt to re-find a trace of a better self in the act of admitting the worse.

'The consciousness of the world is a humiliating consciousness,' wrote Feuerbach in her translation of him. So it often was to her throughout the years. 'The first stone against which the pride of egoism stumbles is the *thou*, the *alter ego*' (Feuerbach, p. 82, part 1, chapter 8):

My fellow-man is my objective conscience; he makes my failings a reproach to me; even when he does not expressly mention them, he is my personified feeling of shame.
(Feuerbach, p. 158, part 1, chapter 16)

Reality, said Feuerbach, was first felt, was primitively encountered as something resistantly physical, an external, unyielding substance like a hard sharp stone. That is how one knew something was *there*, not-oneself, by running up against it in the world. But worse for Mary Ann Evans was the no less painful thought, in course of her evolution, that finally the other person, externally as separate as a stone, was also soft and vulnerable inside, as she was. That was the humiliating and the painful consciousness, an emerging imaginative realization of what was not so solid but immaterial and made of feeling. It was an ostensibly simple thought but a second thought, and a far from simple experience. It was repeatedly undergone in what was called in *The Mill on the Floss*, after Bunyan, the Valley of Humiliation.

'What Shall I Be Without My Father?'

Robert Evans had never really recovered full health after breaking his leg in 1845, causing his daughter to hurry back from a holiday tour of Scotland with the Brays. Sea air was prescribed him, and over the next two or three years of his decline Mary Ann would regularly take him to seaside resorts in Dover, the Isle of Wight, Brighton, and St Leonard's. Through most of 1848 she was still hoping that his frequent attacks of influenza could be staved off, indicating nothing worse. But by 1849 he was showing signs of severe heart problems. His physician would not allow him to climb stairs, and his bed was established in the dining room, Mary Ann sleeping on the nearby sofa.

She was suffering the claustrophobia of her situation. It was like being inside some 'dark damp vault' (GEL 1, p. 265). Sometimes, tired and dispirited, she seemed more ill than her father, with headache or toothache, and was becoming miserably thin. Yet she kept tending to him and reading to him, especially their favourite, the novels of Water Scott, which she read him regularly over the last five or six years of their lives together.

She had begun to read Scott when she was 7 or 8. Then, when she had had to return to a neighbour the copy of *Waverley* that had been loaned to her, before she had finished it, she had first turned writer. She recreated 'in lines that thwart like portly spiders ran'[14] the story as far as she had got before it had been taken from her, and then tried to see the way forward. Maggie Tulliver does the same with Scott's *The Pirate* but cannot make of it the happy ending which she so much wants, however many times she tries (*The Mill on the Floss*, book 4, chapter 1). Later, in the midst of her family duties, frightened by the sudden bursts of anger and even hatred she felt towards father and mother and brother, Maggie would think of some great man— 'Walter Scott, perhaps'—whom she could tell 'how wretched and how clever she was, and he would surely do something for her' (*The Mill on The Floss*, book 4, chapter 3).

When nursing her father, Mary Ann found 'no other writer would serve as a substitute for Scott, and my life at that time would have been much more difficult without him' (GEL 5, p. 175). Yet in his will Robert Evans left his set of Waverley novels to Fanny. Mary Ann had to wait until G. H. Lewes bought her a set on New Year's Day 1860, inscribed to 'Marian Evans Lewes, the best of Novelists, and Wives'.

*

Even on holiday with her father at St Leonard's in June 1848, a better mood would not come. She wrote to Sara Hennell of the fate of poor mortals condemned to wake some fine morning only to find the poetry of the world all gone:

> The hard angular world of chairs and tables and looking-glasses staring at them in all its naked prose. It is so in all the stages of life—the poetry of girlhood goes—the poetry of love and marriage—the poetry of maternity—and at last the very poetry of duty forsakes us for a season and we see ourselves and all about us as nothing more than miserable agglomerations of atoms.   (GEL 1, p. 264)

Her life felt mechanical and determined, like the motion of atoms at one level, of routines at another, with nothing else holding it together. She spoke as though from outside herself of the wretchedly 'poor tentative efforts of the *Natur Princip* to mould a personality', nominally called Mary Ann Evans (GEL 1, p. 264). But she did not think she had a personality, she wasn't a person, she wasn't anyone any more. Her duty was to her father, but it was hard to remember, let alone to feel, the emotion—'the very poetry of duty'—that prompted it. The very thought that she *should* have such feeling, that her situation should make her stronger and more loving, 'has an irritating rather than a soothing effect' (GEL 1, p. 265). Maggie Tulliver was afraid of herself when the pent-up feelings of apparently hard-hearted rebelliousness would 'flow out over her affections and conscience like a lava stream and frighten her with the sense that it was not difficult for her to become a demon' (*The Mill on the Floss*, book 4, chapter 3). But by now Mary Ann Evans did not even feel like a human being with a heart, her life was contracting:

> I feel a sort of madness growing upon me—just the opposite of the delirium which makes people fancy that their bodies are filling the room. It seems to me as if I were shrinking into that mathematical abstraction, a point—so entirely am I destitute of contact that I am unconscious of length or breadth, and by the time you see me again, I shall have lost all possibility of giving you any demonstration of a spiritual existence...
> (GEL 1, p. 264)

In such a dangerously depressed and disturbed vision, she was just part of the room.

In just such a room at home Robert Evans was lingering, sometimes better, often worse, and at times 'she thought he might last for years, in a state of imbecility' (GEL 1, p. 272). She had already been nursing him for two years. By September 1848 Cara was writing in worry to her sister Sara:

> We are very anxious about M. A. and shall be very thankful to hear that all is over. Her father gets rapidly worse. The doctors expect his death to take place suddenly, by a suffusion of water on the chest; and poor M. A., alone with him, has the whole care and

fatigue of nursing him night and day with this constant nervous expectation. She keeps up wonderfully mentally, but looks like a ghost.   (GEL 1, p. 272)

Nonetheless, for all her fears of a lingering imbecility, there was still something admirably strong in Robert Evans. He was still able to rally occasionally as the father:

> It is a great comfort that he is now quite aware of his situation, and was not in the least discomposed when Isaac told him he might die suddenly. It was quite a pleasure to see him sitting in his chair looking so calm just after he had known this; and he takes opportunities now of saying kind things to M. A. contrary to his wont.   (GEL 1, p. 272)

Perhaps she who usually wanted to say everything could not bear to tell her father his fate; perhaps it was Isaac's role as male heir, to which she deferred, and it was easier for him with his sense of stern responsibility and his position outside the home. But howsoever it was, she was more used to coming second to Isaac than to hearing her father say kind things to her, and Cara adds of such acknowledgements: 'Poor girl, it shows how rare they are by the gratitude with which she repeats the commonest expressions of kindness' (GEL 1, p. 272).

Lingering on for months into 1849 Robert Evans was desperately tired—with 'scarcely energy to notice his own children'. What increasingly the daughter was anxiously looking for was no longer signs of precious kindness but basic human indications that he was still there with her, responsively, and wasn't losing his mind:

> His mind is as clear and rational as ever notwithstanding his feebleness, and he gives me a thousand little proofs that he understands my affection and responds to it. These are very precious moments to me; my chair by father's bedside is a very blessed seat to me.   (GEL 1, p. 283)

In the bare offices of the sickroom where now, near its end, human life was at its most minimal and yet fundamental, this woman, nearly 30, encountered what she had sought repeatedly but found only occasionally: the revelation of an irreducible, overwhelmingly primary reality offering at least the freedom from anything lesser. For all her conflicts, doubts, and self-consciousness on other occasions, this was overwhelmingly the thing itself. It lies as a memory behind what she was to write in *Scenes of Clerical Life*:

> Within the four walls where the stir and glare of the world are shut out, and every voice is subdued—where a human being lies prostrate, thrown on the tender mercies of his fellow, the moral relation of man to man is reduced to its utmost clearness and simplicity: bigotry cannot confuse it, theory cannot pervert it, passion, awed into quiescence, can neither pollute nor perturb it. As we bend over the sick-bed, all the

forces of our nature rush towards the channels of pity, of patience, and of love, and sweep down the miserable choking drift of our quarrels, our debates, our would-be wisdom, and our clamorous selfish desires. This blessing of serene freedom from the importunities of opinion lies in all simple direct acts of mercy, and is one source of that sweet calm which is often felt by the watcher in the sick-room, even when the duties are of a hard and terrible kind.   ('Janet's Repentance', chapter 24)

The discourse is general because, however specific, the experience also is. These fundamental offices, she writes, are beyond the to-and-froing of intellectual doubt; they 'demand no self-questionings, no casuistry, no assent to propositions, no weighing of consequences'. All is utterly 'reduced' to the basics of humankind, the shared mortality of the species, 'the moral relation of man to man' even between daughter and father. There is no clashing of different levels of reality, theoretical and practical, or different claims within a family. The difficult daily relation to the familiar person—the sense of past wrongs, differences of opinion or belief, petty clashes of ego—becomes what this most complex of realist writers actually so often sought: a thing, naturally and almost physically, simple and direct and clear. More than any theoretical idea that could represent it, more than any fixed, predictable, or anxious emotion, this tending of the sickbed was, for once, everything in one thing, life reduced to one totally absorbing, indefeasible, and ultimate reality.

Whatever its content, George Eliot's characters know when they encounter such a supreme moment. Maggie feels the fall and ruin of her father 'with that terrible beating of the heart which makes existence seem simply a painful pulsation'. He has suffered a stroke in hearing of his defeat at law:

Her father's eyes were still turned uneasily towards the door when she entered and met the strange, yearning, helpless look that had been seeking her in vain. With a sudden flash and movement, he raised himself in the bed—she rushed towards him, and clasped him with agonised kisses.

Poor child! It was very early for her to know one of those supreme moments in life when all we have hoped or delighted in, all we can dread or endure, falls away from our regard as insignificant,—is lost, like a trivial memory, in that simple, primitive love which knits us to the beings who have been nearest to us, in their times of helplessness or of anguish.   (The Mill on the Floss, book 3, chapter 1)

'Poor child': Maggie Tulliver at this point was aged 13; the woman who had become the writer was 40, ten years on from the death of her own father. But at whatever age its occurrence, the experience itself is called sacred or blessed, because it is what George Eliot would still think of as religious, like being in the hands of God.

It is also called 'strange', with a sense of awe, for not fitting into artificially pre-established categories of normal understanding or response. The 'strange, yearning, helpless look' with which the father seeks sight of his daughter is primitive love close to fundamental death. It was strange, wrote Mary Ann Evans herself in a letter to Charles Bray in May 1849 knowing she was living within a definitive epoch of her existence, with a definite end in ever closer sight:

> Strange to say I feel that these will ever be the happiest days of my life to me. The one deep strong love I have ever known has now its highest exercise and fullest reward— the worship of sorrow is *the* worship for mortals.   (GEL 1, p. 284)

The words 'sorrow' and 'happiest' go together in that 'deep strong love'. Robert Evans was 'the one love'. He died during the night of 30 May, before dawn of the next day, and was buried on 6 June 1849.

On the day before his death, 29 May, Mr Bury, the surgeon, had warned Mary Ann that her father was unlikely to last the night, and Isaac came to be in Foleshill at the end. She sat with the dying man, her hand in his, till four o'clock that morning when he became quieter. There was still one more night to be endured when she wrote to Charles and Cara Bray of the imminent blank future:

> What shall I be without my Father? It will seem as if a part of my moral nature were gone. I had a horrid vision of myself last night becoming earthly sensual and devilish for want of that purifying restraining influence.   (GEL 1, p. 284)

She had humiliated herself before with father figures. What wouldn't she do for love? What would she do without external function, bearings, or ballast? Over the last few months she had been trying to allay her devils, the force of her inner needs and emotions, by reading the work to which she was to have Maggie Tulliver turn, in flight from her own demons: Thomas à Kempis' *Imitation of Christ*. She was nearly 30, self-doubting, at the mercy of her own powerful feelings, and unconvinced of her own stability. Her roots seemed lost. Like her married sister and stepsister, she was left by her father a bequest of £100 in cash and £2000 in trust, bringing in an annual income of £90. It left her in that characteristic middling state she knew so well in so many other ways, neither rich nor destitute.[15] But, supplemented by the proceeds of translating and reviewing, there was at least the material prospect of an independent life, if she could be capable of independence in other terms.

Within five days of the funeral the Brays had taken her abroad, to France, Italy, and Switzerland. She remained in such low tearful spirits that Cara almost regretted taking her away so soon. By the end of July 1849 when the Brays were returning home to Coventry, she decided to stay on alone in Geneva for up to a year, for the sake of restoring her health.

It was not just a matter of her physical well-being. She separated from the Brays and stayed on by herself as if in some terrible test. The precipices of the Alps had terrified her and she had struggled not to spoil the Brays' holiday. Now she seemed determined to try to triumph over her inner fears and sorrow by taking on a physical version of what she truly was, at this point in her life—essentially alone.

When she revisited Bellagio and Lake Como in 1860 with George Henry Lewes, she remembered eleven years back 'with a word of gratitude' to Cara:

> for the past goodness, which came back to me with keener remembrance than ever when we were at Genoa and at Como—the places I first saw with you. How wretched I was then—how peevish, how utterly morbid! And how kind and forbearing you were under the oppression of my company! I should like you now and then to feel happy in the thought that you were always perfectly good to me. That I was not good to you, is my own disagreeable affair... (GEL, 3, p. 321)

This was so often how it turned out in a life not chronologically clear at the time of its unfolding. The ability to see it more fully and feel it rightly came only afterwards, outside ego and immediate feeling, when she could see herself as another person— because to a degree she had become one. Then, in contrition, the mental reversal occurs that could not take place at the time, when trapped in predicament and personality: 'Feel happy in the thought that you were always perfectly good to me. That I was not good to you, is my own disagreeable affair.' There is no getting over 'that'. The terrible asymmetry hurt her, like a flaw deep in nature: that she could not be herself *and* be just to others, at the same time.

Yet she had glimpses of the future. At times, in the very midst of the nursing of her father, she had been able to see an end in sight that inevitably made for a new beginning for her. She wrote to Sara Hennell 23 June 1848 on 'creatures about to moult or to cast off an old skin, or enter on any new metamorphosis': 'I am entering on a new period of my life which makes me look back on the past as something incredibly poor and contemptible' (GEL 1, p. 269). But a year later, alone in Geneva, her position was closer to that she recalled near the beginning of *Silas Marner*:

> Even people whose lives have been made various by learning, sometimes find it hard to keep a fast hold on their habitual views of life, on their faith in the Invisible—nay, on the sense that their past joys and sorrows are a real experience, when they are suddenly transported to a new land, where the beings around them know nothing of their history and share none of their ideas—where their mother earth shows another lap, and human life has other forms than those on which their souls have been nourished. Minds that have been unhinged from their old faith and love, have perhaps sought this Lethean influence of exile, in which the past becomes dreamy because its symbols have all vanished, and the present too is dreamy because it is linked with no memories.
>
> (*Silas Marner*, 1861, chapter 2)

It was the opposite of that ultimate reality experienced in the dying of her father. Without the properly securing framework she always wanted, physical or spiritual, the past seemed hardly real, the future a blank, and she had never been adept at living easily or unreflectively in the sheer present.

'I confess I am more sensitive than I thought I should be,' she wrote to the Brays, 'to the idea that my being alone is odd' (GEL 1, p. 301). She had hoped her old-looking appearance would have saved her from awkwardness. In the boarding house where she first stayed, 'All the world says I look infinitely better,' adding however, 'to myself I seem uglier than ever' (GEL 1, p. 298). But she still needed words from home: 'My nature is so chameleon I shall lose all my identity unless you keep nourishing the old self with letters' (GEL 1, p. 302).

Her anxieties in thinking about her friends at home, and imagining them thinking or not thinking of her, increased with the distance: 'I have not spirit to write of myself until I have heard from you, and have an assurance from yourself that you yet care about me' (GEL 1, p. 304). She thought that she was putting a brave face on it in the letters she did write. But she was shocked to learn that Charles Hennell, reading her letters home to the Brays, still could detect in them the morbid element in her character—'the dwelling on yourself and a loving to think yourself unhappy'. 'Nothing can be truer,' she replies, 'but I am distressed and surprised that this is so very evident from letters in which I really tried to avoid everything which could give you pain' (GEL 1, p. 307). This was always a great fear: that whatever the determination and the changes, a deep, early, and major fault-line would still reveal itself. Even in the future, George Eliot would never wholly get over being Mary Ann Evans, the consciousness of physical plainness still sporadically undercutting the intellectual superiority, the self-doubt and melancholy undermining the fleeting sense of success.

Still, there were moments in Geneva when she could begin to see how best to position herself:

> It jumps admirably with my humour to live in two worlds at once in this way. I possess my dearest friends and my old environment in my thoughts—and another world of novelty and beauty in which I am actually moving—and my contrariety of disposition always makes the world that lives in my thoughts the dearer of the two—the one in which I more truly dwell. (GEL 1, p. 303)

She knew she was homesick and yet would be sick at home. But in such letters this—far more than in any budding capacity for story-telling or description—is the nascent realist novelist: in the ability to live in two worlds at once, whatever the strains and difficulties of relating them.

In fact, in the face of all these testing pressures she also reverted somewhat to type, recreating a familiar pattern. In Geneva she finally took up lodgings for five months with a Swiss artist and his wife, M. and Mme D'Albert-Durade. I can say *anything* to them, she reports to the Brays; she did not have to explain or apologize for herself:

> M. D'A understands everything and if Madame does not understand she *believes*—that is she seems always sure that I mean something edifying. She kisses me like a mother, and I am baby enough to find that a great addition to my happiness.   (GEL 1, p. 322)

Likewise she loves the husband, fifteen years her senior, 'as if he were father and brother both' (GEL 1, p. 316), and he even painted her portrait in oils. But he was not physically attractive: four feet high as a result of a deformed spine, he was in that respect an elderly model for the crippled young man, Philip Wakem, who adores Maggie Tulliver in *The Mill on the Floss*. At any rate, there was nothing of the fiasco with the Brabants. But he did, protectively, accompany her back to England in March 1850 to secure her safe passage, and stayed two months, touring the country. On his return they kept in touch by letter, she addressing him by the familiar form of 'tu', albeit with the permission of Mme D'Albert. Later he burnt these letters, he told Cross, lest posterity should misinterpret their intimacy.

On her eventual return to England in March 1850, she made some family visits but stayed mainly with the Brays at Rosehill. If exile made her feel rootless, returning did little to reassure her that she still had a home or a purpose: 'It is always a shock when vital changes have occurred in one's individual lot, to return to a well-known place, after the absence of some duration, to find it wearing the same unchangeable aspect' (Blind, p. 71). But how had she changed, and, if so, could she sustain whatever might be good in that change, without an external life into which to put it? She could not stay long with her brother and his family: their close childhood past had long been insufficient to hold them together. Defensively perhaps, she wrote of the family members who received her back to what could be no more than a monotonous existence: 'I am delighted to feel that I am of no importance to any of them, and have no motive for living amongst them' (GEL 1, p. 336). Mathilde Blind spoke extensively to Cara Bray and Sara Hennell in working on the early biography. They told her that, staying with the Brays, she was still 'restless, tormented, frequently in tears, perhaps unconsciously craving a wider sphere, and more definitely recognized position' (Blind, p. 76).

It was then that John Chapman came to call.

John Chapman was 29, two years her junior, very handsome, brash, and lively, the London publisher of Mary Ann Evans's anonymous translation of Strauss which had appeared in 1846. She had first met him around that time and was perhaps self-protectively unimpressed by his attempts to be 'interesting'. She was calling herself Marian Evans, in her struggling new epoch of life, and now it was that Chapman

Fig. 6. John Chapman (1821–1894) (George Eliot Fellowship).

came back with the idea of making her his intellectual assistant and taking her to London. In October 1850, he came to visit the Brays, bringing with him Robert William Mackay, whose book, *The Progress of the Intellect*, Chapman had just published. Influenced by Strauss, it offered itself as a critical enquiry into the natural history of religion, claiming that the key to all religious mythologies was their origin in nature worship. It seemed natural to ask the translator of Strauss to write a review of Mackay's book for the *Westminster Review*, the great progressive and reformist quarterly of the age, albeit currently in decline.

Known in his charismatic youth as 'Byron', Chapman had qualities that, in addition to his looks and his charm, were almost irresistible to her. He was earnestly idealistic, bent on self-improvement morally and intellectually, and keen to find a purpose beyond the business world in which he was immersed. He was excitedly forward-looking and radically progressive, as though ready to think anything in the creation of a modern world. He was also open and candid in manner, equally ready to say everything that he did think. Best of all, he needed her intellectual help for his self-education and, in his youthful charm, rather humbly accepted her guidance and tuition. She loved that, and he in turn enjoyed the mix of the ingenuous and the disingenuous mixture in himself, in the tacit power of his attractiveness and the explicit ceding of deference. Looking back on the year of 1850 in his diary entry for 1 January 1851, there is a snapshot of a man who was all over the place, precariously juggling with difficulties on every side, extricating and improvising his way:

> I open the record of this new year with a sad retrospect of the last one—sad in regard to the trying difficulties I have gone through pertaining to my business, sad in regard to the wretchedness I have endured through my affections, sad that I have wasted much time and seem to have made no intellectual progress,—and saddest of all that I have made *others* sad, and have not at all profited by this year, in the very vigour of my manhood, to become a better man.[16]

Mary Ann Evans was to move to London, lodging at the capacious house that was at once Chapman's home and place of business, at 142 Strand. There Chapman lived with his wife, Susanna, fourteen years his senior and the inheritor of her father's fortune as a Nottingham lace-manufacturer, their children, and the children's governess Elisabeth Tilley, a younger more attractive woman, aged 30, and his mistress. Into this complicated, volatile, and indeed often sad household moved Marian Evans.

Almost immediately the pattern of humiliation resumed. Susanna could seemingly tolerate the arrangement with Elisabeth, but neither could bear the clever new interloper, especially when Chapman bought her a piano, to listen to her playing Mozart in her room, or kept visiting that room to learn German from her. At first they fell out on which of the three should accompany Chapman on his walk, but by

18 January 1851 the situation had worsened, as his diary record of the chaos acknowledges:

> S. and E. had a long talk this morning which resulted in their comparing notes on the subject of my intimacy with Miss Evans, and their arrival at the conclusion that we are completely in love with each other. E. being intensely jealous herself said all she could to cause S. to look from the same point of view, which a little incident (her finding me with my hand in M.'s) had quite prepared her for. E. betrayed my trust and her own promise. S. said to me that if ever I went to M.'s room again she will write to Mr. Bray, and say that she dislikes her.[17]

Just 'a little incident' and in brackets too, though two deleted coded symbols in the diary for the following day suggest further intimacies with 'M'. So it went on for nearly three months of suspicions and jealousies, rows and patchings—'S. had a long talk with M. before dinner unsatisfactory to S. from the high tone M. took'; 'after dinner in my presence...M. confessed S. had reason to complain, and a reconciliation was effected'. And all this surrounded a woman whose '*absolute* need' was to have someone to love her and her alone. She had entangled herself in relative shifts and compromises, until compromised completely. Then, on 24 March, Chapman records in his diary a classic tangle:

> M. departed today, I accompanied her to the railway. She was very sad, and hence made me feel so.—She pressed me for some intimation of the state of my feelings,—I told her that I felt great affection for her, but that I loved E. and S. also, though each in a different way. At this avowal she burst into tears. I tried to comfort her, and reminded her of the dear friends and pleasant home she was returning to,—but the train whirled her away very very sad. (Haight, pp. 86–7)

She went back to Coventry and the Brays.

Yet by May he too was back, to woo her return to London as unofficial editor for the *Westminster Review* which he was in the process of purchasing: 'Walked with M. before breakfast, told her the exact condition of things in regard to E. whom on every account I wish to stay at the Strand. She was much grieved and expressed herself prepared to atone in any way she could for the pain she has caused, and put herself in my hands prepared to accept any arrangement I may make' (Haight, pp. 89–90). Unlikely as it seems, perhaps she did not know or want to acknowledge, before this point, that Elisabeth was fully his mistress. What she herself had done or not done, how far their own intimacy had gone, to what extent she was manipulated or at fault, is not to be known. 'My Tina,' says a loving clergyman to a young woman in *Scenes of Clerical Life*, 'we have all our secret sins; and if we knew ourselves, we should not judge each other harshly' ('Mr Gilfil's Love-Story', chapter 19).

Chapman simply sat on the grass with her, remarking on 'all the elements, characteristics and beauties of nature which man and woman jointly present':

> I dwelt also on the incomprehensible mystery and witchery of beauty. My words jarred upon her and put an end to her enjoyment. Was it from consciousness of her own want of beauty? She wept bitterly.   (Haight, p. 90)

But she returned with him to 142 Strand.

Chapman doubtless had his pleas and arguments in place, as he always seems to have had. Years later, in 1857, he told Barbara Bodichon that the strongest reason he felt for wanting to consummate the union between himself and Barbara was derived 'from a consideration of your health' and a conviction 'of the reinvigorating effects on your system of a fulfilment of love's physical desires'.[18] When the affair ended, she told of it to her friend Marian: by then, long since over her own experience with Chapman, she had achieved a second life with George Henry Lewes and as George Eliot.

But back in 1851, at 142 Strand, she ran much of the publishing business. In *The Autobiography of Mark Rutherford* (1881), William Hale White wrote a version of what had been his own work there under her tutelage, making her into Theresa, intellectual niece of the ineffectual proprietor. He had done badly there, inner self-doubt making him an awkward blunderer, forgetting important details and lacking thoroughness. At some point, mishearing, he had passed on the wrong print instructions, and then on realizing how costly was his mistake, burst into tears:

> I told her how nothing I had ever attempted had succeeded; that I had never even been able to attain that degree of satisfaction with myself and my own conclusions, without which a man cannot live; and that now I found I was useless ... I was beside myself, and I threw myself on my knees, burying my face in Theresa's lap and sobbing convulsively. She did not repel me, but she gently passed her fingers through my hair.
> (*The Autobiography of Mark Rutherford*, chapter 9)

She knew this feeling of his in herself. Later, he hurries off to the printer, offering to pay for setting up afresh, only to find Theresa has already been there, 'and had paid herself for the rectification of the mistake, giving special injunctions that no notice of it was to be given to her uncle'. Nor had she said a word about it to the blunderer himself. For that, Hale White writes, 'Blessed are they who heal us of our self-despisings. Of all the services which can be done to man, I know of none more precious' (chapter 9). She could carry out this silent service for others, but who was to heal her of her own self-despisings and her fears of herself?

At the death of her father she had written, 'What shall I be without my father?' Not just 'what shall I do?', but 'what shall I be?' It was as though she had never really had a mother. For all her female relationships, it had always been men, her father, her brother, older teachers and mentors, other women's husbands. There was a terrible foreboding: 'part of my moral nature gone ... earthly sensual and devilish for want of that purifying restraining influence'. And so it might have seemed in 1851.

And yet within months of the death of Robert Evans, in that same year of 1849, she had also written to the Brays, in another glimpse of the future: 'Keep me for seven years longer and you will find out the use of me' (GEL 1, p. 303). In accord with this alternative prophecy, *Scenes of Clerical Life* was published in 1856. But between the two possible futures, her life lay in the balance.

Life says to Self in a poem she wrote towards the end of her time in 1878, 'all thy anguish and thy discontent/Was growth of mine':

> I was no vulgar life
> That, like the water-mirrored ape,
> Nor discerns the thing it sees,
> Nor knows its own in others' shape.

Life says that it was taking her its own way. She was going to see.

Three Translations

In January 1851, at the prompting of both Charles Bray and John Chapman, Mary Ann Evans published her first ever review in the *Westminster*. It took as its subject a work actually published by the canny Chapman himself, Robert William Mackay's *The Progress of the Intellect*. The very title was close to the intellectual ambition of the reviewer, and the review itself so impressed Chapman that it convinced him to make Mary Ann Evans unofficial editor of the *Westminster* when he acquired it within the year.

But by 'progress', Mary Ann Evans insisted that she did not simply mean the utilitarian modernizing agenda. She undoubtedly agreed that 'it is better to discover and apply improved methods of draining our own towns, than to be able to quote Aristophanes in proof that the streets of Athens were in a state of unmacadamized muddiness' (*Essays*, p. 28). But alongside the value of useful practical action in creating a better future, there was something else to be done with the past in the realm of thought. It was nothing to do with academic study of the streets of ancient Athens, but with how the thinking of the past still unconsciously informed the present, providing a ready-made framework of understanding that was increasingly inappropriate to a modern world. 'Our civilization, and, yet more, our religion,' she wrote, 'are an anomalous blending of lifeless barbarisms, which have descended to us like so many petrifactions from distant ages, with the living ideas, the offspring of a true process of development' (*Essays*, p. 28). Working within that confused blending of old and new, the critical challenge was how to work the living thought free of those residual, dead, but still lingering throwback-formations which often inertly contained or obstructed it.

In this way Mackay was not offering a narrative history of the great religions in the erudite spirit of intellectual antiquarianism, but a critical interpretation of what life impulses had lain behind or within those faiths and needed now to be freed from them. He wrote of 'how each race had a faith and a symbolism suited to its need and its stage of development' (*Essays*, p. 29). Mackay's was a grand monolithic theory of what, throughout different ages and lands, and in the face of great natural forces, all religions had provided: a potentially reassuring and consoling explanation of the implacably powerful external world and a capacity to appease or transform it. Mackay sought objectively to show why past forms of belief had flourished and how they were now extinguished. 'Progress' in its further, future 'development' lay in the project of distinguishing the ossified *forms* of past belief from that underlying human *content* which, trapped alive within them, needed the rescue of expression in new terms.

In her review, Mary Ann Evans was close to the spirit of the guiding light of the *Westminster*, John Stuart Mill—in particular in his classic article published in the *Review* of March 1840, comparing the contrasting mentalities of Bentham and of Coleridge:

> By Bentham, beyond all others, men have been led to ask themselves, in regard to any ancient or received opinion, Is it true? and by Coleridge, What is the meaning of it? The one took his stand *outside* the received opinion, and surveyed it as an entire stranger to it: the other looked at it from *within*, and endeavoured to see it with the eyes of a believer in it.[1]

Bentham, the rational modernizer, the utilitarian social reformer, had coolly enquired, ab extra of any proposition, whether, in the eye of reason, it was true or false. If true, the task was how then to put it to present use in serving the sum of general human happiness. If false, what at least was exposed and disempowered were the narrow prejudices and self-interests previously masked in dogmatic opinion. Conversely, Coleridge, the romantic poet and philosopher, enquired instead as to why any long-held belief, whether true or not, could have maintained itself for so long. He sought to imagine, through its history, what needs a belief had struggled to satisfy as an attempted expression of human reality. Though she wanted to learn every possible mental perspective and, like Mill himself, seek some synthesis of their oppositions, to Mary Ann Evans it was this Coleridgean reading 'from within' that appealed most in her commitment to the role of imaginative sympathy in understanding. Her sense of progress involved more than the intellectual project of critically discarding the history of past beliefs, because, for the literary type of reader she was, no past was ever merely past:

> It may be doubted, whether a mind which has no susceptibility to the pleasure of changing its point of view, of mastering a remote form of thought, of perceiving identity of nature under variety of manifestation—a perception which resembles an expansion of one's own being, a pre-existence in the past—can possess the flexibility, the ready sympathy, or the tolerance, which characterizes a truly philosophic culture.
>
> (*Essays*, p. 29)

It is exciting suddenly to see in retrospect how all reading to Mary Ann Evans, even the reading of non-fiction, was nascently a species of novel-reading—or at least of novelist-like reading. She absorbed the books as if they had inner characters of their own; she sought mentally to impersonate the point of view to be found within them, seeking their pre-existence within herself now. She loved the mental change it made in her as she shifted imaginatively from one perspective to another, beyond the limits of an egotism and a rigidity of opinion that so often frustrated, shamed, or annoyed her. The clue for potential novelists in life, in reading, and in thinking, as Nadine Gordimer has said, is an eagerness for a 'change of focus' from an established way of seeing, making for sudden re-alerted interest in life wherever and howsoever it arises.[2] *Middlemarch*'s Dorothea, 'that priggish lioness' so vulnerably open to the need for change, was, Gordimer later added, 'my favourite female character in any fiction'.[3]

What Mary Ann Evans loved above all was when the expansion of meaning happened not laboriously but quickly and immediately, as when she read Rousseau's *Confessions*, which seized her like a whirlwind, she said—or, as she writes in a review of Froude's autobiographical novel *The Nemesis of Faith* for the *Coventry Herald and Observer*, 16 March 1849:

> On certain red-letter days of or existence, it happens to us to discover among the *spawn* of the press, a book which, as we read, seems to undergo a sort of transfiguration before us. We no longer hold heavily in our hands an octavo of some hundred pages, over which the eye laboriously travels, hardly able to drag along with it the restive mind: but we seem to be in companionship with a spirit, who is transfusing himself into our souls, and is vitalizing them by its superior energy, that life, both outward and inward, presents itself to us for higher relief, in colours brightened and deepened.[4]

The Nemesis of Faith was about unconversion: the loss of the Christian God, the loss of supportive family, the mix of burden and freedom in the resultant experimentation in the morality of human relationships, including the risk of sexual attractions across conventional social norms. A young intellectual, Markham Sutherland, loses his belief and falls in love with a married woman, Helen Leonard, who hesitates to leave her loving husband for fear of losing custody of her child. But when the daughter dies of sudden fever, Markham guiltily attributes the death to God's punishment for his sin, fearfully regressing at the very moment when Helen herself, painfully bereft but now free, turns to him to go forward with the new relationship. To Mary Ann Evans, such work, in its intense entanglements, was no longer materially just a book. The contents of an extreme and messy predicament were suddenly made representative of the age's barely expressible transition from one framework to another, and given form by a novel. Transfigured and transfusing are her words: the novel seemed to transmit its verbal code direct and almost unmediated into mind and heart. In similar spirit, she wrote to the Brays at the end of 1849, whilst struggling to translate Spinoza:

> What is wanted in English is not a translation of Spinoza's works, but a true estimate of his life and system. After one has rendered his Latin faithfully into English, one feels that there is another yet more difficult process of translation for the reader to effect.
>
> (GEL 1, p. 321)

She was a remarkable scholar and already had a good reading knowledge of five languages—French, Italian, German, Latin, and Greek—from the 1840s. Later, in the 1860s, for the sake of her work she would add Spanish and finally Hebrew. But it is that second more difficult translation that is always Mary Ann Evans's interest as a reader: the translation of the work into herself, of herself into the work: 'For those who read the very words Spinoza wrote, there is the same sort of interest in his style as in the conversation of a person of great capacity who has led a solitary life, and who says from his own soul what all the world is saying by rote' (GEL 1, p. 321). That is why, for all the difference, she had likewise valued Rousseau, a soul revealing itself as much unconsciously as consciously.

She completed three works of literal translation 'rendered faithfully': David Strauss's *Leben Jesu*, published as *The Life of Jesus, Critically Examined* in 1846, Feuerbach's *Essence of Christianity* in 1854, both of them from the German, and Spinoza's *Ethics* from Latin in 1856.

The Life of Jesus, Critically Examined

It was the Strauss translation that was completed dutifully 'by rote'. The project had come out of her Coventry friendship with the freethinking Brays, Hennells, and Brabants—in particular Charles Bray—against the old family faith. It took her two years to work through the 1500 pages of *Leben Jesu*. What Strauss had sought to do there, by lengthy and minute dissection of the biblical texts, was to separate the historical Jesus from the mythological Christ. By the end, as Caroline Bray wrote to Sara Hennell:

> She said she was Strauss-sick—it made her ill dissecting the beautiful story of the crucifixion, and only the sight of her Christ-image and picture made her endure it.
>
> (GEL 1, p. 206)

She toiled away at a literal translation of Strauss's exhaustive and repetitive investigation into every episode in the life comparatively across the four Gospels—analysing each one in terms of traditional, historical, and mythological interpretations. So much of the life of Christ, according to Strauss's reading, was a myth, a fiction constructed to fit the prophecies of the Old Testament. To Strauss it was not that the Gospels were products of a fact, but the facts were products of ideas held by the earliest followers. She had initially promised herself to manage six pages a day, reckoning on one or two hours per page, eight or nine months in total. But it became 'soul-stupefying labour' that gave her headaches and worse, a sense that in the words of Psalm 106, heaven had sent 'leanness' into her very soul for reviling the Gospels (GEL 1, p. 182). Extraordinarily, as the labour continued well beyond her deadline, and slowed and slowed, in front of her Mary Ann kept the sight of Christ, both in an engraving of a painting by Paul Delaroche and in a twenty-inch cast of the Danish sculptor Thorvaldsen's depiction of his rising. It was as though, in its very soullessness, the de-mythologizing text, together with the ploddingness of translation from a language she had been only gradually mastering, almost reconverted her to Christ. What troubled her was not the thought that Jesus may have been no more than human, and not the Messiah of miracles, but the inhuman and depersonalizing methods by which that conclusion was reached, through a kind of slow and minute subtraction of meaning. It was the opposite of the 'expansion' she always loved. For, as he put it on the opening page of his introduction, Strauss undid what he called the first feeling of 'immediate embodiment' when the divine enters incarnate into the human. In its place, according to 'the progress of mental cultivation', he brought into view the 'mediate links, explanatory chains of cause and effect' hiddenly underlying those initial appearances. It was what would now be called the work of deconstruction. However necessary to the discipline, this progressive critical method, in stepping back from the text, made it impossible to effect that second translation she always craved—from 'rote' back into 'feeling'. It was a long, dry process of drudgery and disenchantment. Though she did not dispute Strauss's idea, what she did dispute was that it was 'a perfect theory in itself', as the sheer self-enclosed length of the book seemed to suggest (GEL 1, p. 203). She was sceptical of complete explanatory systems. What Strauss offered was no more than a negative part of a greater reconstructive purpose.

Nonetheless, although not himself an unbeliever, Strauss as scholarly interpreter was what, at the beginning of her task, Mary Ann Evans may well have thought she herself ought to be: learned, rational, enlightened, emancipated, progressive. But her translation of *Das Leben Jesu* found wanting in the book something that was still essential to her from her upbringing onwards: something signalled by human emotion, here also associated with soul and faith and religion. At this time of her life, she mainly found out what lay beyond the rationalistic framework she seemed to need by these means—back to front, from what was unbearably missing. There was no real person, no sense of human being left in the work of Strauss, neither in Jesus nor in the author himself, and therefore nothing for the thinking to be translated into, to make for a human model of living thereafter.

So it was that no sooner did she finish the work than she turned to what she thought of as the most beautiful passage in the Gospel according to Luke. After the crucifixion Jesus reveals himself again to his bereft and disillusioned disciples at Emmaus, just at the point when the longing that each of them had for their ideal seems to have been destroyed. She imagined what it was like to be a disciple:

> The soul that has hopefully followed its form—its impersonation of the highest and best—all in despondency—its thoughts all refuted, its dreams all dissipated. Then

comes another Jesus—another but the same—the same highest and best, only chastened, crucified instead of triumphant—and the soul learns that this is the true way to conquer and glory...'This was the Lord!'   (GEL 1, p. 228)

That was the second Jesus, the rebirth of life and hope and purpose for which Mary Ann Evans was always looking. If it could not be resurrection, it had to be new birth by translation into a fresh, different, but still living form.

Meanwhile, at a more mundane level, she continued to worry about the publication of the book, and then after that she became anxious about the reviews. 'It is very laughable,' she tried to say to Sara Hennell, 'that I should be irritated about a thing in itself so trifling as a translation.' Only if a work was 'important enough to demand the sacrifice of one's whole soul,' she said, should it be this long and so troublesome (GEL 1, p. 191). The translation of Strauss was not that grand an undertaking and yet it was undermining something that felt like her soul.

In truth, Strauss was more an attack on her post-adolescent evangelicalism and its theology than on the family-based faith she had felt before that. It wasn't that a defence of that simpler faith was unavailable: remarkably it was to be found just where her father might have suspected it was destroyed—in her freethinking Coventry circle itself. Charles Hennell had published, in advance of his own reading of Strauss, his *Inquiry Concerning the Origin of Christianity* in 1838, with further revisions in a second edition of 1841. It was a rationalistic work that sought to distinguish historical facts from the mythological structure imposed around them, and Strauss himself had written to Hennell a letter of congratulation. But in tacit contrast to her experience with Strauss, what Mary Ann Evans experienced as she read and reread *The Inquiry* were feelings of admiration and delight. It was, she thought, a *life's* work in every sense. The difference from Strauss seemed to lie in the way that, after the first requirement that fact be separated from fiction, Hennell made a second more humanly constructive move. Speaking with particular relation to the risen Christ, for example, he gently and tenderly wrote of how 'the most beautiful fictions are those which bring to view the forms of departed friends'.[5] Imagine the sudden loss of such a leader as Jesus at the crucifixion, together with the 'romantic hopes' he had excited, the 'sublime views' to which he had raised the minds of his followers, the

---

Fig. 7. On the Desk—while translating Strauss's *Life of Jesus Critically Examined*. Cara Bray in a letter to her sister Sara in 1846: 'Marian says she is Strauss-sick—it makes her ill dissecting the story of the Crucifixion, and only the sight of the Christ image and picture makes her endure it.' Twenty-inch cast of the Danish sculptor Thorvaldsen's statue of Christ's rising—Herbert Art Gallery & Museum, Coventry; head of Christ, an engraving of a painting by Paul Delaroche given to Marian Evans by John Sibree (courtesy of Nuneaton Library).

feelings of 'veneration and attachment' he had awakened: it was this heartfelt experience that must have prompted in the disciples the 'illusion' of his resurrection, perpetual presence, and future reappearance. Thinking as much like a literary reader as a theological interpreter, Hennell had more to offer than subtraction and scepticism:

> Fictions proceeding from such feelings, and also connected, as they were in the case of the disciples, with the real interests of life, must be of a different character from those thrown out in the mere wantonness of imagination. Hence the appearance of simplicity, earnestness, and reality, which in the midst of palpable inconsistencies, pervade the evangelic histories, and render even their fictions unique.
>
> (*Inquiry Concerning the Origin of Christianity*, 1841, p. 249)

To complete Hennell's second and saving move, the fictions were not only associated with the 'real' in their motivation, but were themselves made into 'facts' of a different kind—valuable facts of cultural influence if not of scientific veracity. For although Hennell continued to insist that imagination and the feelings were 'unsafe guides in an inquiry into facts', and although the real occurrences probably bore 'no proportion' at all to the grandeur of shape they had assumed in the Gospels, nonetheless he concluded of the disappearance of the body of the crucified Jesus:

> [T]he sublime views which it was in part the occasion of bringing forth, and the moral revolution which it contributed to promote, are in themselves deeply-interesting facts.
>
> (*Inquiry Concerning the Origin of Christianity*, p. 250)

The argument was that fictions, believed, became facts and deeds. That such cultural facts were not merely illusions in their effects, even if they had been in their origins. That some richer, warmer way of being in the world was made possible by the work of fiction. And this warmer way need not constitute a sacrifice of mental rigour. These were the underlying emotional concerns of the woman who was to become a fictionalizer in realism.

The Essence of Christianity

Hence it was that her next translation—that of Feuerbach's *Das Wesen des Christentums* (1841)—provided a genuinely more liberating opening for the rebirth of belief in a second, more human form.

What Feuerbach sought to do was not merely negative in the way of shaking belief. Unlike Strauss or Mackay, his interest was not in a factual, historical critique of Christianity but in a psycho-philosophical analysis, such as Mary Ann Evans had found in Charles Hennell. 'I do not inquire what the real, natural Christ was or may have been in distinction from what he has been made or has become in Supernaturalism,' wrote Feuerbach in the words of her translation. 'On the contrary, I accept the Christ of religion, but I show that this superhuman being is nothing else than a product and reflex of the supernatural human mind.'[6] Feuerbach's might have been an approach characterized by the reductive vocabulary of 'nothing else than' or 'nothing but', but for the second use of the word 'supernatural' in that introductory sentence: 'A product and reflex of the *supernatural human* mind.' The superhuman or supernatural God is the result of something superhuman and supernatural, not in the objective world, it is true, but in the nature of the subjective human mind—in its yearnings, its needs, its imagination, and its feelings, all seeking some powerful external object of help, love, and recognition.

Feuerbach's rule of translation was to find the superhuman not above and beyond the human but inside it, in the processes that unconsciously created an unreal entity out of the real needs of human nature. God did not make Man in His own image: it was the other way round. Man created God out of the best human qualities and aspirations, and the most urgent human needs. We ourselves unconsciously projected upon our God our own fragile ideals, in an attempt to give Justice or Mercy or Love a credible, strong, and enduring form, a reassuring place and reality outside and beyond those selves: 'Whatever man conceives to be true, he immediately conceives to be real (that is, to have an objective existence), because originally only the real is true to him' (*Essence of Christianity*, p. 19). Originally, for human creatures, the 'real' is that which must have resistant material substance; they cannot grasp that the immaterial, the invisible, or the subjective has a distinct or separate existence. Hence the creation of a God, a being materialized, albeit in an immaterial spiritual realm, to objectify and assure invisible and uncertain human values. The Greeks and Romans, says Feuerbach, 'deified accidents as substances; virtues, states of mind, passions, as independent beings' (*Essence of Christianity*, p. 21). In the grammar of projected religion, they lifted adjectival qualities such as 'war-like' or 'wise' out of the passing temporal stream of life and turned them into static nouns and substances, solidified gods such as Ares or Athena. In a religious sentence such as 'God is love' or 'God is merciful', the Feuerbachian rule of translation was that it was not the subject that was true but the predicate. The predicates contain the best of human nature projected into the making of a god, and the god who helps spell out those predicates was really us in disguise from ourselves. It meant that the desire to hold onto the feelings of loving and being loved, or the need to be merciful and receive mercy in turn, was truly our highest reality. Again, the nouns were false and simplified: 'In God I make my future into a present, or rather a verb into a substantive' (*Essence of Christianity*, p. 174). Elements and processes *within* the human situation had been dramatized into being independent forces and personified powers *above* it: the work of nineteenth-century prosaic translation was to put the powers above back within the human condition, to work out their place when dissolved into a more truthful and complex human syntax down on earth.

Not transcendence but immanence was the rule: static abstractions were to be turned back around into what they had come out of and what they must now work themselves back into. So in *Middlemarch* there is the young woman Dorothea on honeymoon in Rome, not yet realizing that This is Marriage, that she has project-ively chosen the Wrong Man. Those would be summary abstractions, general formulae, like the easier alternative of describing the experience as the normal one of 'finding one's feet':

> Dorothea was crying, and if she had been required to state the cause, she could only have done so in some such general words as I have already used: to have been driven to be more particular would have been like trying to give a history of the lights and shadows; for that new real future which was replacing the imaginary drew its material from the endless minutiæ by which her view of Mr Causabon and her wifely relation, now that she was married to him, was gradually changing with the secret motion of a watch-hand from what it had been in her maiden dream. It was too early yet for her fully to recognize or at least admit the change, still more for her to have readjusted the devotedness which was so necessary a part of her mental life that she was almost sure sooner or later to recover it.   (*Middlemarch*, chapter 20)

The commas around the clause 'now that she was married to him' to be found in the final published version were not present in the original manuscript: they were added later in clarity. But it would be too steady for Dorothea herself to mark off the phrase or to understand the condition; she is still inside the unnamed experience, in the confused middle of its discovery. 'It was too early yet for her fully to recognize or at least admit the change': '*too* early *yet*' feels the pressure of taking in 'fully'; 'recognize' struggles with 'admit'. It is a syntax that says this woman is in the midst of change, without a sense of form or orientation any more. The 'endless minutiae' of content at the subliminal level of the Victorian novel will gradually mass to create for Dorothea, from below upwards, the conscious message that George Eliot already bears for her: *This is your life and marriage now*. But what fascinates George Eliot, even in apparently small normal life, is the unimaginably precise point which T. S. Kuhn in *The Structure of Scientific Revolutions* (1962) was to describe as a paradigm shift, the moment at which an old framework of understanding becomes so shaken by realized anomalies within itself that it must give way to a successor. But it is that strange place *in between* one damaged paradigm and its unknown future replacement that is most crucial to George Eliot, in the psychological subconscious equivalent of 'the secret motion of a watch-hand'. It is a place called 'yet', as in 'It was too early yet', since human creatures, in the process of going along, can only realize the mental change after it has already happened. Dorothea's is the 'after' that comes sooner or later; but George Eliot, submerged within her, marks the 'already' that is happening in process. Between the two of them, these sentences are almost impossible; they are alarmingly like the total consciousness of our own subconsciousness. 'The new real future replacing the imaginary': but replacing it only gradually, bearably. That is why they are long complex sentences seeking their way, almost in advance of themselves, to be fully realized only in the time to come.

That is to say, the later implications for George Eliot of reading Feuerbach were to be syntactic, from within human predicament. The version of herself in Maggie Tulliver 'wanted some explanation of this hard real life':

> the unhappy-looking father seated at the breakfast-table, the childish bewildered mother; the little sordid tasks that filled the hours, or the more oppressive emptiness of weary, joyless leisure; the need of some tender, demonstrative love; the cruel sense that Tom didn't mind what she thought or felt, and that they were no longer playthings together; the privation of all pleasant things that had come to her more than to others; she wanted some key that would enable her to understand and, in understanding, endure... (*The Mill on the Floss*, book 4, chapter 3)

Every thing there is just part of a list, the sheerly given: there is no syntax to link them. And it was syntax that, in the formation of George Eliot, was to be the mark and the instrument of an underlying understanding in the working out of 'some key', through complex, interconnected relations. Those relations, literal as well as mental, included the people themselves: the father, the brother, and the need for connection. She wanted a relation to the given in life that was more than merely passive. She was, with Feuerbach, a realist, committed to what was in this world and no other, to what was ordinary; but to become an active realist, she finally became a realist writer, making the relationships within her mind as well as seeking them within the world.

It was not that grammar was the solution but it was the process, the planning site, for a complex form of secular thinking that required writing for its working out. The syntax of her sentences constituted a level of praxis at which she could think through the implications of both a secular world-view and the residues of religious meaning. So it is at the end of chapter 4 of *Adam Bede*, on the sudden death of his father, Adam feels a terrible regret at his own harshness towards the drunk and unreliable old man in his latter days. There is one final, decisive sentence:

> When death the great Reconciler has come, it is never our tenderness that we repent of, but our severity.

'Death' is another of those abstract personifications that needed translating not only on the page but in the imagined life: if only we could translate what all too belatedly is seen as important at the very end of life and have it 'wrought back' into the unheroic ordinariness, the so-called accidents, of life's middle. That is how Feuerbach's project was another version of what became realism, not at the expense of idealism but by revision and reincorporation of it. Feuerbach reduced meaning at one (higher) level in order to rescue and exalt it at another (lower) one.

For the moment, for Marian Evans now living in London as a writer and editor, thinking was what enabled her to continue her life through all the practical difficulties and emotional entanglements. 'With the ideas of Feuerbach I everywhere agree,' she wrote to Sara Hennell (GEL 2, p. 153), though his actual phraseology, she added, was not hers and not what she would employ. She could immerse herself in the translation, inside a work whose content gave her a spirit and a courage that otherwise could waver. Where translating Strauss was a terrible labour in which she almost turned against the book, the translation of Feuerbach took what she had experienced, and what she had failed to experience, to a new intellectual level of life. At least she could fight for her existence, with some dignity, on that front, when she could hardly advance it on any other.

In fact, as we shall see in Chapters 4 and 5, those other concerns—the relationships with Chapman and, later, Spencer and finally Lewes—were never tidily separate, but in mingling intellect and Eros for a long time could not be properly ordered. 'Serially rejected,' writes the novelist Zadie Smith, 'Marian grew convinced that the life of the affections would never be hers. Finally she gave up on experience and settled for the comforts of the intellect: reading, translating, reviewing.' Nonetheless, she adds, 'it was theory that brought her to practice'.[7] But it was also practice in the shape of painful experience that had brought her to theory, in order to work out her life mentally and retrospectively. Feuerbach himself knew how theory came second in the natural order of experience: 'The copy follows the original, the image the thing which it represents, the thought its object.'[8] In breathing, he said, I need the air, I depend upon it; but in thinking of breathing the relationship is reversed and the air becomes the object of thought (*Essence of Religion*, p. 40). The movement into thinking could turn around a life, could make someone who feels like a mere object among other objects in the world into a subject again. But still one must return to living and breathing. Always there are these movements between levels in the life of this woman, from concrete experience raised into abstract thinking, from abstract thinking wrought back to concrete experience.

What she sought through reading and reviewing and translating the works she cared about was not only an income and a position in the world, vital as that was, but (to use Feuerbach's own term) a *sublimation* of autobiographical matter. Indeed, above all it had to do still with Robert Evans: 'What shall I be without my father?'

The Essence of Christianity offered this new Marian Evans in 1854 the equivalent on the intellectual level of what, back home as Mary Ann Evans, she had undergone at the level of experience in the 'Holy War' against Robert Evans in 1842. It gave her a strong theoretical justification for what otherwise might just have seemed a weak daughterly compromise of her rebellious beliefs or unbeliefs. In Feuerbach she found the compromise she had made in returning to church with her father, defended now with the uncompromising rigour of a formal philosophy. Janet in 'Janet's Repentance' found herself in crisis 'every moment slipping off the level on which she lay thinking, down, down into some depth from which she tried to rise again with a start' (chapter 16). It was not going to be like that for Mary Ann or for Marian: she would hold on mentally, she would rise above what could have sunk her.

That decision to recommence going to church was not in worship of a non-existent Father above but for the sake of the feelings of the obstinate and vulnerable father below. That was itself the Feuerbachian turnaround, in action. The large issue was not really the ostensible principle of going or not going to church: it was the apparently smaller matter, the matter of her father's feelings, that should have been seen, and was eventually seen, as of greater significance. This was to put into practice the revision of the scales offered in her essay on the poets Young and Cowper: the apparently small in the provincial Cowper might be really greater than the ostensibly large in the grandiose Young.

So in thinking of her hurt but obdurate father, it did not sufficiently matter—as she must have said to herself—that he as a father should have been looking after *her* feelings; that it was at least as much his responsibility to imagine her point of view as she his; *and* that he would not even appreciate all that she had had to go through seemingly to placate him. These were understandable thoughts but demeaning ones—and realized as being such when, like Dorothea complaining in solitude about her treatment by Casaubon, the woman could hear that what she was saying to herself was really crude and childish. The fact was that hers was the larger intelligence and the deeper understanding, and with that came responsibilities which transcended at a moral level the appearance of defeat or the concern for unfairness at the mundane one. The real work went on inside those appearances, in search of the true size and proportion of things. As Rufus Lyon says in *Felix Holt*, 'The right of rebellion is the right to seek a higher rule, and not to wander in mere lawlessness' (chapter 13).

'The relations of child and parent, of husband and wife, of brother and friend—in general of man to man—in short, all the moral relations are per se religious' (*The Essence of Christianity*, p. 271). This was not mere piety in Feuerbach, it was translation in excitement. It was not making the human and the moral a substitute for the divine and the religious: the human and the moral *were* divine and religious if we could see it, and nothing else was or needed to be. 'What yesterday was still religion,' wrote Feuerbach, 'is no longer such today,' adding, 'and what today is atheism, tomorrow will be religion' (*Essence of Christianity*, p. 32).

This was the new secular religion, hidden within unheroic, flawed, mundane, and secular settings. For Feuerbach, those human feelings for good that previously had gone into the old forms of religion were themselves religious: they needed nothing more to be worthy of the word religious, for that was why they had been cherished in God in the first place. And yet in any new religion of humanity, Mary Ann Evans had still to see the un-ideal faults and frailties of her father and know that he was no god. And the faults and frailties on her own side too, as though in rebellion she had had to create and exacerbate his pain before she could feel the reality of his predicament and recognize her love again. There were no single thoughts, simple solutions, or pure unmixed principles. She had to recognize that she could find only within herself the higher moral recognition which enabled her to do what she did and which made it far more than mundane. That was the hard, hard work of morality when no one else was there and everything must be thought and thought again.

In *Freud and Philosophy* (1970), the philosopher Paul Ricoeur characterizes sceptical enquiry and disillusioning interpretation as a hermeneutics of suspicion. Suspicion is occasioned by the gap between the apparent meaning of a text and its real meaning, often to be uncovered in and despite the text's own (frequently subconscious) defences, self-interests, omissions, and illusions.

Nineteenth-century biblical criticism was involved in creating that hermeneutics. But even more, a psychoanalyst, the founding psychoanalyst, would be adept at such work in unmasking unconscious motivations and mechanisms. Freud, with Marx and Nietzsche, was one of the great nineteenth-century destroyers, in defence of the reality principle against fantasy and illusion, and in preparation for a new world of stark modern liberation. And certainly in Marian Evans, as she developed away from her younger evangelical self, there was the intelligent force of what William Hale White called one of the most critical, sceptical, unusual, and unconventional creatures he had known. She had what he called in *The Autobiography of Mark Rutherford* (1881) a 'spice of bitterness and flavour of rudeness' so that when he said something foolish, she told him he did not mean what he said but 'spoke from the head or teeth merely' (chapter 9). Again, she was not merely loving.

She felt a corrosive fury at the denigration of ordinary earthly life adopted by the parochially narrow-mindedly religious, in order only to lift their own beliefs proudly above such mundanity. In her essay 'Evangelical Teaching; Dr Cumming' in the *Westminster Review*, October 1855, she writes of how this populist minister, Cumming, took up a dogmatic creed of fire and brimstone, original sin, and ever-lasting damnation 'that often obliges him to hope the worst of men, and to exert himself in proving that the worst is true' (*Essays*, p. 189). What was 'hope' doing in that sentence, in that mentality, that it had so lost its way in hoping for the *worst*? Why were exertions employed only for the purpose of proving the worst the most true?

Life was being misplaced, displaced, and devalued by such fundamental inversions of meaning. The very sincerity of Cumming's belief would make him say anything to his purpose, however unscrupulous, and ignore everything inconveniently good, to fit in with a theology which was a crude reductive system, a 'scheme rather than...an experience' (*Essays*, p. 162). He is one of those Christian teachers who believed that Man is a compound of the angel and the brute:

> The brute is to be humbled by being reminded of its 'relation to the stalls', and frightened into moderation by the contemplation of death-beds and skulls; the angel is to be developed by vituperating this world and exalting the next. (*Essays*, p. 338)

By this 'double process' of human denigration, she concludes both angrily and wittily, you get *the Christian*—the so-called 'highest style of man' made up of so little of the life of Christ himself. For little trace is there in such so-called Christians

> of really spiritual joys, of the life and death of Christ as a manifestation of love that constrains the soul, of sympathy with that yearning over the lost and erring which made Jesus weep over Jerusalem, and prompted the sublime prayer, 'father, forgive them', of the gentler fruits of the Spirit, and the peace of God which passeth understanding—of all this, we find little trace in Dr. Cumming's discourses. (*Essays*, p. 163)

There was not much of what was really higher in 'the highest style of man', only the lowering of what he put beneath him. Good deeds were done by such not out of the spontaneous overflow of feeling but for the unloving sake of spiritual pride now and heavenly reward hereafter.

This then is what her angrily witty critical essays existed to do—to see into the secret places of her subject's psychology, to expose the semi-conscious backstairs skulduggery going on behind the shallow theological front. But as an early critic, George Willis Cooke, put it of those critical writings, 'She could attain the highest range of her power only when something far more subtle and intrinsic was concerned':

> That she could dissect and explain the inner man, [her essays] made apparent enough; but her genius demanded also the opportunity to create, to build up a life of high beauty and purpose from materials of its own construction.[9]

'For years I wrote reviews,' she said of herself rather harshly to the American journalist Kate Field, 'because I knew too little of humanity.'[10] Intrinsic work was what she sought, in the thick of the human, not outside it. Criticism was less than half the work of a novelist whose first task was to bring into being the characters she only then also analysed, judged, or pitied.

By the time of her last essay for the *Westminster*, January 1857, Marian Evans was almost dismayed to have to look back with contemptuous suspicion at what she had once loved in the otherworldly poetry of Young's *Night Thoughts*: 'When a poet floats in the empyrean, and only takes a bird's eye view of the earth, some people accept the mere fact of soaring for sublimity, and mistake his dim vision of earth for proximity to heaven' (*Essays*, p. 367). She had been one of these people in her youthful enthusiasm. But now she saw that this was the sort of false transposition—heaven's height raised upon the lowering of earth—that a reading of Feuerbach unmasked. It was, however unconsciously, a deception that made for what Marian Evans called the 'radical insincerity' of a poet able to treat of vague and lofty abstractions instead of concrete realities and specific emotions. Marian Evans quotes Young's lines:

> Far beneath
> A soul immortal is a mortal joy

She then picks up on that condescending word 'beneath':

> Happily for human nature, we are sure no man really believes that. Which of us has the impiety not to feel that our souls are only too narrow for the joy of looking into the trusting eyes of our children, of reposing on the love of a husband or wife,—nay, of listening to the divine voice of music, or watching the calm brightness of autumn afternoons? But Young could utter his falsity without detecting it, because, when he spoke of 'mortal joys' he rarely had in his mind any object to which he could attach sacredness. (*Essays*, p. 368)

To write words and not to have simultaneously in mind the felt presence of the real subjects to which they referred was, to Marian Evans, the very definition of both insincerity in writing and unreality in thinking. That list of hers—the eyes of the children, the love of a spouse, the divine music, and the beautiful landscape—though still only a list in correction of false poetry, was sufficient for the moment to justify her scathingness. It was not she and her mentors who were reductive of meaning but the proponents of a so-called higher world.

What she really admired in her essay on Young was the contrast with the poet Cowper, not seeking the grandly remote and sublime but cherishing things in proportion to their nearness, however small. Cowper gently loved what lay about him: the heart is hard and dead, she quotes, 'that is not pleased / With sight of animals enjoying life' (*Essays*, pp. 382–3). A hermeneutics of suspicion would be, for Marian Evans, no more than a stage in a corrective journey. What Feuerbach offered her was not only the exercise of a sceptically critical interpretation but the opportunity to recover even from within criticism the hermeneutics of what Ricoeur himself calls recollection or charity, and what she called sympathy or love.

Feuerbach helped her in this constructiveness. It was not religion, said Feuerbach, that was the object of his attack but theology. And Feuerbach got the ontological order right: the inspiriting impulse for religion came in the first part of *The Essence of Christianity*, the hardened faith called theology only later in the second. Theology, he argued, occurred at that moment when what initially had been creative projections became reified and then separated from their human sources. The first thought 'There is a God' is inspiring, writes Feuerbach; but 'just in proportion as this existence becomes a prosaic, an empirical truth, the inspiration is extinguished' (*Essence of Christianity*, p. 201). The instinctive need for a larger life becomes institutionalized and dogmatized. It was this bitterly ironic idea of 'alienation'—the projecting upon another of what really belonged to ourselves, the giving of our good only to leave us feeling bad and passive—which later so attracted Marx to Feuerbach. For when distinctions within human nature are 'hypostatized' as nouns marking distinct substances and divine persons, then there follows all the separated, dead fixity of rules and systems and laws (*Essence of Christianity*, p. 232). Marian Evans was frustratedly bored with and angry at 'laboured obedience to a theory or rule' (*Essays*, p. 379). Morality at its best, she claimed, should manifest itself not through a person's dutiful recognition of a secondary system but in genuine emotion set free, like a practical and intuitive form of art, to express itself 'in direct sympathetic feeling and action', in specific individual occasions (*Essays*, p. 379). At its most radical this was a challenge to what, in the great tradition of Western philosophy, was deemed 'higher' knowledge, which all too often sought to subsume the particular and the transitory under an already-existent and apparently permanent conception of the universal. An inversion of that order of thought was more excitingly alive: a lifetime's general knowledge and experience to be brought to, tested, or realized in a specific inductive encounter with an individual occasion. But it remained to be seen that this thinking could only be shown finally in the thinking of the realist novel, at once both generous and sceptical. All Marian Evans knew for the moment was her aversion to general and static systems of literal-minded enforcement:

> Love does not say, 'I ought to love'—it loves. Pity does not say, 'It is right to be pitiful'—it pities. Justice does not say, 'I am bound to be just'—it feels justly. (*Essays*, p. 379)

Ontologically, the verbs come directly before the didactic nouns. And when love does not come naturally, as it would not come when Mary Ann Evans first confronted her father's attempted dominion over her beliefs, then it is that morality 'is dependent on the regulation of feeling by intellect' (*Essays*, p. 166). But still

Feuerbach insisted that even in moments of self-reproach, we should not be alienated from ourselves:

> I acknowledge what I am not, but ought to be, and what for that very reason, I, according to my destination, can be; for an 'ought' which has no corresponding capability does not affect me, is a ludicrous chimera without any true relation to my mental constitution. (*Essence of Christianity*, p. 28)

Like the feeling of God, the sense of 'ought' can still be me and mine, even if a lost or suppressed or resented part of me: 'I can perceive sin as sin, only when I perceive it to be a contradiction of myself with myself—that is, of my personality with my fundamental nature' (*Essence of Christianity*, p. 28). Human nature at that fundamental level, adds Marian Evans, 'is stronger and wider than religious systems, and though dogmas may hamper, they cannot absolutely repress its growth: build walls round the living tree as you will, the bricks and mortar have by and bye to give way before the slow and sure operation of the sap' (*Essays*, p. 187).

Indeed, to Feuerbach, one of the ways to learn what was the deep unconscious nature of the human species was to see how it had formed and conserved itself in the creation of religion. At its origin, religion instinctively arises out of two apparently opposite but related human drives: the sense of lack and therefore of dependence, and the power of emotionally driven imagination. For Feuerbach, human beings are not the first things in the world but the latest inhabitants, the most needy and the most complicated. As a species we come second into a world of nature already existent before us and indifferent to us. We typically think afterwards: initially we are just biological creatures, products of a world in which we have evolved, trying to work from below upwards. The human species begins therefore with feelings of vulnerable dependence and inadequacy, of limitation and weakness and insecurity. We have a physical, emotional, and mortal sense of much that is lacking, and, correspondingly with that, a poignant need for external recognition and protection, for help from somewhere. That is why these poor struggling human creatures needed religion and unconsciously created a God for themselves. 'This need is alone the spring of culture' (*Essence of Christianity*, p. 160). The creatures' creation of their God is the human race's most magnificent imaginative invention, a strength made out of weakness for the sake of psychological survival. But if we had consciously made and had known we were making this God, it could not be a God to us, it could not be a help to us from outside and above. That is why the human species has to hide from itself its own power of imagination: 'Something is wanting to him without his knowing what it is—God is this something wanting'; God is 'the compensation for the poverty of life, for the want of a substantial import' (*Essence of Christianity*, pp. 195–6). God, writes Feuerbach, is 'the substitute for the lost world'—a first ideal world which actually we never had.

It was the idea of the incarnation of God within Man through Jesus Christ that disclosed the secret workings of religion. For here, half-admitted within orthodoxy itself, was the true process: what Man had given to God, God gave back to Man, His Son, as by an inevitable return. Heathen philosophers, said Feuerbach, celebrated activity; but Christians consecrated passivity, included even in the suffering of God's Son for the sake of Man. Christianity was a religion of the human heart, it was not in lofty control or in power: it was *moved*: 'All that proceeds from it seems to it given from without', 'The heart overcomes, masters man' (*Essence of Christianity*, p. 59). Man is mastered here by what is actually his own power, not felt to be his own: the power of feeling for the world, for others. But Feuerbach could not simply regret the paradox of the strength of feeling felt as vulnerability. He concludes: 'The Christian religion is so little superhuman that it even sanctions human weakness' (*Essence of Christianity*, p. 60). Christ was not the impervious divine, but shed tears and suffered; Christ prayed for the cup of sorrow, the fate of crucifixion, to pass from him; Christ cried of his Father, why hast thou forsaken me? This deep acceptance of so-called weakness was what most moved Marian Evans in her Christian inheritance. It was what God was for.

But at the same time there is, for Feuerbach, an active demand in human beings as well as an insecure neediness. Constantly in the very process of writing, reading, or translating *The Essence of Christianity*, human beings seem to move to and fro between that realm in which they have to feel weak and insecure, and some other place where they can find and use their strength. Fuelled by feeling, imagination is the faculty in humans that drives the shift from passive to active. At its strongest, imagination in Feuerbach always wants and believes in 'more'—more than the finite and beyond the limited. Imagination embodies, he said, something of the human *essence* that struggles within human *existence*, as though that existence, albeit real, were too narrow a container for all that is in it. That essence is felt as a longing, a yearning, never at home in the world yet ever still seeking a home for itself there, through every failure: it is not static or definable but it shows its presence by its irresistible perseverance through different forms and circumstances. This is where Feuerbach is emphatically not sceptical precisely because human beings cannot be, in origin. The feelings and the imagination cannot help finding ways of believing and creating what they stand for. They must claim existence and reality for themselves, whatever the later compromises and adjustments and defeats. They insist on some human surplus, a vulnerable unruliness still worthy of a place in the world: 'No man is sufficient for the law which moral perfection sets before us; but for that reason, neither is the law sufficient for man, for the heart' (*Essence of Christianity*, p. 47).

So it was that *The Essence of Christianity* itself was a book of excited repetitions trying to stabilize themselves, of one major thought seeking to realize itself again and again through a variety of situations and utterances. For all her personal self-doubt and life's own apparent discouragement of her instincts, Marian Evans found herself translating formulations from Feuerbach that, under her pen, seemed revelatory—not ponderous like Strauss's but absolutely, innocently brave:

> It is a general truth, that we feel a blank, a void, a want in ourselves, and are consequently unhappy and unsatisfied, so long as we have not come to the last degree of a power...so long as we cannot bring our inborn capacity for this or that art, this or that science, to the utmost proficiency. For only in the highest proficiency is art truly art; only in its highest degree is thought truly thought, reason. Only when thy thought is God. dost thou truly think, rigorously speaking. (*Essence of Christianity*, pp. 36–7)

It is natural for us that we cannot help first thinking that what we do is the most important thing in the world, if we do anything wholeheartedly. We have to assume first of all that what we think is the truth, if we are at all to get out the thought. There is an involuntary but indispensable egoism naturally inherent in the organism, in its hunger and its work, and that egoism, in seeking the best from and for itself, was quite different from any later and more self-conscious version:

> He who is skilful in his profession, in his art, he who fills his post well, and is entirely devoted to his calling, thinks that calling the highest and best. How can he deny in thought what he emphatically declares in act by the joyful devotion of all his powers? If I despise a thing, how can I dedicate to it my time and faculties? If I am compelled to do so in spite of my aversion, my activity is unhappy one, for I am at war with myself. (*Essence of Christianity*, p. 171)

'That which exists has necessarily a pleasure, a joy in itself...to blame it because it loves itself is to reproach it because it exists. To exist is to assert oneself, to affirm oneself...there also is religious power' (*Essence of Christianity*, p. 63). This was exhilaratingly celebratory in a way that Strauss was not, offering unashamed defence of intuitive belief, promotion of the happiness of being, acknowledgement of the irresistibly recurrent tendency of human beings to expand and maximize themselves. The chastening and corrective realization that what one did was relative not absolute, that what one thought and felt was partial not infallible, that intense vitality also made for intense pain, came later, in what the Bible called the Fall, like a return of the external check and limit of the world. Then it was like a different world, and you became a different person, more object again than subject. But what came before that, even amongst creatures so secondary to the planet, was religion to Feuerbach. Religion meant the human faculties could not help but believe in themselves, both in order to be and within the very act of being. 'What is finite to the understanding is nothing to the heart', and for the heart, said Feuerbach, 'it is impossible to feel feeling limited, to think thought limited' (*Essence of Christianity*, p. 6). That is why, in the original moment of religion and creation, human beings can have no scepticism, whilst they are living so powerfully from within outwards; no sense, for example, of a distinction between what God is in himself and what he is for me:

> I cannot know whether God is something else in himself or for himself than he is for me; what he is to me is to me all that he is. (p. 16)

> God is not seen, not heard, not perceived by the senses. He does not exist for me, if I do not exist for him; if I do not believe in a God, there is no God for me.... the addition 'for me' is unnecessary. (*Essence of Christianity*, p. 200)

Feuerbach loved this state of vital freedom precisely because it was so dynamically involuntary in its affirmations. It was a state relative to us, to the human point of view; but what else was there? was Feuerbach's retort. What else was there for us but the human point of view if we were to do work in the non-human world and impose our human will and potential upon it? 'Faith is nothing else than confidence in the reality of the subjective' (*Essence of Christianity*, p. 126); it is 'the conviction of man of the infinite value of his existence... the faith of man in himself' (*Essence of Christianity*, p. 105) in the heart's need to make a world out of our own aims. Imagination is the means by which faith would not deny to what it believed in 'the bliss of existence' (*Essence of Christianity*, p. 112). It was not that these human qualities had now to prove themselves worthy of the name 'religion' in place of the old structures: they were what had created the old faith, and had only to prove worthy of themselves.

It was Kant who had written of the unknowable thing as it was in itself—the noumenon—while the things we human beings knew could be known only through their appearances to us, as phenomena. But to Feuerbach, Kantian thought when thus applied to God as He was in Himself and not as He was for us, was not religion but was what had become rigidified into 'theology': 'When religion becomes theology, the original involuntary and harmless separation of God from man becomes an intentional, exaggerated separation' (*Essence of Christianity*, p. 197). To say God was unknowable was, Feuerbach, argued, to give God no more than a negative existence, 'an existence without existence' (*Essence of Christianity*, p. 15), effectively denying the God one instinctively believed in, through one's flesh and blood and feelings. By such ghostly abstractions, Theology punished and intimi-dated human beings with the shadow of the Unknowable, the resultant uncertainty deterring them from securing any position, any independent foothold. Mystery as unreachable absolute truth was converted into a system of dogma that made humans passive and obedient, in denial of their gifts and efforts. It cruelly contrasted the phenomena of experience with dauntingly unreachable abstractions of what was called Truth; it reified and alienated reality as always something other than ourselves, questioningly distinct from whatever we thought we saw or felt. But for

Feuerbach, everything has its own world: 'What God is to me is to me all that he is', 'The leaf on which the caterpillar lives is for it a world, an infinite space' (*Essence of Christianity*, p. 8).

Always, whether as Mary Ann or Marian Evans, she required from persons and from thoughts all the encouragement she could obtain to create and construct in the face of external fixities, and to give of herself despite fear of rejection. This courage Feuerbach offered at the level of the huge potential that the species contained for any individual member of it. It meant that the human mind in the face of reality was such as not only to find and face what was there, and adapt to it. It also had the capacity to do, as well as to know, to create things out of itself— and it could not help insisting on that capacity, to change and to add to what was given. It was hard for her to learn and relearn that, and to have personal confidence in it.

In any individual endeavour, there was always a 'discrepancy between the power of conception and the power of production' (*Essence of Christianity*, p. 8). But this sense of never being able to manage to achieve all that at some level one felt the possibility of doing was not simply personal failure, said Feuerbach. The power of conception was still maintained through the inadequacy of any individual actual-ization of it: 'He who having written a bad poem, knows it to be bad, is in his intelligence, and therefore in his nature, not so limited as he who, having written a bad poem, admires it and thinks it good' (*Essence of Christianity*, p. 8). This conscious-ness which told the individual that his or her particular production was less than good, still gave individuals a general sense of the good, even though they individu-ally might not fully attain it. It was the existence of that general level of possibility and potency, correspondent to the species *within* the individual, which Feuerbach encouraged, beyond the accidents of the personal lot. Yet the poem still remained bad, where ignorance might have been bliss. But this situation was like what Daniel Deronda said to the despairing Gwendolen Harleth many years later when she wants to give up singing on finding she will never be the great performer she had hoped to be:

'For my part,' said Deronda, 'people who do anything finely always inspirit me to try. I don't mean that they make me believe I can do it as well. But they make the thing, whatever it may be, seem worthy to be done. I can bear to think my own music not good for much, but the world would be more dismal if I thought music itself not good for much. Excellence encourages one about life generally; it shows the spiritual wealth of the world.'

'But then if we can't imitate it?—it only makes our own life seem the tamer,' said Gwendolen, in a mood to resent encouragement founded on her own insignificance.

'That depends on the point of view, I think,' said Deronda. 'We should have a poor life of it if we were reduced for all our pleasure to our own performances. A little private imitation of what is good is a sort of private devotion to it...to understand and enjoy what the few can do for us.'   (*Daniel Deronda*, chapter 36)

That valuing of 'life generally' went deeper than self-disregarding admiration. It was rather what Feuerbach insisted upon: that whatever was in your 'intelligence' was in your 'nature' too, not alien but part of you. This was the power of thought, and the vitality of the so-called intellectual life for Marian Evans: that what you thought, at some level you became—even when the thoughts were not originally your own, or personally and finally not quite realizable. It was a broad religious impulse that made Deronda take up the rich meaning of the word 'devotion'.

In his resistance to abstraction, and his genuinely excited immersion in sudden mental twists and turns often cryptic or repetitive, Feuerbach was not the sort of thinker to create a whole formal argument, distinct and measured, out of his thoughts. Nor could he quite conclude what those thoughts finally meant for what he called a philosophy of the future, shorn of false names and structures.

What he left instead was a dynamic and a dialectic: 'Man—this is the mystery of religion—projects his being into objectivity, and then again makes himself an object to this projected image of himself thus converted into a subject' (*Essence of Christianity*, pp. 29–30). If our creation of God was a projection from within outwards, the seeing of ourselves as through the eyes of God was a taking of that projection of ourselves back inside again. That dialectical 'return' immersed in the processes of living was inevitable: what was ours always came back to us, albeit in another form or at another level. This was an immanent universe: everything apparently transcendent was in fact its product and needed to be turned back into its intermixture. This tolerance of mixedness rather than abstract purity was what Feuerbach called love: 'Love recognises virtue even in sin, truth in error' (*Essence of Christianity*, p. 257). Yet if Feuerbach had now 'un-converted' God, turning Him back into a version of the human species, did it mean that what the species had once done for itself via Him, it could now more directly do for itself?

It was not that straightforward a translation from the religious to the secular, though it seemed that it should be so. For surely what we had given to a fictitious God we could now give to ourselves in reality since it was actually ours in the first place. Everything in Christianity—prayer, help, judgement, mitigation, grace, understanding—already unconsciously corresponded to some human instinct or need from which it came and to which it could return. But, on the other hand, did we really believe we would be as ruled by what we now know to be our own consciences as we used to be under the all-seeing eye of an undeceivable God? This was the case against Feuerbach and his representative in George Eliot that was made by commentators such as W. H. Mallock in *Is Life Worth Living* (1879).[11] To what or whom would prayer now turn if there was no one or no thing responsively out there to pray to? You could not simply give to yourself the help you may have given to others; nor could you expect from such others all that we had once received from being able to believe in God. Secularization was not a simple transfer, without loss.

Nor could human beings simply undo the dialectical mental process that Feuerbach described as the equivalent of the heart contracting and expanding in the pulsating circulation of the blood, out into the arteries and then back in again:

> As life in general consists in a perpetual systole and diastole, so is it in religion. In the religious systole man propels his own nature from himself, he throws himself outward; in the religious diastole he receives the rejected nature into his heart again.
>
> (*Essence of Christianity*, p. 31)

The inventive human capability, said Feuerbach, is nothing without an object: only in creating an object for itself can it begin to see what it is and do what it can. It has to be done that way, in terms of what Feuerbach calls 'returns', receiving back from what first of all was given out. As Feuerbach put it, addressing the race with his usual erratic mixture of brilliance and opacity: 'Feeling is thy own inward power, but at the same time a power distinct from thee and independent of thee' (*Essence of Christianity*, p. 11). It is never a power simply under its user's command or control.

Perhaps Feuerbach's best example is one close to Marian Evans's heart: listening to music. There it feels as though the listener is getting back something, consciously, which he or she has felt in a different, often unconscious, form or setting before: 'What, then, is it which acts on thee when thou art affected by melody? What dost thou perceive in it? What else but the voice of thy own heart? Feeling speaks only to feeling' (*Essence of Christianity*, p. 9). What the listeners hear is the feeling of their own feeling, as though returned to them. And it counts more, in a way, for coming back and, as it were, re-minding. For the music of sorrow is heard with feelings that now involve more than sorrow precisely in the feeling of it. It includes the accumulation of human experience in the whole cultural tradition of art doing something with, and making something of, what is otherwise passive experience. That is why Marian loved the collective human voice in Handel's great choruses (GEL 1, p. 247): they seemed to transform the shrieks of individual sorrow into the great sympathetic solidarity of species consciousness. As Feuerbach puts it rapturously: 'Pain must give itself utterance; involuntarily the artist seizes the lute . . . He soothes his sorrow by making it audible to himself, by making it objective . . . by communicating it to the air, by making his sorrow a general existence' (*Essence of Christianity*, pp. 121–2). When what people have given out into the world comes back to them objectively, then that for Feuerbach is like the human meaning of God.

George Eliot would know what that somewhat tricky formulation, the feeling of a feeling, could really mean.

Here is an example from 'Janet's Repentance'. A woman, Janet Dempster, has been abused by her alcoholic husband till, ironically, she turns to alcohol herself. Even after Lawyer Dempster dies, her own alcoholism remains. She has begun to conquer her demon, but there comes a moment in recovery when, looking for some papers, she finds a small decanter half-full of brandy, left hidden in her late husband's desk. She barely manages to stop herself drinking from it, only at the last second hurling it to the floor, and then running out of the house until she reaches the churchyard where at last she can think:

> She tried to remember those first bitter moments of shame ... the deeper and deeper lapse; the oncoming of settled despair ... And then she tried to live through, with a remembrance made more vivid by that contrast, the blessed hours of hope and joy and peace that had come to her of late, since her whole soul had been bent towards the attainment of purity and holiness.
>
> But now, when the paroxysm of temptation was past, dread and despondency began to thrust themselves, like cold heavy mists, between her and the heaven to which she wanted to look for light and guidance. The temptation would come again—that rush of desire might overmaster her the next time—she would slip back again into that dark slimy pit from which she had been once rescued, and there might be no deliverance for her more. Her prayers did not help her, for fear predominated over trust; she had no confidence that the aid she sought would be given; the idea of her future fall had grasped her mind too strongly.   ('Janet's Repentance', chapter 25)

The whole scene is still written within a religious vocabulary that Marian Evans had herself outgrown. There are desperate thoughts of soul, blessing, heaven, deliverance, temptation, pitfall, and prayer, in a struggle to find help from within, to little avail. But it is that more secular psychological word 'confidence'—'she had no confidence'—that in its want destroys faith. Before and even after she became George Eliot, it was such occasions of insecurity, in relation to where one was in reality, that were of most unsettling concern. What Janet Dempster feels here, even amidst her success in barely avoiding temptation, is a sense of continuing failure. This fear and shame are her only reward, like renewed punishment, and if that is an injustice, it is created by the unbreachable skin-of-the-teeth paradox of her equivocal achievement. Hers is a feeling which, within that world, a reader can imaginably share: realism means there is no simple dramatic solution for once and all, but no sooner is temptation barely overcome then the thought is 'the temptation would come again' and then 'next time ...'. But acting as external witnesses from their own world rather than as imagined protagonist in hers, readers may surely feel Janet has done well, is doing well here, precisely when she fears she is not. The desperate struggle against relapse feels almost heroic. But, crucially, not to Janet herself. And the reader of course does not exist in Janet's world to offer Janet the encouragement which there is no one else there to provide. This is her power, her precarious achievement, felt as weakness; a power seemingly not under her command, in need of the help she can barely muster within or find without. But she could not possibly see all she did as she did it; like most humans, she could not know her own worth. What she felt was the fear, not just as an emotion but as an intimation of a perilously ongoing state otherwise too painful for her steadily to contemplate. Meanwhile there is the reader, the author—and even another character such as Janet's mother, helplessly looking on from a picture of herself on the mantelpiece whilst actually living in a separate house of her own: all these are the witnesses, not quite beside her, standing in lieu of a lost, missing, and impossible God who knows the value of what is private and hidden.

What is the place of such vicarious feeling?[12] The realist novel gives it room and value. A reader with such feeling is what Feuerbach would call the species—a representative of the species-consciousness—looking at a particular lonely version of itself, as a human god might. In this way, the feelings akin to Janet's that such witnesses have had before in their own lives come movingly back to them from outside. They return with a pity and respect which at the time they themselves could not possibly feel in Janet's panic-stricken situation, any more than she could: 'In the religious diastole he receives the rejected nature into his heart again.' That is the feeling of the feeling, as it returns to us from outside back in again. We do for others through that feeling what we cannot manage in feeling for ourselves.

Yet there has to be *somebody* for Janet herself, in that human call of hers which in an older language would be prayer. There was some deep primal part of Mary Ann Evans and Marian Evans alike that, irrepressibly, could not but believe that whatever was thought must be spoken and heard, and that whatever was needed ought to be found and given. Janet suddenly thinks of the evangelical minister whom she has heard speaking not simply as a clergyman but as a fellow human: 'Alone, in this way, she was powerless. If she could see Mr Tryan, if she could confess all to him, she might gather hope again. She *must* see him...' ('Janet's Repentance', chapter 25). It was like turning to a version of George Eliot in Janet's own world.

In her early career, George Eliot was content to show the humanizing work of religion going on still within the partially distorting framework of theology. The truth of a belief was far less important than what it enabled. Tryan, not Tryan's God, would serve. In Janet Dempster's provincial town of Milby, back in the 1830s, evangelicalism was a new moral movement amongst the common people—and in the hands of Tryan it was very different from what it was to be so narrowly in Dr Cumming. The difference is based on the Feuerbachian principle of 'by his God thou knowest the man, and by the man his God' (*Essence of Christianity*, p. 12):

Religious ideas have the fate of melodies, which, once set afloat in the world, are taken up by all sorts of instruments, some of them woefully coarse, feeble, or out of tune, until people are in danger of crying out that the melody is detestable.

('Janet's Repentance', chapter 10)

George Eliot, here at the beginnings of her maturity, grants that some of Tryan's hearers had 'gained a religious vocabulary rather than religious experience', that (as she puts it with satiric wit) a weaver's wife, once a silly slattern, was by evangelicalism no more than converted into 'that more complex nuisance', a silly *and* sanctimonious slattern. When 'the mental atmosphere is changing, and men are inhaling the stimulus of new ideas', then even so, 'folly often mistook itself for wisdom, ignorance gave itself airs of knowledge, and selfishness, turning its eyes upwards, called itself religion'. George Eliot unfussily expected in humans such compromised mixtures, such impure messiness. The development of a strenuous intelligence in her served to make the tolerance of impurity not a merely complacent or careless benignity but a carefully discriminated and patient understanding.

'One would like one's life to be borne on the onward wave and not the receding one—the flow and not the ebb,' wrote Marian Evans to Barbara Bodichon in 1859, amidst talk of war and social unrest, 'Yet somebody must live in the bad times' (GEL 3, p. 228). By 'must live' she did not just mean a stoical acceptance but a resistant fight for the life still left in things that seemed otherwise reduced or damaged. In the ebb tide of faith of all kinds, Feuerbach had helped teach her to rescue whatever she could of life's content from the forms and frameworks that contained it. And in that content, George Eliot looked for the little pieces that remained from the great syntheses of the past, which still might serve for new growth. Evangelicalism was one such fragment of the great religious tradition refound amidst the ebb tide. For all its fundamental flaws, its sectarian distortions, and its mixed effects, evangelicalism had 'brought into palpable existence and operation' in the little town of Milby

> that idea of duty, that recognition of something to be lived for beyond the mere satisfaction of self, which is to the moral life what the addition of a great central ganglion is to animal life. ('Janet's Repentance', chapter 10)

It is a metaphorical analogy but more than just metaphor or analogy. The central ganglion of the brain was considered to provide hitherto diverse nervous activity with an organizing centre, directing or inhibiting action, as the physical underpinning for the evolution of consciousness, attention, and choice. In the same way, ideas for George Eliot were cluster centres, pulling thoughts together, making the creature into a human being of more centred consciousness. This was what came to be of interest to

William James in both psychology and religion—'the shifting of men's centres of personal energy within them and the lighting up of new crises of emotion': 'When ripe, the results hatch out, or burst into flower.'[13] By subconscious processes, at such moments of need or crisis, an habitual centre of energy was displaced by a new configuration, nervous and mental, which the religious tradition had known as the experience of 'conversion'. Feuerbach's rules of translation were modernized versions of conversion. The idea of duty and of higher responsibility, when felt as religious in the dynamic sense offered by Feuerbach and, later, by William James, was revitalized into something more like a new faculty than an old moralism.

Feuerbach himself became like a vital new faculty in the nervous system of Marian Evans. It was crucial to George Eliot that within and beneath the language and behaviour of common life there were other levels of life, parallel languages, and codes. Feuerbach was one thinker who helped Marian Evans to see these unconscious secrets and dynamics. What he stood for was key for acts of translation and conversion, such that she could look beneath the ostensibly dull surface appearance of a person or an institution and rewrite the script of what was really there. That translation, revision, and alternative language still went on within the ongoing terms of the ordinary, George Eliot staying as loyal to the life she was seeking to transform as Mary Ann Evans had to her father.

Spinoza's *Ethics*

The third translation went unpublished until 1981. In 1849, Mary Ann Evans had told her Coventry friends she was translating Spinoza's *Tractatus Theologico-Politicus* from the Latin and while that task was never completed, between 1854 and 1856 she returned to Spinoza to translate his *Ethics*. It never appeared in print because George Henry Lewes, who had himself begun and then handed over the translation and was by now acting as her agent, fell out with the proposed publisher, Henry George Bohm, much to her dismay. This was part of the pattern, the translation of Strauss prompted by Charles Bray, of Feuerbach by Charles Hennell, and finally of Spinoza by Lewes. Yet it was not only chronologically that Spinoza (1632–1677) preceded Strauss and Feuerbach; in the *Tractatus* he was the intellectual origin for freethinking criticism of the Bible and for the replacement of religious superstition and dogmatic theology by pure philosophic reason.

Matthew Arnold summarized in *Essays in Criticism* (1875) what the *Tractatus* had meant for the nineteenth century. It offered what was another act of revised reading, of retranslation—a recognition of the natural laws and rational truths previously hidden within the form of divine rules and commands. Ideas were expressed as precepts because of the ignorance of the ancient multitudes, in need of obedience for want of reason. So it was in the New as well as the Old Testament:

the apostles, like Christ, spoke to many of their hearers 'as unto carnal not spiritual'; presented to them, that is, the love of God and their neighbour as a divine command authenticated by the life and death of Christ, not an eternal idea of reason carrying its own warrant along with it.[14]

It was that sense of 'its *own* warrant' that offered active freedom in one intrinsic move, rather than the heavy two-step mechanism of stern commandment followed by dutiful obedience. This marked the crucial difference between the traditional morality of transcendence, where commands came from above, and Spinoza's ethics of immanence where laws were discovered from within the world. Because the whole immanent order had nothing outside itself, was itself 'its own warrant', it was ungraspably nameless and infinitely extensive from within. Spinoza and his translators simply offered a proliferating variety of names, calling 'it' God or Nature, the universe, creation, world, or order. In the *Ethics*, the immanent order is refracted into multiple versions and instances of itself—this creature, that occurrence, this configuration—in an interacting web of differences and similarities arising out of the same essential substance. Everything was a part of the great 'it', of God or Nature, the same basic material in different combinations.

That an idea of reason could carry within itself its own warrant also made for the difference between what Spinoza called 'adequate' as opposed to 'inadequate' ideas. Spinoza, Arnold said, 'has made his distinction between adequate and inadequate ideas a current notion for educated Europe' ('Spinoza and the Bible', p. 181). The adequate idea is one that is logical in its explanatory force, truly representing from within itself the order and connection of things. But the inadequate idea is more like something psychological, a false or confused consciousness, attached to a fortuitous or willed ordering, without clear relation to its own hidden premises. Consciousness of this latter kind registers only effects, and is itself an effect, not turning back upon itself to discover from within its own causes. So, for example, humans think themselves free because they are conscious of their actions, when actually it is only because they are ignorant of those actions' real causes: 'Their idea of liberty is, that they do not know any cause of their actions.'[15] But as Spinoza wrote in a letter, quoted by William Hale White in his own essay on Spinoza: 'I call that thing free which exists and acts solely from the necessity of its own nature.'[16] That the truly 'free' was related to 'necessity' of nature was a mark of the distinctive vision offered by the *Ethics*.

Spinoza offered an analogy for the sort of correction of normal human vision that was essential to right thinking:

> When we look at the sun, we imagine it to stand about 200 feet distant from us; an error which does not consist in this imagination solely but also in the fact that when we imagine it we are ignorant of its true distance and of the cause of this imagination.

> For although we afterwards know, that it is more than 600 diameters of the earth distant from us, we shall not the less imagine it to be near ...
>
> (*Ethics*, pp. 71–2, part 2, proposition 35, scholium)

What we appeared to see and feel directly was not the truth, the non-human reality. The truth lay with adequate thinking, disinterested reason, which performed the non-physical form of seeing. Through what Spinoza called 'the eyes of the mind' (*Ethics*, p. 232, part 5, proposition 23, scholium), such thinking involved the recognition of what was needed in the second place to revise the illusions of apparently immediate experience. And this difficult mental corrective was even more necessary in relation to non-visual phenomena—especially the field of human emotional interests.

Psychologically, humans were naturally self-aggrandising, putting themselves at the centre of the universe, as though they were the earth's sun. This was the natural first drive of life that Spinoza called *conatus*, the illusory need to be special that each creature must have in its self, to help fight for its own continuance and welfare. But conatus could be channelled into something other than ego, that speck in the eye that disabled the beholder from seeing anything clearly outside the self: 'Will not a tiny speck very close to our vision blot out the glory of the world, and leave only a margin by which we see the blot. I know no speck so troublesome as self' (*Middlemarch*, chapter 42). By analogy to astronomical orbits and the revolution created by Copernicus, Galileo, and Kepler that took the earth out of the centre of the universe, there had to be for humans too a recognition of the necessary, difficult movement from centre to circumference—without any corresponding loss of purpose. What was loss for the ego might be precisely what created another level, a level of further developed thinking which began to see the world from outside ego's limits, where the creature no longer had to fight for its own assertion of life in abrasive relation to others. These were the liberating transformations of 'conatus' in which Spinoza was most intently involved—the same basic material turned into working at a different level, 'the *eyes* of the *mind*'.

Arnold argued that 'a philosopher's real power over mankind' resided not just in his 'throw[ing] into circulation a certain number of new and striking ideas and expressions' but in 'the spirit and tendencies which have led him to adopt those formulas' ('Spinoza and the Bible', p. 175). To be truly great, 'he must have something in him which can influence character, which is edifying' ('Spinoza and the Bible', p. 180). This was, in its own terms, close to what Marian Evans had meant when she said that, because of its complexity and its method, Spinoza's *Ethics*, in particular, needed two translations—the first of the literal text, the second of its meaning, even though contained within the first. It is that second translation that we shall see in operation later within the novels of George Eliot, not always through separate conscious influence, but transfused into a working element within the mind that developed out of the literal translator.

Most nineteenth-century commentators, included George Henry Lewes, were content to find something of that second translation in the impressive way that Spinoza had led his life. Excommunicated by the Jewish community as a heretic, he was thereby also freed, as an obscure exile, to live outside any orthodoxy. This was an austere philosopher who sought to make of himself a man of impartiality, without resentments, with an intellectual love for the forms and ways of the universe, beyond his own tribal self-interests. For him a philosophy that could not heal the soul was no better than a medicine that could not cure the body. In *Fortnightly Review* 1866, George Henry Lewes wrote of the quarrel with the Jewish elders in ways that might have reminded the then Marian Lewes of her own more minor struggles at home. The rabbis had urged the young scholar, 'If you are not with us, do at least pretend to be with us; give us your countenance, if not your heart'—to which Lewes responds: 'To some sensitive consciences this is an appalling request.'[17] Spinoza's was a sensitive conscience: he 'not only would not pretend to believe what he did not believe; he was hurt at the supposition that he could be bribed into hypocrisy' (*Lewes*, p. 274). But he had waited until after his father's death to speak his mind. Then he sought calmly to understand and accept the opposition he had created, and transform his painful exclusion into an inner independence of any partial sect or pressurizing influence.

The *Ethics* was not written in a personally human form. Its method was forbiddingly geometric—in the style of Euclid with definitions of first principles, then axioms, propositions, proofs or demonstrations, corollaries, and finally down to notes or scholia, derived each from other in a tight impersonal web of relations designed to be a map of the world. It was a method developed for the specific purpose of demonstrating truth, like the definition of triangle, beyond any distortions of personal human interest. For creation itself did not exist simply or finally for the sake of man, its laws being other and greater than human wishes. Arnold quoted from the *Tractatus*, 'Our desire is not that nature may obey us, but, on the contrary, that we may obey nature' ('Spinoza and the Bible', p. 176)—which became in his own poem 'Empedocles on Etna': 'Born into life! 'tis we / And not the world, are new', 'To tunes we did not call our being must keep chime' (1.2 lines 202–3, 196). What impressed Arnold was that, in Spinoza, this largeness in denial of wholly human ends was liberating, rather than, as so often in Arnold himself and Arnold's century, demoralizing or melancholic. Thinking at this universal level was, for Spinoza, humanly expansive, in denial of mere projection.

In this respect, translating the *Ethics* was like turning Feuerbach on his head for Marian Evans, as though shifting from one character to another in a novel called 'philosophy'. Where Feuerbach was fast and revelatory, Spinoza was careful and slow; where Feuerbach inhabited the early world of intuition and feeling, Spinoza represented the later world of corrective reason and full consciousness. They were like different parts of the brain, offering alternative world perspectives. In particular,

Spinoza located the subjective human world within a wider objective one and, in place of the Feuerbachian drive to impose the subjective, sought instead through reason a fundamental re-education of the human perspective.

But, above all, was Spinoza's extraordinary presumption: that through his definitions and propositions Nature would unfold itself in his book, as in his mind, according to the very logic of the universe. 'The order and connection of ideas is the same as the order and connexion of things' (*Ethics*, p. 47, part 2, proposition 7). Nothing could make reading more important because if Spinoza was anything like right, then what was being read—even for just a moment—was the text of the universe itself. It was an extraordinary visionary possibility for thinking and writing. Einstein was to sign the visitors' book at the home of Spinoza in Rijnsburg, 2 November 1920, in the spirit of his own ambition to find what he called God's thoughts, through his own mathematical language in the theory of relativity developed in obscurity in 1905. To unite through thinking with what was permanent in the universe was, for its thinker, to become part of what was permanent, regardless of personal mortality. It was to become one of the modes through which 'it', the immanent system called God or Nature, thought of itself by means of some part of it. That extraordinary sense of mental union is why there was always a controversy as to how far Spinoza was the first man to live by an essentially secular philosophy instead of an irrational religion, or whether his was the pantheistic philosophy of what Novalis called a God-intoxicated man.

Two novelists, not for the moment George Eliot herself, may help explain, succinctly and from an easier starting point, something of what is at stake in this endeavour at pure objective thinking. The novelist and philosopher Rebecca Goldstein writes imaginatively of Spinoza and the adequate idea: 'He loves it when an explanation fits firmly into place, leaving no space at all. When he understands why something is the way it is, why it has to be that way, the knowing feels like pleasure to him.'[18] Religions looked outside the world for explanations of it, but here the world was made to think, through human reason, from within itself. When an explanation did not fit, when it seemed forced or distorted or unintegrated, then, as a figure in another novel, Herzog, eponymous troubled protagonist of our second novelist, Saul Bellow, says direct to the spirit of Spinoza: 'Thoughts not causally connected were said by you to cause pain. I find that is indeed the case.'[19] Pleasure and pain mean here the very expanding or contracting of a life, its sense of either flourishing health or poisoned diminishment in the space available to it. The verbal formulations in that mental space were not merely stylistic issues, but indices of greater or lesser mental health, of more or less vitality of ordered being finding its place in the understanding of the universe. It is these novelists who help us see how this visionary grandeur is related to an individual's intense experience of finding a thought fitting or not fitting into place—and all the more so in the inner life of a writer's intimate experience of thinking. There was something important here for

Marian Evans in her search to overcome the mental pains of separation and anomaly.

Lewes himself knew well the only truly autobiographical passage in the works of Spinoza. It concerns what was, for Spinoza, the personal origin of his philosophy, in his effort to get out of the cycle of pleasure and pain, out of the life of continual inadequacy of thought and purpose, in the search for some unfailing good:

> I finally resolved on inquiring if there was anything truly good in itself... which if possessed could give supreme and eternal happiness. I say, *I finally resolved*, because at first it seemed inconsiderate to renounce the good which was certain for a greater good which was uncertain. I pondered on the advantages which accrued from reputation and wealth, all of which I must renounce if I would seriously undertake the search after another object, and which, if happiness chanced to belong to these advantages, I should necessarily see escape me... I therefore resolved this in my mind; whether it were possible for me to regulate my life according to a new rule, or at any rate ascertain the existence of such a rule, without changing the actual order of my life—a thing which I have often in vain attempted. For those things which most frequently occur in life, and in which men, judging from their acts, think supreme happiness consists, may be reduced to three, *riches, honours,* and *pleasures of the senses.* (*Lewes*, p. 279)

For Spinoza, the history of these three was as follows. Of sensuous pleasures there follows, after their fruition, only sadness, and, if not repentance, then deadness and dullness until the next occasion arising. Of riches, the more we possess, the greater the pleasure, and then the greater the desire to increase them, on and on tormentingly. And in the attainment of honour and reputation, we must direct our lives according to the wishes and standards of others outside ourselves, seeking only what the mass of men believe in. These passions were not adequate and self-sufficient solutions: they were the continuing causes of the problems they purported to resolve. Spinoza could feel the contradictions within his very syntax. This was why sentences were experimentally vital: they were like laboratory tools by means of which the mind could create further tools, mentally to reorder itself. The change was vitally necessary:

> I saw I was in the greatest danger, which forced me to seek a remedy, even an uncertain one; as a man in sickness, seeing certain death before him unless something be done, will seize at any remedy, however vague, for in that is all his hope. (*Lewes*, p. 280)

It was very difficult wholly to renounce a normal human life without guarantee of anything surer replacing it, but that life was killing Spinoza. His understandably evasive effort to continue with the old partial comforts, however flawed and unsatisfactory, whilst also trying to find a higher rule, was incoherent and contradictory, in shape and sense and feel. The struggle to have it both ways was, in his more precise sense, an 'inadequacy' that spoke powerfully to those in the midst of life, trying to reform ill-shaped ways of being. Marian Evans may herself have been one of those who would not or could not give up on the so-called norms for the sake of something higher; out of a mixture of both strength and weakness, of neediness and determination, loyalty and fear, they still tried to keep and run the two together. If she loved the idea of sacrifice even when she had little to give up, equally she remained greedy for life. She was not, finally, a pure thinker. But Spinoza was: for him, uncompromising reason meant that he would not wait for his life's narrative to tell him, usually too late, that he had nothing left to lose in taking the solitary's path of worldly renunciation. With a discipline dependent on the stern power of reason to resist easy temptations, Spinoza finally resolved to seek a greater good without prior guarantees as to its existence. What was contained here was also something that Deronda was to say to Gwendolen: that the law, implicit in the order of things, required effort and commitment ahead of any certainty of success.

George Henry Lewes said that he first had a sense of what Spinoza meant through an amateur Jewish philosopher, by day a watch-mender, whom he knew from a discussion club held in Red Lion Square in Holborn in the 1830s. It was this learned but obscure man, Cohn or Kohn, who first took Lewes through Spinoza, as though himself a minor version of the outcast lens-grinding philosopher, and, nearly fifty years later, became a partial model for Mordecai in George Eliot's *Daniel Deronda*.

But for Marian Evans, as for Matthew Arnold, it was the poet Goethe who first offered that second translation of Spinoza which, in Arnold's formulation, 'humanized' knowledge, even knowledge as disinterested and purified as Spinoza's own. In her case, Goethe's testimony was confirmed and intensified by her relation to George Henry Lewes, who was writing his *Life of Goethe* at the very time that she was translating Spinoza and that the two of them were forming their partnership. For Goethe, Spinoza was a thinker who might help free one from the frenzied bondage of the passions, from the mangled and distorted shape that a human being all too often made of a life and a mind, and create in its place a being of universal calm and clarity, of unegotistical acceptance of the order of things. In 1773 Goethe, aged 24, was suffering the loss of his beloved Lotte Butt to another man, in the turmoil that led to the writing of *The Sorrows of Young Werther*. It was then, in trouble, that he had discovered himself through Spinoza, by coming at the philosopher from what he thought of as the opposite or other side of formal thinking:

> The all-equalising calmness of Spinoza was in striking contrast with my all-disturbing activity; his mathematical method was the direct opposite of my poetic style of thought and feeling, and that very precision which was thought ill adapted to moral subjects made me his enthusiastic disciple, his most decided worshipper. Mind and heart, understanding and sense, sought each other with eager affinity, binding together the most different natures.[20]

The poet found the philosopher, as though they might want and need each other. The heated emotions on one side found in Spinoza, on the other, translation into a language of understanding. It was a kind of philosophic medicine for the psyche, through which the 'I' was also able to look at itself as 'he'. As George Henry Lewes had made clear in an article on 'Goethe as a Man of Science' for *Westminster Review* (October 1852), this was part of Goethe's great holistic ambition: to be a new Renaissance man combining art and science, moving constantly from one viewpoint to another, from theory to practice, from creating to observing, from synthesis to analysis and back again: 'The systole and diastole of human thought were to me like a second breathing apparatus—never separated, ever pulsating' (*Westminster Review*, 58, p. 485). As Lewes could well see, Goethe's greatest ambition was to develop as many separate powers as possible and still to bring those powers back together again in a unity that was itself enlarged by what it sought to integrate:

> The more imperfect a being is, the more do its individual parts resemble each other, and the more do these parts resemble the whole. The more perfect the being, the more dissimilar are the parts. In the former case the parts are more or less a repetition of the whole; in the latter case they are totally unlike the whole. The more the parts resemble each other, the less subordination is there of one to the other. Subordination of parts indicates high grade of organization.   (*Westminster Review*, 58, p. 499)

This was the law of higher creation: it emerged when the first law of simple repetition or sameness—the basic law of constantly created and recreated life— became gradually and increasingly involved in a second development, the law of individuation or evolved differentiation. Knowledge grows, wrote George Eliot similarly in an unpublished essay on 'Form' in 1868, 'by its alternating processes of distinction & combination' (*Essays*, p. 433). The alternation of sameness and difference, the process of non-identical repetition, was fundamental to the evolution of the world, the advancement of knowledge, and the development of the individual, alike—to properly complex 'organization' at every level.

Lewes remarked on how Spinoza's austere method made it barely possible for Goethe to study him systematically. Goethe himself admitted that he could not be sure how much he had read *in* the *Ethics* and how much he had read *into* it. But Lewes knew from his own experience how a single phrase, a partial thought could work on a reader, encountering 'some entirely novel and profoundly suggestive idea, casually cited from an ancient author' without necessity for a full understanding of every other part within the whole. A study might be fruitful without being systematic, a phrase let fall might fructify in the mind, said Lewes, and so a fragment might help recover, from within, an active sense of the whole to which it was found to belong. Thus it was with Goethe, in his regular returns to Spinoza's system: 'He studied it to draw therefrom food which his own mind could assimilate and work in to new forms' (Lewes, *Life of Goethe*, p. 177).

So likewise did Marian Evans, though systematically translating Spinoza. But it was as ever with her: the translation, though picked up at the will of another, became a cover for the studying of ideas close to her own needs and experience, without her yet having to submit them to independent publication. What she herself was assimilating in the search for new forms of organized being was her ability to be Spinoza to her own Goethe, philosopher to poet.

William Hale White had already seen something of it when he worked with her at John Chapman's. In the transmuted version of her in *Mark Rutherford's Autobiography*, the formidable Theresa—'she was a constant study to me...she was not a this or a that or the other'—admonishes his protagonist for disparaging the role of love in life. She says that though foolish and inane sentimentality makes her sick, nonetheless love is *the* subject of subjects, what keeps the world straight and human nature from division or despair:

> Her brain seemed to rule everything. This was an idea she had, and she kindled over it because it was an idea. It was impossible, of course, that she should say what she did without some movement of the organ in her breast, but how much share this organ had in her utterance, I never could make out.   (chapter 9)

How much was to do with herself she never wanted him to know.

It meant 'heart' seeking 'mind', even in herself. That is why Spinoza's insight into psychology was particularly vital to her, though itself only one part of his own wider concerns in establishing within his book atom by atom, element by element, the building blocks of creation in its increasingly complex codes and combinations. In the preface to part 3 of the *Ethics*, on the origin and nature of the emotions, the great principle behind the method was for once made utterly explicit in common language—here again in Marian Evans's translation:

> Many have written on the emotions and actions of man as if they were not treating of natural things which follow the common laws of nature, but of things which lie beyond the domain of nature; they appear indeed to regard man in nature as an *imperium in imperio*—a state within a state.   (*Ethics*, p. 91)

There were not two kingdoms in the universe—nature's and man's; no more than within man there were two separate realms—mind and body. What Spinoza's immanence and his monism meant, as opposed to transcendentalism or pluralism or dualism, was *one* whole interrelated universe and nothing standing outside or above it; the variety of existing things explained within one reality and one substance comprising a vast series of interlocked similarities and differences. From that perspective human beings could be seen as natural creatures, life forces within the greater life force, striving to maintain and if possible extend themselves, expanding with pleasure, contracting with pain.

For Spinoza there was in reality no supernatural personal God to reward or punish the individual; no individual who was simply a special thing, created whole by a separate fiat; no basis for an artificially coercive or compensatory morality: 'Blessedness is not the reward of virtue, but is virtue itself; and we do not delight in it because we conquer our passions, but because we delight in it, we are able to conquer our passions' (*Ethics*, p. 242, part 5, proposition 42). A Dorothea in George Eliot's *Middlemarch* at her best did not do right in order to be happy, but despite pain in the process, found herself happy in doing right. And equally a Bulstrode did what conventional morality condemned as utterly alien and abhorrent for reasons that psychologically were entirely natural and explicable:

> Passions such as hatred, anger, and the like, considered in themselves, follow from the same necessity and power of nature as other phenomena; and consequently they have determinate causes whereby they may be understood, and determinate qualities, which are as well worth our study as the properties of any other object on which we are pleased to destine our exclusive attention. I shall therefore treat of the nature and powers of the Emotions and the power of the mind over them according to the same method as I have used in the preceding books...I shall consider human actions and appetites as if the subject were lines, surfaces, or solids.   (*Ethics*, p. 92)

There could be a science of psychology, a natural philosophy of the emotions, as of any other enquiry into the laws of states and objects in the universe. The human arena was not especially separate but was its own version of the workings of the universal force of Nature. And within it the material that went wrong was the same as that which went right, only worse ordered. To Mary Ann Evans, even at her first reading in 1849, this did not seem merely cold and impersonal work, as Strauss's had seemed, but rather something like 'the conversation of a person of great capacity who has led a solitary life, and who says from his own soul what all the world is saying by rote' (GEL 1, p. 321).

By rote, the world thought it knew what was meant by 'love' and by 'hate'. But here was Spinoza analysing these emotions by means of a long slow chain of careful logic. He began at the beginning with the fundamental drive in all living things called, as we have seen earlier in this chapter, 'conatus': 'the effort by which every thing strives to persevere in existing' (*Ethics*, p. 100, proposition 7). Then he went on via intermediate steps to the added note: 'the mind can undergo great changes, and pass at one time to a higher at another to a lower degree of perfection; and these vicissitudes or passions explain to us the motions of pleasure and pain' (*Ethics*, p. 102, scholium to proposition 10). Thus, by 'pleasure' he means the passage to a higher degree of perfection in being, by 'pain' the movement to a lower degree of fulfilment—such that the mind strives to seek pleasure and avoid pain in the attempt to maintain and expand its existence. For in the process of regularly 'passing' from one state to another, in the movement from joy to sorrow, from passion to action, Spinoza saw the continual increase or subtraction of a creature's sheer energy. Joy, for example in 'the definition of emotions' in part 3 is described as 'pleasure accompanied by the idea of something past, which has had an issue beyond our hope': it is not a fixed state, but dynamically relative in that sudden surprising shift beyond even hope itself; it shows life as more alive than could ever have been imagined from the emotional situation preceding it. In the course of life's passage one could feel one's vital strength—or in the ancient sense of the word 'virtue'—coming or going, expanding or contracting. 'From this,' Spinoza concludes in a note to proposition 13, 'we clearly understand what love and hatred are':

> Love, namely, is nothing else than joy accompanying the idea of an external cause; and hatred is nothing else than sadness accompanying the idea of an accompanying cause. We see further, that he who loves necessarily strives to have and keep present with him the thing he loves; and on the contrary, he who hates strives to remove and destroy the thing he hates.   (*Ethics*, p. 104, scholium)

The idea of an external cause creates gratitude or resentment. There is no judgemental moralism on Spinoza's part here; this is 'necessarily' the internal logic of the emotions. For example, in what we call by rote 'jealousy':

> If we imagine the being we love united to another with the same or a stronger bond of friendship than that which hitherto attached him exclusively to us, we shall feel hatred towards the beloved being and envy towards our rival.   (*Ethics*, p. 118, proposition 35)

Or, conversely, another combination of emotional atoms may emerge finally as 'revenge':

> If we imagine a person as causing pleasure to the being we love, we shall love this person. If, on the contrary, we imagine him as causing pain to the beloved being, we hate him.   (*Ethics*, p. 109, proposition 22)

Emotion when suffered as a passion is, said Spinoza, 'a confused idea' (*Ethics*, p. 219, part 5, proposition 3, demonstration). In that state you do not have the emotion so much as the emotion seems to possess you. Moreover, the external object of the emotion seems not just the occasion for the feeling but its actual cause, leaving the emotion-bearer powerlessly at the mercy of the beloved, or vulnerably in the hands of fortune, when in fact the real cause was within the self. Yet even in this confusion and distortion there is a hidden internal logic—a psycho-logic—by which these intense emotions work unthinkingly. That is why the passions were not merely irrational phenomena to be disdained and discarded by a rationalist, but rather contained in them the raw and ragged stuff of human life—the struggles of *conatus*—for thought to work upon in order to create a higher, clearer level of understanding.

Here, in such thinking, was the training for a deep psychologist, such as George Eliot became in a second translation of Spinoza, amidst all the other elements of her thought and experience. 'Conatus' looks like this through the eyes of the novelist. On the surface, the normal human world might only see from the outside an ageing but still solid and formidable woman. But what is really there is a creature struggling to maintain its existence:

> Under protracted ill every living creature will find something that makes a comparative ease, and even when life seems woven of pain, will convert the fainter pain into a desire.   (*Felix Holt*, chapter 1)

Her name is Mrs Transome but at the subterranean biological level is a thin-skinned nervous organism, painfully sensitive to whatever touches it. Observers and neighbours

> never said anything like the full truth about her, or divined what was hidden under that outward life—a woman's keen sensibility and dread, which lay screened behind all her petty habits and narrow notions, as some quivering thing with eyes and throbbing heart may lie crouching behind withered rubbish.   (*Felix Holt*, chapter 1)

That internally quivering thing is as the nucleus of a life that through forces of attraction and aversion must expand or contract in relation to its immediate environment. Casaubon in *Middlemarch*, faced by what his vulnerability thinks to be the criticism of his young wife, almost literally 'shrinks' (a favoured word of George Eliot's) from her pity and the judgement implicit in it (chapter 29). Yet Dorothea still reaches out expansively towards him, even though he continually repels her. Maggie in *The Mill on the Floss* 'writhes' under the adverse judgement of Tom, rebelling against it for its 'incompleteness' while at almost the same time justifying her brother through her 'self-blame' (book 5, chapter 5). This was where a novelist might begin her work—in the world of humans struggling for life, beset by their emotions as confused ideas.

Conatus thus means that creatures must naturally seek to live, but often do so by means that, in the process, threaten their existence. A man, for example, naturally seeks to escape the consequences of sexual misdemeanour, making his very existence dependent on his secret never being discovered. In *Silas Marner*, Geoffrey Cass hardens himself in this way, in the desperate gambler's risk of relying upon contingency. Writes George Eliot in her own authorial voice:

> Favourable Chance, I fancy, is the god of all men who follow their own devices instead of obeying a law they believe in. Let even a polished man of these days get into a position he is ashamed to avow, and his mind will be bent on all the possible issues that may deliver him from the calculatable results of that position. Let him live outside his income, or shirk the resolute honest work that brings wages, and he will presently find himself dreaming of a possible benefactor, a possible simpleton who may be cajoled into using his interest, a possible state of mind in some possible person not yet forthcoming. Let him neglect the responsibilities of his office, and he will inevitably anchor himself on the chance, that the thing left undone may turn out not to be of the supposed importance. Let him betray his friend's confidence, and he will adore that same cunning complexity called Chance, which gives him the hope that his friend will never know. (*Silas Marner*, chapter 9).

'Possible' fights against 'calculatable', as 'betray' to 'never know'. This is what happens when human beings try to get away with what they have done, when they rely upon luck, desperate possibility, and event, instead of the order of reason and law and truth. What is depicted here is natural but it is also frightening. The fearsome perspicacity of George Eliot's external diagnosis summons the internal experience that tries to evade it: mind sees the secrets of that heart, that heart fears such a mind. The betrayed friend may never know; but George Eliot does. She knows too how the narrative of a life goes on and on, growing away from the straighter line of law and truth, taking a man with it.

Here is another man, who is frightened of the consequences of blaming his wife for the unhappiness of a marriage which has gone beyond the point of easy repair. George Eliot does not simply write 'Lydgate reluctantly saw that his wife was unkind and unhelpful to him', or 'Lydgate tried to hide from this thought'. Instead, in the brilliance of free indirect discourse George Eliot hears, as it were, what deep down he is secretly saying to himself, what his emotions are trying not to think:

> she had still a hold on his heart, and it was his intense desire that the hold should remain strong. In marriage, the certainty 'She will never me love me much' is easier to bear than the fear, 'I shall love her no more'. (*Middlemarch*, chapter 64)

To a conventional rote language this might be called 'weakness', or 'fear', or 'cowardice'. But here it is rather the deep human need to hold onto love, his own for her, if not hers for him. It is the right thing which, finding itself in the wrong place, at least tries to make its situation better. 'Never much' from her is *easier* than 'no more' in me, and still very hard to bear. That is how most human beings had to live.

*

Marian Evans knew she had suffered, and often not very nobly so, in the confusion and turmoil of her feelings. However puritanically inclined, she also learnt to know how suffering was not some martyr-like good desired by a challenging God but was, as Spinoza said, a subtraction and diminishment of her capacity for life. How to turn what she was suffering *under* into something she could more clearly think *about* was the mental somersault she sought. It converted what was depressively passive into active usage, without change of material but change of relation to it.

It was always the same material throughout life, throughout nature: what changed was only the forms, the combinations, uses, and the understandings of it. Experience that was unlearned from, and unthought of, would lie toxically passive in human beings, taking life from them. But 'an emotion which is a passion, ceases to be a passion, as soon as we form a clear and distinct idea of it' (*Ethics*, p. 219, part 5, proposition 3). 'As soon as' is the phrase that speaks of the escape from psychological slavery: one did not think in order to be more free, one was inherently more free in simply being able to do the thinking, to rescue the idea from the emotion within which it was confused and confined.

Always Spinoza stressed the damage, the diminution of the life of the self that sadness not only caused but itself constituted. It included the sadness of guilt as well as depression, for, in a radical passage from Spinoza's *Tract on God, Man, and Happiness* that William James was also to seize upon as an expression of the truest mental healthiness, it was said of the occasions when humans made mistakes:

> One might perhaps expect gnawings of conscience and repentance to help to bring them on the right path, and might thereupon conclude (as every one does conclude) that these affections are good things. Yet when we look at the matter closely, we shall find that not only are they not good, but on the contrary deleterious and evil passions. For it is manifest that we can always get along better by reason and love of truth than by worry of conscience and remorse. Harmful are these and evil, inasmuch as they form a particular kind of sadness.   (*Varieties of Religious Experience*, p. 128)

Marian Evans knew the damage that the puritan in her caused her. Philip Wakem and Stephen Guest both plead with Maggie Tulliver—not altogether disinterestedly—to stand against her morality for the sake of the greater life instinct which they say exists in sexual love. But for entangled young women such as Maggie or Dorothea what their imperfect ethics was fighting *against*—the egoism and the harm to others too often inherent in the appetites—was much worse than the flawed and faulty means desperately employed in the battle. In their imperfection the children of Israel had had to receive as forcible divine commandments what in truth were freely rational perceptions; but the guilt or the obedience were the fallen human means of having what only the exceptionally enlightened might possess at a different level, more purely, more disinterestedly. That was the beauty of Spinoza's life, as G. H. Lewes and others saw it—the capacity to rise above the turbulent emotions and transcend personal grudge or anxiety. But Marian Evans, for all her intelligence, still felt herself one of the stubbornly erring children of Israel; writing as George Eliot was the nearest she got to finding a place above the mangled and inefficient movements of the beleaguered woman. Still she remained both: half author; half all that the author worked from and worked upon. And it was still from within the puritan tradition, through *work*, that she came the nearest she could to anything like creative happiness, to turning passive to active, and Marian Evans into George Eliot.

Her reading of Spinoza was therefore not just another apprenticeship step in becoming 'a novelist of ideas'. What she found were notes towards the act of mental self-transformation. Nothing, said Spinoza, could overcome an emotion but a stronger emotion. What Spinoza offered was not cold inhuman reason but an implicitly passionate act of analysis, emotion taken up into thought of itself, into the capacity to think. Amidst all the necessary daily drudgery involved in the translation and magazine work, what Marian Evans most wanted was what mattered to Daniel Deronda in his own increasing crisis—active not passive knowledge, emotional understanding:

> He was ceasing to care for knowledge—he had no ambition for practice—unless they could both be gathered up into one current with his emotions; and he dreaded, as if it were a dwelling-place of lost souls, that dead anatomy of culture which turns the universe into a mere ceaseless answer to queries, and knows, not everything, but everything else about everything... (*Daniel Deronda*, chapter 32)

What mattered after all was not thinking *about* a subject so much as thinking *within* it; thinking that might not just eventually lead to, but itself immediately constituted change and action.

For Spinoza, a person did not do good *in order to* receive a reward, did not employ reason *in order to* be more calm, as in two distinct steps. For the enlightened, the reward was truly intrinsic to, beautifully at one with, the frame of mind created by the doing good, the thinking well; a frame of mind that, by thinking from the perspective of the universal order, became lifted into being an expression of it. So it was that the novelist saw that the work that got her closest to careful thinking about reality was that which went on *within* the immanent texture of writing—thinking inside the subject rather than thinking about it; knowing through creating. Immersed in that way, she might see her characters like different possible versions of her imaginative self, but by that very act be free from being permanently tied to the point of view of any one of them. All this is part of what, from Chapter 4 onwards I will describe as the biography of the writing, encrypted within the writing.

Writing of the long apprenticeship of George Eliot, the Victorian man of letters, Leslie Stephen concluded:

> I do not think that any one who has had a little experience in such matters would regard it as otherwise than dangerous for a powerful mind to be precipitated into public utterance. The Pythagorean probation of silence may be protracted too long; but it may afford a most useful discipline: and I think there is nothing preposterous in the supposition that George Eliot's work was all the more powerful because it came from a novelist who had lain fallow through a longer period than ordinary.'[21]

In the ancient school of Pythagoras, five years of purification were required instead of ready talk and easy opinion. It was not that Mary Ann or Marian Evans, for more than thirty years, was ever silent. But hers was an apprenticeship. Her education could have been just a jumble of thoughts and viewpoints, books and thinkers, as so much mid-Victorian thinking seemed to be: what Alasdair MacIntyre in *After Virtue* (1982) calls an incoherent post-religious Babel of many languages, in ill-digested muddles and contradictions, and baggily enforced syntheses. But, eventually, writing would have to create the experimental testing ground to find what was genuinely needed in the immanence, process, and content of human life, in search of what was right, and when and where.

CHAPTER 4

The Two Loves of 1852

1. Herbert Spencer

It was Christmas Day 1887. The old philosopher sat in his chair, 'not daring to move body or mind', waiting somehow for sufficient strength to complete his *System of Philosophy* for which he had sacrificed his life. The young woman, sitting beside this old family friend and mentor, 'can give him no help'. 'If he would only give up his self-preserving policy and be content to make the most of every hour without considering the cost ...' But he was bunkered down within his system, not only his book but the scheme of mental economy in which he has set himself to write it. He was living a sort of spider-like existence, 'sitting alone in the centre of his theoretical web'—a theory of evolution within which everything was to be explained. When suddenly he moaned 'Why suffer more todays?', she could give him no answer. He felt lonely, fearing the world would judge him as a defunct thinking machine from a bygone age rather than any sort of man.[1]

This was not quite Dorothea and Casaubon in *Middlemarch*. She was the 29-year-old Beatrice Potter, later to become Beatrice Webb, sociologist and socialist. He was, as she put it, 'poor Herbert Spencer', aged 67, due to live on for another sixteen etiolated years. Beatrice reminded him, he said, of George Eliot, whom he had first met over thirty-five years previously, in 1851 at the house of John Chapman. He had thought Marian Evans to be, mentally, the most admirable woman he had ever met. It was even rumoured that they had briefly been engaged in 1852. But physically he had no desire for her.

Reading the proof of his *Autobiography*, Beatrice Potter was disturbed that he never seemed to have felt the sacrifice he had made in devoting himself solely to his work. 'I was never in love,' he told her. His was, she wrote in her diary, a mental deformity caused by the excessive development of one faculty, the intellectual, at the expense of the sympathetic and the emotional.

Beatrice Potter will have read in the *Autobiography* Spencer's report of what Marian Evans had said to him back in the spring of 1852:

> Considering how much thinking I must have done, she was surprised to see no lines on my forehead. 'I suppose it is because I am never puzzled,' I said. This called forth the exclamation—'O! that's the most arrogant thing I ever heard uttered.'

He had replied, 'Not at all, when you know what I mean,' explaining that his way of thinking did not involve the sort of mental effort associated with the wrinkling of the brows:

> It has never been my way to set before myself a problem and puzzle out an answer. The conclusions at which I have from time to time arrived, have not been arrived at as solutions of questions raised; but have been arrived at unawares—each as the ultimate outcome of a body of thoughts which slowly grew from a germ. Some direct observation, or some fact met with in reading, would dwell with me: apparently because I had a sense of its significance.... Little by little, in unobtrusive ways, without conscious intention or appreciable effort, there would grow up a coherent and organized theory. Habitually the process was one of slow unforced development, often extending over years; and it was, I believe, because the thinking done went on in this gradual, almost spontaneous way, without strain, that there was an absence of those lines of thought which Miss Evans remarked.[2]

This was the thinker whom one reviewer in *The Leader* of 12 April 1851 had called the English Spinoza. Spencer seemed be able to recreate within his mind the emergent formation of the world itself. He did not solve problems but, tuning in to what he felt were the patterns of nature, let his thoughts evolve in ways correspondent to the evolution of natural laws. On the other hand, his opponents argued that all he did was fit any fact that suited within his ready-made abstract system. For Spencer, said T. H. Huxley, the definition of a tragedy was a theory spoiled by a fact. Marian Evans herself reported that when she and Spencer went out together on a scientific expedition to the Royal Botanic Gardens at Kew, if a flower did not correspond to his theories, then too bad for the flower.

The reviewer who likened Spencer to Spinoza was George Henry Lewes. The acquaintance that subsequently arose with Spencer, wrote Lewes, 'was the brightest ray in a very dreary *wasted* period of my life':

> I had given up all ambition whatever, lived from hand to mouth, and thought the evil of each day sufficient. The stimulus of his intellect, especially during our long walks, roused my energy once more, and revived my dormant love of science. His intense theorizing tendency was contagious, and it was only the stimulus of a theory which could then have influenced me to work.[3]

Lewes's life was in pieces at the time. His wife Agnes was having an affair with Thornton Hunt, his editor at *The Leader*. She had a baby by Hunt in 1850, though Lewes registered the boy as his own, and subsequently three more children by Hunt. Lewes himself was drifting towards literary hackwork. The grand theory that gave him renewed intellectual stimulus was eventually set out most distinctly in Spencer's *Westminster Review* essay of 1857, 'Progress: Its Law and Cause'. It was the work of his that Marian Evans herself most admired, incorporated three years later into the opening part of *First Principles*.

Spencer's key principle, which he took from the embryologist Von Baer, was the evolution of structure throughout the universe from what he called an initial indefinite and incoherent homogeneity to a definite, coherent heterogeneity. The first movement in the development of a simple seed into a tree or a simple ovum into an animal was thus the appearance of a difference, a new variation or division, which, in the drive towards individuation, was then continuously repeated in different forms of increased complexity. Hence the increase of distinct and stable heterogeneity. According to the Nebular Hypothesis, postulated by Swedenborg, Kant, and Laplace, the solar system itself began as an indefinitely extended nebulous medium, a great hot cloud of almost complete uniformity or homogeneity. But at some point, through a slight variation in gravitation forces, the cloud began to contract and condense, leaving a difference between the space into which the concentrated mass had now collapsed and the space it had previously occupied, occupied by residual rings of gas. Between the interior and the exterior of the mass there were now changes of density and temperature, and different rotational velocities, dependent on distance from the centre. These differentiations increased in number and degree until there was an organized group of sun, planets, and satellites, consisting of numerous contrasts of structure and action amongst its members. Such was the generation of heterogeneity: the increase in differentiation *and* interrelationship at once.

In the same way human society, argued Spencer, began with the tribe whose members all perform the same actions for themselves and culminates in the civilized community where, by a more economical division of labour, members perform different actions for each other. The society is then not so much a sum of similar aggregated parts as a complex of differing parts forming a web-like whole. There are more individuals and, equally, a greater need for collaboration between them.

In art, the change from homogeneity to the heterogeneity of different dimensions and points of view is clear, says Spencer, if we compare

> an Egyptian statue, seated bolt upright on a block with hands on knees, fingers outspread and parallel, eyes looking straight forward, and the two sides perfectly symmetrical in every particular, with a statue of the advanced Greek or the modern school, which is asymmetrical in respect of the position of the head, the body, the limbs, the arrangement of the hair, dress, appendages, and its relations to neighbouring objects.[4]

So too in the generation of human language: what probably began as mere exclamatory cries developed into nouns and verbs as the basic primary elements. An initial template of names roughly applied to ill-defined classes was able to be refined and adapted, making branches, derivatives, and compounds from the same roots or elements. It was a process that Coleridge had called de-synominization, in the movement from like to subtly unlike meanings. Where at first the names for objects were few, and their range therefore unspecific and wide, similes and metaphors had to be employed to suggest ideas that could not be expressed directly. So too in grammar. Hebrew Scriptures offered an aggregation of sentences of single subject and predicate, few qualifying terms, and the links between the serials and parallels often left implicit. But the writings of modern times exhibited a far greater degree of complex integration through subordinate prepositions, modificatory conjunctions, and qualifying clauses in which the parts become mutually interdependent—extricable only with damage to the meaning of the rest of the whole. And as with the development of subordinate clauses in language, so it was with the evolution of counterpoint in music, creating complex alternatives to simple serial melody, with different voices, instruments, and sequences co-operating to the enrichment of interrelated human meaning. The same process of differentiation went on both within and across all the branches of endeavour. Spencer concludes of language:

> In the gradual multiplication of parts of speech out of these primary ones—in the differentiation of verbs into active and passive, of nouns into abstract and concrete—in the rise of distinctions of moods, tense, person, of number and case—in the formation of auxiliary verbs, of adjectives, adverbs, pronouns, prepositions, articles—in the divergence of those orders, genera, species, and varieties of parts of speech by which civilised races express minute modifications of meaning—we see a change from the homogeneous to the heterogeneous. (*Spencer Essays*, p. 165, 'Progress: Its Law and Cause')

Perhaps nothing was as important to the creation of the mind of George Eliot as the availability for deployment of an evolved syntax. The development in the formation of grammatical sentences was not merely a specialized artistic flourish of style. It was a vitally useful tool in the creation of a complexity of thought to match the evolved complexity of human life.

But what Marian Evans especially loved in this grand theory was how differentiation simultaneously revealed relationship, an increased individuation involving a subtler mutuality and integration. In much the same way, every gain in the known was also at once an increase in the positively unknown. 'The explanation of that which is explicable,' wrote Spencer near the close of his essay, 'does but bring out into greater clearness the inexplicableness of that which remains behind' (*Spencer Essays*, p. 196). The sense of a limit is simultaneously an imagination of what lies beyond it. The lack of clear knowledge as to *what* something is becomes at once a recognition *that* something is, really existent beyond our knowing (*First Principles*, pp. 76, 72). This is the sense of the Unknowable which Spencer took from the theologian

H. L. Mansel and which Mansel took from Kant, and the idea of the noumenon, the thing in itself which humans could only know as a phenomenon relative to themselves. As Spencer elaborated in *First Principles*:

> Besides that *definite* consciousness of which Logic formulates the laws, there is also an *indefinite* consciousness which cannot be formulated. Besides complete thoughts, and besides the thoughts which though incomplete admit of completion, there are thoughts which it is impossible to complete, and yet which are still real.[5]

At the end of 'Progress: Its Law and Cause', Spencer wrote that the sincere man of science finds himself in the midst of perpetual changes of which he can discover neither the beginning nor the end. That was a fundamental realism beautiful to Marian Evans: that in the middle of life was a constant regulative sense of there always being something outside their terms to which our flawed conceptions gesture and point even in their felt partiality. She wrote to Sara Hennell on this sense of the Unknowable, 'Didn't you like the conclusion of Herbert Spencer's article in the W R? There was more feeling in it than we generally get in his writing' (GEL 2, p. 341). What Marian Evans loved was the possibility of somehow thinking incomplete thoughts and not making them look completed. In the end this was not what Spencer the systematizer wanted. It was to be George Henry Lewes, not Henry Spencer, who took most note of such inherent limitations, who felt their presence, and for that he paid the price of looking conceptually fuzzy and messily unsystematic.

In Spencer, it was the customary want of such feeling in the writing that troubled Marian Evans just as later it also disturbed Beatrice Webb. It was the emotional equivalent of the lack of a furrowed brow. For what Spencer sought in every realm was a form of untroubled smoothness. This included his essay 'Philosophy of Style', published by Marian Evans in the *Westminster Review* in October 1852.

The 'Philosophy of Style' was an attempt to consider language as an apparatus of symbols, the purpose of which was as immediate a conveyance of thought as was possible. 'The force of all verbal forms and arrangements is great,' argued Spencer, 'in proportion as the time and mental effort they demand from the recipient is small' ('Philosophy of Style', para. 45). The economy of mental energy was a paramount priority:

> How truly language must be regarded as a hindrance to thought, though the necessary instrument of it, we shall clearly perceive on remembering the comparative force with which simple ideas are communicated by signs. To say, 'Leave the room' is less expressive than to point to the door. Placing a finger on the lips is more forcible than whispering, 'Do not speak'. A beck of the hand is better than 'Come here'. No

phrase can convey the idea of surprise so vividly as opening the eyes and raising the eyebrows. A shrug of the shoulders would lose much by translation into words.

('Philosophy of Style', para. 4)

When oral language is employed, Spencer goes on, the strongest effects are produced by interjections 'which condense entire sentences into syllables': the use of single words such as 'Beware!', or words like 'Bang' sonically close to the things symbolized, carry more direct force than expansion into a proposition. He concludes of language as a vehicle that its 'friction and inertia' deduct from 'its efficiency'. Thus, when we do have to use sentences, the parts should be stated in such a sequence that 'the mind may not have to go backwards and forwards in order to rightly connect them' ('Philosophy of Style', para. 11). Each part should be capable of being understood as it occurs without waiting, without need for correction, in encouragement of the mind's capacity to anticipate what is coming and thus to make swift progress. Language, for Spencer, was a signalled message to be translated as quickly and easily as possible from physical mark to mental realization, from word to concept, from the page into the head.

In pursuit of this economy, he gives direct examples of the different order of similarly worded sentences, arguing that, as a norm, the circumstances surrounding the subject should be given *first* when they crucially determine the mode in which that subject is then to be conceived. That way the mind can go forward without check or delay. Look what happens when the contextual conditions are put in an awkward place, says Spencer ('Philosophy of Style', para. 24), commenting on a complicated sentence from a piece on the uses of historical evidence:

A modern newspaper-statement, though probably true, would be laughed at if quoted in a book as testimony; but the letter of a court gossip is thought good historical evidence, if written some centuries ago.

Now see, he says, the superior effect of rearrangement of the 'though' and the 'if':

Though probably true, a modern newspaper-article quoted in a book as testimony, would be laughed at; but the letter of a court gossip, if written some centuries ago, is thought good historical evidence. ('Philosophy of Style', para. 24)

This was a man who needed to get the thought from the books into his mind as quickly and painlessly as possible. By 1856 Spencer was 'unable to read more than a quarter of an hour together' (GEL 2, p. 233). He could barely stand the effect of thought on his nervous system unless it was the thinking which he described to Marian Evans—growing gradually in 'unobtrusive ways, without conscious intention or appreciable effort', subsuming particulars within manageable generalizations.

But Spencer knew that the first intimation of consciousness arose from the instantaneous effect of tiny nervous blows, as though the sensitive organism was indeed 'struck' or 'hit' by the sensation of a response or the feeling of a thought before it could ever comprehend or assimilate it:

> The subjective effect produced by a crack or noise that has no appreciable duration, is little else than a nervous shock. Though we distinguish such a nervous shock as belonging to what we call sounds, yet it does not differ very much from nervous shocks of other kinds. An electric discharge sent through the body, causes a feeling akin to that which a sudden loud report causes. A strong unexpected impression made through the eyes, as by a flash of lightning, similarly gives rise to a start or shock...The state of consciousness so generated is, in fact, comparable in quality to the initial state of consciousness caused by a blow (distinguishing it from the pain or other feeling that commences the instant after); which state of consciousness, caused by a blow, may be taken as the primitive and typical form of nervous shock.[6]

This was evolution's economy, that mental phenomena should be registered through the same nervous processes as physical phenomena, functioning as adaptive responses to the world taken to another level. In Spencer's physiologically based psychology, the mind worked *between* brain and world, mediating organism and environment, to try to secure equilibrium of the overload of nervous shocks and blows. In embodied structures like our own, he wrote in *Principles of Biology*, 'a slight change initiated in one part will instantly and powerfully affect all other parts'—convulsing muscles, contracting blood vessels, awakening a crowd of ideas accompanied by a violent gush of emotions, affecting heart and lungs and stomach.[7] No human being could stand the full force of those shocks, but Spencer kept his own level of receptiveness as low as he could in mental self-protection. 'We may be thankful,' wrote Charles Bray of the filters and defences we can muster, 'for if as George Eliot says we had a keen vision and feeling for all ordinary life, it would be like hearing the grass grow and the squirrel's heart beat; and we should die of that roar that lies on the other side of silence.'[8] Spencer wadded himself around not with stupidity, as it is said in *Middlemarch* that most of us do in the face of the utmost reality, but with generalization, with law and system. What made his situation more complicated was that these generalizations were not simply or wholly mistaken. As Marian Evans wrote in her essay on Sophocles' *Antigone*, the most painfully important conflicts are not those between right and wrong but right and right, right in one way causing harm in another: 'A man must not only dare to be right, he must also dare to be wrong' (*Essays*, p. 265).

There was little of Spencer's self-protection in George Eliot's own, more implicit philosophy of style. Adaptation—'the continual adjustment of internal relations to external relations' as Spencer put it[9]—might be the way of evolution but it was not always or ultimately the goal she considered most worthy of human beings. She took from Keats the phrase 'a fine excess', to mean something more than the correctness of easy adaptation: an energy of feeling that might be in vain in terms of immediate outcome and yet attempted more than conformity or utility. What is the point of such extra feeling? Answer: 'The generous leap of impulse is needed too to swell the flood of sympathy in us beholders'—beyond the course of normal action, as a fresh stimulation of human possibility—'that we not fall completely under the mastery of calculation, which in its turn may fail of ends for want of energy got from ardour' (*Essays*, p. 451).

Her philosophy of style was to hear within her prose the grass grow, the squirrel's heart beat, and something of that struggling inner roar on the other side of human silence. 'We hardly know what it is to feel for human misery until we have heard a shriek,' writes Mary Ann Evans, 'and a more perfect hell might be made out of sounds than out of any preparation of fire and brimstone' (GEL 1, p. 247).

In such a medium, smooth and effortless precision was impossible, unless one shut one's ears and closed one's eyes. Falsehood, wrote George Eliot, is so easy even when there is no motive to be false, truth so difficult: 'Examine your words well, and you will find... it is a very hard thing to say the exact truth, even about your own immediate feelings' (*Adam Bede*, chapter 17). 'Watch your own speech, and notice how it is guided by your less conscious purposes' (*The Mill on the Floss*, book 6, chapter 13). In *Middlemarch*, a thought ever so slightly out of place at its commencement puts an investigation onto a trajectory ever further off target: 'What was the primitive tissue? In that way Lydgate put the question—not quite in the way required by the awaiting answer; but such missing of the right word befalls many seekers' (chapter 15). The sensitive reader, like the sensitive writer, can feel from within the lines the minute jolts and shocks and leaps, the false moves and sudden turns en route, and is meant to feel them, as though the linguistic medium were itself a form of the nervous system: 'Not *quite* in the way required by the *awaiting* answer.'

George Henry Lewes also took up his position from Spencer. Lewes began his *Principles of Success in Literature* (1865) by saying that just as the ever-increasing development of the Nervous System was crucial to the evolution of animal organisms, so equivalently, it was Thought that was vital to the next level of our development by creating a mental network to bring together through the Language System the diverse threads and elements of existence. That network was not fixed but must vibrate and mutate, and it was language—in particular a non-specialist language that could work across the whole range of meaning—which enabled this liveness of relation and response: 'Language is to the Social Organism very much what the Nervous System is to the Body—a connecting medium which enhances all its functions.'[10] The 'connecting' was, at the micro level, between thoughts in a mind, and then at the macro between minds in a society. For George

Eliot, the language itself was to be a heightened nervous system in the web of her novels, connecting both thoughts and persons at a level far deeper than the coarsely naming language of ordinary description and explanation.

George Eliot was talking about this level of neural sensitivity even from the earliest, in *Scenes of Clerical Life*:

> The keenest eye will not serve, unless you have the delicate fingers, with their subtle nerve filaments, which elude scientific lenses, and lose themselves in the invisible world of human sensations.   ('Janet's Repentance', chapter 11)

She is thinking here about how hard it is to understand another person's motives, how much it requires beyond ordinary blinkered sight and clumsy fingers. So: why does a woman as essentially kind-hearted and dutiful as Janet get so angry with her good-hearted mother? It is because she cannot seem to prevent herself from passing on to her sympathetic mother the pain she has suffered at the hands of her alcoholic husband: 'For the wrong that rouses our angry passions finds only a medium in us; it passes through us like a vibration, and we inflict what we have suffered' (chapter 13). That is what the prose is at its finest: a sensitive medium for human vibrations.

It requires what Herbert Spencer did not want—friction, or what Henry James called a 'retarding persuasiveness' (*Critical Heritage*, p. 276). George Eliot cannot simply go forward. When, for example, Janet finds herself thrown out of the house by her husband in the middle of the night, one paragraph begins, 'For a short space it seemed like a deliverance to Janet.' But then after that short space, the next paragraph goes: 'This, then, was what she had been travelling towards through her long years of misery!' (('Janet's Repentance', chapter 14). It is now read *back* from 'towards'. It is like Lydgate not putting his question 'quite in the way required by the *awaiting* answer': something at the sentence end goes back right to left even as the sentence travels left to right. Or a sentence goes forward, still leaving something behind that is unresolved—like this from *Middlemarch* on why on earth Dorothea, for all her intelligence, could not see from the start her mistake in marrying the dreary old scholar:

> How was it that in the weeks since her marriage, Dorothea had not distinctly observed, but felt with a stifling depression, that the large vistas and wide fresh air which she had dreamed of finding in her husband's mind were replaced by anterooms and winding passages which seemed to lead nowhither? I suppose it was that in courtship everything is regarded as provisional and preliminary, and the simplest sample of virtue or accomplishment is taken to guarantee delightful stores which the broad leisure of marriage will reveal. But the door-sill of marriage once crossed, expectation is concentrated on the present.   (*Middlemarch*, chapter 20)

Though in truth George Eliot's were the only novels he admired, Herbert Spencer might hardly bear how the subordinate clause in the first sentence could get on his nerves: 'How was it that...Dorothea had not distinctly observed / *but felt with a stifling depression,* / that...' That barely admitted feeling of depression cuts across the forwards movement, like a version of the subconscious coming from a different angle, waiting to re-merge only much later in the marriage as a main clause of her consciousness. As the second and third sentences make wincingly clear, Dorothea is in the midst of a reconfiguration of the very experience of time itself, the vague future turned into the new present. Nothing is now simply linear. Each sentence, almost each cause within a sentence, is like a different pen-stroke, coming from a different angle:

> Make a stroke with your pen which represents the first train of thought or mood, or the first group of thoughts you deal with. Then make another pen-stroke to represent the second, which shall be proportionally long or short according to the number of words or pages occupied, and which, connected with the first pen-stroke as one articulation of a reed is with another, will deflect to the right or left according as it contains more or less new matter; so that if it grew insensibly from stroke number one, it will have to be almost straight, and if contain something utterly disconnected, will be at right angles. Go on adding pen-strokes for each new train of thought, or mood, or group of facts, and writing the name along each, and being careful to indicate not merely the angle of divergence, but the respective length in lines. And then look at the whole map.[11]

This is the thinking of the novel, forming its web, making its own mind, in the culmination that is *Middlemarch*.

Something always cuts across simple straight lines. In *The Mill on the Floss* there is a crucial moment when Maggie is torn between her family and her new love for an already entangled Stephen Guest:

> 'O it is difficult—life is very difficult. It seems right to me sometimes that we should follow our strongest feeling; but then, such feelings continually come across the ties that all our former life has made for us—the ties that have made others dependent on us—and would cut them in two. If life were quite easy and simple, as it might have been in Paradise, and we could always see that one being first towards whom...I mean, if life did not make duties for us before love comes—love would be a sign that two people ought to belong to each other. But I see—I feel it is not so now...'
>
> (*The Mill on the Floss*, book 6, chapter 11)

In the latent biography of the writing itself, the reader can hear the raw emotional stress points crying *inside* the rationalizing syntax that surrounds them. The grass is growing and the squirrel's heart beats audibly in the subdued and unavailing tonal cries of 'first' ('always see that one being *first*') being cut across by 'before' ('if life did not make duties for us *before* love comes'). Life here is 'difficult', not 'easy and simple': what within strong feeling is 'right *sometimes*' is also what '*continually* comes across' other forms of emotional right or need or requirement. '*If* life were', '*if* life did not', '*might* have been' and '*could* always see', '*would* be a sign... [of] *ought*': these are the jarring signs of a lost paradise, having to meet that final 'But' of realism—'But it is not so now.' Cadence, inflection, and tone are, as Spencer himself said quite rightly, 'the commentary of the emotions upon the propositions of the intellect' (*Spencer Essays*, p. 329, 'On the Origin and Function of Music'). In George Eliot the apparently little words and signs and phrases, like articulate shrieks prior to categorical naming, are the emotion that must accompany the required ways of adult life. A half-hidden emotion, that is to say, which has to function in counterpoint to, or in conflict with, the sheer discipline of making sense and doing duty. Such almost 'unspeakable vibrations', as George Eliot wonderfully calls them, are the effects of strong emotional experience like powerful music 'searching the subtlest windings of your soul, the delicate fibres of life where no memory can penetrate' (*Adam Bede*, chapter 33). In the hidden inner biography of this prose there may be no one specific or articulate memory perhaps, but there are within its shape and texture windings and fibres which themselves *are* memory lodged as at the deepest level of emotional recognition in a human being. It is a dynamic version of what Mrs Cadwallader says satirically of Mr Casaubon's thin scholarly blood: 'Somebody put a drop under a magnifying glass, and it was all semicolons and parentheses' (*Middlemarch*, chapter 8).

The network of such intricate windings and fibres explains why there are no Spencerian straight lines or unfurrowed brows in George Eliot's fallen world. The syntax is not single and straightforward because the mind is not simple, because the experience of life's chronology is not straightforward, because one thought cuts across another. At the beginning of chapter 29 of *Middlemarch*, she begins to write conventionally enough, 'One morning some weeks after her arrival at Lowick, Dorothea—'. Then immediately she stops the completion of the simple sequence line with the interjection, '—but why always Dorothea?' 'Was her point of view,' George Eliot goes on, 'the only possible one with regard to this marriage? I protest...' That protest is part of a language of 'checks' in George Eliot, one key term within that informal lexicon of hers which emerges in practice to make up the novelist's implicit equipment for human thought. In the face of crass modern generalizations, what is fundamentally necessary is, she argues in her essay 'The Natural History of German Life' (1856), a knowledge of ordinary people not only 'to guide sympathies rightly' but also 'to check our theories' (*Essays*, p. 272)—where 'check' means primarily to arrest, stop, or retard automatic motion or easy onward passage. This revisionary advice—including the caution to examine your words well, to watch your own speech—applies also to the characters in the fiction as well as their author, checked by a thought or by a fear. Alone, Dorothea bursts out angrily against the thought of Casaubon's treatment of her and then 'she began to hear herself, and was checked into stillness' (*Middlemarch*, chapter 42). Or, when Janet becomes a part of her community again and not just the beaten wife of an alcoholic, there was now 'no check to the full flow of that plenteous current in her nature—no gnawing secret anguish—no overhanging terror—no inward shame' ('Janet's Repentance', chapter 25). Yet as friendly faces beam on Janet in her recovery, George Eliot adds: 'And she needed these secondary helps'—which might almost be an epigraph for the whole human process of multiple considerations in George Eliot, against simple one-sidedness. Complexity is the implicit cry: 'There is no general doctrine which is not capable of eating out our morality if unchecked by the deep-seated habit of direct fellow-feeling with individual fellow-men' (*Middlemarch*, chapter 61); 'Moral judgements must remain false and hollow, unless they are checked and enlightened by a perpetual reference to the special circumstances that mark the individual lot' (*The Mill on the Floss*, book 7, chapter 2). In the midst of running away with Stephen Guest, Maggie Tulliver turned back to her family, only to be more disgraced by neither going through with the elopement nor wholly rejecting it from the first. All people of broad and strong sense, says George Eliot, instinctively detest 'the men of maxims' whose clear-cut formulas allow them so easily to pronounce Maggie Tulliver a disgrace to her sex, regardless of the specific complexities:

> And the man of maxims is the popular representative of the minds that are guided in their moral judgment solely by general rules, thinking that these will lead them to justice by a ready-made patent method, without the trouble of exerting patience, discrimination, impartiality, without any care to assure themselves whether they have the insight that comes from a hardly-earned estimate of temptation or from a life vivid and intense enough to have created a wide fellow-feeling with all that is human.   (*The Mill on the Floss*, book 7, chapter 2)

This is the sentence and the sequence of one who knows what it is to have gone through experience, without ease; who realizes the checks and obstacles that are needed to refine general assumptions to particular situations. Thinking at its best is a flexibly self-correcting two-way movement, up and down, to and fro. 'A correct generalization gives significance to the smallest detail, just as the great inductions of geology demonstrate in every pebble the working of laws by which the earth has become adapted for the habitation of man' goes one essay (*Essays*, p. 31). But, equally, in another essay it is written, 'Emotion links itself with particulars ... Generalities are the refuge at once of deficient intellectual activity and deficient feeling' (*Essays*, p. 371). The key is to find the syntax, and underlying that the character of mentality, which can do justice through both particulars and generals, thoughts at different times in different contexts, without simple contradiction. It is manifest in self-checking sentences that begin like this, again from the fine protesting passage in *The Mill on the Floss*:

> The great problem of the shifting relation between passion and duty is clear to no man who is capable of apprehending it...

It is a sentence that is like a definition of complexity for this author, brilliantly turning round to admit its own problems. And it was such problems that drove Marian Evans to the 'medium of art': 'My writing is simply a set of experiments in life ... I become more and more timid—with less daring to adopt any formula which does not get itself clothed for me in some human figure and individual experience' (GEL 6, pp. 216–17). 'More and more timid', 'less daring': these are the words not of cowardice but of the sort of compunction that creates the writer of realist novels. The deeper understanding comes back to front through the friction of bafflements and mistakes, like Mr Tulliver's: 'for getting a strong impression that a skein is tangled there is nothing like snatching hastily at a single thread' (*The Mill on the Floss*, book 1, chapter 8). 'Every mistake, every absurdity into which poor human nature has fallen may be looked on as an experiment' (*Essays*, p. 31). In chapter 85 of *Middlemarch* Bulstrode faces the judgement of the mob, and George Eliot says that he would be like one of John Bunyan's persecuted martyrs in *The Pilgrim's Progress*, save for one thing: he is not innocent. He has not that interior protection against what is nonetheless still ugly and unjust in the mob. 'The pitiable lot is that of the man who could not call himself a martyr,' she writes: it is that quiet word '*not*' which bears the weight of the biography of writing, the almost physically painful shock-place the writing comes out of, turning it round upon itself. 'He could not call himself...': the friction point is where one simple old word like 'innocent' or 'martyr' is denied and disabled, and there is required the evolution of many more words in mitigation and qualification instead. When she writes 'not', it remembers all this.

No popular maxims, no crowd prejudice, no easy sentence will serve but '*individual* experience'. In 'Mr Gilfil's Love-Story' from *Scenes of Clerical Life*, Maynard Gilfil is a clergyman who falls in love with Tina Sarti, the young daughter of an Italian singer adopted by Gilfil's patron. But Tina has her heart broken by Captain Anthony Wybrow, his patron's heir, and in a vengeful frenzy takes a knife to him, only to find him already suffering a heart attack. In the aftermath of his death and in her remorse for what she intended, she confesses to Gilfil. His reply needs to be carefully lengthy in the face of over-simple punitive self-judgement:

> He would not speak long, lest he should tire her, and oppress her with too many thoughts. Long pauses seemed needful for her before she could concentrate her feeling in short words.

'But when I meant to do it,' was the next thing she whispered, 'it was as bad as if I had done it.'

'No, my Tina,' answered Maynard slowly, waiting a little between each sentence; 'we mean to do wicked things that we never could do, just as we mean to do good or clever things that we never could do. Our thoughts are often worse than we are, just as they are often better than we are. And God sees us as we are altogether, not in separate feelings or actions, as our fellow-men see us. We are always doing each other injustice, and thinking better or worse of each other than we deserve, because we only hear and see separate words and actions. We don't see each other's whole nature. But God sees that you could not have committed that crime.'   ('Mr Gilfil's Love-Story', chapter 19)

It is Feuerbach who enables George Eliot still to do her work through a language of God. But it is not the subject of the sentences—God—that is her concern; it is the predicates, in respect of what God sees, and what needs to be seen in humans, even if it is beyond humans themselves always to see it. The check that Gilfil gives to Tina is a cautionary top-down generalization against generalizing or simplifying; a necessary background for the understanding of a particular crisis that, lived from down below, is straining to raise upwards the thought of itself. We could think almost anything, but it is what specifically happens, what we actually do or do not do in any individual encounter, that matters. Gilfil begins from better 'or' worse—'we are always...thinking better or worse of each other than we deserve': the two together, equally possible and plausible, but neither of them infallible or quite accurate, neither wholly or simply right on its own. The syntax has to be better than the vocabulary: our thoughts are often worse than we are, *just as* they are often better than we are; we intend to do the good that we never actually do *in just the same way* as we think we mean to do the bad but do not. It is the same natural set of dispositions and possibilities, from two quite different directions and in two opposite ways, that must be held in mind as the human matrix. To hold it together, that repeated 'just as' is the crucial connective in the syntax of a full mind.

This wider intelligence of Gilfil's is like a formula for the novel as an experiment in life that could go either way, take many ways, in any specific individual outcome. That is to say, it is the work of adding layer after layer: situation, people, change of context, dialogue, unspoken background, difference of speakers, difference in motivations, presence of their differing pasts, and so on—all in the generation of a densely complex interacting model of life, 'not in separate feelings or actions, as our fellow-men see us'.

Nor 'in separate words' either. Gilfil knows he cannot speak long lest he should tire the already worn-out girl with too many thoughts, but still he speaks slowly 'waiting a little *between* each sentence'. The whole intensity of the passage is about how to get something 'long' into something 'short', and in that context the spaces left between the sentences are not empty, as they formally appear, but implicitly full of what it takes to get from one to another. This is the biography of a text, its under meanings and connections. George Eliot knows she has recreated something of reality when she has made the text such a medium as, within which, in the words of Herbert Spencer himself, 'it is difficult to detect the multiplication of effects which is elsewhere so obvious' (*Spencer Essays*, p. 184, 'Progress: Its Law and Cause'). She knows she has got close to the Real when the text is become too dense for simple extrapolation. 'Every Real,' wrote George Henry Lewes, 'is the complex of so many relations, a conjuncture of so many events, a synthesis of so many sensations, that to know one Real thoroughly would only be possible through an intuition embracing the Universe.'[12]

'We don't see each other's whole nature.' George Eliot is less interested when, earlier, Tina goes into a jealous frenzy as a result of Captain Anthony's ill-use of her. George Eliot knows that reactive humiliation as well as the chronic unfaithfulness of men such as John Chapman; she knows the cruelly simple cause and effect of passion. As Gilfil will say to Tina, 'And wrong makes wrong. When people use us ill, we can hardly help having ill feeling towards them. But that second wrong is more excusable.' That second wrong is how the organism begins to become what the external situation is making it be. But, for George Eliot, the essential human question is how far one such as Tina will simply receive, conduct, and pass on these transmitted pressures linearly, or how far she can hold them back within herself, resist them, and transmute them in the act of making herself more character than victim.

Because a character is a denser medium. When Lydgate gives his hand to Bulstrode to help him out of the public meeting which has exposed his disgrace, it is as though to the crude gossips, putting two and two together, Lydgate were admitting his complicity as one of Bulstrode's party. And Lydgate knows that, even as, reluctantly, he still offers his hand: 'What could he do? He could not see a man sink close to him for want of help.' He is still a doctor, making a swift diagnosis: 'Lydgate felt sure there was not strength enough in him to walk away without support.' But with one stroke of the pen George Eliot writes, 'this act which might have been one of gentle duty and pure compassion . . .', and then with another stroke, from a different angle, 'was at this moment unspeakably bitter to him' (*Middlemarch*, chapter 71).

It is Dorothea who becomes like Gilfil to a Lydgate who 'had so often gone over in his mind the possibility of explaining everything . . . and had so often decided against it':

> 'Tell me, pray,' said Dorothea, with simple earnestness; 'then we can consult together. It is wicked to let people think evil of any one falsely, when it can be hindered.'
>
> Lydgate turned . . . and saw Dorothea's face looking up at him with a sweet trustful gravity. The presence of a noble nature, generous in its wishes, ardent in its charity,

> changes the lights for us: we begin to see things again in their larger, quieter masses,
> and to believe that we too can be seen and judged in the wholeness of our character....
> He gave himself up for the first time in his life, to the exquisite sense of leaning entirely
> on a generous sympathy, without any check of proud reserve.   (*Middlemarch*, chapter 76)

It is the great thing that George Eliot could do, it seemed, for anyone. 'We are always
doing each other injustice...We don't see each other's whole nature', but she could
see. And so what a difference it made 'to believe that we too can be seen and judged
in the *wholeness* of our character': that is, the different medium and mass called
character rather than story. It is that little phrase 'we too' that bespeaks the previous
lack, loss, and yet need of belief. For beneath the sophistication of evolved intelligence, there is so often at the heart of George Eliot the simple little raw cry: behind
'we *too*' there is the meaning—me, even I. Only her father had taken her part. Here it
says: he *gave* himself *up* for the *first* time in his life *without* any *check* of proud reserve:
again the little words, like blows reversed and wounds healed, have contrapuntal
depth even as the sentence goes on lineally through them. Such breakthroughs
would change the very medium—the lights, the width and depth, and soundscape—
of life, making the world more of a place in which what was on the inside could
come outside and be better received there. Farebrother had earlier warned the ever-
earnest Dorothea that even an honourable man such as Lydgate might be swayed
and corrupted by money—admitting, from another angle of the pen, that he has
often felt 'that weakness in myself'. When she characteristically replies how fine it
would be to stand against the rest of the world as the one person who believed in
another man's innocence, Farebrother adds ruefully: 'Character is not cut in
marble—it is not something solid and unalterable. It is something living, and
changing, and may become diseased as our bodies do' (chapter 72). In all these
interlocked processes George Eliot is *both* Dorothea, seeking to take not one part for
the whole but recognize instead the wholeness of a character, *and* Lydgate, the
defensive hider of shameful secrets, vulnerably unconfident of true interpretation
even in himself, *and* also Farebrother in reluctant and self-implicated corrective. That
complex is itself the syntax and network of her creative imagination.

  This is the paradox. That in the making of herself as a writer, George Eliot owed
almost everything to the evolution of syntax, but finally almost nothing to the idea's
chief proponent, Herbert Spencer. And that was because she used its form of
thinking as a nervous-feeling mental instrument, in a way that was almost the
opposite of Spencer's own unemotional and frictionless ideal. It made what was
true at the personal level the expression of something also deeper in the contrast
between them. That is to say: she—or, at any rate, what 'she' turned out to be—
could never have married him. Or like Dorothea with Casaubon, should never.

*

But Marian Evans did not know that in 1852.

Until it was finally released from the British Museum where Spencer had lodged it with instructions that it not be made public for a hundred years, no one knew of the letter that Marian Evans had written and handed to Spencer in July 1852 after he had rejected her love:

> I know this letter will make you very angry with me, but wait a little, and don't say anything to me while you are angry. I promise not to sin any more in the same way.
>
> My ill health is caused by the hopeless wretchedness which weighs upon me. I do not say this to pain you, but because it is the simple truth which you must know in order to understand why I am obliged to seek relief.
>
> I want to know if you can assure me that you will not forsake me, that you will always be with me as much as you can and share your thoughts and feelings with me. If you become attached to some one else, then I must die, but until then I could gather courage to work and make life valuable, if only I had you near me. I do not ask you to sacrifice anything—I would be very good and cheerful and never annoy you. But I find it impossible to contemplate life under any other conditions. If I had your assurance, I could trust that and live upon it. I have struggled—indeed I have—to renounce everything and be entirely unselfish, but I find myself utterly unequal to it. Those who have known me best have always said, that if ever I loved any one thoroughly my whole life must turn upon that feeling, and I find they said truly. You curse the destiny which has made the feeling concentrate itself on you—but if you will only have patience with me you shall not curse it long. You will find that I can be satisfied with very little, if I am delivered from the dread of losing it.
>
> I suppose no woman ever before wrote such a letter as this—but I am not ashamed of it, for I am conscious that in the light of reason and true refinement I am worthy of your respect and tenderness, whatever gross men or vulgar-minded women might think of me.   (GEL 8, pp. 56–7)

Was she beautiful or not beautiful? are the opening words to *Daniel Deronda*, and it may be asked somewhat similarly of this letter: Is it brave or is it humiliating? But though 'separate words' might well suit gross men or vulgar-minded women, it is as ever both these things, brave and humiliating—and more shades of things too. It is what happens when primary needs within—'my *whole* life must turn upon that feeling'—have to meet secondary considerations in the outside world—'be satisfied with *very little*'; when—to deploy what the philosophic terms of Spinoza and Spencer really mean to the life and feelings of this woman—the demands of 'conatus' met the necessities of 'adjustment'. 'Always as much as you can...I can with very little' is the shorthand of compromisedness here from which Spencer, unsurprisingly, still withdrew. After all, how could it work? The letter is saturated with the repressed need still for everything: 'always be with me', 'not sacrifice anything', 'to renounce everything', 'entirely unselfish', 'utterly unequal', 'loved thoroughly my whole life', 'no woman ever before'. The complications are immersed in a syntactic medium of 'if' and 'but'—and it is no surprise that Marian Evans had to write this and give it to Spencer, to read at a distance, rather than be able say it to him direct, through all those difficulties of communication: 'If you can assure me, if I had your assurance', 'Not forsake me, as much as you can, I can be satisfied', 'If you become attached, until then, if only I had you, if ever I loved, if you will only', 'But I find myself unequal, but I am not ashamed, whatever [they] might think of me.' This is what William James meant when he said that below the surface level of simply nameable emotions there were deeper shaped contours of feeling known only in the feeling of *if*, the feeling of *but*.[13] It is not necessarily about the memory of specific events, memories, or emotions but these things wrought into the very nerve and fibre of the writer's being, at a level of subtle unconsciousness unrecallable in ordinary autobiography. At that level, the woman who became George Eliot does not write (as Spencer might just about have preferred—at least stylistically), 'If I am delivered from the dread of losing it, you will find that I can be satisfied with very little'; but more magnificently, more terribly, and more like the George Eliot to come: 'You will find that I can be satisfied with very little, if I am delivered from the dread of losing it.' She cannot move that dread of broken emotional investment, can do nothing with it on her own, and can see nothing that comes after placing love and trust in someone and then losing him. By his avoidance of blows, there was in Herbert Spencer no underlying biography, no irrepressible life, the brow was clear.

But Marian Evans can still write starkly, almost nakedly, of 'the simple truth' in her letter to Spencer, even in complex form: 'it is the simple truth which you must know in order to understand why I am obliged to seek relief'. In that commitment to the truthful, the raw, the needy, the discreditable, and even the stupid, all of which remain beneath the level of defensive intelligence and acceptable presentation, there lies what, in the future, would be a double force of realism. First, that in the biography of the writing, the sympathetic reader who is so sought, encouraged, and educated by George Eliot, can always hear the simple first cries that the sentences arise out of and have to negotiate: 'The secret of our emotions never lies in the bare object, but in its subtle relations to our own past: no wonder the secret escapes the unsympathising observer' (*Adam Bede*, chapter 18). Second, that as the intelligence and the complexity come out of something primally and emotionally simple, so too they seek to return to it from a higher level, and deliver something solid, simple, and normal back to the world, as the complexities of a Henry James, say, perhaps rarely do.

The failed scholar Casaubon will not let Dorothea near him. 'His experience,' George Eliot writes finally, 'was of that pitiable kind which shrinks from pity' (*Middlemarch*, chapter 29). 'Pitiable' is one of those visceral words with George Eliot, biographical to the writing, as it was said of Bulstrode, 'The pitiable lot is that of the man who could not call himself a martyr.' The word is George Eliot's rewrite of 'pitiful' or 'pathetic', and it is the sound of that original underlying version which Casaubon instinctively shrinks from: the inherent judgement in which contempt can hardly be denied a role in the complex formation of the pity that transmutes it. 'That pitiable kind which shrinks from pity': again it is the word order of the sentences that is vital, and the check that prevents easy responses. For 'pitiable' here—up front and yet turned adjectival—knows within itself how the man will shrink from what it offers; yet finds that response to be even more a ground for pity, and is able still to try to give itself, even if more indirectly, as an adjective adjusting itself in place of the nounal force it still retains. Still pitying, though almost helplessly, those who cannot bear pity, and yet always ready to try again, is why 'pitiable' remains there, marking what remains undauntedly *simple* at heart, in the face of pain, paradox, complexity, helplessness, and discouragement. If then, ironically, it still can find no place to act in the world, and is not sufficient, it has to go into the world of literature, held there as otherwise lost human potential. For there in the fiction it is as if, under cover of the sophisticated modifying syntax, the author is silently saying to Dorothea: keep pitying even so. Keep imagining—even though it was your imagination that made you idolize him in the first place—the man who seems to have no imagination, as Dorothea with Casaubon and Marian Evans with Herbert Spencer. Keep trying to sympathize with what seems unsympathetic, for that is the purpose not the irony of sympathy: 'The last refuge of intolerance is in not tolerating the intolerant, and I am often in danger of secreting that sort of venom' (Cross, 1, p. 471).

So it is for Dorothea after the doctor has left, wanting to know her husband's diagnosis and bear it with him:

> Dorothea had been aware when Lydgate had ridden away, and she had stepped into the garden, with the impulse to go at once to her husband. But she hesitated, fearing to offend him by obtruding herself; for her ardour, continually repulsed, served, with her intense memory, to heighten her dread, as thwarted energy subsides into a shudder; and she wandered slowly round the nearby clump of trees until she saw him advancing. Then she went towards him ... (*Middlemarch*, chapter 42)

The 'impulse' first 'to go at once', and then the new secondary hesitation; the original ardour, turned by that recently learnt fear of obtruding herself into intense memory and increased fear instead; then the aimless wandering that results from the loss of first things; and yet despite the fear and the discouragement, finally the renewed turn she makes towards him—only to receive another blow, a further rebuff. The twists and turns of the narrative here are like the nervous turns of syntax elsewhere. And they bespeak what Saul Bellow in *More Die of Heartbreak* meant by *keeping the first heart* through all life's vicissitudes. It is the turns in this passage that are what is most autobiographical—the shaped commitments and not just the contents of George Eliot's thinking.

But Casaubon has been given his death sentence and all he does in the face of Dorothea's renewed effort is turn away, and turn her away, as she almost predicted and certainly feared. Alone in her room afterwards, she thinks she will never again turn to him, her pity is overthrown. Yet after thinking alone for hours she tries once again before nightfall, going down the stairs even as he comes up them:

> When her husband stood opposite to her, she saw that his face was more haggard. He started slightly on seeing her, and she looked up at him beseechingly, without speaking.
> 'Dorothea!' he said, with a gentle surprise in his tone. 'Were you waiting for me?'
> 'Yes, I did not like to disturb you.'
> 'Come, my dear, come. You are young, and need not to extend your life by watching.'
> When the kind quiet melancholy of that speech fell on Dorothea's ears, she felt something like the thankfulness that might well up in us if we had narrowly escaped hurting a lamed creature. She put her hand into her husband's, and they went along the broad corridor together.   (*Middlemarch*, chapter 42)

Waiting up, going downstairs, joining hands, speaking kindly. This is the return of the ostensibly simple in the simply moral, just as surely as it is for Lydgate when he accepts from her the support that Casaubon still mainly cannot. It is a return to what still may be possible, though limited, within the world. That 'thankfulness' in not harming an already lamed, aged, and dying 'creature' has no object—in the world according to Feuerbach there is no God to deserve or receive it, and it is not to or for herself that Dorothea can be grateful. And 'creature' is like 'pitiable', admitting the painful, the sad, and the loving in complex measures but at least all in one. Still, thankfulness is a feeling that will not be gainsaid. Beatrice Webb admired that other faculty besides cold reason, 'which George Eliot calls the emotive thought' (*My Apprenticeship*, p. 199).

Earlier in that terrible month of July 1852, Marian Evans had written Herbert Spencer from a holiday in Broadstairs, saying she was doing nothing, reading little, with a loathing 'for all tagging together of sentences,' adding jokingly, 'You see I am sinking fast towards "homogeneity" and my brain will soon be a mere pulp unless you come to arrest the downward process' (GEL 8, p. 51). More than twenty years later she would write, 'Of Mr. Herbert Spencer's friendship I have had the honour and advantage for twenty years, but I believe that every main bias of my mind had been taken before I knew him. Like the rest of his readers, I am of course indebted to him for much enlargement and clarification of mind' (GEL 6, pp. 163–4).

Marian Evans was, like Spencer, a rationalist, a fellow thinker in the evolutionary progress from a simple homogeneity to the complex heterogeneity that culminated in human beings and their societies. But in unlikeness, it was not just that she was more simply emotional, more humanly concerned than the intellectual male, though it is true that hers was a commitment to that many-sided and integrated development which Spencer preached but could not practise. It was also that what she became most interested in, as George Eliot, was when human existence pushed reason to a reasoning outside its familiar categories and beyond its normal limits. Her very sentences register that pressure and that struggle in the face of individual experiments in life. Rather than the syntax of fitting in with a grand theory, her syntax was the creation of more than she could easily explain, whilst at the same time still committed to trying to understand it.

CHAPTER 5

The Two Loves of 1852

2. George Henry Lewes

George Henry Lewes had first met Marian Evans in October 1851 when John Chapman introduced him to her as a desirable contributor for the *Westminster Review*. They met again infrequently at Chapman's parties. But as often was the case with him, in his brash and flippant manner, Lewes did not make a good first impression. It was through another of her infatuations, Herbert Spencer, that she really began to know Lewes, just over a year later, early in 1853. 'Being with Lewes one afternoon when I was on my way to see her,' Spencer wrote in a letter 3 February 1881, 'I invited him to go with me (they were already slightly known). He did so':

> This happened two or three times; and then, on the third or fourth time, when I rose to leave, he said he should stay. From that time he commenced to go alone, and so the relation began—(his estrangement from his wife being then of long standing). When I saw the turn matters were taking it was, of course, an immense relief to me. (GEL 8, p. 43)

Spencer had for some time suffered 'qualms as to what might result' from his constant companionship with this woman whom he admired morally and intellectually without physical attraction. There was friendship but, as he put it with detachment, 'I could not perceive in myself any indication of a warmer feeling.' He had tried to warn her—he had taken what he called the 'strange', almost 'absurd' step of writing to her directly of his fears. He was relieved when she did not seem to take as a humiliating insult his admission that 'while I felt in no danger of falling in love with her, she was in danger of falling in love with me'. Instead she took it 'smilingly', he believed, 'understanding my motives and forgiving my rudeness'. And so their intimacy had carried on as before through the summer of 1852 into the beginning of 1853 in the form of an agreed friendship, until 'just what I feared might take place, did take place. Her feelings became involved, and mine did not.' So badly did Spencer feel at involving her, albeit 'involuntarily, or rather, against my will', that he had even hinted at the possibility of recompense by marriage but she herself had seen that it could 'only lead to unhappiness' (GEL 8, pp. 42–3). Then Lewes had come along; it was a relief, a good turn of events.

Lewes was a small, bold, bright, and ugly man with a past, a reputation for sexual looseness. 'Imagine a very short slender man,' wrote Marian Evans's friend, Bessie Parkes in 1854, 'with blue eyes, large & full of meaning & feeling; very large mouth, expressive but quite too coarse; plain features deeply pitted with the small-pox, long dark hair waving into his neck; his face always reminded me of a Lions, & the hair was like a mane.'[1]

Born in 1817 of illegitimate birth and having experienced an irregular education abroad, Lewes, with his excellent French and love of theatre, was no conventional Englishman. An enthusiastically wide-ranging journalist for the periodicals, he was an actorly showman, freethinking bohemian, and witty mimic and storyteller. Thomas Carlyle described him as the '*dramatic* G. H. Lewes', airy, loose-tongued, merry-hearted, 'with more sail than ballast' (Ashton, p. 96). He could seem like a conceited and rather vulgar dandy at first sight, but in his defence John Stuart Mill insisted:

> [W]hat gives him that air is precisely the buoyancy of spirits which you have observed in him, & he is so prompt & apparently presumptuous in undertaking anything for which he feels the slightest vocation (however much it may be really beyond his strength) only because he does not care at all for failure, knowing & habitually feeling that he gets up stronger after every fall & believing as I do that the best way of improving one's faculties is to be continually trying what is above one's present strength.   (Ashton, p. 40)

Mill concluded, 'He is confident but not at all conceited, for he will bear to be told anything however unflattering about what he writes'. This buoyancy of Lewes, the sailing onwards, the not caring about failure were all precisely the opposite of Marian Evans, heavy-laden and self-doubting. For all that Mill said Lewes lacked the first-class abilities necessary for the highest work, he had published a much-read four-volume *Biographical History of Philosophy* in 1845–6, which sold 10,000 copies in a single year, and *Comte's Philosophy of the Sciences* in 1853, as well as plays, periodical articles, and literary reviews, and a semi-autobiographical novel, *Ranthorpe* (1847), about a romantic young writer, struggling between dreams and reality. In particular, his writings on drama, on actors, and on acting, which he loved, were alert to the emotional liveness and dynamic psychology of performance, and especially to the close interaction of body and mind in the actor's sensitized nervous system. He was the first, said the critic and playwright William Archer, to introduce the word 'psychology' into the language of dramatic criticism, and when later he turned to writing on psychology itself, the actors became models for his physiological writings on vibration, tremor, and discharge.[2] His motto was 'What we did we were. What we can we are.'[3] But he did too much, it was said, and spread himself too widely.

1853, the year of their coming together, was also the year in which Charlotte Brontë's *Villette* was published. The alliance between Marian Evans and George Henry Lewes was almost as unlikely as that between Brontë's Lucy Snowe and Monsieur Paul, as they both half-humorously acknowledged. In exile in Villette, which was based on Brussels, Lucy was the plain, cold, pale English spinster without hope, vainly trying to deny her passion and give up on any belief in love and happiness; Paul the small, proud, exuberantly volatile French professor who goadingly would not let her do so. Lewes had met Charlotte Brontë in 1850 and found her a sickly-looking old maid but Marian Evans knew, as did he, the fire and passion she gave out through her work. As Lewes wrote in a review of Brontë's characters in the *Westminster Review*, April 1853 (vol. 117, p. 254):

> They outrage good sense, yet they fascinate. You dislike them at first, yet you learn to love them. The power that is in them makes its vehement way right to your heart. 'Propriety', ideal outline, good features, good manners, ordinary thought, ordinary speech, are not to be demanded of them. They are the 'Mirabeaus of Romance'.

Whereas Herbert Spencer had never learned to love Marian Evans, she herself had long since got over her unfavourable first impressions of Lewes, seeing something deeper behind the mask. Mirabeau was the ugly fiery energizing force of the Revolution in France: it was as 'a miniature Mirabeau in appearance' that Marian Evans had described Lewes to Charles Bray in October 1851 when she first met him with Chapman (GEL 1, p. 367). Their union was to offend the 'propriety' of conventional forms. They had to believe in it, and make it strong, against the outer world. By April 1853 she was writing to Cara Bray:

> Mr. Lewes especially is kind and attentive and has quite won my regard after having a good deal of my vituperation. Like a few other people in the world, he is much better than he seems—a man of heart and conscience wearing a mask of flippancy.   (GEL 2, p. 98)

This was becoming characteristic experience: that real as opposed to fantasy events were slow in preparation, revealing themselves only gradually through the work of time, through reappraisals on second thought in place of first impressions. That was what was so powerful about *Villette*: the return of hope after youth, the possibility of happiness long since lost and abandoned, the unexpectedness of people turning out better not worse than had been supposed.

Though no one knew it, the unlikeable Monsieur Paul was modelled on M. Heger, a married man with whom, in her youth in Brussels, the unattractive Charlotte Brontë had fallen unhappily in love. Here, equivalently, for Marian Evans was Lewes, a married man, separated from his wife, and either unable to obtain a divorce because he had accepted another man's child as his own and thereby condoned the adultery, or unwilling for fear of publicity. Amidst all the fecklessness of his wife's lover Thornton Hunt, Lewes was still taking generous financial responsibility for Alice and for the children—both those who were his and those who were not. But the need to work and the accompanying unhappiness was making him ill. It was during one of those bouts of exhausted illness in April 1854, when he was ordered not to work for a month, that Marian Evans tended him, carrying out for him the tasks of writing and editing he undertook for *The Leader*. Whenever it was that they had first become lovers, this act of care was a decisive culmination.

Charles Bray understood something of this, and tried to defend her going abroad with Lewes on account of his health and her determination to look after him. As in his own conduct, Bray tried to mask the sexual element for the sake of conventional morality. Against those urging her to return at once without Lewes, 'she replies that his health will not permit it at present, that she is absolutely necessary to him, and she refuses to do what she would consider wrong out of deference to the opinion of the world'. Bray stresses the continuity of her character in this:

> People must be allowed to come to their own conclusions as to the right or wrong of her conduct. She also must be allowed to satisfy her own conscience. As a daughter she was the most devoted I ever knew, and she is just as likely to devote herself to some *one* other, in preference to all the world, and without reference either to the regularity or legality of the connection. (GEL 8, p. 128)

It was not just theoretical freethinking, it was the same quality of devotion she had showed her father; only she who could be called daughter could not now be called wife. Had Marian Evans read this letter, or George Eliot existed to think about it in a novel, either would have known just how poignantly ironic it was that such continuity of devoted feeling meant that the break she averted with her father over religion became now decisive with her brother Isaac over extra-marital love. The continuity at one level destroyed continuity at another. In the family rejection that followed, she tried to make herself see

> how much of the pain I have felt concerning my own family is really love of approbation in disguise...If I live five years longer, the positive result of my existence on the side of truth and goodness will outweigh the small negative good that would have consisted in my not doing anything to shock others, and I can conceive no circumstances that will make me repent the past. (GEL 2, p. 342)

Negative good in not doing anything was no real good. This was what was impressive about her courage—that its risk was tied fast to her fears and to her weaknesses, and had to struggle in a day-to-day continuance that looked to the future to redeem itself. It was never a straightforward story for her: she was vulnerable to what people thought of her. It took her nearly three years to bring herself to tell her brother of the relation with Lewes; in another five years she had published *Adam Bede, The Mill on the Floss,* and *Silas Marner.*

Eloping together in their 30s to seek second lives, these were two desperate people, though their desperation took different forms: he struggling almost manically to hold out by carrying on; she in recurrent despair of anything heartfelt to go on with. Lewes wrote of himself to Carlyle, in explanation of his separation from his wife:

> My separation was in no-wise caused by the lady named, nor by any other lady. It has always been imminent, always *threatened*, but never before carried out, because of those assailing pangs of anticipation which would not let me carry resolution into fact. At various epochs I have explicitly declared that unless a change took place I could not hold out. (Ashton, p. 155)

That was what it was like for Lewes, busily trying to maintain his broken life, immersed in hyperactive effort, until illness and the fear of further illness created crisis and almost breakdown. That was why he had admired Spencer for offering an overarching theory in place of this living merely hand to mouth. But after Lewes had left his wife, he could not 'hold out' alone, either.

Near the beginning of 1852, suffering over Herbert Spencer, Marian Evans had been writing to friends as though no new turn of life was possible:

> For you must know that I am not a little desponding now and then, and think that old friends will die off, while I shall be left without the power to make new ones. You know how sad one feels when a great procession has swept by one, and the last notes of its music have died away, leaving one alone with the fields and the sky. I feel so about life sometimes. It is a help to read such a life as Margaret Fuller's.[4] How inexpressibly touching that passage from her journal—'I shall always reign through the intellect, but the life! the life! Oh my God! shall that never be sweet?' (GEL 2, p. 15)

It was not a musical procession that was passing her by but life itself, leaving her in silence. The secondary compensation of reigning through the intellect was, to her, hardly compensation at all if there were no real emotional fulfilment beneath it. It was Lewes who was 'the life! the life!' It was he who believed in her when she did not believe in herself, and who came to believe she could become a novelist. He knew from the first, as did so many, that she was a considerable intellect. But what he discovered and helped her to discover was that she could write story and dialogue, human drama and human feeling—in short, could write 'the life' itself.

That was still to come. By June 1854, they had left together, a couple, for Weimar, which she, writing enigmatically to Sara Hennell, called 'Labassecour' (GEL 2, p. 165). It was the name Charlotte Brontë had given for Belgium in *Villette.*

It was an elopement that, as she had said of Lewes himself, was much better than appeared at first sight to others surrounding them. Only when Carlyle sent him a word of generous encouragement did Lewes let out some of the pain he usually silenced. 'One must have been, like me, long misjudged and harshly judged without power of explanation, to understand the feelings which such a letter creates,' he wrote:

> I sat at your feet when my mind was first awakening; I have honoured and loved you ever since both as teacher and friend, and now to find that you judge me rightly, and are not estranged by what has estranged so many from me, gives me strength to bear what must yet be borne! (GEL 2, p. 176)

To be understood and rightly judged, amidst partial distortions and the incapacity for full explanation and rebuttal: how much the desire for that was a drive in the psyche of Marian Evans too. It was what drew her to Lewes himself. At much the same time, she was writing resolutely to her former beloved, the less than resolute John Chapman:

> I do not wish to take the ground of ignoring what is unconventional in my position. I have counted the cost of the step that I have taken and am prepared to bear, without irritation or bitterness, renunciation by all my friends. I am not mistaken in the person to whom I have attached myself. He is worthy of the sacrifice I have incurred, and my only anxiety is that he should be rightly judged. (GEL 8, pp. 124–5)

There is no simple unhurt defiance in this. In both her and Lewes, for themselves and for each other, there was a vulnerability to being judged in the effort to found a relationship in the midst of scandal. One of Lewes's contributions to psychology was his constant insistence that the organism must live within a medium, the individual in a surrounding society.

And in that surrounding society it was the philanderer John Chapman of all people who was insisting that, though of the two of them Lewes was much more blameworthy than she, 'Miss E' had put herself foolishly at risk. Chapman was worried for her, he said: 'Now I can only pray, against hope, that he may prove constant to her; otherwise she is *utterly* lost' (GEL 8, p. 126).

Of course, Marian Evans never knew what Chapman wrote. But in the imagination of George Eliot more than twenty years later, there is created the cry of the heiress Catherine Arrowpoint in *Daniel Deronda* in response to the charge of throwing herself away on an upstart bohemian Jewish composer:

> 'Why should I not marry the man who loves me, if I love him?' said Catherine. To her the effort was something like the leap of a woman from the deck into the lifeboat...
>
> (*Daniel Deronda*, chapter 22)

When Klesmer himself expresses doubt and fear that he may not be worth the sacrifice, she replies, 'Is it the accusations you are afraid of? I am afraid of nothing but that we should miss the passing of our lives together.' It is what Marian Evans would have said, albeit in her different circumstances. It was the great leap, to save her life.

She wrote to Cara Bray in September 1855, in defence of moral vows unsanctioned by any church: 'Light and easily broken ties are what I neither desire theoretically nor could live for practically. Women who are satisfied with such ties do not act as I have done—they obtain what they desire and are still invited to dinner' (GEL 2, p. 214). But the novelist Charles Kingsley had called her Lewes's concubine, the sculptor Thomas Woolner a sort of whore, the phrenologist George Combe thought some insanity had taken over the brain of one he had previously so much admired. Even her friend Bessie Parkes, who did not take to Lewes, had written to her at the lodgings they shared as man and wife, addressing her as 'Miss Evans'. It could have caused their removal. As to 'Miss Evans' herself: 'I have renounced that name, and do not mean to be known by it in any way' (GEL 2, p. 384). As she was to put it in *Felix Holt* in characteristic revision of conventional reality, 'It is not true that love makes all things easy; it makes us choose what is difficult' (chapter 49).

In *The Mill on the Floss*, Maggie Tulliver did not finally take that leap in eloping with Stephen Guest. Drawn on by sexual passion, halfway along she nonetheless decides to return home, which is, to her, the more difficult choice. But it is the same condemnation by the men of moral maxims that she suffers as Miss Evans, and it arouses the fierce indignation of George Eliot. For that is what the novel does, in offering the inner and not just outer story of something individually other than the normal world's formulaic summaries. But still it registers what is the worst condemnation, that of her brother. 'Tom,' Maggie says to him, 'I am come back to you— I am come back home—for refuge—to tell you everything—' To which Tom retorts in the very tones of Isaac Evans, not hesitating to use the memory of their dead father: 'You will find no home with me.... You have disgraced us all—you have disgraced my father's name. You have been a curse to your best friends.... I wash my hands of you for ever. You don't belong to me' (*The Mill on the Floss*, book 7, chapter 1). In life it was different. Isaac Evans had responded to his sister's announcement of her union only via his solicitor. She could not have borne, she said, to hear in him a tone she could not recognize.

The complexity of life 'is not to be embraced by maxims': 'to lace ourselves with formulas of that sort is to repress all the divine promptings and inspirations that spring from growing insight and sympathy'. It is not that that great cry against unjust and reductive judgement in book 7, chapter 2, of *The Mill on the Floss* is 'really about' the scandal of its author joining with George Henry Lewes, or derives mainly from its painful memory. On the contrary, by the novelist's act of writing, the personal scandal and the private pain were turned into being no more and no less than a tacit part, or a hard-earned example, of the great achieved protest, and were creatively used for that purpose. When Milton wrote in defence of divorce, it was argued against him that he was really pleading his own cause, as a man in an unhappy marriage, whilst seemingly advancing a general argument. But Marian Evans, now Marian Lewes, writing on the 'Life and Opinions of Milton' in Lewes's *Leader* for August 1855, responded: 'There is much unreasonable prejudice against this blending of personal interest with a general protest. If we waited for the impulse of abstract benevolence or justice, we fear that most reforms would be postponed to the Greek Kalends' (*Essays*, p. 156). There was no such division of time known to the Greeks; it meant it would never happen. This realist understanding was what went into the making of a George Eliot who would say in *Scenes of Clerical Life* that she was not writing from 'a lofty height' but 'on the level and in the press with' her flawed and besieged characters. The work of 'helping the world forward,' she wrote, does not wait to be done by pure, disinterested, and perfect human beings. Neither Luther nor John Bunyan, nor John Milton for that matter, 'would have satisfied the modern demand for an ideal hero, who believes nothing but what is true, feels nothing but what is exalted, and does nothing but what is graceful' ('Janet's Repentance', chapter 10). Amidst their mess, chaff, and failings, they have earned their one or two hard-won truths 'by long wrestling with their own sins and their own sorrows'. If there is even in them such a 'blending' of personal interest with general protest, of fixed and obstinate opinion with finer and deeper insight, then that too is part of the flawed human struggle to do something with integrity.

Lewes was to know more than anyone else what was going through her mind as she wrote. He knew the tacit and mingled memories that were both creative of and released by the power of literary language:

> Genius is rarely able to give any account of its own processes. But those who have had ample opportunities of intimately knowing the growth of works in the minds of artists, will bear me out in saying that a vivid memory supplies the elements from a thousand different sources, most of which are quite beyond the power of localisation, the experience of yesterday being strangely intermingled with the dim suggestions of early years, the tones heard in childhood sounding through the diapason of sorrowing maturity; and all these kaleidoscopic fragments are recomposed into images that seem to have a corresponding reality of their own.
>
> (*Principles of Success in Literature*, chapter 3, part 4)

Lewes wrote this in 1865, with ample opportunity of intimately knowing 'the growth of works' in the mind of the artist he had loved, lived, and worked with for eleven years.

*

Lewes had chosen Weimar for their temporary refuge abroad because he also wanted to pursue research there for his *Life of Goethe*. It was a hallmark of their love that theirs was a union made further substantial by the work and the intellectual collaboration that surrounded it. In the words of Thomas Hardy near the end of *Far from the Madding Crowd*, this was one of those rare solid unions achieved through the association of man and woman not merely in their pleasures but through their labours too (chapter 56).

In the *Life of Goethe*, published the following year in 1855, there is a telling moment when Lewes has to deal with Goethe's sexual behaviour as a young man—in particular his jilting of the young Friederike Brion, the 16-year-old daughter of a priest. 'The thoughtlessness of youth, and the headlong impetus of passion,' Lewes writes, out of his own earlier free-living experience, 'frequently throw people into rash engagements.' Then it is that 'the *formal* morality of the world, more careful of externals than of truth, declares it to be nobler for such rash engagement to be kept, than that a man's honour should be stained by a withdrawal'. Yet to marry in that way, for all the remorse, was to let the letter take precedence over the spirit, in particular the spirit of both Goethe and Shelley in defence of Romantic freedom and sincerity of feeling. But the older Lewes, becoming settled in partnership with Marian Evans, now goes on in a very different note:

> [Goethe] had experienced, and he could paint (no one better), the exquisite devotion of woman to man; but he had scarcely ever felt the peculiar tenderness of man for woman, when that tenderness takes the form of vigilant protecting fondness. He knew little, and that not until late in life, of the subtle interweaving of habit with affection, which makes life saturated with love, and love itself become dignified through the serious aims of life. He knew little of the *companionship* of two souls striving in emulous spirit of loving rivalry to become better, to become wiser, teaching each other to soar. He knew little of this... (*Life of Goethe*, book 3, chapter 1)

But Lewes did now know it—the seriousness, the teaching each other to become better, the fusion in the very words 'vigilant protecting fondness', like an image of that subtle interweaving of experience blending elements of life into what was in every sense a relationship. It was Lewes who not only encouraged the novel-writing but protected it from the criticism which otherwise might have led her to give up writing at the least adversity. He had had his doubts not about her intellect but about whether she could combine it with dramatic power. 'You must try,' he had told her from their earliest days together; 'I deferred it, however, after my usual fashion' she recalled (GEL 2, p. 407), but then a title came to her one morning, lying in bed. 'The Sad Fortunes of the Reverend Amos Barton'. It was a great day when, in October 1856, Lewes went to town on purpose to leave her a quiet evening to finish 'Amos

Barton' with the death of Amos's wife, Milly: 'I read it to G. when he came home. We both cried over it' (GEL 2, p. 408). He had come back to find that she was a novelist after all. She chose the pseudonym George Eliot, not least because of the scandal around her own name, as well as her concerns about the treatment of lady novelists. But it was above all 'George' after Lewes, and though Eliot was chosen as a good solid name, some later readers guessed it was a secret pun: 'To L— I owe it'.

'In my buoyant confidence,' writes Lewes to the publisher John Blackwood while the gender and identity of George Eliot were still unknown, 'I try in vain to give him some of my hopefulness, but Nature is too strong' (GEL 2, p. 372). The author's nature was to say, 'I never think what I write is good for anything till other people tell me so, and even then it always seems to me as if I should never write anything *else* worth reading' (GEL 2, p. 260): 'We want people to feel with us,' she concludes in her need for kindness and confirmation, 'not to act for us.' But Lewes did both— 'with' and 'for'—as her loving companion and increasingly her literary agent, transmitting his life and his hope into her as she became, increasingly, the leading writer in the partnership.

It was as though Lewes took over the insecurities of Marian Evans—made her Marian Lewes—in order to let her become George Eliot. And as he was seeking to fuse his hope into her, she was transfusing her life into her novels. For this is where any biography must begin to leave her life—or rather pursue it, as she did, innerly through the writing.

Lewes himself knew how much she was reusing what had once seemed the useless experience of her own past. Away from her desk Lewes called her a perfect woman, but 'writing—writing—writing', '*at* the desk—oh!—my!—God!!!' (GEL 5, p. 282). This was Lewes's parody of Goldsmith's praise of the actor Garrick—that on stage he was natural, it was only off-stage that he was always acting. Settled with Lewes, she had turned her life into work, for which she was the 'vehicle'. She could be kind and loving, but away from the desk it was increasingly a life off-duty, residually waiting and planning to write again. All the time there was a sort of nervous overload: hypochondria, anxiety in maintaining the existence of 'George Eliot', and a fearfulness of the hubris of being God-like in her novels whilst only human outside them. It was Lewes who was asked out to dine when, in the early years of their union, she was still not respectable company. Later at the Sunday gatherings they held at their house, the Priory, she was transformed into the Madonna, the great author unveiled by Lewes to whom each supplicant approached for dialogue. But she was almost nothing in herself at times, tired, troubled with headache and toothache, worried. As she herself was to write in her journal, November 1868, on her dedication to work: it was making 'a higher life for me', 'a life that is young and grows, though in my other life I am getting old and decaying' (GEL 4, p. 490). One was feeding off the other. That is why, increasingly, in what follows, the chapters of her life—a second life—will bear the names of the novels she wrote.

Yet the transfusion from one life to another higher one was never quite secure. Back at the start in November 1856, Lewes had had to warn Blackwood against expressing the slightest reservation even in accepting the 37-year-old's first ever story:

> my friend...is unusually sensitive and unlike most writers is more anxious about *excellence* than about appearing in print—as his waiting so long before taking the venture proves. He is consequently afraid of failure though not afraid of obscurity; and by failure he would understand that which I suspect most writers would be apt to consider as success—so high is his ambition. (GEL 2, p. 227)

And it was no better, many apparently successful years later, when he wrote to Blackwood, 13 February 1872, in the midst of her writing of *Middlemarch*:

> Reading 'Felix Holt' the other morning made her *thin* with misery, so deeply impressed was she with the fact that she could never write like that again and that what is now in hand is rinsings of the cask! How battle against such an art of ingeniously self tormenting? (GEL 5, p. 246)

This was perhaps as near exasperation as Lewes ever allowed himself to express. *Middlemarch* was to be, many times over, a far greater novel than *Felix Holt*.

He was quite opposite in character, as she knew with some wonder. Even as the publication day loomed for the first volume of his culminating project, *Problems of Life and Mind*, she noted how 'calmly certain' he was 'that very few will care about its discussions': 'No human being can be more happily constituted than he in relation to his work. He has quite an exceptional enjoyment in the doing, and has no irritable anxieties about it when done' (GEL 5, p. 450).

At no time was this capacity for enjoyment more apparent than in the three months, away from their London lodgings, that they spent together in Ilfracombe and Tenby during the summer of 1856. His *Life of Goethe* was finished, while her first venture into fiction was planned to commence on their return to London. It was like a belated and extended English honeymoon. Lewes had borrowed a microscope in his fresh enthusiasm for scientific investigation and was writing up articles entitled 'Sea-Side Studies' for *Blackwood's Magazine*. His companion gamely went about with him in barely suitable clothing, gathering molluscs and anemones, and feeling stronger in mind and body, she said, than ever before. It was lovely that his articles appeared adjacent to 'Scenes of Clerical Life' in *Blackwood's* during 1847 and that the two works were each published as separate books within weeks of each other the year following. It was a companionship and a marriage. *Sea-Side Studies* was, said Lewes years later, 'the book of all my books which was to me the most unalloyed delight', whilst Marian told Bessie Parkes that this work of her husband's was 'a pet book of mine: there is so much happiness condensed in it! Such scrambles over rocks, and peeping into clear pool, and strolls along the pure sands, and fresh air mingling with fresh thoughts' (GEL 6, p. 226; 3, p. 134). The private life was now shared with Lewes: there is henceforth less immediate evidence of it in her letters.

It is in *Sea-Side Studies* that some of the feel of what it was to be George Henry Lewes is best conveyed. At the time of its writing, he said, the microscope and the scalpel took possession of his whole intellectual existence. Even when he was relaxing by reading literature a phrase like 'throbbing heart' would send him hurrying off to study the heart of some embryo. A play of light would make him think of the image of a mollusc or a polyp: 'The things I have seen in tapioca pudding...!'[5] There is no missing the voice and gusto of the popularizer, the personal enthusiast unabashedly vulnerable to Mill's or Carlyle's dislike at any hint of breezy facetiousness. But he speaks also of a thousand problems and a thousand strange thoughts arising from his observations: 'Here was an animal without a heart; there, one without a liver... Here was an animal breathing by means of its legs; and here one not breathing at all' (*Sea-Side Studies*, p. 55). The happiness lies not merely in the fascination but deep in the act and effort of knowledge—'knowledge which ever opens into newer and newer vistas, quickening our sense of the vastness and the complexity of Life' (p. 56). It is common, says Lewes, to speak of the effect on the human mind produced by the experience and study of 'Nature', but his excitement is very specifically to do with the microscopic view taking him further and further beyond normal, external generalizations: 'Here the Microscope is not the mere extension of a faculty, it is a new sense' (p. 57). The microscopic view reveals 'something of the great drama which is incessantly enacted in every drop of water, on every inch of earth' (p. 58)—this from a critic who had previously thought theatre the epitome of the dramatic. 'Even with a microscope directed on a water-drop,' wrote George Eliot later, 'we find ourselves making interpretations which turn out to be rather coarse': under a weak lens a creature appears to be voraciously attacking its prey, but a stronger lens 'reveals to you certain tiniest hairlets which make vortices for these victims while the swallower waits passively' (*Middlemarch*, chapter 6). That was what George Eliot was to seek: the human equivalent of stronger and subtler lenses to get beneath the surface of coarse vision, coarse language, coarse interpretation. Increasingly, with Lewes, she was on the lookout for new instruments, fresh senses, greater faculties and organs, to create at once a deeper sense of life and a finer person involved in the examination of it. It was Lewes who gave Marian Evans an increased sense of *life*, even through the lens of the microscope:

> Then and only then, do we feel how full of Life, varied, intricate, marvellous, world within world, yet nowhere without space to move, is this single planet, on the crust of which we stand... (*Sea-Side Studies*, p. 58)

This sense of plenteous life made Lewes himself feel more alive:

> And if with this substitution of definite and particular ideas for the vague generalities
> with which at first we represented Nature—if with increase of knowledge there comes,
> as necessarily there must come, increase of reverence, it is evident that the study of Life
> must of all studies best nourish the mind with true philosophy.   (*Sea-Side Studies*, p. 58)

He was tired of revising his *Biographical History of Philosophy* for new editions, though
the couple needed the money: 'Metaphysics is dry biscuit—especially for a man
hungry for zoology' (Ashton, p. 173). It was a mood that fitted with the philosophy
of Comte on which he had written in his early association with Mill: namely, that the
world was now in a third age, after the age of religion, after the age of philosophy
and metaphysics, an epoch of science. And in the journal she wrote on holiday with
him at Ilfracombe, Marian Lewes began to look at the surrounding world through
Lewes's practical scientific gaze:

> I never before longed so much to know the names of things as during this visit to
> Ilfracombe. The desire is part of the tendency that is now constantly growing in me to
> escape from all vagueness and inaccuracy into the daylight of distinct vivid ideas. The
> mere fact of naming an object tends to give definiteness to our conception of it—we
> have then a sign that at once calls up in our minds the distinctive qualities which mark
> out for us this particular object from all others.   (GEL 2, p. 251)

It is part of a movement to a second, clearer life that Lewes, both in his person and in
his work, helps make possible for her. It is as though, psychologically, to her great
relief, an emotional mist had lifted. Instead of endless intellectual vocabulary, there
was this physical sense of a reality, offering a definiteness—something concrete to
be pointed to—around which efforts at investigation must gather and be tested.
Lewes wrote of 'the true spirit of inquiry' in his *Physiology of Common Life* (1859–60),
with all the new-found discipline of a careful moral scrupulosity:

> we must resolve, in a loving, seeking, earnest spirit, to keep our minds open to the
> reception of Fact; and calmly to acquiesce in it, when presented, instead of opposing it
> by presumptions of our own.... If we ask Nature a question, we must listen patiently to
> her reply; should that reply perplex us, we must ask again, putting the question in
> another form; and should again, and again, the same reply be elicited, we must accept
> it, be it never so destructive of our theories and anticipations. We must not dictate an
> answer to the Oracle we consult.   (*The Physiology of Common Life*, vol. 2, chapter 9)

He called it 'Nature' or 'Life' but it was equally to do with that realism, in its
broadest commitment, which both Lewes and his companion would bring to their
questioning in their different ways. This is where, intellectually, the marriage was

also possible: that is to say, it was precisely Lewes's commitment to empirical findings that left room for 'answers' which, being more like replies than solutions, challenged the questions and frameworks that prompted them. She could not have lived with the closed-minded equivalent of a Strauss or a Spencer, reducing meaning by the narrow interpretation of it.

What was at stake here was what, in his long essay of 1865, *The Principles of Success in Literature*, Lewes called 'sincerity', a quality necessary to the pursuit of both art and science. However, the essay itself was concerned essentially with art, and we shall turn later to its application in science.

In *Principles of Success in Literature* Lewes endorsed Goethe's insistence on at least having one's own voice, however small or mistaken, rather than being someone else's echo. It had been that for which he had praised Charlotte Brontë in *Villette*. To be truly sincere in relation to thought, style for Lewes cannot be the application of fine phrases of surface ornament, of secondary dress, and borrowed manner. Sincere style is whatever means are necessary *through* which to get out symbols that intelligibly express the matter in the author's mind. It is not an aim or end in itself. Do not try to be beautiful or affecting, says Lewes, but 'endeavour to be faithful, and if there is any beauty in your thought, your style will be beautiful; if there is any real emotion to express, the expression will be moving' (*Principles of Success in Literature*, chapter 4). Style cannot be imitative, it must be personal: 'Personal experience is the basis of all real Literature. The writer must have thought the thoughts, seen the objects (with bodily or mental vision), and felt the feelings... Importance does not depend on rarity so much as authenticity' (chapter 1). In such formulations one can feel the fundamental confidence—to use a simple word for a complex phenomenon—he had long before this striven to instil into the creation of George Eliot out of Marian Evans. What was required was not something extraordinarily beyond her. It was a matter not of rarity but authenticity. Imagination was in the service of realism not fantasy. Or, as he magnificently put it, 'Fairies and demons are not created by a more vigorous effort of imagination than milk maids and poachers' (chapter 3).

Emerson had said in his *Essays*, 'Those facts, words, persons which dwell in a man's memory without his being able to say why, remain because they have a relation to him not less real for being as yet unapprehended. They are symbols of value to him, as they can interpret parts of his consciousness which he would vainly seek words for in conventional images' ('Spiritual Laws'). Lewes himself quoted Emerson similarly on 'Self Reliance' in support of such personal cues and clues, found in the midst of life without one's yet knowing their meaning or purpose, origin or end. This was the sort of thick empiricism Lewes and George Eliot both respected: resonant 'answers' half-offering, half-seeking—as though from back to front—the right question or context for themselves. Something rang a bell, touched or struck a nerve, seemed a possible new centre of organization or exploration. But too often, said Emerson, individuals, refusing to *be* individual, dismissed these sudden special gleams of thought—only because they were their own and not those of some authority. Yet if we do not acknowledge and put to use such thoughts, says Emerson, there is at least another way in which they can return to us: 'In every work of genius we recognize our own rejected thoughts; they come back to us with a certain alienated majesty' ('Self-Reliance'). That is what Marian Evans had learnt in her own way from Feuerbach on alienation: that communications picked up and received from outside were also messages that, hitherto unrecognized, were dimly felt or wanted within. She loved reclamation through consciousness: the finding of a hitherto unthought thought, as Spinoza had urged; the creation of a subject matter which could be thought about where previously it had been an unacknowledged part of the stream of life. Emerson had admired Miss Evans back in Coventry in 1848 when introduced by the Brays—he thought hers a 'calm, serious soul', while she thought him 'the first *man*' she had ever met (GEL 1, pp. 270–1). Now she wanted no longer to lose but use and reclaim those rejected, lost, or wasted thoughts, and, through her work, to offer back to others their own latent capacity for understanding.

But sincerity also involved a demand upon the writer in faithful responsibility towards that individual vision:

> Many of those who unhesitatingly admit Sincerity to be one great condition of success in Literature find it difficult, and often impossible, to resist the temptation of an insincerity which promises immediate advantage. It is not only the grocers who sand their sugar before prayers. Writers who know well enough that the triumph of falsehood is an unholy triumph, are not deterred from falsehood by that knowledge.
>
> (chapter 4)

In the secluded privacy of the act of writing, it is all too easy, says Lewes, to yield to the immediate pressure of temptation—the momentary makeshift phrase that gets past difficulties and keeps the work going; the easy or grandiloquent sentiment that creates a shortcut. Misgivings are set aside, he argues, because in all likelihood no one will ever detect the means, the minute sleights-of-hand by which the effect is created. 'To make belief [into] practice', Lewes had had to learn from his partner, and in *Principles of Success in Literature* he actually acknowledges his debt to Marian Evans's essay on the poet Young, written eight years earlier. Young's systemic insincerity was unarrested by any sense of a demanding reality, grandiose words heaped one upon another, not in fidelity to their subject but to produce an easy effect on an admiring audience. Lewes himself, in the years he spent with the work of George Eliot going on beside him, became less and less willing to write rapidly, but increasingly involved himself in more careful revisions.

Those revisions were not always for the sake of greater simplicity. Significantly enough, Lewes acknowledges what Herbert Spencer has to say in 'The Psychology of Style' as to the value of reducing friction and avoiding redundancy, economizing on energy and reducing retardation. But he was always scrupulously flexible—sincere, himself, in not merely sticking to a fixed position—when detecting important exceptions to a general rule. He respected instances when the rule was suspended or revised by an individual venture that, like his own partner's, went beyond the constraints of the norm. 'Economy, although a primal law, is not the only law of Style':

> That man would greatly err who tried to make his style effective by stripping it of all redundancy and ornament, presenting it naked before the indifferent public. Perhaps the very redundancy which he lops away might have aided the reader to see the thought more clearly, because it would have kept the thought a little longer before his mind, and thus prevented him from hurrying on to the next while this one was still imperfectly conceived.... Redundancy... is beneficial when its retarding influence is such as only to detain the mind longer on the thought, and thus to secure the fuller effect of the thought. For rapid reading is often imperfect reading.
>
> ('The Laws of Style 1, The Law of Economy')

In particular, it is the novelist who may 'linger where the dramatist must hurry; he may digress, and gain fresh impetus from the digression, where the dramatist would seriously endanger the effect of his scene by retarding its evolution' ('The Laws of Style 2, The Law of Simplicity'). The slow deep reasoning of a George Eliot exists not merely to illustrate the thought for better effect but to show more of the sheer thinking that has gone into it, and that it contains, until such thought itself creates another equivalent thinker deepened by the having of it.

Lewes states as a general rule, 'Economy dictates that the meaning should be presented in a form which claims the least possible attention to itself as form'; but then adds, '*unless* when that form is part of the writer's object' ('The Laws of Style', my italics). He is not going to lay down theoretic laws on form for such as George Eliot, but see how those principles must be expressed, revised, or even defied inside the secret work of actual writing. In *Middlemarch* the deliberately obtrusive authorial image of a web in the midst of the novel—'I at least so much to do in unravelling certain human lots, and seeing how they were woven and interwoven, that all the light I can command must be concentrated on this particular web' (chapter 15)—was to mean that awareness of every single strand in the novel (character, predicament, thought, or theme) involved a near-simultaneous awareness of the existence of every other strand in relation too. This was form conspicuous as *meaning*: 'Composition is to the structure of a treatise what Style,' says Lewes, 'is to the structure of sentences' (*Principles of Success in Literature*, chapter 5). It takes human consciousness to a higher level than is managed by humans normally: 'Has it not by this time ceased to be remarkable—is it not rather what we expect in men, that they should have numerous strands of experience lying side by side and never compare them with each other?' (*Middlemarch*, chapter 58).

Like so many terms for Lewes, 'Simplicity is a relative term' ('The Laws of Style 2'). The scientific psychologist in Lewes was alert to the fact that when the mind rejects all needless complexity, what it recoils from is not the complexity but the needlessness. What is sought is not simplicity in fixed preference to complexity, but, in any situation, the most adequate means to achieve the fullest necessary effect. For both George Eliot and George Henry Lewes, in the face of a complex reality and an always necessarily limited perspective upon it, what was characteristically required was not one simple absolute thought, but two or three or four thoughts, modifying and developing each other.

The sort of 'success in literature' with which Lewes is concerned is therefore not any superficially airy acclaim. It is, most remarkably, to do with psychological success: the ways in which minds may reach other minds through the act of symbolic representation. It is here that Lewes also shows how emphatically moral a man he was in his recognition of the need for a conscientious verbal care for thought in reaching the object of enquiry and, through it, the mind of others. Precision, in the checks and exceptions, in the very syntax of scruple, was demanded by a true sense of his craft:

> The obscure workers who, knowing that they will never earn renown yet feel an honourable pride in doing their work faithfully, may be likened to the benevolent who feel a noble delight in performing generous actions which will never be known to be theirs. (*Principles of Success in Literature*, chapter 4)

Morality in writing had relation to morality outside it. Lewes was better in his nature, said Marian Evans—more generous, less egotistical or jealous, more quietly forgiving, not least in complicated relation to his wife and children—than people could ever at first see. But her own nature was not so easy, her form of tolerance often being achieved more through repentance than forbearance. The epistemological doubt that warned of the need for mental scrupulosity, for revised acceptance and generosity of point of view, always hurt her far more than it did him. As she wrote in the person of Theophrastus Such towards the end of her life, even mere acquaintances

> are probably aware of certain points in me which may not be included in my most active suspicion. We sing an exquisite passage out of tune and innocently repeat it for the greater pleasure of our hearers.... How can a man be conscious of that dull perception which causes him to mistake altogether what will make him agreeable to a particular woman, and to persevere eagerly in a behaviour which she is privately recording against him? (*Impressions of Theophrastus Such*, 1879, chapter 1, 'Looking Inward')

This is how Gwendolen Harleth came to be humbled before the musician Klesmer in *Daniel Deronda*; it is how, in *Adam Bede*, Adam could not know in the moment of its happening that the blushing Hetty was not thinking of him but of another. But it went further than the contingent psychological pain of particular exposed instances of mistake: there was a more inherent epistemological possibility of perhaps never even knowing these misapprehensions for most of life. Knowing where it was that you could never be sure was crucial to the work of this couple.

There was this kind of scrupulous sincerity in the science too. There Lewes was as good as his word in seeking 'Fact'. He carried out substantial and careful scientific work throughout his life—on the nervous system of both simple and complex organisms, on the importance of the spinal cord as a volitional centre. He wrote papers for the British Association for the Advancement of Science and for the newly created periodical *Nature*, and helped to found the equally illustrious *Mind* as his ever-growing interests crossed from physiology into psychology.

He was always anxious to prove his worth as more than an amateur, as a true disciple of his beloved Goethe, a man of science as well as letters. But his sincere enthusiasm was itself a hostage to fortune with the professional establishment. Alexander Bain, psychologist disciple of Mill, wrote of Lewes to George Croom Robertson, professor of philosophy at University College London, 'His affectation being always beyond his powers, and always after the appearance of novelty, it is hard to give him the credit he expects' (Ashton, p. 243). It would have hurt Marian Lewes had she heard such remarks: it was precisely the sort of painful, doubt-creating criticism that struck at the roots of personality and achievement, and from which, in her own case, Lewes himself had protected her. After his death, knowing his bravely subdued longing for acceptance, she established a physiology student-ship in Lewes's name at Cambridge, as well as preparing for publication the last two volumes of *Problems of Life and Mind*.

Up to his demise in 1878, aged 61, Lewes worked for over ten years on the five-volume *Problems of Life and Mind*.[6] He had jokingly called it his 'Key to all Psychologies' after the impossibly ambitious 'Key to all Mythologies', the failed life's work of Casaubon in *Middlemarch* which was never published and barely written up from compendious notes. Like Casaubon too, he said ruefully, he would have to bequeath its completion to his poor wife. The spirit of comedy and self-deprecating irony was part of Lewes's personal style. It fitted well with his lightening resilience, the actor's playful and resourceful mastery of subtle tonal messages and half-revealed disguises. Increasingly he played second fiddle in a partnership where at first he had been the better-known literary figure. But the income generated by the sale of the novels, on which he kept a careful eye in all negotiations, enabled him finally to work and write more for himself, in extended and almost private contemplation, away from the

literary field in which his wife dominated. *Problems of Life and Mind* has that feeling—
that the work became, for Lewes, his own voluminous world of fluid investigation
and open venture, of wide-ranging conjecture and correction, in thinking of the
unpredictable and the uncertain. It made a world at once complementary to hers and
alternative to it. Reviewing the second volume in the *Atlantic Monthly* in 1875, William
James felt it was helping to make a ferment in the creation of a new philosophic
future in which he was himself involved.

Lewes had never been naïvely empirical about 'Fact' but in *Problems of Life and Mind*
he became increasingly philosophical in thinking about its status. He thought Life
itself was a fact, but the 'ultimate fact', and not susceptible to final explanation.
'What Thought is we do not know, perhaps we never shall,' he had acknowledged in
The Physiology of Common Life, 'We do not know what Life is. But the realm of mystery
may be reduced to one of "orderly mystery"; we may learn what are the laws of Life,
and what are the laws of Thought' (p. 55). In his *Biographical History of Philosophy* he
had already stated the view of ancient sceptics:

> The world apart from our consciousness, i.e. the non-ego *qua* non-ego—the world
> *per se*—is, we may be certain, something utterly different from our world as we know it;
> for all we know of it is derived through our consciousness of what its effects are on *us*,
> and our consciousness is obviously only *a state of ourselves*, not a copy of external things.[7]

Light, colour, sound, pain, taste, and smell do not exist in the universe without the
presence of creatures to feel them. In itself, Nature is an 'eternal Darkness—an eternal
Silence'. Both George Henry Lewes and George Eliot had that sort of imaginative awe
which saw everything human as approximative and provisional, at once wonderfully
inventive and poignantly vulnerable in the attempt to make a home upon the planet.

This meant a radical revisionist view of reality. *Foundations of a Creed* was the first
volume of the series of *Problems of Life and Mind*, published in 1874. There Lewes
argued that it is not that 'the phenomena of Nature' are '*determined by Law*' as is almost
universally supposed; on the contrary, 'This must be replaced by the more accurate
conception of the *Law being determined by the phenomena*' (PLM 1, p. 273, chapter 5).
Similarly, he is sceptical as to the explanatory power of the idea of a distinct and
merely static 'cause' in simple linear relation to a resultant effect:

> In cause and effect there are not two things, one preceding the other, but two aspects
> of one phenomenon successively viewed.... The two things which may be said to
> co-operate are the two related terms of the operation; but we must not isolate these
> terms and consider the one to be cause or antecedent, the other effect or consequent:
> since *isolated*, the terms lose all causal significance, and *related*, the one is not the product
> of the other, but both must co-operate in the causal relation.
>
> (PLM 2, pp. 323–4, problem 5, Force and Cause, chapter 1, para. 19)

The cause *is* the effect in another aspect. And 'every cause,' Lewes concluded, 'is a plural—the symbol of complex conditions, co-operant factors' (para. 20). As George Eliot put it in the epigraph to chapter 64 of *Middlemarch*:

> All force is twain in one: cause is not cause
> Unless effect be there.

A cause only becomes known as such in retrospect, and is as much made cause by its effect as vice versa. 'We separate, for convenience,' says Lewes: we separate mental and physical phenomena as if between inner and outer worlds, and then within that inner world separate again mental from neural phenomena. But mind and body are, he says brilliantly in one of his powerful images, 'as the convex and concave surfaces of the same sphere, distinguishable yet identical' (*PLM* 1, pp. 104–5). Even the slightest reflex action involves mental attributes or attributes that will become mental, as every mental state likewise involves physical workings. The language that best reflects the working of the whole organism *as* a whole is not therefore a language of separation:

> Words are not like iron and wool, coal and water, invariable in their properties, calculable in their effects. They are mutable in their powers, deriving force from very trifling changes of position; colouring and coloured by the words which precede and succeed; significant or insignificant from the powers of rhythm and cadence.
>
> (*Principles of Success in Literature*, 'The Laws of Style 1')

The words here are not straightforwardly separate and linear, but more subtly and more organically literary even when functioning outside literature, offering instead 'influence reflected back and influence projected forward' ('The Laws of Style 3').

In all this, it is not a matter of simply trying to decide who most affected whom in the Lewes–Eliot partnership, and in what particular aspects or measurable proportions. It is about the development of a way of thinking, in and around them both, that indicates the nascent emergence of a changing world-view. What excited the Lewes–Eliot partnership was not a narrow explanatory rationalism but a thinking that worked on the verge of knowing, 'or, more strictly, at the edges of ignorance'. Theirs was a commitment not simply to discover the details of the known world but to explore 'the very terms under which [that world] might be conceived'.[8] That is why Imagination was vital in all realms:

> Were all the qualities of things apparent to Sense, there would be no longer any mystery. A glance would be Science. But only some of the facts are visible; and it is because we see little, that we have to imagine much.
>
> (*Principles of Success in Literature*, chapter 3)

Human minds have to employ secondary abstractions and constructions, imaginative fictions and hypotheses in order to get some hold on these phenomena in reality. But philosophers have been wary, says Lewes, of stating what he himself dare boldly affirm: 'the introduction of Fiction to be a necessary procedure of Research' (PLM 1, p. 272, chapter 5). Their fear was that such an admission would throw doubt over the certainty of any conclusions thus attained. But if scientists had limited their efforts solely to the collection of separate facts, 'Science would have been only a sterile nomenclature... Without Hypothesis no step could be taken. Our very perceptions involve it' (PLM 1, p. 291, chapter 7). Imagination is as vital in science as it is in art: it is the same process used in different forms. And that is what George Eliot says in the famous epigraph to the opening chapter of Daniel Deronda: there always has to be 'the make-believe of a beginning', the work of pre-supposition, in science as in poetry, for everything actually begins in the 'middle' of things and has to 'reckon backwards as well as forwards'. What is distinctive to science, said Lewes, is some form of experimental test towards verification or falsification of those hypotheses.

It was Lewes himself who made an important imaginative breakthrough in using the term 'emergent' in contrast to 'resultant', when thinking about the concept of 'effects'. He wanted to make a distinction between the mere regrouping of pre-existent materials—which was the simple mechanical resultant; and, on the other hand, the emergent evolution of something dynamically new, unpredictable at its first appearance because not immediately known in advance. A measurement simply results from the sum of its units: $1+2=3$. But there are other products which are not quantitatively aggregated but embody a quality not seen separately, beforehand, in any of the elements that came together to create it. An emergent effect, says Lewes 'cannot be reduced' either to the sum or to the difference of its components (PLM 1, p. 369, problem 5, chapter 3).

Without that distinction between the mechanically resultant and the dynamically emergent, science would have held no importance for George Eliot in the study of the highest and most subtle combinations. It could not have been part of her mental language. Lewes had found an account of chemical as compared to mechanical composition in J. S. Mill's System of Logic, but it was Lewes who coined the key term 'emergent'. In mechanical composition, says Mill, we can compute in advance the effects of a combination of causes by deduction from the laws which we know to govern those causes when acting separately. But by chemical composition there is produced out of two substances 'a third substance with properties different from those of either of the two substances separately, or of both of them taken together. Not a trace of the properties of hydrogen or of oxygen is observable in those of their compound, water' (A System of Logic, 1843, book 3, chapter 6). Working inductively, we are unable to foresee what result will follow from any new combination, until we have tried the specific experiment. Mill concludes:

> If this be true of chemical combinations, it is still more true of those far more complex combinations of elements which constitute organized bodies; and in which those extraordinary new uniformities arise...It is certain that no mere summing up of the separate actions of those elements will ever amount to the action of the living body itself. (*A System of Logic*, book 3, chapter 6)

He is thinking finally of the study of human beings, the greatest of all emergent phenomena.

Unlike as water is to oxygen and hydrogen, their combination regularly makes water come to be—even though we remain currently ignorant of the invisible process by which each quits its gaseous state to assume something so utterly different as liquid. That is what Lewes meant by 'orderly mystery', in which there remains an epistemological gap in the very process of transformation. It is that gap—filled only by the recognition of change and difference when automatic action ceases—which best characterizes the emergence of human consciousness itself in response to difficulties of understanding.

Emergence is therefore, for Lewes, a model of the most powerful and exciting cognition, in the face of complex forms of reality. He loved it when, in writing, for example, a sentence was suddenly crystallized, bursting into consciousness, by the identifying use of the copula, the verb 'to be':

> The words float suspended, soulless, mere sounds. No sooner are these floating sounds grasped by the copula, than in that grasp they are grouped into significance: they start into life, as a super-saturated saline solution crystallizes on being touched by a needle-point. (*PLM* 2, pp. 128–9, problem 3, chapter 2, para. 17)

'Start into life' is in every sense a phrase characteristic of the dynamism Lewes felt when something comes into being and truly *is*. Repeatedly in *The Principles of Success in Literature*, he refers to 'the evolution of meaning' in the unwinding course of a sentence, coming into fuller and fuller organization of itself. The mysterious transition from one state into another, the moment of emergently changed organization, were always of deepest interest to Lewes. And in George Eliot, human beings were the most transitional of all beings. She it was who gave human treatment, subtly combined use, to the ideas the couple lived amidst. This chapter is finally about seeing what future emerged out of this vital strand of her life and work.

It comes to this: Who but George Eliot—and even she only partially—could trace out 'the suppressed transitions which unite all contrasts' in ordinary human life

(*Middlemarch*, chapter 20)? By what process did George Eliot's Bulstrode get from his early piety to an act of wrongful deception without ever acknowledging the wrong: 'for himself...the fact was broken into little sequences, each justified as it came by reasonings which seemed to prove it righteous' (*Middlemarch*, chapter 61)? Through what 'endless minutiae', operating at microscopic level, did Casaubon and Dorothea come to find within weeks that the marriage they had anticipated was not at all the marriage they were to have, altering as it did 'with the secret motion of a watch-hand' (*Middlemarch*, chapter 20)? How had a naturally candid young man such as Arthur Donnithorne 'brought himself into a position in which successful lying was his only hope'?

> Are you inclined to ask whether this can be the same Arthur who, two months ago, had that freshness of feeling, that delicate honour which shrinks from wounding even a sentiment, and does not contemplate any more positive offence as possible for it?—who thought that his own self-respect was a higher tribunal than any external opinion?
>
> (*Adam Bede*, chapter 29)

In his secret affair with Hetty, an intensely hidden experience of two months can suddenly have done the inner work of years:

> Our deeds determine us, as much as we determine our deeds...There is a terrible coercion in our deeds, which may first turn the honest man into a deceiver, and then reconcile him to the change; for this reason—that the second wrong presents itself to him in the guise of the only practicable right. (*Adam Bede*, chapter 29)

These things—the course of a young life, career, or a marriage—were emergent not resultant, were fluid, unpredictable, and barely visible to the naked eye—until they finally surfaced to become almost inexorably hardened. It is Lewes's microscopic process transferred to the study of human beings: like Lydgate in *Middlemarch*, George Eliot 'wanted to pierce the obscurity of those minute processes which prepare human misery and joy, those invisible thoroughfares which are the first lurking-places of anguish, mania, and crime, that delicate poise and transition which determine the growth of happy or unhappy consciousness' (*Middlemarch*, chapter 16).

It required an extraordinary language, or wide-ranging mix and shift of languages. In *Principles of Success in Literature*, Lewes himself was sensible and clear as to the two main philosophical types, and psychological usages, of general thoughts:

> If my object is to convince you of a general truth or impress you with a feeling, which you are not already prepared to accept, it is obvious that the most effective method is the inductive, which leads your mind upon a culminating wave of evidence or emotion to the very point I aim at. But the deductive method is best when I wish to direct the light of familiar truths and roused emotions, upon new particulars, or upon details in

unsuspected relation to those truths; and when I wish the attention to be absorbed by these particulars which are of interest in themselves, not upon the general truths which are of no present interest except in so far as they light up these details. A growing thought requires the inductive exposition, an applied thought the deductive.

(*Principles of Success in Literature*, chapter 2)

At first, it may look like an applied thought, giving new light to a particular dark instance of itself, when George Eliot offers general sentences signalled by the first-person plural, such as: 'Our deeds determine us ... There is a terrible coercion in our deeds.' But often 'our' may change, for example, to 'him', and 'him' becomes both general and specific at once—as in: the bad deed that turns the honest man into a liar 'then reconciles him to the change for this reason—that the second wrong presents itself to him in the guise of the only practicable right'. Then, with psychological drama, the sentence spells out precisely what Arthur, and the Arthur-hidden-in-the-reader, is trying to avoid. The words are more like personal wounds symbolically reopened—the wince of '*reconciles*' to further desperate '*wrong*' as if 'the *only* practicable *right*'—rather than resultantly known truths. In this way, the apparently applied thought comes more and more active and alive, becoming a *growing* thought lodged between particular and general, a particularized generalization, a generalized particular, coming from the two directions at once. This painfully growing induction into a general truth is hard to take, leading us where we hardly want to go, towards truths that psychologically (in Lewes's phrase) 'you are not already prepared to accept'. Not *prepared*, that is, in almost any sense—across the spectrum from not willing, or not ready, to not psychologically equipped in advance. George Eliot loved that interaction or alternation of the inductive 'uphill path' and the deductive 'high road' (*Essays*, p. 153), always switching point of view, melding different dimensions and processes in the density of complex thinking. It is close to what Will Ladislaw believed it was to be a poet: 'a soul in which knowledge passes instantaneously into feeling, and feeling flashes back as a new organ of knowledge' (*Middlemarch*, chapter 22). It was then, in the midst of those multiple movements, that she knew she was in the thick of her material.

In her early work, 'George Eliot' as narrator can at times seem intrusively to speak an overly explicit language, especially when she is anxiously trying to reach and change her audience and create her own reception. Turning outwards to the limits of her influence, she exerts herself to find the right place for her story and its ideas to be received within, that she may be able even to continue to write it. So in 'Amos Barton': 'What mortal is there of us, who finds his satisfaction enhanced by an opportunity of comparing the picture he presents to himself of his own doings, with the picture they make on the mental retina of his neighbours? We are poor plants buoyed up by the air-vessels of our own conceit...' (chapter 2). But unlike Herbert Spencer, George Eliot does not want the book to give itself up as quickly as possible to the mind that reads it; she wants the mind to be slowly immersed in the book as if *there*, at least for the while, and not outside, could be the marks of reality itself, immanent in the very sentences. It is within those sentences, in their interstices, that she can begin to find out and realize what thinking is going on at the micro level. That is what the voiced mind of George Eliot is at best and ever increasingly: not a heavily didactic imposition ab extra but the suddenly emergent bursting out of what has been intricately contained within the biography or genesis of the writing. She wants to translate further into language what art can find out from within the very midst of art; a translation not afterwards but from the microscopic midst of its own texture. She wants to make the small implicit motions of the mind as large as they feel to their writer in the discovery of something important en route. That is where the emergent happens, in the transits of writing, when the writer knows most intimately the intervolved workings of the thinking and seeks to bring it further out into the world.

She had to feel her way. Writing, said Lewes, was a higher form of the evolution-ary method of 'trial and error'. He quoted Alexander Bain: 'The first steps of our volitional education are a jumble of sputtering, stumbling, and all but despairing hopelessness. Instead of a clear curriculum, we have to wait upon the accidents, and improve them when they come' (*Physiology of Common Life*, p. 150). George Eliot knew a version of that 'all but despairing hopelessness' at the mental level but came also to appreciate the importance of never fully knowing but working her way forward. In the course of a creature's struggles, said Bain in *The Emotions and the Will*, 'the animal accidentally makes one movement which is followed by an alleviation or cessation of the pain; this makes it discontinue all the other movements, and continue that which alleviates' (quoted in *Physiology of Common Life*, p. 148). In the writer, the accident was improved, taken as a sign for further expansion or contraction, transmuted or revised into a possible turn or opening. As Lewes had said, in literature words were not discrete entities but offered 'influence reflected back and influence projected forward'. Exploratory thinking was like stumbling and correcting, but even in that, as Lewes explained, the development of a natural human process:

> Personality corresponds psychologically with what physiologically is the guiding influence of the centre of gravity. Every part of the body has its weight; the whole has its centre of gravity, and the movements are regulated by that. 'Our walking,' says Goethe, 'is a series of falls'; but the series is co-ordinated by the feeling of central equilibrium. The position of the centre of gravity is a continually shifting point. The attitude of the Personality is likewise a continually shifting point.   (PLM 3, p. 197)

George Eliot could turn from one centre of her novel to another ('But why always Dorothea? Was her point of view the only possible one?'), but she could also make the very turn of her paragraphs a way of using the power of stumbling, the work readjusting its balance even as it was pushing along. So it is in *Scenes from Clerical Life* with Janet, at the beginning of a new chapter, as she lies shocked and still in a neighbour's bed, after having been thrown out of her husband's house in the middle of the preceding night:

> Her ideas had a new vividness, which made her feel as if she had only seen life through a dim haze before; her thoughts, instead of springing from the action of her own mind, were external existences, that thrust themselves imperiously upon her like haunting illusions. . . . Her husband had so long overshadowed her life that her imagination could not keep hold of a condition in which the great dread was absent and even his absence—what was it? only a dreary vacant flat, where there was nothing to strive after, nothing to long for.
>
> At last the light of morning quenched the rushlight, and Janet's thoughts became more and more fragmentary and confused. She was every moment slipping off the level on which she lay thinking, down, down into some depth from which she tried to rise again with a start.   ('Janet's Repentance', chapter 16)

George Eliot loved to put her own nervous system into that of her characters, in search of new emergent terms through which to get hold of complex mental situations. Everything in such a deeply mixed and fully ranging language, as much science as it was art, was like metaphor: a series of linguistic trials and errors in search of an approximative precision within the resistant field of human experience. Here Janet can hardly awake to this reality in the dawning signalled by that second paragraph, but is constantly on the verge of belatedly falling back asleep and then starting up, with no sense of how to either carry on the same or begin afresh. Thinking is like falling here, the mind working within physical terms for itself—'her imagination could not *keep hold of* a condition', 'she was every moment *slipping off the level on which* she lay thinking'—in search of some new centre of orientation and balance.

The biography of writing—the inner story of what goes into and comes out of its composition, the mental life of the writer in the very act of writing—is signalled most clearly in the evidence of manuscripts. There we can see George Eliot herself at key moments seeking the orientation and the knowledge her characters themselves can barely find on their own. Here, for example from chapter 50 of *Middlemarch*, Dorothea finding out that Casaubon's will forbids her to marry Will Ladislaw on pain of losing her fortune. She had never had the thought, and can scarcely comprehend that her husband, now deceased, had had such suspicions in life. It is a crisis which, like Janet's, was hard to absorb, needed time, and demanded painful and uncertain transition. This is the published text with the significant revisions made at manuscript stage numbered and in italics:

(1) She might have compared her experience at that moment to the vague, alarmed consciousness that *(2) her life was taking on a new* form, that she was undergoing a metamorphosis in which memory would not adjust itself to the stirring of new organs. Everything was changing its aspect: her husband's conduct, her own duteous feeling towards him, every struggle between them—and yet more, her whole relation to Will Ladislaw. Her world was in a state of convulsive change; the only thing she could say distinctly to herself was, that she must wait and think anew. One change terrified her as if it had been a sin; it was *(3) a violent shock of repulsion from her departed husband,* who had had hidden thoughts, *(4) perhaps perverting* everything she said and did. Then again *(5) she was conscious of* another change which also made her tremulous; it was a sudden strange yearning of heart towards Will Ladislaw. Her world was in a state of convulsive change; the only thing she could say distinctly to herself was, that she must wait and think anew.

In general there are more dashes than semi-colons or colons in the manuscript, fewer commas and more fluidity—the living signs of emergent thinking, as she rapidly goes along. But specifically (1) 'She might have compared her experience at that moment' was an insertion in the manuscript: she deleted her simpler first thought 'It seemed to her as if she had at that moment the vague, alarmed consciousness...', because the haunting possibility of the recognition of what is happening to her is even further away from consciousness, is even harder to take on board in the midst of the change, than the original formulation suggested. Then (2) 'her life was taking on a new form' had multiple revisions: she deleted the less traumatic 'she was entering on a' and also her next thought 'her life was changing its' as still too summary, in order instead to offer the process of something more strangely, gradually, and disturbingly emergent. 'A violent shock' (3) was originally 'the violent shock' and it came not 'from her' but 'towards her' as if from him: now it comes from her in a suddenly instinctive repulsion against her husband that is simultaneously a guilty shock to her. It was not just that he had hidden thoughts (4) 'in his mind'; she crosses out 'in his mind' and puts in 'perhaps perverting everything she said and did', as if going into that mind a terrible step further. Nor is it simply what she first wrote (5) 'Then again there was another change...' but 'Then again she was conscious of another change': less summary, more the interior stun of realization, more sheer overload in consciousness. This is not just George Eliot revising her manuscript, it is George Eliot getting into the nervous system of Dorothea in an almost insupportable revising of her own life.

*

After long illness, Lewes died of cancer on 30 November 1878, aged 61. What was left to his devastated partner, who had tried not to see what was coming, was the revision of the last two volumes of *Problems of Life and Mind*. It was the only work

Marian Lewes could undertake in the midst of her mourning, as her final collaboration. As a result of research into the manuscripts undertaken by K. K. Collins, we can see what she added, to what extent she even made differences, in the very act of loyally completing Lewes's work.

She made over three hundred often minor amendments to Lewes's text, but in particular rewrote and expanded two paragraphs on the emotions in volume 5 (problem 3, chapter 11) and, most significantly, a whole sub-chapter on the moral sense in volume 4 (problem 1, chapter 8).[9] It is as though through the revisions one can see—and see her seeing—an ur-text or coarser vestige of the general tendency of mind that went early into Lewes, shorn of nuance and development. It was a mental attitude that came from the influence of Herbert Spencer and from Auguste Comte's system-building.[10] And it still bore traces of the quintessential or stereotypical nineteenth-century Man of Science and Sociology—that is to say: a commitment to naturalistic, evolutionary explanations of human behaviour; and an emphasis on the pre-eminence of the social world over its individual parts and subjects.

On the formation of the moral sense in human beings, this rationalist tendency was to stress as primary the interaction between, on the one hand, brute animal nature, in its naturally egoistic appetites of hunger and sexuality, fear and pleasure; and, on the other, the counter-checking effect of the social medium, in terms of punishment and reward, approval and disapprobation, as evolved public versions of caresses and blows. Aggressive and defensive needs in the individual inherently contained the sense of a vulnerable dependence upon external forces while at the same time having to face the threat of collision with the equivalent competitiveness of others. This fundamental primitive structure of competing forces was what George Eliot found in Lewes's manuscript account, and she thoroughly accepted it. 'All emotions in the beginning,' she emphasizes for him in a final revision, 'are egoistic.' Such 'reduction' to 'primary manifestations', she writes in carefully discriminated justification of her husband's position, 'is not merely useful, it is indispensable to a true analysis of and natural history of morals' (*PLM* 4, p. 147, problem 1, para. 111a). Without it the parts played by 'impulse, cognition, and habit' in the complex development of a moral life would be impossible.

But, she insists, the further moral life is not simply a resultant of egoism and the social checking of egoism through enforced self-interest. It is 'wrought out of innumerable closely interwoven threads of feeling and knowledge'. It is made from complex combinations of conscious judgement and immediate impulse which, moreover, come out in different forms in different individuals—in one through terrible struggle, say, or in another by heroic reflex (*PLM* 4, p. 147, problem 1, para. 111a). She concludes in words Lewes never wrote:

The different strands of human experience which combine to create moral sentiment act in various proportion on individual minds, and hence it happens that some formulas of ideal motive which have an intense reality for one mind have little force for another. (*PLM* 4, p. 151, para 113)

It is like the threads and strands of *Middlemarch* when, in response to her husband's desperate plea for help in their domestic finances, Rosamond replies, 'What can I do, Tertius?' and George Eliot comments:

That little speech of four words, like so many others in all languages, is capable by varied vocal inflexions of expressing all states of mind from helpless dimness to exhaustive argumentative perception, from the completest self-devoting fellowship to the most neutral aloofness. (*Middlemarch*, chapter 58)

'What can I do?' is like the basic template, a genetic grammar for human nature: the minute tonal variations mark the difference that the individual makes within the core linguistic matrix of the social range of possible meanings. 'What can *I* do?': in Rosamond her voice is like a shrug; in Dorothea it would have created the life of a moral emotion. This is when the voice of George Eliot herself unmistakably enters into her late husband's work in this revised interpolation:

The Moral Sense, which, in the first instance, was moulded under the influence of an external approbation and disapprobation, comes at last, in the select members of a given generation, to incorporate itself as protest and resistance, as the renunciation of immediate sympathy for the sake of a foreseen general good, as moral defiance of material force, and every form of martyrdom. (*PLM* 4, pp. 146–7, para. 111)

At last is not the same as it was at first. At last morality is individual and internal, not merely externally determined or socially compliant, but free and even defiant, 'incorporated' into a single voice and its particular personal nuances. And then again:

Kant's fine phrase—'Man refuses to violate in his own person the dignity of humanity'—may represent an abiding efficient response in the consciousness of a given person, the musical keynote, as we may say, to which his other sentiments are adjusted.
(*PLM* 4, p. 151, para. 113)

One human being can represent humanity even in defiance of the current norms of society: that was how morality had become a power. It is Kant's absolute sense of duty, the categorical imperative, treating human beings as an end in themselves, acting according to a maxim which, rather than being an incoherent passing whim, is such as can be made into a universal law. 'What can I *do*?' in Dorothea's voice rather than Rosamond's is a 'musical keynote, as we may say', or as Spencer had said, 'the commentary of the emotions on the propositions of the intellect.'[11] It is what makes for what is crucial to George Eliot: the *emotional* and *individual* difference to the basic meaning—the gentle note or personal emphasis of intonation, 'the dignity', instead of the neutral, reductive, or dead touch. When Casaubon was alive, even amidst the pain he in his misery caused her, Dorothea struggled 'that she might be the mercy for those sorrows' (*Middlemarch*, chapter 42). Not merely the adjectival form—that she might be 'merciful' towards—but the awkward-fitting noun ('*the* mercy'), the otherwise abstract ideal of the categorical imperative which, called into substance by being incorporated in her, would not otherwise be there were she not there to be it. Dorothea is one of those 'select members of a given generation'. She finds morality as a separate force in herself, evolved beyond social conditioning, distinct from the pressure of her marriage.

It was Kant who, in his *Critique of Pure Reason* (1781), made the distinction between the 'a priori' and the 'a posteriori', meaning respectively: necessary conclusions taken from first principles prior to and independent of sense observation; and conclusions worked up from sense impressions, experience, and empirical evidence. According to Edith Simcox, a youthful Mary Ann Evans had wished to make a synthesis of the two, to reconcile German idealism working deductively from above downwards with British empiricism working inductively from below upwards: 'It was in this early period [at Foleshill] that in the course of a walk with a friend she paused and clasped her hands with a wild aspiration that she might live "to reconcile the philosophies of Locke and Kant!" Years afterwards she remembered the very turn of the road where she had spoken it.'[12] But the reconciliation lay with her philosopher friends. In his *Principles of Psychology* (1855) Spencer had argued that what is a priori for the individual had been a posteriori for the whole species: that is to say, that what a person might experience as an undoubting intuition of first principles was transmitted from the immense antecedent accumulation of slowly organized and consolidated experience in the race, bequeathed through the inheritance of a gradually evolved human nervous system. Evolution transmuted that which had been derived from long hard experience into what was eventually handed down to be felt immediately as innate and intuitive. Or, as Lewes himself had put it, back in the very first volume of *Problems and Life and Mind*:

> Respecting the so-called Mental Forms both schools are right, though standing at different points of view. The *psychological* fact tells us that the Forms are connate, therefore *a priori*; the *psychogenetical* fact tells us that the Forms are products of ancestral Experience, and therefore *a posteriori*. (PLM 1, pp. 202–3)

Then he had quoted George Eliot herself from *The Spanish Gypsy*:

> What! shall the trick of nostrils and of lips
> Descend through generations, and the soul,
> That moves within our frame like God in worlds,
> Imprint no record, leave no documents
> Of her great history? Shall men bequeath
> The fancies of their palates to their sons,
> And shall the shudder of restraining awe,
> The slow wept tears of contrite memory,
> Faith's prayerful labour, and the food divine
> Of fasts ecstatic—shall these pass away
> Like wind upon the waters tracklessly?

It is with the mind as with the body, down the generations. The Moral Sense evolves from the outward conditioning of social forces to the inner autonomy of individual conscience. What had derived from social forces was now, Marian Lewes insisted, a priori able to resist social forces. It was a wonderful loop of evolved achievement. She drove life upwards.

But what her husband had written was also true. Humans can be like dogs, 'running away and hiding after a conscious misdemeanour, having more fear of the stick than belief in forgiveness'. So analogously in the lower human stages of what we have come to call Remorse, there is still primitively 'the misdoer's mere terror of the vengeance he has incurred from supernal powers'. In one who does not understand, or want to understand, what is the true nature of the wrong in wrong-doing, the desire is simply to get away with it and escape public censure. And if that does not work, then 'forgiveness is contemplated as a heal-all' (PLM 4, p. 150, problem 1, chapter 8). In *Middlemarch* Bulstrode was one such creature, made primitive again in the face of exposure and disgrace for sins past:

> A great dread had seized his susceptible frame, and the scorching approach of shame wrought in him a new spiritual need. Night and day, while the resurgent threatening past was making a conscience within him, he was thinking by what means he could recover peace and trust...if he spontaneously did something right, God would save him from the consequences of wrong-doing.   (*Middlemarch*, chapter 61).

The external threat of shame and punishment is making a conscience within him. But it is there only in a subordinate clause, the right matter—the making of conscience—still not quite admitted to its right place; while his default mentality remains central to his identity in its attempt still to do some deal with God. If the guilt had been able to move to the centre, it would have been released like a new organ or faculty within him; it would have made him the different human being he could not bear belatedly to try to be. That is what sentence-making almost genetically stands for in George Eliot: the specific combination of different factors, places, balances, and possibilities in any one given individual. 'Turn your fear into a safeguard' is what Deronda urges upon Gwendolen in her dread of what she might do within her trapped marriage:

> 'Keep your dread fixed on the idea of increasing that remorse which is so bitter to you. Fixed meditation may do a great deal toward defining our longing or dread. We are not always in a state of strong emotion, and when we are calm we can use our memories and gradually change the bias of our fear, as we do our tastes. Take your fear as a safeguard. It is like quickness of hearing. It may make consequences passionately present to you. Try to take hold of your sensibility, and use it as if it were a faculty, like vision.' Deronda uttered each sentence more urgently; he felt as if he were seizing a faint chance of rescuing her from some indefinite danger.   (*Daniel Deronda*, chapter 36)

That is the great 'turn', strength made out of weakness, the same matter changed in the changing of its place, till it is made a new faculty. It is what turned Marian Evans into George Eliot.

It was Lewes himself who wrote in his final volume that the use of verbal ideas was like the use of algebra as a notation for carrying out high-level operations on certain relationships: 'Algebra cannot exist without values, nor Thought without feelings. The operations are so many blank forms until the values are assigned. Words are vacant sounds, ideas are blank forms, unless they symbolise images and sensations, which are their values' (*PLM* 5, p. 470, problem 4, chapter 5, para. 32). The algebraic formulae must be eventually cashed in; the abstractions have to be translated back into their reality in the human mix. The words and their grammar likewise have to become realized as feelings again, particular and individual in order to be real.

But as Marian Evans had known even back in 1856 when she wrote her essay 'The Natural History of German Life', human language was always more than algebra and allowed for more subtle translations, even from within itself—translation of its meaning through further words, added nuance and refinement, different kinds of vocabulary:

> It must be admitted that the language of cultivated nations is in anything but a rational state...one word stands for many things, and many words for one thing; the subtle shades of meaning, and still subtler echoes of association, make language an instrument which scarcely anything short of genius can wield with definiteness and certainty. Suppose, then, that the effort which has been again and again made to construct a universal language on a rational basis has at last succeeded, and that you have a language

which has no uncertainty, no whims of idiom, no cumbrous forms, no fitful shimmer of many-hued significance, no hoary archaisms 'familiar with forgotten years' [Wordsworth]—a patent de-odorized and non-resonant language, which effects the purpose of communication as perfectly and rapidly as algebraic signs. Your language may be a perfect medium of expression to science, but will never express life, which is a great deal more than science. (*Essays*, pp. 287–8)

George Eliot used science as she did everything—for the sake of life, for deeper human purposes of existence. And in this she was more committed to the emotional and the individual in her thinking than even her partner.

She could not go back to religion for that emphasis on 'the great deal more'. As we saw in Chapter 3, she did not admire the mindless dogmatic moral language of narrowly unkind and unthinking evangelicals like Dr Cumming, with all their stupidly simplified rules. She early insisted instead that the highest moral habit, in its constant preference for truth, must demand thinking—'the co-operation of the intellect with the impulses', 'the regulation of feeling by intellect' (*Essays*, p. 166). But for all its checks and prompts and arguments, intellect alone was also insufficient. 'In proportion as morality is emotional,' she had written in her essay 'Worldliness and Other-Worldliness', 'it will exhibit itself in direct sympathetic feeling and action, and not as the recognition of a rule' (*Essays*, p. 379). And in so far as morality is emotional, she had added in parenthesis (p. 379), it also 'has affinity with Art'.

Lewes was not an unemotional man but his childhood was so different from hers—born illegitimate, living with a stepfather he hated, emotionally rootless and wandering, educated in a wide and informal variety of settings. No wonder he wrote of the importance of the individual defying the social norms in personal, political, and intellectual life: 'for all originality is estrangement' (*PLM* 1, 'Psychological Principles', para. 72, p. 161). But despite his own early attempts at novel-writing, and however much his other writings added to her language, he could hardly have written of, or with, the rich language that formed the culmination of chapter 5 of *The Mill on the Floss*:

> Life did change for Tom and Maggie; and yet they were not wrong in believing that the thoughts and loves of these first years would always make part of their lives. We could never have loved the earth so well if we had had no childhood in it,—if it were not the earth where the same flowers come up again every spring...What novelty is worth that sweet monotony where everything is known and loved because it is known?...
> Such things as these are the mother tongue of our imaginations, the language that is laden with all the subtle inextricable associations the fleeting hours of our childhood have left behind them.

Lewes had little of such rooted language, however much within her own it secretly pained George Eliot to know what, in loss and in gain, lay behind that phrase '*mother* tongue'. This is why she emphatically did not want her thinking to go on in abstract language alone. It is true that Lewes had himself condemned the abstractions of metaphysics, and hoped instead to transform their content into a new science which combined physiology and psychology and sociology for a new age and a better world. But, for her, the deeper motivation was not thus anonymously social or political or scientific: it lay first, still, in the emotional inheritance and emotional neediness of the girl who lost her mother, and who found a love with her father and brother which in later life she had hardly hoped to find elsewhere, until Lewes himself came along. For such a person, no thought was sufficient unless it came out of and went back into the affective life which for her marked the deeper language system of the real. Philosophically Lewes agreed: 'The emotional temperament is that which is most energetic... Character is not measured by Intellect, for Intellect can only prompt in company with Emotion' (*PLM* 5, problem 3, chapter 11, para. 157). But George Eliot wanted that philosophy to be a philosophy in feeling and morality and action. It was, for her, the realist novel, above all other forms and languages, that was the vehicle by which to find particular and individual emotional places, humanly saturated solutions, to make philosophic thinking do a deeper work. There, at its most dense, language became the instrument which, as she had said, 'scarcely anything short of genius can wield with definiteness and certainty'.

It served to 'express life, which is a great deal *more* than science'. Guilt was likewise 'more' than what doubtless it evolved from and was often still mixed with—the threat of punishment and shame. Conscience was not simply or finally the same as the fear of social disapprobation. Indeed, morality was creative of the individual, and most characteristically so not in submission to but in defiance of social pressures, in resistance to social determinants. The felt sense of right offered a different centre of being, an innerly felt responsibility registered within the evolved nervous system, like a higher command whatever else was within or around. That is the spirit of what George Eliot insisted upon in a language fuelled by love of her husband, in the editorial work she was doing for him in the aftermath of mourning, as a last revision. She knew too the inferior murkier versions of herself, that she had finally come out of.

The final clinching piece of major revision she carried out on behalf of her husband's work made room for some lines from Wordsworth. It was an implicit insistence on the need for a literary language to give reality to argument:

> Remorse has no relation to an external source of punishment for the wrong committed: it is the agonised sense, the contrite contemplation, of the wound inflicted on another. Wordsworth has depicted a remorse of this kind—
>
>> Feebly must they have felt
>> Who, in old time, attired with snakes and whips
>> The vengeful Furies. Beautiful regards

Were turned on me—the face of her I loved;
The wife and mother, pitifully fixing
Tender reproaches, insupportable!

The sanction which was once the outside whip has become the inward sympathetic
pang.   (PLM 4, chapter 8, para. 112)

Wordsworth's man is haunted in his solitude by the imagined face of the wife he let
down: at some point of sensitive development, silent loving reproach internal to
the individual becomes worse than being externally pursued by the avenging
Eumenides. That is the point at which, for George Eliot, the novel takes over from
the ancient Greek drama—when the external whip may turn into the internal pang,
in its stead; when the genuinely individual may emerge out of the homogeneously
social; when initial egoism may become sympathetic to equivalent other egos,
knowing how they too must feel. It is the transformation Deronda wished upon
Gwendolen in her fear and remorse. There it was, in the novel's work both within
and between individuals, that the social realm was no more and no less than the
testing ground for the capacity of individuals to translate themselves—to translate
what was in them, as potential and as need—into the real, into the ordinary, and
thus transform it.[13]

It was a flawed and partial translation of imperfect individual effort, since (as she
painfully knew) no individual life went undetermined, undamaged, or unthwarted
by the social medium. But within that effort, George Eliot acted defiantly as
interpreter and intermediary, to try to carry through into the world as much
human effect as she could. She offered mitigation and rescued ideals, she rewrote
faulty scripts, she revised the erring and the ordinary. She was still doing it in putting
her husband's own work into the press.

In her revisions and her experiments alike, what she offered was 'emotional
intellect' and its recognition of the power of raw human content. She wanted and
she therefore eventually had to create

the more comprehensive massive life feeding theory with new material, as the
sensibility of the artist seizes combinations which science explains and justifies.
(Daniel Deronda, chapter 41)

That comprehensive massive life was the novel in all its burgeoning complexity. It
made theory, science, mind, and society itself always take in a great deal more—the
more that humans were[14]—than could be easily accommodated or presently
explained. And yet always, however much she too had influenced him and had
her own inner differences, she still thought in sundry different ways: to George
I owe it.

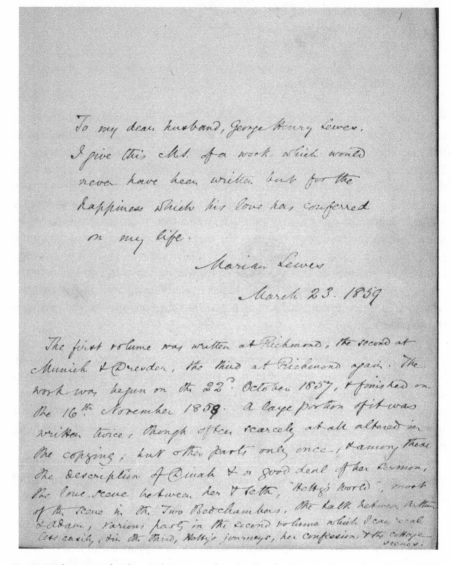

To my dear husband, George Henry Lewes.
I give this M.S. of a work which would
never have been written but for the
happiness which his love has conferred
on my life.

Marian Lewes

March 23. 1859

The first volume was written at Richmond, the second at
Munich & Dresden, the third at Richmond again. The
work was begun on the 22ᵈ October 1857, & finished on
the 16ᵗʰ November 1858. A large portion of it was
written twice, though often scarcely at all altered in
the copying; but other parts only once, & among these
the description of Dinah & a good deal of her sermon,
the love scene between her & Seth, 'Hetty's World', most
of the scene in the Two Bedchambers, the talk between Arthur
& Adam, various parts in the second volume which I can recal
less easily, &in the third, Hetty's journeys, her confession & the cottage
scenes.

Fig. 8. Dedication of _Adam Bede_ to 'my dear husband, George Henry Lewes' (© British Library).

CHAPTER 6

'The first time' in the 'new era'

Scenes of Clerical Life, 1856–7

Looking back in 1874, George Eliot wrote a letter to Sara Hennell that mentioned Francis W. Newman, the younger brother of John Henry Newman, as an almost forgotten figure: 'I have a sort of affectionate sadness in thinking of the interest which in far-off days I felt in his "Soul" and Phases of Faith . . . How much work he has done in the world, which has left no conspicuous mark, but has probably entered beneficently into many lives!' (GEL 6, p. 34). In *The Soul*, which, published by John Chapman, she had read as her father lay dying in May 1849, Newman had written of 'two families of children on this earth: the once born and the twice born' (chapter 4.2). Marian Evans knew—particularly as her first life was coming to an end with her father's death—that she had now to be a twice-born soul. She was not one who easily, happily, and naturally found a home on the earth but had to remake herself through hard experience, through work and effort and complex invention—all that realist art meant to her. *The Soul* was favourably reviewed by George Henry Lewes in *The Leader*, where he said that it created a path of possibility for a reformation of spirit. William James was further to develop the idea of the 'twice-born' in his *Varieties of Religious Experience* (1902). What was at stake was the creation of a second life.

For Marian Evans this second life and second self had, for once, a specific starting date: September 1856. Thereafter, so much of Marian Evans could be seen in retrospect to have contributed to the making of George Eliot, though it was also the making of George Eliot that redeemed and justified the life of Marian Evans. In that two-way movement running both forwards and backwards, blending experience and invention, autobiographical memory with imaginative thinking, there was to be no isolatable time in which it was ever clear how much a particular present was leading to a future or owed its achievement to its past. But there is an underlying story from 1819 to 1880 even if it cannot be told lineally, and there was at least one date in it that holds sufficiently firm to make it definite even amidst her uncertainties: the date of the creation of 'George Eliot' as author:

September 1856 made a new era in my life, for it was then that I began to write Fiction.

(GEL 2, p. 406)

Fig. 9. George Eliot, 1858, photograph by Mayall (© National Portrait Gallery).

To write a novel had 'always been a vague dream of mine', though 'always' has to be another approximative term: 'my shadowy conception of what the novel was to be, varied, of course, from one epoch of my life to another'. Finally a title came to her in a dreamy doze as she was lying in bed one morning: 'The Sad Fortunes of the Reverend Amos Barton'. But it was the actual writing that gave awakened focus to the vague dream, substance to the shadowy conception, whilst needing that tacit and cumulative background behind it for its sources. The nearest she had got years before was 'an introductory chapter describing a Staffordshire village and the life of the neighbouring farm-houses': 'It happened to be among the papers I had with me in Germany and one evening at Berlin, something led me to read it to George...He began to say very positively, "You must try and write a story"' (GEL 2, p. 407).

In the same month she was sending off to Chapman at the *Westminster Review* her essay 'Silly Novels by Lady Novelists' which she had been mulling over since July. Hers, if she could write them, were not to be of that ilk. She hated sentences like 'In order to forgive we must have been injured', however much they had been doubly or triply underscored in pencil by previous admiring readers. Instead, to the breathless question posed in one novel when Lord Rupert suddenly enters its heroine's life like a picture stepping out of its frame: 'Is this reality?', she wrote underneath, 'Very little like it, certainly' (*Essays*, pp. 308–9).

Less certainly, 'something led' her, she says, to read to Lewes the writing she had left discouragingly incomplete years earlier. It was as though that 'something' were waiting to be turned into a thing more definite. But it was never wholly definite until the hand picked up the pen again and actually made its mark. And then at the very moment of its own epoch-making emergence, for all her sense of there being eras which finally come to the surface in a life, the fiction itself knew the strange indefiniteness of the inner reality of lived time, gradual and invisible. In the greatest of the early work, 'Janet's Repentance', a woman cannot say just where, at any one specifiable time, her life and marriage first went wrong:

> The seeds of things are very small: the hours that lie between sunrise and the gloom of midnight are travelled through by tiniest markings of the clock: and Janet, looking back along the fifteen years of her married life, hardly knew how or where this total misery began; hardly knew when the sweet wedded love and hope that had set for ever had ceased to make a twilight of memory and relenting, before the oncoming of the utter dark. (*Scenes of Clerical Life*, 'Janet's Repentance', chapter 13)

This was the 'hardly knowing' of the experience of reality itself. The absolute loss ('set for ever') is folded within ongoing time, day after day. That makes for a double dimension within the realism—the sense of elusively near-absolute moments hidden but persistent within the relative and temporal. No one could put a finger on precisely what had caused this, and exactly when.

But now, even in writing this, for Marian Evans, become Marian Lewes, become George Eliot, the seeds of things were coming into fruition.

Yet it was typical that she only began to value *Scenes of Clerical Life* after she had completed the works that turned out to have followed from it. Writing to her publisher, John Blackwood, early in 1860, after the great success of *Adam Bede* and with *The Mill on the Floss* about to appear, the worrier in George Eliot was now fearful that her first work, *Scenes from Clerical Life*, would become neglected in the wake of the other two. 'I think it is of importance to the estimate of me as a writer that "Adam Bede" should not be counted as my only book,' she wrote, adding her most personal concern:

> There are ideas in these stories about which I care a good deal, and am not sure I can ever embody again. (GEL 2, p. 240)

It is not that she ever wholly outgrew the first emotional ideas in her fiction any more than in her life. But the form in which they were cast in *Scenes of Clerical Life* was preliminary, and relatively unprotected, allowing an earliness of both vulnerably raw and delicate expressions.

Three *Scenes*

The *Scenes* were not so much 'sketches' as she first called them, but short stories that, en route to novels, she was outgrowing even in the process of writing them. After 'The Sad Fortunes of Reverend Amos Barton', the second story, 'Mr Gilfil's Love-Story', 'grew longer than I expected under my hands'; the third, 'Janet's Repentance', showed in its very strength 'the want of a larger canvas'; and a fourth in fact turned from the 'limitations' of 'Clerical Life' into the 'large canvas' of a novel, becoming *Adam Bede* (GEL 2, pp. 269, 300, 378, 381).

First published in *Blackwood's Magazine* between January and November 1857, the three *Scenes*, appearing as a two-volume set at the beginning of 1858, owed their existence not only to the direct encouragement of George Henry Lewes but to the indirectly interwoven influence of two other men, inner to her life: William Wordsworth and Ludwig Feuerbach.

'I have never before met with so many of my own feelings, expressed just as I could like' (GEL 1, p. 34). She acquired the six-volume collected edition of Wordsworth in 1839 and read him throughout her life, taking more epigraphs for her work from him, in the background of her reading, than from any other author save Shakespeare. He was to her what the finally defeated leader of the Haitian Revolution, Toussaint Louverture, was to him:

> Thou hast left behind
> Powers that will work for thee; air, earth, and skies;
> There's not a breathing of the common wind
> That will forget thee; thou hast great allies;
> Thy friends are exultations, agonies,
> And love, and man's unconquerable mind.

'I don't know where there is anything finer' (GEL 7, p. 262).

It was, first of all, the Wordsworth of *Lyrical Ballads* who had insisted on the importance of prose and prosaic subjects to his radical reinvention of what was poetry. His was the prophetic effort to free art from a degeneration into artifice which, he believed, had made poetry a secondary specialism no longer in touch with the first things—the primary feelings and real concerns—of human life. *Lyrical Ballads* offered a poetry which dared to be simple and elemental. As he put it in the 'Preface to Lyrical Ballads':

> [O]ne circumstance which distinguishes these Poems from the popular Poetry of the day...is this, that the feeling therein developed gives importance to the action and situation, and not the action and situation to the feeling.[1]

The mundane subject matter may hardly seem much, but it is feeling that knows it does matter. 'Feeling,' Feuerbach was to write, similarly, within his own register, 'knows no other necessity than its own, than the necessity of feeling.'[2] It cannot believe that what it feels is not important. 'Emotion, I fear, is obstinately irrational,' protests George Eliot ('Janet's Repentance', chapter 22). It cares for the one among many, she went on, when Pharisees can hardly accept how 'there is more joy in heaven over one sinner that repenteth, than over ninety and nine just persons that need no repentance'. It 'absolutely refuses' to deny the real existence of individuals or to accept that value can be settled by the balance sheet of mathematical loss and gain. In order to be read as she wished to be read, and as she wished her common-place people to be understood, she felt she had first to write, explicitly, even obtrusively:

> These commonplace people—many of them—bear a conscience, and have felt the sublime prompting to do the painful right; they have their unspoken sorrows, and their sacred joys; their hearts have perhaps gone out towards their first-born, and they have mourned over the irreclaimable dead....
>
> Depend upon it, you would gain unspeakably if you would learn with me to see some of the poetry and the pathos, the tragedy and the comedy, lying in the experience of a human soul that looks out through dull grey eyes, and that speaks in a voice of quite ordinary tones.   ('Amos Barton', chapter 5).

In this way, the realist novel was, for George Eliot, a continuation of what Wordsworth had done to literature. It involved for her a double change: the recognition that within ordinary and neglected lives lay what was sublime or sacred was crucial also to the transformation of Marian Evans into George Eliot. Her lowly figures at such moments of disclosure paradoxically stood for more than they themselves would ever know. It was that sense of paradox that also helped create George Eliot.

She well knew how traditionally, ideally, the local clergyman was at the very centre of the community, acting in Feuerbachian terms as a humane agent. As Theophrastus Such's father said, 'A clergyman should feel in himself a bit of every class' (*Impressions of Theophrastus Such*, chapter 2). But the memories were also specific, the examples flawed because themselves human. A number of the characters and situations in *Scenes from Clerical Life* were taken from Nuneaton childhood recollections and local folklore. The prototypes of Amos Barton and Milly Barton were the Reverend John Gwyther and his wife Emma, with their six children: he was curate of Chilvers Coton ('Shepperton') during Mary Ann Evans's childhood and presided over her mother's funeral. Mr Gilfil was based on Bernard Gilpin Ebdell, the vicar who baptized Mary Ann Evans. He had married Sally Shilton, a young girl with a beautiful voice brought up by Lady Newdigate of Arbury Hall, who was the original of Caterina (or Tina). Sir Roger Newdigate, on whose estate Mary Ann Evans had been brought up, became Sir Christopher Cheveral; his wife Hester, Lady Henrietta. Janet Dempster was a version of Nancy Buchanan, wife of the lawyer J. W. Buchanan and friend of Mary Ann's evangelical teacher, Maria Lewis. The evangelical minister Tryan derived from the Reverend J. E. Jones, though, as in many other cases, George Eliot denied any exactness of influence, in defence of her artistic integrity. But local people recognized the stories, just as later, even in their estrangement, Isaac Evans, reading *Adam Bede*, was still able to recognize his sister in print through the portrayal of their father.

The sources in local and childhood memory must have given the unconfident new writer a belief in the reality of her fiction, a subject matter which, though lowly and unremarkable, had claims on existence. Yet the re-creation of these characters in *Scenes of Clerical Life* also depended upon their being cleared in the act of writing from the real-life detritus of superficial gossip surrounding them. In the first story, an unattractive spinster compensates herself by claiming that the beautiful Countess who has imposed herself under the roof of his family house is having an affair with the unprepossessing Amos Barton. If nothing else, so-called morality can make the common gossipy woman feel superior to the noble beauty. The ladies in Milby needed, says George Eliot, to distort faults into vices in order to create and justify a 'wide distinction' between themselves and the Countess ('Amos Barton', chapter 4). Marian Evans knew keenly the force of such gossip, not least of all now, in all that was said of her relationship with George Henry Lewes. But realism required something correctively finer in the making of human connections and distinctions: 'It is so much easier to make up your mind that your neighbour is good for nothing, than to enter into all the circumstances that would oblige you to modify that opinion' ('Amos Barton', chapter 4)

Wordsworth's figures are best when primary—free of secondary social relations and ascribed personality, silent not talkative, marginal, minimal, and elementally

near-anonymous. The old Cumberland beggar is one whom the poet has known
since childhood:

> He travels on, a solitary man,
> So helpless in appearance...

All the time, as people move around him, the bent old man hardly looks up from
the little bit of earth on which his gaze has become so narrowly set, as he walks the
parish. It is like what Wordsworth wrote of in a letter to Sara Hutchinson, 14 June
1802, of the poet's encounter with an obscure aged leech-gatherer in 'Resolution and
Independence':

> What is brought forward? 'A lonely place, a Pond', 'by which an old man *was*, far from
> all house or home'—not stood or sat, but '*was*'—the figure presented in the most naked
> simplicity possible.... '*How came he here* thought I or what can he be doing?'

In the removal of all extraneous ornament, 'was' is one of those basic words of being
which mark Wordsworth's committed return to unadorned human life, at a primary
level of existence. It was not only common realism that was being championed here
but a sense of the real which, in the residual effect of its bare unspokenness,
stimulated the imagination into thinking and verbalizing on its behalf. The leech-
gatherer, the old Cumberland beggar, the deserted wife, or bereaved father—these
were Wordsworth's common muses. What the villagers see in such figures is 'a
record', 'a silent monitor': people carrying with them unconsciously the good which
their plight habitually calls out in others. Call not this old beggar useless, says
Wordsworth, do not create new poor laws to help or restrain him. Even the poorer
villagers, seeing one worse off than themselves,

> can know and feel that they have been
> Themselves the fathers and the dealers out
> Of some small blessings, have been kind to such
> As needed kindness, for this single cause,
> That we have all of us one human heart.

This deep human link is what the beggar gives those others in return for what they
give to him, without ever his recognizing it or, in the poet's eyes, his even needing to
do so. His is like an original version of a transmitted life, unconscious and pre-
verbal, working below the level of normal human intercourse.

It is something of what the Reverend Amos Barton finally gives his community
as a result not of his direct and rather ineffectual ministry but of his helpless
predicament on the sudden death of his lovely and loving wife—a wife better, it

had been said in the community, than this mediocre man ever deserved. And now she is to be buried:

> There were men and women standing in that churchyard who had bandied vulgar jests about their pastor, and who had lightly charged him with sin; but now, when they saw him following the coffin, pale and haggard, he was consecrated anew by his great sorrow, and they looked at him with respectful pity.   ('Amos Barton', chapter 9)

This outward change in his neighbours' silent attitude cannot counteract the deep inner sorrow of the man, but as a result of his troubles rather than his sermons 'cold faces looked kind again, and parishioners turned over in their minds what they could best do to help their pastor' (chapter 9). Feuerbach would know this was the real religious work, below the level of deliberateness. Yet it is also part of realism that, so far from gaining much direct benefit from the change in his neighbours, Amos does not even get to stay in the parish. There is no simple doctrine of sentimental compensation found in all this. 'I have long wanted to fire away at the doctrine of Compensation, which I detest considered as a theory of life,' she had written to John Chapman, 5 July 1856 (GEL 2, p. 258). On the termination of his curacy, the bereft man has now to give up his place, leave behind his wife's graveyard, for the sake of some preferred candidate:

> At length the dreaded week was come, when Amos and his children must leave Shepperton. There was general regret among the parishioners at his departure: not that any one of them thought his spiritual gifts pre-eminent, or was conscious of great edification from his ministry. But his recent troubles had called out their better sympathies...   ('Amos Barton', chapter 10).

That 'called out' is in the very voice of Wordsworth and, being without conscious intent or definite object, is what Wordsworth thought of as Nature's call. It creates the personal fellow feeling of the truly social in place of that previously uncaring gossip, even though it can never be wholly expressed. It is the same with George Eliot's great cries of generalization in the book: they are most achieved and best understood when they are themselves called out by the emotional triggers found in those specific small human moments in the tales which would otherwise be neglected. As Marian Evans's essay on the poet Young had it:

> Wherever abstractions appear to excite strong emotion, this occurs in men of active intellect and imagination, in whom the abstract term rapidly and vividly calls up the particulars it represents, these particulars being the true source of the emotion; and such men, if they wished to express their feeling, would be infallibly prompted to the presentation of details. Strong emotion can no more be directed to generalities apart from particulars, than skill in figures can be directed to arithmetic apart from

numbers. Generalities are the refuge at once of deficient intellectual activity and deficient feeling.   (*Essays*, p. 371)

Genuine concrete generalizations 'call up', like poetry itself, the particulars that they 'represent' at a different level of mind, even as they may also be called up by them. There has to be something primary, something deeply felt behind them. Wordsworth himself in the 'Preface to Lyrical Ballads' spoke of thoughts as the 'representatives' of past feelings, memory made into intellect. In turn those particulars are themselves lodged emotionally in the 'presentation' of irresistible details. With those who possess strong emotion and active intellect and imagination, that 'presentation' is always implicit within any 're-presentation'.

So it is in the account of Amos paying a last visit to his wife's grave before leaving the parish:

> He stood a few minutes reading over and over again the words on the tombstone, as if to assure himself that all the happy and unhappy past was a reality. For love is frightened at the intervals of insensibility and callousness that encroach little by little on the dominion of grief, and it makes efforts to recall the keenness of the first anguish.
>
> ('Amos Barton', chapter 10)

'Reading over and over again the words' is the very signature of the particular. It calls up the second more general sentence about 'love frightened' as the cry of what Feuerbach called the species, the human heart within the individual man, the something large that tries to resist the 'little by little' diminutions of mundane time. The influence of Feuerbach and Spinoza, shaken down to instinct again within the formation of George Eliot, would help her transpose the feeling in the first sentence into the different level of thought in the second, even though—especially because—the man feeling it could hardly make it articulate. Wordsworth himself knew this vocation of literature, in thinking and speaking on behalf of those who cannot, when in the great 'Preface to Lyrical Ballads' he speaks of the poet as one who 'thinks and feels *in* the spirit of the passions of men', who 'should consider himself as in the situation of a translator' (*Wordsworth Prose Works*, 1, pp. 142, 139). In the still simple spirit of George Eliot's early prose fiction there is, equivalently, a call for 'reality'—'reading over and over again the words ... to assure himself that all the happy and unhappy past was a reality', 'frightened at the intervals of insensibility and callousness'. In these minute and ill-fitting places that human beings could hardly bear to inhabit, all this raw and baffled matter was, as Feuerbach again might have pointed out, the human basis for the creation of prayer. But here in the language of psychological and intellectual generalization, the cries are raised only to the level of poignant knowledge and unanswered law: 'love is frightened...' There the general plight remains.

At the death of his wife Amos Barton is no longer a known, small, mediocre personality in an unappreciative community, but suddenly becomes, through bereavement, a bare and limited man in a limitless situation, the unlikely representative of the primary and the original and the fundamental. That is why, throughout *Scenes of Clerical Life*, George Eliot turns at crucial points to moments when characters *come to*, as it were, after sleep or fainting—when consciousness is on the verge of re-entry into the human face, as if for the first time again:

> It is a wonderful moment, the first time we stand by one who has fainted and witness the fresh birth of consciousness spreading itself over the blank features...A slight shudder, and the frost-bound eyes...for an instant show the inward semiconsciousness of an infant's; then, with a little start, they open wider and begin to *look*, the present is visible, but only as a strange writing, and the interpreter Memory is not yet there. ('Mr Gilfil's Love-Story', chapter 15)

This is the starting again of the human story that Wordsworth sought in poetry. It marks why the poet turned to the basic, ordinary life of a peasant or a child. It is also why finally, in the writing of *Silas Marner*, and the unconscious educative effect of a child on the life of the traumatized adult who adopts her, George Eliot thought of Wordsworth as her ideal reader.

In the same spirit Janet waits by the bedside of the comatose and dying husband who had so ill-treated her in their daily life, in a language sunk deep into basic biology:

> [T]he eager straining gaze of her dark eyes, and the acute sensibility that lay in every line about her mouth, made a strange contrast with the blank unconsciousness and emaciated animalism of the face she was watching. ('Janet's Repentance', chapter 24)

She was watching 'for a moment in which her husband's eyes would rest consciously upon her, and he would know that she had forgiven him'. It never happens.

These are primal moments. As Amos kneels by the bed of his own spouse, holding her hand as she passes away, George Eliot writes simply: 'He did not believe in his sorrow. It was a bad dream. He did not know when she was gone' ('Amos Barton', chapter 8). That is 'belief', lost and yearning, unable to find reality. It does not matter that Amos Barton is nominally still a believing clergyman: the thought of Feuerbach, of the basic human need for explanatory consolation in the midst of pained bewilderment, is lodged behind that shock. And the words, like Wordsworth's, are basic too but subtly and sensitively so. 'Gone' is not answered by 'where': it is 'when' that he does not know, as he cannot believe or locate that it happened. George Henry Lewes had not known, any more than his partner herself, whether she, an intellectual, could write story, or could tell of sorrow in simple moving detail. But in *Scenes* George Eliot convinced him.

'There is much pain that is quite noiseless; and vibrations that make human agonies are often a mere whisper in the roar of hurrying existence...seen in no writing except that made on the face...Many an inherited sorrow that has marred a life has been breathed into no human ear' (*Felix Holt*, introduction). This almost tangible silence, with its vibrations of fellow feeling, is what called forth George Eliot to hear and make quietly audible those whispers through her own vocation as writer. It can be heard and felt even in the suppressed aftermath of the life of Mr Gilfil, an obscure stoically decent clergyman George Eliot looks back upon thirty years after his death. For she is the great articulator of the otherwise unknown or neglected human background to any human being, without which context a sense of meaning and understanding is all too easily lost.

Forty years before that, Gilfil had saved the life of the beautiful young Tina after a breakdown caused by her secret relationship with Captain Wybrow. Wybrow was one of those handsome men called 'the charmers' who, taking advantage, could not understand why women became angry with them and could hardly bear it when they did. Marian Evans knew something of the type from John Chapman. With Tina, Wybrow carelessly 'had inflicted a great and unrepented injury on her', only then to assume 'an air of benevolence towards her' ('Mr Gilfil's Love-Story', chapter 11), as though there was no external reality to a secret from the past. Gilfil rescues her and marries her, as he had anyway long wished to do, but then finds the reality of the damage still left in her. Still broken by the affair and in fragile health, Tina dies in trying to give birth. No one would know such a love story to look at Gilfil in his after-years, but this is the background:

> Alas, alas! we poor mortals are often little better than wood-ashes—there is small sign of the sap, and the leafy freshness, and the bursting buds that were once there...I, at least, hardly ever look at a bent old man, or a wizened old woman, but I see also with my mind's eye, that Past of which they are the shrunken remnant.
>
> ('Mr Gilfil's Love-Story', chapter 1)

George Eliot becomes his memory. In the eyes of his neighbours, Amos was 'consecrated' by his great sorrow ('Amos Barton', chapter 9); but when the neighbours are all gone and the old men and women are lost even to themselves, it is George Eliot who recognizes what in millions of human beings she would call sacred—sacred because most deep, most real, even when no one is left to see or know it. She recalls how, at Tina's crisis, Gilfil had been 'almost angry with himself' for feeling so happy while she herself was on the verge of collapse; but he could not help 'the new delight of acting as her guardian angel, of being with her every hour of the day' ('Mr Gilfil's Love-Story', chapter 20). It is characteristic of George Eliot's sense of necessary double bind that the sheer life of the thing cannot be denied—despite oneself, because of oneself—even while the morality of goodness in Gilfil will rightly not tolerate a selfish compensation. This is the density of moral existence, the inextricability of simultaneously multiple considerations. Both the happiness and, even as he helps her, the anger at himself for feeling happiness almost at her expense are forms of love. Only, creatures cannot transcend themselves; from within cannot wholly know what they mean, or how they should be judged from outside or above. That again is the intrinsic way of human life that calls forth the need for others to make good the bewildered needs and unmakeable claims. For a moment Gilfil's life was expanding but it was a moment that died with Tina, and so he withered into living on long after his possible future was buried. It is that sense of the lost and the residual, the imagination of the dwindled 'remnant', and with it the reclamation and revision of what is otherwise left in shrunken prosaic outcome, that creates 'George Eliot' increasingly from such passages in these *Scenes*:

> [I]f you lop off their finest branches, into which they were pouring their young life-juice, the wounds will be healed over with some rough boss, some odd excrescence; and what might have been a grand tree expanding into liberal shade, is but a whimsical misshapen trunk.   ('Mr Gilfil's Love-Story', epilogue)

Such lives had to be *read*, as it were: their hidden language had to be interveningly interpreted to make out the inner growth lost in potential within a final stuntedness that it was too easy to accept as the all-too-literal truth. Human beings were like trees in a landscape of the poets, be it Wordsworth or his forerunner, her also beloved Cowper, writing thus of the oak that once offered shelter to the creatures of the earth but stands now a 'semblance only of itself':

> No flock frequents thee now; thou hast outlived
> Thy popularity, and art become
> (Unless verse rescue thee awhile) a thing
> Forgotten as the foliage of thy youth....
> ('Yardley Oak')

'Unless verse rescue thee awhile': this rereading and rewriting, translation and correction of common life is the task or rescue work for which, in particular after Wordsworth himself, art exists.

*

Otherwise the human call too often goes unheard or is heard unavailingly. And this recognition itself goes into George Eliot's art at the end of chapter 4 of 'Janet's Repentance', where Janet is beaten by her drunken husband. In one of the final paragraphs the beating takes place before the mute portrait of Janet's mother, Mrs Raynor, as though it is almost unbelievable that the mother's steady eyes could not see what was happening: 'Surely the mother hears that cry...' But the next paragraph, as in a split screen-view, turns to the reality of the mother herself in her own home, imagining what is happening in her daughter's. She cannot comprehend how 'this' is what the babyhood and childhood of Janet has come to. 'Weeping with the difficult tears of age', she helplessly dreads what is taking place a little way away. The paragraphs are successive on the page but almost unbearably simultaneous in time. Together they mark George Eliot's instinctive disbelief in what feels to her a paradox: that something terrible should happen in the world, and that no one should be there to see or care for it, or that those who do care can do little to nothing about it. Mrs Raynor stares at the picture she has in her own house, which is of Christ, the sufferer. It hurt the author that even her kindly but cautious publisher, John Blackwood, was disturbed by the portrait of Janet and her husband, the alcoholism, the domestic abuse: compared to the other two stories, 'Blackwood did not like it so well, seeming to misunderstand the characters' (GEL 2, p. 409). As usual Lewes had had to get Blackwood to be more encouraging: 'Your letter . . . considerably staggered me,' wrote Lewes to Blackwood, worrying over the effect on the still unknown author under a male pseudonym—'sensitive, shrinking, refined creature he is' (GEL 2, p. 351).

The same day Blackwood hastily wrote back to George Eliot direct, 'I do not fall in with George Eliots every day and the idea of stopping the series as suggested in your letter gave me "quite a turn" . . . In continuing to write for the Magazine I beg of all things that you will not consider yourself hampered in any way. Of course I will say when I think you are failing to produce the effect you intend or otherwise missing the mark, but unless you write entirely from the best of your own genius or knowledge or observation it would not be worth my while to make any comments at all' (GEL 2, pp. 352–3). As Lewes well knew, this was the greatest achievement in the volume and it was the least appreciated by her chief external supporter. Nothing was worse for her than the effect being separated from the intention, the intention lost in its very movement into the world or come out wrong.

Not often in the reality of common provincial life depicted in the *Scenes* does the right thing happen at the ideal time or in the ideal place. Amos Barton would have been better, says his writer, had he been a cabinetmaker. A tallow candle that serves well enough in a humble kitchen candlestick seems plebeian, dim, and ineffectual in the drawing room. As George Eliot puts it in a sentence vital to her art: 'Alas for the worthy man who, like that candle, gets himself into the wrong place' ('Amos Barton', chapter 2).

Potentially right things found in the wrong place for them are the raw stimulus for the *Scenes*. Though consciously Amos 'thought himself strong' in his profession, really, within himself at foundation level, he 'did not *feel* himself strong' ('Amos Barton', chapter 2). It is again George Eliot who registers these differences between how he thought and how he felt—the angle of deflection between how it should have been and how it was—and then works within those areas of discrepancy and anomaly to make her course corrections. She knew the need for the revision of

Fig. 10. The Publisher: John Blackwood (1818–1879) (courtesy of Nuneaton Library).

faulty human scripts, of things ill said and ill done through failures of imagination and sympathy.

George Eliot could not have got so close to these clerical figures without Feuerbach, or without whatever it was, already within Marian Evans, that responded to him. It was not the sermon but the feeling, not the form but the content, that mattered. And to George Eliot this impulse to save—even from formal religion—what was good within what was not so good, was itself a religious prompting. It had started to become like that even in the days of her Christianity, when she felt remorsefully or charitably. When she wrote to her Methodist aunt and uncle, for example, this clever and proud young woman, too inclined to evangelical harshness, copied from them the Christian kindness that could make amends for human stupidities and inadequacies. 'We are not greatly favoured in our Minister,' she writes of churchgoing in Foleshill in October 1841:

> [T]hough we hear the truth, yet it is not recommended by the mode of its delivery. But there may be as much profit reaped by humble endeavours to derive good under disadvantages, as from the highest privileges, and I would rather narrowly examine my own state of feeling than complain of the lack of outward helps.   (GEL 1, p. 113)

As we saw in Chapter 1, she had had her correction two years earlier, though as ever with her it took time fully to sink in. In early 1837 the uncle and aunt, her father's brother Samuel and his wife Elizabeth, were visiting from Derbyshire. During the course of her stay the aunt, who was recuperating from illness, spoke about a minister she knew who had recently died. Though he had been a drinker, she spoke warmly of the man's good qualities and felt sure that, for all his failings, he must be in heaven: 'This was at the time an offence to my stern, ascetic hard views—how beautiful it is to me now!' (GEL 3, p. 175). It had already had effect earlier, but 'now' was Marian Lewes writing in 1859, the memory of twenty years ago being part of what had made her George Eliot.

By 1857, at the time of the writing of the *Scenes*, she had had not only to rescue the divine message from its flawed human vehicle but to find, within the vehicle itself, the stupid preacher or the alcoholic minister, the unwritten text of hidden human worth, without a heaven to redeem it. This was the act of humanist translation George Eliot needed not just for the sake of her clergymen but in order to see more clearly the Wordsworthian mix of unexpressed sorrow and damaged goodness that was hidden and distorted within the characters of so many people in the ordinary world.

The alcoholic lawyer, Dempster, who brutally beats his wife, has moments when he is still kind to his mother. Son and mother walk together in the garden one sunny morning, with the wife accompanying them. 'In a man whose childhood has known caresses there is always a fibre of memory which can be touched to gentle issues':

> The little old lady took her son's arm with placid pleasure. She could barely reach it so as to rest upon it, but he inclined a little towards her, and accommodated his heavy long-limbed steps to her feeble pace.   (Janet's Repentance', chapter 7)

That slightly awkward 'inclination' towards her is like a moment in *Adam Bede* when the vicar, Irwine, takes off his heavy boots to go gently and quietly to his invalid sister upstairs: 'Whoever remembers how many things he has declined to do even for himself, rather than have the trouble of putting on or taking off his boots, will not think this last detail insignificant' (*Adam Bede*, chapter 5). Meanwhile the mother is still thinking the wife is not 'the right woman' for her son. But it was rather pretty, says George Eliot, yet also sad to see that little group passing out of shadow into sunshine and then back again—because Dempster is not often like this anymore:

> sad, because this tenderness of the son for the mother was hardly more than a nucleus of healthy life in an organ hardening by disease, because the man who was linked in this way with an innocent past, had become callous in worldliness, fevered by sensuality, enslaved by chance impulses; pretty, because it showed how hard it is to kill the deep-down fibrous roots of human love and goodness...
>
> ('Janet's Repentance', chapter 7)

The Wordsworthian language of nature remains there, within the language of biology, just as 'the nucleus of healthy life' itself is, hard still to kill. But it works in George Eliot because of her taking from it two thoughts not one. Not one simply cheering thought of redemption; but two thoughts, called for shorthand 'sad' and 'pretty', which were so inextricably the two sides of the same thing that it was not a matter of choice, attitude, or ingenuity for intelligence to *have to* register them both simultaneously. Thoughts not easy either to hold together or to keep apart constituted for George Eliot a sign that, beyond the power of invention or control, they were coming out of something irreducibly and unconformably real. She admired Ruskin on realism, as she wrote in her review of *Modern Painters* volume 3 in the *Westminster Review* of April 1856. And it was Ruskin who had argued that mechanical repetition in an artist was the sign of unreality, of content too much marshalled by intentional single-mindedness:

> The moment that we trust ourselves, we repeat ourselves, and therefore the moment we see in a work of any kind whatsoever the expression of infinity we may be certain that the workman has gone to nature for it; while, on the other hand, the moment we see repetition, or want of infinity, we may be certain that the workman has *not* gone to nature for it.[3]

This was the nearest George Eliot had to a guarantee of maximum truthful realism: that writer and reader would find the thing before them too much for control by any one easy feeling or simple thought, and turning instead at least two ways: there is sympathy in the pain, pain in the sympathy. In the universe, wrote William James, there were always contradictory elements that did not make for an easy fit. These apparently anomalous elements were, he said, from the point of view of the tidy system-maker, 'so much "dirt", and matter out of place'.[4] But that was just what George Eliot sought: her attention was for whatever was dismissed, excluded, or avoided as dirt, as matter or as people out of place. She wanted not 'a scheme' but 'an experience' (*Essays*, p. 162). And more than that: beyond mere system-making, she sought a framework such as the realist novel that would be a holding ground for these paradoxes and conflicts, anomalies and surprises. So here, what is simultaneously sad and lovely in Dempster's small moment of returning goodness can barely be registered as both, at the self-same time, by ordinary human beings.

Too often people need their fellow creatures to conform to their own standards and ideas '*before* they can accord their sympathy or admiration' ('Janet's Repentance', chapter 10). But the evangelical minister Tryan tells the despairing Janet of how Christ does not require her first to deserve His love, before she can receive it (chapter 18). Her fellow men are not like that. That is why George Eliot had to do 'first' or 'before' work of her own, to clear the way of stereotyping to a deeper understanding in the second place:

> Appeals founded on generalizations and statistics require a sympathy ready-made, a moral sentiment already in activity; but a picture of human life such as a great artist can give, surprises even the trivial and the selfish into that attention to what is apart from themselves which may be called the raw material of moral sentiment.
>
> (*Essays*, p. 270)

The 'surprise' and the access it offers to the emotional 'rawness' necessary to true beginnings goes on inside the scenes, as well as within readers outside them. So Tryan encounters Janet for the first real time:

> The sight of Janet standing there with the entire absence of self-consciousness which belongs to a new and vivid impression, made him start and pause a little. Their eyes met, and they looked at each other gravely for a few moments. Then they bowed, and Mr Tryan passed out.
>
> There is a power in the direct glance of a sincere and loving human soul, which will do more to dissipate prejudice and kindle charity than the most elaborate arguments... ('Janet's Repentance', chapter 12)

That deep emotion is the instinctive mark of *value* found in unlikely persons or places, in situations or emotions that do not seem either normal or ideal. And it is a feeling which even here, if only momentarily realized between two creatures, does a little to reunite the race, shows mutual and original belonging to a species at a level below difference, beyond argument. It is 'new and vivid'; but it takes time for this direct emotional realization to find a place in or have an effect upon the default framework of an individual's fixed understanding. 'Twist and turn their theory as they might,' it is said of the prejudices of his neighbours, 'it would not fit Mr Tryan' (chapter 26). Though powerful, the anomalous moment feels small and transient, unless, like George Eliot, a human being is primed to take maximum notice of such moments of emotion as urgent messengers and not simply sentimental aberrations, and be glad to readjust the focus on life. But for Janet:

> This happened in the autumn, not long before Sally Martin died. Janet mentioned her new impressions to no one, for she was afraid of arriving at a still more complete contradiction of her former ideas.... Janet could no longer think of Mr Tryan without sympathy, but she still shrank from the idea of becoming his hearer and admirer. That was a reversal of the past which was as little accordant with her inclination as her circumstances.   ('Janet's Repentance', chapter 12)

'Shrank'—a common word for George Eliot at such moments—does not just mean 'cowered' but also 'contracted' like a nervous organism diminishing its life in the way that Spinoza suggested, when a vital thought is excluded.

Such was the affective inheritance of George Eliot from Wordsworth or from what it was that artists such as Wordsworth kept alive. The great intellectual in George Eliot believed that the greatest purpose for the existence of intellect was in the service of the emotional recognition of goodness. Ruskin himself admired above all the line in Wordsworth's long poem The Excursion: 'We live by Admiration, Hope, and Love' (4.763). And that is why, in 'Janet's Repentance', George Eliot writes 'The first condition of human goodness is something to love; the second, something to reverence' (chapter 10).

So it is that George Eliot herself is as puritanically moved as is Tryan himself to see Janet forced to speak out of a misery that transforms her. The writer would be simply gladdened by it, were it not at the same time so saddening also:

> While Janet was speaking, she had forgotten everything but her misery and her yearning for comfort. Her voice had risen from the low tone of timid distress to an intense pitch of imploring anguish. She clasped her hands tightly, and looked at Mr Tryan with eager questioning eyes...In this artificial life of ours, it is not often we see a human face with all a heart's agony in it, uncontrolled by self-consciousness; when we do see it, it startles us as if we had suddenly waked into the real world of which this everyday one is but a puppet-show copy. For some moments Mr Tryan was too deeply moved to speak.   ('Janet's Repentance', chapter 18)

When Janet is nearest rock bottom and has 'forgotten' all the normal expedients and secondary defences, her cry to Tryan is, for George Eliot, about as close as can be to the sources of the basically human. The writing here becomes sympathetic in the most intrinsic sense, by responding in so physically sensitive and imaginative a language—the voice, the anxious hands, the eyes, the open face with the heart in it. For this is a language that sees deep into the right thing even through it being in the wrong place.

And the wrong abides. 'Ten years ago,' says Tryan to her, in response to her confession of domestic ruin,

> I felt as wretched as you do. I think my wretchedness was even worse than yours, for I had a heavier sin on my conscience. I had suffered no wrong from others as you have, and I had injured another irreparably in body and soul. The image of the wrong I had done pursued me everywhere... ('Janet's Repentance', chapter 18)

It was a 17-year-old girl from a lower class whose life he helped begin to ruin whilst he was at college. Now it is Janet who faces him. George Eliot was electrified by those moments when the human link was created, as if sparked for the first time again, across differences of person and of time, through despairing doubts and ruinous pains: 'It is because sympathy is but a living again through our own past that confession often prompts a response of confession.' It does not unduly worry George Eliot that sympathy for another begins from something alike in 'me'—any more than it inhibits her to think that divine mercy is really human mercy in disguise. We use what we can, including the so-called impurities—the past errors, the mixed motives, the unsatisfactory human amalgams. When Janet cries, 'I can feel no trust in God. He seems always to have left me to myself', Tryan, even from the midst of his own inadequacies, has to stand in place of both that despairing self and that absent God, as well as Mrs Raynor, the helpless mother: 'The tale of the Divine Pity was never yet believed from lips that were not felt to be moved by human pity' (chapter 18).

Sympathy—that apparently simple term in George Eliot's humane campaign—means startlingly new relations at many levels. When Janet's story triggers Tryan's, it becomes not a one-way but a two-way movement. It means that self and other, memory and imagination, guilt and pity, helper and helped, emerge unexpectedly close together in impure mixtures. Emotion for George Eliot most of all means renewal—renewal of felt importance for what can become cliché, renewal of human links and ties and combinations, sudden and unexpected renewal of a connection that lies deeper than individual differences of temperament or opinion. Indeed, as people age past the time of youthful self-assertion:

> [S]peculative truth begins to appear but a shadow of individual minds, agreement between intellects seems unattainable, and we turn to the truth of feeling as the only universal bond of union. (GEL 1, p. 102)

This is not sentimentality eschewing hard thought or strong belief: it reaches beneath the level of what people self-consciously *think* they think, to thoughts and beliefs held implicit at that level of deep pre-intellectual being which Wordsworth himself marked as fundamental. It is like Janet suddenly coming across a supposed enemy, and through hearing, not seeing, him in the sickroom of the dying Sally Martin, finds another sense in which Tryan is utterly different from what she had supposed.

*

It was very important to George Eliot that Tryan's second life, his vocation as a minister, was not a thing securely separate from or invulnerable to his previous life:

> Mr Tryan was not cast in the mould of the gratuitous martyr. With a power of persistence which had often been blamed as obstinacy, he had an acute sensibility to the very hatred or ridicule he did not flinch from provoking. Every form of disapproval jarred him painfully; and, though he fronted his opponents manfully, and often with considerable warmth of temper, he had no pugnacious pleasure in the contest. It was one of the weaknesses of his nature to be too keenly alive to every harsh wind of opinion, to wince under the frowns of the foolish; to be irritated by the injustice of those who could not possibly have the elements indispensable for judging him rightly; and with all this acute sensibility to blame, this dependence on sympathy, he had for years been constrained into a position of antagonism. No wonder, then, that good old Mr Jerome's cordial words were balm to him. He had often been thankful to an old woman for saying 'God bless you'; to a little child for smiling at him; to a dog for submitting to be patted by him.   ('Janet's Repentance', chapter 8)

The self-locking syntax is vital: 'he had an acute sensibility *to* the *very* hatred or ridicule he did not flinch *from* provoking'. It means that the first nature persists within the second life not only in contradiction but in ongoing need of its own continual overcoming. It is the repeated overcoming that makes and sustains the second life. But the text is a double palimpsest: it contains not only Tryan's early disposition but also George Eliot's own. Edith Simcox knew how these sentences contained Marian Evans's own experience of those 'acute', 'flinching', 'jarring', 'wincing', 'irritated' feelings of tender sensitivity that belong to the thin-skinned:

> Only an obtuse reader of George Eliot's books can fail to discern traces in the author's self of an intensely—just not morbidly—acute sensibility. In one of her later works she speaks of 'the feeling of repulsed tenderness that is almost more of a sensation than an emotion';[5] and it takes little imagination to divine how, in the earlier years of such a woman, the common causes of indifference, shyness, obtuseness, or carelessness, as well as more rare ill-will or misconstruction, must have made this painful sensation only too familiar.[6]

From foolish indifference to unkind misconstruction, Edith Simcox's is a wonderful list—describing with an implicit sympathy, so often wanted at that time, all the pain of the first life. The Marian Evans that remained in George Eliot had always needed, as did Tryan, an answering reassurance to come from without. But where, in the name of his mission, Tryan provoked at one level what at another he could hardly

Plate 1. The Father, Robert Evans (1773–1849), 1842. (courtesy of the Herbert Art Gallery & Museum, Coventry)

Plate 2. The Library at Arbury Hall of which Mary Anne Evans had the run, depicting Sir Roger Newdiate (1719–1806), the original of Sir Christopher Cheverel of Cheverel Manor in 'Mr Gilfil's Love Story'. (by permission of Viscountess Daventry and the Arbury Estate)

Plate 3. The Older Sister, said to be Christiana Evans, Mrs Edward Clarke (1814–1859) by unknown artist. (courtesy of Nuneaton Museum and Art Gallery)

Plate 4a. The Friends: Sara Hennell (1812–1899) self-portrait. (courtesy of the Herbert Art Gallery & Museum, Coventry)

Plate 4b. Charles Hennell (1809–1850), watercolour by Cara Bray. (courtesy of the Herbert Art Gallery & Museum, Coventry)

Plate 5. Caroline (Cara) Hennell, Mrs Charles Bray (1814–1905), watercolour by sister Sara. (courtesy of the Herbert Art Gallery & Museum, Coventry)

Plate 6. The Woman at 30: Marian Evans by François d'Albert Durade, Geneva 1849, copy made by Durade 1881. (courtesy of the Herbert Art Gallery & Museum, Coventry)

Plate 7. The Memories: Robert Evans's spectacles and case and Isaac Evans's satchel. (John Burton and George Eliot Fellowship)

GALLERIE MODERNER MEISTER.

George Eliot

SOPHUS WILLIAMS KUNSTVERLAG BERLIN.
Vervielfältigung vorbehalten.   (E. Linde & Co.)   Déposé. — Registered.

Plate 8. The Woman: Marian Evans in Germany 1854–5, photograph by Sophus Williams. (John Burton and George Eliot Fellowship)

Plate 9. Herbert Spencer (1820–1903). (© National Portrait Gallery)

Plate 10. George Henry Lewes (1817–1878), 1867 pencil sketch by Rudolph Lehman. (courtesy of Nuneaton Library)

Plate 11. The piano, made by John Broadwood and Sons in 1868, was sold on 22 November 1869 to G. H. Lewes Esq., The Priory, 21 North Bank, Regents Park, as a fiftieth birthday present for his partner. On initial inquiry by researchers, the piano company supposed it was not George Eliot's piano because it was only registered with a Mrs Lewes and then in 1880 'Mrs John Cross'. On 15 September 1882 the piano was sent to Charles Lee Lewes, George Henry Lewes's eldest son. (© Herbert Art Gallery & Museum, Coventry)

Plate 12. Griff House Attic—the original of Maggie Tulliver's attic hideaway for her reading and her pain. (courtesy of Nuneaton Library)

Plate 13. Raphael, *Sistine Madonna and Child*. This painting overwhelmed George Eliot in Dresden 1858, during the writing of *Adam Bede*, and is admired by Philip Wakem in *The Mill on the Floss*. (© Gemäldegalerie Alte Meister, Dresden, © bpk—Bildagentur für Kunst, Kultur und Geschichte)

Plate 14. F. W. H. Myers (1843–1901). (© National Portrait Gallery)

Plate 15. George Eliot by Frederic Burton, 1865, a favourite portrait of Lewes's which he hung on his study wall in the Priory. (© National Portrait Gallery)

original penes Mrs. Reginald Allen, NYC.

Plate 16. George Eliot attending a concert, sketched by Princess Louise, a daughter of Queen Victoria, on her programme, 1877. It was an encouragement to George Eliot, after so much early social ostracism, that Queen Victoria admired her work, especially *Adam Bede*, and wanted her autograph. (© Beinecke Rare Book and Manuscript Library, Yale University)

bear, Marian Evans, for want of a formal religious cause, found it less clear how to be brave. Yet, like Tryan, she knew painfully well the contradiction between different parts of self, and the strange experience of releasing into the world forces and energies only to find them coming back to hurt or shame her. Tryan is not like Amos Barton who, for the most of his life, 'had no self-distrust', no capacity to compare 'the picture he presents to himself of his own doings, with the picture they make on the mental retina of his neighbours' ('Amos Barton', chapter 2). But that comparison is the first turn in the making of George Eliot as novelist. It was a function of Spinoza's 'conatus'—the need for self-preservation and self-protection—that such blindness to the view from outside should seem vital to survival, to an illusory but undoubting faith in oneself that was necessary for action. But what Spinoza sought was the recognition that the self that could bear to see more than its own point of view would of itself be expanded as a natural consequence. In the same way, self-distrust, which had been agony to Marian Evans, became in the act of writing an instrument of imagination in George Eliot. When an American correspondent remarked on the difference between her earlier and later work, George Eliot denied that there had been any fundamental 'change in the point of view from which I regard life since I wrote my first fiction—the "Scenes of Clerical Life",' adding, 'though I trust there is some growth in my appreciation of others, and in my self-distrust' (GEL 6, p. 318).

At least Tryan had Mr Jerome, a retired corn-factor who offers kind words that count for more than his wealth. George Henry Lewes thought Jerome was one of the characters that he would have wished George Eliot to have expanded upon had she had the broader canvas of a whole novel (GEL 2, p. 178). For it was as though Tryan himself needed more of Jerome, just as Janet asked so much of Tryan, worn and sickly. No wonder Lewes saw this: he was in his own way his partner's Jerome, even her Tryan, in providing the external support she needed to maintain her second life.

And in that sense, along with Lewes, Edith Simcox and Barbara Bodichon were her ideal readers in everyday life, just as was Wordsworth in the world of her imagination. What her soul thirsted for, more than polite praise, was the deeper recognition,

> the word which is the reflection of one's own aim and delight in writing—the word which shows that what one meant has been perfectly seized, that the emotion which stirred one in writing is repeated in the mind of the reader.   (GEL 5, p. 374)

Writing was an indirect medium through which she nonetheless sought direct contact and direct response, and as far as possible, beneath all the complex intricacy of thought, unmediated communication from the heart to the heart. Still the link was to be achieved through a word, to give some proof and permanence to trust. Psychologically she had need of readers who could return her word with the same emotion in reading that she had had in the writing. Words were alone what might realize feelings, confirm relationships, across human distances. But she also needed the sincere responses of readers for more than personal reassurance—for the fulfilment of her purposes in changing the general social attitude to the hidden and neglected value of common life. It is the early work that most exposes the raw nakedness of that need for sympathetic readers, that honest awkwardness in the effort to create them, which was more subtly avoided, more artistically embedded in the later fiction. The explicit address that is made to readers—'Depend upon it, you would gain unspeakably if you would learn with me to see the poetry and the pathos'—is made for this reason:

> Surely the only true knowledge of our fellow man is that which enables us to feel with him—which gives us a fine ear for the heart-pulses that are beating under the mere clothes of circumstance and opinion.   ('Janet's Repentance', chapter 10)

It signals those moments of appeal which George Eliot boldly tries to write, as it were, from outside her own book, even though she knows they will soon become enclosed again inside the book and read as just another part of it. But she wants to write within literature itself as though from outside the merely literary or aesthetic, to make literature the remedial, preparatory, and cross-border work by which a warmer humane world may come into being.

In the world as it currently is, if commonplace people seem insignificant in comparison with the greater ordering of things,

> is there not a pathos in the very insignificance—in our comparison of their dim and narrow existence with the glorious possibilities of that human nature which they share?   ('Amos Barton', chapter 5)

And it is with 'insignificance' here as it had been in the essay on the poet Young on 'mortality':

> [T]o us it is conceivable that in some minds the deep pathos lying in thoughts of human mortality—that we are here for a little while and then vanish away; that this earthly life is all that is given to our loved ones and to our many suffering fellowmen— lies nearer the foundations of moral emotion than the conception of extended existence.
> (*Essays*, p. 375)

The mute sense of poignant weakness—narrow when it could be glorious; existent for a little while that is not for ever—is what calls forth a corresponding strength of corrective feeling in response. That is what pathos in both passages means—the sense of suffering that arouses sympathy, where the very seeing of the lack creates an obligated effort to mitigate it. She needed her readers to know that thinking a good thought or feeling a good feeling within books created an obligation to be discharged in some way outside them: 'What may be called the raw material of moral sentiment.'

A First Reader and the Fourth *Scene*

It is one of the purposes of this, and the chapters that follow, to turn to the most inward readers of George Eliot and further extend the meaning of biography by giving some brief sense of the afterlife of the work within the lives of those most affected by it. George Eliot wanted an effect on the outside world, and her readers are the beginning of that effect, the meaning of the novelist transmitted not just in a book but through a person reading it. It hurt her when Blackwood could not feel her intention. For however ostensibly sealed off within their aesthetic form and hard covers, the works are never fully themselves until they are needed and used, albeit partially. They are transmitted lives. Sometimes a part of one of the novels means more than, or is not resolved within, the whole in which it figures, and points to a different order or a future time. Sometimes a part is all the human limitation of a reader can manage to take in, the whole being more than can be realized except through a bit of it. George Eliot was well aware of how extracted utterances could become detached and made static, outside the artistic wholes which contained the resonant context of their purpose, but eventually she allowed the young enthusiast Alexander Main, for example, to publish his well-selected anthology of her *Wise, Witty and Tender Sayings* (1875), not least because he spoke of 'the need for you', in 'heart-searching Thoughts which go to the very roots of our being'.[7] That is what her thoughts should finally be—mind-grabbing in their dynamic attraction, heart-searching in the very act of their transfusion.

One such crucial reader from start to finish of her career, whose story begins here, was the literary critic R. H. Hutton, who became editor of the *Spectator*. His reviews were respected by George Eliot herself—unusually, she wrote to him appreciatively of his scrupulously weighed account of both the strengths and the weaknesses of *Romola*, and in the light of his criticism even altered a phrase at the end of *Middlemarch* that seemed too simply to blame Dorothea's failures on the lack of opportunities for women in society.

But between Hutton and George Eliot there was one crucial difference which became more evident as Hutton turned from the immediacy of reviews close upon the publication or serialization of each work, to later essays on the oeuvre as a whole or on Cross's *Life*, offering a more synoptic appraisal. The difference was that Hutton struggled hard to remain a believer in Christianity and counted the cost of George Eliot ceasing to be so. He was the first of her critics to see how much was due to her translating *The Essence of Christianity*. For her, Feuerbach had been the means by which she could live without the opiate of religion, whilst not discarding her belief

Fig. 11. R. H. Hutton (1826–1897), from *Ten Personal Studies*, by Wilfrid Ward (1908).

in religiously motivated feelings and genuinely religious people. But for Hutton, Feuerbach's was 'an *ironic* explanation of the religions of the world': it 'makes the most momentous factor in the history of the world to consist in a grand procession of pure illusions'.[8] For him George Eliot was the great representative test-case of the nineteenth-century turn to modern secularization, in its struggle to retain idealism without a divine mandate. She did not merely stay with 'the given' of the everyday, but transformed 'the given' into 'the meant'—deciphering 'latent and suppressed realities by translating them into other moral situations so as to make them speak for themselves' (*Prospective Review*, vol. 10, 1854, pp. 472–3).[9] Hutton found in the freshly imagined double world of her novels a vital testing of the interrelation between the world within and the world without, in all that went into the formation of reality. We shall see how that testing went on for him in all the novels that followed.

Yet in that great exploratory effort of hers, what Hutton accused George Eliot of being unable to avoid was the one thing she had thought herself resolute against—the idea of compensation.[10] After Feuerbach, it was relatively easy for her to discount the theological notion of rewards in heaven, of blithely asserted blessings to be found in the suffering of adversity. But in articles gathered in his *Essays on Some of the Modern Guides to English Thought in Matters of Faith*, what Hutton critically focused upon was the secular version of compensation—a sentimental tilting of the balance in order to stave off the ever-threatening melancholy of lost meaning or purpose. This was there, he thought, from the start, from the very origins of her attempt to create not only a second self but, in that, a humanist substitute for the primacy of religion. Quoting a letter to Barbara Bodichon, 26 December 1860, in which George Eliot wrote that the greatest calling 'was to do without opium, and live through all our pain with conscious clear-eyed endurance', Hutton made a decisive counter-claim: that at key moments in her life and in her writing she still could not help offering 'minute doses of opium', in amends for her own painful inability to provide adequate consolation (*Modern Guides*, pp. 298–9).What she offered there was not as primary as she had wanted, since salvation was gone; it was second-best and second-order, an emotional human substitute for a lost ideal. Without a grounding faith, a lack that went deeper even than personal want of confidence, she had to lay emphasis from the first to the last of her works on human rescue work. It was what rescued her too. She wanted to use her troubles, to be assured of their use, and to find some abiding alternative to the normal human dependency on life's outcomes. 'How to avoid disappointment' is the heading of one her earliest published essays, written in 1847, in which a painter says that amidst all his misfortunes he loves his pictures still. Its poignant last sentence is a paragraph on its own: 'Who would not have some purpose independent in its value as art is to the artist?' (*Essays*, p. 19). To rescue herself from disappointment, and to rescue her characters from disappointment, she made her life, said Hutton, 'one long strain' (*Modern Guides*, p. 272), in the effort to make through art, human feeling, human kindness, and human morality serve as substitutes for the function of a religion.

Hutton argued that the strain exerted a pressure of undue emphasis that could be seen at unguarded moments within the language—those raw moments to be found especially within the more naked early work or in the practically related issues revealed in other letters. There is a letter to Mrs Bray in 1852 on 'trying to love the glorious destination of humanity, looking before and after', or another in 1870 to Mrs Robert Lytton on trying 'to delight in the sunshine that will be, when I shall never see it any more'. Though not the artistic work itself, such letters gave clues to the rawer underlying concerns that went into it. As a substitute for the afterlife, the idea of an 'impersonal life'—the future of humanity, the continuance of sunshine— involved what Hutton called an '*artificial* strain' in the effort to appease its own inadequacy (*Modern Guides*, p. 297). It was another dose of opium 'in the shape of soothing but thoroughly unreal assuagements of the pain of her own incapacity to help her friends when in trouble' (*Modern Guides*, p. 299). Unreal was a word that Hutton took from a favourite sermon by John Henry Newman and applied to the writer whom he otherwise sincerely admired as the greatest of nineteenth-century realists. He quotes from the sermon 'Unreal Words', preached by Newman on 2 June 1839: 'To make professions is to play with edged tools unless we attend to what we are saying. Words have a meaning whether we mean that meaning or not; and they are imputed to us in their real meaning when our not meaning it is our own fault' (*Modern Guides*, p. 95). It was the worst case of all if literary people, the men and women of words, used their words only artificially, to avoid a want of meaning or cover an abyss.

Where she became unreal, it was not a matter of hypocrisy in George Eliot, Hutton conceded, it was the result of strain and fracture and artifice brought about by lack of faith. The predicament, Hutton concluded not without sympathy, was that of a woman who held God to be a merely human ideal and then had to preach 'that men owe as much obedience to an elevated thought of their own as they could possibly owe to any external inspirer of that thought' (*Modern Guides*, p. 275). It was, says Hutton, at once characteristic and paradoxical of her 'to accept without a murmur a pessimistic estimate of man's nature and capabilities, and then to strain to the utmost all her powers to show that the worse his condition the more imperative is the duty to mitigate its miseries' (*Modern Guides*, p. 306).

The extraordinary thing is that something in George Eliot at times was drawn to this charge. She made an equivalent accusation of her own in the poem 'A Minor Prophet', written in 1865 while she was struggling in the midst of her career to take stock of her position and her best way forward. Hutton speaks of her ironies, her contradictions and paradoxes—being religious-minded without religion, suc- cumbing to pessimism even in her mitigation of it. But George Eliot offers what is perhaps the most dangerous paradox of all in her make-up: namely, the half-repressed puritanical thought that somehow, though it may risk breaking them, people *need* their troubles. It was the sort of outrageously simple and one-sided sentence that she could not possibly say, could not believe to be at all just, and indeed would oppose in those Christian apologists who all too fatuously preached of the uses of suffering in adversity. But it was lodged somewhere fundamental even in her necessary corrections of it. 'A Minor Prophet' looks back at what she calls the 'prejudice' of her own admiration for the failed and troubled, the suffering, the tested, and the incomplete.

Its speaker feels 'bitterly' that every struggling change upon the earth is unjustly 'bought with sacrifice'; yet on the other hand cannot accept the vision of an ideal future offered by the prophet, 'which shows in bird's-eye view a perfect world'. That is not because the speaker thinks a world without pain or struggle wholly impossible; but—far more curiously and somewhat to the speaker's own self-bafflement—she feels that even were such a utopia to come to pass, the people of that more perfect future will also have lost something:

> I fall
> Into short-sighted pity for the men
> Who, living in those perfect future times,
> Will not know half the dead imperfect things
> That move my smiles and tears.

It is an emotional preference for the imperfect over the perfect that does not seem even to the speaker quite morally justifiable. This is the increase in self-distrust in the later work, reflecting backwards over the whole sensibility to human sorrow. It requires a precarious effort to get the combinations and balances right, with a precision of which humans are barely capable. For it is, admits the speaker, 'a paradox' to

> pity future men who will not know
> A keen experience with pity blent,
> The pathos exquisite of lovely minds
> Hid in harsh forms—not penetrating them
> Like fire divine within a common bush
> Which glows transfigured by the heavenly guest,
> So that men put their shoes off; but encaged
> Like a sweet child within some thick-walled cell
> Who leaps and fails to hold the window-bars ...

Where Moses saw the angel of the Lord within the burning bush, it was the pained cry of the child within—the sense of adult humans as still 'children of a larger growth' (GEL 1, p. 23)—that George Eliot heard and felt from *Scenes of Clerical Life* onwards. But it is, the speaker repeats, a 'foolish'—no, worse—it is a 'wicked paradox'; as if George Eliot herself in some terrible sense *needed* the sorrow of her own characters in order to appreciate them:

> For purest pity is the eye of love,
> Melting at sight of sorrow, and to grieve
> Because it sees no sorrow, shows a love
> Warped from its truer nature

But these ambiguous predicaments are explored within the stories. Gilfil was ashamed to feel irresistibly half-delighted in Tina's breakdown, for the opportunity it gave him to tend her. Tryan, a hopeless consumptive, wants to live longer, not deceiving himself that it is now solely for the sake of his religious mission but, more, for love of Janet, for 'the pure human joys which he had voluntarily and determinedly banished from his life . . . that deep affection from which he had been cut off by a chasm of remorse' ('Janet's Repentance', chapter 27). And yet to George Eliot these are not just 'ulterior' motives: emphatically not so, because they honestly look for the right place for themselves in the story, the place to get right within the world, albeit so precariously near to the wrong or the distrusted or the misunderstood. At the end, before his death, Janet and Tryan do kiss: 'The time has not yet come for her to be conscious that the hold he had on her heart was any other than that of the heaven-sent friend who had come to her like the angel in the prison' (chapter 27). 'Any other' is not Victorian sexual reticence but a reverence for what a reductive naming might make too easily fitted in.

These complex self-checking reflections that make people's doubts and limitations and failings an intrinsic part of their value are also like that double-think which made George Eliot value religion for the human benefit that the religious themselves might see as only collateral. Human content finds itself in many different, strange, contradictory, distorted, or constricting forms: 'Every mistake, every absurdity into which poor human nature has fallen, may be looked on as an experiment' (*Essays*, p. 31). George Eliot's answer to her own charge was finally that her love of human feelings, revealed within human failings, was not an opiate; it was the raw material for what a better world might begin to be like—even if she herself could only reach towards it through being moved by sorrows; even if she could hardly imagine or admire a human being of the future who did not need such feelings. She loved the struggling moments of partial self-transcendence, when the painfully raw matter out of which the transcendence was made still surrounded and almost overcame it. That was the flawed achievement of all second lives, including her own, that the second should still have the first life within it, with what was right and what was wrong, in the revision that went on for the sake of lost fundamentals. Those moments of breakthrough were for her the sacred ones, were the fragments of God in a person. Hutton doubted if 'any really great writer of fiction ever thought *up* from his individual characters' (*National Review*, 1, October 1855, p. 338), but George Eliot loved precisely doing that, her people thinking *up* from themselves, in great, great difficulty.

Better to understand this answer is also to explain how *Adam Bede* becomes in a sense the fourth of the *Scenes of Clerical Life*—a scene expanded into the full-blown novel, to test within itself the emotions begun in those first stories. It was begun on 22 October 1857, just thirteen days after the completion of 'Janet's Repentance'.

For it was during the writing of the *Scenes of Clerical Life* themselves that George Eliot remembered a reported incident she had told no one for twenty years. When she did speak of it to George Henry Lewes, he said it was a fine scene for a story. It became known as her 'aunt's story', which she 'blended' with parts of her father's story to make *Adam Bede* (GEL 2, p. 502).

Her aunt, Elizabeth Evans, had told her one afternoon in 1839 of how, as part of her Methodist mission in life, she and another devout woman had visited an unhappy young woman in prison, stayed with her all night, and gone with her to her execution for the murder of her baby. It was an ordinary girl in an extraordinary situation, and of this girl Elizabeth Evans could tell her niece very little. 'In her account of the prison scenes I remember no word she uttered,' Marian Lewes wrote to Sara Hennell in 1859, 'I only remember her tone and manner, and the deep feeling I had under the recital' (GEL 3, p. 176). If the aunt had known more, if the niece had had her exact words and not the tone and the feeling, or had spoken of it much in the years intervening, then the story would have held no such germ of transformation. It was not simply 'the given'; it became the made and the meant. It became a 'clear image' of 'nature's unambitious underwood', to quote the epigraph she used for *Adam Bede* taken from Wordsworth's *Excursion* (book 6). There Wordsworth was writing about Ellen, a young woman deserted by the lover who made her pregnant, and later buried with her baby. Such figures need the tendance, says Wordsworth, of 'something more / Than brotherly forgiveness'—though brotherly forgiveness in the narrower sense was not a given for Marian Lewes.

In her journal she described more fully how she had come to make *Adam Bede*. There was in the beginning the character of Adam and the character of Dinah, wrought of her father and her aunt in new combinations, with the child-murderer Hetty from her aunt's story, and Arthur Donnithorne, the young squire who seduced her: 'Everything else grew out of the characters and their mutual relations' (GEL 2, p. 503). Such was the broader canvas—a network made out of the tacit calls and connections between individuals—towards which the *Scenes* had been working. In the novel that network could then begin to generate of itself, within and between the characters, the evolving interrelationships, and the interrelated thoughts.

The result is two climaxes which complete the earlier work. The first is the sheer demand made by the experience of trouble in George Eliot. It is in chapter 45, where gently but determinedly and over the course of a long night, Dinah Morris *makes* Hetty Sorrel confess her crime in the dark of the prison, as before a presence that grows between them in that dark. She knows that Hetty, for all her despairing reluctance, has to speak of what she is and what she has done, for reasons more than relief, for reasons that, to Dinah, have to do with God and His truth and judgement. Analogously, though without God, George Eliot wants her characters to *utter*—if not to each other, if not even to themselves, at least in and through her. In order to be more than ciphers of 'the given', they must *mean*. They must partly, even momentarily, transcend what they think they have become. Even as the novel moves beyond scenes of clerical life, what Dinah manages with Hetty is crucially what Arthur avoided in his own interview with Reverend Irwine, when naked confession would still have made all the difference to what was to follow. But between Dinah and Hetty, as later between Dorothea and Rosamond at a crucial moment in *Middlemarch* (chapter 81), there is something of what was glimpsed in 'Janet's Repentance' beyond 'this artificial life of ours': 'as if we had suddenly waked into the real world of which this everyday one is but a puppet-show copy'.

'Dinah...help me...I can't...,' cries Hetty, but then: 'I will speak...I will tell...I won't hide it any more' (*Adam Bede*, chapter 45). In these crises what George Eliot was secretly looking for in her people was what became character or soul in its making: a need for truth, an emotional capability of thought, something solid like felt duty, that could stop the shock simply passing through them like a medium—an experiment from which, every time it was repeated, some benefit might come. It is always the shift in her characters from '*I can't*' via 'I must' into '*I will*' that most moved George Eliot:

> By pressure of the dire Impossible
> Urging to possible ends the active soul.
> ('A College Breakfast Party', ll. 523–4)

The Impossible but the Needed was the great human stimulus. But it depended upon the demands of trouble and inadequacy and feeling, beyond the normal, and past competence or confidence. Hence achievement back-to-front, by a sort of double negative as in 'I won't hide it any more.' There was no automatic compensation in this: it was achieved increasingly through human effort going on *inside* the novels, in lieu of any other help, even the author's appeals to her readers.

The second great climax of *Adam Bede* is nearer the end of the novel and speaks even more closely of the equivocal uses of trouble in George Eliot. It marks where Adam himself reaches a position close to his author's own, as a result of the agonizing changes his ill-placed love for Hetty has wrought upon him. Hetty had unthinkingly betrayed and deserted him in the midst of their engagement, had unavailingly gone after the young squire who had made her secretly pregnant, and finally in desperation had left her new-born child to die in the fields. Yet Adam has followed her, and, almost broken, has brought himself to stand by her in court, no longer the old Adam who could judge simply or harshly. In the year or so that follows after Hetty's transportation, Adam comes to love Dinah instead—but without ever forgetting all that has happened beforehand.

The fact is that, through this tortuous process, through the pain it cost him in still feeling for Hetty, Adam is undeniably made a better human being: this in chapter 54 makes George Eliot, as so often at the great moments, think two things almost at once through the medium of Adam. One is that

> it is not ignoble to feel that the fuller life which a sad experience has brought us is worth our own personal share of pain: surely it is not possible to feel otherwise, any more than it would be possible for a man with a cataract to regret the painful process by which his dim blurred sight of men as trees walking had been exchanged for clear outline and effulgent day.

It is done carefully, strugglingly, through the sort of back-to-front double negatives—not ignoble, not possible otherwise—that Wordsworth himself needed in delicate places. 'Deem not useless' the Cumberland beggar; 'not unknown' the less easy or obvious values of complex being: such is in the spirit of the ancient 'via negativa' in which the truly sacred cannot be approached and spoken of directly, but only through what cannot be simply said. Something here that may not be affirmed is not to be denied.

But the other and almost simultaneous thought is this, finally, against opiates, against the fantasy and blasphemy of any second-order compensation. It is that a softened Adam, who finds comfort in Dinah, nonetheless

> could never thank God for another's misery. And if I were capable of that narrow-sighted joy in Adam's behalf, I would still know he was not the man to feel it for himself: he would have shaken his head at such a sentiment, and said, 'Evil's evil, and sorrow's sorrow, and you can't alter its nature by wrapping it up in other words. Other folk were not created for my sake, that I should think all square when things turn out well for me.' (*Adam Bede*, chapter 54)

It is not just he who has suffered. Whatever the eventual effect on Adam, Hetty is Hetty, deported and broken, still. For all the interconnections in feeling, there remain, finally, in realism, terrible and unbridgeable separations at the sheer physical level. The same chapter is saying a strong No to compensation, but No also to the denial of something good and lovely that is imperfectly created from within the harsh forms of failure and suffering.

The two thoughts are not really separate in so far as that to which they refer is a single reality, like 'sad' and 'pretty' with Dempster and his mother. Intervolved, they come out of what Marian Evans called 'the wondrous chemistry of the affections and sentiments, which inevitably gives rise to distinctive forms and combinations' (*Essays*, p. 53). Sorrow, as so often one part of those emotionally founded combinations, showed George Eliot trying to work out, within thoughts that seemed inextricable, what were the guiding signs of life. The suffering of sorrow, that so much moved George Eliot, could not and should not be chosen, was most often cruelly ill-deserved and dangerously damaging, but still there was a chance that it might be rightly used. It resulted from the misdirection of something of value that, in a more just place, should have gone right: it spoke for the better even in its pain. As the Victorian man of letters, Leslie Stephen, author of a study of George Eliot, concluded in an essay on Wordsworth and the transmutation of sorrow, 'Every element of which our nature is composed may be said to be good in its proper place.'[11] Waste not, was his cry, and Art was the search for the proper place of what otherwise was most terribly wasted. But in George Eliot's experiments, the chemistry included the combination of the realist novelist's double task: not only to make first things, lost or defeated human priorities, 'speak for themselves' even from their pain, as Hutton had put it; but also to remain loyal to the unlikely or unglamorous sources of common life, those less than proper places within which the elemental cries were muffled.

It was a chemistry that also went on at the level of individuals, amidst the combinations of Adam and Hetty, of Janet and Tryan: 'There is a simple gravestone in Milby churchyard ... But there is another memorial of Edgar Tryan, which bears a fuller record: it is Janet Dempster, rescued from self-despair ...' ('Janet's Repentance', chapter 28). It is such memories as this, internal to the developing power of the work, that allowed the author of *Adam Bede* to write her boldest message within that novel in chapter 17 ('In Which the Story Pauses a Little'): 'by living a great deal among people more or less commonplace and vulgar of whom you would perhaps hear nothing very surprising,' she says, 'I have come to the conclusion that human nature is lovable'.

Without that conclusion the novels could not have been written, despite all that remained barely loveable still within them. As A. S. Byatt's protagonist, Stephanie, thinks to herself in *Still Life*, 'George Eliot was a good hater. She looked long and intelligently at what she hated, with curiosity to see exactly what it was, and the necessary detachment to imagine it from within and without, these two breeding a kind of knowledge that was love.'[12] It was the opposite of the knowledge the young Marian Evans had found in reading the painful low-life realism of Balzac's novels of the *Comédie Humaine*. For all her later admiration of Balzac's craftsmanship, she had felt she was 'guanoing her mind' in reading him (GEL 1, p. 234). 'Surely the only true knowledge of our fellow man is that which enables us to feel with him—which gives us a fine ear for the heart-pulses that are beating under the mere clothes of circumstance and opinion' ('Janet's Repentance', chapter 10). If *Adam Bede* was the fourth *Scene*, *Silas Marner was*, as we shall see in Chapter 8, a fifth—without the clerical life, but with Wordsworth, and more of Wordsworth, in defence of the primacy of hard-won goodness.

Scenes of Clerical Life was George Eliot's birthright, vulnerably insisting on the need to start from feelings of good. Such feelings can be hard to believe, says one character in a modern novel written by one of the heirs of George Eliot. 'I know that,' replies another, 'Good things are much harder to believe than bad things. Human beings are shockingly bad at believing good things. That's one of the secrets I know.'[13] Writing to Sara Hennell in May 1849 of Francis Newman, in the midst of nursing her father and living what she called 'unspeakable moments', Mary Ann Evans had said, even then: 'There is a sort of blasphemy in that proverbial phrase "too good to be true"' (GEL 1, p. 282).

Adam Bede

'The Other Side of the Commonplace', 1857–9

George Eliot spoke of 'phases' in her mental development, and was clearly glad of her ability to learn and to build as she went along. It is also true that George Eliot worked hard to make each work have its own distinct atmosphere and reality: accordingly, each chapter that follows tries to recreate the singular *life* of the particular novel it describes as though that novel were the equivalent of a personal existence in the world or of a chapter in the author's mental life.

But no study of the mind within the fiction can stick with the idea of mere successive sequence, one novel after another. The very presence of George Eliot herself in the midst of her fictions pointed always to different dimensions. It pointed across novels, forwards and back in the interwoven story of her written life, just as surely as the later writing self goes back to the earlier writing self and brings it forward into imaginative interplay. But above all, that presence inside the novels insisted on the relation to life outside them. She wanted her readers to be emotionally and imaginatively immersed in her works but, crucially, wanted that immersion to provoke in them the equivalent of the George Eliot part of herself—namely the part that extrapolated by bursting into further thought, that was so moved by the importance of the often neglected particular as almost to take it out of the book by registering its resonant application elsewhere.

So it is through a reader that we know, in the biography of writing, some of the passages in *Adam Bede* that most moved the author even as she composed them. George Eliot wrote to her publisher, John Blackwood, on 31 March 1859, praising a forthcoming review of the novel to appear in *Blackwood's Edinburgh Magazine* in April. 'I would like you to convey my gratitude,' she writes of the reviewer:

> I see he is a man whose experience and study enable him to relish parts of my book which I should despair of seeing recognized by critics in London back drawing rooms. He has gratified me keenly by laying his finger on passages which I wrote either with strong feeling or from intimate knowledge, but which I had prepared myself to find entirely passed over by reviewers. (GEL 3, p. 41)

Victorian reviewers often quoted lengthy passages, samples of the essential feel of the work. Which were the passages this reviewer picked out in *Blackwood's* that so pleased George Eliot?

Many derived from feeling for her father—his solidity and straightness, the belief in practical work—not exposed as an old-fashioned idea to be dismissed by the London intelligentsia as crude or philistine, but recreated through art in the living person of Adam Bede himself:

> I like to read about Moses best, in th' Old Testament. He carried a hard business well through, and died when other folks were going to reap the fruits: a man must have courage to look at his life so, and think what'll come of it after he's dead and gone. A good solid bit o' work lasts: if it's only laying a floor down, somebody's the better for it being done well, beside the man as does it.   (*Adam Bede*, chapter 50)

Lives seriously lived were more important than fashions or opinions. This was George Eliot in every sense 'taking the part' of the father who in life had always taken Mary Ann's part in all her difficulties. It was like an expanded version of the moment when, in *The Mill on The Floss*, Maggie Tulliver can for once stick up for her father—now stricken and bankrupt—as he had long stuck up for her. In the face of the harsh criticisms his wife's family make of his folly, it is she and not her usually assertive brother who bursts out angrily: 'Keep away from us then, and don't come to find fault with my father—he was better than any of you—he was kind—he would have helped *you*, if you had been in trouble' (book 2, chapter 3). This is not only a movement in love and gratitude and reciprocated generosity. It was also, for Maggie Tulliver, the movement from passive to active that Spinoza knew to be essential to a humanly flourishing life. And, more, for George Eliot it was the turnaround movement that Feuerbach, in Marian Evans's translation, described as a return,[1] when the feeling she had long ago received was no longer just her father's feeling but was her own feeling too come back upon her as more than memory, a feeling she could now reuse to recreate him independently in a new and second life. It was as though her whole earlier life 'returned to her now as a power' (*Middlemarch*, chapter 80). The movement of Marian Evans to George Eliot was to a George Eliot who still came out of Marian Evans, and, knowing what she owed her in strength and in weakness, wrote for that Marian Evans and her like, on behalf of their struggling loves and pains.

Nothing was better for her than to find that what she cared for in her heart of hearts was also felt and recognized by others than herself. That was why the Liggins affair hurt her. Joseph Liggins was the son of a prosperous Nuneaton baker, rusticated from Cambridge for getting into bad company, who claimed authorship of *Scenes of Clerical Life* and *Adam Bede* to restore his reputation and his finances. At first it was no more than a ludicrous irritant. But as the matter got more serious over two years of continuous gossip, it was not only that Liggins seemed almost to be taking away the one thing she had most earned. It was also that, despite her vulnerability to public opinion through her alliance with Lewes, she was now forced into disclosure of her own authorship. She had wanted at one level to be unknown, in order to be known only at a deeper level: anything that confused those levels or increased her ambivalence disturbed her greatly.

But to see her own privately loved passages re-endorsed in a good review by a sensitive reader was to defy the London drawing rooms from which she was largely excluded as Lewes's illicit partner. Her rooted commitment was to the community of provincial life in the tradition of the Wordsworth of the Lakes and the *Lyrical Ballads*. Her reviewer in *Blackwood's* was, as she suspected, a provincial clergyman, warm in appreciation of human goodness. William Lucas Collins, a lowly curate in Northamptonshire, loved the emotional richness of the book, and admired the courage and the charity of a writer who 'by living a great deal among people more or less commonplace and vulgar', could say, as we have seen, that 'I have come to the conclusion that human nature is lovable' (*Adam Bede*, chapter 17).

This was the writer who, from *Scenes of Clerical Life* to *Impressions of Theophrastus Such*, stood out against any damage done to what Wordsworth said human beings most needed to live by—'admiration, hope, and love'.[2] Collins himself loved the scenes of Dinah's preaching and of the community's harvest supper, but he kept coming back to Adam, absolute on work, craft, action, and embodied practice in the world:

> '[T]here's such a thing as being over-speritial; we must have something besides Gospel i' the world. Look at the canals, and th' aqueducs, an' th' coal-pit engines, an' Ark-wright's mills there at Cromford; a man must learn summat beside Gospel to make them things, I reckon. But to hear some o' them preachers, you'd think as a man must be doing nothing all's life but shutting's eyes and looking what's a-going on inside him. I know a man must have the love o' God in his soul, and the Bible's God's word. But what does the Bible say? Why, it says as God put his sperrit into the workman as built the tabernacle, to make him do all the carved work and things as wanted a nice hand. And this is my way o' looking at it: there's the sperrit of God in all things and all times—weekday as well as Sunday—and i' the great works and inventions, and i' the figuring and the mechanics. And God helps us with our headpieces and our hands as well as with our souls...' (*Adam Bede*, chapter 1)

In *Culture and Anarchy* (1869), the cosmopolitan Matthew Arnold was to write against judgemental parochialism, narrow provincialism, the over-practical culture of ethics and action based on the Hebrew religious tradition, as opposed to the alternative heritage in the high fineness of Greek philosophy and art. But George Eliot's Adam says, 'I like to read about Moses best...' In another passage selected by Collins, he goes on to insist that 'religion's something else beside notions. It isn't notions that sets people doing the right thing—it's feelings':

> 'It's the same with the notions in religion as it is with math'matics,—a man may be able to work problems straight off in's head as he sits by the fire and smokes his pipe; but if he has to make a machine or a building, he must have a will and a resolution, and love something else better than his own ease....I look at it as if the doctrines was like finding names for your feelings, so as you can talk of 'em when you've never known 'em, just as a man may talk o' tools when he knows their names, though he's never so much as seen 'em, still less handled 'em.' (*Adam Bede*, chapter 17)

Feeling had in it something more like the concentrated reality of actually doing. For all her own intellectual width of understanding, George Eliot was interested in narrowness as a starting point and a focal centre. Too often education began too far up, as a second-order vocabulary, not only without but in place of the 'deep hunger' she was to speak of in *Impressions of Theophrastus Such* as vital to the personal reality of true endeavour, whatever its flaws and partialities (chapter 5).

The novel offered George Eliot both a wider remit and a lesser definiteness. What for Adam was an almost physical principle of life and action from the very first was, for George Eliot, a third thought, a thought inherited, criticized, and then partly revalidated—after her break with her father's faith and, then again, after her return to it at a different level via Feuerbach. She wanted 'notions', she wanted 'names', yet wanted them not as substitutes but as tools for the messages and aims of feeling.

As a reviewer, Collins found this newly developed being called George Eliot, above all, in chapter 17, 'In Which the Story Pauses a Little'. It is the first great extended statement of herself and her purposes, taking off from an account of the imperfect, unideal clergyman, Mr Irwine, as if to make a link forward from *Scenes of Clerical Life*:

> These fellow-mortals, every one, must be accepted as they are: you can neither straighten their noses, nor brighten their wit, nor rectify their dispositions; and it is these people—amongst whom your life is passed—that it is needful you should tolerate, pity, and love: it is these more or less ugly, stupid, inconsistent people...

These people—without whom we 'frame lofty theories' which 'only fit' a world of extremes and ideals. Collins kept saying that he 'must find room' in his review for lengthy quotations from this chapter, and it was like the room that now, after *Scenes of Clerical Life*, George Eliot insistently made for apparently commonplace figures at full and saturated novel length. The reviewer concluded that, beneath the surface-skin of the novel, readers were watching, in the author of *Adam Bede*, 'the operations

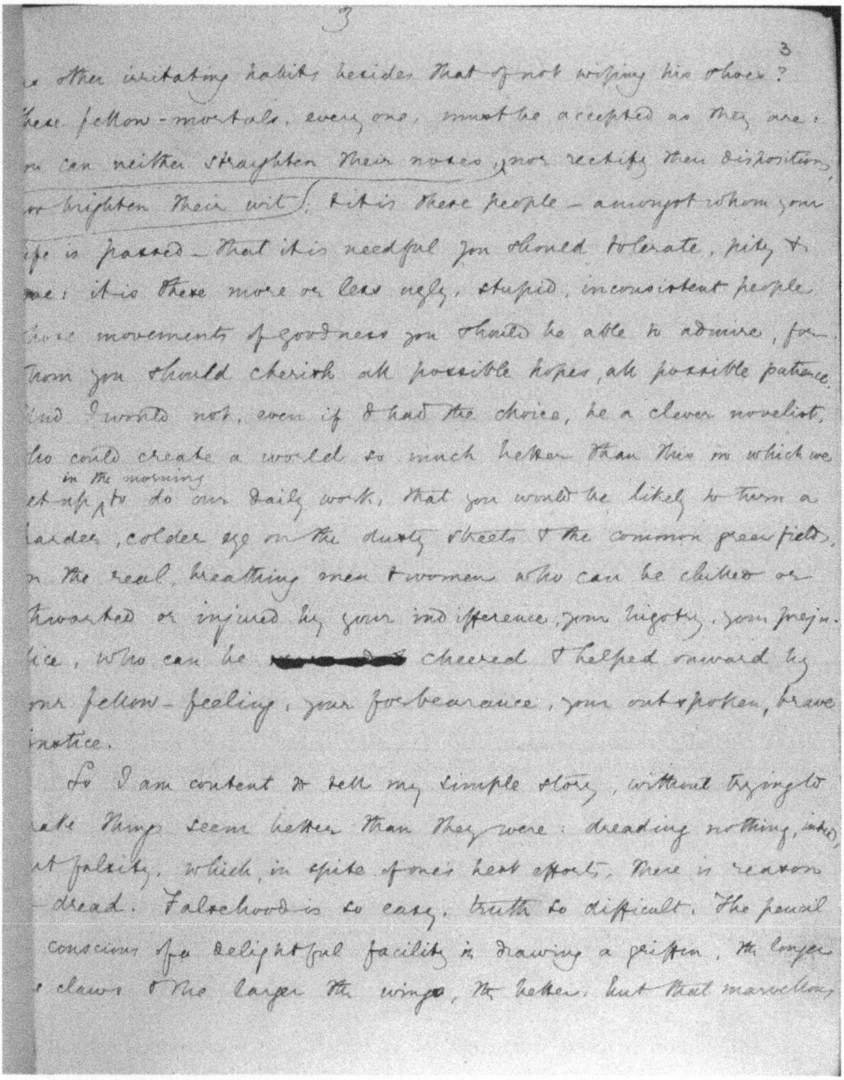

Fig. 12. Three manuscript pages from *Adam Bede*, chapter 17 in defence of realism, Dutch paintings, and human sympathy. 'These fellow mortals, every one, must be accepted as they are...'(© British Library).

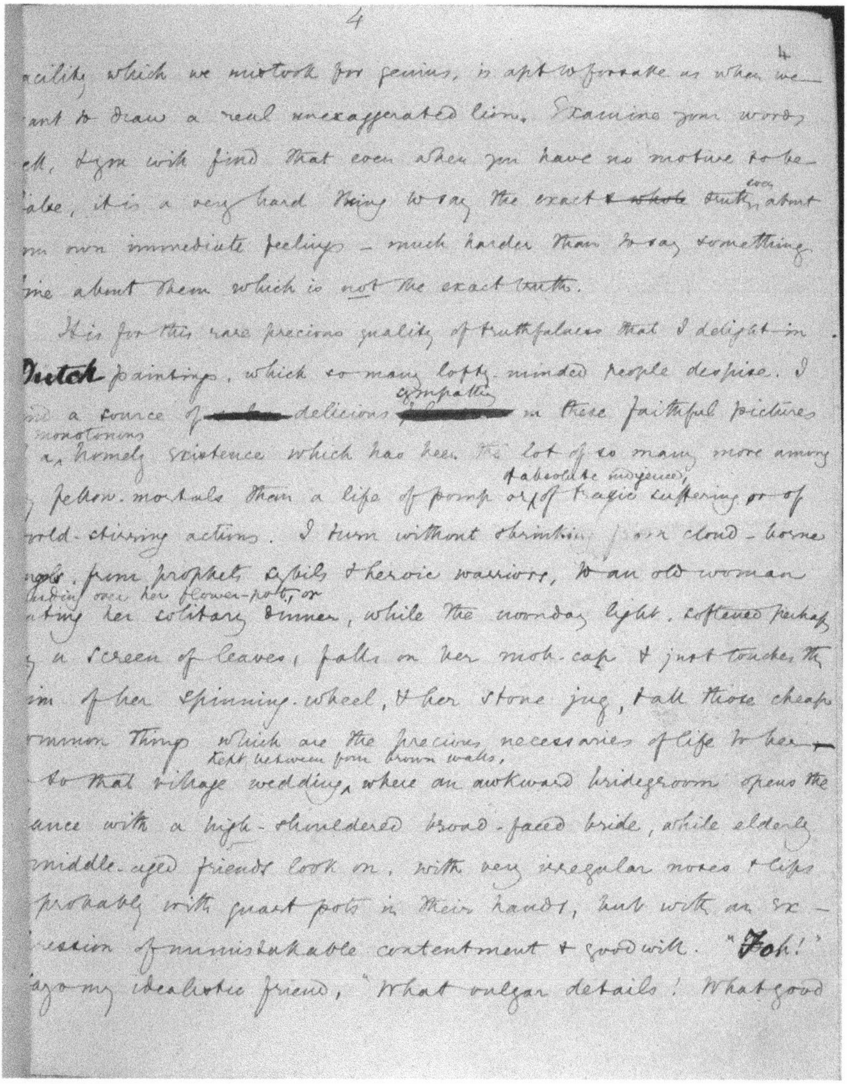

4

...cility which we mistook for genius, is apt to forsake us when we
want to draw a real unexaggerated lion. Examine your words
well, & you will find that even when you have no motive to be
false, it is a very hard thing to say the exact & ~~whole~~ truth, about
your own immediate feelings — much harder than to say something
fine about them which is <u>not</u> the exact truth.

It is for this rare precious quality of truthfulness that I delight in
Dutch paintings, which so many lofty-minded people despise. I
find a source of ~~so~~ delicious *sympathy* in these faithful pictures
of ~~monotonous~~ a homely existence which has been the lot of so many more among
my fellow-mortals than a life of pomp or of tragic suffering or of
world-stirring actions. I turn without shrinking from cloud-borne
angels, from prophets, sibils & heroic warriors, to an old woman
bending over her flower-pot, or
eating her solitary dinner, while the noonday light, softened perhaps
by a screen of leaves, falls on her mob-cap & just touches the
rim of her spinning-wheel, & her stone jug, & all those cheap
common things which are the precious necessaries of life to her,
kept between four brown walls,
to that village wedding, where an awkward bridegroom opens the
dance with a high-shouldered broad-faced bride, while elderly
middle-aged friends look on, with very irregular noses & lips,
probably with quart-pots in their hands, but with an expression of unmistakable contentment & good-will. "**Foh!**"
says my idealistic friend, "What vulgar details! What good

Fig. 12. Continued: 'I find a source of delicious sympathy in these faithful pictures…'

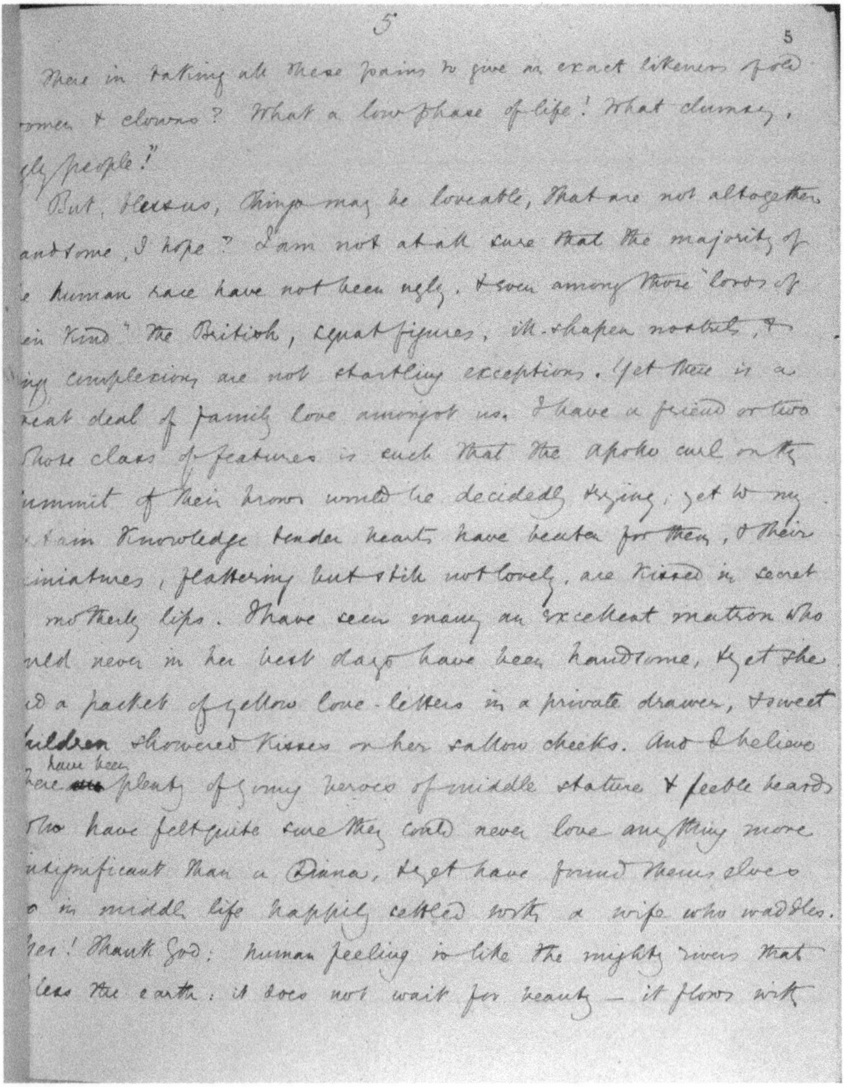

5 5

there in taking all these pains to give an exact likeness of old
omen & clowns? What a low phase of life! What clumsy,
ly people!"
But, bless us, things may be loveable, that are not altogether
andsome, I hope? I am not at all sure that the majority of
e human race have not been ugly, & even among those "lords of
eir kind" the British, squat figures, ill-shapen nostrils, &
ingy complexions are not startling exceptions. Yet there is a
reat deal of family love amongst us. I have a friend or two
hose class of features is such that the Apollo curl on the
ummit of their brows would be decidedly trying; yet to my
rtain knowledge tender hearts have beaten for them, & their
iniatures, flattering but still not lovely, are kissed in secret
motherly lips. I have seen many an excellent matron who
uld never in her best days have been handsome, & yet she
d a packet of yellow love-letters in a private drawer, & sweet
hildren showered kisses on her sallow cheeks. And I believe
here have been plenty of young heroes of middle stature & feeble beards
who have felt quite sure they could never love anything more
nsignificant than a Diana, & yet have found themselves
in middle life happily settled with a wife who waddles.
es! thank God; human feeling is like the mighty rivers that
less the earth: it does not wait for beauty – it flows with

Fig. 12. Continued: 'But, bless us, things may be loveable, that are not altogether handsome, I hope? I am not at all sure that the majority of the human race have not been ugly . . . human feeling is like the mighty rivers that bless the earth: it does not wait for beauty –'

of a skilled anatomist', laying bare the secrets of the human frame yet with a hand that was 'not only sure and steady, but gentle as a woman's' (*Blackwood's*, April 1859, p. 504). Previously only Dickens had deduced from purely internal evidence that the author was a woman. But in that mixture of love and analysis, she was also making room for herself, room for hard thinking, and for her work's effect within a serious reader.

These moments of George Eliot's ostensible generalization of course remained still inside the work, for all their effort of language. But to have the deepest parts of the book's meaning taken away by readers, from within themselves, was as essential to George Eliot's purposes as was the work's own artistic integrity. This is why the chapters of my volume from now on, novel by novel, must still try to move between the works at representatively key moments of cross-cutting significance. And they must also move between the novels and the best readers of them to offer a model of the right use of fiction for life.

An Experiment in Life

Writing at the end of November 1858, she concluded a brief history of the composition of *Adam Bede* by saying, 'I love it very much and am deeply thankful to have written it' (GEL 2, p. 504). But thankful to whom or to what? There were emotions that she could not wholly account for, but in the sheer content of life were too burstingly full not to have some reality in and beyond themselves, some external referent or significance, however unspecifiable. Like Adam Bede himself, in order to make something, George Eliot had to have 'a will and a resolution, and love something else better than [her] own ease'. But now, for the sharp anatomist, something more was at stake than in the very earliest writings, involving not love alone, but the critical trials put upon love.

At the foundations of this novel, Adam is a simple, hard, absolute man. But the work of George Eliot upon him, for all her loving sympathy, was ever tending towards the complex, the painfully softened, the relative. What follows in the unfolding of the novel's story is therefore a matter not only of Adam's work, but of what will be called 'that growing tenderness which came from the sorrow at work within him' (*Adam Bede*, chapter 50). It is these little explosive phrases—'at work within'—that mark the inner movements of George Eliot's thinking, the shifting of the field and its centre.

In this way, the story of the softening of the old Adam was not a gentle but itself a hard thing. It lay in emotionally binding Adam, disproportionately as it were, to the fate of beautiful thoughtless little Hetty Sorrel:

> Whenever Adam was strongly convinced of any proposition, it took the form of a principle in his mind: it was knowledge to be acted on . . . Perhaps here lay the secret of

the hardness he had accused himself of: he had too little fellow-feeling with the weakness that errs in spite of foreseen consequences. Without this fellow-feeling, how are we to get enough patience and charity towards our stumbling, failing companions in the long and changeful journey? And there is but one way in which a strong determined soul can learn it—by getting his heart-strings bound round the weak and erring, so that he must share not only the outward consequence of their error, but their inward suffering.   (*Adam Bede*, chapter 19)

George Eliot spoke of her 'experiments in life', the endeavour here being 'to see what our thought and emotion may be capable of' (GEL 6, p. 216), across the asymmetry between the 'strong' and the 'weak', the 'higher' and 'lesser' natures:

It is our habit to say that while the lower nature can never understand the higher, the higher nature commands a complete view of the lower. But I think the higher nature has to learn this comprehension, as we learn the art of vision, by a good deal of hard experience, often with bruises and gashes incurred in taking things up by the wrong end, and fancying our space wider than it is.   (*Adam Bede*, chapter 15)

It is not width or height that teaches but the absorption of those dimensions within the felt narrowness of immediate predicament. In being tied by the 'heart-strings', Adam follows Hetty in her journey of desperate escape from home, not only physically, but step by step imagining her fleeing in trouble just ahead of himself. Adam had begun to learn the vocabulary and syntax of change in the sudden death of that drunkard father whom he had grown to view almost with contempt. The two brothers, Adam and the gentler Seth, look at the body of their father, Thias, in a famous passage we read earlier, in Chapter 3:

The wide-open glazed eyes were grey, like Seth's, and had once looked with mild pride on the boys before whom Thias had lived to hang his head in shame. Seth's chief feeling was awe and distress at this sudden snatching away of his father's soul; but Adam's mind rushed back over the past in a flood of relenting and pity. When death, the great Reconciler, has come, it is never our tenderness that we repent of but our severity.   (*Adam Bede*, chapter 4)

From 'pride' to 'shame' is the forwards direction of story, but the turn of mind rushes backwards from 'severity' to a 'pity' that is consciously too late. Now in the unfolding form of George Eliot's first full-length novel, Adam must go on to learn the whole revised language, its outer course, and its inner meaning, generating itself out of the basic letters and building blocks of the human script, from first to last and back again. He learns not as he had learnt in the past directly from a teacher like Bartle Massey or a master such as Jonathan Burge, who knew more than he, but from Hetty who knows far less, in her plight.

'The first glad moment in our first love is a vision'—and so it had been for Adam Bede coming upon Hetty in the garden, amongst the cherry trees, suddenly blushing. Only, as George Eliot will sharply say later, Hetty's beautiful face had 'a language that transcended her feelings':

> There are faces which nature charges with a meaning and a pathos not belonging to the single human soul that flutters beneath them...eyes that tell of deep love which doubtless has been and is somewhere but not paired with these eyes—perhaps paired with pale eyes that can say nothing.   (*Adam Bede*, chapter 26)

In the same way a national language 'may be instinct with poetry unfelt by the lips that use it'. Truth '*not* belonging' to beauty, true feeling '*unfelt*' inside the biologically inherited expression of it: this is the tough other side of that benignly corrective revision in George Eliot through which, from the *Scenes of Clerical Life* onwards, undistinguished features had been shown to conceal *true* hearts. For all her sophistication, it still shocks and threatens George Eliot when *less* is humanly meant than should be:

> Hetty bending over the red bunches, the level rays piercing the screen of apple-tree boughs, the length of busy garden beyond, his own emotion as he looked at her and believed that she was thinking of him, and that there was no need for them to talk— Adam remembered it all to the last moment of his life.
>
> And Hetty? You know quite well that Adam was mistaken about her. Like many another man, he thought the signs of love for another were signs of love towards himself. When Adam was approaching unseen by her, she was absorbed as usual in thinking and wondering about Arthur's possible return: the sound of any man's footstep would have affected her just in the same way—she would have felt it might be Arthur before she had time to see...   (*Adam Bede*, chapter 20)

To the normal, conventional story-reader this might seem no more than the usual irony of love. Adam loves Hetty; Hetty loves Arthur: it is 'you' the reader who, in familiar collusion with the narrator, 'knows quite well' what the poor simple characters do not. But to George Eliot it is more painfully paradoxical than just that shift of point of view. 'And Hetty?': it palpably hurts to turn from Adam to Hetty, and, worse, from Adam's Hetty to Hetty herself and her own dream of being Arthur's. For the two paragraphs are not just successive but are instead almost distinct worlds, mind-spinningly co-existent at the self-same time, in the one world called reality.

She was really thinking about Arthur. It makes a difference that it is not just the juxtaposition 'And Hetty? Adam was mistaken', which is terrible enough; but 'And Hetty? *You know quite well that* Adam was mistaken', as though this is not simply a book, a closed world of mere fiction, but lives transferred by secret communication, the outside world brought inside this one. 'You', the reader like the novelist, exist for this moment in an otherwise humanly impossible dimension, a place of absolute understanding between and above the interrelated separateness of Adam and Hetty and Arthur, each unknowing of the full extent of their own limitation and of their unconscious solipsism within it. That is how a George Eliot paragraph or two begin to wire up a dense neural network.

And, likewise, it makes another kindred difference that it is not just 'he thought the signs of love for another were signs of love towards himself' but 'Like many another man, he thought signs for another were signs towards himself ', so that the reader is at once imaginatively made protagonist as well as witness as if such simultaneity were possible.

Reality is set bending and spinning by such extra twists and formulations. By chapter 26, when Adam has found out his error, these two paragraphs jackknife into one sentence: 'that while he had been rocking himself in the hope that she would come to love him, she was already loving another': it is the painful inner vibration between 'while' and 'already' that marks what I have called the internal biography of George Eliot's novel-writing. In this way 'And Hetty?' is like the mental shorthand of 'But why always Dorothea?' in *Middlemarch*. It is not just a change of point of view, slow and heavy George Eliot spelling it out. That is only what it seems like when 'you' begin reading too far up, not seeing how far down this originally comes from. 'And Hetty?' 'Always Dorothea?' are really the pre-grammatical expressions of nervous shocks arising out of a sudden sense of difference, of asymmetry, of something more than one. *Not* just what Dorothea thought, *not* as Adam thought it to be—jolting correctives and interrupting reappraisals felt suddenly in the midst of going along. This is the task of the George Eliot reader: to feel on the pulses those origins of raw thought lodged within the complexity of intelligence that evolves out of them—visceral, like first life under a sophisticated second.

Yet within a moment, thinking becomes a complex layered activity again—'Adam remembered it all to the last moment of his life'. Adam is wrong about Hetty as the outcome of the story will show, but George Eliot is concerned with something deeper than irony. From another dimension beside the linear and serial, he never forgets the rightness in the moment of thinking himself beloved. Adam remembered as a vision what it would have been all too easy for him to let story cancel and forget as though made non-existent by what followed from it. Experience is stranger than that, story inflected through character, like light through a prism.

This refraction happens most powerfully when a George Eliot novel has gathered so much rich overlapping human matter as to begin to go wild, beyond the boundaries of the known even whilst it seems still sited within them. Then, as she told Johnny Cross, a 'not-herself' took dramatic possession of her best writing and she felt her own personality to be no more than an instrument through which this spirit was acting. Again, this is a step further on from *Scenes of Clerical Life*. In 'Janet's Repentance', Tryan knows there is no simple control or solution. Even after Janet turns away from drink and despair, he knows there is no complete conversion, 'that the hopefulness of the morning would be followed by a return of depression and discouragement'. This is the chastened thinking too of the realist novel. After her initial improvement, Tryan still has forebodings as to the 'unseen elements' within human sums that for better or worse may frustrate even 'the wisest calculations' (chapter 22). But in that uncertainty, Tryan has prayer and can call these unseen or unknown elements the Divine Will: this, for him, 'filled up the margin of ignorance which surrounds all our knowledge with the feelings of trust and resignation'. What George Eliot has, instead, is no more and no less than a profound sense of the margin of ignorance surrounding our apparently secure and familiar knowledge, and of how quickly and perilously the force field changes to reveal that ignorance. 'I know,' says Adam in another passage from chapter 17 of *Adam Bede* singled out by reviewer Collins, 'there's a deal in a man's inward life as you can't measure by the square'

> and say 'do this and that'll follow', and 'do that and this'll follow'. There's things go on in the soul, and times when feelings come into you like a rushing mighty wind, as the Scripture says, and part your life in two a'most, so as you look back on yourself as if you was somebody else.

It is like the moment when, at the sudden death of his father, Adam's mind rushed back over the past 'in a flood of relenting and pity'. Describing how she first came to write fiction, George Eliot said that, as the years had passed:

> I lost any hope that I should ever be able to write a novel, just as I desponded about everything else in my future life. I always thought I was deficient in dramatic power...
>
> (GEL 2, p. 406)

Lewes too, even in his encouragement, 'distrusted—indeed disbelieved in, my possession of any dramatic power' (GEL 2, p. 407). She was a thinker. But even more than the *Scenes*, it was *Adam Bede* that marked the discovery of dramatic force not as merely sensational plot but psychologically erupting into the lives of the characters themselves: 'When feelings come into you like a rushing mighty wind...'

For nearly two hundred pages, comprising the long slow first book of *Adam Bede*, the little village of Hayslope in Loamshire—probably based on Ellastone, Staffordshire, where Robert Evans lived in his youth—seems wholly ordered, everyone knowing their place. But, as reviewer Collins recognized, the whole field, terrain, and climate of the novel is changed—and changed dramatically—by the end of the third and the beginning of the fourth volume, with chapter 27 entitled 'Crisis'. While they were in Munich in April 1858 Lewes had urged Marian to make Adam Bede himself less passive. For all her uncertainties, it is remarkable that she could almost always write when they were away from home. Her response was the fight with Arthur in 'Crisis', which, like a flooding emotional rush of music, came to her 'as a *necessity* one night at the Munich opera when I was listening to *William Tell*' (GEL 2, p. 504). It is like what Adam had called the rushing mighty wind, driving on all that was to come, when in chapter 27 he sees at a distance Arthur kissing Hetty. But what is remarkable is that the subtler shock—the all-changing realization that reveals unrecognized ignorance and underlying chaos—is not Adam's. For this is the subtlety that George Eliot wrought upon Lewes's suggestion: it is Arthur's, at an inner psychological level deeper than the plot in which it is nonetheless simultaneously contained.

Avoidance is what naturally comes first to Arthur, in the effort to keep the world small and safe. He tries to ward off the objective reality of the disclosure, the affair having gone far beyond kissing. Swiftly, mentally, he shifts to and fro between the lost opportunity for openness, the horror of being caught, and the possibility of still getting away with it, almost as if deciding who now he must become. Feeling 'a startled uncertainty how far Adam was speaking from knowledge and how far from mere inference', Arthur seeks to measure and contain the consequence by how much Adam knows and how much Adam will make of what he does know, personalizing the issue: 'He was going to make a serious business of this affair. Confound the fellow!' In the midst of Adam's rebuke, 'Arthur had a sudden relief when Adam was speaking; he perceived that Adam had no positive knowledge of the past and that there was no irrevocable damage done . . .'—the relief of a greedy instinct for life at the back of his mind seeking a wriggling escape route. It is as though avoidance were survival itself—but then the screen erected around the safe ground gives way, when Arthur in turn has a sudden understanding of just why this dalliance of his means so much more to Adam.

Then it is that there is most reluctantly created for him here something greater than survival—morality itself instead, made dramatically real not just as a rule but as an experience, a realized form of being. The proud young squire has initially to hear his social inferior say: 'And you've been kissing her, and meaning nothing, have you? And I never kissed her i' my life, but I'd ha' worked hard for years for the right to . . .' And then the social distinction drops away, and the world changes:

> The discovery that Adam loved Hetty was a shock which made him for the moment see himself in the light of Adam's indignation, and regard Adam's suffering as not merely a consequence, but an element of his error. The words of hatred and contempt—the first he had ever heard in his life—seemed like scorching missiles that were making ineffaceable scars on him. All screening self-excuse, which rarely

falls quite away while others respect us, forsook him for an instant, and he stood face to face with the first great irrevocable evil he had ever committed.   (*Adam Bede*, chapter 27)

It is not only Adam, the solid and undeflectable person that Arthur stands 'face to face with'. It is also in that instant the more impersonal flash of truth that confronts him, the invisible moral element that is for once embodied and made real in the midst of self-exculpation and self-deception. Breaking through the screen of protective human hiding, here is suddenly, even within this reversal and changed relativism of point of view, the presence of the unavoidably absolute, the ultimate and irreversible reality of a life: a young man is 'face to face', for the 'first' time, with the 'ineffaceable' and 'irrevocable'. For that moment Adam himself is not merely outside Arthur in external consequence but 'an element' within what he now sees through Adam's eyes. 'He was only twenty one,' adds George Eliot, in an implicit mixture of horror and mitigation: almost up until this very moment Arthur 'had proudly thought that no man should ever be able to reproach him justly.' But the promised years ahead have disappeared in the acts of moments.

And yet even the feeling of the unbearably irrevocable is, paradoxically enough, itself transient. It shifts off into something else for Arthur almost at the point of his having it—will he now have to fight Adam?—just as it had done earlier, when he failed to confess his sexual temptations to the Reverend Irwine. With Irwine, 'the mere fact that he was in the presence of an intimate friend who had not the slightest notion that he had had any such serious internal struggle as he came to confide, rather shook his own belief in the seriousness of the struggle' (chapter 16, 'Links'). Then Arthur had made it so that there was no one to tell him otherwise, no words or signs outside to prevent him continuing his seduction: this is where the novel comes in instead of normal life's evasions, with George Eliot as that missing figure who unrelentingly believes in the seriousness of the struggle and the necessity for fully facing it. Only now in the person of Adam in the chapter 'Crisis' there is someone close by Arthur who does know, at least some of it. Such moments are what one thinker has called 'miniature death-of-God experiences' when what used to be called God's own truth is evaded through the understandable and almost irresistible instinct for self-preservation; or, if it is momentarily realized, still unconsummated by the sustained finality of external judgement.[3] Morality takes the form here not of convention but of sheer terror in the face of the reality of consequence inflicted on another. 'He was only twenty-one.'

'And Hetty?' She was 17, another young person who would not confide in anyone else, and thus was dangerous to herself from the very beginning of the affair:

She thought of nothing that was present. She only saw something that was possible: Mr Arthur Donnithorne coming to meet her again... That was the foreground of

Fig. 13. Elizabeth Evans, Methodist aunt (1766–1849), source of Hetty's story and model for Dinah Morris in *Adam Bede* (courtesy of Coventry History Centre).

Hetty's picture; behind it lay a bright hazy something—days that were not to be as the other days of her life had been.... Hetty had never read a novel: if she had ever seen one, I think the words would have been too hard for her: how then could she find a shape for her expectations? They were as formless as the sweet languid odours of the garden... (*Adam Bede*, chapter 13)

In (what another chapter calls) 'Hetty's World' she cannot really *think*, as Marian Evans at least could still think even amidst sexual entanglement. Hetty has nothing by which to hold onto or contain her experience. It is George Eliot who provides the background consciousness to her picture in the painting of it. This is what this novel and this novelist can do with a character who herself would never be able to read this work: use mentality of the higher order to imagine someone almost without such mentality; create, within form, the very experience of formlessness and chaos; the work almost overwhelming itself from below and within. The so-called lower nature here begins to take over the knowingly higher by the sheer force of its reality in predicament. This is the great challenging and disturbing loop for the novelist in the strangely demanding twists and turns of the apparently common realist novel— to employ powerful mental faculties paradoxically in the creation of a character who precisely lacks them, yet whose lack produces more revelation for the novelist than adequacy could achieve. Or again, as it is when George Eliot writes, 'Hetty had never read a novel:... how then could she find a shape for her expectations?'—the world is turned inside out until, within the novel, fiction stands for a reality its characters can hardly bear. These turnarounds are not unlike the sheer surprise that began when a non-believer was able to write a great Methodist sermon in the person of Dinah, as George Eliot did in chapter 2 of the novel. But they give the lie to what has been more or less said of realism in the schools of theory for the last forty years—that nineteenth-century realism is conservatively bland and unimaginative, bourgeois and parochial, not truly art at all. As we have heard George Henry Lewes insist, 'Fairies and demons are not created by a more vigorous effort of imagination than milk maids and poachers.'

For Hetty, the incapacity to believe what is happening to her begins to take her to an inconceivable world of intolerable reality:

Reasons why he could not marry her had no existence for her mind; how could she believe in any misery that could come to her from the fulfilment of all she had been longing for and dreaming of? She had not the ideas that could make up the notion of that misery. (*Adam Bede*, chapter 31)

That is the most fundamental use of the word '*ideas*' that an intellectual could ever have—imagining the origin of and the need for such things long before they ever become high-flown or philosophic. To live is to have to think, in some form or other, that the novel can show even in the realms of the implicit or unconscious. It is like a further development of George Eliot's interest in Tina in *Scenes of Clerical Life*. For all her secret relationship with her guardian's nephew, she has now to meet Captain Wybrow's beautiful fiancée and hear how pleased everyone is at the forthcoming betrothal:

> Mr Bates's words about Sir Christopher's joy, Miss Asher's beauty, and the nearness of the wedding, had come upon her like the pressure of a cold hand, rousing her from confused dozing to a perception of hard, familiar realities. It is so with emotional natures, whose thoughts are no more than the fleeting shadows cast by feeling: to them words are facts and, even when known to be false, have a mastery over their smiles and tears.   ('Mr Gilfil's Love-Story', chapter 7)

She has to hear people saying how lovely is the bride-to-be, how happy the family must be, how the two make a beautiful couple. Tina can barely contain her feelings; she cannot stop and hold them sufficiently to make thoughts out of them. She acts and reacts impulsively, in discharge of her powerful feelings, precisely because she cannot think.

Instead of ideas then, Hetty must make desperate movements. She has not learnt, like Arthur, to find a way round things: for her as for a child 'there is no despair so absolute as that which comes with the first moments of our first great sorrow' (*Adam Bede*, chapter 31), and unlike Marian Evans there is no second life of adult adjustment. From the moment that Arthur failed to confess his temptation to Irwine, and, through thought, hold back the sexual impulse within his own person, there was nothing and no one to stop the formation of a chain reaction in the novel. It is the law of consequence, turning individuals into nothing more than parts of circumstance, as Irwine had described to Arthur even at the moment Arthur was trying to evade it:

> 'But surely you don't think a man who struggles against a temptation into which he falls at last as bad as the man who never struggles at all?'
>
> 'No, certainly. I pity him in proportion to his struggles, for they foreshadow the inward suffering which is the worst form of Nemesis. Consequences are unpitying. Our deeds carry their terrible consequences...consequences that are hardly ever confined to ourselves....But I never knew you so inclined for moral discussion, Arthur? Is it some danger of your own that you are considering in this philosophical, general way?'
>
> (*Adam Bede*, chapter 16)

To which Arthur replied 'as indifferently as he could': 'Oh no, no danger.' From that moment forces are passed on, transmitted, conducted in a series of reactions and knock-on effects that are like chemical and physical experiments in the world—until it is Adam, not Arthur, who has to return to Irwine to tell him all that has happened, as though Arthur had handed it on to him as he has also to her: Hetty pregnant, Hetty running away in vain search of Arthur, Hetty arrested for child-murder. Adam waits for his appointment to see the Vicar, with all this on his mind:

> Adam sat looking at the clock: the minute-hand was hurrying along the last five minutes to ten, with a loud hard indifferent tick, and Adam watched the movement and listened to the sound as if he had had some reason for doing so. In our times of bitter suffering, there are almost always these pauses, when our consciousness is benumbed to everything but some trivial perception or sensation. It is as if semi-idiocy came to give us rest from the memory and the dread which refuse to leave us in our sleep. (*Adam Bede*, chapter 39)

This is when George Eliot knows she has done what she meant to do as a realist novelist—released a cumulative reality, a definite something, an overwhelming human content which is irreducibly more than anyone can fully control or name, know or bear—or, even so, quite avoid. It is the moment seemingly close to that terribly increased percentage register of reality which in *Middlemarch* is called hearing the grass grow or the squirrel's heart beat, that roar on the other side of silence to which humans have to try to close their ears: 'Why do you suppose we are all set or most of us for 5 percent, with a few people set to 6 percent and even fewer to 7 or 8? ... Do you think the reason might be that whoever sets us poor little machines knows very well how much we can stand. Because *I* can't stand it, and I try hard not to think about what I know ...'[4]

But it is, above all, through the unthinking Hetty that the chain reaction is driven on beyond the reluctance of thought itself. George Eliot said that the opening of the fifth book—Hetty's 'Journey in Hope', followed by her 'Journey in Despair'—'was, I think, written more rapidly than the rest of the book, and was left without the slightest alteration of the first draught' (GEL 2, p. 504). These are some of the most terrifying chapters George Eliot ever wrote. Books 5 and 6, comprising the whole of the third and final volume of the three-volume novel, were themselves written 'in six weeks, even with headachy interruptions, because it was written under a stress of emotions' (GEL 3, p. 249). The novelist found herself in a new gathering place of inspiration, a necessity of the 'not-herself' beyond mere choice. And it is Hetty's instinctive movements in despair that force the novel and the novelist to reach whirlwind power. For these movements in the wild countryside are equivalent to Arthur's to-and-fro motions of trapped mind in the face of unbearable truth, only now enacted at a more sheerly physical level. Since she cannot think separately of her life within her life, the physical and the psychological are made terrifying one for Hetty, without her knowing it. Pregnant and about to give birth, she runs away in search of Arthur only to discover that his regiment has already departed for Ireland. This is when the world of ordinary purpose abruptly ceases. For this is when she reaches a place, mental within the physical, which George Eliot fearfully calls 'the borders of a new wilderness where no goal lay before her' (chapter 37, 'The Journey in Despair'). She no longer has anywhere to go: she cannot get to Arthur, she cannot go home in disgrace.

As the force of her situation begins to overcome her, it is her body that is carrying out her thoughts—in her 'objectless wandering' to and fro: 'without knowing what she should do with her life, she craved the means of living as long as possible'. Even the petty vanity of the earlier chapters is transformed in the new land in which she finds herself. In the midst of a despair close to suicide, unexpectedly,

> the very consciousness of her own limbs was a delight to her: she turned up her sleeves, and kissed her arms with the passionate love of life.

Tolstoy loved *Adam Bede*: there is no more Tolstoyan moment than that wholly unexpected thinking within the flesh. What before in her bedroom looking-glass had been vanity in her has become, in this stranger world, a form of survival. And with Hetty, George Eliot herself turns from the clever plain woman who despised foolish pretty girls to one who has also entered a very specifically different reality:

> [Hetty] felt a strange contradictory wretchedness and exultation; wretchedness that she did not dare to face death; exultation, that she was still in life—that she might yet know light and warmth again. She walked backwards and forwards . . .

A 'wild woman' now, she is 'clinging to life only as the hunted wounded brute clings to it', walking back and forth desperately in the dark, turning towards home but knowing she cannot return. So it is until, 'driven to and fro between two equal terrors'—of living like this or of finishing herself—she can momentarily fall asleep exhausted in the temporary 'relief of unconsciousness'.

'She must wander on and on, and wait for a lower depth of despair to give her courage'—the courage of suicide. In this, one of George Eliot's greatest narrative sentences, it is that terrifying word 'wait' which marks the shift into a wholly different world of existence: it is the only word that is *like* thinking, if not in stopping physical movement at least in trying to work at a different level within it. This—an abnormal existence with nothing to look forward to but the death to which it still cannot quite give way—is paradoxically her *life* now. What should have been a temporary emotion—panic, despair, the need of someone to turn to—has become a condition, only stable enough to require her to live trapped in her instability, for as long as it lasts. Realism here means unbearable realization, the destroying of any protective function of thought by the commitment of an intellectual to follow in imagination a character almost incapable of thinking. It is like the moment in Tolstoy's *Death of Ivan Ilyich* when death is no longer a cliché to the dying Ivan but a reality, momentarily breaking the very thought that tries to hold onto it. Or as it is when, as George Eliot puts it, 'we feel the truth of a commonplace...when the commonplace "We must all die" transforms itself suddenly into the acute conscious-ness "I must die—and soon"' (*Middlemarch*, chapter 42).

It is life on the *other* side of the commonplace. 'Could she be the same Hetty that used to make up the butter in the dairy?' (*Adam Bede*, chapter 37); 'Are you inclined to ask whether this can be the same Arthur who, two months ago...?' (chapter 29). 'The same, I assure you; only under different conditions. Our deeds determine us, as much as we determine our deeds' (chapter 29). And then there is Adam himself on the eve of Hetty's trial for murdering her new-born baby: 'You would hardly have known it was Adam without being told. His face had got thinner this last week: he had the sunken eyes, the neglected beard of a man just risen from a sick-bed' (chapter 41); 'in the broad sunlight of the great hall, among the sleek shaven faces of other men, the marks of suffering in his face were startling even to Mr. Irwine...' (chapter 43). On this other side of normal life, the art of George Eliot no longer set out Arthur and Hetty and Adam in causal storyline within a settled little provincial location, but saw them also begin to co-exist in the different stranger shape of a non-linear matrix, operating beneath the movements of ordinary time. The com-bined pressure going on within this interlocking force field produces thinking which bends in this manner, as Adam looks at Hetty in the dock, awaiting the verdict:

> Adam had not dared to look at her in the first moments, but at last, when the attention of the court was withdrawn by the proceedings, he turned his face towards her with a resolution not to shrink.
>
> Why did they say she was so changed? In the corpse we love, it is the *likeness* we see—it is the likeness, which makes itself felt the more keenly because something else *was*, and *is not*. There they were—the sweet face and neck, with the dark tendrils of hair, the long dark lashes, the rounded cheek and the pouting lips: pale and thin—yes—but like Hetty, and only Hetty. Others thought she looked as if some demon had cast a blighting glance upon her, withered up the woman's soul in her, and left only a hard despairing obstinacy. But the mother's yearning, that completest type of the life in another life which is the essence of real human love, feels the presence of the cherished child even in the debased, degraded man; and to Adam, this pale hard-looking culprit was the Hetty who had smiled at him in the garden under the apple-tree boughs—she was that Hetty's corpse, which he had trembled to look at the first time, and then was unwilling to turn away his eyes from.   (*Adam Bede*, chapter 43)

A word such as 'corpse', the emphasis on the likeness rather than the change, the association of Adam's love to a mother's love—as we have seen, these are measures of how far into the world of a stranger wildness this novel has had to go. So much of the imagination of Hetty's predicament comes out of Marian Evans's own terrible cry, 'What shall I be without my father?' But Hetty had neither father nor mother, nor anything like her creator's intelligence. Only, Marian Evans knew in herself the fears of a wild life, of a sudden sexual chaos. Adam was her father, Robert Evans, made first into Hetty's lover, then transmuted here for the moment into Hetty's mother: such is the force of the imaginative changes. And operating within them is the characteristic George Eliot set of complex layered movements: backwards to the memory of Hetty in the garden which, it had been said, 'Adam remembered ... to the last moment of his life' and then forward again to that of Hetty's loss and ruin; from trembling to look at her to an equal unwillingness to turn away—and all in a single sentence of mind.

It is Adam's final resolve to bring himself to look at Hetty which completes the creation of this terrible matrix between this young woman and her two lovers. What George Eliot most sought for in her whole work was the equivalent of that life-wrenching turn from Adam's view of Hetty to the reality of Hetty herself; from Arthur's self-deceiving denials to his realized imagination of himself through the eyes of Adam; from Adam's pained aversion in the courtroom to his straight look at that Hetty who had once smiled at him in the garden, secretly thinking of Arthur without his knowing it—that shift across psychological boundaries of mind and situation which George Eliot also went through within her characters. It was the great reality-changing turn to 'the other side of silence', to the 'imagination of the other side of death, gazing backward', or to 'that new terrible life on the other side of the deed' (*Middlemarch*, chapters 20, 42; *Daniel Deronda*, chapter 62). So it is that Arthur finds himself in 'that border-land of sin, where he will be perpetually harassed by assaults from the other side of the boundary' (*Adam Bede*, chapter 12), or his equivalent, Godfrey Cass in *Silas Marner*, can 'imagine no future for himself on the other side of confession' (chapter 3). But it is here, on this other side, that morality and goodness must find a place or not truly at all. That is why Adam's love, like that of Silas Marner for the golden-haired little girl who replaces his material gold, is called extraordinarily a *mother's* love, by dint of the strangeness of the world it now has to function within, and for all the entanglements of Eros. All love, as it is said in a modern novel significantly entitled *The Other Side of You*, is basically the *same* thing, only changing its appearance as it enters the terms of reality:

> It simply moulds itself to the person—obviously you don't show love to a babe in arms the way you do to your mistress. But in essence it's the same.[5]

And that is how even morality becomes strange and wild in the later movements of *Adam Bede*.

Consider what something that in the ordinary world might pass for 'forgiveness' looks like in this transformed setting. In chapter 27 Adam strikes Arthur, only immediately to find himself thinking what was the good of it: 'What man of us in the first moments of a sharp agony,' says George Eliot, like a good reader of Spinoza, 'could ever feel that the fellow-man who has been the medium of inflicting it, did not mean to hurt us? In our instinctive rebellion against pain we are children again...' But then Adam must become adult again. For all the blows aimed at his supposed enemy and betrayer, 'He had not rescued Hetty, not changed the past, there it was, just as it had been.' By chapter 48, at the end of the fifth book, Adam is on the other side of this discovery, and everything has come to pass for Hetty, culminating in her trial, conviction, and last-minute pardon. It is then that there is 'Another Meeting in the Wood' to match the meeting with Arthur in chapter 27. In that strange reunion Adam is long past the point of trying to make Arthur suffer something of what he himself has suffered: 'Adam could not help being moved: it was impossible for him not to feel that this was the voice of the honest, warm-hearted Arthur whom he had loved and been proud of in the old days; but nearer memories would not be thrust away' (chapter 48). 'Impossible not to' is crucial to the involuntary power of human feeling in George Eliot. Yet 'impossible not to' is followed equally by 'but... not'—'but nearer memories would not be thrust away'—in the further work of syntax responding to a demandingly complex world that is neither utterly lost nor quite redeemed. Hetty herself is still transported even though Arthur has managed to get her a last-minute reprieve from hanging for child-murder.

But reviewer Collins above all chose the following long, vital passage which, as Edith Simcox later noted in her memorial article in *The Nineteenth Century*, made George Eliot grateful for this reviewer's 'appreciation of the finer and less obvious shades of meaning' in her novel. In the sixth and final book, more than eighteen months after the trial, Adam is now more master of himself, delighting again in his work and even beginning to love Dinah, and yet, as we have seen near the end of Chapter 6, he

had not outlived his sorrow—had not felt it slip from him as a temporary burthen, and leave him the same man again. Do any of us? God forbid. It would be a poor result of all our anguish and our wrestling if we won nothing but our old selves at the end of it—if we could return to the same blind loves, the same self-confident blame, the same light thoughts of human suffering, the same frivolous gossip over blighted human lives, the same feeble sense of that Unknown towards which we have sent forth irrepressible cries in our loneliness. Let us rather be thankful that our sorrow lives in us as an indestructible force, only changing its form, as forces do, and passing from pain into sympathy—the one poor word which includes all our best insight and our best love. Not that this transformation of pain into sympathy had completely taken place in Adam yet. There was still a great remnant of pain, and this he felt would subsist as long as her pain was not a memory, but an existing thing, which he must think of as renewed with the light of every new morning. But we get accustomed to mental as well as bodily pain, without, for all that, losing our sensibility to it. It becomes a habit of our lives, and we cease to imagine a condition of perfect ease as possible for us. Desire is chastened into submission, and we are contented with our day when we have been able to bear our grief in silence and act as if we were not suffering. For it is at such periods that the sense of our lives having visible and invisible relations, beyond any of which either our present or prospective self is the centre, grows like a muscle that we are obliged to lean on and exert.   (*Adam Bede*, chapter 50)

Not 'the same', six times. This is how Adam can live, as it were on both sides of the thought—not like Arthur or like Casaubon, each in their different ways seeking to hide from the external reality of word or thought or memory. In Adam there is transformation *and* remnant, a becoming accustomed but not insensible, a memory within and the living subject of it still living independently outside it. In recognition of these double thoughts, Edith Simcox, creative reader as she was, put together chapter 50 with this from chapter 54:

> That is a base and selfish, even a blasphemous, spirit which rejoices and is thankful over the past evil that has blighted or crushed another, because it has been made a source of unforeseen good to ourselves. Adam could never cease to mourn over that mystery of human sorrow which had been brought so close to him; he could never thank God for another's misery. . . . But it is not ignoble to feel that the fuller life which a sad experience has brought us is worth our own personal share of pain. Surely it is not possible to feel otherwise, any more than it would be possible for a man with cataract to regret the painful process by which his dim blurred sight of men as trees walking had been exchanged for clear outline and effulgent day. The growth of higher feeling within us is like the growth of faculty, bringing with it a sense of added strength. We can no more wish to return to a narrower sympathy than a painter or a musician can wish to return to his cruder manner, or a philosopher to his less complete formula.

This moral growth, going deeper and further than the word 'moral' normally implies, is like an art in life that cannot be *un*known, that cannot go back to its first crude style, but is as an informal philosophy building up within the individual:

> Let our habitual talk give morals their full meaning as the conduct which, in every human relation, would follow from the fullest knowledge and the fullest sympathy—a meaning perpetually corrected and enriched by a more thorough appreciation of dependence in things, and a finer sensibility to both physical and spiritual fact.
>
> (*Impressions of Theophrastus Such*, chapter 16)

But it is for all that an ambivalent growth, almost in two minds within itself. For it says on one side 'never cease to mourn, never thank God for another's misery', like the earlier 'not outlived his sorrow, not felt it slip from him'; but also on the other it is like 'impossible not to' before—'not ignoble to feel', 'not possible to feel otherwise' 'can no more wish to return'. The painful negative force of this experience is not denied but it is repositioned and used, again in careful double negatives on the other side of what would otherwise be too simply and fatuously positive. These are the linguistic markers of how feeling becomes embedded into a complex configuration of experience; how this complex experience itself creates a new 'faculty', like 'a muscle that we are obliged to lean on and exert'; and how this faculty is related to the perceived emergence of a new field and centre of understanding. It was out of those new faculties, created by the serious value of trouble, that George Eliot herself began to be formed on the other side of Marian Evans. But the Marian Evans who was still in her was part of what she kept plunging raw into the imagined experience of her characters, as she moved dialectically in double and redoubled thought between her strengths and weaknesses: 'Because a real artist knows the other side of himself better than the side he's in at the time. You don't paint as you are; you paint as you're not. But you only know what you're not through knowing what you are.'[6] Salley Vickers's *The Other Side of You* (p. 149, part 2, chapter 9) also includes a powerful reference to the words of Thornton Wilder from his preface to *The Angel That Troubled the Waters* (1928):

> An artist is one who knows he is failing in living and feels his remorse by making something fair, and a layman is one who suspects he is failing in living but is consoled by his successes in golf, or in love, or in business.

Deliberately or not, Marian Evans had kept herself largely unconsoled by normal life. But the great representative layman inside the novel, Adam Bede, does not simply congratulate himself on his good fortune. In his own scrupulous way, he has indeed the undeniable consolation of marrying Dinah in his second life, while in a way that also makes him worthy of doing so, never forgetting Hetty from his first.

For Edith Simcox, George Eliot created herself out of the inadequacies of a normal life in order to be able to think and say this sentence which she italicized in her memorial essay: 'It is at such periods that the sense of our lives having visible and invisible relations, beyond any of which either our present or prospective self is the centre, grows like a muscle that we are obliged to lean on and exert.' These are the invisible as well as visible relations I have been tracing in the matrix of *Adam Bede*, a force field of interrelations operative at differing levels whose complexity goes beyond those 'poor words' of connection such as sympathy or society. As was said in relation to Adam at Arthur's moment of unbearable realization, these people exist not just in straightforward external 'consequence' of each other's actions but are become 'elements' of feeling and thought pleated within each other. They are transferred lives held in an inter-responsibility too complex to be easily disentangled.

So it is when Adam cannot initially bring himself to witness the trial and can only bear to hear news brought via his usually rough-tongued aged schoolmaster Bartle Massey: then it looks as though that old misogynist is of all people going to have to take Adam's place in standing by Hetty, even for Adam's sake. Says Bartle Massey of the moment when Hetty's stricken uncle, Martin Poyser, is called to testify: 'But when she heard her uncle's name, there seemed to go a shiver right through her, and when they told him to look at her, she hung her head down, and cowered, and hid her face in her hands' (*Adam Bede*, chapter 42). It is as though Poyser is become her repressed nervous system even as he himself trembles on his own account: 'And the counsellors,—who look as hard as nails mostly,—I saw, spared him as much as they could.' There's one man ought to be there, says Adam bitterly in reply, meaning Arthur, then knowing a second later that it is himself who must now stand up for her.

In such an impossibly difficult world it almost does not matter, finally, what precisely was the individual intention, whose exactly was the initial fault—as, how much in retrospect seems to have become sin more than mistake in Arthur; or just what Hetty did or did not do to the baby in abandoning it. There is never a single cause, never an easy and clear separation of good and bad, never a guarantee against an apparently little matter growing large in unforeseen directions. Realism, I have argued, means the novel created as a site for a sense of reality more ultimate than control or explanation. That is how and why such realization is an art, because almost impossible to bear or to avoid in life itself. Hetty, Arthur, Adam know this, when the normal percentage of realization in them has risen even a very few points on the scale.

Force Fields

What this creation of a realist, indeed almost super-realist, novel means is what, in the work of another of the admirers of George Eliot, is called psychological field theory.

William James, psychologist and philosopher, was the older brother of the novelist Henry James, and it was Henry who directed William to *Adam Bede* in the first flush of his enthusiasm for it, followed by *The Mill on the Floss*. William first read *Middlemarch* in 1872 as part of his recovery from depression, praising its intellectual power and calling it 'the biggest novel ever written'.[7] The largeness of its range and vision of life was vital to him, contributing to his sense of there always being what he was to call, for shorthand, 'a more' to existence. It meant an 'unclassified residuum', the anomalous, unadmitted, often wild material that is not part of the accepted system but is the sign of reality as always in excess of whatever we say it is.[8] In the face of that indiscriminate and disordered richness of existence, human beings have to be selective, have to create partial fields of conscious attention, and then switch and alternate between them. It was like the description of the pier-glass in the candle in *Middlemarch* (chapter 27). The glass is scratched randomly in all directions, but put a lighted candle as a centre of illumination 'and lo! the scratches seem to arrange themselves in a fine series of concentric circles round that little sun.... These things are a parable. The scratches are events, and the candle is the egoism of any person.'

James's field theory derived from Faraday's work on electromagnetic force fields, but there were two figures central to the George Eliot circle to whom he made acknowledgement for its development: to George Henry Lewes himself and his work on emergence; and to her young acolyte F. W. H. Myers on the hidden power of subliminal consciousness.[9] That is James's importance in this story: he was like a descendent of Lewes.

In *Varieties of Religious Experience* lecture 9, the shifting of centres of personal energy within an individual are signalled by the sudden lighting-up of new hot spots of awakened emotion. These are, says James, quite common alterations of character, as when we pass from one aim to another, or one system founded by a predominant and recurrent interest to a momentary doubt about it or distraction from it, or simply shift from one subject of attention to another object of alternative excitement. But, James adds, these ordinary oscillations are no less than minor versions of larger dynamic experiences: of 'conversion', in the radical change from one state of mind to another in a time of crisis; or, alternatively, of a 'divided self' split between opposing centres of energy, neither of which can fully or long establish itself without the counter-attraction of the other. The large changes of mind are of the same basic physics as the small ones, and the latter can very quickly become the former.

In lecture 10 James goes on to describe these states as more or less temporary psychological worlds, which he calls 'mental fields', each with its habitual 'centre of interest' around which 'the objects of which we are less and less attentively conscious fade to a margin so faint that its limits are unassignable'.[10] There is in every field a 'centre', and then a 'fringe', and past that indefinite bound or margin always a sense or feel of a subconscious '*more*' beyond it.[11] The area called the margin 'lies around us like a "magnetic field", inside of which our centre of energy turns like a compass-needle, as the present place of consciousness alters into its successor'. What is more, 'our whole past store of memories floats beyond this margin, ready at a touch to come in', including a felt sense of other 'residual powers, impulses, and knowledges' lying subconsciously in wait for focal activation (*Varieties*, p. 232):

> Some fields are narrow fields and some are wide fields. Usually when we have a wide field we rejoice, for we then see masses of truth together, and often get glimpses of relations which we divine rather than see... At other times, of drowsiness, illness, or fatigue, our fields may narrow almost to a point, and we find ourselves correspondingly oppressed and contracted.
>
> Different individuals present constitutional differences in this matter of width of field.

It is great organizing minds, added F. W. H. Myers, that have vast fields of mental vision, a strong vocational purpose creating from its centre a wide range of diverse interest. George Eliot's was such a mind, and hers was increasingly the widest of fields, developed from *Adam Bede* onwards. For in that development one of her main methods was to see what happened when the narrow had to experience more than it could normally contain. 'More' is what experience always is to George Eliot, just as 'narrow' is what human beings, for the most part, still are.

In his *Physiology of Common Life*, published in the same year as *Adam Bede*, Lewes quoted the psychologist Alexander Bain on James Watt and his singled-minded search to invent the steam engine: 'His intellect and observation were kept at work, going out in all directions for the chance of some suitable combination rising to view; his sense of the precise thing to be done was the constant touchstone of every contrivance occurring to him, and all the successive suggestions were arrested, or repelled, as they came near to, or disagreed with, this touchstone' (vol. 2, pp. 153–4). Watt created a specific field of endeavour. More generally, regarding the range of attention and focus in any individual, Lewes was to conclude, 'It may be likened to the expansion and restriction of the visual field.'[12] What was crucial to its formation was a touchstone or centre becoming the focal hub of a reconfigured nervous system, the organizing principle of a created force field, drawing together the steel filings of life as by magnetic purpose.

But in the novels of George Eliot what was required was, again, always *more* than what was literally sufficient or easily found, in that now total dedication of a life which left the rest of it almost a husk. This involved that realization of 'relations, *beyond* any of which either our present or prospective self is the centre'. And so from *Adam Bede* to *Middlemarch* she created multiple centres, in alternation between differing egos. But that extended field included capacity for movement not only between these differing magnetic centres but also across apparently set lines and conventional boundaries. Hence the complicated interrelations of Adam and Arthur and Hetty across paragraphs, chapters, and books; hence ultimately in *Middlemarch* the simultaneous two-way charge of even a single stunning little sentence concerning Casaubon and Dorothea and their first honeymoon quarrel: '*Both* were shocked at their *mutual* situation' (chapter 20). For this was the setting up of the super brain and the super mind of George Eliot. Her constant complaints about headache in the midst of writing throughout her working life were a mournful side-effect of the need she had furiously to overload her brain in order to become that multi-centred writer on every page. It was like Joseph Conrad in a letter to Edward Garnett (20 March 1898) saying he could feel his brain.

A novelist in the tradition which George Eliot helped to establish is the human being perhaps most primed to let in human matter not easy to fit into normal categories. But ordinary people, said William James, have no such magnificently inclusive view: 'they stumble along, feeling their way, as it were, from point to point and often stop entirely' (*Varieties*, p. 232). For anyone aspiring to be a thinker, James concludes, truth is elusively at any moment like the visible area round a man walking in a fog, or like what George Eliot calls 'the wall of dark seen by small fishes' eyes that pierce a span in the wide Ocean'.[13]

These lines describing life as like swimming through a dark muddy ocean are taken from 'The Spanish Gypsy'. Suddenly in that fog or ocean the *more* comes into the field, almost to its breaking point, forcing in extremis a merely literal language of experience to go beyond its set terms. As Adam says to Dinah,

> 'for it seems to me it's the same with love and happiness as with sorrow—the more we know of it the better we can feel what other people's lives are or might be, and so we shall only be more tender to 'em, and wishful to help 'em. The more knowledge a man has the better he'll do 's work; and feeling's a sort o' knowledge.' (*Adam Bede*, chapter 52).

'The more' and 'the better'.

Marian Evans had believed in the sheer 'quantity of existence' as offering new combinations of vitality just when the great subjects of thought seemed all exhausted (GEL 1, pp. 251, 247). It was a phrase she took from the writings of the essayist John Foster: '*Quantity of existence* may perhaps be a proper phrase for that, the less or more of which causes the less or more of our interest in the individuals around us. The person who gives us most the idea of ample being, interests us the most.'[14] In human beings in this area, sheer quantity could eventually shake down into a change in quality itself. But that 'more' depended not only on the number of emotional experiences but also on the responsive development of an increased capacity for them, extending the fullness of the field of consciousness beyond immediate clear margins. With one part of her brain the novelist needed to find an emotional place of human predicament that was more than her characters could routinely cope with—*that* was the sign of achieved reality; a resonant space created in order to challenge that other part of her brain to try to think out what was going on within it. Hence, a limited creature such as Hetty suddenly finds herself in a limitless situation, still trying to eat bread in the midst of considering suicide. Hence, a man with a secretly discreditable past such as Bulstrode suddenly fears its exposure:

> The terror of being judged sharpens the memory: it sends an inevitable glare over that long-unvisited past which has been habitually recalled only in general phrases. Even without memory, the life is bound into one by a zone of dependence in growth and decay; but intense memory forces a man to own his blameworthy past. With memory set smarting like a reopened wound, a man's past is not simply a dead history, an outworn preparation of the present: it is not a repented error shaken loose from the life: it is a still quivering part of himself, bringing shudders and bitter flavours and the tinglings of a merited shame. (*Middlemarch*, chapter 61)

George Eliot's phrases are no longer general, habitual, or literal in such places but more like those wounds and shudders—what in *Adam Bede* was called 'bruises and gashes'—transposed into mentality, while the past and the fear of its exposure are '*making* a conscience within him', their painful neo-physical pressure forging that organ, that nervous system, that centre of acute consciousness within him that he would want to resist. This is the intense zone, the sensitive field activated in and around Bulstrode. There he sees the past suddenly coming into his normal field of vision, feels it coming between him and everything present outside—

> as obstinately as when we look through the window from a lighted room, the objects we turn our backs on are still before us, instead of the grass and the trees. The successive events inward and outward were there in one view: though each might be dwelt on in turn, the rest still kept their hold in the consciousness. (*Middlemarch*, chapter 61)

He can no longer turn away, or as he does so, what he turns away from returns upon him. This was the dizzying mental demand—seeing one thing outside, whilst at the same time secretly thinking of another to be hidden from it within; recognizing that an internal thought has reference to an object whose reality nonetheless still remains separate, even as the thought tries to cover or master it. This demand, relished by George Eliot but feared by a Bulstrode or an Arthur Donnithorne, was for an impossibly simultaneous perception of all these things—past and present, inside and outside—that existed together. But the bearable human response, within a limited field of vision, could only be an alternate view, one side followed by its other side, and yet the other side never long out of view but clamouring for attention. Such is 'that instantaneous alternation which makes two currents of feeling or imagination seem simultaneous' (*The Mill on the Floss*, book 6, chapter 1).

The great realist experiment in life is created by boundary-breaking questions such as this:

> What if the world proves itself to be quite other than the place we had previously imagined it to be? If fate or our own choice or some unfathomable mixture of both plunges us suddenly into a wholly different context, into a war, a natural catastrophe, a prison, or a hospital?

Then in that place of crisis, writes another modern novelist and critic—Dan Jacobson:

> What is so disconcerting is not so much the other reality in itself, as the mere possibility of its being so near that you only have to make one step to cross over

into a new existence just as self-contained and valid as the previous one; and thus find the thought of the plurality of worlds confirmed with a terrifying suddenness.[15]

The change of context can be the experience of a different place or another mind in suddenly altered existential situation. It is like the overwhelmed Dorothea in *Middlemarch* not knowing what to make of her honeymoon with Casaubon or even if honeymoon or some equivalent is the right name for what is happening to her in this disorienting transition between worlds. It is like Maggie Tulliver carried along by the new experience of sexual attraction, as by the flow of music or a current of water, forgetful of both past and future, of memory or thought—but then coming to, and having to face the status of the reality of her affair with Stephen Guest. It is like Hetty stepping into the wild. What is extra strange is how the new situation seems as 'self-contained', as apparently absolute in its present reality, as the one that it succeeds in the process of time and relativism. It is like being quite normally and unthinkingly healthy, becoming desperately and mysteriously ill, and then becoming well and returning home again—at each point of transition forgetting the previous stage or not seeing how it fits into a whole view of life. The task of Adam Bede, as he returns more or less to normal again through the love of Dinah, is still to retain within the recovery of the realm of what is firmly safe the previous perspective of the traumatically wild and painfully dangerous, and then, as George Eliot herself most strives to do, to recreate the one truth from within the perspective of the other.[16]

Each novel has its own biography, its own feel and field, and its own evolution. Each is a different world made out of the individual inner worlds and various possible other worlds competing and interacting within it, like various flickering candles illuminating the pier-glass. Those dynamic configurations and reconfigurations, culminating in *Middlemarch*, begin in *Adam Bede*. In this way, the creation of a dense complex of multi-dimensions in fiction is the story of George Eliot. A reader will see it being formed through Chapters 6, 7, and 8 in this volume, in the foundations laid in *Scenes of Clerical Life*, in the expansion within *Adam Bede*, and in the development of differing fields and levels in both *Adam Bede* and *The Mill on the Floss*—till through the difficulties described in Chapter 9, there emerges the full-blown multi-channelled realism that is *Middlemarch*.

CHAPTER 8

The Mill on the Floss

'My problems are purely psychical', 1859–60: Psychology and the Levels of Thought

In the midst of her infatuation with her cousin's fiancé, whilst Stephen and Lucy are out riding, Maggie Tulliver turns to the piano. After her father's financial ruin, she no longer has one in her own home—'no piano, no harmonised voices, no delicious stringed instruments, with their passionate cries of imprisoned spirits sending a strange vibration through her frame' (*The Mill on the Floss*, book 4, chapter 3). Now, in Lucy's father house, it was wonderfully pleasant again

> to sit down at the piano alone, and find the old fitness between her fingers and the keys remained and revived, like a sympathetic kinship, not to be worn out by separation—to get the tunes she had heard the evening before and repeat them again and again until she had found out a way of producing them so as to make them a more pregnant, passionate language to her.   (*The Mill on the Floss*, book 6, chapter 6)

The evening before the young people had made music together. At one level what Maggie is doing here is replaying under her touch the secret, barely identifiable, and otherwise transient feelings of a nascent love affair. This young woman has little other 'sympathetic kinship' at this time, more or less separated as she is from her own family, with precious little opportunity for the expression of 'passionate language', in those 'passionate cries of imprisoned spirits'. But then there comes immediately after this a curious mental detail, seemingly distinct from the obvious emotional or psychological associations:

> The mere concord of octaves was a delight to Maggie, and she would often take up a book of Studies rather than any melody, that she might taste more keenly by abstraction the more primitive sensation of intervals.

This exercise comes from a different part of her brain, which tries to see how things are made and done from their basic beginnings ('primitive') and works out in a more austere mode what effects lie tacitly and subtly between the notes ('intervals'), before ever they find fully combined expression in the rich melodies themselves. It works beneath the richness of final composition to bring out the underlying essentials by a kind of subtraction that is nonetheless intense rather than cold. It is mind at the new level called 'abstraction'.

It is not the same as the habit of mind Marian Evans had criticized in the poet Young, whose love of 'abstractions' she associated with a 'telescopic view' of human beings: 'The adherence to abstractions, or to the personification of abstractions is closely allied in Young to the *want of genuine emotion*' (*Essays*, p. 371). Nor is it the same as Feuerbach's own contrast of what is merely abstract with what is real flesh and blood. There God Himself is an abstraction, a projected product of Man thereby alienated from his own best inner qualities. We worship an absolute God of abstract moral rectitude, says Feuerbach, but it is not severe and distant beings who are merciful, only sensuous, living, feeling beings: 'Mercy is the justice of sensuous life'.[1] That is why there had to be a God made flesh in Christ, to forgive by being incarnate and not abstracted. Along with George Henry Lewes, George Eliot herself was profoundly sceptical of abstract intellectual systems, in particular of the abstract thinking called metaphysics.

What Lewes preferred were practical experiments, taken even from the psychology of daily experience. He quotes the eighteenth-century Scots physician Robert Whytt: 'Few persons in health feel the beating of their heart, though it strikes against their ribs with considerable force every second; whereas the motion of a fly upon one's face or hands occasions a very sensible and uneasy titillation.' Lewes goes on:

> In like manner, the various streams of sensation which make up our general sense of existence, separately escape notice until one of them becomes obstructed, or increases in impetuosity. When we are seated a window, and look out at the trees and sky, we are so occupied with the aspects and the voices of external nature, that no attention whatever is given to the fact of our own existence; yet all the while there has been a massive and diffusive feeling arising from the organic process; and of this we become distinctly aware if we close our eyes, shut off all sounds, and abstract the sensations of touch and temperature—it is then perceived as a vast and powerful stream of sensation, belonging to none of the special Senses, but to the System as a whole.[2]

This rightful use of intelligent abstraction is like hearing an inner roar; it temporarily shuts down certain forms of sensuous immediacy in order to switch attention to the inner condition of their working.

Such a shift is a mark of conscious mind; without it the creature has no separate understanding of itself. In *Middlemarch*, Maggie Tulliver's successor, Dorothea, would never have wanted to be as intellectually detached and morally distant as the poet Young but, on the other hand, was 'humiliated to find herself a mere victim of feeling, as if she could know nothing except through that medium' (chapter 20). Even in Feuerbach there is a recognition of the importance of abstraction, rightly employed, in the development of the race. The merely emotional man 'cannot abstract himself from his feelings, he cannot get beyond them', cannot envisage beyond what is immediate the distinction between subjective and objective cognition (*Essence of Christianity*, p. 133). We are for the most part trapped unthinkingly within ourselves and our inevitable partiality: 'I cannot so abstract myself from myself as to judge myself with perfect freedom and disinterestedness' (*Essence of Christianity*, p. 159). But the great abstract thinker who sought to bring mental clarity to 'confused ideas' unthinkingly embodied in practical behaviour, was of course also translated by Marian Evans. It was Spinoza's rationalist ambition to disclose, cleanly and purely, the primal order underlying the psychological tangle and chaos of human emotions.

Yet, for all her musical exercises, it was not usually possible for Maggie, any more than Dorothea, to find in life itself an equivalently useful power of abstraction that sits apart from the medium of feeling. Even so, in the turmoil of her emotions she feels a need, itself emotional, for the capacity to extrapolate, to get at least temporarily above her own life through the power of thinking of it. Otherwise there is terrible confusion played out both behind and before her eyes, as there is for Bulstrode when he stands at his own window at the time of his worst fears. Then he sees before him, coming between him and the landscape like an optic bleed, the sight and the thought of his guilty past. What Maggie wanted, as it were, was to be George Eliot, the George Eliot created only by writing of a transmuted version of Marian Evans—what, as we shall see, Edward Dowden was to call 'a second self' abstracted out of the character of Maggie.[3]

But in the turmoil of this first self, Stephen is not the first of Maggie's emotional entanglements. Before him in the story of her confused entanglements there was Philip, the crippled son of her father's enemy, whom she had been seeing in secret until discovered by her brother Tom. Then Tom had said to her, bruisingly:

> 'I never feel certain about anything with *you*. At one time you take pleasure in a sort of perverse self-denial, and at another, you have not resolution to resist a thing that you know to be wrong.'
>
> There was a terrible cutting truth in Tom's words—that hard rind of truth which is discerned by unimaginative, unsympathetic minds. Maggie always writhed under this judgment of Tom's: she rebelled and was humiliated in the same moment: it seemed as if he held a glass before her to show her her own folly and weakness—as if he were a prophetic voice predicting her future failings—and yet, all the while, she judged him in return: she said inwardly, that he was narrow and unjust, that he was below feeling those mental needs which were often the source of the wrong-doing or absurdity that made her life a planless riddle to him.   (*The Mill on the Floss*, book 6, chapter 4)

The intelligence that knows Tom's limitations cannot wholly abstract itself. It is caught up in her past and compromised by her guilt. Hence what she could say in retort is said only 'inwardly'—as if by *her* failings she had lost the right to speak outwardly of *his* 'in the same moment'. It is an intelligence implicated in its being hers, trapped just as surely as the imprisoned spirits Maggie hears crying out within music. Abstraction hurts here precisely because it cannot fully abstract itself from where it comes from and what it refers to—it hurts to look at oneself as if through another's eyes and yet still connected to what one is looking at; free neither to think with impartial ease nor not to think and remain obliviously uncaring.

The novel here is doing some complicated thinking about being in two or more minds, both across different characters and within single individuals. Maggie had loved her brother, but how can she find and give love outside the family and even against it? To Maggie, the secret friendship with Philip Wakem had been like 'sweet music' but 'athwart it there came an urgent monotonous warning from another voice' (book 5, chapter 1). Tom himself never is in two minds in this way. He always single-mindedly knows where he is and what he stands for: his energies always go into 'the one channel' which George Eliot herself at once admires and fears (book 4, chapter 2). It is he, correspondingly, who can see so clearly and coldly from outside how 'at one time' Maggie is committed to the idea of self-denial and then 'at another' is apparently self-indulgent. But what Tom cannot see is the connection that might be more telling than the contrast: in Maggie there are the same 'mental needs' in the interval, as it were, beneath and between those two opposite drives, blindly unwill-ing as she is to give up on some unknown state that might combine or transcend them. Literal-minded Tom only saw the story of one impulse contradicted by another following it; it would take a contemporary psychologist, James Sully, to say instead: 'Maggie Tulliver...was nothing but a bundle of inconsistencies to her brother. Yet the reader who looks deep enough sees those alternations of passionate longing and renunciation to be the outflow of one complex individuality.'[4]

It is, nonetheless, uncomfortably true that the inconsistency that Tom condemns comes out something deeply ambivalent and divided in Maggie herself: 'she rebelled *and* was humiliated', 'Maggie always writhed under this judgement of Tom's...*and yet, all the while*, she judged him in return'. What cannot be held together at the same time, will break out in different ways at different times.

In consequence, these unresolved dilemmas of need have an effect on the plastic form, on the resultant configurations and reconfigurations of the novel, responding to the human movements of its own content. So it is that Maggie, in fearing what she may do with Stephen in betrayal of Lucy, finds herself messily turning back to Philip as a relatively safer substitute within the world of extra-familial love. Instead of her being in two minds, she is now with two men, using (as Tom might unkindly say) one against the other:

> For Philip, who a little while ago was associated continually in Maggie's mind with the sense that Tom might reproach her with some justice, had now, in this short space,

become a sort of outward conscience to her, that she might fly to for rescue and strength. Her tranquil, tender affection for Philip, with its root deep down in her childhood, and its memories of long quiet talk confirming by distinct successive impressions the first instinctive bias—the fact that in him the appeal was more strongly to her pity and womanly devotedness than to her vanity or other egoistic excitability of her nature, seemed now to make a sort of sacred place, a sanctuary where she could find refuge from an alluring influence which the best part of herself must resist...

(*The Mill on the Floss*, book 6, chapter 7)

In something like Tom's harsh version of single truth, it would mean just this: Stephen is sexually attractive; whereas, modelled as he is on Marian Evans's land-lord, M. d'Albert Durade, in Geneva, Philip has had a hunched back since birth. He is the object of no more and no less than childhood affection and womanly sympathy, not adult sexuality:

This new sense of her relation to Philip nullified the anxious scruples she would otherwise have felt, lest she should overstep the limit of intercourse with him that Tom would sanction; and she put out her hand to him, and felt the tears in her eyes without any consciousness of an inward check. (*The Mill on the Floss*, book 6, chapter 7)

Maggie is not an unkind or manipulative woman, but this is what happens when a form of thinking, in the logic of emotional needs, has almost unthinkingly to go on within desperately improvised behaviour, in the terrible convolutions of circum-stance and event. In the writing of this, the third volume of *The Mill on the Floss*, commencing with book 6, 'The Great Temptation', George Eliot was again, as in *Adam Bede*, 'in a drive of feeling and writing', as Lewes told Blackwood, 'getting her eyes redder and *swollener* every morning as she lives through her tragic story' (GEL 3, pp. 267, 269). The characters gather together, overlap, and interfuse, till the culmin-ation is the great flood in which Maggie drowns with her brother even in trying to come to his recue. At the end of January 1860 George Eliot wrote Blackwood that she was ill, a prisoner in Bunyan's castle of Giant Despair, 'who growls in my ear that The Mill on the Floss is detestable' (GEL 3, p. 254). Lewes told Blackwood a few days later 'there never *was* so diffident and desponding an author, since the craft first began' (GEL 3, p. 258). And yet the third volume was completed at great speed between 16 January and 21 March 1860.

But that final-volume crescendo of books 6 and 7 was partly set up by the countervailing work of retardation in the fourth book, 'The Valley of Humiliation'. In the alternation of the work's rhythms—crisis and aftermath, aftermath and new crisis—that book comprises a crucial section in volume two of the triple-decker novel (books 3–5). Significantly, it comes after the novel's first great disaster in the bankruptcy of Mr Tulliver in book 3—his breakdown following the fall from his horse, and the loss of his mill to Philip Wakem's father, bringing to an end the first volume of early life.

George Eliot's mid-book realism characteristically has to do with that second stage of life that soberly follows upon the sudden firstness of eruptive drama. Living with the day-by-day aftermath is, in its own extended way, every bit as testing through length of time as was the initial instant blow. So it is after the father's partial recovery from his stroke:

> There is something sustaining in the very agitation that accompanies the first shocks of trouble, just as an acute pain is often a stimulus, and produces an excitement which is transient strength. It is the slow, changed life that follows—in the time when sorrow has become stale and has no longer an emotive intensity that counteracts its pain, in the time when day follows day in dull unexpectant sameness and trial is a dreary routine—it is then that despair threatens: it is then that the peremptory hunger of the soul is felt, and eye and ear are strained after some unlearned secret of our existence which shall give to endurance the nature of satisfaction.
>
> (The Mill on the Floss, book 4, chapter 2)

The passage marks a significant generic difference in the development of this novel, moving from first things to an after-stage of slow continuous time in which the novel follows dramatic power with the sobriety of post-dramatic realism shorn of mere events. Then people like Janet or Dorothea have to live on and on, within situations normalized even by unhappiness. The more it goes on, The Mill on the Floss exists as it were *after* 'the first' (which was another candidate for the title of this chapter) in the 'slow changed life that follows' within the second stage of young lives. The writer's own sister Chrissey had died in March 1859, one of the contributing factors to the slowness of the initial composition of this novel, along with a move of house and the excitement of the reception of *Adam Bede*: she wrote to Sara Hennell, 'Chrissey's death has taken from me the possibility of many things towards which I looked with some hope and yearning in the future' (GEL 3, p. 38). There was no future that way. After writing 'The Lifted Veil'—'not a *jeu d'esprit*, but a *jeu de melancolie*' (GEL 3, p. 41)—she had to go back to The Mill on the Floss instead: such is the strangely mixed world within which a realist novelist has to live. She had to travel backwards.

The greatness of the first stage of life lay in the novel's first volume, the two child-time books of The Mill on the Floss. In the rich glow and power of the young Maggie's thin-skinned experience, there is a vulnerably excessive intensity that has vital force in itself. At this level of undeveloped consciousness, there is a 'surplus of passion' felt at the moment of its occurrence, almost independently of its outcome on others or effect on oneself (book 5, chapter 3). Nor is it a matter of precisely what one felt, but how much one felt within it. What is experienced as unhappiness and despair has nonetheless protest, resistance, even vitality within its pains. It is not with the young Maggie as it is with the mature Adam, thinking of Hetty's fate with one part of himself, while he also lives on with what is left him. There is as yet no relative sense of experience, no *second* learned nature such as, say, Dorothea has to begin to acquire, when her first directness of ardour is continually repelled by her aged husband, Casaubon. For the young girl Maggie, there is only an emotionally absolute time, time present—'the strangely perspectiveless conception of life' (*The Mill on the Floss*, book 1, chapter 7), which has neither terrible forebodings nor soothing 'memories of outlived sorrow' (book 1, chapter 9). In her refuge in the attic, unthinkingly the girl will one moment do vengeful violence to her doll for some terrible disappointment inflicted upon herself, the next see a sudden beam of sunshine and irresistibly want to run down to it outside. Such alternating moments call forth what Doris Lessing in her own memoir calls 'real remembering'—which means 'if even for a flash, even a moment—being back in the experience itself. You remember pain with pain, love with love, one's real best self with one's best self'— before the distancing perspectives of compromised adulthood set back in.[5] This is how George Eliot remembers, using Mary Ann Evans as a young Maggie Tulliver in the attic, in the aftermath of her brother's anger, crying aloud to no one:

> What use was anything if Tom didn't love her?...She knew she was naughty to her mother, but she had never been naughty to Tom—had never *meant* to be naughty to him.
>
> 'O he is cruel!' Maggie sobbed aloud, finding a wretched pleasure in the hollow resonance that came through the long empty space of the attic.
>
> (*The Mill on the Floss*, book 1, chapter 5)

It is like recalling a different creature, normally forgotten in adult life, with a different meaning for emotions. At its best 'the outer world seemed only an extension of our own personality' (book 2, chapter 1), and so it was for Maggie till Tom would angrily hurt her feelings, consigning them to the rejected and lonely person she has to become as a result. Then, in the refuge of her alternative little world at the top of the house, Maggie makes everything around her into some quivering hurt resonant organism. Later even these direct raw cries as to what she really *meant* will become consciously subdued and modified; she will check and draw in her feelings, breaking the link between within and without, and leaving the world outside colder and more separate. Only the novelist could still hear the cries on the other side of silence.

But for the young, easily hurt Maggie, even the relationships with father and brother are not simply stable and confident external realities: they come and go like pulsations of mortifying loss and almost unexpectedly joyous renewal. So it is when she unexpectedly succeeds in catching a fish and Tom cries with delight, 'O Magsie! you little duck!': 'It was enough he called her Magsie' (book 1, chapter 5). Or her father defends her for rashly cutting her own hair, 'You was i' the right to cut it off if it plagued you': 'Delicious words of tenderness! Maggie never forgot any of these moments...' (book 1, chapter 7). They are a sort of music to her ears.

But by the end of the first volume Tom and Maggie 'had entered the thorny wilderness, and the golden gates of their childhood had for ever closed behind them' (book 2, chapter 7): it is the realist equivalent of the Fall after the Garden of Eden. Story in the second volume then begins to mean what Maggie fears—that 'everything is going away from us—the end of our lives will have nothing in it like the beginning' (book 3, chapter 6). In the novel's second movement, people (and in particular Maggie) more and more begin to have to live exactly as they do not wish to live, had not meant to live, within a place where relief is scant. 'Now,' comments one reader, 'there will be a new kind of desolation, a steady continuing one, when the intense moment passes and the sorrow remains. It is now no longer the ebb and flow of her own emotions that magically control the world; from now on it will be an increasingly stubborn fact.'[6] That is why, after the great passage on the hard daily grind that follows 'the first shocks of trouble', George Eliot offers two simple sentences ending with little questions:

Tom went to and fro every morning and evening and became more and more silent in the short intervals at home: what was there to say?

And:

Poor Mrs Tulliver, it seemed, would never recover her old self—her placid household activity: how could she?   (The Mill on the Floss, book 6, chapter 7)

And that is the point, that they are questions so subdued as never to rise to the level of being asked out loud at all. This is because they are embedded in hidden resignation, in carrying on precisely by not asking why or how or what, when there is no apparent alternative to their lives. Maggie is one who will still ask such questions of herself, and if the answers do end up in only another form of acceptance, still it must be for her as a result at least of finding a mental 'abstraction'—unearthing 'some unlearned secret of our existence' which is not to be found in passive or unthinking living but becomes an explanatory idea or guiding belief about life. Becoming a sort of second mind above and not just within her existence, the thinking that is sought may not outwardly change that life but may be at least the inner means to 'give to endurance the nature of satisfaction'. Thinking is the adult alternative to the cry out loud. Its syntax, as we have seen in Chapter 3, is not 'easy and simple, as it might have been in paradise' when what comes first stays first. New and disturbing feelings 'continually come across the ties that all our former life has made for us' in the movement from family love to the sexual love that threatens to sever past connections. Then it is that thought has to make second-thought adjustments and reconnections in a new ordering of emotional and ethical experience (book 6, chapter 11).

Maggie had always had 'a blind unconscious yearning for something that would link together the wonderful impressions of this mysterious life' (book 2, chapter 5). Now she consciously needed 'some explanation of this hard, real life... some key that would enable her to understand and, in understanding, endure' (book 4, chapter 3). The need for access to a second level of mind has become explicit, awkward, and almost embarrassingly ironic were it not also urgent and desperate. Why cannot she still live a first life, straightforwardly, without need of these secondary aids towards making a second life? There are no direct answers around her, and, crucially, not even direct questions: something out of the experience of repeated failures had to be inferred instead, as though back to front. That is why the second volume of *The Mill on the Floss*, comprising books 3, 4, and 5 (respectively 'The Downfall', 'The Valley of Humiliation', and 'Wheat and Tares'), is so painful and so equivocal an artistic achievement, in showing all the obstacles to achievement in young adult existence.

It is an old book not a contemporary person that serves Maggie as counsel; but it does not feel like an abstraction, a series of abstract ideas, because it seems embodied in a voice and a presence. The powerful 'vibration' she gets from serious music is something she now finds in coming upon *The Imitation of Christ* by Thomas à Kempis, marked at certain passages by some hand doubtless long dead but giving a pointed direction—'as if she had been awakened by a strain of solemn music, telling of beings whose souls had been astir whilst hers was in stupor'. She is simultaneously listening to a voice with one sense, as well as reading an old book with another:

> it was by being brought within the long lingering vibrations of such a voice that Maggie, with her girl's face and unnoted sorrows, found an effort and a hope that helped her through two years of loneliness. (*The Mill on the Floss*, book 4, chapter 3)

We know that, ten years after first reading *The Imitation of Christ*, George Eliot was rereading the book in November 1859 at the same time as writing this novel, marking and re-marking the passages herself, albeit without the God Thomas à Kempis worshipped: 'It is but little thou sufferest in comparison of them that have suffered so much... If thy little adversities seem but not little unto thee, beware lest thy impatience be the cause thereof' (*The Mill on the Floss*, book 4, chapter 3). For Maggie, was there some scale and perspective outside the ego that allowed her to see, and get, above herself?

As we might have known and have already seen, Maggie rushes to the thought like the 'suddenly apprehended solution of a problem' wonderfully falling into place, to give great personal relief:

With all the hurry of an imagination that could never rest in the present, she sat in the deepening twilight forming plans of self-humiliation and entire devotedness, and in the ardour of first discovery, renunciation seemed to her the entrance into that satisfaction which she had so long been craving in vain. She had not perceived—how could she until she had lived longer?—the inmost truth of the old monk's outpourings, that renunciation remains sorrow, though a sorrow borne willingly.

(*The Mill on the Floss*, book 4 chapter 3)

Again, this is another version of 'the first'—the ardour of 'first discovery'—in need of a second, later, and longer re-embedding of an Idea of life back within lived experience. She did not see this yet, and 'How could she until she had lived longer?' is the interjection of one who, becoming George Eliot only in her 30s, *has* lived longer, knowing the value of sheer 'quantity of experience' (GEL 1, p. 251). But abstracted and adopted ideas of life *are* needed in George Eliot—the experience of life going wrong time and time again implies the need to think, however belatedly or obtrusively, as though all conscious thought were second thought, correctively. Otherwise the young come 'out of school-life with a soul *untrained*', as George Eliot says in particular of girls such as Maggie. Because in the normal world no one tells, no one teaches, no one equips for life, as though there were no problems or the problems are kept secret. Hence the need for the silent inner transmission of complex, hidden knowledge through a book. What Thomas à Kempis is to Maggie is what George Eliot would want to be to equivalent strugglers who have no other form of humane education in the deeper secrets of existence. Her hand points to her own text.

Angry at so-called 'good society' for being able to carry on conventionally as if there were no hidden needs or problems, George Eliot writes of the want of what she insists on calling no more and no less than a felt 'something'—'something that will present motives in an entire absence of high prizes', 'something, whatever it was, that was greatest and best on earth', 'something, clearly, that lies outside personal desires, that includes resignation for ourselves and active love for what is not ourselves' (*The Mill on the Floss*, book 4, chapter 3). There is no acknowledgement of it in the outside world, as though it did not exist, and therefore no training in it, no discipline for what can otherwise barely sustain itself without rewarding prizes or personal satisfactions. Remarkably, the old book provided the extra charge of effort and lift of hope which 'helped her through two years of loneliness', in place of people, teachers, loving friends, and relations.[7] But the transmission of meaning to its reader, to Maggie, is not guaranteed to be automatic or exact—as George Eliot says to her own reader:

From what you know of her, you will not be surprised that she threw some exaggeration and wilfulness, some pride and impetuosity even into her self-renunciation.

(*The Mill on the Floss*, book 4, chapter 3)

'*Threw*' marks the desperately enthusiastic continuance of Maggie's first nature into her second. And as a result, in messy and imperfect praxis, '*even*' is the word that marks biographically the wince at the hidden little discrepancy within. In one way, the idea is too much an ideal abstraction for her; in another it is still inflected with personal desire.

What is being depicted here is a state, so to speak, of half-thinking. John Stuart Mill had described something of its nature in writing of half-truths in the great third chapter on individuality in *On Liberty* (1859):

> As is usually the case with ideals which exclude one half of what is desirable, the present standard of approbation produces only an inferior imitation of the other half. Instead of great energies guided by vigorous reason, and strong feelings strongly controlled by a conscientious will, its result is weak feelings and weak energies, which therefore can be kept in outward conformity to rule without any strength either of will or of reason.

Mill wanted a holistic logic, wanted a definite two-sided integration of mind. But in the more fluid psycho-logic of George Eliot in this novel, half-thinking is the struggling territory human beings mainly occupy, especially at Maggie's nascent stage of development, neither fully one thing nor the other. In the *Genealogy of Morals* (1887), Nietzsche was to describe human beings as amphibious creatures, thrown out of their native sea, onto strange dry land, and forced to walk unsteadily into consciousness. It is as though in Maggie, likewise, the levels of life are being learnt almost separately, with honest awkwardness, one by one. It takes time even for the beginning of their integration.

The raw overcommitment of hers to the idea of self-renunciation produces in Philip a response which (so characteristically of the novel) offers some truth to Maggie while nonetheless psychologically involving ulterior purpose for himself— he cannot abstract the one from the other:

> 'What a dear, good brother you would have been, Philip,' said Maggie, smiling through the haze of tears. 'I think you would have made as much fuss about me, and been as pleased for me to love you, as would have satisfied even me. You would have loved me well enough to bear with me, and forgive me everything. That was what I always longed that Tom should do. I was never satisfied with a *little* of anything. That is why it is better for me to do without earthly happiness altogether...'
>
> 'Maggie,' he said, in a tone of remonstration, 'Don't persist in this wilful senseless privation. It makes me wretched to see you benumbing and cramping your nature in this way. You were so full of life when you were a child—I thought you would be a brilliant woman—all wit and bright imagination. And it flashes out in your face still, until you draw the veil of dull quiescence over it.'
>
> (*The Mill on the Floss*, book 5, chapter 3)

That 'flash', like a visual vibration, is also written across the face of the prose. In the inner biography of the writing, the reader can see and feel the verbal spark of the girl still in a word or phrase within the young woman's sentences: 'never satisfied with a *little*' goes with both the earlier 'I always longed' and the later 'better do without altogether'. The flash of feeling is there also in the sudden reference to Tom, in the deflected desire to make Philip her substitute sibling when, as the novel's force field of reference shifts and oscillates, Philip is really to be second-best not to Tom as brother but to Stephen as lover. But the passage goes on over all these electrical flashes and subliminal links:

> 'Why do you speak so bitterly to me, Philip?' said Maggie.
> 'Because I foresee it will not end well; you can never carry on this self-torture.'
> 'I shall have strength given me,' said Maggie, tremulously.
> 'No, you will not, Maggie: no one has strength given to do what is unnatural. It is mere cowardice to seek safety in negations. No character ever becomes strong in that way. You will be thrown into the world some day, and then every rational satisfaction of your nature that you deny now, will assault you like a savage appetite.'
>
> (*The Mill on the Floss*, book 5, chapter 3)

The 'double impression' felt by Maggie at this moment 'corresponded to the double impulse of the speaker': the novel's mixture is of abstract impersonal truth but with a passionately personal motive in offering it. It is as though a reader could measure by just such a literary kind of accounting—'strength' she says but 'tremulously'—the loss of the first life, the entanglement of the single way. There are instead multiple colliding and overlapping experiments—inchoate philosophies, adopted ideas, mental adjustments and compensations—going on in the heads of all the young ones in partial defiance of parts of themselves and of the older generation around them. It is there in Tom's determination to see how far rigidity and rightness can take him in repairing his father's loss; in Maggie's neo-religious effort at absolute self-denial; in Philip's hungered attempt at a natural authenticity desired so poignantly by those whom George Eliot, thinking also of herself, called the 'ugly and deformed'.

This novel, then, is *younger* than *Adam Bede*, even though it comes after it. It is a step back, crucial to further development, in the story of a young 'soul' still desperately seeking 'a sense of home' in life (*The Mill on the Floss*, book 2, chapter 5). Struggling at the beginning of what was eventually to become *Sylvia's Lovers*, Mrs Gaskell wrote in a letter of 1859, 'I think I have a feeling that it is not worth while trying to write, while there are such books as Adam Bede & Scenes of Clerical Life—I set "Janet's Repentance" above all still.'[8] They were works full of a rich and warm goodness, she felt, despite whatever else was in them. In a way this was also to be George Eliot's own situation in the unresolved problems of *The Mill on the Floss*, through the difficult middle years following it, to be discussed in Chapter 9: namely, that it was increasingly difficult to go on from the success of *Adam Bede*, that something in the order of what Wordsworth might have called natural piety or sacred ties was ever more shaken and threatened.

In *Adam Bede* Hetty, hellishly wandering in the countryside, had no aim or end. But Feuerbach said that all humans must have before themselves a God, 'that is to say, an aim or purpose' (*Essence of Christianity*, p. 64). *The Mill on the Floss* is the novel in vulnerably autobiographical search of aim, through the often unwieldy interrelation of abstract thought and concrete experience that marks life's second stage. Its characteristic syntax is that of Maggie when she accedes to Tom's demand that she never see Philip in secret again:

> If she had felt that she was entirely wrong, and that Tom had been entirely right, she could sooner have recovered more inward harmony; but now her penitence and submission were constantly obstructed by resentment that would present itself to her no otherwise than as a just indignation.   (*The Mill on the Floss*, book 5, chapter 5)

There, as it were post-adolescently, in that half-thought-out middle of things, is where George Eliot characteristically now does her work. And always its sign is the unsettling presence of human psychology—the age of psychology magnificently led by George Eliot yet leaving nothing simply pure or clear or abstract, unembodied or uncontextualized. A phrase such as 'it would present itself no otherwise than' marks the contorted pressure of intermingled categories—the ideal of self-renunciation beset by the latent psychological reaction within or against it; moral indignation uncomfortably close to its psychological motivation. It makes Maggie almost sick of herself, sick of everything being messy and personal and psychological and unresolved. It is like Marian Evans at another level—'My problems are purely psychical' (GEL 2, pp. 155–6). And at that level, it is like George Eliot finding her writing only 'a kind of glass in which she beholds her infirmities' (GEL 6, p. 165)—inadequacies both mirrored in her characters and felt in her attempt to write of them.

'You will be thrown into the world some day, and then every rational satisfaction of your nature that you deny now, will assault you like a savage appetite.' But though in the novel's tangle of values Philip's prophecy is indeed realized in Maggie's affair with Stephen, it is not the direct and immediate cries of savage appetite that are her biggest threat. It is something more convoluted in her nature, the product of being caught between two worlds. What finally brings her closest to giving way to Stephen's love is not the new Eros but the old ethics itself, in the sight of Stephen's misery at her principled rejection of him: 'This yielding to the idea of Stephen's suffering was more fatal than the other yielding, because it was less distinguishable from that sense of others' claims which was the moral basis of her resistance' (*The Mill on the*

Floss, book 6, chapter 13). Her resistance, which had seemed the call of conscience on behalf of Stephen's Lucy, is translated into being perhaps no more than another sort of selfishness at *his* expense, in a different usage of self-blame and self-renunciation. The old vocabulary of her moral heritage, it seems, will not stay unthinkingly steady as a general guide to conduct, but its maxims can turn and twist and apply any which way. Then, almost unbearably, if not impossibly, thinking seems called forth to try to work out a correct application in every particular instance.

*

And yet in all this psychological conflict and confusion, it is the bystander, Philip, who retains an emotional clue from the first to last. It is there in the fullness of life he saw in Maggie as a child and still sees in flashes in the woman. That fullness is what characterized the great unexplainable emotions of the novel's first volume. Philip tells Maggie, even in the midst of her later difficulties, that he had always known that she would be the same whenever he saw her again—whatever she had tried subsequently to impose on her nature. He is attuned to her, feels the affinity through all the change and disorientation, from the moment as a schoolboy he first saw her eyes 'full of unsatisfied intelligence, and unsatisfied beseeching affection' (book 2, chapter 5). It is as though she has been his best sign of what life is and can be:

> I do not want to explain that: I don't think any of the strongest effects our natures are susceptible of can ever be explained. We can neither detect the process by which they are arrived at nor the mode in which they act upon us. The greatest of painters only once painted a mysteriously divine child—he couldn't have told how he did it—and we can't tell why we feel it to be divine. I think there are stores laid up in our human nature that our understandings can make no complete inventory of. Certain strains of music affect me strangely—I can never hear them without their changing my whole attitude for a time, and if the effect would last I might be capable of heroisms.
>
> (*The Mill on the Floss*, book 5, chapter 1)

This is a message, otherwise without a place in the world, transmitted in and through himself. It is the other side of the musical studies in abstraction with which this chapter opened. Nothing here is taken apart in order to understand the bare primary basics; everything comes suddenly together in rich live performance or immediate view, creating deep vibrations in listener or spectator out of what is felt as an emotional pre-language, prior to the verbal. It is not the world of normal society that gives a prompt or place to such responses, but something closer to what was best in the undiscriminated feelings of childhood in this novel. The 'oppressive feeling' of bourgeois 'good society' in *The Mill on the Floss*, however roughly decent in its standards, offers 'conventional worldly notions and habits without instruction and without polish': it lacks the earlier warmth loved by reviewer Collins in *Adam Bede*'s depiction of Mrs Poyser's dairy or Bartle Massey's night school, or the harvest feast. It is, writes George Eliot, irradiated by 'no sublime principles, no romantic visions, no active, self-renouncing faith' like Maggie's; it is moved by 'none of those wild, uncontrollable passions which create the dark shadows of misery and crime' as with Hetty; it is marked by none of that 'primitive rough simplicity' that gave to Wordsworth the poetry of peasant life (*The Mill on the Floss*, book 4, chapter 1). Philip's feel for what he took to be essential Maggie, like the sight of Raphael's Sistine Madonna, or like the music of Handel or Haydn or Beethoven, offered a place of emotional origins in the midst of things, instead of that narrow society which stifled the beautiful, great, or noble.[9] It was not about explaining that place of feeling; it was about finding it without knowing in advance, and a deeper self being found in the act of doing so.

As newly Mrs Lewes, she had first seen the Raphael (Plate 13) in Dresden in 1858 whilst writing *Adam Bede*, rushing out of the church almost hysterically overwhelmed. It was perhaps above all the sight of the eyes of the mother and child that made it for ever her most loved painting: heads touching but in different quiet attitudes; both full of unspoken knowing in themselves, the future weight of the world upon her, the deep light of sacred life in his eye. During the same trip suddenly, outside a Nurnberg church, she had heard an organ and congregation, and irresistibly entered: 'How music that stirs all one's devout emotions blends everything into harmony—makes one feel part of one whole, which one loves all alike, losing the sense of a separate self.'[10] The separate self in George Eliot's personal past—Marian Evans made also into Maggie Tulliver—too often felt as though it had no emotional place in the world, no vocation or membership, nowhere in which to be in her element. But here was that element, the feeling without which no great thought could be thought. No character becomes strong, said Philip, through negations. Here was the opposite: positive recognitions felt powerfully as somehow clues to what innerly mattered, to what was loved at an unknown, underused centre.

As a boy Tom Tulliver had struggled with his lessons while his clever schoolmate Philip Wakem had not. It seemed at the time a minor point, but it is said that Tom's faculties failed him in the face of the 'abstractions symbolised' in the pages of the Eton Latin Grammar that Mary Ann Evans had already mastered with the help of Reverend Sheepshanks back in 1840 (*The Mill on the Floss*, book 2, chapter 1). In his direct, practical, and literal-minded intelligence, Tom had no power of 'apprehending signs and abstractions' (book 2, chapter 4). After all, he is the fortunate one in this novel, the determined young male who can accumulate sufficient money to achieve the great purpose of returning the mill to his father before he dies, which his poor idealistic sister simply cannot, not least because of her gender. When Mr Tulliver shakes his son's hand and says what a great thing it is to be thus proud of him for what he has done, Maggie also feels unequivocally for once that 'Tom *was* good', and that 'the faults he had to pardon in her had never been redeemed, as his faults were' this day (book 5, chapter 6). In his own way too, Philip knew his ineffectuality in the world, with gifts that never quite fulfilled what they seemed to offer. If only the transient effect of these fragments of musical resonance would last, says Philip, when they so much seem to give the very *score* of life, the deep notes and chords of felt significance waiting to be performed and re-performed: then, he says, I could try to translate them into something else, then 'I might be capable of heroisms.' But what redemption or fulfilment is there for those who cannot perform a direct heroic act, who can neither create art themselves nor quite find the equivalent of its powers in the action of the world? Though 'passion answers as well as a faculty' and keeps him above 'the dead level of provincial existence', Philip must also acknowledge his 'susceptibility in every direction, and effective facility in none' (book 5, chapter 3). This could have been the fate of Marian Evans. Kept aloof from all practical life as Philip had been, on account of his disability and his father's protective love, his is a nature 'half feminine in sensitiveness', a masculine version of Marian Evans without George Eliot (book 5, chapter 3). Lamed in a different way, Maggie finds herself admitting to Philip that she does not enjoy the happiness of other people as she knows she should: I can only really feel for them, she says, 'when they are in trouble' (book 6, chapter 2). These are young natures who, as George Eliot puts it in characteristic syntax, 'have risen *above* the *mental* level of the generation *before* them, *to which* they have been *nonetheless tied* by the strongest fibres of their *hearts*' (book 4, chapter 1).

At a level higher than the learning of basic Latin but related to it, the artistic language, the painting, and the music that move Philip and Maggie are all, in this specific sense, forms of abstraction—that is to say: signs in lieu of direct actions, awaiting translation back into existence. It is, as we have already seen G. H. Lewes saying, on algebra, in Chapter 5: 'Algebra cannot exist without values, nor Thought without feelings. The operations are so many blank forms until the values are assigned.'[11] In contrast, in ancient and sensuous nations, wrote Feuerbach, to think and to speak were identical, and were unreflectingly immediate: in that stage of development, men and women as they go along 'think only in speaking; their thought is only conversation. The common people, i.e., people in whom the power of abstraction has not been developed, are still incapable of understanding what is written if they do not read it audibly, if they do not pronounce what they read.'[12] The irascible old schoolmaster in *Adam Bede*, Bartle Massey, is moved to unusual gentleness by the spectacle of the illiterate farm labourers at his night school painfully making out 'the grass is green', 'the sticks are dry', 'the corn is ripe' (chapter 21). These—grass, corn—were things they naturally knew and worked with, yet now in poignant alienation struggled with, at the abstract level. But in the full development of reflective writing and silent reading, the abstraction is reintegrated into the world to which it refers. There is a constant inner movement backwards and forwards between word and the thought it tacitly releases, a subtle interval to and fro between felt meaning and the signs necessary to give it extended embodiment. George Eliot loved that movement between abstract and concrete, particular and general, word and feeling, one part of the mind and another. She could read scores and studies and yet, crossing senses, still hear silently inside her their music, just as Maggie Tulliver could innerly hear in her mind her book's thinking voice. These various sign-systems offered a medium or dimension distinct from the conventional norm. They served to reveal what one thinker who admired George Eliot and influenced William James was to call the 'subliminal'.

Another Reader: F. W. H. Myers

It is in identifying the pain of unused or misdirected human potential that F. W. H. Myers becomes important as a reader of George Eliot, seeking in her a guide to the young. An unfulfilled man not quite 30, he wrote to her in 1872 while reading *Middlemarch*, praising her as 'the only person who could make life appear potentially noble and interesting without starting from any assumptions'.[13] 'Without any assumptions' meant, essentially, without fixed religious dogma. But it was not that there could be *no* assumptions; rather, what a George Eliot novel was committed to was questioning its own premises, asking what the psychological predicaments that she created latently stood for. Nor, under her pen, did the secular realist novel have in advance a clear final aim—precisely because of its inner search for such a thing, through its characters' struggles. George Eliot was never fundamentally interested in set beginnings or summary endings at the margins of the self-consciously fictional—they made her nervous, when where she really wanted was to be was in the dense midst of things. But she did want to get somewhere, to create possibilities and see how far they could be actualized. In this way, it was the sense of the word 'potentially' in Myers' letter—'life potentially noble and interesting'—that was most crucial to the young man. He wrote to 'Mrs Lewes' in a vulnerable draft of his final letter, on the unfulfilment of youthful potential in feeling:

> Life has come to such a pass—now that there is no longer any God or any hereafter or anything in particular to aim at—that it is only by coming into contact with some other person that one can be oneself. There is no longer anything to keep an isolated fire burning within one, all one can do is feel the sparks fly from one for a moment when one strikes a kindred soul. Such contact in real life can make one feel for the moment immortal; but the necessary circumstances are so unusual ... Love must be set among great possibilities and great self-sacrifices, and must demand the full strain of all the forces within one. Unless things can so happen the first moment of love is apt to be the best. (*Studies in Myers*, p. 133)

It could almost have been Maggie writing: 'some other person', 'a kindred soul', sparks and fires, possibilities and sacrifices. But what Myers himself focused upon in 1872 was not the early romances of Maggie so much as Will Ladislaw's first vain feelings of love for Dorothea, and then Dorothea's visit to Rosamond in the effort to save her marriage to Lydgate: 'This is the best conception of life that in this stage of the world we can form.' A late Romantic in the later Victorian age, Myers found in Will and in Dorothea, as he found in the love poetry of Wordsworth,[14] the imagination of what great love would look like when its destiny was 'to deny itself at some heroic call' (*Studies in Myers*, p. 174). Otherwise, in the normal course of life, the first great force of love became dissipated into the narrative of workaday marriage. For love in its highest form, he wrote to Mrs Lewes, was a passion 'grossly out of proportion to the dimensions of life' (*Studies in Myers*, p. 215).

Myers regularly attended the Leweses' Sunday afternoon gatherings at the Priory. Increasingly, in his dissatisfaction with the limits of the mundane, he became interested in psychical research—in communication from the other world, personal immortality, and the possibility of love literally surviving death. 'Do you understand,' George Eliot said to him plainly one day, 'that the triumph of what you believe would mean the worthlessness of all that my life has been spent in teaching?' (*Studies in Myers*, p. 214). Virtue for her had no otherworldly rewards. Between the twin poles of the creature's inner desire and the medium's resistant limitation, George Eliot would never give way on either side: that was what made the basic field of endeavour for her, whilst Myers was constantly seeking an escape route to another world. It was to Myers famously that she said, in the fellows' garden of Trinity College, Cambridge, speaking of the three great words, God, Immortality, and Duty, how inconceivable the first, unbelievable the second, and therefore how peremptory and absolute the third. What Myers could not bear to accept was realism's commitment to the time after 'the first'—the vision not of heroic action or sacrifice, of the terrible shock, or the transcendental feeling or reward, but of the slow living on in mundane time by those seeking for *more* than the prosaic to be found only, nonetheless, from within its midst.

At her death, Myers described what he thought was George Eliot's own inner sense of falling short. The complexity her work had generated at one level could find no end or solution for itself at another. 'There is no longer any God or any hereafter or anything in particular to aim at', he had written to her. In that harsh light, Myers spoke of George Eliot's resignation to the probability that, for creatures with no otherworldly future to look to, their advance in moral feeling and spiritual aspiration would also be an advance in felt *pain*. That was too hard. To some who felt such pain—and he includes himself—her consolations seemed insufficient and her resignation premature: 'They could not readily acquiesce in her negations, nor range themselves unreservedly as the fellow-workers of her brave despair.'[15] He then quotes from a letter she wrote to one such bereft sufferer, actually himself, 16 November 1877:

> I only long, if it were possible to me, to help in satisfying the need of those who want a reason for living in the absence of what has been called consolatory belief.
>
> But all the while I gather a sort of strength from the certainty that there must be limits or negations in my own moral powers and life-experience which may screen from me many possibilities of blessedness for our suffering human nature. The most melancholy thought surely would be that we in our own persons had measured and exhausted the sources of spiritual good.   (GEL 9, p. 201)

What she wanted at least was an understanding of her method and its legacy: the garnering in her novels of sufficient inner-human material to overflow the boundaries of conventional concepts; the effort to regenerate out of that rich material strenuously new thinking that pushed art itself beyond the boundaries of autonomous fiction in the search for modern meaning. The psychological material was almost inexhaustible; the novel was the finest instrument for its generation, as close as art could get to recreating life's raw and dense excess of unassimilated material—what William James had called 'human stuff'. And as such, in its super-saturated human spaces, the novel held open as a reservoir for future thought and future resolution those informal potentialities for life and for thought that went unrecognized by philosophy and yet were vital to the race's deeper further sustenance. Some future novelist might be able, must be able, by thought in the midst of art, to make more of all that was held within the experiment called the novel than she had managed in her own single efforts: 'There must be limits or negations in my own moral powers and life-experience.' But the personal limitation and the flawed application were less than the essential method to be passed on. It was like what Matthew Arnold had argued in *Literature and Dogma*: that it was the inner method of Christ that mattered more to a later world than his outer mythic status. Jesus was able, wrote Arnold—'dare one say, like a poet?'—to 'put things in such a way that his hearer was led to take each rule or fact of conduct by its inward side, its effect on the heart and character; then the reason of the thing, the meaning of what had been mere matter of blind rule, flashed upon him'.[16] It was that inward side to meaning, and its secret personal work upon heart and character deep within, that George Eliot honoured, even as her own version of 'religion'. 'Please not to call it by any name,' Dorothea had begged Ladislaw (*Middlemarch*, chapter 39): 'It is my life. I have found it out, and cannot part with it. I have always been finding out my religion since I was a little girl.'

That method—and the sense that the novel could be that important—has never been as fully recognized in the world as George Eliot had wished and intended. But in the later work of Myers himself there is recognition of the creative thought-method that George Eliot, as the great representative of the realist novel, had implicitly bequeathed. It was to do with his invention of the term 'subliminal'—of all that went on *below* the level of what Myers had called ordinary, conscious 'assumptions'.

As William James describes in his essay 'What Psychical Research Has Accomplished', Myers, in a series of articles, had likened ordinary consciousness to the visible part of the spectrum of light, while invisibly beyond it there was also the psychological and psychic equivalent to ultra-violet rays and infra-red energy. Without that recognition of the invisible, the world-view of the nineteenth century was too narrow, too materialistic. Myers argued that in the great reservoir called the human psyche, there was always some part that was unmanifested, some power held in abeyance or reserve: it could never express itself completely. Instead, during the long evolution of human beings, there had been a continual displacement of the threshold—the 'limen'—of consciousness. Natural selection had raised certain faculties above that threshold whenever they were found especially necessary for survival: they became 'supra-liminal', part of the agenda and apparatus for the conscious continuance of normal life, till eventually they could become automatic. But other powers, not called into consciousness as immediately useful, were stored 'subliminally' in unconscious memory, waiting for the need and call of use. So, for example, even when raised into inchoate consciousness in the younger generation, the cultural sensitivity of Philip Wakem or the feelings of Maggie Tulliver seemed powers superfluous to their society. They were unhappy young souls, fervently homeless, as Myers had felt himself to be. But what George Eliot always sought was to *extend* the range of the human—in expansion of social width, through increased inner depth, burrowing into the subliminal and the hidden subconscious. As she put it most famously: 'the greatest benefit we owe to the artist, whether painter, poet, or novelist, is the extension of our sympathies' (*Essays*, p. 270).

To achieve this, George Eliot puts pressure on herself across the limen. So it is that with one part of her mind, she will provoke herself by asking—like a stern moralist, or simply a baffled onlooker—how it was that a sensitive and loving young man such as Philip could urge Maggie to give up her principles and deceive her family, to stay in secret communication with himself. How could it be his wish, one might ask in concern for her, 'to overcome Maggie's true prompting against a concealment that would introduce doubleness into her own mind and might cause misery to those who had the primary natural claim on her'? Then from another part of her mind, she begins to spell it out from within him, in reply. He persuaded himself that he was not being selfish, that he had no self-interested hope of getting her to return his feelings, and that it was better for her to have access through him to books and music and talk. Then suddenly she shifts a level, and now wholly attuned, can think *about* Philip whilst also thinking from deep *inside* him:

> But there was a surplus of passion in him that made him half independent of justifying motives. His longing to see Maggie and make an element in her life, had in it some savage impulse to snatch an offered joy which springs from a life in which the mental and bodily constitution have made pain predominate.
>
> *(The Mill on the Floss*, book 5, chapter 3)

In that sudden realization of this force of partial independence, what George Eliot had found is Philip's subliminal life, that irrepressibly savage will to live, even in an ill-shaped form. It was what, as a 20-year-old reader, she had found in the so-called immoral novels of George Sand: 'I would never dream of going to her writings as a moral code or text-book. I don't care whether I agree with her about marriage or not . . .'; but George Sand could give her reader six pages of human passion such that 'one might live a century with nothing but one's own dull faculties and not know so much as those six pages suggest' (GEL 1, p. 278). The power came from a different mind, and from what was to become a different part of George Eliot's own mind: the power of surplus passion.

In the 1860s and 1870s, John Hughlings Jackson—personally influenced by both George Henry Lewes and Herbert Spencer, and himself in turn an influence upon Myers and William James—was developing the language of the two hemispheres of the brain. In George Eliot it is as though much of what is signified in the pre-verbal right hemisphere, in all its intuitions and gut feelings and even savage impulses, was being translated into the left, that hemisphere which Hughlings Jackson said was the one which alone was conscious in words. To put it another way: in the background to her consciousness there was an intuitive sense of the totality of force at stake in any one moment, and at the front the capacity to work successively through all that it comprised and indicated, writing out part after part. As she works one mind within another in her sentences, Philip's mind in her mind, or right hemisphere within left, a reader can almost see George Eliot moved again, at a new level, by the sense of felt 'surplus' she is unfolding in the very act of writing. We have seen in Chapter 7 that extra life in the latter stages of *Adam Bede* through Hetty, kissing her own arms; we have seen it in Arthur at the moment when another person seemed to become more than a consequence of his life but an 'element' in it. George Eliot would not forget these extra things that burst through conventional understanding and raised the level of it.

The genius among humankind, said Myers, is one who possesses a readier communication between supraliminal and subliminal forces than most ordinary people can achieve. In what is called the inspiration of genius there is a 'sudden creation of new cerebral connections or pathways'.[17] Unseen, unknown latent forces emerged by 'subliminal uprush', breaking through the habits and limitations of the normal field of conscious attention. Then the re-enlivened consciousness of those emergent forces was not something merely in place of unconsciousness but was primed to be the vehicle that secured its passage, alert to translate its emotional transmissions. It was part of the novelist's mental equipment to keep consciousness on that alert, not shut itself up in dry rationalism, but stay close to its own potential sources. George Eliot, wrote the psychologist James Sully, always made her reader 'an unconscious, if not conscious, psychologist', minutely following thought processes rarely known in the individual characters themselves.[18]

For those ordinary people who were less than geniuses, an equivalent, said Myers, was what happened to them in dreams, or was experienced in odd anomalous disturbances and moments of instability, often hard to accommodate:

> We identify ourselves for the most part with a stream of voluntary, fully conscious ideas,—cerebral movements connected and purposive as the movement of the hand which records them. Meantime we are aware also of a substratum of fragmentary automatic, *liminal* ideas, of which we take small account. These are bubbles that break on the surface; but every now and then there is a stir among them. There is a rush upwards as of a subaqueous spring; an inspiration flashes into the mind for which our conscious effort has not prepared us. (*Human Personality*, p. 63)

Liminal ideas were what George Eliot did take account of, did make her readers take account of, as Thought—intrinsically inchoate—in its very making. This breaking of the surface is what sudden turns and bursts of music did for Philip Wakem, as though for him, as for Maggie, they were a blindly felt key to life, beneath the level of normal visible reality.

And at distinct moments, human beings become viscerally aware of such movements. A character may descend from above to below: Maggie, entangled in her sexual desires, remembers how, in the two years of her renunciation, she used to think that 'she had made great conquests, and won a lasting stand on serene heights above worldly temptations and conflict'; but 'here she was down again in the thick of a hot strife with her own and others' passions' (*The Mill on the Floss*, book 5, chapter 5). And equally a character may re-ascend by force of a saving thought: on the verge of succumbing to Stephen, Maggie remembers the resolve of weeks past, imagines what tomorrow will feel like, invokes the sense of something beyond the natural 'inclination of the moment' (book 6, chapter 14). But the language that is superhumanly George Eliot's ascends, turns, and descends within moments; works up from below, thinks back down from on high in swift combinations of thought. It is with her as Lydgate once put it, before he lost his way: the mind 'must be continually expanding and shrinking between the whole human horizon and the horizon of an object glass' (*Middlemarch*, chapter 63). It was out of an equivalent to-and-fro interchange between what Myers called the supraliminal and the subliminal that the complex mind of 'George Eliot' was created: a George Eliot who in one mind produced what could not be simply or wholly explained, and with another continued to make strenuous efforts nonetheless to understand it, at the very limits of understanding.

The Mill on the Floss is, in consequence, not only the biography of Maggie Tulliver or the transmuted autobiography of Marian Evans; it also loops backwards, after *Adam Bede*, to be the autobiography of why and how George Eliot had had to come into being, even through the struggles of Maggie. Riding the influence of Spencer and Lewes, George Eliot comes into fruition at just the point when psychology was becoming free of its previous subjection to philosophy, without yet becoming an independent scientific discipline: it held everything human in solution, as opposed to what in 'Janet's Repentance' was called 'that false psychology which prejudges individuals by means of formulae, and casts them, without further trouble, into duly lettered pigeon-holes' (chapter 8). True psychology becomes a name for all otherwise unclassified potential and residue, secrets and conflicts, emotional scars and messy longings: it is, at once, what Maggie Tulliver at one level could hardly bear unsorted within herself and what George Eliot at another made into the triumph of her art. Thinking across those levels, the critic Edward Dowden was to put the following question in an essay of 1872 which moved Lewes to tears and which he read to his wife:

> When we have passed in review the works of that great writer who calls herself George Eliot, and given for a time our use of sight to her portraitures of men and women, what form, as we move away, persists on the field of vision, and remains the chief centre of interest for the imagination?

It is not, he answers, the near-visible form of Maggie or Dinah or any of the other characters that stays with us so much as the character of George Eliot herself:

> one who, if not the real George Eliot, is that 'second self' who writes her books, and lives and speaks through them. Such a second self of an author is perhaps more substantial than any mere human personality encumbered with the accidents of flesh and blood and daily living. It stands at some distance from the primary self, and differs considerably from its fellow. It presents its person to us with fewer reserves; it is independent of local and temporary motives of speech or silence; it knows no man after the flesh; it is more than an individual; it utters secrets, but secrets which all men of all ages are to catch; while, behind it, lurks well pleased the veritable historical self secure from impertinent observation and criticism. (*Critical Heritage*, pp. 320–1)

Lewes was moved to read of the achievement he knew so well at first hand—how she had managed to both use and secure herself. That second self, in evolving out of the first, is become, wrote Dowden, a great nature, 'which has suffered and has now attained, which was perplexed and has now grasped the clue...possessed of something which makes self-mastery possible' (*Critical Heritage*, p. 321).

As Theophrastus Such says to his fellow creatures, 'the more intimately I seem to discern your weaknesses, the stronger to me is the proof that I share them. How otherwise could I get the discernment?' (*Impressions of Theophrastus Such*, chapter 1, 'Looking Inward'). It was a complex self-mastery, a strongly looped use of weaknesses, that involved what Myers had called 'a sudden creation of new cerebral connections and pathways'. 'George Eliot' may begin as a commenting persona or an anonymous narrator but her existence in the novels was increasingly that of a language-presence which came out of her abstracting from the characters all that they could not say or could not think or could not be, holding that for them when there was no other vehicle or home. And this analytic language became the expression of an intimated person as author and authority, humanly embodying emotional attitudes and mental beliefs otherwise difficult singly to specify or activate. This was what Edward Dowden meant by a 'second self' seeking to retrieve through the second life and second thought of fiction whatever was lost or broken, left neglected or anomalous, from the first life, from the old world order, from the subliminal store of latent human need. In every sense she was giving her life, her biography past and present, over to her work. As she wrote to a fan who supposed that on publication of a novel she must feel triumphant:

> Exultation is a dream before achievement, and rarely comes after. What comes after, is rather the sense that the work has been produced within one, like offspring, developing and growing by some force of which one's life has served as a vehicle, and that what is left of oneself is only a poor husk.   (GEL 8, p. 383)

It was to the writing of transmuted autobiography, in particular a psychological study of a woman such as Maggie who needed more than her own psychology, that her own life was being surrendered. The husk was what was left in the giving of herself almost wholly to her writing, her only offspring, as by a kind of blood transfusion. This was why in her *Autobiography* the novelist Margaret Oliphant spoke with conscious envy of how Lewes's care had allowed George Eliot to live in 'a mental greenhouse', untroubled by real family cares. Mrs Oliphant was left a widow, struggling to support the family by her writing without ceasing to be a dedicated mother. 'I think she must have been a dull woman with a great genius distinct from herself,' she wrote of her luckier rival, 'something like the gift of the old prophets.'[19] But it was not quite true. So much came from Marian Evans still.

And yet hers was a second self not just to the historical first self of Marian Evans but to almost all the characters—a higher meta-self that nonetheless was not simply looking down on them from above, but more as if driven up from below, by force of the complex and unspoken cries of pain and frustration otherwise unheard within a narrow fallen world. As she had first said in *Scenes of Clerical Life*, speaking of Tryan against the cruel and distant 'bird's-eye glance of a critic': 'I am not poised at that lofty height. I am on the level and in the press with him' (Janet's Repentance', chapter 10). Her people needed that second self, needed the feeling and the thinking, the support and the belief that was in it, though they rarely had it. It spoke for them as Thomas à Kempis had once spoken to them, in one of the works that felt to George Eliot to be a *real* book, not some forced, artificial, or insincere thing 'written on velvet cushions to teach endurance to those who are treading with bleeding feet on the stones'. Rather, 'it was written down by a hand that waited for the heart's prompting'. In 'a fashion of speech different from ours', it was, nonetheless, in translation and transmission 'a lasting record of human needs and human consolations' (*The Mill on the Floss*, book 4, chapter 3).

Reader as psychologist, reader in need of counsel, reader becoming his or her own self in the process—such a reader speaks like this: 'Of all the pleasures of reading I rank this the highest—hearing a voice, speaking as it were directly to you—almost as a confidence—of something the writer has come to know at a cost, or as a joy...I believe that the intimate, naked voice of indurated experience is what stays with us after all the paraphernalia of plot and what else has been forgotten.'[20] Such is the voice of George Eliot, arising out of the struggles of human psychology.

CHAPTER 9

'Great Facts Have Struggled to Find a Voice'

The Toll of the 1860s

It had always been difficult. A deeply uncomfortable feeling lay behind her becoming a writer in the first place:

> My troubles are purely psychical—self-dissatisfaction, and despair of achieving anything worth the doing. (GEL 2, pp. 155–6)

But the troubles were still there after the success of her first full-length novel:

> Yes, I *am* assured now that 'Adam Bede' was worth writing—worth living through long years to write. But now it seems impossible to me that I shall ever write anything so good and true again. (GEL 3, p. 66)

She told Barbara Bodichon that everything she wrote seemed to her 'poor and trivial in the doing' and only when it was quite gone from her, 'and no longer my own', did it seem satisfactory: 'That is the history of my life' (GEL 3, p. 366). And so the unbelief went on into *Romola*, even after the good reception of *The Mill on the Floss*, the novel that had managed to succeed *Adam Bede*:

> Will it ever be finished? Ever be worth anything? (GEL 4, p. 17)

Romola was the worst experience, beginning with what turned out to be almost a research trip to Italy from April to June 1860. The extensive reading that went into the writing and the writing itself were not only taking over her life, the whole process was now ageing and draining her. But on completing *Romola* in 1863, the beginning of a new work, *Felix Holt*, only started the whole process up again—writing 'in deep depression, feeling powerless' (GEL 4, p. 401):

> I have no confidence that the book will ever be worthily written ... I am going doggedly to work at my novel, seeing what determination can do in the face of despair. (GEL 4, p. 421)

273

'The old demon tries to get hold of me again whenever an old work is dismissed and a new one is being meditated' (GEL 3, p. 428). And so it was again in struggling with what actually turned out to be her masterpiece:

Sept. 11 [1869]—I do not feel very confident that I can make anything satisfactory out of 'Middlemarch'. I have need to remember that other things which have been accomplished by me were begin under the same cloud. G. has been reading 'Romola' again and expresses profound admiration. This is encouraging.   (Cross, 3, p. 99)

Then again, finally, with *Daniel Deronda* on 25 December 1875 of all days:

Each part as I see it before me *in werden* [potential] seems less likely to be anything else than a failure; but I see on looking back this morning—Christmas Day—that I really was in worse health and suffered equal depression about 'Romola'; and so far as I have recorded, the same thing seems to be true of 'Middlemarch'.   (Cross, 3, p. 271)

Speaking of her journal, she noted, 'I have often been helped in looking back in it, to compare former with actual states of despondency' (GEL 6, p. 439). But despite the partial relief, it clearly bothered her that she had to consult her journal, rather than some more immediate inner resource, to see how she might pull through again, despite or because of herself. She felt as though she had become a paper-woman, someone who could only, barely function through the work of words on a page; otherwise, a figure of moaning and groaning and panic, learning almost nothing from her recurrent fiction-related crises.

The doubt still remained to the very end. The historian Lord Acton reported in his review of Cross's *Life* that ultimately she had melancholy thoughts in looking to the future of her work: 'George Eliot did not believe in the finality of her system, and near the close of her life, she became uneasy as to the future of her fame.[1] She did not know how she would stand with those generations to come on whose favour she relied—we might even say, in the context of this book, with ourselves now. Acton also emphasizes her sense of the disparity between the ideas she conceived in her work and her execution of them. For all her method and her intent, if the execution was partial and the ideas themselves incomplete, what would it all come to? What if, in future, 'that mist that shrouded her horizon should ever rise over definite visions of accepted truth?' She feared that, in some new intellectual dawn, 'her doctrine' would be deemed old-fashioned and makeshift, and 'embarrass her renown'. She knew how, in the great unimaginable changes of future history, it could even be that 'men will have come to be ashamed of things they're proud of now' (*Felix Holt*, chapter 30). The first original work that she had planned to write, in 1853 when completing her translation of Feuerbach, was a book to be called *The Idea of a Future Life*, an idea that stayed with her through to her very last major work, *Daniel Deronda*.

Feuerbach himself had the astronomer Galileo say to Copernicus, like a man of the future world addressing the man of the past: 'Oh if you ... could have lived to see the new additions and confirmations of your system, what delight you would have derived from them!'[2] It is Galileo, born 1564, who makes his predecessor, died 1543, into his forerunner by a powerful loop of time combining indebtedness with reclamation. In *Middlemarch*, the doctor Lydgate takes as his hero the sixteenth-century physician and anatomist Vesalius, as he tells his young wife:

> 'No wonder the medical fogies in Middlemarch are jealous, when some of the greatest doctors living were fierce upon Vesalius because they had believed in Galen, and he showed that Galen was wrong. They called him a liar and a poisonous monster. But the facts of the human frame were on his side; and so he got the better of them.'
>
> 'And what happened to him afterwards?' said Rosamond, with some interest.
>
> 'Oh, he had a good deal of fighting to the last. And they did exasperate him enough at one time to make him burn a good deal of his work. Then he got shipwrecked just as he was coming from Jerusalem to take a great chair at Padua. He died rather miserably.'
>
> There was a moment's pause before Rosamond said, 'Do you know, Tertius, I often wish you had not been a medical man.'   (*Middlemarch*, chapter 45)

There was the truth of Vesalius' studies and there was also the struggle and the outcome of his life. But what if, after all, more like Lydgate than Vesalius, George Eliot had no transcendent merit to live on after her life's end? What if she was right in her distrust of her work, right as to the want of a future for the unsystematic system created by her novel-writing?

To W. H. Mallock in *Is Life Worth Living?* (1879), liberal-minded secularists such as George Eliot were no more than a temporary historical hiatus between the old and the new. Encouraged by Feuerbach and Comte, they tried to pour the old wine into new bottles, to paper over great cracks in meaning: that is to say, to translate Christian ethics into a post-Christian context without the theological underpinning on which those ethics had first been founded:

> [Secularists] forget that the ideals that were once active in the world were active amongst people who thought that they were more than ideals, and who very certainly did mistake them for facts; and they forget how different their position will be, as soon as their true nature is recognised.[3]

What could be the prohibition against suicide or euthanasia, against adultery or sexual freedom if marriage was no longer a permanent sacrament and life itself was something lesser, weaker, less significant and dignified than it had been under a Christian world order? How could secularists still emotively use the old language of the sacredness of life, having abolished the sacred? Was it not the case that human beings were more likely to behave well or shun temptation if they believed they were judged by an all-seeing God above, rather than relying upon their own conscience and ideals? There is no point comparing the present situation, said Mallock, to that which existed before Christianity, and saying it was the same. It was through the felt loss of a Christianity which Western men and women had depended upon throughout so much of their history that we found ourselves now living bereft. It was an age unparalleled in the history of human experience, a modern Babel of competing standards and confused purposes, made out of broken fragments of old and new in uneasy amalgamation. Life had now to have intrinsic value since there was no other any more to support it; it must be, in and of itself—with all its lonely difficulties and despite its transience—somehow worth living. What is it all for? was the suppressed cry of a race haunted by transience, finitude, and death.

The secularist 'has to make demands upon human life that were never made before; and human life is, in many ways, less able to answer to them' (*Life*, p. 19). It is true that a painter inspired with a great conception may have a week of intense fulfilment, employed upon his picture, such that it seems an end in itself; but the value of that week, said Mallock, depends upon his belief that he will realize his vision and finish his painting and have it recognized. If life is actually more like an unfinished painting, then all the people who try to live their life, paint their picture, will die cut short in disillusion, employed in temporary pastimes without an achieved end. Life must change its very shape in a modern world without a permanent goal, without a complete and final fulfilment, like the Heavenly City at the end of Bunyan's *Pilgrim's Progress*. But Mallock quotes George Eliot's great resistant cry, 'I desire no future that will break the ties of the past.' Holding on between two worlds, she would not accept that life had either had to go back to the foundationally old or forward to something more radically new. In *Is Life Worth Living?* Mallock at the end turns back to the old, to Roman Catholicism, in the spirit of John Henry Newman's own conversion. But there was another figure, a German of whose work Mallock was among the first English readers, who ruthlessly pointed to the new.

It was Nietzsche. To him, near the end of the century, George Eliot was no more than a Victorian secular hangover, still suffering from the death of a God she had helped to kill. Ambivalently, even at this late hour, she was seeking to stem the tide of modern doubt by replacing a Christian religion with a still Christianized morality, a compromised and insecure sense of humane decency shaken from its divine underpinnings. This, to Nietzsche, was decadence, already dying. In 1889, in *Twilight of the Idols*, the German polemicist famously proclaimed:

> G. Eliot.—They have got rid of the Christian God, and now feel obliged to cling all the more firmly to Christian morality: that is *English* consistency, let us not blame it on little

blue-stockings *à la* Eliot. In England, in response to every little emancipation from theology one has to reassert one's position in a fear-inspiring manner as a moral fanatic.[4]

English secular moralists were hidden cowards, scared at what they had half done. They tried to forget the genealogy beneath their morality, how much it relied on Christian belief for its origin and on the Christian God as its guarantee. That is why psychologically they were so dutifully and unremittingly moral in compensation: morality was itself a form of guilt for the destruction of the old belief; duty was the will to replace God by showing no loss of human goodness resulting. It was ironic that it was another German, Ludwig Feuerbach, who had helped George Eliot to effect this.

The point at issue, wrote Nietzsche in *The Genealogy of Morals* (1887), was 'the value of the non-egotistical instincts, the instincts of compassion, self-denial, and self-sacrifice'. These values were made things transcendent and absolute by liberal humanists, yet it was these very same selfless instincts that aroused first Nietzsche's suspicion and finally his contempt:

> It was here, precisely, that I sensed the greatest danger for humanity, in sublimest delusion and temptation—leading it whither? into nothingness? Here I sensed the beginning of the end, stagnation, nostalgic fatigue, a will that had turned *against* life.[5]

Stagnation was resistance to a new dawning future. It contained within it the restraining ethics of pity—a softening and a corrective weakening turned into a moral strength. What was being made was a second nature—only second natures, warned Nietzsche, are customarily weaker than the first.[6] Look what mankind has done to its first nature, says Nietzsche, speaking like a reverse edition of Feuerbach:

> In such psychological cruelty we see an insanity of the *will* that is without parallel: man's will to find himself guilty and unredeemably so . . . his will to erect an ideal (God's holiness) in order to assure himself of his own absolute unworthiness. What a mad, unhappy animal is man! (*The Genealogy of Morals*, p. 226, second essay section 22,)

The depression and unhappiness, the inability to resist the sickness of guilt and duty and self-disparagement, were the most telling signs of the loss of naturalness as a birthright: powerful desires became covert under the threat of social punishment. Without external discharge, feelings turned back inward, till punishment itself was unhealthily interiorized as shame and then bad conscience. A now divided and deformed creature had been violently severed from the old outward animal world of freedom and roaming, of contest and wilderness, and made to have a demeaning inner life of psychological consciousness, in place of action.[7] A tame social morality, the revenge of the weak herd massing together against the strongly divergent, was, to Nietzsche, all too boringly predictable. Abstract principle was mechanically applied to achieve rigidly consistent behaviour towards everyone, regardless of difference and in suppression of vitality.

What Nietzsche sought to bring into being was the Übermensch, the post-Christian superman beyond the second-rate tameness of the common world. A strong first nature is, in Nietzsche, 'the condition in which one is the *least* capable of being just'. It is a nature that breaks through second-order fair-mindedness whenever one is seized by a vehement, one-sided, all-surpassing, and unashamedly subjective passion—for a cause or an action, for an idea or person. The inspired person may be blind and narrow-minded, and yet

> this condition—unhistorical, anti-historical through and through—is the womb not only of the unjust but of every just deed too; and no painter will paint his picture, no general achieve his victory, no people attain its freedom without having first desired and striven for it in an unhistorical condition . . . As he who acts is, in Goethe's words, always without a conscience, so is he always without knowledge; he forgets many things so as to do one thing, he is unjust towards what lies behind him, and he recognises the rights only of that which is now to come into being and no other rights whatever. Thus he who acts loves his deed infinitely more than it deserves to be loved: and the finest deeds take place in such a superabundance of love . . . (*Untimely Meditations*, p. 64)

There are people who are morally just and sympathetic in relation to others, are conscious of historical and social context, rational as to likelihoods, and capable of impartially seeing every side of a question. It may not be fair that they—themselves the fair-minded—should be *less* capable of having an effect upon the life of the world than the person who ignores many things to do one thing; but that is what Nietzsche emphatically believed. From an external point of view, the unfair people of one obsessive idea might well be misguided or deluded. But they were buoyed up by unselfconscious convictions, and as such they could be the effective ones, capable of creating a possibility, only recognized as such in retrospect, by its very accomplishment. George Eliot in contrast belonged with the wide and many-sided minds, unwilling to be selfish and unjust because knowing themselves already too prone to be so; undertaking instead convoluted reflections upon the duties of self in relation to others, however unreciprocated. And yet there was still in her the voice that was heard in *The Mill on the Floss*: '"But I can't give up wishing," said Philip, impatiently. "It seems to me we can never give up longing and wishing while we are thoroughly alive. There are certain things we feel to be beautiful and good, and we must hunger after them"' (book 5, chapter 1).

Yet Nietzsche hated the voice of weak longing. I am no person, human all too human, he wrote at the end of *Ecce Homo* (1888); but rather 'I am dynamite'.[8] The explosion in him lay in three words and then their after-effect:

God is dead. But given how people are, it might be that there will be caves in which his shadow appears for another thousand years. And we—we must also conquer his shadow.[9]

George Eliot was, for Nietzsche, no more than a representative of those who tried to linger on amidst the shadows, refusing a radical revaluation of traditional Christian values. No wonder Dorothea would not and could not say what her religion was, and did not want it given a name. In *Daybreak*, against the shadows, Nietzsche had thought to blow away the last refuges of secularized religion, of unhealthily self-denying ideals, by casting the light of a deliberately cruel eye on the subterfuges of the pious.

And yet George Eliot saw some of this herself, in her own way. She knew, for example, the disablement as well as the conflict that accompanied the commitment to moral altruism. Of Daniel Deronda, above all, she wrote in culmination:

> His early-wakened sensibility and reflectiveness had developed into a many-sided sympathy, which threatened to hinder any persistent course of action: as soon as he took up any antagonism, though only in thought, he seemed to himself like the Sabine warriors in the memorable story—with nothing to meet his spear but flesh of his flesh, and objects that he loved. His imagination had so wrought itself to the habit of seeing things as they probably appeared to others, that a strong partisanship, unless it were against an immediate oppression, had become an insincerity to him....He hated vices mildly, being used to think of them less in the abstract than as part of mixed human natures having an individual history, which it was the bent of his mind to trace with understanding and pity. (*Daniel Deronda*, chapter 32)

The Sabine women, abducted by the Romans to be their wives, threw themselves between the Romans and the Sabines in the war that followed, women in the middle of conflict imploring their old fathers on one side and their new husbands on the other. In scrupulously trying to see as others saw, in thinking of vice not in the simple abstract but as part of complex individual histories, Deronda was like a classically female mediator, was like the novelist herself. Edith Simcox said that George Eliot's own 'instinct to make allowance for the other side' accounted for what 'may easily have been personal sympathy in her descriptions of Deronda's difficulty about the choice of a career'.[10] Nietzsche thought such liberalism a weakness, even a sickness; but whatever it was called, George Eliot knew, in particular through Deronda, its subtle threat to direct force and action:

> A too reflective and diffusive sympathy was in danger of paralysing in him that indignation against wrong and that selectness of fellowship which are the conditions of moral force; and in the last few years of confirmed manhood he had become so keenly aware of this that what he most longed for was either some external event, or some inward light, that would urge him into a definite line of action, and compress his wandering energy. (*Daniel Deronda*, chapter 32)

His impulse is to say, as he says to the young woman he rescues from suicidal despair, that anybody would have been glad to do as he had done. But Mirah replies, 'It was *you*, and not another, who found me.' *Saint Anybody*—as another character puts it in chapter 32—is the alias for someone hardly able to bear thinking of himself as a real person, a true I.

But, for Nietzsche, the worst deceivers were the writers who found in the refuge of civilized language an elaborate artifice for hiding devastatingly simple motivations, basic wants, and flaws, by the contriving of complex considerations arising out of them. Even the admission of their weaknesses became grist to their own mill. But he saw through their devices:

> *The eye that is feared*—Nothing is feared more by artists, poets and writers than the eye which sees their *petty deceit*... which sees through all the deception of their art the idea as it was when it first stood before them, perhaps as an entrancing being of light but perhaps too as a theft from the world, an everyday idea which they had to stretch, shorten, colour, swathe up, season, so as to make something of it instead of letting it make something of them... [11]

Apply all this to George Eliot: her fear of her ego and yet her doubts of her own worth; her self-distrust and her self-blame; her recurrent inner depression and her obsession with altruistic duty; her guilty consciousness that what she could do in art she could not do in life, that compensation was too often a form of cheating; even while resistance to cynicism and to melancholy was nonetheless necessary on behalf of life: 'What a mad, unhappy animal!' There was always Marian Evans, already like a damaged and inadequate first thing, groaning behind every second move made by George Eliot. To the cruel eye of a Nietzsche, what was being subconsciously admitted at those moments of chronic self-doubt was that writing was a form of cheating, a desperate effort to fabricate a second self upon an unsatisfactory first, and to substitute a vulnerably makeshift patchwork of morality over a yawning abyss of meaning.

And indeed, psychological deflections, camouflages, and secrets fascinated George Eliot.[12] Her interest in psychological secrecy could be just as ruthless as Nietzsche's. Our everyday confidence and certainty, she wrote in *The Spanish Gypsy*, is only built on knowing all 'that is *not* secret' (book 1 1807, my italics): it is the secret uncertainties that can really shake us, which is why they are kept secret. So even as she wrote, the question nagged at her: What would it be like if your writerly gift, your attempted safeguard, was taken away—what would be left of you?

That is why she produced the fine poem 'Armgart' after the painful death of Lewes's son Thornie in October 1869.

The stepfamily of three sons had marked a new epoch in mid-life. Cast out from one family by her own brother, she was now surrogate mother to another, once Lewes's boys could no longer be away at school. Charles was 16 in 1859 when he finally learnt that his parents' marriage had been over for five years. On leaving their school in Switzerland, the three boys would now be under the care of their father and Marian Evans, now Marian Lewes, the famous author of *Adam Bede*. Charles was always the simply steady, loyally decent ordinary boy, the one the couple could bear to have at home. For one thing, he shared a love of music with the woman they called 'Mutter' or 'Mother', while Agnes Lewes was 'Mamma'. Names were always difficult in the readjustments of her life. But Charles helped make the adjustment. Marian Lewes saw in him 'one of those creatures to whom goodness comes naturally. Not any exalted goodness, but everyday serviceable goodness such as wears through life' (GEL 4, p. 177). Even after Lewes's death, Charles proved to be touchingly supportive of the marriage to Johnny Cross, knowing his father would have wanted her to be protected.

It was the younger two boys who were problems for a couple who wanted to devote themselves to each other and to their work, and yet felt strong emotional obligations to the earlier family. Edith Simcox recalled George Eliot speaking 'half in self-reproach of the people who live in so many relations that their lives must be always full, whereas she always sent the strength of her feelings in the channel that absorbed it all. It has been so with her father' (GEL 9, p. 266). But Marian Evans's father had not made his one channel that of writing of the ordinary lives of others at one level whilst separating herself from them at another. It might indeed seem that writing was too close to cheating, to hypocrisy, to artificial life. The separation from the outer world had been partly forced upon the couple as a painfully conscious result of their irregular union, an ostracism that created 'a sort of dual egoism' in living for each other. But the concentration of that relationship was ever increasingly on her work. And that meant the equivocal and self-doubting state of being a writer, and in particular a realist novelist, placed uneasily between fiction and the world. The stepfamily was only a practical version of this tension between life and work, between self and others, but though perhaps a simple issue when compared to the great questions of life and mind, it would not simply go away.

The trouble was that neither of the younger brothers could find a steady career, though repeatedly sent away at considerable expense on different projects. Thornton, two years younger than Charles, was the ebullient enthusiastic one, noisy and hopeful, but unable to settle to anything but wild ideas of action, adventure, or war. When he left for Natal in 1863 his stepmother described him as 'at once amiable and troublesome, easy and difficult to manage', causing both her and Lewes considerable anxiety (GEL 4, p. 117). He had failed his exams for the Indian civil service, and in South Africa involved himself instead in wildly unsuccessful schemes for working the land and making money. Bertie, two years younger still, was rather helplessly dim in such a family. He joined his brother in South Africa in 1866 after a failed attempt at farming in Scotland, until Thornie returned home in 1869 suffering badly with what he thought was kidney stone. It was a spinal complaint that killed him. Marian Lewes for once left off her novel-writing, from May to October 1869, whilst she helped nurse him, and he died in her arms. 'Death,' she wrote to her fellow novelist Harriet Beecher Stowe, 'had never come near me through the twenty years since I lost my Father, and this parting has entered very deeply into me. I never before felt so keenly the wealth one possesses in every being to whose mind and body it is possible to minister comfort through love and care' (GEL 5, p. 71). Across the years, both the 'unconventional intellectual daughter and the exiling stepmother' were able for once, as one critic puts it, to assert the precedence of 'womanly nurturance' over 'the will to autonomous mental work'.[13]

'Armgart' is thus about a great female opera singer who has lost the extraordinary voice which had excused her everything, and has to become an ordinary human being, just like a million others, instead. She will not take consolation or medication at her loss—her doctor only wanted, she says, to

> Drug me to sleep that I may wake again
> Without a purpose, abject as the rest
> To bear the yoke of life. He shall not cheat me
> Of that fresh strength which anguish gives the soul,
> The inspiration of revolt, ere rage
> Slackens to faltering.
>
> (585–90)

Like a figure out of Nietzsche she had wanted to exist (in the title of one of his works) 'beyond good and evil'. But living on after the death of her superhuman gift, whether in defiance or despair, hers is, she says:

> A power turned to pain—as meaningless
> As letters fallen asunder that once made
> A hymn of rapture.
>
> (564–6)

What happened if the sentences fell apart? What if, in George Eliot's own case, the realist novel was no more than a means of disguising its author's hidden need and overwhelming ambition within the depiction of the ordinary? But another part of George Eliot, closer to Marian Evans, cries out almost angrily, through Armgart's lamed and loyal cousin Walpurga. To the superwoman who has suddenly lost her special powers and mourns the loss, she retorts: Why should the wheels of destiny run over many lives 'but yours they must keep clear of' (822)? If you are no longer special, then turn your lost gift into a new concern for helping others, who never even had such gifts in the first place. 'Who has need of me?' says Armgart. To which Walpurga replies, 'Love finds the need it fills' (808).

George Eliot's great admirer, Edith Simcox, knew that even in the later years when she recreated herself as the wise Madonna, and was trying to transfer into life something of the complex balance she had been seeking in fiction, she could still be as dangerous as she could be compassionate. It is the vital paragraph I quoted first in the Introduction:

> [I]n spite of the tenderness for all human weakness that was natural to her, and the scrupulous charity of her overt judgments, the fact remained that her natural standard was ruthlessly out of reach, and it was a painful discipline for her friends to feel that she was compelled to lower it to suit their infirmities. The intense humility of her self-appreciation, and the unfeigned readiness with which she would even herself with any sinner who sought her counsel, had the same effect upon those who could compare what she condemned in herself with what she tolerated in them.[14]

Though George Eliot 'would *even* herself', Edith Simcox still felt herself silently judged from a higher standard, like Gwendolen before Daniel Deronda. What was involved was an unbearably complex amalgam of checks and balances: George Eliot's own fear of the potential cruelty of her intelligence—an intelligence that did much to combat a deep lack of self-confidence but also encouraged a critical pride that was itself a ground for self-reproach; the threat of condescension, nonetheless, implicated in the very effort at kindness, to its detriment; the asymmetry between the benevolent tolerance of others and the unpityingly rigorous demands she had to make on herself in order to achieve it; the tension between judgement and mitigation, between what felt natural and what correctively must go against the natural grain; the high moral standard that seemed so charitable as to abolish all ordinary standards in offering a tenderness that felt almost unmerited; the sympathy with error and sin that came out of her own lashed conscience too; the resolve to treat others as the products of antecedent circumstances, and yet oneself as responsibly, accountably free. And so on, and so on went the tensions and paradoxes, there seemed to be a thousand such inter-volved considerations. Logic could not hold them together, only something like a person could do so—an extended exceptional person sustained within writing, and made up of a combination of relations too subtle separately to list or wholly to explicate.

But if Nietzsche ever suspected that George Eliot was frighteningly dangerous or wonderfully complex, he dismissed the danger as the cruelty of moralism and the complexity as a form of evasion. In *Thus Spoke Zarathustra*, Nietzsche's protagonist, the Prophet, comes upon the Ugliest Man in the world. Do you know who I am, the

Ugliest Man asks him—to which the Prophet suddenly gives an explosive reply of terrible realization:

> 'You are the murderer of God...You could not endure him who saw you—who saw you unblinking and through and through, you ugliest man! You took revenge upon the witness!'

To this in turn the figure of Ugliness then says, in defence of shame and in resistance to pity:

> But he—had to die: he looked with eyes that saw everything—he saw the depths and abysses of man; all man's hidden disgrace and ugliness. His pity knew no shame: he crept into my dirtiest corners. This absolutely-curious, too-intrusive, over-compassionate god had to die. He always saw me: I desired to have revenge on such a witness—or cease to live myself. The god who saw everything, even man: this god had to die. Man could not endure that such a witness should live.[15]

George Eliot is not for once the ugly one here, however much the Marian Evans in her knew the power of personal shame and secrecy, or sought some resistance to the old dogmas. It is rather as though, just as the Ugliest Man murdered God, a Nietzsche would kill off a George Eliot, in terms of the mental types they each represent in the later movements of the nineteenth century. For just as the Ugliest Man describes it, is the pain of her god-like analyses. She saw everything. So it is for a reader in the very introduction to Felix Holt on private stories ostensibly too small or too secret to be known to the world:

> There are glances of hatred that stab and raise no cry of murder; robberies that leave man or woman for ever beggared of peace and joy, yet kept secret by the sufferer— committed to no sound except that made on the face by the slow months of suppressed anguish and early morning tears. Many an inherited sorrow that has marred a life has been breathed into no human ear.

There are, she concludes, at deep human levels the 'quivering nerves' of 'sleepless memory' which continues its watch through all dreams. By literary communication, itself secret, the prose uses the force of verbal generalizations to drive out of hiding the specific sleepless memories, sub-vocal and subconscious, held perilously secret within almost every reader. The words seem to examine the reader even as the reader examines them, caught as readers are between seeing the language out there and registering it as feelings, shames, scars, and pains, in here. No wonder human beings turn away from such terrible scrutiny, within and without. With George Eliot, wrote the Victorian man of letters John Morley, the reader with a conscience must open the book as though putting himself into the confessional.[16]

Unlike Mallock, George Eliot did not read Nietzsche, while Nietzsche, never much interested in mere fairness, hardly read George Eliot with much thoroughness. But local cautions aside, there is a bigger issue in the mental battleground created between what George Eliot and Friedrich Nietzsche represent. It lies in the urgent concerns that their rival traditions bequeath to the modern world, and in the anxieties each symbolically constitutes for the other. I have put down Nietzsche's challenges, together with George Eliot's painful awareness of what, within her own terms, was their translated substance, in order to set the tangled scene for the terrible struggle that went on in the writings of the 1860s, in the different sub-genres of her experimentation. A history novel, a fable, a drama or long poem, a political novel— but none of them wholly or clearly what they purported to be: these were the challenges of new territories. Hers was increasingly now a series of experiments in the 'mixed condition of things': there the distinction that was attempted in *Romola* between 'hopeless confusion' and 'struggling order' could not yet be clear (chapter 57). To Nietzsche it would be the former, where George Eliot hoped it was the latter.

The Historical Novel: *Romola* and 'a transition in her life' (1860–3)

This is the period of the writing's middle age. Of the composition of *Romola* in 1862–3, John Cross recalled his wife's account of that time:

> The writing of 'Romola' ploughed into her more than any of her other books. She told me she could put her finger on it as marking a well-defined transition in her life. In her own words, 'I began it a young woman,—I finished it an old woman.' (Cross, 2, p. 352)

This had much to do with all that went into the switch from the warm familiarity of the Midlands of the early nineteenth century to the challenge, set by Lewes himself in 1860 during an Italian holiday, of fully depicting Florence in 1492. It fitted with her own admiration of the historical novels of Walter Scott. But with it went all that heavy research George Eliot required of herself in order to acquire 'as full a vision of the medium in which a character moves as of the character itself' (GEL 4, p. 97). It made her feel like the aged scholar she was to depict in *Middlemarch*, Casaubon, lost amongst the archives of research, and it added tension to the supportive relationship Lewes provided. She read over 150 books in preparation—Dante, Boccaccio, Petrarch, Machiavelli, Cellini, Pico della Mirandola, as well as lesser-known Renaissance writers, the complete works of Savonarola, historical novels, histories and biographies of the period, art and literary histories, plus 25 period sources from

Florentine chroniclers.[17] But the struggle was not just with the historical material. She began it as a young woman, fresh from going back to write of Maggie; but now a process of ageing took place in the wearing course of the writing itself. A startling offer of £10,000 from George Smith (nearly a quarter of her earnings across a whole successful writing career), plus a consulting editorship of the *Cornhill Magazine* for Lewes, lured her away from the supportive Blackwood. But Smith required serialized publication in twelve (eventually fourteen) monthly parts in the *Cornhill* when she had only the first eight chapters, less than two parts, already completed. Privately John Blackwood blamed Lewes for his acquisitive management of her affairs ('It is too bad after all the kindness she has experienced but I am sure she would do it against her inclination' (GEL 4, p. 38)), though she too was relieved to be free of money worries with Lewes's family to support. Towards her, the decent man was dignified and magnanimous: 'I am of course sorry that your new Novel is not to come out under the old colours but I am glad to hear that you have made so satisfactory an arrangement' (GEL 4, p. 35). At any rate, she was left anxious, depressed, and often ill, with headache and toothache and stomach-ache, colds and insomnia, and biliousness, perhaps menopausal symptoms. By November 1861, in the midst of trying to get help by reading Scott's *The Pirate*, she was tempted to abandon the whole thing.

But the pressures were also internal to the novel. In the work of this middle period in her life, what was painful to her was the increased *indirectness* she had to register between her characters. It was a loss of the youthful directness that Maggie Tulliver always wanted though never entirely found, the absolute openness that Dinah brought to Hetty in her cell, out of belief of the need finally to tell everything. A fellow novelist, Mrs Humphry Ward, said of George Eliot how 'impossible' it was 'for her to "talk" her books': 'she was too self-conscious, too desperately reflective, too rich in second thoughts for that'.[18] Writing began where the ability for direct speaking ran out, just as George Eliot came into existence increasingly in those silent spaces between her characters where she could almost hear the subconscious thoughts they suppressed. So much would not come out as feelings expressed in direct words but was forced back in as thwarted energy, as though at the very origin of human psychology, only to come back out again in devious or misshapen forms: 'It was the final departure of moral youthfulness... something was gone' (*Romola*, chapter 22).

What was gone is what is felt by the aged in such a way as to age them further. In *Felix Holt* Mrs Transome 'felt herself loveless; if she was important to any one, it was only to her old-waiting woman Denner' (chapter 35). But when in extremis Denner asks her stricken mistress that characteristically direct George Eliot question, what can she do, how can she help, it is only to hear this: 'No, good Denner... You can't help me'—to which Denner replies, 'That's the hardest word of all, madam' (chapter 50).

The greatest achievement of this hard middle-age period is the creation of the handsome young Greek outsider in fifteenth-century Florence, Tito Melema, like an evil threatening genius inside her. It says everything that the most compelling subject has become the deep loss of trust and of love and of help. For Tito, taken further than the portrayal of Arthur Donnithorne in *Adam Bede*, is the cheater of truth, the betraying denier of emotional claims, the most indirect of all her characters. Concealment in the earlier work came out of a single catastrophic happening—with Hetty, say—but now it becomes a persistent, psychological form of existence, close to George Eliot's own deepest fears and insecurities.

Where Romola is devoted to her blind and demanding father, Tito last knew of his own foster father—to whom he has owed everything—as a man captured and enslaved by the Turks, and probably now dead. In his youth and strength, with new opportunities before him, Tito was not going to go back now, he tells himself, for the sake of a lost old man:

> After a long voyage, to spend months, perhaps years, in a search for which even now there was no guarantee that it would not prove vain...Any maxims that required a man to fling away the good that was needed to make existence sweet, were only the lining of human selfishness turned outward: they were made by men who wanted others to sacrifice themselves for their sake. He would rather than Baldassarre should not suffer: he liked no one to suffer; but could any philosophy prove to him that he was bound to care for another's suffering more than his own? To do so he must have loved Baldassarre devotedly, and he did *not* love him... (*Romola*, chapter 11)

There are, that separated mind knows, obligations which can never be proved as existent in the absence of feeling. And what Tito has done, gradually and inexorably, is deaden those sensibilities in himself, in the liberation of disinheritance. When Baldassarre turns up in Florence after all, it is only for Tito to deny all knowledge of him. Confronted by the old man's pleas, Tito immediately blurted out, 'He is a madman': had he not, he could have made some extenuation of his past behaviour, how he had thought there was no chance, and so on. But instead he is shocked to find that that 'sudden' denial was something that he had 'prepared' for himself, without knowing it was preparation (chapter 23). George Eliot herself knew she had wanted to be like a Romola to Robert Evans and did love him. But on the other side of herself she also knew what might go into the fight for her own life. What fired her own imagination of Tito was the terrifyingly autonomous rationality of the blank negation: 'and he did *not* love him', the simple 'and' and 'not' the hardest words of all in creating the matter of fact.

Poised at the beginning of his new-found Florentine career, Tito now must fear that Romola, his betrothed, is on the verge of discovering how he has denied and betrayed Baldassarre. It is so close to her finding out:

> There was a strange complication in his mental state. His heart sank at the probability that a great change was coming over his prospects, while at the same time his thoughts were darting over a hundred details of the course he would take when the change had

come; and yet he returned Romola's gaze with a hungry sense that it might be the last time she would ever bend it on him with full unquestioning confidence.

(*Romola*, chapter 13)

It appeared to be 'the last moment in which she would love him without suspicion', and 'at the same time' the quick mind is made to see the present as already becoming the past in a sickeningly looming future; 'and yet' in the very midst of alternative realities he persists in acting the same within this present. It has to be expressed in one sentence, covering all the shifts that still are held together.

This is not the good little bluestocking George Eliot who is mocked by Nietzsche, but someone every bit as deadly as he in the exposing work of an all-seeing psychology. She knows that Tito, the charmer and hedonist who always tries to avoid what is unpleasant, has made his own safety his 'god' (chapter 60): 'he had no sense that there was strength and safety in truth' (chapter 23). He has cut himself adrift from any tradition of faith or ethics, dismissing any form of the all-seeing god. Nietzsche might have asked why George Eliot had to make such a figure at best amoral, why she had to see him as increasingly immoral. But to her, as just occasionally to Tito himself, it is frightening that he is so, and that a vision of a world without morality might be so plausible, so possible. That fear—which George Eliot calls 'dread' and Nietzsche 'cowardice'—may be morality's own last cry of the need for itself.

Romola's brother, Dino, may know the truth about Tito but he is dying. In the crosscurrents of fifteenth-century Florence, in the complex mixture of cultural Renaissance and religious Reformation, the brother had turned from the classical learning of their scholar father, despite the old man's blind neediness for a successor, and deserted his family to become the austere monk, Fra Luca. Romola explains to Tito why she must go to him despite their long and bitter separation and the feelings she has of betrayal, even though to Dino, in his own world, his conversion was a hard act of conscience:

> He is very ill, and he has abjured me to go and see him. I cannot refuse it, although I hold him guilty; I still remember how I loved him when I was a little girl, before I knew that he would forsake my father. And perhaps he has some word of penitence to send by me. It cost me a struggle to act in opposition to my father's feeling, which I have always held to be just. I am almost sure you will think I have chosen rightly, Tito, because I have noticed that your nature is less rigid than mine, and nothing makes you angry: it would cost you less to be forgiving; though, if you had seen your father forsaken by one to whom he had given his chief love—by one in whom he had planned his labour and his hopes—forsaken when his need was becoming greatest— even you, Tito, would find it hard to forgive. (*Romola*, chapter 13)

'I still remember how I loved him when I was a little girl, before...' is pure George Eliot in relation to the early life with a brother—the loss and the continuing claim. But equally Romola's 'if you...' is a vital and much-used second gear in George

Eliot's mental equipment: What if it were *you*? is always a question for herself. Only here, even while Romola seeks justification for the apparent weakness of forgiveness, the secret inner identification lies for Tito in the quite different way in which he himself forsook and denied a father, for reasons less justifiable than Romola's brother. Of course, Tito would like to stop Romola from seeing her brother; for his first thought is to avoid the danger of Dino giving him away. But the reader hears in the silence that follows her speech the indirectness of Tito's suppressed inner response, as though it measured the angle of his deflection from the straight way:

> What could he say? He was not equal to the hypocrisy of telling Romola that such offences ought not to be pardoned; and he had not the courage to utter any words of dissuasion.

He says out loud instead, after that missed beat:

> 'You are right, my Romola; you are always right, except in thinking too well of me.'

And then at once, at the word 'except', George Eliot appears in the human tangle with her own characteristic word 'really':

> There was really some genuineness in those last words, and Tito looked very beautiful as he uttered them, with an unusual pallor in his face, and a slight quivering of his lip . . .
> > (*Romola*, chapter 13)

This is the family damage that Marian Evans knew so painfully, played over again with all the problems of fathers and brothers and unreliable lovers, in a different variation. But what is most disturbingly frightening here are the lingering remnants and residual possibilities of real goodness in the chancer who is Tito—in the inability as yet of a more complete hypocrisy; in the almost involuntary genuineness of what might indeed have been 'last words' had not the exposure of his sin been luckily averted by the brother's death. It is not a simple distinction between ugliness at one level and beauty at another, when good and evil are still too close to each other and not yet fully formed as irrevocably distinct. The reader feels simultaneously existent in one world of morality where badness is made plain—infidelity, untruthfulness, cheating—and in another of psychology where it is wholly imaginable and temptingly understandable. And yet those two worlds somehow overlap, must interrelate, are troublingly co-existent.

Such is the territory of George Eliot's troubled middle period, already in her own terms dense with the problems which Nietzsche later represented. It is where Romola finds herself stranded when she turns from thinking of her brother to looking up to see Tito, from the pale of Fra Luca's dying face to the sensuous warmth of a handsome living one, as if across wholly different worlds:

> Strange, bewildering transition from those pale images of sorrow and death to this bright youthfulness, as of a sun-god who knew nothing of night! What thought could reconcile that worn anguish in her brother's face—that straining after something invisible—with this satisfied strength and beauty, and make it intelligible that they belonged to the same world? Or was there never any reconciling of them, but only a blind worship of clashing deities, first in mad joy and then in wailing? Romola for the first time felt this questioning need like a sudden uneasy dizziness and want of something to grasp; it was an experience hardly longer than a sigh, for the eager theorising of ages is compressed, as in a seed, in the momentary want of a single mind. (*Romola*, chapter 17)

That is where, for George Eliot, the thinking of the ages comes from or goes into: the barely visible point of individual need, fractionally opening a tiny space for thinking in the transition between alternations, at a level beneath the muffling continuance of mundane time. And then the momentary dizziness and felt lack of something to grasp are gone again, unresolved and as if they had never been:

> But there was no answer to meet the need, and it vanished before the returning rush of young sympathy with the glad loving beauty that beamed upon her in new radiance, like the dawn after we have looked away from it to the grey west. (*Romola*, chapter 17)

A framework of understanding is missing, such that without it the anomalous thought and the empty transition can scarcely be remembered, let alone formulated, giving way to what more happily may come next. To Nietzsche, in his extreme and impatient demand, it was timidity and laziness that left unheard something that cried out in the situation of a life, as to every youthful soul: 'Be yourself, all you are now doing, thinking, desiring, is not you yourself.' There exists, he says, no worse creatures than those who, neglecting that cry, have thus 'evaded [their] genius and now look furtively to left and right', lost and empty inside. The best artists are those who, above all people, hate this evasion and betrayal, and it is these artists who 'reveal everyone's secret bad conscience': namely, the law that every man is a 'unique miracle' and must take him or herself seriously, and largely dares not and does not (*Untimely Meditations*, pp. 127–8). Again, that is why many readers of George Eliot go and have gone to her work—in that bad conscience of not bearing to think hard enough in their lives. It was what Marian Evans had feared of herself; it was what George Eliot still feared the future would say of her writings.

And still Tito hides from Romola, now his wife, the existence of Baldassarre, the guardian he left for dead. As a result he finds himself involuntarily shrinking from her even whilst the deceit is outwardly successful:

> The terrible resurrection of secret fears, which, if Romola had known them, would have alienated her from him for ever, caused him to feel an alienation already begun between them—caused him to feel a certain repulsion towards a woman from whose mind he was in danger. That feeling had taken hold of him unawares... (*Romola*, chapter 27)

'Already' marks the characteristic loss of straightforwardness. The syntax here figures not only the content of Tito's thoughts but the pattern and the internal wiring of his ethical character. It leads Tito, in the midst of his continuing marriage, to find secret relief in the arms of the pretty, undemanding Tessa instead: 'He wanted a refuge from a standard disagreeably rigorous, of which he could not make himself independent' (chapter 34). There is in marriage, says Dorothea to Rosamond in *Middlemarch*, 'something even awful in the nearness it brings', but Tito's 'nearness' to Romola serves as a means only to work apart from her even from within their relationship. When we do turn to someone else apart from our marriage, continues Dorothea, 'it murders our marriage—and then the marriage stays with us like a murder' (*Middlemarch*, chapter 81). But Tito is all about getting away with murder— not only of the marriage but of the very sense of an overarching truth such that if it is not seen and not known, it is made non-existent. That too is a tiny early modern version of the killing of God:

> His mind was destitute of that dread which has been erroneously decried as if it were nothing higher than a man's animal care for his own skin: that awe of the Divine Nemesis which was felt by religious pagans, and, though it took a more positive form under Christianity, is still felt by the mass of mankind simply as a vague fear at anything which is called wrong-doing. Such terror of the unseen is so far above mere sensual cowardice that it will annihilate that cowardice: it is the initial recognition of a moral law... (*Romola*, chapter 11)

Tito is lawless. His relationship with the pliable Tina means, terribly to him, 'there would *always* be a risk of betrayal' (chapter 18), when all he wants to do is live in the immediate present. But that is to believe only in a life of chance and risk. George Eliot, in the words of R. H. Hutton, as we have seen in Chapter 6, suffered the inordinate stress of having to be 'a law to herself', her sense of scrupulous moral duty without an overseeing God creating in her an 'artificial' character, the second nature of a woman who—non-pejoratively speaking—'was her own God'.[19] In this, the Christian Hutton was making the same point as the post-Christian Nietzsche: that is how it is for those in the high Victorian age who are too little religious for the religious, insufficiently secular for the secular. The point for both critics was that morality as previously conceived was unsustainable without the Judaeo-Christian God as a reality; and that George Eliot was the quintessentially strained product of a cruelly transitional, in-between age, neither wholly emancipated from the old faith nor devoutly assured by it. The loss of a divine judge outside man resulted, for George Eliot, in a tension between the temptation to an easy self-absolution—letting oneself off in relation to conduct that, if you believed in an external spiritual judge, you would probably condemn—and the countervailing impulse to apply the corrective upon oneself too sternly, too unremittingly, too anxiously if there is no other power in creation which can be relied on but the moral efforts of your own untrustworthy self. Tito comes out of that tension and intensifies it.

But George Eliot's wager is that the great agnostic space she occupies between faith and unbelief is not merely historical and transitional—in Victorian England any more than in Renaissance Florence—but a recurrent in-between place lodged deep in the configuration of the human psyche as the source of its thinking. It was thinking that arose out of the subliminal reservoir of tensions, paradoxes, ambivalences, and conflicting needs that still held life in solution by their instinctive refusal to yield to easy resolution. And in that equivocal area of being lies also George Eliot's great discovery: the spectrum of psychological response which, fluctuating between unconscious and subconscious, she calls in *Adam Bede*—speaking of Arthur and his sexual temptations—

> a sort of backstairs influence, not admitted to himself...In a piece of machinery...a small unnoticeable wheel which has a great deal to do with the motion of the large obvious ones. (*Adam Bede*, chapter 16)

One register—the non-conscious or unspoken—is translated into another—the consciousness of George Eliot, where it is shocking to find it admitted and articulated.

Faith and security are shaken, and religion too is unmasked. To so many around him Savonarola, monk, prophet, politician, and leader, had seemed to be a kind of superman who, by expelling the corrupt Medici dynasty, would create in republican Florence a new Jerusalem. But though meant to become unified again through his agency, politics and religion are secretly becoming two different worlds in him: he is a man in whom 'irrevocable errors and lapses from veracity' are now become neurologically entwined 'with noble purposes and sincere beliefs'; whose 'self-justifying expediency' is inwoven with the 'tissue of a great work' as one organic body (*Romola*, chapter 64). At a crucial moment he has to be tested as no modern man or woman of George Eliot's own age would ever have to be. He must face Ordeal by Fire in order to show he is indeed miraculously a chosen one. And that it is when, for all his self-proclaimed divine mission, Savonarola finds it 'impossible to believe' that he or any man can walk through flames 'unhurt'; impossible, even if he resolved to attempt it, that he would not 'shrink' involuntarily at the last moment. This is still a creature, one who at basis is revealed as essentially biological. And equivalently at such moments George Eliot herself shifts from cultural humanist to scientific biologist in another move across differing world-views. When Savonarola imagines a human being entering the fire, 'he felt it with shuddering vibrations to the extremities of his sensitive fingers'.

Mentally he cannot wholly explain this sudden recoil, even to himself:

> Our naked feelings make haste to clothe themselves in propositions which lie at hand among our store of opinions, and to give a true account of what passes within us something else is necessary besides sincerity, even when sincerity is unmixed.
>
> (*Romola*, chapter 64)

That even sincerity cannot go sufficiently deep into the psyche, is again the sign of this area and this period for George Eliot, when nothing seems to hold. Even as he kneels in audible prayer, seeking belief to transcend the fire, Savonarola no longer hears the words on his lips but other voices in his head, rehearsing a way out: 'The appeal to Heaven for a miracle by a rash acceptance of a challenge, which is a mere snare prepared for me by ignoble foes, would be a tempting of God, and the appeal would not be responded to' (*Romola*, chapter 64).

In this way Savonarola evades the Trial but in so doing loses the support of the people. But then, as his authority gives way, he is seized by the Medici faction, to face torture unless he confesses to the duplicity of using God for political ends:

> [I]nstead of eyes that venerated and knees that knelt, instead of a great work on its way to accomplishment, and in its prosperity stamping the agent as a chosen instrument, there came the hooting and the spitting and the cursing of the crowd; and then the hard faces of enemies made judges; and then the horrible torture, and with the torture the irrepressible cry, 'It is true what you would have me say: let me go: do not torture me again: yes, yes I am guilty.' (*Romola*, chapter 71)

It was not only the sheer pain of torture that forced this submission, says George Eliot. It was also the inner devastation of self-belief in the face of the mocking crowd, and, with that, the psychological reversal that followed his own horrified recognition that he cannot prove himself through trial or torture. The sheer force of the real-world outcome shakes and then confirms his loss of faith in himself, confidence in his own subjective reality gone as if it had never been, except as delusion. It was

> that wavering of belief concerning his own impressions and motives which most human beings who have not a stupid inflexibility of self-confidence must be liable to under a marked change of external conditions. (*Romola*, chapter 71)

I cannot have been right is the sudden naked feeling behind the terrible intelligence that comes out of that inability to be simply stupid. This was why, at a far lesser level, George Eliot herself was vulnerable even to reviews: they exposed a long-feared but suddenly opening gap between the internal and the external worlds, when the idea or conception she had had in her writing and in her self seemingly had no actualized reality in the world outside her head. It is not just that 'self-confidence' goes, but everything else of the evolved self can disappear with it and the world become inhospitably bare again.

Yet after her inevitable disillusionment with the faithless Tito, Romola had psychologically needed to believe in Savonarola. It was a complicated substitution because it was Savonarola who had made her give up on the idea of leaving her husband. But the earlier threat of papal excommunication against her mentor had removed Romola's subtle feeling for what George Eliot calls those 'finer shades of fact' which 'soften the edge' of simple antitheses of good and evil. It was easier if her image of Savonarola could be purified through his being seen as the victim of a corrupt church. For in her own predicament 'Romola required a strength that neutrality could not give':

> [T]his Excommunication, which simplified and ennobled the resistant position of Savonarola by bringing into prominence its wider relations, seemed to come to her like a rescue from the threatening isolation of criticism and doubt.   (*Romola*, chapter 55)

But, like the 'sincere', the 'simple' and the 'noble' are no longer innocent. They belong to what, 'in the struggle of the affections, seeking a justification for love and hope' (chapter 52), Nietzsche would again harshly call a form of cheating, and Spinoza, more neutrally, *conatus*. But like confidence, this needy trust can disappear suddenly in the face of too many new and disillusioning discoveries. So it is when Romola begins to see all too clearly Savonarola's excesses of ego, and amorality in politics:

> With the sinking of high human trust, the dignity of life sinks too; we cease to believe in our own better self, since that also is part of the common nature which is degraded in our thought; and all the finer impulses of the soul are diluted. Romola felt even the springs of her once active pity drying up, and leaving her to barren egoistic complaining.   (*Romola*, chapter 61)

'Degraded' and then 'barren': this is the worst that the creator of Janet and Adam and Maggie had come to, the very 'we' language turning against faith in 'us' at bottom. 'We cease to believe in our *own* better self.' What George Eliot here does is place herself and her people in situations that risk allowing the hidden and the murky and the disillusioning to emerge and be exposed. And that is her toughest sincerity in *Romola*, working against the tricks and feints of sincerity itself. You can feel there human creatures 'wavering' from internal conviction in the face of external pressures; 'darting' their thoughts towards possibilities of future escape in the fundamental effort to seek pleasure or avoid pain; 'shrinking' away from 'the threatening isolation of criticism and doubt'—all as though by minute antennae and tiny feelers that the organism does not want to acknowledge at the larger upper level of conscious conventional character.

It comes to a crisis when Savonarola denies Romola's plea to spare the life of her godfather. Bernardo del Nero was a friend of the late Lorenzo de' Medici, the Magnificent, and remains faithful to Lorenzo's sons. But he takes no part in the Medicean counter conspiracy against Savonarola, though equally he will not expose it to the other side. He is an in-between man not out of indecision but out of commitment to both sides, or aspects in them. But partly through Tito's treachery in acting as a double agent, del Nero is arrested as a conspirator and summarily executed with other conspirators, despite Romola's appeal. Romola hears the condemned men leaving for an execution she will not witness:

> She needed no arm to support her; she shed no tears. She felt that intensity of life which seems to transcend both grief and joy—in which the mind seems to itself akin to elder forces that wrought out existence before the birth of pleasure and pain. Since her godfather's fate had been decided, the previous struggle of feeling in her had given way to an identification of herself with him in these supreme moments: she was inwardly asserting for him that, if he suffered the punishment of treason, he did not deserve the name of traitor; he was the victim to a collision between two kinds of faithfulness. It was not given to him to die for the noblest cause, and yet he died because of his nobleness. He might have been a meaner man and found it easier not to incur this guilt. Romola was feeling the full force of that sympathy with the individual lot that is continually opposing itself to the formulae by which actions and persons are judged.
>
> (*Romola*, chapter 60)

With Tito and with Savonarola, Romola as woman has to be the sensitive human receptor of whatever the men leave behind them in their wake. And this is the moment that picks up what had seemed lost when earlier, in chapter 17, Romola had been unable to think how her devout brother in his death and her carefree lover in his beauty could belong to the same world. Now comes to Romola through her second father an individually felt reality that will not fit the conventional formulae, is neither wholly of one party nor of the other, and defying the simple language of names and categories needs a finer syntax to work through the shades of meaning: 'If he suffered the punishment of *treason*, he did *not* deserve the name of *traitor*'; 'it was *not* given to him to die for the *noblest* cause, and *yet* he died because of his *nobleness*'. What erupts is more than liberal sympathy or sincerity but a radical isolated identification—and that at a supreme moment of transcendent reality breaking down the norms of life precisely by manifesting itself through an unjust death that has no place within them. Yet it is even in that death an 'intensity of life'. It belongs with those 'elder forces' that are beyond joy or grief and before pleasure and pain, with nothing now socially to lose; forces which are to George Eliot kin to the very origins of human feeling. In the manuscript she first wrote merely 'elder forces than pleasure and pain' but then went deeper: 'elder forces that wrought out existence before the birth of pleasure and pain'. For the feeling is like a surge of protesting life unreconciled to the present conditions of existence. This woman who has been so selflessly supportive to all around her is left alone here, suspended, unable to give help—'there was dead silence. As she saw [Savonarola] standing motionless before her, she seemed to be hearing her own words over again' (chapter 59): she does not know what to do with that strange aloneness which nonetheless is poised, not needy. This lies in the area adumbrated by Goethe on Shakespeare, as quoted by Lewes:

> His plots, to speak according to the ordinary style, are no plots, for his plays all turn upon the hidden point (which no philosopher has yet seen and defined), in which the peculiarity of our *ego*, the pretended freedom of our will, clashes with the necessary course of the *whole*. But our corrupt taste so beclouds our eyes, that we almost need a new creation to extricate us from this darkness.   (*Life of Goethe*, book 2, chapter 6)

It is this 'hidden point' that Romola occupies here, seemingly without effect on the whole remorseless outer story. Yet for her this is the place where the social realm, while effectively stronger than the lone ego, the defiant I, is also morally less than it; where, as a result, the individual apprehends the necessity for a universal order that transcends the corrupt social one but remains nonetheless in clouded darkness. It is like a momentary vertical dimension even while the horizontal work of time goes on. And always, even in the midst of story, George Eliot exists to try to find a right place for the thoughts that arise out of it, their importance too often suppressed or neglected within the stifling medium and the unthinking sequence of human lives. Story is becoming like the social context itself in *Romola* as also in *Felix Holt* after it: too often an ill-measure of, or a detrimental force in, the expression of existence.

It is not clear how to employ this ancient emotional force or, specifically, what Romola herself can do with this breakthrough to make a future. And yet, however helpless it was in saving Bernardo, however much it was indeed the product of that deep helplessness, it constituted a moment as near the absolute as George Eliot could attain. Such points reveal, as W. H. Mallock put it, 'the part to be greater and more complete than the whole' (*Critical Heritage*, p. 455). The whole, the Christian form or framework, was going or gone. What Feuerbach had done was show the form itself was no more than a projection of the content. Now there was only the content, albeit with residual assumptions, conventions, traditions, and needs still strongly adhering. But for George Eliot, the best form and holding place for that human content was the realist novel because it allowed the most powerful parts of life—such as Romola's response to the execution of her godfather—an uncategorized place in the described world. To leave room for the anomalous and unresolved and inconsistent, for betrayed faith and lost belief, and for the failed transcendence of moments that should have been transcendent, did not make for perfect organic composition, But George Eliot would sacrifice the aesthetic completenesss, and risk the autonomy of a book for the intense immediate interest of whatever might be learned from it: that is why she was present, as thinker, in the work.

From now on, amidst almost intractable and uncertain matter, this was always George Eliot's predicament: 'We almost need a new creation to extricate us...' But there was not a wholly new creation perhaps until *Daniel Deronda*. With *Romola*, as she wrote to R. H. Hutton in appreciation of his review, 'my predominant feeling is—not that I have achieved anything, but—great, great facts have struggled to find a voice through me, and have only been able to speak brokenly' (GEL 4, p. 97). This chapter is about those parts, moments, and stammerings that, throughout the work of this stage, are neither easily assimilated nor easily ignored.

But in *Romola*, wonderfully, all that resolves the novel is accident. Romola, fleeing Florence by boat, finds herself in a plague-stricken village. There she is taken to be the Virgin Mother though she knows full well that she is not—the woman who, used everywhere to fill the gaps and heal the wounds of the male world, had devoted herself to her blind father, had been obliged by her mentor Savonarola to return to her faithless husband—only to be further disillusioned by husband and mentor alike, and finally bereft of godfather as well as father. But for once the right thing in George Eliot is no longer in the wrong place for itself—whether it is the right word, the right utterance, the right action, or above all perhaps, the good man or woman in search of a vocation. Romola can help the sick and dying just by accidental change of place, a solution simpler than the problem it solves. It enables Romola to return to Florence to what otherwise would have seemed the greatest of anomalies still: her care of Tessa and the children, left by the now dead Tito.

'Successive Mental Phases': The Mixed Genre of *Silas Marner* (1860–1)

Writing to her publisher, John Blackwood, before she left him for George Smith, George Eliot had expressed the wish for early publication of *Silas Marner* because 'I like my writings to appear in the order in which they are written, because they belong to successive mental phases' (GEL 3, pp. 382–3). When they were published a year behind me, she continued, 'I can no longer feel that thorough identification with them which gives zest to the sense of authorship'. Nothing ever meant so much to her once the feeling of it had passed and gone cold. She often *liked* the work better at a distance, but then it might just as well have been written by someone else. Before that, it mattered that it had been written by her, that it had an inner story for her in the act of writing it, even amidst the pain. But the succession of mental stages was far from simple now.

So much of the work of this decade was aborted or interrupted. Lewes at one point took away from her *The Spanish Gypsy*, a long verse drama which she had begun working on after *Romola* and before *Felix Holt*, because he was afraid it was making her ill. It was resumed two years after *Felix Holt* and probably is best read in relation to *Daniel Deronda* later. But what it shows is a symptomatic double failure.

Two lovers—one a Spanish nobleman, the other discovering herself to be a gypsy—are unable to remain together because of the conflicting demands of the wider world. The gypsy girl, Fedalma, then turns back to Zarca, the parent she had not previously known, but only for the gypsy cause itself to fail, once the lover kills the father.

The cry of the gypsy chief to his long-lost daughter had been of a man seeking to be for his race what Moses was to the Jews, and out of himself create a tradition for them:

> So abject are the men whose blood we share:
> Untutored, unbefriended, unendowed;
> No favourites of heaven or of men.
> Therefore I cling to them! Therefore no lure
> Shall draw me to disown them, or forsake
> The meagre wandering herd that lows for help
> And needs me for its guide ...
> Because our race have no great memories,
> I will so live, it shall remember me.
>   (*The Spanish Gypsy*, book 1, lines 2755–61, 2763–4)

It was almost George Eliot's own hidden thought, that hubristic desire to *create* a new tradition. It made her write the poem 'O May I Join the Choir Invisible', in the desire to become one of those human beings who, after death, might 'live again / In minds made better by their presence', urging man's future 'search / To vaster issues'. But by the poem's close Fedalma, the daughter left to carry on the work, only 'saw the end begun' (*The Spanish Gypsy*, book 5.75), the fire that might have glowed for half a century and beyond slowly going out. Since in great and terrible moments 'space widens in the soul' (book 4.975), she can see the future track of the legacy paradoxically dwindling in front of her. The whole poem is an image of incomplete beginnings, of a lost future for what should have become a past heritage. It was Maggie Tulliver's fear that the end of our lives will have nothing in it like the beginning (*The Mill on the Floss*, book 3, chapter 6).

Silas Marner was a story of parent and child that belonged to a wholly different, earlier era in the novelist's development. It did not come about in due order, but was something that interrupted the pained early stages of working on *Romola* and got between its start and its completion.

In *Romola*, George Eliot, blocked, was struggling to get a sense of her medium, could not 'hear' her Italian characters as she could the voices of her Midlands novels. She and Lewes had moved to London in September 1860, to help his eldest son Charles settle in his new career at the Post Office, aided by the recommendation of Anthony Trollope. 'The loss of the countryside has seemed very bitter to me,' she wrote in her journal for 28 November. Suffering from 'physical weakness and mental depression' she feared for her work.[20] The only thing she had written was an oddly bitter tale of sibling cheating, 'Brother Jacob'. But then came a memory from her countryside childhood, the image of a man walking with a stoop, a linen-weaver bearing a bag on his back with the expression of one who seemed to feel himself an alien in the world. The involuntary idea, like a free gift in the midst of grinding research, 'thrust itself' between her and the copious research into *Romola*, 'came *across*' her new plans with what turned out to be the last of her Wordsworthian tales of old-fashioned village life (*Journals*, p. 87; GEL 3, p. 371). It is the story of a man who becomes, as it were, a stepmother, in a way that actually strengthens a sense of natural relationships. For it is a further measure of the lost emotional directness of the writings of this period that they have often to do with problems of false parentage, struggles of second-hand stepparenthood, and the trauma of filial betrayal. All this *Silas Marner* overcomes, like a brief vision reconsolidating a ground first established in *Scenes of Clerical Life*, before it has to be gone over and over again in the works that follow.

The mythically burdened and diminished man in George Eliot's memory becomes clarified in story as one has lost faith in God and trust in humans as a result of betrayal by his best friend and fellow believer, and who now lives like an alien, in exile from his homeland. It becomes a bold mix of fable and realism, in search, by any combination of means, for anything that might survive disillusionment, even in its midst.

Traumatized, inarticulate, shut down, and closed in within himself, Marner makes his repetitive work as a weaver his only life for the next fifteen years, the hoarded gold he gains from it his only love, until the money is mysteriously stolen during a moment of blackout.[21] Then it is that, without his treasure, he finds he needs help at some almost primitive creaturely level: 'Left groping in darkness, with his prop utterly gone, Silas had inevitably a sense, though a dull and half-despairing one, that if any help came to him it must come from without...' (*Silas Marner*, chapter 10) Before, he secluded himself; now, in vain hope of the return of his treasure, he must leave his door open:

> During the last few weeks, since he had lost his money, he had contracted the habit of opening his door and looking out from time to time, as if he thought that his money

might be somehow coming back to him, or that some trace, some news of it, might be mysteriously on the road, and to be caught by the listening ear or the straining eye. It was chiefly at night, when he was not occupied in his loom, that he fell into this repetition of an act for which he could have assigned no definite purpose, and which can hardly be understood except by those who have undergone a bewildering separation from a supremely loved object.   (*Silas Marner*, chapter 12)

It is always a clue in George Eliot when a phrase such as 'no definite purpose' or 'no good reason' is inserted, not dismissively but in search of the deeper thought beneath mere conscious rationalism. The literary equivalent of the door now left open is that little verbal sign 'except' in letting in imaginative understanding—'can hardly be understood *except* by those who have undergone a bewildering separation from a supremely loved object'. In place of direct exhortation, it was the word of subtle back-to-front appeal that George Eliot was to use in the great introduction to *Felix Holt*—of those secret human sufferings 'seen in no writing *except* that made on the face by the slow months of suppressed anguish . . .' But Silas Marner himself is not exceptional; he cannot read the signs of life in himself or others. What he has instead is that terrible linked severance between 'supremely *loved* (object)' and '*bewildering* (separation)': as so often, the feeling is conveyed not so much in the individual words as between them in the way they aided each other.

'You cannot help me,' Mrs Transome was to say to her faithful servant. With Silas it is, 'If any help came to him, it must come from without.' But at another level, formal composition is also itself the work of *help*, as Ruskin argued in his commitment to making technique in art something humanly more than just technical. It is the 'help' of everything in the work by everything else, otherwise 'hurt' by omission; the complex co-operation by which life itself comes into being, through its constantly rediscovered laws. In the human terms which composition thus represents, the slow working forwards of a work of art towards its integration depends upon 'trust' in its gradually coming together.[22]

'We mun trusten' is the simple watchword of the good peasant woman, Dolly Winthrop, who helps Silas bring up the golden-haired little child who mysteriously comes through his open door to replace his lost gold. But that bringing of trust to life again is a very frail thing within the actual content of *Silas Marner*; it comes cautiously and gradually to Marner himself, and first of all only through his dawning sense of fundamental human need exposed in a state of felt dependence.

So, *there* is the little girl, aged 2, a sudden part of life that Marner can hardly make out—where again, as with the literal symbol of the open door, the weaver's myopia serves a more than physical purpose in registering the difficulty of the sight:

The heap of gold seemed to glow and get larger beneath his agitated gaze. He leaned forward at last, and stretched forth his hand; but instead of the hard coin with the familiar resisting outline, his fingers encountered soft warm curls. In utter amazement, Silas fell on his knees and bent his head low to examine the marvel: it was a sleeping child—a round, fair thing, with soft yellow rings all over its head. Could it be his little sister come back to him in a dream—his little sister whom he had carried about in his arms for a year before she died, when he was a small boy without shoes or stockings? That was the first thought that darted across Silas's blank wonderment. *Was it a dream?*

(*Silas Marner*, chapter 12)

Bewilderment and now amazement, blankness and wonderment, and—in that realist blend of physical meaning with what is more than physical—the man on his knees. One framework gives way—the hard gold coinage; another from the long-repressed past is instinctively summoned instead—the little sister whom he cared for when only a youth himself and who died. This is Wordsworth's territory, as George Eliot well knew: human life close to the inarticulately primitive, instinctive, and basic; sudden memory like a 'first thought' adding a crucial dimension to a creature's struggling present. But it is an experience made all the more powerfully complicated first by the weaver's traumatic exile from his first known life, and then again by his recurrent cataleptic absences often resulting from shock—both factors leaving great gaps, holes, and discontinuities in his consciousness and in his story of himself. Into those 'chasms' or 'blanks' as George Eliot repeatedly calls them, comes the child, felt as anomalous and inexplicable, yet accepted. Was it his little sister come back to him? Was it a dream? Stirring into inchoate life himself, looking for points of resemblance or contact, Marner cannot fit the child into his implicit framework of wide-awake reality, and it is the framework not the little girl that must be set aside. It is not, as the cynic might say, that it is simply 'too good to be true'; more, paradoxically, Marner cannot *imagine* that *this* is *reality*. For it is reality, not fantasy, that is the truly hard work for imagination. And what from the outside might seem generically a mere fairy story now has its status realistically tested from within itself, from inside the mind of its baffled protagonist. This is George Eliot's own self-doubt transmuted, the work asking questions of itself creatively from within. It means that, in that bafflement, there open up new feelings, strange thoughts, and old memories that dart 'across' Silas's mind just as the thought of *Silas Marner* itself had creatively come 'across' George Eliot even while she was slogging on with the researches and aborted rehearsals for *Romola*.

It makes for a relationship that does not fit with conventional gender types nor with simplified accounts of selflessness—'"This" is come and I've a *right* to keep it,' insists the old bachelor: 'It's a lone thing—and I'm a lone thing'; 'I want to do things for it myself,' he tells Dolly, in fear of her kindly offered help, 'else it may get fond o' somebody else' (*Silas Marner*, chapters 13, 14). The weaver, unlike the anxious novelist, does not mind when the child interrupts his work. It is trust that revives and grows by a complication of chronology characteristic of George Eliot: 'As the child's mind was growing into knowledge, his mind was growing into memory: as her life unfolded, his soul, long stupefied in a cold narrow prison, was unfolding too, and trembling into full consciousness' (chapter 14). What makes this the great Wordsworth benchmark of life in George Eliot is that nobody is doing this, neither one of them is consciously and deliberately *making* it happen since it is more than either of them, something travelling backwards and forwards in complicated directions. It defines life as what goes on beyond cause and effect, beneath clarity of intention or plan: 'Our consciousness rarely registers the beginning of a growth within us any more than without us: there have been many circulations of the sap before we detect the smallest sign of the bud' (chapter 7). As R. H. Hutton said, what George Eliot did was give a 'strong intellectual impress' to a story that was deliberately 'unintellectual' (*Critical Heritage*, p. 176): that was the purpose of intellect, always for her, to speak for what was not itself. The natural goodness of the relationship, growing outside the normal bonds of normal family structures, serves as a Wordsworthian legacy.

Baffled by the 'incompatible claims of love', Silas can hardly bear to discipline his little Eppie, named after his mother and his sister, even for her own supposed good. His tenderness makes it 'painful to him to hurt her' (*Silas Marner*, chapter 14). But the composition of *Silas Marner* needs something tougher in it too. As though already in anticipation of the works to come, it needs the 'help' of a testing contrast offered by a darker presence. It is the presence of Godfrey Cass that takes George Eliot forward from Arthur Donnithorne towards Tito Melema.

He is the child's real father, out of his clandestine marriage to Molly Farren, a once sexually attractive lower-class woman turned opium addict who dies in the snow outside Silas Marner's house. He needed to keep his secret, for in his other life further up the social scale, Godfrey has long been wanting to marry Nancy Lammeter, the beautiful but high-principled daughter of a wealthy landowner. He takes a chance on secrecy when the results of honest confession leave no chance of anything but certain discovery. He makes the lawlessness of contingency his god. So he can hardly help feel something of a terrible relief at the convenience of Molly's death. Yet he is also shocked at the terror he feels when he thinks that Molly, found in the snow, might *not* be dead. That 'not', that thought

> was an ugly inmate to have found a nestling-place in Godfrey's kindly disposition; but no disposition is a security from evil wishes to a man whose happiness hangs on duplicity. (*Silas Marner*, chapter 13)

Godfrey is not simply a bad man: there is an 'ugly inmate' in a 'kindly disposition'. But, as we go along the sentence, what was a thought in its 'nestling-place' then starts to take over that disposition from within and becomes its recipient's moral character—and this in marked contrast to the almost identical life process by which the seed and the sap rising in Marner's subconsciousness begin to form a new bud. What are finally and decisively called good and evil come out of the same human material, the same developing processes, and are thus so disturbingly near to one another. This then is a language which, more alert to reality than normal, shows the peril of the good within the bad: '*happiness*' implicated in 'duplicity' has no '*security*' from 'evil wishes'. Reading here becomes a process as close as humans can get to the processes of the thinking mind in all its jolts and layers. A mind trying to be pure, writes George Eliot, is as uneasy in the presence of its lies 'as a great artist under the false touches that no eye detects but his own' (chapter 13). That is why some of the words hurt as they pass. George Eliot is that great artist who, through her sentences, makes the processes of the aesthetic feel analogous to the acutely precise perception also of the moral and immoral: 'Deeper down, and half smothered by passionate desire and dread, there was the sense that he ought not to be waiting on these alternatives, that he ought to accept the consequences of his deeds ... But he had not moral courage enough' (chapter 13). 'He ought not' but 'he had not' are painful in their telegraphese.

The psychologist James Sully wrote that what was most distinctive in George Eliot's treatment of characters was that she showed them 'in the making'.[23] But what increasingly also interests George Eliot in her own middle period is the sense of a sort of stuckness in characters who, no longer fully in the making, have to live with the consciousness of what they have made and become, what they have done and what they have failed to do. It is the point at which the loose rich possibilities of psychology become straitened and hardened by their consequences within what we call the realm of morality—as it was to be with Tito:

> Under every guilty secret there is hidden a brood of guilty wishes, whose unwholesome infecting life is cherished by the darkness. The contaminating effect of deeds often lies less in the commission than in the consequent adjustment of our desires—the enlistment of our self-interest on the side of falsity; as, on the other hand, the purifying influence of public confession springs from the fact that by it the hope in lies is for ever swept away, and the soul recovers the noble attitude of simplicity.   (*Romola*, chapter 9)

There is a potential moment of transition—perhaps repeatedly on offer but often quite missed and negated—when a life in the midst of gathering entanglements goes either into contamination or purification, secrecy or confession, gradual degeneration or partial recovery. That is the point at which it has to go one way or the other, with finality.

Silas Marner itself goes two ways—back to the early work, forward to the later. And this is never clearer than at the moment when Godfrey first saw Marner with the unowned baby. Then, in the subtlety of thinking that goes into the very form of this book, the two stories of Godfrey and of Silas are, for the first time, brought closely together, to be decisively separated:

> She was perfectly quiet now but not asleep—only soothed by sweet porridge and warmth into the wide-gazing calm which makes us older human beings, with our

inward turmoil, feel a certain awe in the presence of a little child, such as we feel before some quiet majesty or beauty in the earth or sky—before a steady glowing planet, or a full-flowered eglantine, or the bending trees over a silent pathway. The wide-open blue eyes looked up at Godfrey's without any uneasiness or sign of recognition: the child could make no visible audible claim on its father; and the father felt a strange mixture of feelings, a conflict of regret and joy, that the pulse of that little heart had no response for the half-jealous yearning in his own, when the blue eyes turned away from him slowly, and fixed themselves on the weaver's queer face, which was bent low down to look at them, while the small hand began to pull Marner's withered cheek with loving disfiguration.   (*Silas Marner*, chapter 13)

In what is perhaps George Eliot's most formally perfect work, at the very point of decisive equipoise, this is another of those great near-absolute, vertical moments, turning from the child's blue eyes, up to the sky above, and down again to a small flower, in a movement that, like Wordsworth's, almost makes up the whole universe again. Through a recreation of the earliest of languages—the sight of the child's 'wide-gazing calm' compared to the inner turmoil of us adults—it silently establishes the pre-articulate feeling, those underlying bonds and attachments, which are the basis for life in George Eliot. But at the same time (and in the manuscript George Eliot works hard to make the complex syntax of the last sentence register the twists and turns of comparison), this is the precise moment when, amidst the conflict of feelings, Godfrey lets himself become an adult damagingly separated from innocent being by not admitting 'the father'. Even with Molly, raising the drug to her lips at her last moment despite the baby in her arms, 'the mother's love pleaded for painful consciousness rather than oblivion' (chapter 12). *The* mother, *the* father, *its* father: this is like the unvoiced plea of ancient functions of biological life trying to find their way back into the human world again. It is the call that saves Romola near the end when she responds to the cry of an unknown baby, needing someone's help. But here 'the child could make no visible audible claim on its father': there is not even a comma between the adjectives in this strange negatively expressed persistence of a claim. This is Godfrey's moment of damning choice, in not choosing; but there is also an intuitive life in the child, turning to Marner instead, that does the choosing, as though it were the truth itself. That truth is a thing rarely 'visible' or 'audible' and, like the claims of 'the father' and 'the mother' when denied or unacknowledged, it can be turned to nothing. But then it becomes like murdering a family, easily done for temptingly plausible reasons, with no one there at the time to say how important it was.

So it is that by the second half and the second mental phase of *Silas Marner*, after a sixteen-year time gap like Shakespeare's *The Winter's Tale*, the story of Godfrey Cass has wholly diverged from Marner's, like a branching of the work into two different ways of being. On the death of Molly, Godfrey became free after all to marry Nancy

Lammeter, but the union with Nancy turns out, ironically, to be a childless marriage. Now, in a disappointed middle age, again characteristic of this period of writing, Godfrey seeks belatedly to adopt his own daughter, offering her the opportunity of a supposedly better life. Why let his mind fly to 'that void', as if the lack of a child 'were the sole reason why life was not thoroughly joyous to him'? Because, as George Eliot knows from her reading of Spinoza, we have to try to fill in the gaps in life with something definite: 'I suppose it is the way with all men and women who reach middle age without the clear perception that life never *can* be thoroughly joyous: under the vague dullness of the grey hours, dissatisfaction seeks a definite object, and finds it in the privation of an untried good' (*Silas Marner*, chapter 17). Eppie becomes that object to Godfrey. But if in the Cass story this is an attempt at contrition and recovery, it is, by a triumph of form, simultaneously a test upon the Silas–Eppie relationship, upon trust and softened human feeling, by tempting the young woman to a second life amongst the gentry. A man who is not simply bad can still think secretly like this, in reclaiming his lost girl and inducing her to leave the old weaver: 'Was it not an appropriate thing for people in a higher station to take a charge off the hands of a man in a lower?' George Eliot calls this class-talk from the supposedly higher party 'coarse', though the words are in fact coarser than his intentions: 'he had not had the opportunity, even if he had had the power, of entering intimately into all that was exceptional in the weaver's experience' (chapter 17). He does not know enough to put his feelings into the right place or form; ever since his first great evasion of life before the baby in Marner's arms, he has not that sense of over-brimming human content by which to challenge himself and his stereotypes; he has not read, as it were, that other side of this compressed novel. For there are no novels in real life that allow Godfrey to see what readers of *Silas Marner* have felt so intimately, or urge him to undertake what the novelist exists to model as intelligent and imaginative sympathy in human beings.

Marian Evans had known something like this back in Coventry in 1846. Charles and Cara Bray, childless, had adopted Bray's daughter Nelly, by his mistress. But the women of the family had made a difference, as they seek to do throughout the life and work of George Eliot. In 1864, with a stepfamily of her own, Marian Lewes writes to Cara's sister Sara Hennell of how good Sara was with Nelly, how much better than her own was Sara's sense of childhood. 'These,' she goes on, writing in the terrible midst of Nelly's terminal illness, 'are the lasting things—the true thoughts, the true feelings, the good deeds' (GEL 4, p. 158).

But if the true and the good and the lasting belong to the story of Silas and Eppie, the Cass story is the saddened alternative. Like lies to the pure, like faults to the artist, the reassuring words Godfrey speaks to Marner—'Eppie, I'm sure, will always love you and be grateful to you: she'd come and see you very often'—are such as can only 'fall gratingly on susceptible feelings'. 'Why didn't you say so sixteen year ago, and claim her before I'd come to love her?' is Marner's just cry. Still looking for the easy graft in place of the deep roots, Godfrey says placatingly, 'She'll feel just the same towards you.' 'Just the same?' retorts Marner, 'Just the same? that's idle talk. You'd cut us i'two' (*Silas Marner*, chapter 19). That riposte from her true if not natural father was no idle talk but heartfelt reality; it was the life and the sheer feeling for life that Godfrey has crudely, sadly lost for himself long ago: 'Our deeds are like children that are born to us; they live and act apart from our own will ... they have an indestructible life both in and out of our consciousness' (*Romola*, chapter 16).

When finally, knowing they can never have a child of their own, Godfrey does confess to Nancy what he failed to do back then, Nancy asks him why he did not tell her about Eppie from the very start. 'Do you think I'd have refused to take her in, if I'd known she was yours?':

> 'And—O, Godfrey—If we'd had her from the first, if you'd taken her to you as you ought, she'd have loved me for her mother—and you'd have been happier with me: I could better have bore my little baby dying ...' (*Silas Marner*, chapter 18)

It is not hard to imagine the childless stepmother Marian Lewes in the background here, as it were reading what George Eliot wrote from the front of her mind. But 'you wouldn't have married me then' is Godfrey's only response, left as he is with what has become reduced to the negatively pragmatic. As George Eliot says, there was in Nancy an anxiety and a respectability inevitable to one 'shut out from its due share of outward activity and of practical claims on its affections—inevitable to a noble-hearted, childless woman, when her lot is narrow' (chapter 17). This decent but conventional woman refused the idea of adopting a child in place of her lost pregnancy, until Godfrey explained the real nature of his relationship with Eppie. But now that narrowness of hers has to take in more than it has ever known—a vital thing in George Eliot. She replies to her husband:

> 'I can't say what I should have done about that, Godfrey. I should never have married anybody else. But I wasn't worth doing wrong for—nothing is in this world. Nothing is so good as it seems beforehand—not even our marrying wasn't, you see.' There was a faint sad smile on Nancy's face as she said the last words. (*Silas Marner*, chapter 18)

This is when the part in its rich and dense detail is almost more than the whole which contains it; this is the moment in George Eliot when the authority of deep quiet feeling creates an almost autonomous sense of life that cannot be simply managed or bargained with. It is not just abruptly and flatly, 'I wasn't worth doing wrong for' or 'Nothing is so good as it seems beforehand.' George Eliot loved the musical-like dashes in her work that the printers most often turned into formalized colons and semi-colons according to the house style. Here they remain—'I wasn't worth doing wrong for—nothing is in this world. Nothing is so good as it seems—not even our marrying'—marking what, more than flat concept, is vital to the specific inner life and tone of an individual in the realist novel. In the midst of the sadness of what Nancy says to Godfrey, there is the extra novelist detail of that faint smile amidst the gentle tone of beauty, which no longer fits within any easy framework of explanation or outcome but is tacitly significant. It is a strange sad and ageing loveliness that Godfrey himself possesses, when refused by Eppie he quietly leaves the Marner homestead, with Nancy following him out. On the other side of the door, a little while on, is this:

> That quiet mutual gaze of a trusting husband and wife is like the first moment of rest or refuge from a great weariness or a great danger—not to be interfered with by speech or action which would distract the sensations from the fresh enjoyment of repose.
>
>   But presently he put out his hand, and as Nancy placed hers within it, he drew her towards him, and said—
>
>   'That's ended.'   (*Silas Marner*, chapter 20)

'The first' once again even near the end. But that almost formal loveliness, however peaceable, belongs with something coming not 'first' but only afterwards—'ended' before the end of life itself, in finally accepted stasis. At least, nothing is secret anymore; it is, after all, a marriage. But as the epigraph from Wordsworth's 'Michael' puts it, 'for declining man'—in a life without children, lived instead with regretted consequences—there are 'no forward-looking thoughts'.

Felix Holt, the Almost Political Novel (1865–6)

What Nietzsche saw in George Eliot was stagnation, no future. Go forward or if not, as W. H. Mallock and R. H. Hutton seemed to urge, at least go back. A religious conservative such as the novelist Charlotte Yonge had admired the early work but, writing in the *Monthly Packet* in May 1885, saw in George Eliot's later work untutored 'religious sentiments' without a religious belief to support them. After the failure of the spiritual phase of feeling in Maggie and the exposure of Savonarola, what was left in George Eliot's work, said Yonge, was only the ineffectual yearnings of emotional women. Merely clinging on to the remnants of a lost past left the damaged and vulnerable individual struggling to have an effect within a powerfully entangling but diminished world, without an extra uplifting dimension any longer available. Hutton believed what he felt George Eliot knew but could hardly bear to admit: that what was left was an increasingly limited and limiting social and political medium as the sole place for human effort, with that effort almost doomed to failure.

In *Felix Holt*, the novel that followed *Romola* in 1866, Felix Holt is a social reformer in a version of Nuneaton, at a period just after the Great Reform Bill of 1832, whereas Savonarola had been meant to be the religious revolutionary over three hundred years earlier. But just as the key character in *Romola* is Tito, the true protagonist of *Felix Holt* is Mrs Transome, as though, for shame, neither of them were worthy of the title of hero or heroine of the novel in which they appear.

Mrs Transome is a formidable woman, married to an aged man who has lost his wits, and haunted by a secret sexual past. Walking with her former lover, her lawyer, she feels indignation at the practised blandness in him that allows him to ignore her worries and 'all that was truly in her heart':

> But no sooner did the words 'You have brought it on me' rise within her than she heard within also the retort, 'You brought it on yourself.'   (*Felix Holt*, chapter 9)

It is that killer second-thought that smothers the first voice of her core self, forcing it back in upon itself before it can blurt out its feelings and its secrets. She had so looked forward to the return of her son Harold, absent for fifteen years, now an established and talented man, a widower with a young son of his own. But secretly, unknown to himself, he was her son by adultery with her lawyer, Jermyn. His return is her last dared hope, when for once she might be able to get ahead of her past, might recover some primary, pure, and happy feeling: 'Could it be that now...she was going to reap an assured joy?—to feel that the doubtful deeds of her life were justified by the result?' (*Felix Holt*, chapter 1). And then she has to find, within half an hour, the crushing disappointment of his being a mere indifferent stranger to her: 'The moment was gone by; there had been no ecstasy, no gladness even.' How could she ever have thought again that there would be? To her servant Denner Mrs Transome says that she was 'afraid of ever expecting anything good again'; that could she choose now, she would wish that Harold had never been born. And when Denner tries to remind her of her happiness at the time of his birth, again the comfort is rejected:

> I don't believe I felt the happiness then as I feel the misery now. It is foolish to say people can't feel much when they are getting old. Not pleasure perhaps—little comes. But they can feel they are forsaken—why, every fibre in me seems to be a memory that makes a pang. They can feel that all the love in their lives is turned to hatred or contempt.
>
> (*Felix Holt*, chapter 39)

'They', 'their lives turned': this is the transformation that most bitterly defines this period at its lowest. Everything is turning to its opposite, as if final disappointment is all that the good things, and the hope for them, serve to set up in human nature. The young woman in the novel, Esther, staying in the house of Mrs Transome, and tempted into marrying the wealthy widower son, sees in her hostess the effect of choosing wrongly in youth:

> Pretty as this room was, she did not like it. Mrs Transome's full-length portrait, being the only picture there, urged itself too strongly on her attention: the youthful brilliancy it represented saddened Esther by its inevitable association with what she daily saw had come instead of it—a joyless, embittered age.... (*Felix Holt*, chapter 49)

It seems to take George Eliot back to her own childhood, perhaps to that mysterious unhappy mother: 'And many of us know how, even in childhood, some blank discontented face on the background of our home has marred our summer mornings. Why was it, when the birds were singing, when the fields were a garden, and when we were clasping another little hand just larger than our own, there was somebody who found it hard to smile?' (chapter 49). In one thing alone Mrs Transome was still young and ardent: 'her terrors'. The youthful passions of her past were living now only in 'her dread' that that past would finally catch up with her, in the tangled chronology of her life (chapter 34). What is so terrifying to young Esther is how the dynamic potential of a life can become so apparently static.

In reviewing *Daniel Deronda*, the critics George Saintsbury and R. H. Hutton both complained about what they considered pedantic words and cerebrally overladen phrases such as 'dynamic quality', 'emotive memory', 'cancerous vices', and 'coercive types' (*Critical Heritage*, p. 369). But for George Eliot these were often terms that contained within them traces of her intellectual biography. 'Dynamic' was one such, used in the novel's first sentence, in relation to the force of Gwendolen's glance. It came from the work of Auguste Comte, many years earlier.

It was Comte who, in the 1840s, created the new discipline of sociology, borrowing from physics and biology the distinction between its two major parts—the static and the dynamic—and applying the science to human phenomena. Social *statics* consisted in the analysis of the action and reaction of the different elements of the social system at any given moment of its existence. Social *dynamics*, however, took the separately frozen frames of society at the various definable stages of social development and recast them as continuous movements in time, as history. It was a distinction that, as in biological evolution, corresponded to that between order and progress: order consisting in the stability of co-existent conditions that enabled the formation and maintenance of social organization at a point of equilibrium; progress consisting in the emergent social change that, through succession, fuelled the further evolution of collective human life. In Darwinian terms, the two aspects were like the work of descent and variation, species and gradual modification, creating, over long periods of time, the transmutation of existing material. In sociology as in biology, the interaction of *both* sets of laws was necessary. But though to Comte statics were the essential base, it was dynamics that were of most interest, creating qualitative change out of a quantity of matter through the work of energy at a subterranean level of being. 'My gratitude increases continually for the illumination Comte has contributed to my life,' she wrote in January 1867 (GEL 4, p. 333). He offered rational hope for a better social future. In her final illness, she asked John Cross to read to her Bridge's translation of the *Discours Préliminaire* so that she might share with him one of her favourites.

In the biography of her intellect, Comte meant, for her, J. S. Mill and the *Westminster Review*, meant Herbert Spencer and George Henry Lewes himself.[24] Yet when John Blackwood asked her to take the character of Felix Holt out of the completed fiction and reuse him eighteen months later to address the working class in non-fictional form, it was not to them she turned. It was the need for order as much as progress, for Edmund Burke and the instinctive conservatism of her father as much as Comte and the progressiveness of her friends, that influenced what she wrote not only explicitly in Felix's 'Address' but also previously and more implicitly in the novel itself.

The Felix Holt who is turned into real life in the 'Address' writes that it is thoughtlessly dangerous for a man, even a selfless radical, to 'tug and rive' for his objectives 'without caring how that tugging will act on the fine widespread network of society in which he is fast meshed' (*Essays*, p. 419). Felix is a radical who loyally contains his middle-class capacities and learning within a working-class life, refusing to move upward. He is an agent of moral change who endeavours to make what is dynamic within him do its work *inside* the order he occupies, as in the irrigation of a country: 'there are the old channels, the old banks, and the old pumps, which must be used as they are until new and better have been prepared, or the structure of the old has been gradually altered' (*Essays*, p. 421). Set in the period of the first Reform Bill of 1832 but written in the context of the second bill of 1866–7 that further widened the franchise, *Felix Holt* offers a protagonist whose radicalism, nonetheless, is not simply to do with contemporary progressive politics—with the vote, the distribution of wealth, the protest against unjust injury that can become injurious in its turn. That version of politics offers Felix nothing by which to break the circle of power, or stop the knock-on effects of action and reaction in society. Rather, the first condition of social regeneration, argued Comte, was that politics must again be subordinated to morality. So, in his visionary ambition to educate and reform human nature within society, Felix Holt has a radicalism that seeks rather to reach 'some roots a good deal lower down than the franchise' (*Felix Holt*, chapter 27). It was in this way a novel that suited John Blackwood. This time Lewes could not persuade George Smith to buy it for £5000 after he had lost money on *Romola*, and she herself, rather guilty over what had happened, was glad to go back to the loyalty of the old firm for the rest of her career.

'Where great things can't happen, I care for very small things,' says Felix to Esther Lyon, 'such as will never be known beyond a few garrets and workshops.' He goes on:

'If there's anything our people want convincing of, it is that there's some dignity and happiness for a man other than changing his station' (*Felix Holt*, chapter 45). Felix Holt wanted to make the public world closer to the good and real stored, in little, within the private and personal one. George Eliot, equivalently, wanted thinking about society to be closer to the humane thinking that went on within the complex network of the realist novel. The massive achievements of the Industrial Revolution in creating a larger, faster world in turn encouraged in public and political life an overlarge mode of thought, a too high level of hastily anticipated possibility: 'a coarse indiscriminatingness obstructive of more nicely-wrought results', 'an exaggerated expectation inconsistent with the intricacies' (chapter 16). Precisely because 'there is no private life which has not been determined by a wider public life' (chapter 3), it is deep within the private that, for George Eliot, the experiments of life are to be conducted, testing how far down the feared determinism may actually reach.

Felix Holt needs his ideas and ideals to be static. Without them, as had happened once before in his own dissolute youth, 'I should become everything that I see now beforehand to be detestable' (chapter 27). George Eliot will not scorn that need for some higher mental hold or order, for the principles that, in the midst of confusion, must function top down. But it is outside the public realm that life can succeed in this novel, finding a niche for its development only 'by making itself very small'.[25] It is not so much Felix's grand ideas that matter as the energy of their personal impact as transmitted through Esther Lyon.

Esther is, like so many beautiful young women in George Eliot, seemingly too materialistic and superficial to make for much in the world. But then one day she is taken aback to discover that she is not after all the daughter of the learned and pious Nonconformist minister, Rufus Lyon (who was modelled on the father of Mary Ann Evans's teachers, the Franklins, back in Coventry). Twenty-two years before the story of *Felix Holt* begins, a French woman came into the minister's life, left, by the death of her English husband, penniless, with a young baby, in a strange land. In spite of his community, Lyon fell in love with her, married her with her child, and gave up his calling. Only when Annette died did he return to the ministry, bringing up Esther as his own. None of this Esther had known, and for once the sudden disclosure comes to a stepdaughter less as a trauma than an enlargement of vision. Lyon had seemed to her a rather tedious nobody working in low society, but in that sudden astonishing resolution to love that mother, he had been, Esther now sees, what George Eliot calls a passionately 'quick soul' in impulsive action, for all his customary slow and careful study:

Through these spasmodic leaps out of his abstractions into real life, it constantly happened that he suddenly took a course which had been the subject of too much doubt with him ever to have been determined on by continuous thought.

(*Felix Holt*, chapter 16)

After the abstract endlessness of the plausible, the possible, or the doubtful, these abrupt actions seem like openings suddenly creating future reality.

But in the subsequent grind of life, warns George Eliot, the vision is most frequently 'left farther and farther behind, vanishing for ever even out of hope in the moment which is called success' (chapter 6). That is why she needs to see human beings disclosing themselves *as* fuller human beings. That is why, inside this novel, she has Felix burst upon Esther in an unconventional language of courtship that in its unapologetic demand for life is comedy in the deepest sense:

> Not enough, Miss Lyon....I want you to change. Of course I am a brute to say so. I ought to say you are perfect. Another man would perhaps. But I say, I want you to change.
>
> (*Felix Holt*, chapter 10)

It is what Feuerbach called a real *Thou* that he wants, and like some early version of a character in D. H. Lawrence, that he seeks to provoke out of the conventionalism of social standing. It is not simply 'I want you' but 'I want you to': 'I want you to see what shallow stuff that is', 'I want you to see that the creature who has the sensibilities you call taste, and not the sensibilities that you call opinions, is simply a lower, pettier sort of thing—an insect', 'I want you to change.' It tries to be a language that is the direct opposite of the hiding, the secrecy, and the unreachable separateness that so often characterizes this stage of the fiction, in an effort to break through the denial of help. 'Through all her mortification,' says George Eliot after all this, 'there pierced a sense that this exasperation of Felix against her was more complimentary than anything...' (chapter 10). The novels need women to be a human force. It was crucial to Comte in his utopian vision for the progress of society that women should be the influential guardians of a fundamental felt reality in life, the active re-callers of a human caring prior to the development of the world of business or the work of mental abstraction.[26] It was what, as surrogate mother, Silas Marner had stood for, because, as ever in George Eliot, it was not the specific historical form, the gender, that finally mattered so much as the content preserved within it, the feeling transferable by imagination, sympathy, and love. George Henry Lewes said that it was his own partner who had helped him to see the vision in Comte's female utopia. And here it is Eros that is powerful.

But story is beginning to be insufficient a vehicle for meaning in these novels, as *Felix Holt* turns into the story of a riot and the tale of an inheritance. What George Eliot was looking for is something that, at moments before story or in its interstices, becomes physically present in human beings. It is that transfiguration which can be seen in Esther when 'the consciousness of her superiority amongst the people around her was superseded' and something else has passed into her through the influence of Felix (chapter 24). Then, when the spark of mischief or vanity was gone from her eyes, and 'the large look of abstracted sorrow was there', even her father was 'surprised by a certain grandeur which the smiles had hidden' (chapter 37). This is the 'abstraction from objects of mere personal vanity or desire' (chapter 30) which makes the face no longer socially conscious but shows instead, *without* the creature knowing it, something behind that face, a subject thinking and being at a level deep within itself before ever it resumes the level of habitual involvement in the stories of the world. It shows what one philosopher has called the 'pathos' of our condition,[27] and that what George Eliot calls 'the sightless beauty which tells that the vision is all within' is visible even so to almost any onlooker: it is an image of intensely conscious innerness at the same time still existent, unconsciously, in the outside world (chapter 45). This is in emphatic contrast to Tito in *Romola* who, in all his bland beauty, has no true face: 'The strong, unmistakable expression in his whole air and person was a negative one, and it was perfectly veracious; it declared the absence of any uneasy claim, any restless vanity...' (*Romola*, chapter 10). What is *there*, going on behind that forehead?

The novelist A. S. Byatt, writing on the first chapter of *Daniel Deronda*, notes how (like Esther) Gwendolen would sooner have the disapproving attention of this handsome stranger, Deronda, than be disregarded 'as one of an insect swarm who had no individual physiognomy'. She then refers to a work which Marian Evans had reviewed in her Coventry days, *L'Insecte*, in which the French historian Jules Michelet describes spending a long time torturing an ant by placing it under a glass and taking away its oxygen till 'it began to rub its head with its feelers and felt great pain': 'And Michelet then has an immense page on how an ant has no face, you cannot meet its eye, you can't understand what it is.'[28] Creatures without faces: such could make no appeal for human sympathy at that deep biological level which makes of sympathy something more than the sentimental. But with Esther, what is going on within and behind that newly unselfconscious face of hers is, as in the regeneration of Silas Marner, the making not just of a character in a novel but of a human being in the world—'a *new* fineness sending wonderworking vibrations through the heavy mortal frame' (*Silas Marner*, chapter 19). It naturally symbolizes something vital to this middle period of experiment in vision and in concealment, in biology, psychology, and morality, in anomaly and reordering: namely, changes in the very *configuration* of the characters' psychological worlds, shifting patterns in the complex interrelation of within and without.

But it is also part of the experiment in *Felix Holt* that this fineness of vibration turns only into terrible shudders in the moral thickening of the older generation. When Mrs Transome tries to prevent the risk of Harold antagonizing Jermyn by exposing his financial irregularities, Harold asks her flatly, in his ignorance of the past, 'Why do you wish to shield such a fellow, mother?' Harold simply will not do what she almost begs him, adding with a significance he cannot know as she does: 'It has been chiefly through him that you have had to lead such a thrifty miserable life—you who used to make as brilliant a figure as a woman need wish.' Then:

> Mrs Transome's rising temper was turned into a horrible sensation, as painful as a sudden concussion from something hard and immoveable when we have struck out with our fist, intending to hit something warm, soft, and breathing, like ourselves. Poor Mrs Transome's strokes were sent jarring back on her by a hard unalterable past. She did not speak in answer to Harold... (*Felix Holt*, chapter 36)

This is a world become, as in a second, inhuman for her, not warm or soft or breathing. What is hard and immoveable in its ringing vibration is not just Harold but the past itself, the situation suddenly made physical. And the worst of it is the silent inner realization of how slow and gradual and inexorable was the process of self-entrapment by her own actions. It feels like a mental illness.

But then the life of the novel changes again. Harold has threatened to replace Felix as Esther's lover, offering her the temptation of an easier, richer life in society. But when Harold discovers the truth of his parentage, he resolves to go to Esther to tell her that he cannot now offer her the life he has promised and must instead withdraw:

> He had been occupied with resolute thoughts, determining to do what he knew that perfect honour demanded, let it cost him what it would. It is true he had a tacit hope behind, that it might not cost him what he prized most highly: it is true he had a glimpse even of reward; but it was not less true that he would have acted as he did without that hope or glimpse. It was the most serious moment in Harold Transome's life: for the first time the iron had entered into his soul... (*Felix Holt*, chapter 49)

Before this Harold was not half the man Felix Holt is; he is, sneers George Eliot in chapter 8, like the two-dimensional map of a man, formed out of those set qualities, 'unspeculative, unsentimental, unsympathetic', that the world would think made for an agreeable enough person. But this is the iron moment, as when Adam Bede knows how Hetty's suffering continues long after his own, or when Maggie finally turns back from eloping with Stephen Guest: 'It is true...it is true...but it was not less true.' That shift from still continuing psychological concessions ('tacit' and 'behind'), to moral imperatives which are wholly different in feel to the conventional morality he has usually adopted, is what marks 'the first' and the 'most serious' real moment in the life of Harold Transome, the extra dimension he has as a fully human being. Esther had learnt to see Harold increasingly through Felix's eyes, critically, but now Esther herself was 'keenly touched': 'With a paradoxical longing, such as often happens to us, she wished at that moment that she could have loved this man with her whole heart' (chapter 49). What is offered for that tiny second is a different story or the felt loss of one such, revived as an imaginative alternative in the very moment of its impossibility. Adding another layer of richness beyond factual story and in the midst of its turns, this momentary regret is like Harold's 'glimpse of a reward' that never happened, right up until the moment when it could not. For only then in relinquishing Esther was Harold temporarily worthy of her. But even as Esther is moved to think of what might have been, and even as she bids it farewell, still there is (to use a key term of George Eliot's) no real *'room'* for that momentarily retrospective glimpse of a possible future, to be made into the present. Yet it is a deeper Harold, and a better Esther in response to him. Though no one has any measure for this, they, like George Eliot at another level, are at that moment creating the world, making it more human, even though falling short of complete continuance.

It was not only great anomalous facts that were struggling to find a right voice, it was also micro-moments like this that were able to speak only intermittently; but above all it was the relation between the two that sought its passage. 'What is "common" about common life?' asked Saul Bellow, 'What if some genius were to do with "common life" what Einstein did with "matter"?'[29]

CHAPTER 10

Middlemarch

Realism and Thoughtworld, 1869–71

The great simple fact about *Middlemarch* is that it began as two quite separate novels, two worlds, and ended as woven into four or more together. Published serially every one to two months in eight book parts between December 1870 and December 1871, each part was not a separate novel, taking one story or one principal character at a time: rather, to maintain the readers' width as well as depth of attention, each part had to contain within itself, in varying combinations and emphases, the strands of the whole. But it really began in putting together two nascent novels as though initially they were two separate mindsets.

In the previous rather desultory two years George Eliot had been mainly working on her poetry, in particular *The Spanish Gypsy*. Looking ahead to the year to come on 1 January 1869, the writer, always nervous of beginnings, envisaged a novel called 'Middlemarch' which she commenced in July, in a return to the provincial tradition of 'the gradual action of ordinary causes, rather than exceptional' (GEL 5, p. 168) before the *Romola* years. 'The various elements of the story,' she wrote Blackwood, 'have been soliciting my mind for years—asking for a complete embodiment.' But speaking with reference to her frequent and lengthy European holidays with Lewes, she added 'between the beginning and the middle of a book, I am like the lazy Scheldt; between the middle and the end I am like the arrowy Rhone' (GEL 5, p. 16). By the beginning of September she had written an introduction, mainly concerning the new doctor in town, Lydgate, and three chapters centring on the Vincy family and Featherstone. But the work was set aside while she and Lewes tended to his dying son Thornton. He had become paraplegic and was 'strangely indifferent about everything now' (GEL 8, p. 467). He died on 19 October and she wrote in her journal, 'This death seems to me the beginning of our own' (GEL 5, p. 60). Lewes's health, never good and now worse for his loss, alarmed her, and they took yet another trip to Germany and Austria, and later the English East Coast, for recuperation.

More than a year later, in November 1870, she began a different novel instead, 'Miss Brooke', and by the end of the month had written a hundred pages, though she reassured herself it was only an 'experimenting' undertaken 'without any very serious intention of carrying it out lengthily'. The story was of an ardent young woman Dorothea Brooke, a modern St Theresa though 'foundress of nothing', seeking, without the structure of a clear faith, a vocation and an epic life in the modern world This was 'a subject which has been recorded among my possible themes ever since I began to write fiction' (GEL 5, p. 124). But she added that the project would 'probably take new shapes in the development'—'shape' and 'development', together with the recurrently related idea of 'seeds', being crucial to the processes of her writing.[1] By the end of the year the beautiful young Dorothea was married to the ageing scholar Casaubon and embarking on her honeymoon: the die was cast, and the story was now to continue at length in the tightening hold of that ill-chosen marriage upon the protagonist's youthful, inchoate potential.

But at some point early in 1871 'development' took a different turn, as she turned back to try to fuse the new 'Miss Brooke' story with the halted work on 'Middlemarch'. It was the moment when she moved beyond the sense of stuckness felt in and around the work of her troubled period. By mid-March she had joined the two separate beginnings and had the first eighteen chapters in order. George Eliot loved fusion or what she called blending, the moment when one thing was no longer awkwardly obtrusive or static but became part of two or three or more interacting elements in a form of life. By putting together different stories, they had ceased to be stories. As D. H. Lawrence said of George Eliot to Jessie Chambers when they were still youthful readers in provincial working-class Eastwood, 'It was she who started putting all the action inside.'[2] What was salutary was the sense of separateness, two different lines of direction, before any meeting or blending. This was the largest formal movement since the expansion of *Adam Bede* upon *Scenes of Clerical Life*. Always she had wanted to move backwards and forwards and across, into particulars and back out into speculations, without getting lost. Narrative had now taken on a new interrelated form, an interwoven web in which George Eliot was even more central in holding the work together from within its midst. As a result there is a sort of buoyant authorial release in the writing when beginnings are made closer to middles. So, by the opening of chapter 15, reincorporating some of the old introduction to the first 'Middlemarch', she can share openly her writer's insider sense of having 'so much to do in unraveling certain human lots'—even though she was also putting them together—and 'seeing how they were woven and interwoven'—such that 'all the light I can command must be concentrated on this particular web...' So it was later in chapter 27 when she wrote the parable of the pier-glass and the cradle. And so it is again, near the beginning of chapter 10, when she protests against the reader too readily accepting the views of the other characters on Casaubon without turning 'from outside estimates' to imagine 'the report of his own consciousness'. That

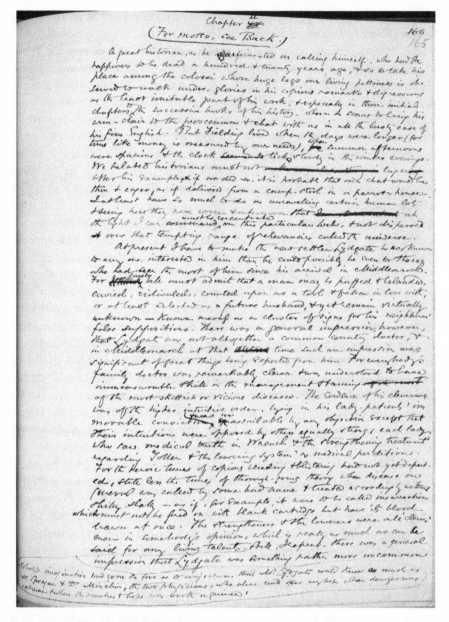

Fig. 14. Manuscript of *Middlemarch*, chapter 15: 'all the light I can command must be concentrated on this particular web' (end of first paragraph) (© British Library).

turn was, as we shall see, a vital part of the mobile, rotational geometry that was the essence of this novel's multidimensional capacity.

In the midst of all this, in November 1870, she writes to her friend Barbara Bodichon about one of those characteristic moments of hers when, awake in bed, she lay worrying over her mistakes and inadequacies:

> Lying awake early in the morning according to a bad practice of mine, I was visited with much compunction and self-disgust that I had ever said a word to you about the faults of a friend whose good qualities are made the more sacred by the endurance his lot has in many ways demanded. I think you may fairly set down a full half of my alleged grievances to my own susceptibility and other faults of mine which necessarily call forth less agreeable manifestations from others than as many virtues would do, if I had them. I trust to your good sense to have judged well, in spite of my errors in the presentation of any matter. But I wish to protest against myself, that I may as much as possible cut off the temptations to what I should like utterly to purify myself from for the few remaining years of my life—the disposition to dwell for a moment on the faults of a friend. (GEL 5, p. 123)

She always wanted to revise the past for the better, to rewrite her own script for the future, and not just on paper. But it is on paper—in the very novel to which she was going to return to writing that very day, when she rose from her letter to Barbara Bodichon—that we can see how 'eating my own words' created the self of the novelist, doing better to others than Miss Evans had often done:

> If to Dorothea Mr Casaubon had been the mere occasion which had set alight the fine inflammable material of her youthful illusions, does it follow that he was fairly represented in the minds of those less impassioned personages who have hitherto delivered their judgments concerning him? I protest against any absolute conclusion, any prejudice derived from Mrs Cadwallader's contempt for a neighbouring clergy-man's alleged greatness of soul, or Sir James Chettam's poor opinion of his rival's legs,—from Mr Brooke's failure to elicit a companion's ideas, or from Celia's criticism of a middle-aged scholar's personal appearance... (*Middlemarch*, chapter 10)

'I *protest against* any *absolute* conclusion': George Eliot's is a world of self-corrective relativism, of revisions made out of her own past mistakes, in a realist novel's arduous effort of 'provisionally framing its object and correcting it to more and more exactness of relation' (chapter 16). Suppose we do indeed turn 'from outside estimates of a man, to wonder, with keener interest, what is the report of his own consciousness about his doings or capacity: with what hinderances he is carrying on his daily labours; what fading of hopes...' This was the fear of hubris: that she could not sit omnisciently writing *Middlemarch* all day and then in her 'other life' simply continue to make those same moral mistakes she judged of in her fiction (GEL 4, p. 490). But she knew she did.

The work was all-encompassing, using her life, taking over her life, and yet still judging her life. 'When a subject has begun to grow in me,' she wrote Alexander Main in November 1872 when finally she had finished *Middlemarch*,

> I suffer terribly until it has wrought itself out—become a complete organism; and then it seems to take wing and go away from me. That thing is not to be done again—that life has been lived.   (GEL 5, p. 324)

That is how each novel had its individual demanding life, possessing her, taken from her life, like a separate being she is forced to become, with a biography of its own. 'I could not rest with a number of unfinished works on my mind,' she continues: '[W]hen a conception has begun to shape itself in written words, I feel that I must go on to the end before I can be happy about it.' Only when she had finished *Middlemarch* could she turn to read Lewes's manuscript for one of the volumes of *Problems of Life and Mind*. 'I have found my strength hardly enough for "Middlemarch". I easily sink into mere absorption of what other minds have done, and should like a whole life for that alone' (GEL 5, pp. 324–5). But until the novel was complete, those other minds and her capacity for total imaginative absorption in them had to be served within *Middlemarch* itself.

Driven by that superhuman demand that *Middlemarch* constituted, this is now George Eliot as a full-fledged character amidst her own characters in the novel. By the end of chapter 10 she has introduced Mr Vincy, Bulstrode, Lydgate, and other characters from 'Middlemarch' at a dinner party, just before Dorothea's honeymoon departure. Then two paragraphs into chapter 11, after she has introduced Lydgate to Dorothea, without Lydgate registering any sense of her importance, she writes: 'But any one watching keenly the stealthy convergence of human lots, sees a slow preparation of effects from one life on another, which tells like a calculated irony on the indifference or the frozen stare with which we look at our unintroduced neighbour.' As R. H. Hutton had said, in reviewing *Romola*, George Eliot's best work did not produce an immediate or straightforward effect by scenes that were complete in themselves. On the contrary it was slow cumulative work, like life's itself: 'You have to unroll a large surface of the picture before even the smallest *unit* of its effect is attained.'[3] This was even truer now. In that gradual build-up of interrelations in *Middlemarch*, backwards and forwards and across, form had found a voice and a purpose in George Eliot at the maximum of herself now, not as some cosily old-fashioned narrator but as a writer in person.

By chapter 34, long past the point of initial writerly anxiety, the linking of the Featherstone story of an old man's legacy with the Miss Brooke narrative can go on fluently at another level within the head of Dorothea herself, as the novel performs one of the great processes so characteristic of its capability—switching channels, doing the same things at different levels:

> But for her visitors Dorothea...might have been shut up in the library, and would not
> have witnessed the scene of old Featherstone's funeral, which aloof as it seemed to be
> from the tenor of her life, always afterwards came back to her at the touch of certain
> sensitive points in memory...Scenes which make vital changes in our neighbours' lot
> are but the background of our own, yet, like a particular aspect of the fields and trees,
> they become associated for us with the epochs of our own history, and make a part
> of that unity which lies in the selection of our keenest consciousness.
>
> (Middlemarch, chapter 39)

Even the lack of connection connects, subtly. What she saw in the cold scene was at once the dismal outer sight and the lonely thought within of someone dying and leaving no love behind. Set within the ordinary provincial world, this is the strange psychological landscape of *Middlemarch* experienced in an alternating multiplicity of backgrounds and foregrounds, centres and peripheries, in shifting fields. The reader has to 'see' almost simultaneously that what is in the foreground for one character serves only as a background for another. It is simple and obvious at one level but dizzyingly complex in practice. Immersed in the world of one couple, Dorothea and Casaubon, the reader, within a chapter or two, may become equally immersed in the marriage of another, Lydgate and Rosamond, and then have a third thought, at once startling and poignant: that all the time that the one relationship was at the absolute centre of vision, another was still going on alone and unattended to, and so it will be always, in the name of human limitation and human relativism. Even the reparative shift back to what was forgotten has temporarily, then, to neglect what it has just come from. It is a sort of realist illusion of course, between chapters and across books, that what is being narrated successively was actually going on simultaneously; that the forward move to remembering one relationship that the reader was considering some chapters ago retroactively recreates what was happening in it all the time we were attending elsewhere. In this the idea of the all-seeing God revives and dies again, springs out of human need, in imagination of that impossible all, and subsides again into the realism of necessary partiality.

In one of the two volumes of George Henry Lewes's *Problems of Life and Mind* that Marian Lewes prepared for the press after his death, Lewes registers powerfully in his own terms the reciprocal mix of felt limitation, impossibility, and richness that is involved in the very intertexture of human life and the human faculties that seek to register it. We have two eyes, two ears, two hands, and in the brain two hemispheres, he writes. But in correction of the work of one of Lydgate's heroes, the French physiologist Bichat on the symmetry of animal organs, Lewes insists that, structurally and functionally, the organ pairs are, within their similarity, also slightly different, offering a certain specialist independence of power and action together with a community and convergence. So the eyes separately offer somewhat different points of view in coming together to work towards a maximum integration of focal

Fig. 15. George Henry Lewes c.1865 (© National Portrait Gallery).

efficiency. And this is the case in all sorts of movement between subjective and objective, foreground and background, centre and circumference. What goes into the composition of our reality, what reality is, is ultimately a mystery to us. To our eyes and minds, says Lewes, differentiated experiences 'must be regarded as a *series*; but the true comparison for sensorial reaction is that of a *web*'. That is *Middlemarch*, itself a sort of social super-brain, composed as a series in sequence, but increasingly conceived and formed as a web. Its scanning focus, to continue with the words of Lewes,

> successively traverses and retraverses all the positions of the sensorial field, and...
> thus successively brings now one and now the other point into the daylight, leaving
> the others momentarily obscured though still impressing the sentient organism; we
> can understand, then, how among the numerous impressions many are so rapidly
> brought into focus that they seem simultaneous.[4]

So within the retina, says Lewes, the macula gives central vision of high acuity by combining at a deep physiological level 'two or more strands of different impressions'. And conversely at the psychological level, though when we monitor our *own* internal changes we know that the watcher and the watched are the same person, we are obliged to experience them as two almost different personalities. Succession and alternation are our only tactical access to simultaneity. Unless, that is, we were creatures of a wholly different scale:

> If our sense of hearing were but a thousand times quicker than it is, how would a
> perpetual noise distract us. And we should in the quietest retirement be less able to
> sleep or meditate than in the middle of a sea-fight. Nay, if that most instructive of
> senses, seeing, were in any man a thousand, or a hundred thousand times more acute
> than it is by the best microscope, things several million of times less than the smallest
> object of his sight now would be visible to his naked eyes, and so he would come
> nearer to the discovery of the texture and motion of the minute parts of corporeal
> things: and in many of them, possibly get ideas of their internal constitutions; but then
> he would be in a quite different world from other people: nothing would appear the
> same to him and others.[5]

It would be like seeing the grass grow or hearing the squirrel's heart beat. This is the seventeenth-century enlightenment philosopher John Locke, praised by Lewes himself in his *Biographical History of Philosophy* as the classic type of the English mind: the well-balanced empiricist who knew the limits of understanding, and, refusing the madness of trying to go beyond them, worked within them to discover whatever was adapted to its capacities. But again there is the woman in Doris Lessing's *Shikasta*, a novel of science fiction or space fiction as she calls it, who knows the norm of the human mind is to register safely only 5 per cent of reality and yet risks her sanity in seeking an extra 1 or 2 per cent of vision. Emotionally Marian Evans was another such, extending her mind through the writing of Middlemarch.

As we have constantly seen in these pages, she worried constantly, almost pathologically, about her effect on others across the gulf of ignorance, the selfish blunders, inattentive unkindnesses, the sins of omission, as well as her own vulnerability to criticism. For though she may have had less to hide and to rue than her own Mrs Transome, her imagination felt like a skin almost unbearably sensitive to the human touch—as was said of the old woman in Felix Holt: 'The finest threads, such as no eye sees, if bound cunningly about the sensitive flesh, so that the movement to break them would bring torture, may make a worse bondage than any fetters' (chapter 8). Those threads were George Eliot's own nerve ends, where her thoughts were first registered. They are also present in that 'hampering threadlike pressure of small social conditions' which marks the felt environment of Middlemarch (chapter 18) in little wincing moments so often denoted in that novel by the almost biological verb 'shrink' in its combination of aversion and diminishment: 'his was the worst loneliness which would shrink from sympathy', 'his was a mind which shrank from pity'; 'he shrank, as from a burn, from the utterance of any word about his private affairs'; 'she shrank from the words which would have expressed their mutual consciousness, as she would have shrunk from flakes of fire', 'he seemed so withered and shrunken' (chapters 10, 42, 77, 74). One day in the future, says the author of Impressions of Theophrastus Such, human beings may mutate into creatures for whom consciousness is 'no more than a mere stumbling of our own organisms on their way to unconscious perfection'. Then automatically, without the struggle and pain of the bare nervous fibres of human sensitivity,

> the planet may be filled with beings who will be blind and deaf as the inmost rock, yet will execute changes as delicate and complicated as those of human language and all the intricate web of what we call its effect, without sensitive impression, without sensitive impulse... ('Shadows of the Coming Race', chapter 17)

As it is, however, human language for George Eliot is the nervous system of her writing, and the medium of Middlemarch becomes that intricate vibrating web within which the language operated.

The psychologist James Sully, a young attendant at the Sunday afternoon intellectual gatherings at the Priory, said George Eliot 'had a clairvoyant insight into mind and character, which enabled her to get at once into spiritual touch with a stranger, fitting her talk to his special tastes and needs, and drawing out what was best in him'.[6] Sceptical of colleagues such as William James and F. W. H. Myers who were interested in psychical research of phenomena beyond the grave, Sully was not one to use the word 'clairvoyant' lightly. But in a realist rather than supernatural sense, he felt she was indeed telepathic. As he was to make clear in the article on 'George Eliot's Art' that he wrote for *Mind* after her death, what George Eliot was, above all, was a mind-reader, working in a multi-channelled sympathetic medium that transmitted its messages between her own mind, the minds of her characters, and the minds of her readers.[7] She famously remarks of Lydgate, who was constantly aware of the limited means of his poorer patients and yet neglected his own domestic economy: 'is it not rather what we expect in men, that they should have numerous strands of experience lying side by side and never compare them with each other?' (*Middlemarch*, chapter 58). But that is what *Middlemarch* itself is as a whole: an interrelated network of numerous comparative threads and strands of experience, of sundry silently transmitted inner cries from the almost insupportable babel of mankind. Those strands, remarkably, are not only thoughts in the minds of individual people, but also those individual people as themselves different thoughts within the mind of George Eliot: 'Why always Dorothea?', 'Poor Lydgate! or shall I say, Poor Rosamond!' (*Middlemarch*, chapters 29, 16). The novel was the super-connected brain for which, at another level, George Eliot was the conscious mind and spokesperson.

And yet, for all its felt demands to have a separate life, the work was still drawing upon *her*. It is a definitive moment when F. W. H. Myers asked her direct, 'from whom, then, did you draw Casaubon?' Casaubon, the failed scholar who never finished his great book, the desiccated old man who probably could not consummate his marriage. She might have answered, externally, old man Brabant back in the 1840s; or Mark Pattison, rector of Lincoln College Oxford who wrote a learned book on the sixteenth-century scholar Isaac Casaubon and married a woman twenty-seven years his junior, who took George Eliot into her unhappy confidence; or even Herbert Spencer himself. But:

> George Eliot, with a humorous solemnity, which was quite in earnest, nevertheless, pointed to her own heart.[8]

She was Casaubon, in her heart: 'Impossible to conceive any creature less like Mr. Casaubon than my warm, enthusiastic husband, who cares much more for my doing than for his own, and is a miracle of freedom from all author's jealousy and suspicion. I fear that the Casaubon-tints are not quite foreign to my own mental complexion...' (GEL 5, p. 322). The Marian Evans—even the happier Marian Lewes—who remained vulnerably present behind and within George Eliot, was the one the work still and always pointed towards, at source. It was another great Feuerbachian return: you went away in imagination only finally to come back home again in memory, but it could not be done direct. It was a translated life. And that was the turn for readers too, she hoped: that the work should finally point to their heart and be taken to heart accordingly. A life transferred.

Science Fiction

In *Middlemarch* George Eliot is not satisfied by a conventional account of the effect of Dorothea on Will Ladislaw as she walks in on him. Instead she writes:

> When Mrs Casaubon was announced he started up as from an electric shock, and felt a tingling at his finger-ends. Any one observing him would have seen a change in his complexion, in the adjustment of his facial muscles, in the vividness of his glance, which might have made them imagine that every molecule in his body had passed the message of a magic touch. And so it had. For effective magic is transcendent nature; and who shall measure the subtlety of those touches which convey the quality of soul as well as body, and make a man's passion for one woman differ from his passion for another...The bow of a violin drawn near him cleverly, would at one stroke change the aspect of the world for him... (*Middlemarch*, chapter 39)

The electrically changed molecular structure of the body, the changed nature of the phenomenological world, the magical and musical made scientific and neurological: that is why, at the end of Chapter 9, it was hinted that George Eliot had already begun to carry out, under cover of the common world, what Saul Bellow meant by the work of physics and chemistry and biology.

As though working from within a human science of mind, George Eliot loved terms equivalent to transmitter, receptor, medium, reactor. Even as a young essayist in Coventry in 1846 she referred to a friend of promise, one whose make-up even so fatally contained 'elements which would too probably operate as non-conductors, interposed between his highly-charged mind and the negatively electrified souls around him' (*Essays*, p. 15). In the *Westminster Review*, October 1854, she writes of Madame de Sablé and the literary influence of quick-witted women of seventeenth- and eighteenth-century France, passing 'like an electric current through the language'. They introduce a feminine element into 'the wondrous chemistry of the affections and sentiments, which inevitably gives rise to distinctive forms and combinations'. In contrast, she speculates, women of more heavy Teutonic origins tended to 'absorb' ideas rather than recharge them with 'the energy required for spontaneous activity'. That type of mentality lacked sufficient electric power 'to produce crystallization' and give the 'phantasms of great ideas' that 'float' through the mind a definite 'fixity' (*Essays*, pp. 54, 53, 56). These cultural-physiological theories may be most questionable but it is the terms used that are telling. Combination, conduction, absorption, reaction, electrical energy, crystallization: these created a language from chemistry and physics that gave George Eliot insight into the vitality of human forces below the level of normal human descriptions. They were communications that felt more like the passing of inner secrets than the giving of moral lessons. It was these dynamics, these different dimensions, that she sought to reach in her writing and in her readers, and most powerfully so in this novel. As she had already put it in 'Silly Novels by Lady Novelists' at the commencement of her own career in 1856:

> No educational restrictions can shut women out from the materials of fiction, and there is no species of art which is so free from rigid requirements. Like crystalline masses, it may take any form, and yet be beautiful; we have only to pour in the right elements—genuine observation, humour, and passion. But it is precisely this absence of rigid requirement which constitutes the fatal seduction of novel-writing to incompetent women. (*Essays*, p. 324)

Far more than merely competent, the new amalgam she was now forming might be called George Eliot's *science* fiction. As John Tyndall, another of the Sunday afternoon guests at the Priory, put it in his famous Belfast Address 1874, the crucial shift in the history of knowledge was from theology to science, and from above to below. Theory was to work not at the level of the supra-sensible but of the sub-sensible, treating not of gods but of chemical atoms and biological cells.

It is a different world of reality, even acoustically. When his young bride innocently asks Casaubon at what point is he going to stop writing volume upon volume of notes and finally bring them all together in a book for publication, it is as though the very soundscape has altered, amplified to shrieking point:

> In Mr Casaubon's ear, Dorothea's voice gave loud emphatic iteration to those muffled suggestions of consciousness ... hearing in hard distinct syllables from the lips of a near observer, those confused murmurs which we try to call morbid, and strive against as if they were the oncoming of numbness! And this cruel outward accuser was there in the shape of a wife—nay, of a young bride. (*Middlemarch*, chapter 20)

He wanted a young bride who would be uncritical—even at the very moment that she herself didn't know she *wasn't* being. Somewhere he knows he will never finish his great work—because it is not in the least that. He will never even really start it. 'I suffer terribly,' George Eliot had said of any subject of her own, 'until it has wrought itself out ... I feel it must go on to the end ...' But here she imagines the other side, her related opposite. The sentences she writes are, she knows, the sentences Casaubon himself flinches from: what was hidden and obscured inside turned to 'hard distinct syllables' without, just as the young bride assumes in his eyes 'the shape' of a cruel accuser. And it might be like this if, impossibly of course, George Eliot characters had to read her own hard distinct syllables about them—as her readers have to in their stead. Of Dorothea meanwhile George Eliot writes, 'She had not yet learned those hidden conflicts in her husband which claim our pity. She had not yet listened patiently to his heart-beats, but only felt that her own were beating violently': that characteristic and repeated 'not yet' of George Eliot's bends time forwards and back again, needs time in the midst of a transition that cannot even know itself to be so. That is what transitions are in the underworld of experience beneath the microscope: holes in the fabric of reality, revealed as transitions only in retrospect when they have helped complete the passage into what succeeds them, and therefore never fully revealed at all. Dorothea entered into marriage with the abstract idea of self-devotion, projecting upon the old man her own youthful need for idealism:

> but yet it had been easier to her to imagine how she would devote herself to Mr Casaubon, and to become wise and strong in his wisdom and strength, than to conceive with that distinctness which is no longer reflection but feeling—an idea wrought back to the directness of sense, like the solidity of objects—that he had an equivalent centre of self, whence the lights and shadows must always fall with a certain difference. (*Middlemarch*, chapter 21)

A notional ideal that beforehand seemed so high and selfless is now turned back down and immersed in a life of complex considerations. It is these great mental turnarounds—the right thing in the wrong place now trying to find the better framework through which to reinterpret and revise itself—that were vital to the woman who became George Eliot through her own self-reappraisals. In the process, the cross-mixture of physical and mental vocabularies, the multi-directional forces, the sense of some centre for an alternative model of reality hidden within this one— all this is almost dizzying. Those mentally syntactic shifts come in the wake of traumatic crisis: cognitive overload, stretched being, the demanding sense of a high-percentage Reality that is almost impossible or unbearable, inexpressible or unplaceable: 'the point at which the formal structure, as it were, falls into its content'.[9] Expectations and defences collapse.

In George Eliot, such experiences, absorbed within the system, become like the stirrings of new organs; convulsive feelings become metabolically realized eventually as new faculties in the very effort to survive their own force. Here with some future Dorothea, as Howard Jacobson rehearses it, 'an *idea* is wrought back to sense, an abstraction is alchemised into concreteness, until the thing we call sympathy is discovered, not in an act of voluntary loving kindness, but as an actual sense perception'.[10] Many of the hidden and indirect deeds and misdeeds in *Middlemarch* are 'like the subtle muscular movements which are not taken account of in the consciousness, though they bring about the end that we fix our mind on and desire' (chapter 68). For true consciousness, it takes a long time physically to emerge out of first-person stupidity and ignorance, to see the change to which past memory has had to adjust itself, and to recognize in the name of imagination both equivalence and difference at once: Casaubon 'had an equivalent centre of self' as Dorothea did, but within it always 'a certain difference' from hers. George Eliot writes in another of her great syntactic loops of mind across the pronouns: 'She was as blind to his inward troubles as he to hers.' It is as much human physics as it is biochemistry, wherein the invisible presence of the unknown is deduced only through its intricately disruptive effects on the known.

Space changes, time changes, sound changes, and the sensitivity of heartbeats with it; thin-skinned, the psychic shapes of bodies seem almost contorted with emergent or repressed thoughts. In such a world George Eliot's sympathy was never simple or single: in a recent novel based on the creator of *Middlemarch* and *Daniel Deronda*, one character is amazed at the way in which George Eliot, the unbeliever, can sympathize at one moment with the struggling birth of Christianity, at the next with the resistance of those seeking to maintain the old Roman faiths: 'He gave up trying to follow the Sibyl's sympathies' in their bewildering succession.[11] Within that many-sided, ever-shifting, and unconflicted sympathy, what George Eliot was always really asking was: In what possible world could this thought be true, or that point of view comprehensible? In one world Sir William Herschel was the great astronomer who broke the barriers of the heavens, but back on earth he was a provincial organist, giving music lessons to novice pianists (*Middlemarch*, chapter 15). Not knowing what he was to become, neighbours of the sublime Milton offered him, through the mirror of their views, unfavourable reflections of himself (*Middlemarch*, chapter 10). But equally, and more often, in another version of that world, a provincial Casaubon aspiring to find the great Key to All Mythologies despite the scorn of his contemporaries, turned out to be indeed a lost pedant, sticking to a hopelessly old and inflexible idea in a field where points of view were changing rapidly. Nor did the up-to-date man of science, Doctor Lydgate, ever become the heroic discoverer he had hoped to be. And yet it was not wholly impossible for such aspirants; their failures could have contained still the partially distorted traces of a future success: 'a vigorous error vigorously pursued has kept the embryos of truth a-breathing: the quest of gold being at the same time a questioning of substances, the body of chemistry is prepared for its soul, and Lavoisier is born' (*Middlemarch*, chapter 48). Out of the delusion of alchemy came the science of chemistry through its founder. But it is the future achievement that retrospectively redeems a past which had an altogether different outcome in mind or prospect. Or as we may recall George Eliot brilliantly putting it in her epigraph to chapter 64: 'All force is twain in one: the cause is not cause / Unless effect be there.' It is a strange loop of time to know how Herschel's future was utterly to transform what had seemed the banality of his past; how he riskily borrowed from his sense of that possible future the energy to create it. These thoughts belong with the mathematics of probability. There, for every Herschel, there are vast numbers of Casaubons or Lydgates whose past sense of the future never came to be at all:

> For in the multitude of middle-aged men who go about their vocations in a way determined for them ... there is always a good number who once meant to shape their own deeds and alter the world a little. The story of their coming to be shapen after the

average and fit to be packed by the gross, is hardly ever told even in their own consciousnesses; for perhaps their ardour in generous unpaid toil cooled as imperceptibly as the ardour of other youthful loves, till one day their earlier self walked like a ghost in its old home...

Lydgate did not mean to be one of those failures... (*Middlemarch*, chapter 15)

That last sentence can be read at once both forwards and backwards: confident aim, ironic intention. It is that word 'imperceptibly' that is the human science of those subtly gradual processes even of normalization itself. Another of the habitués of the Priory Sundays, the mathematician W. K. Clifford noted that between any two points on a line, you can always put more points of division and 'there can be no end to this process... Between any two points of the line there is an infinite number of other points'. Or put a drop of water under a powerful microscope, and you see its granular structure; yet even if you increase the power of the microscope again and again and again, you never know anything more than that the structure is 'too fine-grained for us to perceive its discontinuity, if it has any'.[12] George Eliot knew that theoretically she could go on and on and on seeking the precise point or final moment of transition and never locate it, only locate at best something that came after it, whilst finding the infinitely minute process of focusing and refocusing taking her further and further away from the perception of the solid world of common human experience. Reality went on being mysterious; for every gap filled, another deeper one opening, even as a result. As Ruskin said, in another thought experiment: place an object as close to the eye as you like, 'there is always something in it which you *cannot* see' and yet sense as missing; place the object as far away as you can until it becomes a mere spot, still 'there is always something in it which you *can* see' even in a hinted way.[13] What George Eliot can do is work between the two parallel processes, the diagram and the portrait, the micro- and the macro-vision, and maintain, through sufficient variation of focus and interaction, the identity between them.

There is, then, something more in all this than George Eliot's own psychological uncertainty as to whether she was closer to Herschel than to Casaubon. That uncertainty was no more and no less than the personal fuel for the vertiginous sense of various possible fates and diverse dimensions for any entity. Clifford himself had written of curved space, extra dimensions, hidden irregularities and asymmetries in post-Euclidean geometry—matters as mind-bending as they were space- and time-bending. Lydgate, in his former life in Paris, had fallen in love with a dangerously beautiful actress; asking her to marry him was, he knew, 'the sudden impulse of a madman' but 'No matter! It was the one thing he was resolved to do':

Strange, that some of us, with quick alternate vision, see beyond our infatuations, and even while we rave on the heights, behold the wide plain where our persistent self pauses and awaits us. (*Middlemarch*, chapter 15)

Within the same person here, there are the two selves—one the bystander, the other hurtling on, in the bewildering (lack of) relation between almost different worlds that only George Eliot, it seemed, could embody in herself.

This then, developing out of the force-field movements of *Adam Bede*, is George Eliot's relativity—different worlds going on even within the same world. It makes encounters with others, across great unseen gulfs, stranger than human beings could normally bear to know. After exiling himself from Dorothea in London, Will Ladislaw, on a return visit to Middlemarch, is in danger of becoming entangled with Lydgate's wife instead, at the same time as his friend Lydgate, knowing nothing of this, is feeling himself being dragged down by Rosamond into the distracting minutiae of economic difficulties:

> The two men were pitying each other, but it was only Will who guessed the extent of his companion's trouble. When Lydgate spoke with desperate resignation of going to settle in London, and said with a faint smile, 'We shall have you again, old fellow', Will felt inexpressibly mournful, and said nothing. Rosamond had that morning entreated him to urge this step on Lydgate; and it seemed to him as if he were beholding in a magic panorama a future where he himself was sliding into that pleasureless yielding to the small solicitations of circumstance, which is a commoner history of perdition than any single momentous bargain.
>
> We are on a perilous margin when we begin to look passively at our future selves, and see our own figures led with dull consent into insipid misdoing and shabby achievement. Poor Lydgate was inwardly groaning on that margin, and Will was arriving at it. (*Middlemarch*, chapter 79)

These are different men on different journeys. But there is potentially in common the matter of London and Rosamond, which Lydgate speaks of in the tones of the normal world but Ladislaw hears transmitted with a sort of terrible groaning cry in it. The magic panorama was a device to show a series of pictures exhibited a frame at a time but made to pass so rapidly before the audience as to seem continuous, like an early version of film, the discontinuities absorbed in the overall imperative to make sense. Yet at these moments of mental crisis, what goes into the making of the structure of ordinary life and is normally taken for granted becomes less integrated, more obtrusive upon consciousness. In the accelerated vision demanded here, Will is already ahead of Lydgate, domiciled in London, and seeing Rosamond coming on towards him. But at that same time Lydgate is almost gone past that terrible boundary into the world of hopeless determinism which Will is fast approaching. Meanwhile it has already been said of Rosamond and Lydgate that, even though to the common eye they looked as though they were wholly together, 'Between him and her indeed there was that total missing of each other's mental track, which is too evidently possible even between persons who are continually thinking of each other' (chapter 58); 'Each

331

lived in a world of which the other knew nothing' (chapter 16). There are times when Lydgate turns to Rosamond, as Dorothea had turned to Casaubon, and the appeal goes straight through the partner as though he or she were not 'there', were not part of the same expected world of human values. This is that 'half-maddening sense of helplessness which comes over passionate people' when their passion is met by no apparent feeling in response: 'What place was there in her mind for a remonstrance to lodge in?' (chapter 65). When what had been supposed to be universal feelings were not felt by one's nearest partner, then there was no absolute universe after all; the smaller world resulting became, for lack of reciprocity of feeling, unstable, unreliable, peculiarly lonely, and discomforting. It seemed to Lydgate 'that she had no more identified herself with him than if they had been creatures of different species' (chapter 58). It seemed to Dorothea that the hand she had offered Casaubon never really touched him: 'It is in these acts called trivialities that the seeds of joy are for ever wasted' (chapter 42). Such cries and gestures of possibility or need went off as if into infinity, into a no-world that could or should have been, and yet in waste or limbo was not. Marian Evans had met the mathematician Charles Babbage, father of the modern computer, at Chapman's house, considering him an ugly man and a poor speaker but a great authority (GEL 2, p. 23). In his *Bridgewater Treatise*, Babbage had spoken remarkably of infinitesimal vibrations of 'all the accumulated words pronounced from the creation of man'. Nothing was ever wholly obliterated even over centuries but present still 'in aerial pulses, unseen by the keenest eye, unheard by the acutest ear, unperceived by human senses':

> The air itself is one vast library, on whose pages are forever written all that man has said or woman whispered. There stand for ever recorded, vows unredeemed, promises unfulfilled.[14]

Precisely because she may not have believed in its objective existence as Babbage did, George Eliot, in occupying a stratospheric dimension within *Middlemarch*, was that library of lost sounds.

But out of the triangular force field created between Lydgate, Ladislaw, and Rosamond, a chain reaction, an unbearably extended human sensitivity, results from the increased strain cast upon conventional present-time from different directions. The catalyst is a fourth factor or element, in Dorothea. Just before Will talked with Lydgate, Dorothea had found Will and Rosamond together in seemingly intimate discussion. As Dorothea rushes off, Rosamond seeks sarcastically to placate Will's horror by saying he can quite easily go after her and simply 'explain' that his 'preference' is still for Dorothea if he likes. Furiously, Will drives her words off their mental track, as though to stop that future-rushing journey of hers in which she is involving him:

I had one certainty—that she believed in me.... That's gone.... Explain! Tell a man to explain how he dropped into hell! Explain my preference! I never had a *preference* for her, any more than I have a preference for breathing. No other woman exists by the side of her... (*Middlemarch*, chapter 78)

Overborne at hearing this, Rosamond is nearer one of those moments of max-imum percentage of bearable reality than she has ever been, and the effect is head-spinning. She 'was almost losing the sense of her identity, and seemed to be waking into some new terrible existence'. It is not she who matters to Will, it is Dorothea: that is what her whole body registers in shock. What Will, 'another nature', felt was being burnt into the very place of that identity of hers, with the devastating force of an alternative point of view which is not the effect of deliberate liberal-mindedness but, again, an almost violently bio-chemical recon-figuration of self and self's unthinking world: 'She felt a new terrified recoil under a lash never experienced before.'

It is from Dorothea, when she returns the following day after a night of lonely anguish, that Rosamond, like a dying particle, suddenly receives a burst of pre-egoistic energy. Dorothea is to her an utterly unlikely kind of woman, one who, on the rebound from secret inner hurt, seeks not to complain or rebuke but make herself of some external help to those other three, Lydgate, Rosamond, and Ladislaw:

Rosamond, taken hold of by an emotion stronger than her own—hurried along in a new movement which gave all things some new, awful, undefined aspect—could find no words, but involuntarily she put her lips to Dorothea's forehead which was very near her, and then for a minute the two women clasped each other as if they had been in a shipwreck....

'When you came in yesterday—it was not as you thought.... He was telling me how he loved another woman, that I might know he could never love me,' said Rosamond, getting more and more hurried as she went on... (*Middlemarch*, chapter 81)

The acceleration—'hurried along...more and more hurried as she went on'—results from being overtaken, taken over, by an alternative reality, leaving her own reality behind as a mere dreamworld. It was a chapter that was written in a whirlwind, possessing George Eliot herself. In it at this moment Rosamond is a happening, not a person, something undefined and without normal identity that, precipitated out of the explosive concatenation of overlapping interests, must go fast forward to seek some realization of itself before it dissipates. This is what happens when 'we have to do with a simultaneity of destinies and a coexistence of a host of different narratives'.[15]

More Science Fiction: Thoughtland

It was at the Priory in 1875 that yet another young aspirant, E. A. Abbott, was sympathetically encouraged by George Eliot, for all her unbelief, to take up again the religious novel *Philochristus* he had been trying to write for years. He had previously written to her, pleading for a novel from her hand that expressed the Gospel message shorn of the language of miracle. Instead, she said, he had to try to write his own novel, and finally in 1878 he did so, managing it from the perspective of a disciple trying to understand Christ, not as he was in himself—since that seemed wholly beyond him—but through Christ's effect on the history of the disciple's own life. The measure of the greater thing could only be sensed through its effect within the lesser. But at the Priory, Abbott also met John Tyndall over dinner, Tyndall being part of an intellectual climate that, with Lewes and Clifford, included within it an interest in the brilliant German physicist and polymath Hermann von Helmholtz. It was Helmholtz, with his expertise in sound and sight and space, who imagined what it was like to be a two-dimensional being, confined to the surface of a world. Years later, in 1884, Abbott found a better solution to his interests by the writing of the science fiction, *Flatland: A Romance of Many Dimensions.*

What it offers is an imaginative subhuman template for the geometry of creation. Abbott's protagonist, a creature shaped as a square, lives in Flatland. But in his experimental journeying he must first descend to Pointland, where inhabitants live as points in a straight line they themselves cannot see; then re-ascend to the three-dimensional world of Spaceland, to become by that process a thinker between two worlds. The creatures of Pointland live in a closed world, unable to form any conception of another geometric dimension. But if the figure from Flatland can literally see the limitations of Pointland below his two-dimensional vantage point, then by analogy he can begin to imagine, in turn, Spaceland's higher perception of his own framework. However easy it is for creatures in one dimension to look down on the level below them, so commensurately hard it is to imagine their own dimension is not the ultimate one. But Abbott's protagonist bears a mind now straining to think outside and beyond its own dimensions by means of what he calls the inner world of Thoughtland. There he tries to hold on to his imagination of an extra invisible dimension through the sheer force of language, repeating the blind mantra 'Upwards and yet not Northwards' where north would only take him along his line not above it. It is in this way that this work of creative geometry recasts the idea of Christ incarnate, existing beyond the realist understanding of his disciples. For Abbott, outside the Bible, it was Shakespeare and then George Eliot who were the great natural explorers of extra dimensions within existing ones. And for him, what *Flatland* did was to expose the underlying diagram, the existential geometry, and the implicit allegory, contained within the pictures of life

W. & D. DOWNEY,   57 & 61, Ebury Street, London.

THE REV. DR. ABBOTT.

Fig. 16. Edwin Abbott Abbott (1838–1926) (© National Portrait Gallery).

made animate first in the Elizabethan and Jacobean drama and then again in the nineteenth-century realist novel.

It is a powerful abstract language, braille-like, that gets the creature out of Flatland, out of his conventional framework, into Thoughtland: 'Upwards and yet not Northwards.' In *Romola*, Baldassarre, a traumatized old man once a scholar, now a refugee deserted by his own adopted son, stares at an old text he formerly knew well, by the second-century Greek historian and geographer, Pausanias. It seems only a flat unmeaning thing now: '*ΜΕΣΣΗΝΙΚΑ. ΚΒ*':

> In old days he had known Pausanias familiarly; yet an hour or two ago he had been looking hopelessly at that page, and it had suggested no more meaning to him than if the letters had been black weather-marks on a wall...

Then suddenly something comes back to his brain, releases a third dimension called the meaning, realized and felt—

> but at this moment they were once more the magic signs that conjure up a world....
> He snatched up the book, but the light was too pale for him to read further by. No matter: he knew that chapter; he read inwardly.... The words arose within him, and stirred innumerable vibrations of memory. He forgot that he was old: he could almost have shouted.   (*Romola*, chapter 38)

It is suddenly opened inward, as if reading itself began again, by a series of translations: outer letters turn into inner sounds, mere marks into nerves and feelings; these bodily vibrations are themselves made mental, triggering thoughts and releasing memories. It is like the famous opening of *Adam Bede* where 'a single drop of ink' turns like magic into a vision of the past: George Eliot has an implicit sense of the movement from brain to mind, the work of transmission exploding across realms, between the ink marks and the human meanings they create. There is even, in her own words on the reading of Pausanias, a vibration of the brain to be picked up across the back marks—between 'in *old* days he had known Pausanias familiarly' at the beginning and at the end 'he *forgot* that he was *old*', as though once inside the act of reading there is a different universe of time for Baldassarre, a forgetting of the externally 'old' for the moment and a more innocent meaning for 'forgot'.

Only in a Flatland were there simple literal and static facts. In his own sphere, in relation to scientific thinking, George Henry Lewes had changed from being, in his early days, a follower of John Stuart Mill. Mill had believed that inductive discoveries were no more than the sum of the observations of facts already existent, empirical reports that merely copied and corresponded to what was simply waiting to be found in the world, without anything added. But in *Problems of Life and Mind* Lewes became increasingly more persuaded by the Kantian philosopher William Whewell as to the initiating role of imagination and invention in having to create the framing ideas and modifying conceptions by which facts were revealed in the act of their being bound together. A new 'point of view' made the facts assume a different 'aspect' (another key word for George Eliot), and, though therefore partial and relative, a theoretical view was confirmed by what it helped to reveal which might not otherwise have been seen without it. A true theory, argued Whewell in his *Philosophy of the Inductive Sciences*, is 'a Thought which is contemplated distinct from Things and seen to agree with them; while a Fact is a combination of our Thoughts with Things in so complete agreement that we do not regard them as separate'.[16] It is easy to forget that in a Fact the Ideas 'are applied so readily and familiarly, and incorporated with the sensations so entirely, that we do not see them, we see through them' (Whewell, 1, p. 40). In reality there are two things working in dialectical relation to each other—Thought and Fact—not one. But in reading the world just as in reading a book, mental interpretations for the most part go unrecognized: 'Most men are unconscious of this perpetual habit of reading the language of the external world, and translating as they read' (Whewell, 1, p. 24). All the more so when the language seems so clear and customary as not to have to be 'seen' but rather can be 'seen through':

> If the inscription were entire and plain, in a language with which we were familiar, we should be unconscious of any mental act in reading it. We should seem to collect its meaning by the sight alone. But if we had to decipher an ancient inscription, of which only imperfect marks remained, with a few entire letters among them, we should probably make several suppositions as to the mode of reading it, before we found any mode which was quite successful; and thus, our guesses, being separate from the observed facts, and at first not fully in agreement with them, we should be clearly aware that the conjectured meaning, on the one hand, and the observed marks on the other, were distinct things, though these two things would become united as elements of one act of knowledge when we had hit upon the right conjecture.   (Whewell, 1, p. 8)

George Eliot's is deliberately not that flat, transparent language uninvolving of consciousness: rather, what she seeks is a version of Baldassarre's experience, of finding static black marks suddenly having a *physical* effect in their conversion into mentally dynamic meanings. The reader can feel the thought going into the sentences, into the hidden interstices. As she was to put it in *Daniel Deronda*:

> [T]he subtly-varied drama between man and woman is often such as can hardly be rendered in words put together like dominoes, according to obvious fixed marks. The word of all work, Love, will no more express the myriad modes of mutual attraction, than the word Thought can inform you what is passing through your neighbour's mind.   (*Daniel Deronda*, chapter 27)

There is an extra dimension in her language and in her form that allows both persons and ideas to *rotate*, enabling the manifestation of different aspects of each phenomenon, and the movement from one phenomenon to another different one. It is a serious version of what she says satirically when Dorothea baffles her uncle: 'woman was a problem which ... could be hardly less complicated than the revolutions of an irregular solid' (*Middlemarch*, chapter 4). Hers is not the Euclidean geometry of Spinoza but, within a rotational setting called *Middlemarch*, a living model of ever-shifting structures forming and reforming at microscopically deep levels—as Lewes himself puts it:

> There is an incessant formation of neural groups; there is also an incessant disaggregation and reformation of groups....*The group is never a fixed structure*; it is only a disposition of the elements which is easily re-formed; just as in a Kaleidoscope there are certain groups of the separate pieces of glass which combine now in one way and now in another. (*PLM* 5, pp. 140–1, problem 2, para. 110)

What George Eliot grew ever more used to doing was shaking that kaleidoscope of neural groupings, shifting the centre. Realism in George Eliot is not a world flatly taken for granted where the nature of experience can be simply congruent with habitual linguistic formulae, nouns 'put together like dominoes': it is a world taken somewhat apart, coming somewhat apart, in which Thought must seek to decipher the inner workings of the world's variety even as it is still externally ongoing. What position in space has the inner life as it looks out on the three-dimensional world? How and where does it achieve contact with the invisible inner life of another human life? What is going on in the movement between one phase or configuration of reality and another? Language itself was a two-way movement between the mind creating the page and the mentality created on it, in a rich and often emotionally charged holding ground for thinking. When George Eliot could make a verbal entry point into the encoded secrets of experience, the words returned to her the thought of fresh unwritten matter for further verbal exploration in a now denser medium. She did not simply write of the young Dorothea in relation to Casaubon, 'She had not learned his hidden conflicts', but immediately revised the manuscript to read 'She had not *yet* learned' and 'She had not yet learned *those* hidden conflicts *in* her husband *which* deserve our pity.' Little words, like microscopic particles, carry her forward to penetrate further, till she changes the pious 'deserve our pity' into the deeper '*claim* our pity', as if within another dimension she could hear the inner cries crying to her. In a deeper world it is precisely the claims that are not made—that cannot ask for themselves because not expecting to be answered, knowing nowhere where they could be met—which are the greatest claims of all. That is how pity or sympathy are odder than we customarily think they are, for not being complete healing love, for not being magical cures: so far from being merely what Nietzsche called 'human, all too human', they are like something, consciously and imperfectly, in lieu of what we need to fill the gaps, paper the cracks. They are vicariously displaced feelings in awkward search for a place in the world where they might still offer a little help when (and because) nothing else can.

Nowhere is this deeper insight into a sub-reality more powerful than in the depiction of those who do not want to admit they are living secretly separated within a continuingly bad marriage, who try not to think of the hidden fissures and fault lines. After years of a lonely studious bachelorhood, Casaubon had every reason to think that he *ought* to feel rewardingly elated by the devotion of the beautiful young Dorothea. That was how it was meant to be, but

> now he was in danger of being saddened by the very conviction that his circumstances
> were unusually happy: there was nothing external by which he could account for a
> certain blankness of sensibility which came over him just when his expectant gladness
> should have been most lively... (*Middlemarch*, chapter 10)

In his book on *Pessimism*, inspired by George Eliot's own resistance to hopelessness, James Sully wrote on the instinct to measure the value of the world in terms of human feeling. But the problem lies in the relativism of the measurement: 'There is a constant tendency to measure the dimensions of any given feeling, not from an absolute zero-point, but from the point of our most frequent, customary, or habitual emotional states.'[17] Happiness and unhappiness are not absolute states with set quantities of pleasure or pain, but relative movements between one and the other, up and down from a baseline default that is itself put in place without thought. Hence Casaubon is saddened by finding himself unaccountably not happy when he somehow should be. In time, in space, in relation to other people, in relation to their own feelings, the humans of *Middlemarch* may know where they want to be or are expected and supposed to be in the apparently normal, solid, predictable three-dimensional world; but they do not know where they are in reality: 'He could not account for a certain blankness...' He is being at once disrupted and reorganized by motions of inchoate proto-thought below the reach of his entire control. Consciousness, seemingly set up to be orderly and linear, is reset within a bending, warping tension.

Lydgate is a gifted 29-year-old medical man with a beautiful wife, who insists on 'not saying angrily within himself that he had made a profound mistake':

> [B]ut the mistake was at work within him like a recognized chronic disease,
> mingling its uneasy importunities with every prospect, and enfeebling every thought.
> (*Middlemarch*, chapter 58)

By a kind of natural law the doctor cannot diagnose himself in this uncharted area even as he tries to deny and then palliate the shock of 'chronic disease'. In the aftermath of a marital row, in a situation in which marriage is no longer an ideal state of fixed equilibrium, the new human physics of George Eliot is become frighteningly unpredictable,[18] as the man tries to hold the union steady at a sought level of resolved normality:

> It was as if a fracture in delicate crystal had begun, and he was afraid of any movement that might make it fatal. His marriage would be a mere piece of bitter irony if they could not go on loving each other. (*Middlemarch*, chapter 64)

George Eliot and George Henry Lewes admired the imaginative etymologies offered in Horne Tooke's *Diversions of Purley* (1786, 1805). What they read there was the implicit biography of thinking, the history of the micro-thought-processes implicit within words. So: 'If' was what Horne Tooke called a supporter of Plutarch's 'tripod of truth', linking consequent to antecedent in search of an 'if-then' conclusion. But in 'if they could not go on loving each other', the 'if' is not allowed to derive, as Horne Tooke said, from 'given that', but is rather 'lest', in Tooke's definition an attempted lessening or shrinking. The awkwardness of the formulation is to do with the sheer difficulty of trying to 'go on' out of fear of the opposite, back-to-front, outside-in now, when it is 'he' who is having to take upon him all the work of keeping a 'they' together. These are the strange in-between worlds fleetingly but recurrently glimpsed—thought that is not quite thought, life that is not quite life, in the unacknowledged lacunae between husband and wife, wife and husband, caught somewhere between unreachable depths and inadequate surfaces, in the breaking of the usual unthinkingly swift links between perception and action, thought and speech, cause and effect. The wild chaos of a Hetty Sorel is not taken out of the normal landscape but found in semi-suppressed and muffled explosion, in swerves and gaps and bumps within it. All that is straight, said the dwarf in Nietzsche's *Thus Spake Zarathustra*, tells lies; all truth is crooked. But in *Middlemarch* it is not good that so much has ceased to be straight, that a sense of pristine orientation is lost or overlaid in the compromised worsening of relationships:

> His marriage seemed an unmitigated calamity; and he was afraid of going to Rosamond before he had vented himself in this solitary rage, lest the mere sight of her should exasperate him and make him behave unwarrantably. There are episodes in most men's lives in which their highest qualities can only cast a deterring shadow over the objects that fill their inward vision: Lydgate's tender-heartedness was present just then only as a dread lest he should offend against it, not as an emotion that swayed him to tenderness. (*Middlemarch*, chapter 73)

Here is the language that needs to say 'lest' twice: 'solitary rage lest ... dread lest'. We have seen in Chapter 3 just how well George Eliot knew Spinoza's geometric method, designed to recreate through the clarity of logic on the page the multi-dimensional plan of the world beyond it. This included the demonstration of a genetic architecture in humans that generated a multiplicity of complex emotions out of core elements of pleasure and pain, joy and sorrow. But what has happened in Lydgate's 'lest' is an extra warping convolution as a result of the deteriorating context to which his emotions find themselves adapting—a marriage through which tender-heartedness, made almost unrecognizable to its own bearer, is turned into the fright of losing itself. An emotion that naturally should have been expansive has become a shadow of itself, what Spinoza called a sad passion, in another version of life shrinking and contracting. It is here with the element of tenderness as it was said earlier of conceitedness: 'all conceit is not the same conceit, but varies in correspondence with the minutiae of mental make in which one of us differs from another' (chapter 15). Universals take intricately different shapes, blended into the make-up of differently combined individuals under pressure of their whole environment. Hence the bends and distortions, the internal struggles and compromised defences, without which lives are not manageable. The traditional way of formal philosophy, said William James, was to aspire to stasis, to permanent general and universal laws, top down; but 'why, from Plato to Aristotle downwards, philosophers should have vied with each other in scorn of the knowledge of the particular, and in adoration of that of the general, is hard to understand'. For those who add psychology to philosophy as he himself did, 'the only value of universal characters is that they help us, by reasoning, to know new truths about individual things'. The recognition of the intricately particular, he added, may require 'even more complicated brain-processes' than high-flying metaphysics.[19] George Eliot used general characters—'There are episodes in most men's lives in which...'—for the sake of furthering her recognition of the importance lodged within specifics, and in turn used those specifics further to extend and refine her general understanding.

But in order for ordinary human beings to be normal, sane, and effective in the world of action, conscious perception has to make subtractions from the overload of incoming and underlying surpluses of sensory material. It has to make a selection from all that William James meant by the raw, undifferentiated, unscreened stuff, inside and out, which, beneath the threshold of visibility and conventionally named feeling, made one great dissonantly buzzing confusion of primordial experience (PP, 1, p. 488). In *Middlemarch* it is the grass growing, the squirrel's heart beat, the roar. The world feels full—a continuum, a plenum. If its roar is not partially sealed off, then it is like what it is for the strange protagonist of 'The Lifted Veil', doomed to hear amidst his own thoughts the noise of the thoughts of others all around him. The veil is necessary, to cover the gaps and the defects, to hide the million underlying micro-forces, even by a false but protective sense of approximate completeness. Otherwise, as in a novel by one of George

Eliot's foremost modern admirers, human beings can find themselves fearing imminent madness.

A. S. Byatt's strange young schoolboy, Marcus, is crossing some playing fields—sensing the boundaries of the pitches, the railway tracks, the morning sun—when a shift of light suddenly creates a geometric grid, a mathematical landscape, with strange lines of force:

> The light was busy. It could be seen gathering, running and increasing along the lines where it had been first manifest. Wild and linear on the railway tracks, flaming, linking, crossing on the tennis-court mesh, rising in bright intermittent streams of sparks from glossy laurel leaves and shorn blades of grass. It could also be seen moving when no object reflected, refracted or directed it. In loops, eddies, powerful direct streams, turbulence and long lines proceeding without let through stones, trees, earth, himself, what had been a condition of vision turned into an object of vision.
>
> Things were newly defined by it....a presence, and a presence with purpose...He was both saved (from bright blinding, from annihilation) and prevented (from losing himself) by a geometric figure...He saw intersecting cones, stretching to infinity, containing the pouring and rushing. He saw that he was at the, or a, point of intersection, and that if it could not pass through it would shatter the fragile frame to make a way. He must hold together, but let it go through... [20]

He had tried to stop, in parts, first his body, then his attention, but 'there was a sickening moment when the inside of the head seemed to be striding on beyond his own eyes' (Byatt, p. 120). The boundaries, physical and geographical, have all altered utterly.

At moments of great crisis, there is in George Eliot a sudden widening of the world, when a person can no longer hold thoughts in his or her own head but is forced into a multi-dimensional way of thinking in a dizzyingly changed world. It was so from 'Janet's Repentance', as we have seen in Chapter 3:

> Her thoughts, instead of springing from the action of her own mind, were external existences, that thrust themselves imperiously upon her like haunting visions....She was every moment slipping off the level on which she lay thinking, down, down into some depth from which she tried to rise again with a start.
>
> ('Janet's Repentance', chapter 16)

to *Daniel Deronda*, as we shall see again in Chapter 11:

> That was the sort of crisis which was at this moment beginning in Gwendolen's small life: she was for the first time feeling the pressure of a vast mysterious movement, for the first time being dislodged from her supremacy in her own world, and getting a

sense that her horizon was but a dipping onward of an existence with which her own was revolving.   (*Daniel Deronda*, chapter 69)

And it includes difficult little words of spatial orientation—'the *level on which* she lay thinking', 'her horizon but a dipping *onward*'—which force strange equivalent movement in the reader's own head. In *Middlemarch* it happens with Dorothea on her honeymoon in Rome—'an alien world', 'the vast wreck of ambitious ideals' jarring her young sense 'as with an electric shock', 'that ache belonging to a glut of confused ideas which check the flow of emotion':

> [I]n certain states of dull forlornness Dorothea all her life continued to see the vastness of St Peter's . . . and the red drapery which was being hung for Christmas spreading itself everywhere like a disease of the retina.   (*Middlemarch*, chapter 20)

This is where the world, as though oscillating across within and without, changes its dimensions and its boundaries, making the retina, the inner source of outward vision, itself an object and an external sight. *Middlemarch* is so often like a great mind in which its people live and move, crossing through mental pathways; but here it is like a bleeding brain.

It is said in relation to Casaubon that a tiny speck close to the eye can blot out the glory of the whole world, leaving only a margin by which to detect the blot itself, and in Casaubon that speck was his own inner self, past which he could hardly see (chapter 42). But eyes are also opened and made wider. For Dorothea, in the night after finding Will and Rosamond together, the grid of reality changes once again. It does not matter that eventually, happily, she will be proved wrong; it is not a scene undercut by the irony that Will still loves her and not Rosamond, that what she has witnessed she has partly misunderstood. What matters to George Eliot is the change in reality now, inside Dorothea if it were true, regardless of later story:

> 'Oh, I did love him!'
> Then came the hour in which the waves of suffering shook her too thoroughly to leave any power of thought. She could only cry in loud whispers, between her sobs, after her lost belief which she had planted and kept alive from a very little seed since the days in Rome . . .
> In that hour she repeated what the merciful eyes of solitude have looked on for ages in the spiritual struggles of man—she besought hardness and coldness and aching weariness to bring her relief from the mysterious incorporeal might of her anguish: she lay on the bare floor and let the night grow cold around her.   (*Middlemarch*, chapter 80)

This is a world turned as strange for Dorothea as it was wild for Hetty in the fields. The eyes—'the merciful eyes of solitude'—are felt as outside. The loved man, 'moving wherever she moved', is at once both a belief and the person seemingly betraying that belief to hardness, coldness, and tired loneliness in its stead. But the speck and the bleed both begin to retract as Dorothea awakes in morning twilight 'to a new condition':

> [S]he felt as if her soul had been liberated from its terrible conflict; she was no longer wrestling with her grief, but could sit down with it as a lasting companion and make it a sharer in her thoughts. For now the thoughts came thickly.... (*Middlemarch*, chapter 80)

Reactively, she could have turned on Will as a betrayer, and even more easily she might have turned on Rosamond in his stead: that is the sort of mechanical psychological process of deflected transfer that is not of the very greatest interest to George Eliot. But instead Dorothea stops, holds tight the reaction within herself as a moderating force of being, until the situation itself seems to look back at her: 'She began now to live through that yesterday morning deliberately again, forcing herself to dwell on every detail and its possible meaning. Was she alone in that scene? Was it her event only?' So it was before in chapter 42 during her most threatening break with Casaubon: the recalled scene now is 'like a shadowy monitor looking at her anger with sad remonstrance' (perhaps the finest use of 'sad' in literature, silently pleading a simple 'Don't do harm' beneath the verbal sophistication). Augustine described looking at certain texts in the Bible, when they seem obscure or unfelt, as being as though the eyelids of God are closed in them, the face of God hidden; but whenever they clear, the eyelids open and the meaning looks out and into its reader.[21] In place of the eyes of God here it was the merciful eyes of solitude. And here too, in another great shift of reality, it is grief that suddenly and remarkably changes both its position from inside to out and its nature from foe to companion and sharer: 'She could sit down with it ...' This is a human being trying to find for an innerness that transcends the ego within which it nonetheless remains contained, some place and arrangement *outside*—and she senses how paradoxical, almost impossible, that actually is:

> All the active thought with which she had before been representing to herself the trials of Lydgate's lot, and the marriage union which, like her own, seemed to have its hidden as well as evident troubles—all this vivid sympathetic experience returned to her now as a power: it asserted itself as acquired knowledge asserts itself and will not let us see as we saw in the day of our ignorance. She said to her own irremediable grief, that it should make her more helpful, instead of driving her back from effort.
>
> (*Middlemarch*, chapter 80)

In that last sentence she wants 'it' to make a place back inside 'her' for what it is right then to do, reforming the geometric lines of one life in relation to those three other lives. But what is also vital here in these complex lines and shapes is the insertion of just three words in a subordinate clause: 'the marriage union which, *like her own*, seemed to have its hidden as well as evident troubles'. This is autobiography put to use, no longer in the foreground like the speck of self, or a main clause, but in the great mental background now actively giving itself to an imaginative understanding of others. It may be called sympathy in the normal world but here, in the way it 'returns' as a power and 'asserts itself' as acquired knowledge, it is the making of an extra dimension, the molecular remaking of a human being. It is also like what George Eliot's verbal ability achieved: her language itself turned back upon her to offer her help. Given out in the act of writing, the words came back to her as a power that itself gave *her* a further sense of deep meaning.

'Wrought Back to Sense'

It is a terrible thing to lose an extra dimension. For Lydgate, what is commonly called vocation meant the existence of a whole intellectual world within him. But as 'scientific conscience had got into the debasing company of money obligation and selfish respects' (chapter 73), he can no longer contain 'that' extra world within 'this' mundane one:

> '*This* is what I am thinking of; and *that* is what I might have been thinking of' was the bitter incessant rumour within him, making every difficulty a double goad to impatience.... It was the sense that there was a grand existence in thought and effective action lying around him, while his self was being narrowed into the miserable isolation of egoistic fears, and vulgar anxieties for events that might allay such fears.
>
> (*Middlemarch*, chapter 64)

'This ... That ... It': in that shift of boundaries again, the man has ceased to embody a world which now instead lies outside and beyond him, and he has become the mere shell of a person within a material existence.

Without an extra dimension the world is as it is for Dorothea's bland sister Celia—two-dimensional:

> When people talked with energy and emphasis she watched their faces and gestures merely. She never could understand how well-bred persons consented to sing and open their mouths in the ridiculous manner requisite for that vocal exercise.
>
> (*Middlemarch*, chapter 3)

Or even as it is with Rosamond, reproducing her music master's performance 'with the precision of an echo':

> It was almost startling, heard for the first time. A hidden soul seemed to be flowing forth from Rosamond's fingers; and so indeed it was, since souls live on in perpetual echoes, and to all fine expression there goes somewhere an originating activity, if it be only that of an interpreter. (*Middlemarch*, chapter 16)

While the music lasts, at least the first time it is heard, the missing dimension is temporarily present in the world, even though its borrower does not internalize it and hardly knows it. Only much later, at the point of crisis, does Dorothea's wavelength pervade her.

It is in Dorothea that thinking becomes a multi-dimensional world which George Eliot can see forming. When she looks out of her window in the midst of her own sorrows and sees the distant primal figures of a man with a bundle on his back (like Marian Lewes's first early vision of Silas Marner) and a woman carrying a baby, suddenly 'she felt the largeness of the world':

> She was a part of that involuntary, palpitating life, and could neither look out on it from her luxurious shelter as a mere spectator, nor hide her eyes in selfish complaining.
>
> (*Middlemarch*, chapter 80)

Across that 'neither' and that 'nor' is the in-between area in middle earth that George Eliot loves to see created and recreated, in the continual working-out of life. As in *Adam Bede*, this vision 'will not *let* us see as we saw in the day or our ignorance'. *It* will not let *us* ignore it, however little we know of that 'it'— involuntary life, accumulated experience, acquired knowledge: the claims it makes, the thoughts it triggers and requires, the independent value it seems to demand, without clearly ascribable cause or intent. Everything that has somehow here got made into 'it' goes on within the sheer lines of George Eliot's prose; but with all the double negatives, the layers and levels and loops and turnarounds within the syntax, this is not Abbott's simple two-dimensional Lineland. It rotates in the mind. It is true that had Dorothea got closer to the man and the woman, all the difficulties of intimacy and relatedness would begin again in a different dimension or perspective. And she knows also that, from such a distance, Casaubon and herself might have been seen by an equivalent bystander as husband and wife simply standing beside one another for life. If that anonymous couple with their baby unknowingly gave Dorothea the feeling of something larger than her own troubles, perhaps too the sight of Dorothea, herself so often unhappy, at other times gives others hope. In its complex and shifting relativism the moment is all part of that 'involuntary, palpitating life' which, too large for any simple conclusion, takes the place of God in this novel.

Thus it was not for Dorothea simply, lineally, to become wise and strong in Casaubon's wisdom and strength. What she needed for herself was a better and higher idea of what was going on, which, through separate thinking, could take the place of personal dependence. But the idea must then become 'an idea wrought back to the directness of sense, like the solidity of objects'. For in all this micro-movement and transference of palpitating energy, what stands out for George Eliot finally is the return from thought back to feeling, to make for a 'solidity' again within the world. For all the strange geometry and physics, it is the solidity to which she is finally committed.

That is why the presence of the ordinary and decent Garth family is vital to the composition of *Middlemarch*, not only as a memory of *Adam Bede* and of the place of her father in her work and in her life, but as a common-world reminder of the ongoingness of solidity, for all the complexities and possibilities contained within it. As Caleb says in down-to-earth terms to the feckless young Fred Vincy, brother of Rosamond, 'You must not always be saying, There's this and there's that—if I had this or that to do, I might make something of it' (*Middlemarch*, chapter 56). Or his wife to Fred on his vow to pay back the money he has borrowed from them 'ultimately': '"Yes, ultimately," said Mrs Garth...having a special dislike to fine words on ugly occasions' (chapter 24). And so there is their daughter, Mary, when Fred tries to say to her that indeed he 'could be better' if he were sure of his being loved by her—Would it be any use for a man to say that? he asks; to which she replies: 'Not of the least use in the world for him to say he *could* be better. Might, could, would—they are contemptible auxiliaries' (chapter 14). In much the same way, that simple and conventional woman, Mrs Bulstrode, sister of the head of the Vincy family, can do every bit as well by her disgraced and erring husband as the more noteworthy Dorothea would wish for herself. Here she is in transition— that vital in-between moment—taking a brief but strange moment of time out in her own room before re-entering the reality of her now changed life. For once in these novels, the secret is out in the world, but she knows in a 'mere flash of time', as by a kind of pre-vision, that she will still stand by him. That moment contained within itself 'that concentrated experience which in great crises of emotion reveals the bias of a nature, and is prophetic of an ultimate act which will end an intermediate struggle':

> A new searching light had fallen on her husband's character, and she could not judge him leniently: the twenty years in which she had believed in him and venerated him by virtue of his concealments came back with particulars that made them seem an odious deceit...
>
> But this imperfectly-taught woman, whose phrases and habits were an odd patch-work, had a loyal spirit within her. The man whose prosperity she had shared through nearly half a life, and who had unvaryingly cherished her—now that punishment had befallen him it was not possible for her in any sense to forsake him. There is a forsaking which still sits at the same board and lies on the same couch with the forsaken soul, withering it the more by unloving proximity. She knew, when she locked her door, that she should unlock it ready to go down to her unhappy husband and espouse his sorrow, and say of his guilt, I will mourn and not reproach. But she needed time...
>
> (*Middlemarch*, chapter 74)

And in that time, between the suddenly changed past and the anticipated future of still returning to him, she finally brings herself to readjust in solid, material ways. But it takes two long pages of preparation, for the thing must be done twice—once in the microscopic speed of that strange pre-vision, but once again more slowly by the translation of it back into realism's ordinary solidity, that she might become that loyal person again for the rest of her life:

> When she had resolved to go down, she prepared herself by some little acts which might seem mere folly to a hard onlooker; they were her way of expressing to all spectators visible or invisible that she had begun a new life in which she embraced humiliation. She took off all her ornaments and put on a plain black gown, and instead of wearing her much-adorned cap and large bows of hair, she brushed her hair down and put on a plain bonnet-cap. Which made her look suddenly like an early Methodist.
>
> (*Middlemarch*, chapter 74)

Immediately the next paragraph begins,

> Bulstrode, who knew that his wife had been out and had come in saying that she was not well, had spent the time in an agitation equal to hers. He had looked forward to her hearing the truth from others . . . as something easier to him than any confession . . .

Nothing shows more clearly the turn from successiveness into simultaneity in this novel, the way in which the characters occupy different relative worlds within the same time and space. And for all Mary Garth's scorn for 'might and could and would', still Mrs Bulstrode might have been as Rosamond, forsaking even while living in unloving proximity. 'There is a forsaking which still sits at the same board and lies on the same couch with the forsaken soul, withering it the more by unloving proximity': it is like a thought in the novel's brain waiting for a reader's mind to catch and apply it. What Mrs Bulstrode might have been, or could have done and did not, is, for the reader and the author (those 'invisible' mental spectators), part of what she was and did, in what would normally be unrated or unrecognized achievement. It looks just like carrying on, though shamed; but underneath in the tiny traces of language 'espousing' his sorrow and 'embracing' humiliation mark the inner renewal of vows, which, in the wearing of the old black gown, solemnizes a second marriage within the first that it also mourns for.

It is this return to realist solidity to which George Eliot herself remains constant. That hard solid line is still drawn between physical bodies. What Mrs Bulstrode's damaged fidelity to her husband achieves for the reader in contrast to Rosamond's relation to Lydgate does nothing in the reality of the world of *Middlemarch* to help Lydgate or Rosamond themselves. And it remains a still half-broken fidelity, just as sympathy at one level changes the world in ways neither Celia nor Rosamond can imagine and yet at another can never wholly help or cure the one pitied. At such points, and at that level, a different philosophy—a philosophy of stern dualism between one and another, between within and without—still asserts its necessity in George Eliot, for all the underlying geometric changes, for all the parallel worlds of possibility, the extensions of consciousness beyond self, and the complex micro-connections. That was the great advantage of being an intellectual polyglot: she could see how different philosophies, shaken down into her like differing forms of available thought, suddenly applied to the changed fields or worlds of experience that come upon us.[22] But still there was a commitment to a profound common sense. She once wrote her dear friend Barbara Bodichon a brief note for thoughtlessly not repaying the shilling she had borrowed from her servant: to that servant, it was a considerable sum (GEL 5, p. 3).

There is a little final image of the goodness of the loyalty to common realism in the depiction of Farebrother. He is the lackadaisical bachelor clergyman whom Lydgate, at the start of his *Middlemarch* career, somewhat looks down upon for not loving his vocation as he himself does. When Fred Vincy is most in danger of losing Mary Garth because of his indiscipline, Farebrother speaks to him of his own feelings for her. He thinks she could be his if Fred continues to go wrong. 'I thought you were friendly to me,' says Fred in alarm:

> 'So I am; that is why we are here. But I have had a strong temptation to be otherwise. I have said to myself, "If there is a likelihood of that youngster doing himself harm, why should you interfere? Aren't you worth as much as he is, and don't your sixteen years over and above his, in which you have gone rather hungry, give you more right to satisfaction than he has? If there's a chance of his going to the dogs, let him—perhaps you could nohow hinder it—and do you take the benefit."'
>
> (*Middlemarch*, chapter 66)

There is a pause, then a change in tone 'like the encouraging *transition* to a major key' in this great acoustic novel:

> 'But I had once meant better than that, and I am come back to my old intention. I thought that I could hardly *secure myself* in it better, Fred, than by telling you what had gone on in me.... If there is any chance that word of warning from me may turn aside any risk to the contrary—well I have uttered it.' (*Middlemarch*, chapter 66)

This is solid and secure in being committed to 'come back' to all the directness of sense. What might once have been secretly hidden in free indirect discourse—'Why should you interfere... Aren't you worth as much...'—is here made direct, honestly articulated, out there in the difficult common world. George Eliot knows all the hard underlying things that could also be suspiciously thought: that this moment of sacrifice would not have happened *if* there had been more to sacrifice, *if* Farebrother had been a man of greater passion, *if* there had been more chance for him of Mary, or *if* there had been less weakness and sorrowful ageing in himself. But like Farebrother himself, George Eliot settles for what is there in him as he is, for all the intelligent hypotheticals and qualified possibilities of a complicated and imperfect world. It is still an utterance subtly rendered, indirect even in its directness by being a warning to Fred simultaneous with a securing of himself. It is, that is to say, a speech in translation, transmitted to help make a transferred life. For when he speaks to Fred of the 'temptation', Farebrother is disguised—but disguised only as himself. It is like a good version of the deviousness of Tito Melema in *Romola*. Staying himself, without ever ceasing to be the limited man he is, Farebrother, by that means, makes use of himself, even against himself—transferred on behalf of Fred and, even more perhaps, for the sake of Mary's happiness. It is an inventive use of his own sadness, his deficiencies, and his limited resources. As with Mrs Bulstrode, it has to be done twice, once in the inner world of murky temptations, and once again in the outer world of more stark and practical commitment. Farebrother will not help undo Fred's chances, even by doing nothing. It is like the great double negative of Lydgate's final moral act as a doctor and as a human being, when he cannot let the staggering Bulstrode leave the meeting room, scene of his public disgrace, unaided and unsupported. Bitterly he sees what it must look like in the eyes of onlookers already suspecting him of collusion with Bulstrode; but with reluctance, 'What could he do? He could not see a man sink close to him for want of help' (*Middlemarch*, chapter 71). He could not *not* do it: these are the great double binds. So it was said of Farebrother earlier: 'by dint of admitting to himself that he was too much as other men were', he had become 'remarkably unlike them', in that very acceptance (chapter 18). For however much George Eliot sought analytically to prise apart apparent facts or set attitudes and see what they were truly composed of, there was another creative part of her that knew the inseparability of strengths and weaknesses, even within a single strand. That distinct inextricability which formed a singly blended person in the experiments of life, that final agnosticism as to how far that person could do something else without having to be someone different, *was* art for her: it meant a character was become simply more existent than explicable, as in life itself. Then she had put together something with one part of her brain that she could not wholly take apart with another.

That is why, in *Daniel Deronda*, she will not have to do with the theoretic intellect which, like a poor version of Spinoza, creates its own illusory systems 'in the shape of axioms, definitions, and propositions' that nonetheless exclude fact. An 'emotional intellect' is capable of including in its passionate vision

> the more comprehensive life feeding theory with new material, as the sensibility of the artist seizes combinations which science explains and justifies.
>
> (*Daniel Deronda*, chapter 41)

As we saw at the end of Chapter 5, this is life feeding theory by being more than is easily digested; emotion forcing thought to understand it; art challenging science with the complex material that makes cognition raise the level of its response.

In the midst of her flight into the unknown with Stephen Guest, Maggie Tulliver had turned back through a courage that would seem cowardly, through a compunction that would make her look shameful. It was, I have argued, a crucial moment in the working life of George Eliot. In *Fear and Trembling*, Kierkegaard said it could be a great thing to try to go beyond the common world, to find a higher reality; but it was a greater still to return with the intimation of it to *this* world, in the second place. So in *Daniel Deronda* there is a 'nobler partiality' that exchanges for its 'bird's eye reasonableness' the more 'generous reasonableness of drawing shoulder to shoulder' (chapter 63). It is that comradely moral return after all the insight into the invisible and immaterial, that final unflinching concern for the solid human state in which possibilities do or do not find their fate, which makes George Eliot unsurpassed in the *use* of art, whatever the great fictional experiments that followed her time. For George Eliot, whatever the new and future visions of reality, however experimentally exciting might be their energetic potential, they had still to be transferred back into a form of human life that could feed its mundane course.

CHAPTER 11

Daniel Deronda

The Great Transmitter and the
Last Experiment, 1873–6

A poem by Goethe, known to George Henry Lewes, describes the secret of existence made manifest in the structure of the gingko leaf, shaped as it like a walnut or, as we may say, the two hemispheres of the human brain:

> Does it represent One living creature
>   Which has divided itself?
> Or are these Two, which have decided,
>   That they should be as One?
>
> To reply to such a Question,
>   I found the right answer:
> Do you notice in my songs and verses
>   That I am One and Two?

For Goethe the finest work, closest to the fundamental structures of creation, is such that works both ways: One dividing itself into Two, Two realizing affinity in One. In *Middlemarch*, Lydgate should have been the embodiment of the integration that George Eliot most sought within life and within work, and between them. He had first gone into his studies with 'the conviction that the medical profession as it might be was the finest in the world; presenting the most perfect interchange between science and art; offering the most direct alliance between intellectual conquest and social good' (chapter 15). This was the blend of two-in-one as if the two sides indeed belonged together:

> There was fascination in the hope that the two purposes would illuminate each other: the careful observation and inference which was his daily work, the use of the lens to further his judgment in special cases, would further his thought as an instrument of larger inquiry. (*Middlemarch*, chapter 15)

Practical reality would inform intellectual theory; microscopic investigation would reform social welfare at the macro level. As Goethe put it of his scientific studies,

'There is a delicate empiricism [*zarte Empirie*] that makes itself in the most intimate way identical with its objects, and thereby becomes actual theory.'[1] Such thick empiricism must have felt to George Eliot like an analogy, not so much with 'songs and verses' as for Goethe, but with the art of the realist novel where close verbal description turned very quickly into that rich sense of things which prompted burgeoning thought and higher speculation.

Near the culmination of all that *Daniel Deronda* means in her oeuvre, there comes to Deronda the point at which he can at last say, 'I am a Jew.' That is 'one of those rare moments when our yearnings and our acts can be completely one, and the real we behold is our ideal good' (chapter 63). The integration is *that* way round, rather than 'and we behold our ideal good become real'. The fact that reality can contain the ideal good, after all; that what one had intuitively hoped for becomes *more* than was even hoped: this is what realization truly feels like, rather than the implemented achievement of a target plan. In *The Spanish Gypsy* it is what happens at the moment Fedalma dances instinctively to something felt within the music of the people that speaks to her of her unknown descent. 'Feeling and action flowing into one':

> The spirit in her gravely glowing face
> With sweet community informs her limbs,
> Filling their fine gradation with the breath
> Of virgin majesty; as full vowelled words
> Are new impregnate with the master's thought.
> (*The Spanish Gypsy*, book 1 1324, 1330–3)

As the last two lines suggest, it is like the moment in composition when George Eliot's thinking finds the right words for itself, even as the words receive what brings them fully to life—both ways at once in interchange. Imagine, says Deronda, the stolen offspring of a mountain tribe brought up in exile within the city of the plain, or someone with an inherited genius for painting but born blind: at a deep level of the nerves, it would be 'like a cunningly-wrought musical instrument, never played on', 'an intricate structure that, under the right touch, gives music' (*Daniel Deronda*, chapter 63). Suddenly it sounds and resounds, a hidden inner score is released in performance, two things fit: 'I am a Jew.' But when Deronda repeats this to Gwendolen, who only cares about their possible love for each other, there is a jarring tonal vibration in her response:

'A *Jew!*' Gwendolen exclaimed, in a low tone of amazement, with an utterly frustrated look, as if some confusing potion were creeping through her system.... 'What difference need that make?'

'It has made a great difference to me that I have known it,' said Deronda, emphatically; but he could not go on easily—the distance between her ideas and his acted like a difference of native language.... (*Daniel Deronda*, chapter 69)

So often this novel's is a language seeking relation to what is not to be seen and cannot be easily pointed at. That is what language is finally for George Eliot now when in her final novel she is interested not in the manifest and the obvious, but rather in the secret notes that Maggie Tulliver blindly sought, to chime with some different way of being. Remarkably, it can open huge distances, across different dimensions—the felt 'distance between her ideas and his...'

Or it can close and conjoin them, as in one of the novel's most moving moments when Mirah finally meets her long-lost elder brother. Instinctively, the first word with which she greets him is in the tone that has been her only cherished memory: 'Ezra'. Mordecai, responding to that family name of his, replies in recognition: 'That was our mother's voice.' It was less their own presence they felt, says George Eliot, than another's, the dead mother who still unites them: 'They were meeting first in memories' (*Daniel Deronda*, chapter 47).

The novel is written in part against ignorant prejudice such as Gwendolen's. George Eliot wrote in protest at such reactions to Harriet Beecher Stowe because, in *Uncle Tom's Cabin* (1852), Stowe had done in resistance to black slavery what she herself sought to do in sympathy for the Jews:

> Towards the Hebrews we western people, who have been reared in Christianity, have a peculiar debt, and whether we acknowledge it or not, a peculiar thoroughness of fellowship in religion and moral sentiment. Can anything be more disgusting than to hear people called 'educated' making small jokes about eating ham, and showing themselves empty of any real knowledge as to the relations of their own social and religious life to the history of the people they think themselves witty in insulting? They hardly know that Christ was a Jew. (GEL 6, pp. 301–2)

This is again the voice of an unbridled George Eliot refusing to tolerate what she calls 'stupidity' however 'educated'—where intelligence is far more than intellectual prowess. But there is more than the enlightened liberalism of J. S. Mill's *On Liberty* involved in *Deronda*; it is also written in fierce memory of lost kinship and forgotten origins, in an enlarged vision of the sudden recognition that Mordecai and Mirah, and Deronda and Mordecai, shared between them: 'Christ was a Jew.' England in this novel is a complacently tired and decaying society: the provincial challenge to London drawing rooms mounted in the earlier fiction was not sufficient. For any future at all, what was needed was an even deeper, more articulate, historic sense of a civilization's lost roots, of what belief and mission, values and purposes had been like and what they might be like again. The risk of a radically imaginative movement backwards before ever forwards again was the last chance now, in yet another challenge to the idea of straightforward chronology or simple progress.

*

After *Romola* Again

But most often, in the early parts of *Daniel Deronda*, what is painfully revealed is that disturbing sense of an ill-founded or broken confidence so prevalent in the *Romola* years. It occurs when, for example Gwendolen Harleth, so sure she is exceptional on account of her beauty, thinks she is cutely outscoring Mrs Arrowpoint, a squat, unattractive, and rather ludicrously dressed heiress, but also something of a writer:

> 'I wish I could write books to amuse myself, as you can! How delightful it must be to write books after one's own taste instead of reading other people's! Home-made books must be so nice.'
> For an instant Mrs Arrowpoint's glance was a little sharper...
> 'Imagination is often truer than fact,' said Gwendolen, decisively, though she could no more have explained these glib words than if they had been Coptic or Etruscan.
> (Daniel Deronda, chapter 5)

The sharply ironic writer, who is at once Mrs Arrowpoint *and* George Eliot, sees through Gwendolen, overacting her witty naïveté: 'with all her cleverness and purpose to be agreeable, [she] could not escape that form of stupidity: it followed in her mind, unreflectingly, that because Mrs Arrowpoint was ridiculous she was also likely to be wanting in penetration, and she went through her little scenes without suspicion that the various shades of her behaviour were all noted'. The dualism between the confident feeling within and the unsuspected exposure of oneself outside is painfully glaring. But the extended extra consciousness that might include awareness of that divide is something Gwendolen can hardly bear and must suppress even at the cost of her intelligence: she needs a separate self, but a separate self that has a controlled effect on the world, without being caught up in its consequences.

'Stupidity' is a hard word characteristic of this novel. In *Daniel Deronda*, secretly penetrating criticisms beyond the bounds of the self's control do not remain tacit for long but become spoken direct to their object. In particular there is another more serious artist beside Mrs Arrowpoint in the novel, transposing judgement into strict musical terms. So, Gwendolen unluckily elicits from the composer and pianist Klesmer his estimation of her drawing-room singing:

> Woman was dear to him, but music was dearer. 'Still, you are not quite without gifts. You sing in tune, and you have a pretty fair organ. But you produce your notes badly; and that music which you sing is beneath you. It is a form of melody which expresses a puerile state of culture...without any breadth of horizon. There is a sort of self-satisfied folly about every phrase of such melody; no cries of deep, mysterious

passion—no conflict—no sense of the universal. It makes men small as they listen to it. Sing now something larger. And I shall see.'

'Oh, not now—by-and-by,' said Gwendolen, with a sinking of heart at the sudden width of horizon opened round her small music performance.   (*Daniel Deronda*, chapter 5)

This sinking and opening is the enlargement of scale, the extension of world-view that marks George Eliot's final experiment in life, made also urgently much closer than any previous novel to the present in which it is written. The attack by the German artist and secularized Jew, Klesmer, on the self-confidence of Gwendolen holds within it the undeflectable assault of George Eliot herself upon the narrow and puerile state of contemporary English culture. This is the sharp satiric contempt of which Hale White had seen dangerous glimpses in Marian Evans. But her sarcastic attack on the stupidity of 'the average man'—'with the utmost respect for his knowledge as the rock from which all other knowledge is hewn' (chapter 37)—is not made out of intellectual snobbery; on the contrary, it is made on account of the demeaning damage done to unconventional people, subtle possibilities, and passionate concerns too easily made small or deemed ludicrous by ignorant dismissiveness. Twenty years earlier she had adopted Goethe's term for 'philistine', as Matthew Arnold was to do:

> The *Philister* is the personification of the spirit which judges everything from a lower point of view than the subject demands—which judges the affairs of the parish from the egotistic or purely personal point of view—which judges the affairs of the nation from the parochial point of view, and does not hesitate to measure the merits of the universe from the human point of view.   (*Essays*, p. 297)

'The subject demands': now, she really meant that verb. There is an extraordinary piercing intelligence that raises the level, the standard, the stakes of this novel in light of the struggles and challenges of the middle period from *Romola* to *Felix Holt*. When, for example, Gwendolen can hardly bear Klesmer to be unimpressed by her, what does George Eliot say? She offers a mind-spinning comparison as fast as it is unexpected and demanding: 'vanity is as ill at ease under indifference as tenderness is under a love which it cannot return' (*Daniel Deronda*, chapter 10). Nothing is safe, nothing is unrelated. But the intelligence is most terrible when allied to that insight and judgement which Edith Simcox dreaded in her mentor even when it sheathed its claws, and now the claws are out. It is a mark of the shift from *Middlemarch* to *Daniel Deronda*—from mitigation and tolerant sympathy, to passionate and terrible Old Testament judgement—that Farebrother is, as it were, replaced by Klesmer in terms of the minor character who sets the major tone.

There are fierce human standards that Klesmer can preserve only through the artistic demands and intensities of his music. What makes them fierce is what

George Eliot puts alongside them—the unthinking confidence that Gwendolen has in the ability of her beauty to produce an 'effect' upon the social world, as though it were an accomplishment of genius. That belief in her own specialness, almost to the point of omnipotence, was 'like a bit of her flesh—it was not to be peeled off readily, but must come with blood and pain' (*Daniel Deronda*, chapter 23). But that deep-seated fantasy is what she has to take to Klesmer a second time, for tearing out. Her mother's financial hardships force her to make a living by singing or acting, if she is not to become a mere teacher or governess. Even as she approaches him, needing to know if she can do it, she feels that terrible shift to dependence on another's opinion, on grounds disturbingly other than the familiar security of her social rank or beauty: 'She dreaded Klesmer as part of that unmanageable world which was independent of her wishes' (chapter 23). At best he tells her, after much strict training, personal setbacks, and material hardship, she might eventually achieve something hardly more than 'mediocrity'. The words brand themselves on her: 'too old', 'people no longer feigning not to see your blunders', 'mortifications', 'glaring insignificance', 'indignities': such is the cruel form that Klesmer's genuine compassion for her ignorance had had to take within the register of this final driving work of George Eliot's. This is the splitting and tearing force that comprises the felt reality of dualism in this book, where an implicit dualism is always the philosophy triggered by most traumatic pain in George Eliot: the separation of subject from object; the unsuspected chasm opening between inside and outside self like a contradiction of reality; the crossing from what Feuerbach called the interior independence of thought to the felt dependence on the unmanageable life of the world outside, leaving the hitherto confident self an exposed and diminished thing. It is a breaking in two of the structures of reality in a way that Goethe hated:[2]

> For the first time since her consciousness began, she was having a vision of herself on the common level, and had lost the innate sense that there were reasons why she should not be slighted, elbowed, jostled—treated like a passenger with a third-class ticket, in spite of private objections on her own part.   (chapter 23)

There were no reasons why she should not be so treated; it made no difference that it was she herself. It is like going through to the other side of life, leaving an evacuated self vulnerably behind her.

The verb of fear that constantly recurs in *Daniel Deronda* is no longer 'shrink' as it was in *Middlemarch* but 'dread'—the challenge to be felt in Nietzsche, in Kierkegaard, in Heidegger here made into English. 'She dreaded Klesmer' (*Daniel Deronda*, chapter 23); 'dreaded the unpleasant sense of compunction toward her mother, which was the nearest approach to self-condemnation and self-distrust that she had known' (chapter 9); 'among the forces she had come to dread was something within her that troubled satisfaction' (chapter 29). What Gwendolen has long feared is what her 'crude self-confidence' is in denial of and protection from: a sense of an underlying emptiness and meritlessness. To her, how could a self survive its own 'self-condemnation and self-distrust'? Mary Ann Evans had done so, but, as it is said in a tacit authorial note early in the novel: 'It is possible to have a strong self-love without any self-satisfaction', it is possible to combine self-love with 'a self-discontent' all the more intense because of one's own 'little core of egoistic sensibility' (chapter 2): Gwendolen was unlike her creator in knowing no such inner conflict; hard criticism was banished.

But her secret insecurities are why, from childhood, Gwendolen, like the young Mary Ann Evans, was liable to sudden mortifying attacks of unexpected and inexplicable panic: alone at night away from her mother; in the face of great open spaces offering 'an undefined feeling of immeasurable existence aloof from her' (chapter 6); in the sudden opening of a secret panel to reveal a picture of a dead face and a fleeing figure that petrifies her, like 'a statue into which the soul of Fear had entered' (chapter 6). Gwendolen never really knew her own father. There are four younger half-sisters from her mother's second marriage to an absentee Captain, now dead, of whom, again, Gwendolen can hardly bear to think. Once as a young girl she had even, suddenly, strangled her younger sister's canary-bird when its shrill notes had repeatedly jarred with her own singing. Though she tried to make up for it afterwards and smooth it over, the thought of it always made her wince. In all this she is related not so much to the equally beautiful provincial princess, Rosamond Vincy in *Middlemarch*, who knows no fears and suffers no doubts, but to the unrooted, charismatic Cynthia in Mrs Gaskell's *Wives and Daughters* (1864), who says to her own half-sister of the emotional damage of her own upbringing:

> 'But I know it; and what's more,' continued she, suddenly ashamed of her unusual exhibition of feeling, 'I try not to care, which I daresay is really the worst of all; but I could worry myself to death if I once took to serious thinking.'
>
> (*Wives and Daughters*, chapter 40)

'I daresay', in its worldly tone, is not primarily real in the way that the original 'I dare say' would have to be. It is the trying not to care, or not to appear to care, that is helping to create second-order creatures here: in particular, a generation of beauti-fully distracting but damagingly disinherited young women who half-know that even in their displayed vitality they lack something fundamentally securing that, however unexciting, should have come first. That is why, when it comes to serious thinking, Marian Evans had cried out, at his death, 'What shall I be without my father?' But Cynthia, overhearing her mother telling a friend how this girl of hers had by now quite forgotten her dead father, bit her lips to prevent herself crying out, 'Papa, papa, have I?' (chapter 19).

But in the culminating reworking and the austere heightening of previous work, it is not simply the memory of Rosamond in *Middlemarch* or Hetty in *Adam Bede*—or any other beautiful and stupid young woman so irritating to Marian Evans—that Gwendolen pays for in *Daniel Deronda*. With bolder imagination, there is instead, across the gender divide, something in her make-up that is in memory of Arthur Donnithorne, Godfrey Cass, and Nicholas Bulstrode in their crises, and above all of Tito Melema—those lawless male transgressors who had tried to get away with hiding and screening and pretending and cheating, in psychological defence against any possible realization of truth:

> 'It is good,' sing the old Eumenides, in Aeschylus, 'that fear should sit as the guardian of the soul, forcing it into wisdom—good that men should carry a threatening shadow in their hearts under the full sunshine; else, how should they learn to revere the right?' ... Tito felt himself too cultured and sceptical for that.   (*Romola*, chapter 11)

For all his cleverness, Tito is like a *Philister* in judging everything from a lower level than the subject demands. For such nonsense as moral law Tito was too 'cultured', too 'sceptical', culture being made synonymous with scepticism; while the question of what was truly Good was to him no more than a source of intellectual debate, conveniently left unresolved, says George Eliot, as a matter of relative 'taste'. Without her emotional roots, a merely intellectual Marian Evans could almost have been something of that: clever, sceptical, patronizingly liberated, as her father in his own way had feared she might be. But *Daniel Deronda* is against a too thin and easy version of enlightened modern progressivism: as in Romola herself, 'the subtle result of culture which we call Taste was subdued by the need for deeper motive; just as the nicer demands of the palate are annihilated by urgent hunger' (*Romola*, chapter 49). Hunger came before Taste. That is how *Daniel Deronda* drives beneath the neat surface that Gwendolen tries to preserve. It is why George Eliot wanted, first, underlying impulses to be seen again through all the layers of her writing, because she believed in facing the need and the shame and the humiliation of the raw human material, prior to class, beauty, gift, or luck. That is what the Valley of Humiliation had taught her in her own life.

Tito's is only the fear of being found out by some outer law, at a cost to his life of easy pleasure. As a man, a man of the world, he can find recourse in action and improvisation, always compulsively seeking to do something, anything, to avert disaster and prevent thought or discovery catching up with him. His activity is itself a kind of dread, but one easier to live with than the locked state of inner consciousness from which Gwendolen suffers in the unhappy marriage she had undergone to escape poverty for her mother and herself:

> In Gwendolen's consciousness Temptation and Dread met and stared at each other like two pale phantoms, each seeing itself in the other—each obstructed by its own image; and all the while her fuller self beheld the apparitions and sobbed for deliverance from them.   (*Daniel Deronda*, chapter 54)

It is not even two but three forces here—Temptation, Dread, and the helplessly fuller Self caught between their mechanism; it is five if it includes, at another level, 'each seeing itself in the other': the Dread of itself that comes upon Temptation even as it stirs, and the Temptation still felt even more excitedly within the Dread of it; six even, were there anything that could answer the self's sobbing cry for deliverance. It is clear that George Eliot had long brought to her work an underlying theory of mental states which she never makes wholly explicit but which is triggered and modified by the depiction of specific predicaments. Had she been a male intellectual, with a conventional education and a clear career path, she might well have been more content to create a system of mind in the manner of Herbert Spencer, with Spinoza at one end of that scale, and Casaubon at the other. But Marian Evans's situation was actually closer to what she creates in Daniel Deronda himself, across the gender divide, within a different sort of outsider: 'He was ceasing to care for knowledge—he had no ambition for practice—unless they could both be gathered up into one current with his emotions' (chapter 32). As we have seen in Chapters 3 and 4, it makes the reading of George Eliot so different from reading Spencer or Spinoza. In them the order of ideas in the book is meant to correspond with the order of things outside it: it is an immanent experience, to stay within the book's argument as though within a plan of the universe. In George Eliot, the mix of levels and vocabularies in complex forms of translation and approximation, the crying language of human appeal or yearning or sorrow, are precisely the sign of the need for reference elsewhere; for application and return inside and out, backwards and forward between literature and life; for the text to be at once entity and vehicle, two in one, reused for thinking in different contexts, forms and patterns, languages, lives.

That is how, across the works, there is a hidden genealogy of feeling linking Gwendolen and Tito, for all their differences, as the two most fearfully disturbing creations in the oeuvre. They are both about urgent need: they alike know what it is to have to look after and protect themselves, whereas Rosamond, in contrast, is only about the blithe avoidance and denial of any such anxiety. Gwendolen and Tito make their denials of law in terms of grave misdoings and the terrifying refusal to see them, in the ego's attempted manipulation of its own psychological processes: yet still they know at some involuntary level of mentality the truth of things beneath all that. Reading *Romola* with equivalent awareness, the American realist novelist William Dean Howells wrote of his early reading life:

Tito Melema was not only a lesson, he was a revelation, and I trembled before him as in the presence of a warning and a message from the only veritable perdition. His life, in which so much that was good was mixed with so much that was bad, lighted up the whole domain of egotism with its glare, and made one feel how near the best and the worst were to each other, and how they sometimes touched without absolute division in texture and color. The book was undoubtedly a favorite of mine, and I did not see then the artistic falterings in it which were afterward evident to me.[3]

The young Howells found, he says, the chief part of his ethical experience in reading novels. Here, the moral terror he feels in reading Tito is like the dread Gwendolen feels when increasingly she is forced to face the lurking and volatile possibilities of her own self. It is like the fear, in turn, that a reader may well feel in reading Gwendolen. When they are more than literal, when they are more like the mental work characteristic of a novelist, the connections and combinations that a reader such as Howells makes across the works are finally far more important in reassembling what is George Eliot than the critical perception of artistic falterings of composition in any one novel as a whole. In the story of George Eliot's equivocal relation to psychology, as told in particular in Chapters 8 and 9, it is Tito and Gwendolen who are the culmination of the terrors and horrors of the psychological, of all that finds room to get lost and go wrong in that disorderly holding ground of human complexity.

R. H. Hutton writes of the great 'struggle between evil and good' in Gwendolen,[4] but Howells adds a second layer of George Eliot's thought when he speaks of how Tito made him feel 'how near the best and the worst were to each other, and how they sometimes touched without absolute division in texture and color'. George Eliot knew what Spinoza stood for in her thinking, and not least important was the illusion discussed in the appendix to the first part of the *Ethics* as to an absolute separation of 'good and bad, merit and sin, praise and blame, order and confusion'. This was how it had to be practically for the children of Israel, at the level of sharp moral injunction; but at the deeper level of reason, it was clear that these things were not absolutes, were not even distinct realities, were often the expression of individual psychology in need of firm distinctions. They come from the same stuff, differently organized. It is precisely that closeness of good and evil in the midst of chaotic psychological confusion that provokes not only Howell's but Gwendolen's fear. It is this disorientation that Howells calls perdition and Deronda a dwelling place for lost souls. It is why George Eliot repeatedly quotes from Dante throughout *Daniel Deronda* as though the mundane world could suddenly become a psychological hell or a purgatory on earth for its inhabitants, without even the ability for them to call it such. It is the nightmare maturation of what Marian Evans had written nearly thirty years earlier in a letter to the Brays and Hennells, 'I feel that society is training men and women for hell' (GEL 1, p. 267). Part of the germ for *Daniel Deronda* was the Leweses seeing Byron's granddaughter feverishly losing £500 at roulette when, after the completion of *Middlemarch* in October 1872, they went to Homburg to take the waters: hence the opening scene of Deronda watching Gwendolen gamble.

A further part of the psychological hell lies in Gwendolen's marriage to the heartless and soulless Grandcourt—who, prematurely aged and living a bored and outworn life, is like an absorbant of human energy in the physics of this novel, far worse than anything in Dorothea's marriage to the sterile Casaubon. A languor of intention would come over Grandcourt, for example, 'like a fit of diseased numbness', whenever 'an end seemed within easy reach':

> [T]o desist then, when all expectation was to the contrary, became another gratification of mere will, sublimely independent of definite motive. (*Daniel Deronda*, chapter 14)

There are no motives to which to be tied, no ends worth pursuing. Like an alien creature, Grandcourt can simply stare blankly at the means other people employ, making them pointless and unmeaning. It is a vision of an end-of-the-world remnant of what human nature used to be, a cold instrumental will for power, in place of imagination, sympathy, and feeling.

His pleasure is to create in Gwendolen thoughts and feelings that she can only repress. That Gwendolen has been brought to accept him unwillingly without loving him, secretly knowing of his previous liaison with Mrs Glasher, who bore him four children, and still going ahead despite herself: that is Grandcourt's enjoyment achieved, as a killer of life, precisely through Gwendolen's loss of any natural vitality. She cannot forget that she, who had always thought she could do as she liked, had promised Mrs Glasher she would not marry this man. Her instinctive horror at Grandcourt's secret sexual past and her sense of justice to Lydia Glasher 'had at first come as the undoubting movement of her whole being' (chapter 28). No more can there be that first moment of a whole undivided being; she has split herself in an act of betrayal that is also, oddly to her, a self-betrayal at the same time. She 'had just taken a decisive step which she had beforehand thought she would not take'; 'she was appalled by the idea that she was going to do what she had once started away from with repugnance': a syntax far beyond Herbert Spencer's rationalism. 'It was new to her that a question of right or wrong in her conduct should rouse her terror' (chapter 28). Morality is no longer conventional; on this other side of silence, it has all the psychological force of existential dread. This is hell, with the knowledge that she deserves it, but without the theological framework to know where she really is.

In such binds, her vocabulary is almost destroyed, 'definite *and* vague' being a much repeated pairing. Thus, where Deronda can simply praise Mirah, the young woman he has saved and befriended, for her commitment to 'duty', Gwendolen knows that in her own marriage hers is not duty but 'submission to a yoke drawn on her by an action she was ashamed of' (chapter 45). Again, complex syntax takes her past simple moral words, beyond pure or straight thought. It is shaped like all that bound Mrs Transome by tight poisonous threads—the secret no longer being Grandcourt's family so much as her knowledge of it even in accepting him, compromising her in collusion for ever after: 'All she had to do now was to adjust herself so that the spikes of that unwilling penance which conscience imposed should not gall her. With a sort of mental shiver, she resolutely changed her mental attitude' (chapter 29).

The letter that Mrs Glasher sends her after her wedding night, to accompany the jewels Grandcourt has commanded to be given up to his new wife, is even worse than the remembered words of Klesmer's judgement. It fills her previous inner sense of emptiness with real desolation. She destroys the letter only to find its words returning to her, repeatedly, as if they were set within the jewels clasping her neck: 'You will have your punishment. I desire it with all my soul' (chapters 31, 35). Thinking of *The Mill on the Floss* in particular, W. D. Howells thought George Eliot would naturally have preferred to be a romantic writer, in the sense of powerful emotions seeking extraordinary imaginative outlets: but it was, he said, her ethical conscience that forced her to be realistic (*Literary Passions*, p. 194). Gwendolen is equivalently forced: 'Her confidence in herself and her destiny had turned into remorse and dread' (*Daniel Deronda*, chapter 35).

Of Ideas and Jews

The Wordsworthian influence so potent in the writing of *Scenes of Clerical Life*, through *Mill on the Floss* to *Silas Marner*, is felt most powerfully in *Daniel Deronda* by its absence, in the loss of strong emotional birthright and intuitive inheritance. Little had taken root in Gwendolen's life:

> A human life, I think, should be well rooted in some spot of a native land, where it may get the love of tender kinship for the face of earth, for the labours men go forth to, for the sounds and accents that haunt it, for whatever will give that early home a familiar unmistakable difference amid the future widening of knowledge.
>
> (*Daniel Deronda*, chapter 3)

In memory of *The Mill on the Floss*, this is not some supplementary sentimentality, insists George Eliot; it is something grown to be almost physically encoded as 'a sweet habit of the blood', an internal language-network of feeling. But *Daniel Deronda*'s is the language of disinheritance and the fundamental cost involved: 'At five years old, mortals are not prepared to be citizens of the world, to be stimulated by abstract nouns, to soar above preference into impartiality...The best introduction to astronomy is to think of the nightly heavens as a little lot of stars belonging to one's own homestead' (chapter 3). For George Eliot—and for the Mary Ann Evans still to be found in the intellectual adult—it was always important to start again from a particular location and a felt situation, to have a background to meaning in the warmth of good emotions felt, as Wordsworth said in 'Tintern Abbey', 'in the blood and along the heart'. Without that beginning—however checked and modified in later years—any subsequent knowledge would be a thing cut off and dead, cold knowledge like that of a Casaubon *about* the violet but without 'the scent itself' (*Daniel Deronda*, chapter 32). But this ultimate and culminating novel sets itself to think about the development of those who do not start right. And in that plight, what is marred is the capacity to carry out the kind of abstract thinking which can still work back down again from the lofty subject of 'astronomy' to the 'little lot of stars' most people know with love from the beginning. To Gwendolen, in contrast, 'the little astronomy taught her at school used sometimes to set her imagination at work in a way that made her tremble' (chapter 6). She sees herself at such moments in the novel's sudden cosmic expansion of perspective as merely one among many unnoticed and unprotected small creatures on the planet.

Now in the troubled development of later life, that higher, abstract, impartial, and extended level of consciousness is what fear and trembling demand of Gwendolen. It is what Deronda has himself already acquired, but in ways that Gwendolen, thinking him an aloof intellectual, does not understand. Talking of the family preservation of old inherited buildings, he says to her that 'affection is the broadest basis of good in life':

> 'Do you think so?' said Gwendolen, with a little surprise. 'I should have thought you cared most about ideas, knowledge, wisdom, and all that.'
>
> 'But to care about *them* is a sort of affection,' said Deronda, smiling at her sudden *naïveté*. 'Call it attachment, interest, willingness to bear a great deal for the sake of being with them and saving them from injury. Of course it makes a difference if the objects of interest are human beings; but generally in all deep affections the objects are a mixture—half persons and half ideas—sentiments and affections flow in together.'
>
> 'I wonder whether I understand that,' said Gwendolen, putting up her chin in her old saucy manner. 'I believe I am not very affectionate...' (*Daniel Deronda*, chapter 35)

Half-person, half-idea recalls the earliest model for the relation of Deronda to Gwendolen, that of Tryan to Janet in 'Janet's Repentance'. With that chin of hers, Gwendolen loves to charm and be thought of admiringly; but she can hardly bear to be touched, for the flirtation to become physically real and consummated as sexual: 'The perception that Rex wanted to be tender made her curl up and harden like a sea-anemone at the touch of a finger', 'I shall never love anybody,' she cries to her mother in her younger days, 'I can't love people. I hate them' (*Daniel Deronda*, chapter 7). But what Deronda here speaks to her of is what is still a human love for what she supposes merely non-human or inhuman entities—for buildings, natural objects, or ideas. This, if she but knew it, is his way of responding to his own version of rootlessness and disinheritance, an apparently illegitimate child brought up in unexplained mystery by an aristocratic uncle whom he gradually, but mistakenly, has come to suspect to be his father. For him, 'the moment of finding a fellow-creature is often as full of mingled doubt and exultation as the moment of finding an idea' (chapter 17). *Daniel Deronda* is not only a final explanation of what lies within George Eliot's own love of ideas. It is also, through Deronda and the Jewish half of the novel, a last attempt to see how far ideas themselves, in representing the human, can go ahead of the human as it currently is, to make a higher and warmer human future. As one of the debaters in Mordecai's club puts it in chapter 42, there are ideas already 'mixed with' all the other elements of life—as sowing seed or baking clay, working within the material that makes a medium for them. The other kinds of ideas are those either looking for material and medium, in the name of change, or are already silently and subliminally at work within the social atmosphere.

It was Emanuel Deutsch who first gave George Eliot the Jewish idea. The first mention of the possibility of *Deronda* is made by Lewes in a diary entry made shortly after Deutsch's death. Deutsch (1829–1873) was an assistant cataloguing books in the British Museum from 1855, after leaving his native Silesia. He was a scholar across cultures who knew his Virgil as well as his Old Testament, but became well known in London intellectual circles as a result of an article he wrote in the *Quarterly Review* in 1867, introducing English readers to the Talmud, the book of laws that he insisted had an extended meaning of the word law, comprising everything from the Mosaic code to the study of seeds. It was the work that resulted from Exile when words had to take the place of a homeland, when literature, study, reading, and interpretation preserved a people's memory in lieu of more material advantages. But the chief aim and end of all this learning was doing: the Talmud was practical in its creation of a way of life. It was the glory of Christianity, wrote Deutsch, that it had taken what was hidden amongst the silent community of the learned Jews, and communicated its faith and wisdom and morality to the wider world. Increasingly what the exiled Deutsch sorrowfully yearned for was a Jewish national home.

All this was irresistible to George Eliot. But even as she got to know him, taking Hebrew lessons from him to further the basic work she had done when studying Strauss, his health was failing. As, to his despair, his cancer painfully advanced, she had to urge him against suicide. Rabbi, she wrote to him:

> Hopelessness had been to me, all through my life, but especially in painful years of my youth, the chief source of wasted energy with all the consequent bitterness of regret. Remember, it has happened to many to be glad they did not commit suicide, though they once ran for the final leap, or as Mary Wolstonecraft [sic] did, wetted their garments well in the rain hoping to sink the better when they plunged...
>
> (GEL 5, pp. 160–1)

It was Deutsch, along with Lewes's own memory of Cohn reading Spinoza in Holborn in the 1830s, that formed the model for the ailing prophet Mordecai in *Daniel Deronda*. It was his writing that set George Eliot in pursuit of further reading almost as extensive as she had undertaken in the research for *Romola*. She sent Lewes off in search of obscure Jewish books, and read widely in Jewish history and literature, and the history of anti-Semitism.[5] But this time she had in Deutsch a personal guide in her research, and a guide who offered inspiration for the present and future purpose of all the history and all the knowledge. And in Mordecai equivalently within the novel she had (as she had not had in *Romola*) someone consciously to shape, complete, and unify all the disparate historical materials to purpose, just as at another level she herself had artfully to bring together her own past in the service of meaningful work. Yet still George Henry Lewes himself was doubtful if anyone would ever fully appreciate the Jewish part of the novel, in all its un-English risk and contentiousness.

Unsurprisingly perhaps, one of the readers and reviewers who most favoured George Eliot's Jewish idea in the novel was himself a Jew. Joseph Jacobs was born in Australia of English parents and moved to England, aged 18, to study at Cambridge, going on to become expert in two worlds, both English folklore and Hebrew literature. With George Eliot and Spinoza as his early heroes, Jacobs was another version of the outsider who had come back into a mainstream society. He was 23 when, in 1877, he wrote an enthusiastic review of *Daniel Deronda* in *Macmillan's Magazine*, as a result of which Lewes invited him to the Priory. He met George Eliot just once more, after Lewes's death, when 'she spoke of one of her favourite themes, the appeal of the circle in which one is born even if one has in certain ways grown beyond or outside it'.[6] It is this theme—to be in a circle and yet not wholly of it, to have grown beyond it but still to have the feel of it within you—which is another, not fully integrated, version of the two-in-one, of two things within one person.

It is of particular pertinence to a novel, *Daniel Deronda*, which critics have long assumed to be in two halves, English and Jewish, for all George Eliot's avowed effort to make 'everything in the book to be related to everything else there' (GEL 6, p. 290). For what is at question within the form, as indeed a form of enquiry, is the very nature of realism itself, in so far as increasingly here it contains within it actual needs and fears, again vague but definite, which are not satisfied by it. That theme is in turn related to the diaspora, to the role of Jewish idealism exiled within a land not its own, in the debate between the extremes of complete assimilation and total separatism. Ultimately, says the prophetic Mordecai, what is at stake is the monotheistic unity which is the Jewish legacy to the world: in that complex unity, 'a part possesses the whole as the whole possesses every part' (*Daniel Deronda*, chapter 61).

These two ideas—the need for a right way of abstract thinking, and the problem of an integrated two-in-one—are in complicated relation in George Eliot's austerely bold effort at creating a last innovation of incarnate ideas, for the future. They are

Fig. 17. Joseph Jacobs (1854–1916) (© National Portrait Gallery).

made present as Deronda himself internally confronts the problem and the challenge that Mordecai constitutes for the book as well as for him. I have said that George Eliot had developed an implicit theory of human workings: it is here that it is tried out, in practice, at its most austere and necessarily abstract, as the dying Mordecai fervently claims Deronda as his prophetic heir, to whom is to be handed on his message and his spirit. It was the figure of Mordecai that fascinated Jacobs.

Is this dying man, as seems most probable, no more than a crazy fanatic? What Deronda brings to the question is the thinking equipment that we have seen George Eliot employing layer by layer, dimension by dimension in all the previous work. Here it concerns a drawing of destiny by another German,[7] Moritz Retzsch (1779–1857), a sketch for his painting depicting Mephistopheles playing chess with Man for the prize of his soul. The devilish adversary draws his opponent's defensive pieces away from the disguised point of true attack, convincing him, until it is too late, that he is successfully beating back wave after wave of predictable aggression. It is like persuading us against our best safeguards, says George Eliot, when the cunning one repeatedly urges us always to take our waterproofs with us, knowing full well that the sky is clearing, until after repeated fine days we begin to think waterproofs unnecessary on any day, regardless of the actual weather signs: 'It is a peculiar test of a man's mettle when, after he has painfully adjusted himself to what seems a wise provision, he finds all his mental precaution a little beside the mark, and his excellent intentions no better than miscalculated dovetails, accurately cut from a wrong starting-point' (chapter 37). When finally it does rain, we have long since left behind our protection. Accurate, rational thinking, but from the wrong starting point, leaves the final course crucial degree-points wide of the projected target. Can the thinker readjust?

The greater test of mettle lies in the individual case of Mordecai, when, in a novel which begins with Gwendolen's desperate gambling, the safer bet lies in his being a deluded crank. But Deronda is bored by the so-called men of the world whose common sense is always to know what to think. Moved by Mordecai's offering him a mission in place of his rootlessness, he is resolved to rescue possibility where the greater probability is all too like dying in a culture of the shallowest realism. And yet at the same time he will not simply relinquish the demands of reason in the face of vision, or sacrifice to enthusiasm his loyalty to the rational tradition of human beings. In that tight double bind, the thinking works in a fervent abstraction, within which good and evil, genuine and fake, true neglected prophet and sincerely deluded dreamer are always dangerously close together:

> While Mordecai was waiting on the bridge for the fulfilment of his visions, another man was convinced that he had the mathematical key of the universe which would supersede Newton, and regarded all known physicists as conspiring to stifle his

discovery and keep the universe locked; another, that he had the metaphysical key, with just that hair's-breadth of difference from the old wards which would make it fit exactly. Scattered here and there in every direction you might find a terrible person, with more or less power of speech, and with an eye either glittering or preternaturally dull, on the look-out for the man who must hear him; and in most cases he had volumes which it was difficult to get printed, or if printed to get read.

(*Daniel Deronda*, chapter 41)

So many desperate cranks and madmen: 'Deronda's ear caught all these negative whisperings; nay, he repeated them distinctly to himself. It was not the first but it was the most pressing occasion on which he had had to face this question of the family likeness among the heirs of enthusiasm...' It is like looking at an identikit, in search of the real thing:

Reduce the grandest type of man hitherto known to an abstract statement of his qualities and efforts, and he appears in dangerous company: say that, like Copernicus and Galileo, he was immovably convinced in the face of hissing incredulity; but so is the contriver of perpetual motion. We cannot fairly try the spirits by this sort of test. If we want to avoid giving the dose of hemlock or the sentence of banishment in the wrong case, nothing will do but a capacity to understand the subject-matter on which the immovable man is convinced, and fellowship with human travail, both near and afar, to hinder us from scanning any deep experience lightly. Shall we say, 'Let the ages try the spirits, and see what they are worth?' Why, we are the beginning of the ages, which can only be just by virtue of just judgments in separate human breasts—separate yet combined. Even steam-engines could not have got made without that condition, but must have stayed in the mind of James Watt. (*Daniel Deronda*, chapter 41)

This is not the usual, gradual and increasingly complex build-up of a George Eliot character, but almost its opposite, the undoing of the normal work of the novel, the reduction to skeleton form that awaits the fleshing out of its actual life. This thinking takes place after the character who is its object exists; but it also takes place before he is known, in the very process of being imagined, in abstract, plausibly first one way and then another. Everything has then to come down to the individual chance, the particular instance, the specific judgement, not so much of the person, plausible or tormented, but of the separate value of his or her project.

In this experiment, George Eliot consciously adopts what W. H. Mallock was subsequently to consider to be two of her failings. One is that the explicit voice of George Eliot presents 'the raw material of artistic fiction', 'inviting us to see how the quality of her material has been manufactured, allowing us, perhaps a little unwisely, to examine its quality when in that condition'. Two is that, at the other end of her writerly process, there is equally an incompletion, a failure of realization of potential that stands as 'a chrysalis does to a butterfly, just before the change', leaving works 'quivering with a life that demands some further development'.[8] This is the very biography of the novel-writing.

Daniel Deronda says of its own content: What germ of life is here and how may it develop? It was the transmission of life of which reviewer Jacobs was in search. In relation to Mordecai specifically, the novel knows the possible alternatives: every crank thinks himself one of the great misunderstood; every one of the great misunderstood has been dismissed as a crank. What must follow must again be like 'that arduous invention which is the very eye of research' for Lydgate, 'provisionally framing its object and correcting it to more and more exactness of relation' (*Middlemarch*, chapter 16). For what it also involves, in the outside chance that Mordecai stakes his very life upon, is Whewell's sense that, in science as well as art, there must be the risk of an imagining in advance which will only be proved to have been inspired or delusive in retrospect. Most likely, at its unspeakable in-between time, it seemed to others impossible. This is how truly inventive thinking has to work in time. In contrast to that knowingness-in-advance which is really not thinking at all, imaginative inventiveness is a form of anticipation ahead of itself, in a visionary hypothesis whose very status in reality is yet undecided at the moment of its formation. That is the austere ontological excitement of this novel as it conceives itself in all its workings out, in all its attempted forecasts so riskily different from mere arrogance or complacency. From the moment that Gwendolen senses something in Deronda, from the point that Mordecai does the same, this novel risks believing in something very close to predestination, in George Eliot's last effort towards the future:

> The inspirations of the world have come in that way too: even strictly-measuring science could hardly have got on without that forecasting ardour which feels the agitations of discovery beforehand, and has a faith in its preconception that surmounts many failures of experiment. (*Daniel Deronda*, chapter 41)

'Faith' is the word, pre-conception, forecasting. When Mordecai finds the confirmation of his vision in Deronda, 'His exultation was not widely different from the experimenter, bending over the first stirrings of change that correspond to what in the fervour of concentrated prevision his thought had foreshadowed' (chapter 40). This is science transformed into science fiction even more than in *Middlemarch*. *Daniel Deronda* believes in the existence of things *before* they are known, and in their existence whether or not they are ever quite known. It even thinks that belief in their existence may itself create nascent possibilities. None of this is probable, it is always against the odds. But finally, after being duly weighed, the constant safety of caution seemed contemptible to Deronda when he felt, in contrast, the reality of lives that 'burn themselves out in solitary enthusiasm'. He is thinking of martyrs of obscure circumstance, exiled in the rarity of their own minds, whose deliverances in other ears are no more than a passionate soliloquy—unless perhaps at last, when they are nearing the invisible shores, signs of recognition and fulfilment may penetrate the cloud of loneliness; or perhaps it may be with them as with the dying Copernicus made to touch the first printed copy of his book when the sense of touch was gone, seeing it only as a dim object through the deepening dusk.

(Daniel Deronda, chapter 43)

Characteristically, once she had emotionally located an ontological reality in a person or situation, George Eliot would stay within the feel of it, producing thought after thought after thought, without ever fully exhausting its significance. But here she is spinning an imaginative possibility almost out of thin air, before the idea finds secure incarnation in a person, before the possibility has definite proof, publication, or embodiment. Yet Copernicus turned out to have changed the universe. Take just the phrase 'exiled in the rarity of their own minds': remarkably, it brings the great Jewish collective theme of long external exile back inside the mind of any thinker of any creed. That is the force of the Jewish idea beyond its Judaism; this is the way the novel can make one of its parts suddenly exist within another, apparently smaller one. Those with faith in their mental project endure by knowing 'it is a truth in thought though it may never have been carried out in action. It lives as an idea' (chapter 37). So much of the earlier fiction is haunted by the terrible thought of human waste—of the feeling in Gray's 'Elegy' that 'Full many a flower is born to blush unseen / And waste its sweetness on the desert air.' But here there is more possibility of a faith that there is no waste, that something of value exists even when there is no eye to see it, no crowd yet formed to recognize it. Yet still Mordecai must seek to pass his vision on.

In admiration of chapters 40 through to 43 of *Daniel Deronda* in particular, Joseph Jacobs quoted Hegel: 'The heritage a great man leaves the world is to force it to explain him', adding 'We may say the same of a great work of art.'[9] But *Daniel Deronda* was too easily dismissed by those who did not trouble to think of this work of art with anything like the same seriousness with which, inside it, Deronda had tried to think about Mordecai. And George Eliot had foreseen that rejection, and still had gone ahead with the dangerous material in despite of her own doubts and fears. 'I expected from first to last in writing it, that it would create...resistance, and even repulsion' (GEL 6, p. 301), as indeed it has to the present day.

Excited desperation required it. For Deronda, the fact is that, if nine times out of ten, the likelihood of experimenting with Mordecai was indeed delusion and failure, still the one-in-ten shot, or worse, could come right on *any* of those occasions in real time. And what is more, on a different scale, the rarer option is the more valuable, more worth the odds and risk to a desperate Deronda, than the safe and narrow norm, with its own certain dangers of a boringly predictable and reduced life. In a declining England, the extraordinary venture is with something contained in Judaism.

Deronda himself had previously assumed, with most of his contemporaries, that Judaism was 'a sort of eccentric fossilised form', an anomalous and irrational survival to be left only to the study of specialists (*Daniel Deronda*, chapter 32). As Deronda looks for Mirah's lost brother amidst the Jews of London, he fears the pawnbrokers, the pushy shopkeepers—the novel itself fearlessly exposing both the traces of anti-Semitism in otherwise decent English men and women, and the signs of a people's own degeneration into commercial materialism. For those who saw history as an engine of simple evolution, of two-dimensional linear progress, the Jews scattered amongst different countries were the mere remnant of an anachronistic faith superseded first by Christianity and then again by Enlightenment rationalism. The monotheistic God of Israel, Feuerbach had argued, was no more than the personified egoism of the Israelites, claiming to be specially chosen, exclusive of all other peoples. It was only out of a continuing stubbornness which itself provoked persecution that, even in exile, the Jews had adhered to their ancient law and their separate language, and to the transcendental otherness of their unknowable God.

That is why, in chapter 42, in the working men's debating club, Mordecai has intensely to take on the question of what is progress, and why nineteenth-century minds should ever have such faith in it. 'Woe to the men who see no place for resistance in this generation!' he cries. Resistance externally to an unthinking acceptance of the march of modernization and to the appeasement of fashionable mindsets; but resistance also internally to the decline and degeneration of older forces lodged within a traditional practice. This is the toughening of those who, as the poet Heine said, had fought and suffered on the battlefields of thought. To Mordecai, if in quasi-Darwinian terms the Jews are shamed into thinking of themselves as a modern relic, it is because they have forgotten the older biblical meaning of the term: remnant—a saving remnant of ancient first principles for the human race, a living memory unswervingly embodied in a few good, faithful, and just souls. Mordecai admits

'there may come a check, an arrest; memories may be stifled, and love may be faint for the lack of them; or memories may shrink into withered relics—the soul of a people, whereby they know themselves to be one, may seem to be dying for want of common action. But who shall say, "The fountain of their life is dried up, they shall for ever cease to be a nation?" Who shall say it? Not he who feels the life of his people stirring within his own. Shall he say, "That way events are wending. I will not resist"? His very soul is resistance, and is a seed of fire that may enkindle the souls of multitudes, and make a new pathway for events.' (*Daniel Deronda*, chapter 42)

The Jews are 'the heart of mankind,' says Mordecai quoting the poet Jehuda Halevi. The poet meant by 'heart' the core of affection, unabashed by its own emotional intensity in a cooler world, forming bonds of overflowing feeling in families and communities, making for mercy and tenderness to the poor and weak. That heart, wrote Halevi, was at once emotionally sensitive and physiologically vulnerable—it could be damaged by visitations of sadness, anxiety, or enmity, strengthened by love or purpose.[10] It could live healthily in the world, or it could be broken and damaged and wither there without a second life. In terms of all that may be meant by assimilation, for Mordecai it is one thing for Jews merely to 'melt gradually into the populations we live among', but it is quite another for Judaism to give its qualities back to the world, and continually recall them, to be shared amongst different lands and cultures in renewed transformation. The Jews are not left behind, are not at a standstill, as some of Mordecai's opponents—including secular Jews— argue in the chapter's great debate. On the contrary, Mordecai retorts, they have actively stayed and solidly resisted, as a displaced minority in defiant existence; they have retained and waited. 'When the hand was hacked off, they clung with the teeth'; they held on through the Book and through their writings when there was no other physical form or home.

Deronda has his own careful argument to make. In that properly rational concern of his for accurate distinctions, he notes that there are 'degrees' of wisdom in the decision either to hasten or to retard 'what is deemed inevitable progress'. And in the closeness of one thing and its opposite in human concerns, 'there will still remain the danger of mistaking a tendency which should be resisted for an inevitable law that we must adjust ourselves to'. But if we look back to the history of efforts to make really great changes, he continues, it is astonishing 'how many seemed hopeless' in their beginning. What is more, a sentiment 'may seem to be dying and yet revive into strong life'.

The Jews in their history had represented strong life. At the opening of chapter 42 the novelist quotes and translates from the nineteenth-century Jewish historian Leopold Zunz: 'If there are ranks in suffering, Israel takes precedence of all the nations...' Where, for George Eliot, Christianity in its latter days was effecting a debilitating divorce between humans and this world by its pious emphasis on otherworldliness, the strong root that was in Judaism was the insistence on the two-in-one: the religious in the practical, the practical in the religious, the faith enacted in moral conduct, in deeds and actions on earth. This was Deutsch's committed realism of *doing* truth, in the Hebraic sense that the 'true' was what could be *relied upon*—real, trusted, steadfast, performed in truth, sincerely—even in the face of trouble and change. The calling of the prophet was carried out over the head of contemporary society: not simply to foresee the future, as was often vulgarly supposed, but to remind a lost people of the old first principles, the ancient covenant. In the work of felt ethics over theoretic politics, prophecy was not only to recall but freshly to recreate the past as a living force, symbolically marking a return from exile and from wandering to make a new land again. In this way, for George

Eliot in *Daniel Deronda*, Judaism stood to the world as the individual to an over-standardized society. Citing John Stuart Mill near the end of her essay 'The Modern Hep! Hep! Hep!' in *Impressions of Theophrastus Such*:

> A modern book on Liberty has maintained that from the freedom of individual men to persist in idiosyncrasies the world may be enriched. Why should we not apply this argument to the idiosyncrasy of a nation?

It was crucial to the thinking prior to the production of *The Spanish Gypsy* that it was *not* the Jews who were to be the subject of a poem about a lost tribe and the call of unacknowledged inheritance. The gypsy race precisely lacked and needed to create the internally absorbed and transmitted tradition through which Judaism survived. The Jews, the Christians, the Moors 'were slaves lost, wandering, sunk beneath a curse / Till Moses, Christ, and Mahomet were born': Zarca, the gypsy chief, needs to create almost from nothing what Mordecai has to recreate from Abraham, Moses, and David: a memory for the future. ''Tis that compels the elements and wrings / A human music from the indifferent air. / The greatest gift the hero leaves his race / Is to have been a hero' (*The Spanish Gypsy*, book 1, 3149–52). It is the personal spirit of the heroic master, constantly to be revived by the prophet figures, that prevents the teaching implicit in his example becoming wholly transformed into the established institution it both needs and must resist.

Left in *The Spanish Gypsy* is the memory of the contrast with the tribe of Israel, when the Jewish astrologer Sephardo frankly tells his Spanish master that he will serve Spain only in so far as he also loyally maintains within him his separate identity. 'I am a Jew,' he insists and warns, not 'the pale abstract, Man' (book 2, 888–90). It is not Enlightenment man that is the ideal here, deploying the gift of human reason impartially, impersonally, and universally, across all nations as from above. It is something narrower that seeks embodiment in an initially local and personal form. That is the law of authentic rather than theoretic growth for George Eliot: 'A human life, I think, should be well rooted in some spot of a native land' *before* a human being can develop into a 'citizen of the world, stimulated by abstract nouns'. It was not simply a matter of selecting the rationally ideal good as an end; what was important was the order or sequence of things through which, in life as lived historically and organically, that end could most genuinely and thus stably emerge. Otherwise, excellent intentions were again no better than miscalculated dovetails in carpentry—'accurately cut from a wrong starting-point'. That is yet another risk that George Eliot took: to see the future developing not in some rationally straightforward linear progression but as a result of first turning back to a secure emotional starting point in family, nation, and race. To use the apparently un-ideal example of the gypsies or the Jews was precisely to defy English prejudice in the name of what otherwise could be too easily dismissed as racial prejudice itself.

But it is not advocacy made in the name of narrow Jewish separatism, it is not, as the modern *Philister* might say, George Eliot's defence of racialism, nationalism, or Western imperialism: Jew or gypsy in her writings, while never ceasing to be themselves, are also existent metaphors for what is more than themselves, living analogies for a human need, experienced particularly in Deronda himself as the search for a future. But 'a common humanity', as George Eliot summarized it in 'The Modern Hep! Hep! Hep!', 'is not yet enough to feed the rich blood of various activity which makes a complete man':

> The time is not come for cosmopolitanism to be highly virtuous, any more than for communism to suffice for social energy.

In writing and in thinking, in art as in science, she would always look for where the living energy was, the raw material for later translation.

But so much of Deronda's own energy was blocked and entangled in his pained consciousness of not knowing his own origins. He had not 'the full guidance of primary duties'. To 'angry self' he would characteristically say 'Never mind.' He scorns the escape route of 'a critic outside the activities of men' but, lacking an internal sense of strongly guiding feelings, he can make no more than 'an arbitrary selection where he felt no preponderance of desire'. The novelist feels for Deronda but, in another of this novel's self-testing loops, it is Deronda's own feeling for others that becomes a problem remarkable in a writer devoted to sympathy: 'Persons attracted him...in proportion to the possibility of his defending them, rescuing them.' 'Tolerance was the easiest attitude to him' and 'there was another bent in him also capable of becoming a weakness—the dislike to appear exceptional or to risk an ineffectual insistence on his own opinion' (chapters 33, 37, 28, 16, 43). Without being reactively dismissed, humanist values such as tolerance and sympathy, so greatly cherished at other times and in earlier novels, were demoted in the urgency of *Daniel Deronda* whenever they were in danger of being 'easiest'. It is unabashed ardour, in the face of social proprieties which repress the exceptional, that is demanded of Deronda, instead of 'weakness'—just as surely as dread is the terrible agent of the least easy path for Gwendolen. But the demanding severity here is not Nietzsche's; it is Mordecai's.

It was the value of Mordecai that Joseph Jacobs championed. Jacobs was very aware of Matthew Arnold's fundamental distinction in *Culture and Anarchy* (1869) between the two traditions of Hellenism and Hebraism as rival centres for the Western mind. He knew Arnold preferred the culture of the Greeks, many-sided and disinterested, calmly open to the free and fluent play of rational thought wherever it led, drawn by whatever was contained in beauty. Its sense was of a world of light prior to the downward pull of sin and unhappiness or transcendent of them. The Hebrew way was more to do with one idea, one God, with commitment to mental fixity and earthly practicality amidst the tense difficulties of human struggle. Hebraism committed itself to obedience of the law, to ethical conscience and conduct. What Jacobs wanted to add to this deliberately simplified model of rival influences was what he believed Hebraism had brought into the West from the East. To the Greeks, said Jacob, feeling was intensely personal and egoistic. In response, through the Western tradition of reason they established, it was higher intellect that viewed the universe impersonally through clear mental sight, overcoming feeling. But to the Jews it was the other way round. The God of the Jews was a God not of intellect but of emotion. The universe was charged with personal conceptions, the commandment of the Maker to the individual or to the race was felt directly, subjectively and within. But it was that personal call which then demanded impersonal acts, deeds on earth that were altruistic. The Jews' was not a world of distanced sight, of clear separate and objectified entities spread out for contemplation. It was a world of physical involvement, a series of interrelated motions flowing through individuals, forces passing through them in shocks and waves and vibrations, till at certain critical moments those individuals became the focal point and human representative for the working out of those processes in the actions of the world. Then there were new or reclaimed gifts in the world whose name and whose purpose were only revealed in what their bearers could do as a result of them.

So it is with Mordecai in his unrestrained yearning to embody those unrecognized powers within himself and pass them on. 'Even if his ideas had been as true and precious as those of Columbus or Newton', it was to conventional English minds 'an insane exaggeration' in Mordecai 'to proclaim what seemed to be his own importance'. The 'sublimer part' in a politely liberal, ostensibly selfless Christianized world was not actively to cry out 'I...' but rather more humbly to say, as Deronda might say, 'if not I, then another':

> But the fuller nature desires to be an agent, to create, and not merely look on: strong love hungers to bless, and not merely to behold blessing. And while there is warmth enough in the sun to feed an energetic life, there will still be men to feel, 'I am lord of this moment's change, and will charge it with my soul' (*Daniel Deronda*, chapter 38)

Deronda has had his own share of being 'anybody', of shamed anonymity and self-disparaging passivity. As the rescued Mirah herself puts it, when Deronda says anybody would have done as he had done: 'That is not the right way of thinking about it. I think of what really was. It was you and not another' (chapter 32). The demand here is not as it is seen to be from the conventional world, as though 'I am the lord...my soul' were no more than ego: rather, it comes from the realization of a different world-view which it also helps create. In it, the I is the interconnecting point in a matrix from which some new event and act is coming into being in the public arena: 'Visions are the creators and feeders of the world' (chapter 40). That charging of the moment is the human action fed by an enlarged vision of individual possibility, and when it occurs, it means that the great psychologist who is George Eliot almost gives up on the need for psychology. Deronda felt it first when he knows that somehow 'reverence' must be shown to the girl he has rescued, and that he must not press Mirah to sing for him or tell him anything:

> Why? He gave himself several good reasons; but whatever one does with a strong unhesitating outflow of will, has a store of motive that it would be hard to put into words.

Strong, unhesitating, yet never *too* hard for George Eliot to put into words, except that here:

> Some deeds seem little more than interjections which give vent to the long passion of a life.   (*Daniel Deronda*, chapter 20)

It is a deed, she insists—not just a thought or a non-action, but the definite expression of the purposiveness of a massed life behind it. That life is no longer simply that of a person, a bundle of psychological complexities, but that of an agent charged with a function the world otherwise lacks. Those 'interjections' are, then, eruptions expressive of a world-view of personal action that George Eliot most wanted. They offer a sense of purpose and unity in place of the dualism and the splitting which she feared and hated. 'Action, choice, resolved memory,' says Mordecai, are opposed to the blasphemy of being a mere passive onlooker (chapter 42). They come out of the fuller nature needing to discharge its force, that dense fullness that Ruskin praised when an artist no longer merely repeated himself; the way that *Middlemarch* was, to William James, fuller of human stuff than any novel that was ever written. That fullness of urgent and assertive life bursts the confines of everything but the novel itself.

Compared to that imagination of possibility, and the belief in making that possibility come into being even through oneself, doubt is the easier option. 'Your doubts,' says Mordecai to Deronda, 'lie as light as dust on my belief':

> 'Say my expectation of you has grown but as false hopes grow. That doubt is in your mind? Well, my expectation was there, and you are come.... What are doubts to me? In the hour when you come to me and say "I reject your soul: I know that I am not a Jew: we have no lot in common"—I shall not doubt. I shall be certain—certain that I have been deluded. That hour will never come.'   (*Daniel Deronda*, chapter 40)

For Mordecai and the state of being he represents, doubt is not reality, compromise is not reality, they are halfway houses of safe mental refuge from the risks of involvement. Reality is either the full realization of the truth he foresees or the total defeat he will suffer as a consequence of its not coming true. Your deepest feelings are always *more* than you are, thinks Mordecai, and that 'more' comes from somewhere, wants to go somewhere else, is a message seeking an act. Where did I get this from? is Deronda's question when he has strange feelings of recognition in the shabby Frankfurt synagogue he enters by chance on the Day of Atonement. It was a synagogue the Leweses had visited for the purposes of the novel in July 1873. Here Deronda listens to the austere music of the prayers and cries, as of the human species bringing itself and all its feelings together—'both the yearning and the exaltation gathering their utmost force from the sense of communion in a form which has expressed them both, for long generations of struggling fellow-men':

> He wondered at the strength of his own feeling; it seemed beyond the occasion—what one might imagine to be a divine influx in the darkness, before there was any vision to interpret. The whole scene was a coherent strain, its burden a passionate regret, which, if he had known the liturgy for the Day of Reconciliation, he might have clad in its authentic burden: 'Happy the eye which saw all these things; but verily to hear only of them afflicts our soul. Happy the eye that saw our temple and the joy of our congregation; but verily to hear only of them afflicts our soul. Happy the eye that saw the fingers when tuning every kind of song; but verily to hear only of them afflicts our soul.' (*Daniel Deronda*, chapter 32)

He too is like a man in exile who can hear and feel the great emotional resonance, 'a remote, obscure echo', but not see what it means in its foreign tongue or find a place for its translation into his own existence. Blindly he tries to locate what type of world or creed or people those feelings in him stand for, the human tradition for whatever it is. As he begins to work it out, Deronda must carry forward that tradition felt and living and modified in him, to create a future for what otherwise would become no more than a lost or inert past.

That is the ethos of development that Mordecai seeks to pass on to Deronda, to be his transmitted second life. In Christian Ginsburg's commentary on Kabbalah, which George Eliot read, it is said that the failed soul finds in whoever may take over its purposes its mother. But in Mordecai it is the other way round, and there is something like a maternal transference of self to Deronda, like Adam Bede looking at Hetty in the dock, like Silas Marner with his child. There was in his 'yearning consumptive glance something of the slowly dying mother's look when her one loved son visits her bedside... "My boy"' (*Daniel Deronda*, chapter 40). Life is no longer a fixed given: its mundane terms themselves become metaphors, taking familiar emotions into unfamiliar places in a novel where Deronda seems motherless; where Gwendolen herself, like Marian Evans and despite all Mrs Davidow's comfortings, lacks the strong mother that Mrs Tulliver suddenly becomes in

Maggie's crisis; where Mirah and Ezra are brought together in memory of a maternal voice. What could these lost or wonted things become in a new ordering? The surroundings were in modest parts of London or Frankfurt, but what Deronda hears is a voice that 'might have come from a Rabbi transmitting the sentences of an elder time' to make what is called 'marriages': 'for by marriages the speaker means all the wondrous combinations of the universe whose issue makes our good and evil' (*Daniel Deronda*, chapter 62). Whether it is maternity or marriage, in this work there is no simple turning back: ancient memory is to be carried forward in new forms, missing out the period of over-familiarization of meaning in between. When Deronda finally meets his own mother, now mortally ill—the great singer who, in another version of 'Armgart', sacrificed her family and her faith for her talent—he finds her still rejecting him and, even in her sickness, his vulnerable offer of last help and affection: 'Deronda turned pale with what seems always more of a sensation than an emotion—the pain of repulsed tenderness' (chapter 51).

In this hard and unflinching novel, that sensitive-skinned pain is felt at the prospect of repelling as well as being repelled. Just as he has uncomfortable thoughts about fanatical madmen or about vulgar Jews, Deronda also has a terrible compassionate fear both of bitterly disappointing *and* of falsely feeding the dying Mordecai's final belief. He knows in himself, in relation to Mordecai's claim, 'the repulsion that most of us experience under the grasp and speech which assume to dominate' (chapter 40); he knows of his own need 'to preserve himself from the bondage of false concessions' (chapter 41). He knows the danger of over-commitment with Mordecai just as he knows the hazardous mix of attraction and pity in his relation to Gwendolen, 'as if he were putting his name to a blank paper which might be filled up terribly' (chapter 56). But he also knows what George Eliot speaks of: 'Columbus had some impressions about himself which we call superstitious, and used some arguments which we disapprove; but he also had some true physical conceptions, and he had the passionate patience of genius to make them tell on mankind' (chapter 41). However partially flawed and distorted and illusory in its conception, there may still be something important within the relationship itself: 'Great heaven! What relation has proved itself more potent in the world than faith even when mistaken—than expectation even when perpetually disappointed?' (chapter 40). That is not an argument for deliberately making mistakes. But Mordecai, like Columbus, may be one of those natures who can use what is both ill- and well founded in the human makeshift of themselves, such that 'a wise estimate of consequences is fused in the fires of that passionate belief which determines the consequences it believes in' (chapter 41).

If the novel cannot make Mordecai convincing, as their own novels could not fully realize Felix Holt or Romola, nonetheless great facts struggle for articulation through those experiments in life, and, in returning to those imperfect efforts, *Daniel Deronda* goes further than its predecessor novels in transforming partial failures into flawed templates. It establishes the groundwork for envisioning that *someone*, of whom Mordecai is but one version, could still, in a different cause and in another time, make beliefs become realities. For what is at stake here, in the makeshift of a beginning, is not so much Mordecai, as the open struggle of Deronda's attitude towards him. It is not from early Wordsworth in his commitment to simple, fundamental human feeling but from the visionary Wordsworth of *The Prelude* and *The Excursion* that the epigraph to chapter 40 is taken. 'In the soul a faculty abides' even amidst the cloudy 'interpositions' that seem to hide and darken it. That soul, which Daniel seeks, is for Wordsworth like the moon which

> In the deep stillness of a summer even,
> Rising behind a thick and lofty grove,
> Burns, like an unconsuming fire of light,
> In the green trees; and kindling on all sides
> Their leafy umbrage, turns the dusky veil
> Into a substance glorious as her own,
> Yea, with her own incorporated . . .

It is distinguished only in what it helps reveal, the two-in-one. As Mordecai stands on the bridge over the river at Blackfriars in the dying light of one fading evening, he sees Deronda rowing towards him out of a golden background. They glimpse something in each other in that setting, to do with what is called souls recognized in recognizing. So much in George Eliot cannot be like this visionary Wordsworth, where Wordsworth has the non-human world as a primal place for the solitary mind to work upon—as though he were the first human being again at the first dawn or the first eve on the planet, and thoughts had natural objects for themselves. But in George Eliot's crowded human medium, like some fallen second life with its mass of set routines and competing interests, individual inner efforts are all too often pushed back and stifled by the surrounding force of external pressures and solidly unmoved objects. Or individuals find themselves mufflingly absorbed and lost in objects—situations, people, habits, projects—unworthy or demeaning of them. In the face of that restrictive external world, for example, Dorothea can rarely muster an 'active force of antagonism' save in defence of others whom she sees wronged; for the most part in her own difficulties, in claustrophobic marriage, she no sooner felt the power of any sort of freedom than she felt it subside by 'a quickly subduing pang' (*Middlemarch*, chapter 77). In *Daniel Deronda*, George Eliot at least finds some asocial, pre-social, or outsider spaces from which to try to re-begin the world.

Looking around his dingy debating club of obscure working men, Mordecai thinks of the great tradition of attempted transmission of thought wrought even within common life: 'I have pleased myself with a faint likeness between these poor philosophers and the Masters who handed down the thought of our race—the great Transmitters, who laboured with their hands for scant bread, but preserved and enlarged for us the heritage of memory' (chapter 42). That is what George Eliot had sought to be, especially now near the last.

Henry James quoted Klesmer's angry denunciation of the 'puerile state of culture' that passes for contemporary civilization:—'no sense of the universal'. He said of such great scale-changing phrases that, in their conscious risk of idealism, they give readers of this novel

> the feeling that the threads of the narrative, as we gather them into our hands, are not of the usual commercial measurement, but long electric wires capable of transmitting messages from mysterious regions. (*Critical Heritage*, p. 363)

But what is it that George Eliot finally does transmit?

Finding Pathways

Gwendolen had been aware of Deronda from the moment she had felt him looking at her while she was recklessly gambling—a man regarding her not with customary admiration but in judgement and with irony: 'measuring her and looking down on her' (*Daniel Deronda*, chapter 1). She does not want to feel that extra knowing consciousness—not just his inferred consciousness of her, but her own necessarily involved consciousness of it—because she does not see how to live easily with it. Consciousness of this kind feels to her like being caught—caught gambling, caught pawning her necklace, caught marrying a man whom she knows to have a hidden sexual past. It is the suppressed third element that acts as a paradoxical hidden connective within the dualism that apparently separates within and without. In one respect Gwendolen does not want to believe in or acknowledge that split: she simply wants her inner view to command the outer world. In another way, she fears the loss of inner control, if, say, those young men with whom she flirts want to go further. Then it is as though her inner life is being caught up in the outside world, and that what she has started without wish to continue is being tested out in front of her eyes, as though it had become her self outside her, unless she can still pull back. The ultimate vision of this is when she sees Grandcourt drowning before her eyes as though she had killed him in her thoughts: 'I only know,' she says in horror at herself, that 'I saw my wish outside me' (chapter 56). Inside and outside is a false distinction. For all her efforts at control and separation, the very boundaries of being are disturbingly unsteady and shifting.

But why should great terms of philosophy be applied to the mere psychology 'of a girl, busy with her small inferences of the way in which she could make her life pleasant'? (chapter 11). The criticism made by the more sophisticated Henry James was that, in George Eliot's novels, there was an obtrusive awkwardness of over-stressed meaningfulness that threatened the art itself: 'We feel in her, always, that she proceeds from the abstract to the concrete' (*Critical Heritage*, p. 498). But in *Daniel Deronda*, I have argued there is a deliberate attempt in the portrayal of the relation of Deronda and Mordecai to test out the development of abstract into concrete—of idea to realization, of possibility and plausibility to what may or may not be the case, of the need for general idealism to find relation to specific identity in practical purpose and vocation. But equally, the book turns itself the other way too, from Mordecai back to Gwendolen, to see within the predicament of a specific concrete creature the increasing demand of unthought thoughts and unacknowledged structures—the confused idea of what needs to have an austere abstract language in order to purge its confusion. In this mirroring, Deronda seeks to be to Gwendolen something of what, in the novel's other world, Mordecai simultaneously is to him: a guide and a transmitter.

And increasingly Gwendolen complains that, even in this way, Deronda makes things feel only worse for her. This is also in her an implicitly sexual plea to make life better by loving her. It would be a refuge at the personal level from what otherwise she feels he makes her think, beyond that. What is the good, she cries, of his urging her to an intense commitment to music if it only gives her a greater sense of her own particular musical inadequacies? What is the point of knowing more if knowing only makes what was previously a vaguely unsatisfying life clarified as even less happy? When she says that the world is dull, he replies in a way again devastatingly characteristic of the critical nature of this book, 'I think what we call the dullness of things is a disease in ourselves' (chapter 35).

It is not that she simply, childishly, rejects his idealistic seriousness. She recognizes something she lacks and needs, and painfully feels it, yet then comes the devastating sentence that nearly breaks the heart of the book: 'But one may feel things and not be able to do anything better for all that' (chapter 45). This perhaps would be the worst for George Eliot—outside the book as well as in it:—not that people wouldn't care for the idealism of *Daniel Deronda* but that even in caring, they, like Gwendolen, would not know what to do with it in their own lives, leaving them consciously even shorter of purpose. Since F. R. Leavis, critics have long complained that, for all its linkages and mirrorings, *Daniel Deronda* falls into two separate halves—English and Jewish, Gwendolen and Mordecai, realist and visionary—which the translating intermediary figure of Deronda is inadequate to bring together in one. Yet that is the very point of this resolutely inconclusive novel: it is precisely the pain of their separation, felt differently still in each world, that austerely links them. The felt lack in one realm creates the need for another, even as, at another level, the two halves of the book struggle to find a way to each other. So with Deronda:

He had lately been living so keenly in an experience quite apart from Gwendolen's lot, that his present cares for her were like a revisiting of scenes familiar in the past, and there was not yet a complete revival of the inward response to them.

(*Daniel Deronda*, chapter 56)

The novel shirks nothing in such transitions, in its felt deficiencies as well as demanding intensities. It has not the beautiful symmetry of Goethe's gingko leaf, but it *uses* its own difficulties and failures in a way *Felix Holt* and *Romola* could not.

'One may feel things and not be able to do anything better for all that': 'for all that' marks an invisible fault-line across which, at one level, the demanding conscious-ness that there must be 'more' seems only to make for the feeling of their being even 'less', personally and practically, at another. At such moments there is released into the world a terrible sense of helpless human despair, an immediate pessimism and depression, that is felt not just within either Gwendolen or Deronda separately. It is what is called a third presence that arises like a silent echo between them immedi-ately after they cease speaking:

> For the moment she felt like a shaken child—shaken out of its wailings into awe, and she said humbly—
>   'I will try. I will think.'
>   They both stood silent for a minute, as if some third presence had arrested them,— for Deronda, too, was under that sense of pressure which is apt to come when our own winged words seem to be hovering around us,—till Gwendolen began again— ...
>
> (*Daniel Deronda*, chapter 36)

It is more than idea or mood or atmosphere, bigger than the people involved in it can control or manufacture, a breakthrough amidst the normal reality of the world where, in struggling response, 'try' and 'think' are synonyms and mark the shift from the puerile and childish to the adult and serious. It is, in its, hovering a form of consciousness felt outside the mind, in which the words just spoken seem to have an afterlife, or bear a contagious threat, or suffer a felt fading hollowness of their own that hangs in the air—like the presence or the absence of George Eliot herself in the world. That, I want to conclude, is part of the difference this writer makes and stands for—in seeking to be a third presence.

Here in this novel, at moments in crisis talk, the characters can feel that strange serious presence in the room—coming or going, lifting or depressing spirits—for themselves. So it is when Gwendolen speaks to Deronda of her life with Grandcourt, of her fear of what she might do to be rid of the marriage—'If feelings arose—there are some feelings—hatred and anger...':

> She broke off, and with agitated lips looked at Deronda, but the expression on his face pierced her with an entirely new feeling. He was under the baffling difficulty of

discerning, that what he had been urging on her was thrown into the pallid distance of mere thought before the outburst of her habitual emotion. It was as if he saw her drowning while his limbs were bound.   (*Daniel Deronda*, chapter 36)

This again in its aftermath is itself not just a 'mere thought'. It reveals a sense of reality, a conscious space and vision of meaning, beyond the end of human speech. Or it is there again later in the novel, between Mordecai and Deronda when the visionary's spirit meets renewed consciousness of 'the fixed indifference of men familiar with the object of his enthusiasm'—men wholly unaffected by it as though it had no place in the world (chapter 42). Then, thinking of the failures of communication:

Mordecai let his hands fall, and his head sink in melancholy: for the moment he had lost hold of his hope. Despondency, conjured up by his own words, had floated in and hovered above him with eclipsing wings. He had sunk into momentary darkness.

(*Daniel Deronda*, chapter 40)

Deronda tries to lift this feeling of abandonment by speaking the language of sympathy: 'I feel with you.' 'That is not enough,' replies Mordecai: he wants not just Deronda's hand but his soul.

So it is when Gwendolen sees the visible effect of herself on the face of Deronda, suddenly struck by the hopeless vision of her as though she were drowning and he helpless to save her. It is more than her usual vain appreciation of being looked at, of being lovely; it is more even than a sudden recognition of the pained impression she makes on him. It is, rather, a simultaneous and almost vertiginous consciousness of her being at once a subject to oneself, and an object effecting others, *and* a further or higher consciousness, like a reincorporated third presence, that contains the independent realization of both positions and of both herself and Deronda within a common world:

The pained compassion which was spread over his features as he watched her, affected her with a compunction unlike any she had felt before, and in a changed imploring tone she said—

'I am grieving you. I am ungrateful. You *can* help me. I will think of everything. I will try. Tell me—it will not be a pain to you that I have dared to speak of my trouble to you? You began it, you know, when you rebuked me.' There was a melancholy smile on her lips as she said that, but she added more entreatingly, 'It will not be a pain to you?'

'Not if it does anything to save you from an evil to come,' said Deronda, with strong emphasis, 'otherwise it will be a lasting pain.'

'No—no—it shall not be. It may be—it shall be better with me because I have known you.' She turned immediately, and quitted the room.   (*Daniel Deronda*, chapter 36)

It only normalizes it to say that she feels sorry for him in turn, sorry for his being so sorry for her, across the physical divide of their lives. She had been capable of something of this large-mindedness before this. With Klesmer earlier she had unthinkingly put aside the egoistic wounds made by his criticisms as soon as she felt the power of his playing: she had 'fullness of nature' enough to turn 'her inward sob of mortification into an excitement which lifted her for the moment into a desperate indifference about her own doings' (chapter 5). Again when Klesmer offers an even harder judgement, Gwendolen's better self, conscious of ingratitude, 'made a desperate effort to find its way above the stifling layers of egoistic disappointment and irritation' (chapter 23). But with Klesmer that compunction had happened on delayed second thought, and this with Deronda is now much more nearly a simultaneous effect, as though the simultaneity in time matched the inseparability in existence. This extended consciousness of hers, resultant from the recursive effect *on* her feeling of her feeling's effect on him, is what George Eliot's Feuerbach would call the God in her. Though a movingly frail achievement, it comes out of those hidden workings and structures within and beneath consciousness that undermine crude dualism. And for those underlying mental processes to come more fully into consciousness, it requires and makes more of the human being in whom they take place. Those humans are still less than full natures when they do not know that *they* are doing such things from within themselves, and not simply the Deronda figure who stands outside in attempted help. Which is why George Eliot has finally to take Deronda away from Gwendolen, close as that feels to deserting her:

> Would her remorse have maintained its power within her, or would she have felt absolved by secrecy, if it had not been for that outer conscience which was made for her by Deronda? It is hard to say how much we could forgive ourselves if we were secure from judgment by another whose opinion is the breathing-medium of all our joy—who brings to us with close pressure and immediate sequence that judgment of the Invisible and Universal which self-flattery and the world's tolerance would easily melt and disperse. In this way our brother may be in the stead of God to us, and his opinion which has pierced even to the joints and marrow, may be our virtue in the making.   (*Daniel Deronda*, chapter 64)

But George Eliot again takes away an external God. And in austere requirement she takes away also the temptation of the sexual escape route for Gwendolen, as Deronda makes another world with Mordecai and with marriage to Mirah: 'Much of our lives is spent in marring our own influence and turning others' belief in us into a widely concluding unbelief which they call knowledge of the world, while it is really disappointment in you or me' (chapter 64). It is not disillusionment that Deronda causes Gwendolen. The extra consciousness in this book refuses that simple equation of disappointment with unbelief, even when its thinker is left, like Gwendolen, bitterly hurt or horribly alone. It is not simply Deronda's fault that he cannot be with Gwendolen, and she has to think and know that, ahead of any possible resolution or even instead of any: 'I will try... It shall be better...'

Even though it is full of pre-visions—of what, before they ever really know each other, Mordecai and Gwendolen sense in Deronda and he in them—there are no guarantees or solutions in advance in this book. Gwendolen had said despairingly to Deronda, 'I must get up in the morning and do what everyone does. It is all like a dance set beforehand.... You say I am ignorant. But what is the good of trying to know more unless life were worth more?' (chapter 36). Yet the law of this novel is: that 'trying to know' must exist ahead of any secure recognition of the outcome or value of that effort. Otherwise, indeed, it is 'all like a dance set beforehand'. Often it feels as George Eliot says, when she half-comically describes 'the famous recipe for making cannon': 'to first take a round hole and then enclose it with iron, whatever you do keeping fast hold of your round hole' (chapter 32). Extra inner consciousness is like the hole, easily dismissed as nothing in itself yet keeping the more solid and visible form of things together from inside, filled with the incomplete sense of potential belief or vocation and, equally, with the sense of there always being something more to think or to consider.

The great idealist philosophers of George Eliot's century thought that *the* difficulty of difficulties was the union in one individual of the personal self and a wider-than-personal consciousness. As soon as the self sees the distinction between itself and others, between itself and the world outside, a consciousness is released by that perception, a second consciousness which can no longer be solely self-centred. That is the extra consciousness, so much the subject of this mental biography, that frightened Gwendolen: she tried not to think of it or with it, as if it was not to do with her. It felt like a cause of insecurity, a fear not a capability. But it is what Deronda called a 'faculty', 'like vision' or 'like quickness of hearing', which made consequences present before they happened (chapter 36). And yet increasingly that consciousness seemed trapped within Gwendolen's ego, within her stifled married life, until desperately the 'help of conscience' from which previously she had struggled away becomes what 'she prayed and cried for' (chapter 69).

Like so much in this novel, the so-called higher values, so hard to sustain, must be tested from below and in situ. When Grandcourt tells her that Deronda must be taking sexual advantage of Mirah as her rescuer and protector, Gwendolen has to go to Mirah to try to find out the truth. There are obvious personal motivations for this, in terms of trusting Deronda or even knowing his potential availability, and there came too 'the sudden perception, how very slight were the grounds of her faith in Deronda—how little she knew of his life—how childish she had been in her confidence' (chapter 48). But hers is also the need to know that Grandcourt's narrowly imprisoning, disillusioning view of the world is not truly *the* world. 'How little she knew...how childish she had been': this is the protracted story of how long it takes human beings to grow up, well beyond the time of physical adulthood. And within it, such a visit of Gwendolen to Mirah or of Dorothea to

Rosamond is philosophy in action—implicit philosophy in its original human needs, struggling within the living impulses of human being. In such ways begins the problem of 'how to combine the perspective of a particular person inside the world with an objective view of the same world, the person and his viewpoint included'.[11] The subjective without any uneasy apprehension of the objective beyond it, the objective without any inclusion of the subjective in its view: these perspectives are not long sustainable. Hence Kant's famous formulation in his *Critique of Pure Reason*: thoughts without content are empty, intuitions without concepts are blind. In *Daniel Deronda*, nonetheless, the struggle is at times to hold onto the near empty, at others to abide with the almost blind.

So it is with Mordecai and with Deronda, but also as translated into Gwendolen, in her own more mundane fashion. 'Men can see what is his relation to her,' says Grandcourt cynically of Deronda and Mirah; 'Men who judge of others by themselves,' Gwendolen replies. Yet on her defiantly informing him of Mirah's own subsequent denial, his sneering response is still, 'She told you so—did she?' Gwendolen continues to resist his perspective but so far from that being 'her faith come back again', it is rather, says George Eliot, 'the desperate cry of her faith' (chapter 48). She is like a woman crying 'I want to believe' but tacitly fearing the want is driving the attempted believing; or 'I do believe in Deronda' but not knowing what that means beyond something precariously personal. Yet 'his opinion...may be our virtue in the making'.

George Eliot never believed that idealism, either philosophical or informal, came down simply from above, a priori. Its seeming transcendence was paradoxically generated from below upwards, in both need and difficulty, in the hidden structural possibilities of the human mind and the workings of the human situation—it was all 'in the making'. We have seen earlier in this chapter that extraordinary higher consciousness in one of the greatest moments in George Eliot—when almost involuntarily Gwendolen sees Deronda feeling for her with a distress that makes her feel for him at almost the same time: 'For the moment she felt like a shaken child—shaken out of her wailings into awe..."I am grieving you. I am ungrateful."' That shock of a greater reality allowed, required, and enabled that higher perception which made George Eliot most proud of human beings—because it was a capability, almost regardless of whether what they saw by it was good or bad, painful or encouraging. Whatever it registered, it had become a form, a capacity, which might not always be at the mercy of its own content. And this evolved human increase had a place within the expanded dimensions of time and space that *Daniel Deronda* also creates, from the heights of astronomy to the further reaches of geography, and to visions of a greatly different future.

A higher, wider, extra consciousness may have needed a literary language to give it maximum reality when it could not fully express itself in action, but George Eliot could still explicate it in ordinary educated conversation. The psychologist James Sully reported: 'She could not understand, she said, how any one who had the ability and the opportunity to better the lot of others could sink into pessimism.'[12] The very capacity to see misery, with pain, contained within it the thought of trying to do something in amelioration of it. That is why, even in the midst of a lowering trouble, it could not be long before all the 'active thought', all the 'vivid sympathetic experience' of a Dorothea 'returned to her as a power'—asserting itself 'as acquired knowledge asserts itself and will not let us see as we saw in the day of our ignorance' (*Middlemarch*, chapter 80). Will *not let* us is vital to the work of thought becoming responsibility. George Eliot on pessimists was like the idealist Kant on the Stoics. The transcendent courage involved in their not fearing death, of their knowing there was something more than submission to intolerable life, said Kant, ought to have been a motive to the Stoics not for passive indifference or for disdainful suicide but for the strength of mind that will not let us give up on a return to living.[13] It was what George Eliot had urged upon poor Deutsch. As she put it to Harriet Beecher Stowe, a sense of responsibility to life and to others sprang 'from sympathy with that which of all things is most certainly known to us, the difficulty of the human lot' (GEL 5, p. 31). This again was George Eliot the mediator and translator in the middle of things, syntactically using one human quality called 'sympathy' to combine with, counter, and mitigate another called 'difficulty'. This raised and re-formed consciousness is what sited George Eliot, as James Sully noted, 'midway between the optimist and the pessimist, to which she gave the name of Meliorism' (*My Life and Friends*, p. 264). Midway is the realist novelist's position, not letting life give way on either side.[14]

George Eliot herself, in the novels, stood in proxy for that form of almost transcendent and yet still vulnerable consciousness. She did so whenever her characters could not sustain it in their lives or persons but felt it collapsing into the pain that so often it had to register. That is why this final novel ends without knowing how Gwendolen will manage that extra consciousness within her changed life, because there is no certain knowing of how human beings can. It is the persistent transmission of it that counts and continues, seeking forms and purposes for itself.

R. H. Hutton believed that *Daniel Deronda* was more unequal than *Middlemarch* but in parts greater than it: 'Its average level of power is very much lower' but 'its summits are higher.' 'It rises at certain points definitely above that great book,' he concluded, having once called *Middlemarch* 'one of the great books of the world' (*Critical Heritage*, pp. 376, 302). But sometimes the part—flawed, unfinished—is where the most hinted significance is, in containing a future potential whole. And that is why the reader exists to take away those transmitted parts, the corollary of which may be the sheer capacity of individuals to think more thoroughly within the world by that means:

Man finds his pathways: at first they were foot-tracks, as those of the beast in the wilderness; now they are swift and invisible: his thought dives through the ocean, and his wishes thread the air: has he found all the pathways yet? What reaches him, stays with him, rules him: he must accept it, not knowing its pathway.

(*Daniel Deronda*, chapter 40)

That is the role of the receptive reader of George Eliot, from beginning to end, to pick up what seem to be prints or traces and try to make them into further tracks of life.

The End

George Henry Lewes died on 30 November 1878. On 31 December 1877, to mark the close of the year, Marian Lewes had already written a final note in her journal—'the only record I have made of my personal life for sixteen years and more'—resolving to write no more in it, perhaps hardly to write any more at all. Looking back on the diary markings of her past struggles had encouraged her in her present ones. But now, even though she still had thoughts opening up vistas of possible projects, the future was physically running out: 'Many conceptions of work to be carried out present themselves, but confidence in my own fitness to complete them worthily is all the more wanting because it is reasonable to argue that I must have already done my best' (GEL 6, p. 440). The confidence was never great, but the death of Lewes was virtually the end, leaving her desolate and alone again. The servants heard terrible screams of pain and despair, and for weeks she would see no one, shrinking from even the most tenderly attempted touch. She barely weighed 100 pounds. She had only Tennyson's *In Memoriam* to read, copying out stanza after stanza in the void:

> Tears of a widower, when he sees
>   A late-lost form that sleep reveals,
>   And moves his doubtful arms, and feels
> Her place is empty, fall like these...

But there were Lewes's final volumes to edit, and gradually she admitted support from Charles Lewes and from John Cross. Cross had been like a nephew. He lost his own mother ten days after Lewes's death. Together they read and studied Dante's *Divine Comedy* in the original.

She wrote to him, 'the sun it shines so cold, so cold, when there are no eyes to look love on me' (GEL 7, p. 211). In May 1880 she married him. Cross was 40, twenty years the junior of the woman he had called Aunt. Some friends were shocked, but Charles Lewes said it was what his father would have wanted, someone to look after her, and with typical defiance Barbara Bodichon insisted that she would have married her herself, had she been a man. To add to the mix, after such long and cold silence, brother Isaac wrote his note of congratulations on what was at least her first formally respectable relationship.

But on the honeymoon in Venice, Cross seemed to go mad, perhaps with the heat and the bad air, and some intestinal infection—throwing himself from their balcony into the Grand Canal, to be rescued by the gondoliers. There have always been some who thought the cause was sexual, his horror at her need for consummation.[1] If so, it was the Valley of Humiliation again, the second life gone in the return of those old miseries, ugly needs, and lonelinesses of which, for so long, her writing had been able to make something better.

She died, in part through kidney disease, on 22 December, just seven months after her marriage. At her funeral, Edith Simcox said a child had asked her if it was George Eliot's wife who was going to be buried, and she had vaguely replied yes (GEL 9, p. 23). The writer of *Silas Marner*, and before that of the funeral scene with the bereft children in 'Amos Barton', might have appreciated it.

Such was the death. I have tried to bring out in this book what George Eliot would call 'epochs' in the life, most particularly in the second life constituted by the work. In the individual character of each novel, moments stand out as though they made a breakthrough into a greater percentage of reality than human beings can normally bear. What finds you stays with you, says Mordecai, in varying returns: Adam in prosperity still thinking of Hetty's existence in exile; Maggie deciding not to run off with Stephen, halfway through doing so; Romola on the execution of her godfather; Dorothea with Casaubon when he learns that his condition is fatal, or with Rosamond so close to murdering her own marriage; Gwendolen finding herself about to do what, in marrying Grandcourt, she had said she never would, or Gwendolen again, feeling suddenly sorry for Deronda's sorrow over her. What is more, pivotal moments like these reach out also in making and remaking potential links across the works, as though what the several different stories were in the formation of *Middlemarch*, the various novels are in the creation of the mind of George Eliot—a mental network of varying combinations and sudden connections, showing a way for thinking about existence. Thus: Arthur not confessing to Irwine, and Godfrey not claiming the baby in front of him; the secret terror involved in reading of Gwendolen and of Tito, of Mrs Transome and of Bulstrode; the need for help from Janet through Maggie to Gwendolen; the necessity of thinking always more than one thing at a time. These are not just 'themes' or 'characters': they are experiments in life, techniques and instruments in novelistic thinking, structures, predicaments, and states of being that enable and require readers to put into their mentality a part or byte of what it is that George Eliot makes for in the development of human mind and feeling.

When I first finished reading *Middlemarch*, more than forty-five years ago, I remember thinking as never before on completing a book: now I am going to be lonely again, back out in life without the help of a George Eliot behind me. It was like being without what Dorothea had been to Lydgate in backing him when no one else would, making him believe that he too could be seen and judged in the 'wholeness' of his character. In contrast, Rosamond had spoken just four or five cool words to Lydgate when he most needed her. But those spoken words 'What can I do, Tertius?' had beneath and behind them seventy more unspoken, the sub-vocal presence of George Eliot offering the background to human meaning, even in the felt loss or lack of it. That is what George Eliot felt and still does feel like: the great human background, the added dimension and context for human understanding, so often needed or missing or uncounted in the lonely foreground of life.

But after the books end, the continuing task of realism is to try to think like a novelist *outside* the novels, even by means of them. It is to try to provide from some other part of oneself—from the silent inner novelist of life—what one needs but cannot find from elsewhere: an interior support for meaning and understanding. The great and paradoxical shift in realism is the flip from naming the situation to knowing its reality. That naming is complex but it is all to do with the difference— whatever the situation—between knowing we must all die and, as it said of Casaubon, the acute consciousness 'I must die—and soon.' It does not have to be death, it can be any realization of seriousness for the reader. It happens in the text but it also happens between the text and what it is that it refers to, outside it, on the other side, transmitted and transformed. That is what I take Virginia Woolf to mean when, in *The Common Reader*, she called the George Eliot of *Middlemarch* almost the first novelist who was writing for grown-up people—as though sometimes it seems that everything afterwards is in danger of appearing to be just fiction again. What the demanding presence of George Eliot represents within these novels, in both heart and method, is necessary for an adult existence that ups its standards without either denial of or surrender to its less adult, more undignified needs. I close with a last look at what this transmitted life of George Eliot feels like, bringing back some vital moments for the last time.

In moments of loss, particularly in *Middlemarch*, a woman seeks an empty room. It is as though she is moving back into the surrounds of her own mind, without much in the way of the normal screens to protect her now from the force of a silently roaring reality. It is so with Mrs Bulstrode in that in-between time after she has learned of her husband's past and before she resolves to go back down to him again. Likewise Dorothea, after seeing Will and Rosamond together, has to take time in solitude over a long night to live with her grief and know what to make of it. Or again, when Dorothea needs to go to her room between yet another rejection from Casaubon and another attempt to be of kindness to him. These are the moments in between a first and second life, a movement that is not once and for all, but constantly repeated and reconfigured in different forms and efforts throughout a life. Those in-between moments in crisis or transition hold more of subterranean life than almost any others—like the almost agnostic place that, at another level, historically, George Eliot herself occupies between religion and secularization, between optimism and despair, between competing philosophies, top down and bottom up, in search of future forms of purpose. These in-betweens are a realist's holding ground for whatever in human nature is coming out of one place before it goes into another, the best glimpse we have of the raw or half-fashioned material of human life 'in the making'—in the need of something more from and for itself. At such a point Dorothea, beneath the merciful eyes of solitude, can look direct into the eyes of sorrow, as if these things—solitude, sorrow—had real dimensional existence in the world, and were as important as people themselves. Grief is another such state of being, when Dorothea 'was no longer wrestling with her grief, but could sit down with it as a lasting companion and make it a sharer in her thoughts' (*Middlemarch*, chapter 80). Sit with *it* as companion, make *it* a sharer, saving *it* for human purpose. Without that 'it', without all that is meant by thought and experience and the means to use them, humans are two-dimensional. This then in Dorothea is like making George Eliot—what she stands for and holds onto, the bit in oneself that she represents—also a sharer in one's thoughts, against mere passive suffering and frightened loneliness.

So it is when 'acquired' knowledge struggles to use and incorporate itself—to turn the 'it' of its solitude, sorrow, grief, and the thought of these things, back into a 'me' who can commit oneself to re-entering ordinary life, with something greater than before, however uncertainly. 'It' is then what Dorothea does with herself that she might be 'the mercy' for Casaubon's 'sorrows' when otherwise something humanly needed, like mercy, will go missing in the world: an idea 'wrought back' into feeling and being. It is like the amalgam of demand and compassion that lies behind almost every character in these novels. It is like that 'third presence' felt between Gwendolen and Deronda after they cease speaking and register the seriousness between them. Or that thought of Casaubon's vulnerable mortality that comes to Dorothea's mind 'like a shadowy monitor, looking at her anger with sad remonstrance' (*Middlemarch*, chapter 42). 'It' is George Eliot.

She had dared hope, in the poem 'O May I Join the Choir Immortal', to be one of those influencers who might live again 'in minds made better by their presence'. If there is no God, my teacher, the novelist Stanley Middleton, once said to me wryly but in earnest, then George Eliot will do, will serve instead—as the best version of what a novel's omniscient narrator might really stand for, beyond the technical. She at least is the human-sized God, the idea of God wrought back to human instantiation, as Feuerbach had urged. 'To think is to be God' was how he put it.[2]

She wanted to leave nothing unsaid or at least unwritten. But compare her to what, in one of his thought experiments, a neuroscientist, committed also to literature, envisions as a 'Giantess' encompassing the whole infinite, non-human Universe. This is a sort of super-Gaia, on whom or on which humans can make little personal impression, for all their mass effects on the environment:

> We discovered that we can communicate with her, but we cannot communicate meaningfully. We are of insufficient size. What can we say to her? What question

could we ask? How could she communicate an answer back to us?... And if she told you what was of importance to her, could you understand her answer? Do you think it would have any meaning at all if you displayed one of your Shakespeare plays to a bacterium? Of course not. Meaning varies with spatial scale.[3]

George Eliot, sensing more beyond and beneath, still holds to a middle earth in which, however tentatively, we *can* communicate. She knew, relativist as she was, that for human beings absolute truth was an unknowable and almost non-existent entity. But even as such, it was a sense of truth that humans could neither live with nor do without. In between those two, George Eliot represents the approximate effort at that truth, which human reality needs and fears. That is why inside the novels she is both there and not there—not there as far as her characters can ever know; utterly there for her readers to have to think with; placed between fiction and an extra-literary reality in order to work across them. She is the great transmitter— and the right size for us, to help make us those few percentage points more. As she wrote after *Middlemarch*:

> I have finished my book and am thoroughly at peace with it—not because I am convinced of its perfection, but because I have lived to give out what it was in me to give and have not been hindered by illness or death from making my work a whole, such as it is. (GEL 5, p. 324)

Notes

Introduction

1. Robert D. Richardson, *William James: In the Maelstrom of American Modernism* (Boston, MA: Houghton Mifflin, 2006), p. xiii; hereafter cited as Richardson, *James*.
2. Robert D. Richardson, *Emerson: The Mind on Fire* (Berkeley and Los Angeles, CA: University of California Press, 1995), p. xi.
3. Edith Simcox, 'George Eliot', *Nineteenth Century* (May 1881), p. 787; hereafter cited as '*Nineteenth Century*'.
4. *The George Eliot Letters*, ed. Gordon S. Haight, 9 vols (New Haven, CT: Yale University Press, 1954–78), vol. 2, p. 9; hereafter cited throughout each chapter as 'GEL'.
5. David Carroll (ed.), *George Eliot: The Critical Heritage* (London: Routledge 1971), p. 321; hereafter cited as *Critical Heritage*.
6. Mark Edmundson, *Why Read?* (New York: Bloomsbury, 2004), pp. 45–6.
7. Mark Edmundson, *Why Teach?* (New York: Bloomsbury, 2013), p. 23.
8. To put George Eliot into historical context was the aim of my volume in the Oxford English Literary Series, *The Victorians*, where it is argued that almost everything in that literary history culminates in the writing of *Middlemarch*. I seek not to replicate that approach in making this attempt from a different angle.
9. J. W. Cross (ed.), *George Eliot's Life*, 3 vols (Edinburgh and London: William Blackwood & Sons, 1885), vol. 2, pp. 36–7; hereafter cited throughout each chapter as 'Cross'.
10. GEL 3, pp. 63–4; see also Cross, 2, p. 106.
11. Quoted in K. K. Collins (ed.), *George Eliot: Interviews and Recollections* (London: Palgrave Macmillan, 2010), p. 144; hereafter cited as '*Interviews and Recollections*'.: including William Hale and George W. Smalley.
12. John Morley, 'The Life of George Eliot', *Macmillan's Magazine* (February 1885), reprinted in *Nineteenth-Century Essays*, ed. P. Stansky (Chicago: University of Chicago, 1970) p. 309. Tacitus was a classical Roman historian (AD 56–117).
13. W. H. Hudson, *Far Away and Long Ago* (London: J. M. Dent, 1918), p. 3.

Chapter 1

1. *Westminster Review*, April 1859, p. 508.
2. In *George Eliot and Intoxication* (London: Palgrave, 1999), Kathleen McCormack argued that the mother was alcoholic, as in the remarkably original portrait of Janet as female alcoholic in 'Janet's Repentance', and as with characters such as the troublesome father, Thias, in *Adam Bede*.
3. Mathilde Blind, *George Eliot* (Boston, MA: Roberts Brothers, 1883), p. 19.
4. Quoted in George Willis Cooke, *George Eliot: A Critical Study of Her Life, Writings and Philosophy* (Boston, MA: Osgood, 1883), p. 7.
5. Cooke quoting Edith Simcox, p. 8.
6. Mathilde Blind, *George Eliot* (London: Allen, 1883), p. 18.

7. Here and elsewhere I am indebted to the collaborative manuscript work done with my former PhD student, Melissa Raines, published in her *George Eliot's Grammar of Being* (London: Anthem Press, 2011).

8. Quoted in Gordon S. Haight, *George Eliot: A Biography* (Oxford: Clarendon Press, 1968), p. 5.

Chapter 2

1. Mathilde Blind, *George Eliot* (Boston, MA: Roberts Brothers, 1883), pp. 54–5; hereafter cited as 'Blind'.

2. Rosemarie Bodenheimer, *The Real Life of Mary Ann Evans* (Ithaca, NY: Cornell University Press, 1994), p. 40.

3. *The Varieties of Religious Experience* (1902), ed. Martin E. Marty (London: Penguin, 1985), p. 162 ('The Sick Soul').

4. John Henry Newman, *Apologia pro Vita Sua* (1864; London: Everyman, 1912), p. 164 (part 6).

5. From Müller's lecture on Darwin's philosophy of language, reprinted in *Fraser's Magazine* (May 1873).

6. See, for example, Jonah Lehrer, *Proust Was a Neuroscientist* (Edinburgh: Canongate, 2007), pp. 25–52.

7. Thomas Pinney (ed.), *The Essays of George Eliot* (London: Routledge & Kegan Paul, 1963), p. 317; hereafter cited throughout each chapter as '*Essays*'.

8. Ludwig Feuerbach, *The Essence of Christianity* (1841), translated by Marian Evans 1854 (New York: Harper & Row, 1957), p. 40 (part 1, chapter 2); hereafter cited as 'Feuerbach'.

9. Cf. Hannah Arendt: 'Whatever the fallacies of the two-world theories might have been, they arose out of genuine experiences. For it is true that the moment we start thinking on no matter what issue we stop everything else, and this everything else, again whatever it may happen to be, interrupts the thinking process; it is as though we moved into a different world'; quoted in Adela Pinch, *Thinking about Other People in Nineteenth-Century British Writing* (Cambridge: Cambridge University Press, 2010), p. 18.

10. See Gillian Beer's classic essay on the relation of the protagonist of 'The Lifted Veil' and the narrator of *Middlemarch* in terms of the anxiety of omniscient authorship: 'Myth and the Single Consciousness', in '*This Particular Web': Essays on Middlemarch*, ed. Ian Adam (Toronto: University of Toronto, 1975), pp. 91–115.

11. See Edith Simcox, *A Monument to the Memory of George Eliot: Autobiography of a Shirtmaker*, ed. C. M. Fulmer and M. E. Barfield (London: Routledge, 1998), p. 224.

12. Peter Bayne, 'Shakespeare and George Eliot', *Blackwood's Magazine* 133 (April 1883), p. 525.

13. Shakespeare, *Troilus and Cressida*, 3.3.223.

14. From motto to *Middlemarch*, chapter 57.

15. See Fionnuala Dillane, *Before George Eliot* (Cambridge: Cambridge University Press, 2013). In her working life, it was estimated that Eliot earned over £45,000—where Trollope earned nearly £70,000 and Dickens over £80,000 by his novels alone. Dillane notes that, to earn £50 per annum with the *Westminster Review*, Eliot had to review over a hundred books, whereas the publication of *Scenes of Clerical Life* brought her £443 in 1857 (p. 104).

16. Quoted in Rosemary Ashton, *142 Strand* (London: Chatto & Windus, 2006), p. 86.

17. Quoted in Gordon S. Haight, *George Eliot: A Biography* (Oxford: Clarendon Press, 1968), p. 84; hereafter cited as 'Haight'.

18. In Pam Hirsch, *Barbara Leigh Smith Bodichon* (London: Chatto & Windus, 1998), pp. 62, 112.

Chapter 3

1. J. S. Mill, *Collected Works*, ed. J. M. Robson (Toronto: University of Toronto 1963–), vol. 10, p. 121.
2. Nadine Gordimer, *The Lying Days* (London: Virago, 1983), p. 163.
3. Nadine Gordimer, *Telling Times* (London: Bloomsbury, 2011), p. 140.
4. George Eliot, *Selected Critical Writings*, ed. Rosemary Ashton (Oxford: World's Classics, 1992), p. 15.
5. Charles Hennell, *An Inquiry concerning the Origin of Christianity*, 2nd edition (London: Allman, 1841), p. 248.
6. Ludwig Feuerbach, *The Essence of Christianity*, translated by Marian Evans (London: Chapman, 1854), p. xli; hereafter cited as *Essence of Christianity*.
7. Zadie Smith, *Changing My Mind* (London: Penguin, 2011), pp. 30, 33.
8. Ludwig Feuerbach, *The Essence of Religion*, translated by Alexander Loos (New York: Prometheus Books, 2004), pp. 23–4; hereafter cited as *Essence of Religion*.
9. George Willis Cooke, *George Eliot: A Critical Study of her Live, Writings and Philosophy* (Boston, MA: Houghton, Mifflin & Company, 1883), p. 39.
10. K. K. Collins (ed.), *George Eliot: Interviews and Recollections* (London: Palgrave, 2010), p. 178.
11. See Chapter 9 for later development of the importance of Mallock's objections.
12. I am indebted here and elsewhere to the work on George Eliot by my colleague, Josie Billington.
13. William James, *Varieties of Religious Experience* (1902), ed. M. E. Marty (London: Penguin, 1985), p. 223 (lecture 10); hereafter cited as 'Varieties of Religious Experience'.
14. *Complete Prose Works of Matthew Arnold*, ed. R. H. Super (Ann Arbor, MI: University of Michigan, 1960–77), *Essays in Criticism: First Series*, 'Spinoza and the Bible', vol. 3, p. 165.
15. Benedict de Spinoza, *Ethics*, translated by Marian Evans, ed. Thomas Deegan (Salzburg: University of Salzburg, 1981), p. 71, part 2, proposition 35 scholium; hereafter cited as 'Ethics'.
16. Mark Rutherford, *Pages from a Journal: With Other Papers* (London: Oxford University Press, 1910), p. 41.
17. Rosemary Ashton (ed.), *Versatile Victorian: Selected Critical Writings of George Henry Lewes* (London: Bristol Classical Press, 1992), p. 274; hereafter cited as 'Lewes'.
18. Rebecca Newberger Goldstein, *Betraying Spinoza* (New York: Schocken Books, 2006), p. 200.
19. Saul Bellow, *Herzog* (London: Penguin, 1964), p. 189.
20. George Henry Lewes, *Life of Goethe* (1855; London: Dent, Everyman Library, 1938), p. 176.
21. David Carroll (ed.), *George Eliot: The Critical Heritage* (London: Routledge, 1971), p. 466.

Chapter 4

1. Beatrice Webb, *My Apprenticeship* (1926; London: Penguin, 1971), pp. 54–9.
2. Herbert Spencer, *An Autobiography*, 2 vols (London: Williams & Norgate, 1904), vol. 1, pp. 462–3.
3. Lewes's journal quoted in Gordon Haight, *George Eliot: A Biography* (Oxford: Clarendon Press, 1968), pp. 271–2.
4. Herbert Spencer, *Essays* (London: Dent, Everyman, 1911), p. 170; hereafter cited as 'Spencer Essays'.
5. Herbert Spencer, *First Principles* (1860; London: Watts, The Thinker's Library, 1937), p. 71.

6. Herbert Spencer, *The Principles of Psychology*, 2 vols (1855; London: Williams & Norgate, 1881), vol. 1, p. 151.

7. Herbert Spencer, *Principles of Biology*, 2 vols (New York: D. Appleton, 1866), vol. 2, p. 375.

8. Charles Bray, *Phases of Opinion and Experience during a Long Life: An Autobiography* (London: Longmans, Green, 1884), p. 261.

9. Herbert Spencer, *Principles of Psychology*, 2nd edition (London: Williams and Norgate, 1870–2), vol. 1, p. 293.

10. George Henry Lewes, *Problems of Life and Mind* (London: Trubner, 1880), vol. 5, p. 495: the manuscript was corrected and overseen by Marian Lewes after his death.

11. Vernon Lee, 'On Literary Construction' (1895), quoted in Nicholas Dames, *The Physiology of the Novel* (Oxford: Oxford University Press, 2007), p. 187.

12. Lewes, *Problems of Life and Mind*, vol. 2, p. 313.

13. William James, *Principles of Psychology*, 2 vols (New York: Henry Holt, 1890), vol. 1, pp. 245–6.

Chapter 5

1. Quoted in Rosemary Ashton, *G. H. Lewes: An Unconventional Victorian* (London: Pimlico, 2000), p. 159; hereafter cited as 'Ashton'.

2. It was Coleridge who best conveyed the Romantic sense of the dramatic that Lewes inherited: 'To see Kean act was like reading Shakespeare by flashes of lightning.' This is quoted in Cynthia Ozick, *The Puttermesser Papers* (London: Jonathan Cape, 1999) p. 136, in her account of a modern-day couple seeking to reproduce the relationship of the two Georges, Lewes and Eliot.

3. Quoted in Hock Guan Toja, *George Henry Lewes: A Victorian Mind* (Cambridge, MA: Harvard University Press, 1977), p. 1.

4. Margaret Fuller (1810–1850), American critic, journalist, and advocate of women's rights. Marian Evans wrote a review of her *Memoirs* in the *Westminster Review*, April 1852, and an essay on her feminism in the *Leader*, October 1855. She particularly stressed the power of Fuller's sympathy to overcome her inclination to despise others, whilst also seeking more room for her nature's full development.

5. G. H. Lewes, *Sea-Side Studies*, 2nd edition (London: William Blackwood & Sons, 1860), p. 37.

6. G. H. Lewes, *Problems of Life and Mind*, 5 vols (London: Trubner, 1874–9). The volumes were complicatedly divided into three 'series' and numerous 'problems'. Citations are given by page number, volume number, chapter and paragraph reference, for relative ease of reference amidst different editions and reprints. Hereafter cited as '*PLM*'.

7. G. H. Lewes, *A Biographical History of Philosophy* (London: Routledge, 1891), p. 283 (series 1, eighth epoch, chapter 4).

8. Rick Rylance, 'Convex and Concave: Conceptual Boundaries in Psychology', *Victorian Literature and Culture* (2004), pp. 449–62, p. 455.

9. K. K. Collins, 'G. H. Lewes Revised: George Eliot and the Moral Sense', *Victorian Studies* 22 (summer 1978), pp. 463–92.

10. The influence of Comte is more fully discussed in Chapter 9.

11. Herbert Spencer, *Essays* (London: Dent, Everyman, 1911), p. 329, 'On the Origins and Function of Music'.

12. Edith Simcox, 'George Eliot', *Nineteenth Century* (May 1881), p. 780.

13. 'At the limit, society imposes the obligation on even the most interior or recalcitrant of events to take place in the terms of the community, to translate themselves, as passion does into marriage, into public forms to which the self feels as loyal as, or even more

loyal than, it does to the source in private need and satisfaction. To imagine society is to imagine the possibility of this translation. Equally, it is to imagine that the moral life, with its vocabulary, can be viably interpreted by institutions ... to believe, or at least to hope, that the public judgments of criminal and hero, good man or pariah, stand close on the whole to moral truth', Philip Fisher, *Making Up Society: The Novels of George Eliot* (Pittsburgh, PA: University of Pittsburgh Press, 1981), p. 3.

14. Our field of experience like our field of vision is 'fringed forever by a MORE that continuously develops ... as life proceeds' (William James, *The Meaning of Truth* (London: Longmans, 1909), ch. 4: 'The Relation between Knower and Known').

Chapter 6

1. *The Prose Works of William Wordsworth*, ed. W. J. B. Owen and Jane Worthington Smyser, 3 vols (Oxford: Clarendon Press), vol. 1, p. 129; hereafter cited as 'Wordsworth Prose Works'.
2. Ludwig Feuerbach, *The Essence of Christianity*, translated by Marian Evans (London: Chapman, 1854), p. 146.
3. John Ruskin, *Modern Painters* (London: Smith, Elder, 1843), vol. 1, part 2, section 3, chapter 3, para. 22.
4. William James, *Varieties of Religious Experience* (1902), ed. M. E. Marty (London: Penguin, 1985), p. 133.
5. Deronda at the hands of his mother, *Daniel Deronda*, chapter 51.
6. Edith Simcox, 'George Eliot', *Nineteenth Century* (May 1881), p. 789.
7. See Rebecca Mead's excellent account of Main in *The Road to Middlemarch: My Life with George Eliot* (London: Granta, 2014), pp. 230–8.
8. R. H. Hutton, *Essays on Some of the Modern Guides to English Thought in Matters of Faith* (London: Macmillan, 1891), pp. 298–9; hereafter cited as 'Modern Guides'.
9. See Malcolm Woodfield, *R. H. Hutton: Critic and Theologian* (Oxford: Clarendon Press, 1986), p. 158, to which I am indebted.
10. 'The doctrine of Compensation, which I detest, considered as a way of life', GEL 2, p. 258.
11. Leslie Stephen, 'Wordsworth's Ethics', in *Hours in a Library*, 3 vols (London: John Murray), vol. 2, p. 279.
12. A. S. Byatt, *Still Life* (London: Penguin, 1986), p. 42 (chapter 3).
13. Salley Vickers, *The Other Side of You* (London: Harper Perennial, 2007), p. 125.

Chapter 7

1. Ludwig Feuerbach, *The Essence of Christianity*, translated by Marian Evans (London: Chapman, 1854), pp. 160–1.
2. Quoted in *Impressions of Theophrastus Such* (1879), chapter 10 ('Debasing the Moral Currency') from Wordsworth's *The Excursion*, book 4, lines 763–5.
3. Adam Phillips, *On Balance* (London: Hamish Hamilton, 2010), p. 205.
4. Doris Lessing, *Shikasta* (London: Jonathan Cape, 1979), p. 187.
5. Salley Vickers, *The Other Side of You* (London: Harper Perennial 2007), p. 236 (part 4, chapter 1).
6. Vickers, *The Other Side of You*, p. 164 (part 2, chapter 10). Salley Vickers believes that the nineteenth-century novelists are still the greatest psychologists we have: speaking of the work of George Eliot: 'It makes anything I do seem very inadequate', (<http://www.salleyvickers.com/pages/books/garnet/other/us_conversation.htm>).

7. Robert D. Richardson, *William James: In the Maelstrom of American Modernism* (Boston, MA: Houghton Mifflin, 2006), p. 152.

8. 'What Psychical Research Has Accomplished', in *The Will to Believe and Other Essays* (London: Longmans, Green, 1897). Our field of experience like our field of vision is 'fringed forever by a MORE that continuously develops...as life proceeds' (William James, *The Meaning of Truth* (London: Longmans, 1909), ch. 4, 'The Relation between Knower and Known'). Something always escapes.

9. For more on Myers see Chapter 8.

10. William James, *Varieties of Religious Experience* (1902), ed. M. E. Marty (London: Penguin, 1985), p. 231, lecture 10; hereafter cited as '*Varieties*'.

11. 'My present field of consciousness is a centre surrounded by a fringe that shades insensibly into a subconscious more. I use three separate terms here to describe this fact; but I might as well use three hundred, for the fact is all shades and no boundaries. Which part of it properly is in my consciousness, which out? If I name what is out, it already has come in. The centre works in one way, while the margins work in another, and presently overpower the centre and are central themselves.... Our *full* self is the whole field, with all those indefinitely radiating subconscious possibilities of increase that we can only feel without conceiving, and can hardly begin to analyze. The collective and the distributive ways of being coexist here, for each part functions distinctly, makes connexion with its own peculiar region in the still wider rest of experience and tends to draw us into that line, and yet the whole is somehow felt as one pulse of our life,—not conceived, but felt so', William James, *The Pluralistic Universe* (1909; Cambridge, MA: Harvard University Press, 1977), p. 133.

12. G. H. Lewes, *Problems of Life and Mind* (London: Trubner, 1880), vol. 5, p. 203. See also Alice Jenkins, *Space and the March of Mind* (Oxford: Oxford University Press, 2007).

13. James, *The Meaning of Truth* (New York and London: Longmans, Green & Co., 1909), lecture 3: 'Humanism and Truth'.

14. *The Life and Correspondence of John Foster*, ed. J. E. Ryland, 2 vols (London, 1846), vol. 1, p. 208.

15. Andrey Sinyavsky quoted in Dan Jacobson, *Adult Pleasures* (London: Andre Deutsch, 1988), pp. 83–4.

16. Dan Jacobson, *Time and Time Again* (London: Flamingo, 1986), p. 213.

Chapter 8

1. Ludwig Feuerbach, *The Essence of Christianity* (1841), translated by Marian Evans 1854 (New York: Harper & Row, 1957), p. 49 (part 1, chapter 3); hereafter cited as '*Essence of Christianity*'.

2. George Henry Lewes, *Problems of Life and Mind* (London: Trubner, 1879), vol. 3, p. 474 (problem 4, chapter 1, 'The Physical Basis of Mind').

3. David Carroll (ed.), *George Eliot: The Critical Heritage* (London: Routledge 1971), p. 321; hereafter cited as '*Critical Heritage*'.

4. James Sully, 'George Eliot's Art', *Mind* 6(23) (July 1881), p. 382.

5. Doris Lessing, *Under My Skin* (London: HarperCollins, 1994), p. 218.

6. John Freeman, 'George Eliot's Great Poetry', *Cambridge Quarterly* 5(1) (1970), p. 31.

7. It is the novelist A. S. Byatt who, editing *The Mill* for Penguin, substituted, for the first edition's vague 'years', the manuscript's poignant precision 'two years' after first writing 'many years'.

8. *The Letters of Mrs Gaskell*, ed. J. A. V. Chapple and A. Pollard (Manchester: Mandolin, 1997), p. 581.

9. Though George Eliot told Emily Davies that her own experience of people like the Dodsons, Maggie's aunts and uncles on her mother's side, was 'so much worse' than she had depicted in the novel—in their willingness to blame, their materialism, their narrow values—she nonetheless would not take the easy route of reactively ignoring what they did offer: 'we owe much to them for keeping up the sense of respectability, which was the only religion possible to the mass of English people. Their want of education made a theoretic or dogmatic religion impossible, and since the Reformation, an imaginative religion had not been possible' (GEL 8, p. 465). An imaginative religion was Maggie's need.

10. Margaret Harris and Judith Johnston (eds), *The Journals of George Eliot* (Cambridge: Cambridge University Press 1998), p. 308.

11. G. H. Lewes, *Problems of Life and Mind*, 5 vols (London: Trubner, 1874–9), vol 5, p. 470, problem 4, chapter 5. Hereafter cited as *PLM*.

12. Ludwig Feuerbach, *The Essence of Christianity*, translated by Marian Evans (London: Chapman, 1854), pp. 83–4.

13. Quoted in John Beer, *Providence and Love: Studies in Wordsworth, Channing, Myers, George Eliot, and Ruskin* (Oxford: Clarendon Press, 1998), p. 134, to which I am indebted. Hereafter cited as '*Studies in Myers*', it is not wholly insignificant that this book is dedicated to the novelist and George Eliot reader A. S. Byatt.

14. Especially in the Lucy poems and 'Laodamia', discussed in his book on Wordsworth, 1881.

15. F. W. H. Myers, 'George Eliot', *Century Magazine* 23 (November 1881), p. 63.

16. *The Complete Prose Works of Matthew Arnold*, ed. R. H. Super, 11 vols (Ann Arbor, MI: University of Michigan, 1960–77), vol. 6, p. 219.

17. F. W. H. Myers, *Human Personality and Its Survival of Bodily Death* (London: Longmans, Green & Co., 1903), pp. 82, 85 (chapter 3); hereafter cited as '*Human Personality*'.

18. See Vanessa L. Ryan, *Thinking without Thinking in the Victorian Novel* (Baltimore, MD: Johns Hopkins, 2012), p. 159.

19. *The Autobiography of Margaret Oliphant*, ed. Elisabeth Jay (Oxford: Oxford University Press), 1990), pp. 15, 17.

20. Howard Jacobson, 'It's the Thought that Counts', *The Reader* 31, p. 23 (Autumn, 2008).

Chapter 9

1. Donald Carroll (ed.), *George Eliot: The Critical Heritage* (London: Routledge, 1971), p. 462; hereafter cited as *Critical Heritage*.

2. Quoted in Hans Blumenberg, *The Legitimacy of the Modern Age*, translated by Robert M. Wallace (Cambridge, MA: The MIT Press, 1985), p. 445.

3. W. H. Mallock, *Is Life Worth Living?* (London: Chatto & Windus, 1879), p. 20; hereafter '*Life*'.

4. Friedrich Nietzsche, *Twilight of the Idols* and *The Anti-Christ*, translated by R. J. Hollingdale (London: Penguin, 1968), p. 69.

5. Friedrich Nietzsche, *The Birth of Tragedy* and *The Genealogy of Morals*, translated by Francis Golffing (New York: Doubleday Anchor, 1956), preface 5, pp. 153–4; hereafter cited as *The Genealogy of Morals*.

6. Friedrich Nietzsche, *Untimely Meditations*, translated by R. J. Hollingdale (Cambridge: Cambridge University Press, 1983), p. 76; hereafter '*Untimely Mediations*'.

7. See Nietzsche, *The Genealogy of Morals*, second essay 16, pp. 217–18.

8. Friedrich Nietzsche, *Ecce Homo*, translated by R. J. Hollingdale (London: Penguin, 1979), p. 126 ('Why I Am a Destiny').

9. Friedrich Nietzsche, *The Gay Science*, translated by Josefine Nauckhoff (Cambridge: Cambridge University Press, 2001), book 3, pp. 108, 109.

10. Edith Simcox, 'George Eliot', *Nineteenth Century* (May 1881), p. 796.

11. Friedrich Nietzsche, *Daybreak: Thoughts on the Prejudices of Morality*, translated by R. J. Hollingdale (Cambridge: Cambridge University Press, 1982), p. 137 (book 4, section 223).

12. See Alexander Welsh, *George Eliot and Blackmail* (Cambridge, MA: Harvard University Press, 1985): interested in blackmail for reasons that went beyond the plot of the sensational novel, George Eliot had her own secrets, knew guilt and the fear of exposure, and was vulnerable to public judgement of her private life with Lewes.

13. Rosemarie Bodenheimer, *The Real Life of Mary Ann Evans* (Ithaca, NY: Cornell University Press, 1994), p. 219.

14. Simcox, 'George Eliot', p. 785.

15. Friedrich Nietzsche, *Thus Spoke Zarathustra*, translated by R. J. Hollingdale (London: Penguin, 1969), pp. 276, 278, with minor adaptions (part 4, 'The Ugliest Man').

16. John Morley, *Nineteenth-Century Essays*, ed. Peter Stansky (Chicago: University of Chicago Press, 1970), p. 309 ('The Life of George Eliot' also reprinted in Morley's *Critical Miscellanies* (London: Macmillan, 1888), vol. 3).

17. See Avrom Fleishman's indispensable work 'George Eliot's Reading: A Chronological List', a supplement to *George Eliot–George Henry Lewes Studies*, no. 54–5 (September 2008), especially for the years 1861–2, and also his *George Eliot's Intellectual Life* (Cambridge: Cambridge University Press, 2010), pp. 112–14.

18. Mrs Humphry Ward, *A Writer's Recollections*, 2 vols (London: Collins, 1918), vol. 1, p. 108.

19. R. H. Hutton, *Essays on Some of the Modern Guides to English Thoughts in Matters of Faith* (London: Macmillan, 1888), pp. 296, 274.

20. *The Journals of George Eliot*, ed. Margaret Harris and Judith Johnson (Cambridge: Cambridge University Press, 1998), pp. 86–7; hereafter cited as '*Journals*'.

21. See Melissa Raines, *George Eliot's Grammar of Being* (London: Anthem Press, 2011), pp. 21–37 on the restoring of life in Silas Marner after suspended animation by an almost biological recreation of the creature in relation to the new child: 'what rises to the forefront is the living pulse—the very basis for the ability to feel—and the importance of the awakening of that pulse in an effort to open the pathways of emotional response' (p. 37).

22. See John Ruskin, *Modern Painters* (London: Smith, Elder, 1860), vol. 5, art. 8 (chapter 1, 'The Law of Help').

23. James Sully, 'George Eliot's Art', *Mind* 6(23) (July 1881), p. 385.

24. In *George Eliot's Intellectual Life*, Avrom Fleishman argues, with some justice, that the influence of Comte on George Eliot has been somewhat overstated by earlier commentators (chapter 3).

25. Henri Bergson, *Creative Evolution*, translated by Arthur Mitchell (New York: Henry Holt & Co., 1909), pp. 98–9.

26. Lewes recorded how 'one very dear' to him had enabled him to read Comte imaginatively as a utopia presenting hypotheses for the future, rather than rigid doctrines (GEL 4, p. 333, footnote 6).

27. Roger Scruton, *The Face of God* (London: Continuum, 2012), p. 77.

28. A. S. Byatt and Ignês Sodré, *Imagining Characters*, ed. Rebecca Swift (London: Vintage, 1995), p. 85.

29. Saul Bellow, *Mr Sammler's Planet* (London: Penguin, 1972), p. 119.

Chapter 10

1. See also Margaret Harris and Judith Johnston (eds), *The Journals of George Eliot* (Cambridge: Cambridge University Press, 1998), p. 141.

2. *D. H. Lawrence: A Personal Record by E. T. (Jessie Chambers)* (1935; London: Frank Cass, 1965), p. 105.

3. David Carroll (ed.), *George Eliot: The Critical Heritage* (London: Routledge, 1971), p. 199.

4. George Henry Lewes, *Problems of Life and Mind* (London: Trubner, 1879), third series, part 2, p. 217 (problem 2, chapter 11, para. 188); hereafter cited as '*PLM*'.

5. John Locke, *An Essay Concerning Human Understanding* (1689), book 2, chapter 23, para. 12 (quoted in Neil Hertz, *George Eliot's Pulse* (Stanford, CA: Stanford University Press, 2003), p. 40).

6. James Sully, *My Life and Friends: A Psychologists Memories* (London: Unwin, 1918), pp. 263–4.

7. See Helen Groth, 'The Mind as Palimpsest: Art, Dreaming and James Sully's Aesthetic of Latency', in *Mindful Aesthetics*, ed. C. Dant and H. Groth (London: Bloomsbury, 2013), pp. 107–22.

8. F. W. H. Myers, 'George Eliot', *Century Magazine*, 23 (November 1881), p. 60.

9. Slavoj Zizek, *Event* (London: Penguin, 2014), p. 35.

10. Howard Jacobson, 'It's the Thought that Counts', *The Reader* 31, p. 32 (Autumn, 2008).

11. Patricia Duncker, *Sophie and the Sibyl* (Bloomsbury, 2015), p. 52.

12. William Kingdon Clifford, *Lectures and Essays*, ed. Leslie Stephen and Frederick Pollock (London: Macmillan, 1901), pp. 365, 385.

13. John Ruskin, *Modern Painters* (London: Smith, Elder, 1843), vol. 1, part 2, section 2, chapter 5 ('Of Truth of Space'), para. 4.

14. Charles Babbage, *The Ninth Bridgewater Treatise: A Fragment* (London: John Murray, 1838), pp. 164, 110, 112.

15. From Frederic Jameson, *The Antimonies of Realism* (London: Verso, 2013), p. 229: 'what happens to temporality is this: the simultaneous time-lines, as in Einsteinian relativity, keep overtaking each other; their own times overlap, cancel, outleap each other, overtake, fall behind'.

16. William Whewell, *The Philosophy of the Inductive Sciences*, 2 vols (London: John W. Parker, 1847), vol. 1, p. 24 (hereafter cited as 'Whewell'), in Ian Duncan, 'George Eliot's Science Fiction', *Representations* 125(1), pp. 15–39 (Winter 2014).

17. James Sully, *Pessimism* (London: Henry S. King, 1877), p. 276.

18. I am indebted here to William E. Connolly, *Neuropolitics: Thinking, Culture, Speed* (Minneapolis, MN: University of Minnesota Press, 2002).

19. William James, *Principles of Psychology*, 2 vols (New York: Henry Holt, 1890, reprinted by Dover Publications, New York, 1950), vol. 1, pp. 479–80 (chapter 11, 'Attention'); hereafter cited as '*PP*'.

20. A. S. Byatt, *The Virgin in the Garden* (London: Chatto & Windus, 1978), p. 120; hereafter cited as 'Byatt'.

21. See Jean-Louis Chrétien, *Under the Gaze of the Bible*, translated by J. M. Dunaway (Bronx, NY: Fordham University Press, 2015), p. 16.

22. See William James, *Varieties of Religious Experience* (1902), ed. M. E. Marty (Penguin, 1985), pp. 122–3 (lecture 5): 'Why, after all, may not the world be so complex as to consist of many interpenetrating spheres of reality, which we can thus approach in alternation by using different conceptions and assuming different attitudes, just as mathematicians handle the same numerical and spatial facts by geometry, by analytical geometry, by algebra, by the calculus, or by quaternions, and each time come out right?'

Chapter 11

1. Johann Wolfgang von Goethe, *Scientific Studies*, translated by D. Miller (New York: Suhrkamp, 1988), p. 307.

2. 'So much which belongs to us inwardly we must not develop outwardly; what we require from outside for the completion of our being is withdrawn from us; on the other hand, so much is forced upon us which is as foreign as it is burdensome to us', Goethe, *Autobiography*, translated by R. O. Moon (London: A. Rivers, 1932), p. 592.

3. William Dean Howells, *My Literary Passions* (New York: Harper & Brothers, 1895), p. 218. Hereafter cited as 'Literary Passions'.

4. David Carroll (ed.), *George Eliot: The Critical Heritage* (London: Routledge, 1971), p. 366, hereafter cited as 'Critical Heritage'.

5. See Avrom Fleishman, *George Eliot's Intellectual Life* (Cambridge: Cambridge University Press, 2010), especially pp. 190–1, as well as Jane Irwin's *George Eliot's Daniel Deronda Notebooks* (Cambridge: Cambridge University Press, 1996), and the extensive work carried out by William Baker beginning with *George Eliot and Judaism* (Lewiston and Lampeter: Edwin Mellen Press, 1975), to which I am indebted.

6. Joseph Jacobs, *George Eliot, Matthew Arnold, Browning, Newman: Essays and Reviews from The 'Athenaeum'* (London; David Nutt, 1891), p. xvi.

7. See Rosemary Ashton, *The German Idea* (Cambridge: Cambridge University Press, 1980).

8. W. H. Mallock, *Atheism and the Value of Life; Five Studies in Contemporary Literature* (London: Bentley, 1884; Memphis, Tennessee: General Books, 2009), pp. 64, 58.

9. Joseph Jacobs, *Jewish Ideals and Other Essays* (London: Macmillan, 1896), p. 75.

10. See Baker, *George Eliot and Judaism*, p. 110.

11. Thomas Nagel, *The View from Nowhere* (Oxford: Oxford University Press, 1986), p. 7.

12. James Sully, *My Life and Friends: A Psychologist's Memories* (London: Unwin, 1918), p. 264; hereafter cited as 'My Life and Friends'.

13. See, for example, Kant's *Metaphysical Principles of Virtue*, translated by James Ellington (1797; Indianapolis and New York: Library of Liberal Arts, 1964), p. 83.

14. George Eliot believed she invented the term 'meliorism'; William James took it from Sully as a basis for his efforts in pragmatism.

The End

1. See, for example, Cynthia Ozick's novel *The Puttermesser Papers* (London: Jonathan Cape, 1999), 'Puttermesser Paired', on the transmitted lives of the two Georges, especially 'V The Honeymoon', pp. 149–55, and the idea that Cross was trying to be a replica of Lewes (pp. 143–4).

2. Ludwig Feuerbach, *The Essence of Christianity* (1841), translated by Marian Evans, 1854 (New York: Harper & Row, 1957), p. 40 (part 1, chapter 2).

3. David Eagleman, *Sum* (Edinburgh and London: Canongate, 2009), p. 17.

Select Bibliography

Anyone writing on George Eliot is indebted to a great number of scholars and critics from F. R. Leavis, Joan Bennett, Barbara Hardy, U. C. Knoepflmacher, William Myers, and David Carroll, to Rosemary Ashton, Gillian Beer, Felicia Bonaparte, George Levine, K. M. Newton, and Bernard Paris. Specific debts in particular areas are recorded in the Notes. Gordon Haight's great nine-volume edition of *The George Eliot Letters* (Yale University Press, 1954–74) is foundational, as is Thomas Pinney's edition of the *Essays* (Routledge, 1963), and they are constant sources in the text. What follows is a selection of just some of the most vital works in this area.

Biographies. Following the Lives written by Mathilde Blind and J. W. Cross, the standard biography remains Gordon Haight, *George Eliot: A Biography* (Oxford: Clarendon Press, 1968), though significant biographical work has been subsequently provided by Rosemary Ashton (*George Eliot: A Life*, Hamish Hamilton, 1996; *G. H. Lewes: An Unconventional Victorian*, Oxford University Press, 1991; *142 Strand*, Chatto & Windus, 2006), Gillian Beer (*George Eliot*, Key Women Writers, Harvester, Wheatsheaf, 1986), Kathryn Hughes (*George Eliot: The Last Victorian*, Fourth Estate, 1999), Nancy Henry (*The Life of George Eliot*, Wiley-Blackwell, 2012), and Rebecca Mead (*The Road to Middlemarch*, Granta, 2014). Ruby Redinger's *George Eliot: The Emergent Self* (Bodley Head, 1975) remains the most riskily exciting venture, whilst Rosemarie Bodenheimer's *The Real Life of Mary Ann Evans* (Cornell University Press, 1994) is an excellent account of the importance of the letters, particularly in the early life. *George Eliot: Interviews and Recollections*, ed. K. K. Collins (Palgrave Macmillan, 2010) offers a useful selection of material. *The Letters of George Henry Lewes*, 3 vols and forthcoming are edited by William Baker (University of Victoria, 1995–).

Reference Works. The *Oxford Reader's Companion to George Eliot*, ed. John Rignall (Oxford University Press, 2000) is most useful, together with Timothy Hands, *A George Eliot Chronology* (Macmillan, 1989). See also *A George Eliot Dictionary*, ed. I. G. Mudge and M. E. Sears (Routledge, 1924).

George Eliot's Reading. See Avrom Fleishman, *George Eliot's Intellectual Life* (Cambridge University Press, 2010) and his 'George Eliot's Reading: A Chronological List', a supplement to *George Eliot–George Henry Lewes Studies*, no. 54–5 (September 2008). George Eliot's Notebooks have been published: *Quarry for 'Middlemarch'*, ed. Anna T. Kitchel (University of California Press, 1950); *George Eliot's Middlemarch Notebooks: A Transcription*, ed. John Clark Pratt and Victor Neufeldt (University of California Press, 1979); George Eliot's *Daniel Deronda Notebooks*, ed. Jane Irwin (Cambridge University Press, 1996); *George Eliot; A Writer's Notebook 1854–1879*, ed. Joseph Wiesenfarth (University Press of Virginia, 1981); *Some George Eliot Notebooks*, ed. William Baker, 4 vols (Salzburg Studies in English Literature, reprinted by Edwin Mellen Press, 1976–8). See also Jerome Beaty, *'Middlemarch' from Notebook to Novel* (University of Illinois, 1960). *The Journals of George Eliot* were edited by Margaret Harris and Judith Johnson (Cambridge University Press, 1998).

Literary Criticism. Melissa Raines, *George Eliot's Grammar of Being* (Anthem, 2011) is excellent on the revisions. Also stimulating are Josie Billington, *Eliot's Middlemarch* (Continuum, 2008), Alexander Welsh's brilliant *George Eliot and Blackmail* (Harvard University Press, 1985), Andrew H. Miller, *The Burdens of Perfection* (Cornell University Press, 2008), Garrett Stewart, *Dear Reader* (Johns Hopkins, 1996), Neil Hertz, *George Eliot's Pulse* (Stanford University Press, 2003), and the work of Elizabeth Ermarth, starting from *Realism and Consensus in the English Novel* (Princeton University Press, 1983). On free indirect discourse see Derek Oldfield, 'The Language of the Novel: The Character of Dorothea', in *Middlemarch: Critical Approaches to the Novel*, ed. Barbara Hardy (Athlone, 1967), pp. 63–86.

Intellectual Background. 'There are, believe it, passions of the mind': A. S. Byatt's *Passions of the Mind* (Chatto & Windus, 1969) takes its inspiring title from George Eliot and is best supplemented by Iris Murdoch's *Metaphysics as a Guide to Morals* (Chatto & Windus, 1992) and *Existentialists and Mystics* (Chatto & Windus, 1997). Diana Postlethwaite's *Making It Whole* (Ohio State University Press, 1984) is both under-rated and excellent in its intellectual zest. See also Hilary Fraser (with Daniel Brown), *English Prose of the Nineteenth Century* (Longman, 1996), Rosemary Ashton, *The German Idea* (Cambridge University Press, 1980), Stefan Collini, *Public Moralists* (Oxford University Press, 1991) and *Absent Minds* (Oxford University Press, 2006), and the work of George Levine from *The Realist Imagination* (University of Chicago, 1981) onwards. On Darwinism and science, see Gillian Beer, *Darwin's Plots* (Cambridge University Press, 1983) and *Open Fields* (Oxford University Press, 1996), and Sally Shuttleworth, *George Eliot and Nineteenth-Century Science* (Cambridge University Press, 1984). On psychology, see Rick Rylance, *Victorian Psychology and British Culture 1850–80* (Oxford University Press, 2000), especially on George Henry Lewes; Max Scheler, *The Nature of Sympathy*, translated by P. Heath (Routledge, 1970); and Sophie Ratcliffe, *On Sympathy* (Oxford University Press, 2008). Jan-Melissa Schramm, in her dual volumes on Victorian literature, *Testimony and Advocacy* (Cambridge University Press, 2000) and *Atonement and Self-Sacrifice* (Cambridge University Press, 2012), offers valuable cross-disciplinary insights.

Index